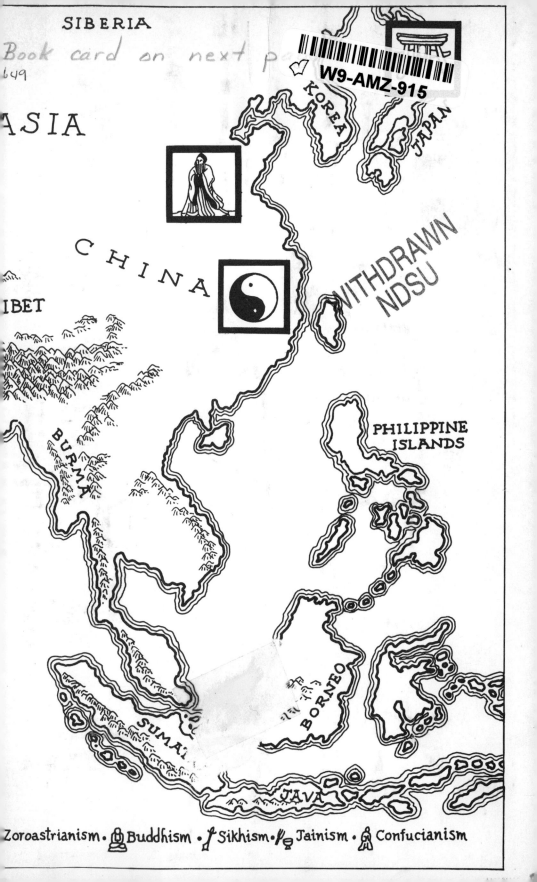

SIBERIA

ASIA

KOREA

JAPAN

CHINA

TIBET

BURMA

PHILIPPINE
ISLANDS

BORNEO

SUMA...

JAVA

Zoroastrianism • Buddhism • Sikhism • Jainism • Confucianism

MAN'S RELIGIONS

MAN'S

RELIGIONS

John B. Noss

THIRD EDITION

The Macmillan Company, New York

Collier-Macmillan Limited, London

The following books from which quotations have been drawn are copyrighted.
(Listed approximately in order of quotation.)

Primitive Man as Philosopher by Paul Radin. Copyright 1927 by D. Appleton and Company.

The Medicine Man by John L. Maddox. Copyright 1923 by The Macmillan Company.

The Native Tribes of South-East Australia by A. W. Howitt. Copyright 1904 by Macmillan and Co., Ltd.

Development of Religion and Thought in Ancient Egypt by James H. Breasted. Copyright 1912 by Charles Scribner's Sons.

The Dawn of Conscience by James H. Breasted. Copyright 1933 by James H. Breasted.

The History of Herodotus, translated by G. C. Macauley. Copyright 1904 by Macmillan and Company.

From the Stone Age to Christianity; Monotheism and the Historical Process by W. F. Albright. Copyright 1940 by The Johns Hopkins Press.

Ancient Near East Texts, edited by James B. Pritchard. 2nd edition. Copyright 1955 by Princeton University Press.

The Religion of Babylonia and Assyria by R. W. Rogers. Copyright 1908 by Eaton and Mains.

To M.B.N.
IN INEXPRESSIBLE
GRATITUDE

And what place is there
in me into which my God can come,
even He who made heaven and earth?
Is there anything in me, O Lord my God,
that can contain Thee? . . . .
Or should I not rather say,
that I could not exist unless I were
in Thee, from whom are all things,
by whom are all things, in whom
are all things?

—AUGUSTINE

Preface to the
THIRD EDITION

THIS EDITION CONSTITUTES A THOROUGH REVISION OF THE TWO PREVIOUS
ones. Not only does it have line drawings and maps for the first time,
but the text itself has been considerably altered both by elision and
enlargement. The written text has about the same length as before, but
it covers the ground more evenly yet with a juster stress on matters of
central importance. Entirely new topics have been introduced, and an
attempt has been made to treat several of the religions in greater depth.
Although this is particularly true of the two chapters on Buddhism,
numerous changes have been made throughout. The section on the religion of the Old Stone Age has been supplemented to bring it up to date;
the general features of the primitive religions have been thoroughly
reconsidered in the light of recent anthropological research, and the
account of them has been rewritten and amplified; additions have been
made to the chapter on the representative national religions of the past,
particularly to the section on Greek religion, the whole chapter having
been revised. The chapter on Buddhism in its first phase now has new
sections on the Chain of Causation and the Wheel of Life. The most
completely revised and rewritten chapter is that on later Buddhism;
this chapter has been restructured and new material has been added
on the Wisdom That Has Gone Beyond (Prajna-paramita), the Trikaya,
Tibetan Buddhism, Zen, and recent developments in Buddhism. The
chapter on Later Hinduism contains added elements concerned with
the Four Permissible Goals of Life, the Vedanta, and Ramakrishna. Al-

ix

though there has been less change in the remaining chapters, more material has been added on the conquest of Canaan by the Israelites, the Dead Sea Scrolls, and recent developments in Christianity; the chapter on Islam has been completely overhauled to ensure more consistency in its orthography, and the section on the Shi'ite sects has been rewritten for greater historical accuracy. The whole text has been altered at many points to introduce new facts, omit expendable sentences and sections, and in general to ensure greater understanding and clarity.

The Preface to the Second Edition, here omitted, contained a pointer to teachers that may need to be repeated. As was the case in the first edition, the Index contains an abundance of cross-references under many major entries. Such entries could prove useful in the assignment of term papers. Entries such as "Ancestor worship," "Angels," "Asceticism," "Atheism," "Christology," "Church," "Creation," "Ethics," "Future life," "God," "Gods," "Heaven," "Hell," "Incarnation," "Magic," "Man (doctrine of)," "Monism," "Mysticism," "Prayer," "Priesthood," and "Sacrifice" contain references to many faiths of the world. A comprehensive essay based on any of these entries, or on any one of many others contained in the Index but not here listed, could prove of great value to the student, especially if he were encouraged to widen his reading in the absorbing literature concerning man's religions, and thus go beyond this book.

Teachers who might want their students to read beyond this book now have a wealth of paperback books at their disposal. Comprehensive treatments of all the religions now appear in this form. In the Suggestions for General Reading immediately following and in the bibliographies appended to each chapter, paperbacks are designated with the symbol "pb" and might well be used by a teacher who may wish a fuller treatment of a particular chapter (as for instance in considering the religions of Greece and Rome) or who may desire to assign term papers on a particular religion or topic. (After all, libraries seldom have enough copies to go around when term papers are assigned.)

This is possibly a large book for a one-semester course. Should it be necessary to do so, or should concentration on specific areas be advisable, the teacher could select for study particular chapters or groups of chapters and ask the student to read further in paperback or hard cover texts. First-rate supplementary reading is now possible in general anthologies and collections of the scriptures of particular religions.

For valuable contributions in their several ways to the improvement of this edition, I wish particularly warmly to thank Professor Charles S. Braden and the young artist who made the line drawings and maps, Mr. Peter Loewer.

JOHN B. NOSS
Franklin and Marshall College

SUGGESTIONS FOR GENERAL READING

Archer, John C. *Faiths Men Live By.* Nelson, 1938

Atkins, Gaius Glenn, and Braden, Charles S. *Procession of the Gods.* Rev. ed., Harper, 1948

Bouquet, A. C. *Comparative Religion.* Rev. ed., Penguin Books pb, 1950

———. *Sacred Books of the World.* A companion source-book to the above. Penguin Books pb, 1954

Braden, C. S. *Man's Quest for Salvation.* Clark, 1940

———. *Modern Tendencies in World Religions.* Macmillan, 1933

———. *The Scriptures of Mankind.* Macmillan, 1952. Available as pb

———. *The World's Religions.* Rev. ed., Abingdon-Cokesbury, 1942. Available as Apex pb

Burtt, E. A. *Man Seeks the Divine.* Harper, 1956

Clemen, Carl, editor. *Religions of the World.* Harcourt Brace, 1931

Eliade, Mircea. *Patterns in Comparative Religion.* Sheed and Ward, 1958

Ferm, Vergilius, editor. *Forgotten Religions.* Philosophical Library, 1950

———. *Religion in the Twentieth Century.* Philosophical Library, 1948

Finegan, Jack. *Archaeology of the World Religions* (illustrated). Princeton University Press, 1952

Frazer, Sir J. G. *The Golden Bough.* Any edition, Macmillan. Available as pb

Friess and Schneider. *Religion in Various Cultures.* Henry Holt, 1932

Hawkridge, Emma. *The Wisdom Tree* (with line drawings). Houghton Mifflin, 1945

Hopkins, E. W. *The Origin and Evolution of Religion.* Yale University Press, 1923

Hutchison and Martin. *Ways of Faith.* Ronald Press, 1953

James, E. O. *History of Religions.* Harper, 1957

Jurji, Edward, editor. *The Great Religions of the Modern World.* Princeton University Press, 1946

King, Winston L. *Introduction to Religion.* Harper, 1954

Moore, George F. *History of Religions.* 2 vols., Scribner's, 1920

Otto, Rudolph. *Mysticism East and West.* Oxford, 1924. Available as Meridian pb

Radhakrishnan, S., chairman editorial board. *History of Philosophy Eastern and Western.* Sponsored by the Ministry of Education, Government of India. 2 vols. George Allen and Unwin, 1952

Smith, Huston. *The Religions of Man.* Mentor pb, 1959

GENERAL ANTHOLOGIES

Ballou, R. O., editor. *The Bible of the World.* Viking, 1939. Available as pb in Viking Portable series

Browne, Lewis, editor. *The World's Scriptures.* Macmillan, 1946. Available as pb

deBary, Wm. Theodore, editor. *Sources of the Indian Tradition.* Columbia University Press, 1958

———. *Sources of the Japanese Tradition.* Columbia University Press, 1958

———. *Sources of the Chinese Tradition.* Columbia University Press, 1960

Lessa, William A. and Vogt, E. Z., editors. *Reader in Comparative Religion: An Anthropological Approach.* Row Peterson, Evanston, Illinois, 1958

Lin Yutang, editor. *The Wisdom of China and India.* Random House, 1942

Preface to the
FIRST EDITION

THIS BOOK HAS BEEN WRITTEN TO MEET TWO SPECIFIC NEEDS: THAT, FIRST, for an introduction to the world's religions containing adequate amounts of descriptive or interpretative details from the original source materials; and that, second, for a presentation of man's most noteworthy faiths in a time-setting that will do justice to their development as well as to their origins. A sufficient number of books now deal with the founders or founding of the great religions; and many others present the various religions as they are or recently have been. This book seeks, as a major aim, to bridge the interval between the founding of the religions and their present state. It is hoped, incidentally, that the frequent quotations from the original source materials—or from authoritative accounts—will make the highly human quality of each religion evident, and thus excite the reader to further reading in a vast field.

Had the author foreseen all that would be involved in his task when he began, he would have been appalled; but he now hopes he would have continued anyway; for the difficulty of the work confronting him over a long period of intensive study and composition has been more than matched by the fascination and enjoyment which have steadily accompanied it. It seems to him a certainty that any sympathetic inquiry into the faith and understanding reflected in man's religions must have such results; and he earnestly prays that readers of his book, not content with what is set down here, may go on to their own greatly rewarding research and discovery. If they find errors in his account, they may then be able to correct him.

It has been a major problem in the making of this book to present an adequate account of the great faiths within what must be called, in spite of many pages, a limited space. To tell the story of religion with as complete objectivity as one can muster, and in accordance with the findings of the latest scholarship, is difficult enough; but to be fair and yet brief, comprehensive and yet concise, interested in the riches of humanizing detail and yet true to proportion and balance of treatment are aims still more difficult, perhaps impossible, to attain. Moreover, the judgment expressed in some reviews of recent books on the world's religions, that no one person can any longer write a competent book on the entire field, since the subject requires for its adequate treatment a panel of experts, is a cause for great diffidence. On the other hand, one may remark, a book by a panel of experts may run into difficulties, too. The chapters may vary widely in the amount of detail which is thought necessary; in spite of every effort to avoid it, there may be overlapping, or the opposite—hiatuses; and there usually are marked differences in pace and literary quality. Not only schematic completeness, but even unity of perspective, may be absent.

Perhaps, then, when there is so much need in our time for books that will broaden our understanding of all peoples, this one needs no further warrant to make its appearance.

It would be impossible here to make the many acknowledgments to the men and books, teachers, fellow-students, and scholars whence this book has drawn everything of value that it contains. The bibliographies at the end of each chapter, the long list of books under copyright from which so many of the quotations have come, and the still longer list of quoted references at the end of the book are inadequate gestures in this direction. To readers for the Macmillan Company, who made many helpful comments on the incomplete first draft of this book, the author owes special thanks. One of them, Professor Horace L. Friess of Columbia University, has since become known to him, and has read the entire manuscript when it was nearing its final form. To his discerning judgment on both general and particular points he wishes to pay special tribute; whatever errors and shortcomings this book still possesses must surely exist despite his aid and counsel, for his scholarship is as exact as it is wide.

Finally, to his wife, who encouraged, sympathized with, and endured him during the summers on Mt. Desert Island, on the coast of Maine, where most of this book was written, the author owes most of all.

JOHN B. NOSS

Note: All numbers in the text following quotations, e.g.[1], refer to Quoted References, pp. 779 ff. For pronunciation of unfamiliar names see Index.

Contents

xv

PART FOUR The Religions of the Near East

PART ONE

Primitive and Bygone Religions

Foreword to
PART ONE

ALL RELIGIONS SAY IN ONE WAY OR ANOTHER THAT MAN DOES NOT, AND cannot, stand alone. He is vitally related with and even dependent on powers in Nature and Society external to himself. Dimly or clearly, he knows that he is not an independent center of force capable of standing apart from the world.

This realization ranges from primitive conceptions of dependence on powers and forces in the immediate social and natural environment to conceptions in the high religions of a first cause of all things, a being personal or impersonal that has produced the universe and is the present basis of its existence and functioning. In either case the religions, as a general rule, relate men closely with the Power or powers at work in Nature and Society.

Although belief in God in the higher religions has sometimes led men to think meanly of the world around them, in the faith that they are pilgrims and strangers here on earth, and heaven is their home, this belief is far from typical of men's religions in general; it is in fact a special sort of belief produced under special conditions. The general attitude is that the relation between man and his world is organic and vital, not accidental and external. If the outer face of Nature is sometimes mistrusted, it is usually in the name of something deeper within that is assigned a higher degree of reality.

Most men, from primitives in the jungles to members of societies far advanced in culture, do not think that men are all that matters. To think this is to run counter to a very deep feeling, namely, that man depends for life and fullness of being on forces outside himself that share in some sense his own nature and with which he must be in harmony. The harmony thus sought is sometimes a harmony in action, as in primitive religions; or it is a moral and spiritual harmony, as in the great religions of the Near East; or the harmony sought is more than a harmony, it is a complete and final identity, as in most of the religions of India and the Far East.

To realize all this is to have sympathy with primitive as well as with advanced religions. The former may say what they have to say mythically, or unscientifically, or in unquestioning acceptance of sense experience or of inherited tradition; but their quest is not unlike that of religions in the larger and more inclusive cultures.

Before we enter on the story of early and bygone religions, we might consider the word "primitive" we have just used. Many careful students of the world's cultures use it with hesitancy, because it connotes lack of development and inferiority. As a matter of fact, primitive cultures are often richly developed and have much to commend them qualitatively. Even more out of favor is the word "savage." This word suggests cruelty, amorality, and barbarism, three terms that are as far from being universally characteristic of preliterate cultures as they are of presumably "higher" literate ones. We can drop its use without loss; but the word "primitive" is hard to replace. "Preliterate" is not satisfactory because it calls attention too emphatically to only one aspect of the cultures to which it applies. With some hesitancy, then, we shall use the word "primitive" hereafter for those smaller, less informed, and more isolated societies whose technology is not as highly developed as in "civilized" societies and whose religious systems are regarded by all in the group, without exception, as indispensable to social harmony and satisfactory adaptation to the immediate environment.

1 Religion in Prehistoric and Primitive Cultures

To one who is confined to it yet does not have the resources of scientific language and description to explain it, the immediate environment is full of mysteries. This is the case of primitive man. His religion has been a necessity to him, for it has provided ways of behaving with the least strain toward mysterious realities—natural forces, ancestral spirits, and the powers felt to be present in men and their social institutions. But when he has acquired the experience to locate his immediate environment in a larger natural setting, he has developed a longer reach of thought and a wider kind of relationship, in which "high gods," "national gods," and "lords of heaven" appear.

In order to understand this, it is well to begin as far back in time as we can go. We turn therefore briefly to prehistoric times.

I   STONE AGE RELIGION

> O ancient cousin,
> O Neanderthaler!
> What shapes beguiled, what shadows fled across
> Your early mind?

4

Here are your bones,
And hollow crumbled skull,
And here your shapen flints—the last inert
Mute witnesses to so long vanished strength.

What loves had you,
What words to speak,
What worships,
Cousin?

Could we find answers to these questions, they might help us to determine when and how religion began. But that is not certain. Since religion is a product of the earliest attempt of the human mind to achieve
a sense of security in the world, the Neanderthaler may not have been
the first religious man. But it is idle to speculate whether he had predecessors. Certainly the story of religion cannot begin in any significant
sense with the first sub-men, like Pithecanthropus, who appeared over
500,000 years ago; for when we consider the remains they left—the
edged flints or eoliths which they used in their difficult struggle for
existence—we can tell very little about the degree of their intelligence,
much less whether they had a religion or not.

As to the Neanderthalers, who, after a long gap, flourished from
100,000 to 25,000 years ago, definite evidence of their religion is in their
graves. The burial of their dead suggests that food offerings (of which
broken bones remain) and flint implements were placed in the grave
during a ceremonial interment. There are signs also of other beliefs.
Evidence has recently accumulated that the Neanderthalers treated the
cave bear with special reverence. They hunted him at great peril to
themselves, and respected his spirit even after he was dead. They
appear to have set aside certain cave bear skulls, with the brains, a
great delicacy, still intact in them, and also certain long (or marrow)
bones, and to have placed them with special care on elevated slabs of
stone or on shelves in their caves, in order to make them the center
of some kind of ritual. Whether their bear-cult was simply a propitiation
of the bear-spirit, or whether it was a form of hunting magic to ensure
the success of the next hunt, or yet again whether it was a sacrifice
or votive offering to some divinity having to do with the inter-relations
of man and bear, is a matter of controversy among authorities.* Another
subject of debate is the Neanderthal treatment of human skulls. Some

---

* See for various views V. G. Childe, *The Prehistory of European Society* (London, 1957) and Johannes Maringer, *The Gods of Prehistoric Man* (ed. and trans.
from the German edition of 1956; New York, 1960).

of the skulls are found, singly or in series, without the accompaniment of the other bones of the body, each decapitated (sometimes even pierced with a round hole) in such a way as to suggest that the brains were extracted and eaten. The evidence is inconclusive as to whether the emptied skulls were placed in a ritual position for memorial rites or whether the Neanderthalers were head hunters who ate in some sacramental way the brains, whether of sacrificial victims, the newly dead, or enemies, to acquire the soul-force in them. In either case it would seem that the Neanderthalers were at least aware of spirit-powers and that animism, a rather advanced mode of thought, had already developed.

When we come to the later and higher culture levels of the Old Stone Age, since 25,000 years ago—to the period of the so-called Cro-Magnon men of Europe and their African peers—we are left in less doubt as to the precise nature of Old Stone Age religious conviction and practice.

The Cro-Magnons were a finely developed race of true men, with skulls somewhat larger than those of modern man. Some anthropologists note a close resemblance to certain groups in the world today, like the Sikhs. The Cro-Magnons were, then, among the taller, more robust members of the human race. They came into a milder climate than that which made so hazardous the existence of the Neanderthalers whom they replaced; and, being free to wander, they lived a more or less nomadic life, although they used caves and shelters during the colder seasons. They lived by gathering roots and wild fruits and by hunting, their larger prey being bison, aurochs, an occasional mammoth, and especially the reindeer and the wild horse. Evidence of their hunting prowess has been found at an open-air camp of theirs discovered at Solutre, in south-central France, where archaeologists have unearthed the bones of 100,000 horses, together with those of reindeer, mammoths, and bison—the remains of centuries of feasting. The Cro-Magnons probably never tamed and domesticated the horse, but they found him good eating. The horse, bearded and small, moved in large herds, was highly vulnerable to attack, and not dangerous.

In somewhat similar fashion as the Neanderthalers before them, the Cro-Magnons buried their dead, choosing the same kind of burial sites, not unnaturally at the mouth of their grottos or near their shelters; and they surrounded the body with ornaments, weapons, and food. Of great interest is the fact that they practiced the custom of painting or pouring red coloring matter (red ochre) on the body, or, at some time subsequent to burial, on the bones.

Paint played a large part in their lives, in fact. The most remarkable cultural achievement of the Cro-Magnons was their painting and modeling. They could draw, paint murals, mold clay figures, carve in the round, or engrave on bone and antlers, with a realism unsurpassed by the art of any known primeval men. Their chief subjects were animals of the hunt, the bison, the horse, the wild boar, reindeers, cave bears, and mammoths. Human figures were comparatively rare; they usually appear in the form of statuettes and are extraordinarily fat and obviously symbolic.

Many of the engravings and paintings were executed on the walls of gloomy caves, by the light of torches or shallow soapstone lamps fed with fat. So far from the cave-mouth and in such nearly inaccessible places did the artists do their work, that they could hardly have had public display of their murals chiefly in view. What then had they in mind?

The answer which seems the most consistent with all the facts is that the practices of the Cro-Magnons included a magical use of the painted and carved figures. That there were medicine men among them is beyond all doubt. A vivid mural in the cavern of Trois-Freres shows a masked man, arrayed in reindeer antlers, bear's ears, and the tail of a horse, who vividly represents a well-known figure in primitive communities, the medicine man or magician. If he was not the actual artist, he conducted the rituals which made use of the paintings and clay figures. Just as among primitive peoples today it is believed that an image or picture can be a magical substitute for the object of which it is the representation, so the Cro-Magnons evidently felt that whoever made an image of an animal subjected it to his influence or somehow brought it into his power. The magical use made of the realistic murals and plastic works of the Paleolithic era is evident in several clear examples. In the cavern of Montespan there is a clay figure of a bear whose body is covered with representations of dart thrusts. Similarly, in the cavern of Niaux an engraved and painted bison is marked with rudely painted outlines of spears and darts, mutely indicating the climax of some primeval hunt; clearly, the excited Cro-Magnon hunters, gathering before the hunt, ceremonially anticipated and insured their success, by having their leaders (medicine men?) paint upon the body of their intended quarry, so vividly pictured on the cave wall, the crude representations of their hunting weapons. They went on the assumptions of sympathetic magic that to foresee is to foreordain, and that like produces like.

Another sort of interest in painting and carving appears in many of the representations of human beings. Tiny sculptured figures of the human female, usually from four to six inches high, are sometimes found in Upper Paleolithic art. Most of them, like the famous Venus of Willendorf, are obviously meant to symbolize fecundity; the extremities of the figures taper away without much attempt at realistic representation; the faces are usually blank and round; while exaggerated emphasis is placed upon fatness, or largeness of hips, breasts, and abdomen. The use of such mother figures in fertility magic seems indicated. In the realm of painting, one mural shows mares painted in foal, and another, in the rock shelter of Cogul, Spain, depicts nine women surrounding a naked male, who seems to be either the subject of a tribal initiation at puberty or the leader in a ritual connected with fertility magic.

It thus appears that Paleolithic man used both fertility and hunting magic, with evident faith in their value as methods of control.

Of direct religious significance are the beliefs implicit in the burial customs of the Cro-Magnons. Since the dead were interred with special ceremonies, near to the shelters in which they lived before death, were flanked in their shallow graves by flint implements, ornaments, and food, and were covered with red paint (symbolizing, no doubt, the redness of the lifeblood), the belief cannot have been less than that the dead survived in some real sense, though there may have been no conception of the survival of a nonphysical spiritual entity; whatever survived had a ghostly corporeality and bodily needs and desires.

Associated with such beliefs there must have been both awe and fear of the dead.* Memories of the dead while they yet lived contributed to both these feelings, and so also did dreams and visions in which the dead appeared. But the determinative factor in creating the sense of something superhuman about the dead was a conception that must have been already well developed—that of a highly potent realm of being or process operative in the forms and forces of Nature.

There are some indications that the Cro-Magnons may have made offerings to powers of nature as well as to their dead. In Germany, at Meierdorf and Stellmoor, young does with large stones placed inside their rib cages were evidently submerged in run-off lakes left by the retreating glaciers of the last ice age; apparently the hunters sacrificed these animals to some nature power on which their success depended. The Cro-Magnons also had a bear-cult, not unlike that of their predecessors, the Neanderthalers; perhaps they wished to propitiate a bear-god;

---

* This would seem to be definitely established by the skeletons of Stone Age dead, which show that corpses were trussed up, bandaged, and buried under heavy stones to keep them from coming back to torment the living.

Cro-Magnon sorcerer dancing in the guise of a bison, with a bow-shaped magical instrument suspended from his mouth, as he pursues a reindeer and an animal suggestive of a bison. (From the Trois Freres Cave)

if so, however, they also applied coercive measures (magic), as is shown by their murals and clay figures of bears, the clay images sometimes punctured with wounds, and the painted figures spouting blood from mouth, nostrils, and body wounds, apparently in the death agony. Clearly, whatever religion they had was inextricably combined with procedures designed to ensure magical success.

This brings us definitely to the Neolithic Age (10,000 to 3000 B.C.), the age in which were developed the art of polishing stone implements like the axe and the arrowhead, the early forms of agriculture, the domestication of animals, the arts of pottery, plaiting and weaving, the building of rude houses and boats, and the first surgery. Marked refinements and improvements were made in religion. The burial rites increased in importance and complexity. Funerals were conducted with elaborate ceremony, including, in some cases, human sacrifice of wives and servants. Burials were made under gigantic boulders, in artificial caves, and in stone chambers, now called dolmens, which were often constructed with incredible labor out of huge stones. Another important development was the cremation of the dead practiced in some regions.

Among the mysteries of archaeological research are the megalithic monuments known as menhirs (single huge stones on end), dolmens (upright stones topped by a cap-stone), and cromlechs and alinements (stones in series, like the Stone Henge). The only certain fact seems to be that they were, in some way not now known, connected with religion, perhaps marking a sacred spot and serving as the center for religious worship and sacrifice on important occasions or at special seasons.

The Neolithic Age is the first to leave us unmistakable relics of nature worship. These include numerous round symbols of the sun and moon. Stones and pillars were venerated. There are suggestions of star and tree worship as well; and the mingling of old fears with a certain sophistication rising from the power obtained by the use of new inventions is shown in the fact that axes, spears, and spoked wheels were venerated as fetishes.

That magic grew into a complex system in the Neolithic Age is suggested by the many painted pebbles which have been preserved, covered with symbols probably having magical significance, though this may not afford a complete explanation of their use.

With this we pause. What have we found? Already developed religious beliefs and practices. But how did religion *begin*? This is the still unsolved problem. It is evident that the relics of the Stone Age form no more than a check or control upon a more fundamental, psychological inquiry—one outside the scope of this volume—that must proceed by a careful use of conjecture. Such conjecture cannot be attempted without a profound knowledge of contemporary primitive religion. Our inquiry also turns in this direction.

II THE GENERAL CHARACTERISTICS OF RELIGION IN PRIMITIVE CULTURES TODAY

Among primitive peoples today, the supernatural scene is infinitely variegated. When we measure the beliefs and practices of any one locality against those of another, almost any particular belief or practice can be matched with its opposite or contradiction. On the surface, generalization would appear to be difficult.

But similarities exist. Primitive men have certain general characteristics and their religious systems have a number of common features.

Some General Characteristics of Primitive Man

A marked characteristic of people in primitive societies is this: with few exceptions, they are so personally identified with the group or community to which they belong that they virtually never fall back upon their own private judgment regarding what may be called public matters. Each man must, of course, make his own choices in the restricted sphere in which he acts in his private capacity, but even there he is not as fully an individual as are men who live in the more highly differentiated, technologically more advanced cultures. In fact, it was not so long ago the fashion to deny him even private thought, under the widely held view that he acted solely in accordance with a mystical or prelogical sense of the group mind; but recent field work in primitive societies proves this view to be extreme. The "group mind" is a convenient fiction of earlier sociology; and there is now ample evidence to show that primitives, while perhaps on the whole unanalytical and nonlogical, are capable of both inductive and deductive reasoning and therefore of a rational ordering of their lives. Moreover, gifted or atypical individuals—the analogues of geniuses and talented eccentrics in other cultures—may in rare instances add new content to the old traditions and thus expand the range of thought and action. On the whole, however, tradition and custom are closely followed.

Another way of putting the matter is to say that for the most part primitives resist change and have what may be called a religious fear of departing even by an iota from the traditional customs and beliefs of the group. The reasons for this may be given briefly.

The old customs and beliefs are adaptive in nature, unifying, comfortable, and sacred. They are adaptive in the sense that they are the means by which primitives have learned, with what they feel to be success, to adapt themselves as individuals and groups to their environment; they are unifying because they are the means by which unanimity in action is attained; they are comfortable because they provide for every individual a not too difficult life pattern that is suited to his status and approved in advance;* and they are sacred because it is felt that the ancestors and the spirits that most affect the well-being of the group have hallowed them.

On closer inspection, these customs and beliefs are seen to be in response to strong biological and psychological demands.

The biological basis of custom and belief is this: the convictions and practices of any one primitive group serve to provide satisfaction

---

* Although it is a fact that in many a primitive group there are "contrary ones" who apparently rebel against the practices of their group (American Indians have called them "crazy horses"), primitives almost universally prefer to run, so to say, on schedules, according to commonly accepted and detailed patterns of behavior. This is a universal human tendency.

of the so-called "basic drives," variously identified and named by anthropologists. (Perhaps Sumner and Keller's list in their *Science and Society* will do as well as any: hunger, love, vanity, and fear; although two qualifications are in order: fear should certainly be interpreted as not itself a drive but the emotional accompaniment of one, namely, the basic impulse to withdraw from situations that threaten pain or death; furthermore, the list should have added to it aggression or the impulse to act to achieve satisfaction or to prevent frustration.) The primitive man has no knowledge of these biologically based drives; nor does he truly understand what happens within him when they are frustrated; but the patterns of culture to which he is bred have, in the manner allowed by environment and social conditioning, risen primarily to satisfy these drives, directly or indirectly, and thus reduce their urgency (as when hunger is reduced by eating); and he senses, without being quite aware of it, that this is the case with himself. His culture, including of course his religion, has no known over-all value for him that he can identify clearly, if asked, unless it be an economic one; but he clings to it tenaciously, until he is forced into change, because it is just that complex of habits and procedures which, in his area and under the economic conditions prevailing, is his best available means of satisfying easily and smoothly the maximum number of his drives, both basic and derived. He is therefore deeply uneasy and anxious if his experiences defy his attempts to construe them as instances of already known processes, to be reacted to in the old, familiar ways.

But the role of the biological factors underlying patterns of culture should not be given too exclusive a stress. Psychological reactions and needs also play a very important role. This could be illustrated by many examples. It is widely true, to take a single case, that the shaman or medicine man is by temperament or through emotional imbalance an introverted type of person who suffers from obscure tensions, anxieties, and frustrations, and is predisposed to solitary reflection and moody abstraction; he therefore comes to believe what he is told—that he is set apart for the experience of spirit-possession, and should let an experienced shaman take him in hand and train him. Such individuals are more likely than others to have religious experiences and to find their true calling in being a mediator between less religiously sensitive people and the spirits. The religious experiences of such psychologically predisposed individuals usually conform to type; that is, they do not widely depart from tradition; but they may take a novel turn and lead to shifts of emphasis in the practice of long-established religious and magical rites. At all events, the more stolid members of the tribe will rely upon their shamans for authentic information concerning the reigning spirits and what is to be done to keep them in a good mood.

But the forms that religion and magic take are affected not only by such peculiarly sensitive individuals but as much or more by group-developments taking a certain turn. A classic example is that of the islanders of Dobu. Here the psychological factors override the biological ones, and induce a biologically unsatisfactory state of public opinion bordering on paranoia: each man's hand is turned against his neighbor in black magic, fraud, and theft; the spirits are uniformly believed to be demonic and sadistic; the priests are dreaded sorcerers; and community life is riddled with fear, suspicion, jealousy and resentment. If it is true that the Dobuan pattern of culture is the local means of satisfying the biological drives, it does this under the severe handicap of psychologically induced hostility, insecurity, and outright terror. The islanders of Dobu are not unique in the primitive world, for other negativistic societies can be cited, such as that of the people of Alor in New Guinea; but it is more common to find tribes of a pacific disposition with comparatively well-disposed spirits and gods.

Perhaps the clue to much that characterizes primitive cultures lies in the fact that primitive man is not often critical of his sensations, because he lives so completely in them. Such sensations are not introspectively analyzed; they are usually accepted for what they are on their surface, whether they spring from firsthand dealings with the realities of the external world, from imaginative reconstructions of such realities, or from interpretations of group experience conveyed through parental instruction and discipline or through tribal tradition and the current beliefs of the group. Psychologists have called this "primitive credulity." It may be said, therefore, that the mental life of primitives is not often complicated by qualifications or hesitancies concerning sense experience. What seems real is real. One authority on primitive cultures says:

> It is one of the salient traits of so-called primitive man, that he allows a full and appreciative expression to his sensations. He is preeminently a man of practical common sense just as is the average peasant . . . This tough-mindedness leads to the recognition of all types of realities, realities which primitive man sees in all their directness and ruggedness, stripped of all that false and sentimental haze so universal among civilized peoples.[1]

The paradox here, however, is this: that the very realism of the primitive in accepting his sensations at their face value, in all their "directness and ruggedness," lends itself to the most fantastic constructions upon experience; all sorts of ideas of life come to be true for him—because his sensations have told him so. And if his group shares his sensations, either directly or through his ability to communicate them; if, that is to say, he and his group feel alike about the truth of some notion or impression, there never is any question: what they all feel to be so, is so.

It is in the light of these facts that we should regard the common features of contemporary primitive religion which we are about to review. However unscientific and fanciful the beliefs and practices which come up for examination are, all have this high practical value: by means of them primitives have arrived at patterns of culture which meet the needs their economic situation, their drives, and their psychological reactions have combined to create in them. Moreover, these practices and beliefs unite the group firmly and provide each person with an approved social role to play.

The Common Features of Primitive Religions

1. *Recognition of the sacred.* An outsider visiting a primitive group would find that the first sign of the religious significance of a place, person, thing, ritual or event is that it is clearly regarded as sacred. A primitive man regards anything sacred or holy with a distinctive attitude uniting respect and caution. The sacred possesses such significance that he never deals with it carelessly or casually, as he may handle his oar and his spear or converse with the members of his family. The sacred signifies supernatural potency, both enlivening and deadly, a power for quick good or bad, and one's attitude toward it may determine whether good or bad will ensue. Anything sacred carries with it the promise of a blessing; but rarely can any but qualified persons, such as chiefs, shamans, priests, and heads of families, deal with the sacred without harm. Impious handling of sacred objects may cause sudden death. The proper approach therefore is with a sense of holy mystery, awe, reverence, and devout "fear of the Lord."

As we proceed, we shall see that the following topics all introduce, in one way or another, the category of the sacred.

2. *Expression of anxiety in ritual.* In the presence of the sacred there is a certain anxiety. Will the holy power be stirred to action? Will this action be favorable? As soon as this anxiety arises, there is a need to act and speak in ways that may promise a favorable outcome. This is the fundamental basis of religious ritual. Malinowski, the famous anthropologist, has put this point well so far as magical rituals are concerned:

In a maritime community depending on the products of the sea there is never magic connected with the collecting of shellfish or with fishing by poison, weirs, and fish traps, so long as these are completely reliable. On the other hand, any dangerous, hazardous, and uncertain type of fishing is surrounded by ritual. In hunting, the simple and reliable ways of trapping or killing are controlled by knowledge and skill alone; but let there be any danger or any uncertainty connected with an important supply of game and magic immediately appears. Coastal sailing as long as it is perfectly safe and easy commands no magic. Overseas expeditions are invariably bound up with ceremonies and ritual.[2]

Religious rituals are similarly conditioned. While it is true that praise, thanksgiving, and desire for communion with divine beings provide much of the content of religious ritual, anthropologists claim that in most religious situations anxiety exists in at least two forms. First, there is a primary anxiety arising from crises or strains in the life of the individual or the community, and this calls forth rituals whose purpose is to provide reassurance; but once these rituals have been firmly established, with their mythical and institutional accompaniments, a secondary anxiety lest the rituals have *not* been promptly enough nor properly performed gives rise to further rituals of purification and expiation.[*] The rituals of primitive peoples therefore not only comfort and reassure but also bind the individuals participating in them to their further performance, for fear that failure to do so will be followed by unhappy consequences.

3. *Inextricable intermingling of religion and magic.* Mention of both religious and magical rites was made in the previous paragraph. There have been many attempts to distinguish clearly between them, with only moderate success. Sir James G. Frazer, for example, saw a chronological as well as formal difference. He believed that magic was early man's attempt to coerce the powers of nature by the use of certain procedures, such as the rituals of sympathetic magic, the effect of which was to establish control over these powers; such rituals constituted a false science, but early man trusted in them. Sometimes, however, he found that the powers of nature were beyond the control of magic; and so he resorted to coaxings and persuasions (prayer), in the hope of favorable response. Religion appeared when magic failed. While this attempt at a distinction has some value, it has been rejected by investigators of primitive societies because (1) no chronological sequence from

---

[*] See pp. 85–118 of Lessa and Vogt, *Reader in Comparative Religion* (Evanston, 1958) for discussion of these points by Malinowski, Radcliffe-Brown, and George C. Homans. The last makes an especially valuable summary statement.

magic to religion can be found, and (2) religious and magical procedures, even when their distinction in definition is allowed, are often
so inextricably combined that they must be seen as at most two aspects
of one ritual. There is some value in saying that where rituals are coercive in intent, they have the character of magic, and where they are
persuasive, they are religious. Value may also attach to Emile Durkheim's view that religious rites are obligatory and magical ones optional;
but this holds true only partially. Much the same thing may be said
of Malinowski's suggestion that magic is a means to a precise end in
view, whereas religion has no immediate practical result in mind but
is an end in itself. The difficulty with all these distinctions is that
instances can be found where no one of them completely applies. For
example, a primitive magician may in the course of a single ritual
coax, beg, peremptorily command, and even threaten the spirits. Frazer's
distinction obviously loses point here; but so do Malinowski's and Durkheim's as well. Perhaps we can say that each of these distinctions has
some use, provided we bear in mind that magic and religion are not
to be classed separately but seen as two distinguishable aspects of the
rituals used in primitive societies.*

4. *Belief in mana.* This is sometimes called *dynamism. Mana* is a
Melanesian term, adopted by anthropologists as a convenient designation for the widespread belief in occult force or indwelling power as
such, independent of either persons or spirits; but it is not the only term
of the kind in circulation among primitive peoples. The same sort of
reaction is closely reflected in various quite parallel terms used by the
American Indians, some tribes of Morocco, the Pygmies of middle Africa,
the Bantu of South Africa, and aboriginal peoples in many other parts
of the world. Taken together all such terms refer to the experienced
presence of a powerful but silent force in things, especially any occult
force which is believed to act of itself, as an addition to the forces
naturally or usually present in a thing. It operates most evidently and
freely through persons and in living or moving things. It is a force that
is thought to be transmissible from objects in nature to man, from one
person to another, or again from persons to things. Hence the importance

---

* It could well be added that even in theologically sophisticated religious systems, religion can seldom be found in a pure state. In the Christian religion, for
example, baptism and the Lord's Supper are often regarded as necessary to ensure,
as if automatically and by magical compulsion or coercion, the worshiper's eventual
entrance into Heaven.

The references for the above distinctions are: Malinowski, *Myth, Magic and
Religion;* Frazer, *The Golden Bough;* and Durkheim, *The Elementary Forms of
the Religious Life.*

it has for primitive folk. Not that primitives, even of today, conceive of nature as being a unified system of energies, but that the whole world is felt to be energy-pervaded. In the last analysis, the concept of *mana* indicates response to the vitally significant or extraordinary in quality, as distinguished from the ordinary, the usual, or the normal in quality. The extraordinary in quality—whether in events or in the character of some forceful man or powerful beast—by its very nature draws attention to itself; and though a primitive fears whatever is eerie or mysterious, he is practical and hard-headed enough to want to have such a mysterious efficacy as *mana* brought to his aid or infused into himself or his spear or the vegetables in his garden. He therefore uses what measures he can to assure himself of these effects, and his heritage in fact provides him with an abundance of magical procedures toward this end.

5. *Animism.* There is general acceptance among present-day primitives of the animistic belief that all sorts of motionless objects as well as living and moving creatures have souls or spirits in them, and that every human being has a soul or souls leaving the body temporarily during dreams and with a kind of finality at death. This notion of souls and spirits has a meaning quite distinct from that of *mana,* the last being in itself impersonal, although a soul or spirit may acquire it or be its outlet in action. Souls and spirits are usually conceived of in a thorough-going anthropomorphic fashion; they have shape, mind, feelings, and will or purpose; they are like living people in being amenable to reason in good moods, and aggressively quarrelsome when angry or upset; they like flattery, devotion, loyalty; they are often not to be trusted out of one's remembrance; eternal vigilance is the price of being on the right side of them, and one must be ever on the alert to continue in their good graces, once obtained. A cardinal fact about the world-view of the primitive peoples is that in their conception, to use the language of E. B. Tylor, "all nature is possessed, pervaded, crowded with spiritual beings." [3] These beings are of the utmost significance and importance to the primitive, because they are power-centers, constantly affecting every man's destiny and interests.

6. *Veneration and worship of spirits.* It has been said truly that man has worshipped everything he could think of beneath the earth, everything between earth and heaven, and everything in the heavens above.[4] Sometimes it is the object itself which is worshipped as living and active, heavily charged with *mana.* Again, the object is not worshipped for itself but for the spirit or soul lodged or inhering in it. Once more, the object is not worshipped at all; it becomes a symbol of the reality which *is* worshipped and which it visibly and tangibly

represents. All three of these modes of worship may at times go on simultaneously, since, as in the case of the worship of idols in India, some ignorant worshipers regard the idol itself as alive, others suppose there is a spirit resident in it, while the cultivated or philosophically-minded devotee makes use of it as a convenient thought-center for symbolizing the reality behind all.

Short of worship, which expresses adoration and is usually accompanied by prayer and praise, are veneration and awe. These include respect and the acknowledgment of the presence of sacred power or quality. Sometimes it is difficult to know where veneration ends and worship begins.

The veneration of *stones* has been widespread. The stones may be of any size, from pebble to boulder, and in any amount, single, in series, or even in heaps. Often they are remarkable in shape or composition. Sometimes they are shaped by human art or skill, as in the case of flint tools or weapons. Aerolites are often venerated, the classic instance being that of the Ka'bah stone at Mecca, which every Moslem pilgrim kisses to acquire its saving virtues. Veneration of shaped stones, and of *any tool* or *implement,* not only existed in prehistoric times, but may be found today in Africa, Oceania, India, Japan, and among North American Indians. Among the primitives of the Philippine Islands the headman's weapons are held to be charged with a vital force that can act of itself. A passage from an account of these people says of one chieftain: "He was no ordinary mortal. . . . His companions insisted that his headaxe and spear killed at his bidding." [5] This sort of belief is not uncommon. The axe is still venerated in the rural districts of Germany and Scandinavia. Veneration of this kind was general in the Graeco-Roman world.

The veneration of *plants* and *trees* is virtually universal among primitive peoples and frequent in more complex cultures. Survivals of such veneration in sophisticated societies are seen in the use of the Christmas tree and of the Maypole. It is said that in Europe, in the Upper Palatinate, woodmen still murmur a plea for forgiveness to a large, fine tree before they cut it down. Not only do trees and plants inspire reverence, but they also represent an exhaustless productivity. Deification of trees, and also of plants and grains, is a natural tribute to the mysterious growth-forces of nature. Trees help crops to grow, assist flocks and herds to multiply, and make women fertile. Barren women are sometimes married to trees in order that they may become fruitful.

Animal-veneration is another almost universal element of primitive religion. It springs up naturally from the feeling that animals are akin to man in unusual degree. So near is the relationship often conceived to be that many peoples have had little difficulty in believing that the soul of a man at death, and even during life, readily passes into the body of an animal, and vice versa. Myths and fairy tales abound in characters such as frog-maidens, bird-women, and vampires who alternately appear in human and bat shapes; while were-tigers and werewolves have contributed a thrill to many a tale of disaster and bloodshed. The lion in Africa; the tiger in Malaya; the eagle, the bear, and the beaver in North America; the bull in Greece and Egypt; the cow in India, Africa, and Scandinavia; the buffalo in South India; the kangaroo in Australia, are among the fierce and strong or gentle and life-sustaining creatures that men have honored with their veneration. Similarly, reverence has been paid to the goose, the dove, and the snake. The last, whether in the form of the sinuous serpent or the winged dragon, has been reverenced under a hundred forms and symbols, of which both the water connections and the phallic associations have been among the chief fascinations for the worshiper.

Rather late in the history of religions comes reverence for the *"elements"* of the world, considered in the abstract—earth, air, fire, and water; though fire, the least abstract because less diffused, has been revered since the dawn of historic times, and probably in the Old Stone Age. The Parsees still honor it. The sky (or space) came at last to be worshipped as the home of the clouds, winds, sun, moon, and stars, themselves regarded as animate. Water, more difficult to conceive of abstractly, was venerated in its discrete forms, fountains, springs, rivers, lakes, and finally the sea, whose hold upon the imagination is such that its worship characterized all early civilizations and continued late into the Middle Ages, when the Doge of Venice was annually married to the Adriatic. In much the same way men have worshipped Earth, the universal mother and grain-bearer.

7. *Recognition of high gods.* This is the natural place to raise the disputed question whether primitive peoples have been widely given to religious relationships with a *high god,* a supreme being. It is common to find among many primitive groups a recognition of the existence of a god far up in the sky or at a great remove, who has made everything, man, earth, sea, and sky, and who at a distance sees all that goes on among men, but, though he sometimes disapproves of what he sees, does not often interfere. Among the lower primitives, like the Pygmies of Africa, the Fuegians of South America, and the Australian bushmen, the belief in such a high god has been even clearer and more definite. It

has been an old belief of these most backward races, that the high god formerly lived on earth, instructed men in their social and moral laws, and then retired to the sky-land, where he keeps an eye on men's doings and sometimes severely punishes their lapses. Lightning is his weapon, thunder his roaring; but he himself is never seen.

A dispute has arisen among anthropologists as to whether this high god has the religious significance of the nearer spirit-powers of the earth. The prevailing opinion is rather negative. Primitive men have not had to be concerned daily about the high god. He is supreme and uncreated, existing from the beginning; but other spirits are much more active as determiners of destiny down on the earth. If there have been any exceptions to this comparative evaluation, we come across them among the Australian bushmen and the Fuegians. The former in some localities address prayers for food to the supreme being, and the latter thought he caused all deaths. Yet the members of one of the Fuegian tribes used to speak of him in the third person, as if he had no direct dealings with them. Moreover, they sometimes issued threats against him, which precludes their having thought him really supreme. But this matter may be left in dispute. Probably, the idea of a great Originator, who has little to do with men in the ordinary course of life, arose very naturally when an answer was attempted to such questions as: "Where did our rituals come from?" or "Who began everything?" or "Who is the First Father?" Unable to think that any of the local powers with which they had daily dealings could have originated or fathered all things, they hit upon a theistic, or better, monotheistic, explanation; but since the being they inferred obviously had not entered their lives, he was in most instances in the nature of a philosophical postulate rather than a present religious reality.

8. *Types of magic.* Magic may be loosely defined as an endeavor through utterance of set words, or the performance of set acts, or both, to control or bend the powers of the world to man's will. It cannot be wholly divorced from religion, as we have heretofore noted, but it is discernibly present when emphasis is placed on forcing things to happen rather than asking that they do.

Sir James G. Frazer has made one type of magic famous. The inclusive name he gave it is *sympathetic magic.* One subdivision of it, which he called "imitative magic," is based on such assumptions as that look-alikes act alike or, more significantly, that like influences or even produces like; therefore, if one imitates the looks and actions of a man or an animal (or even of a thunder cloud), one can induce a like and desired action in the imitated being or object. The hunting magic of

Cro-Magnon man, we can readily see, was a form of imitative magic. Primitive agriculture furnishes another example; it is believed that if the grower goes to his field when the grain is sprouting and, with words of encouragement or command addressed to the emerging plants, leaps again and again as high as he is able, he can induce and even compel the grain to grow at least as high. To cite still another example out of a countless number, primitives often seek an end to drought by going to a steep hill and rolling rocks down its slope while beating drums and shouting boom!; this is done to bring on a rainstorm. (We shall come upon an instance of this before the end of this chapter.)

Black magic has the same basis. If someone, for example, makes an image (imitation) of his enemy, perhaps in wax, and stabs it with pins, the hated one will die. It is frequently quite enough just to describe in detail the terrible things that will happen to an enemy, and then either command (usually by curse) or pray and predict, that they must occur; and they will!

Frazer also found a form of sympathetic magic that he called "contagious." Things conjoined and then separated remain sympathetic with each other. Thus severed hair or fingernails retain a magical sympathy with the person to whom they once belonged, and therefore black magic performed on them causes damage to that person. This type of magic has many ramifications.

These and other practices may be grouped under various headings. It will be helpful here to consider them as exemplifying three *methods of control* of spirit power.

The first is *fetishism*. Fetishism uses the power in inanimate things. It includes the veneration and use of objects into which useful powers do not have to be induced, because they are already there. These are the so-called natural fetishes, the curiously marked pebbles, aerolites, bones, odd-shaped sticks, and the like, which seem from the moment of finding to bring good fortune and to frustrate the evil designs of one's foes. But on its more actively magical side, fetishism involves inducing useful powers into a variety of inanimate objects, stuffed sometimes into an antelope's horn or other receptacle, and confining them there, for the purpose of securing their assistance in a great variety of projects.

Both natural and manufactured fetishes are regarded as possessing a vague sort of personality, at least an active will. This idea accounts for the prevailing attitude taken toward them, especially in Africa. There a fetish is reverenced in the most naively anthropomorphic way. It is first treated as an object of worship, being addressed with prayer, and presented with offerings. This done, a favorable issue is awaited, with hope.

But if the desired result does not follow, the attitude of the owner changes; he passes to coaxing and cajoling, then proceeds to stern commands, next to scolding, and finally to whipping or other chastisement. If there is still no result, the conclusion is either that the spirit has left the fetish, in which case it is useless and another must be found to take its place, or that the spirit, still in the fetish, has been rendered impotent by some more powerful fetish or spirit-power in the neighborhood. In the latter case the magician must be visited and the fetish charged with more power, or substituted with another of adequate potency.

The second method for establishing control over the spirit-powers of the world is *shamanism*. In this case spirits are conjured into or out of human beings by one who is himself spirit-possessed. The shaman of Siberia has been selected to give his name to this practice because he is typical of all witch-doctors, medicine men, exorcists, and sorcerers. It is his function to work himself up to a frenzy of spirit-possession; that is to say, he must lift himself up to the spirit-level, in both consciousness and power, and when in that state establish control over certain spirits, especially those of disease and death, in order either to drive them into people (bedevilment or bewitchment), or expel them from people (exorcism). The following account of an American Indian medicine man vividly describes shamans elsewhere.

The medicine man of the Black Feet Indian tribes, when exercising this art upon a sick person, arrayed himself in the most absurd costume which the mind of man ever conceived. For a coat he wore the skin of a yellow bear. The skin of the head was formed into a mask, which entirely hid the features of the enchanter. On his person in addition to the skin of the yellow bear—an article exceedingly rare and, therefore, in itself a powerful medicine—were the skins of various wild animals which were also anomalies or deformities and hence, in the savage estimation, medicine. There were also skins of snakes, frogs, field mice, snails, the beaks and tails of birds, hoofs of deer, goats, and antelopes, in a word, the odds, and ends, the fag-ends and tips, of everything that swims, flies, or runs. In one hand he held a magic wand, to the clatter, din, and discord of which he added wild startling jumps and Indian yells, and the horrid and appalling grunts, growls and snarls of the grizzly bear, calling on the bad daimon to leave the patient. It was necessary to see the dress of that medicine man before a person could form a just conception of his frightful appearance.[6]

If the sick person had any chance of recovery at all, likely as not he pulled himself together, in full faith that the evil spirit causing his illness had been exorcised. The medicine man on his part usually had no doubt that in the frenzy of his performance he himself had been spirit-possessed, and had been able to establish direct relations with the evil spirit, so as to frighten it off.*

The third method of control—*popular magic*—is not confined to magicians or priests, but is diffused through the group. It is the endeavor of the common folk (with or without the aid of fetish-spirits and shamans, but always by definite procedures) either to prevent the spirit-powers from doing harm to the individual or the group, or to make them serve private or group interests. One set of procedures, which goes under the name of *aversive magic*, is innumerable in its forms; it is perhaps best typified by the ritual by which the community rids itself of an accumulated weight of guilt by transferring it magically to a "scapegoat" or other carrier, e.g., a boat which drifts out to sea. The almost infinite number of procedures working toward social and individual well-being, specifically by promoting fertility in field and flock and in womankind, is often called *productive magic*. The past is rich in instances. Bare mention only can be made here of the corn dances in many parts of the world, fertility rites at sowing based on sympathetic magic, human sacrifice followed by planting of the flesh or pouring of the blood in the fields, and performances magico-religious in character, such as the offering of the first-fruits and firstlings of the fields and flocks to the gods, the worship of bulls and he-goats, ceremonial marriages of fertility gods and goddesses represented by human actors, and the offering of human victims to vegetative and corn deities in order to insure the growth of an adequate food supply.†

9. *Divination.* There is a close connection in primitive religions between shamanism and divination, that is, between rapport with spirit-powers and insight into what is obscure and hidden in the present and future. Such insight is thought to occur during specific divination rites. Shamans may use their own inherent power (magic) or may establish

---

* The psychology of the shaman has been noticed before. His fitness for his office has been undoubtedly determined in most instances by his own susceptibility to trance or seizure. Once recognized as the right sort of person to be a shaman, he shares with others of the same calling the secrets of the profession: a knowledge of powerful drugs, methods of autohypnotism, dance patterns inducing vertigo and frenzy, and techniques resulting in trance states, visions, and hysteria—all of which are interpreted as valuable forms of spirit-possession and control, an interpretation which the shaman, except in rare cases, himself accepts.

† The student is referred to Sir James G. Frazer's *The Golden Bough* (Macmillan), the one-volume abridgement, for fascinating descriptions of these procedures. The unacceptability of the central thesis does not destroy the value of these descriptions.

dependent prophetic relations with the supernatural (a situation that is primarily religious). The general primitive belief is that the shaman or necromancer possesses the power to make contacts in the spirit-world, including communion with the spirits of the dead, and thus gains otherwise inaccessible information about things and events on, above, and under the earth. Often he is believed to be the "familiar" of a single spirit or soul that puts him "in the know." In some contexts divination has an explicit religious aspect. It is made possible by divine inspiration, either through dreams and visions or through oracles, such as those in which the ancient Greeks believed: words whispered by the oaks of Dodona speaking for Zeus or entranced utterances muttered by the priestess at Delphi when Apollo communicated through her. Another aspect of divination is the reading of omens in the flight of birds, the sound of thunder, the appearance of comets, eclipses, "signs in the stars," accidents, sudden death, and like phenomena. Divination seems to be such a necessity to primitives that it is virtually universal.

10. *Taboo.* The placing of taboos is also practically universal. The chief's person is nearly always taboo, as long as there is any vigor or leadership in him.* He is thought to be so heavily charged with power that to touch him, or his clothes, or his cooking utensils, or even the carpet or floorspace upon which he walks, is highly dangerous; immediate steps must be taken to counteract the fatal consequences to the intruder which will ensue. When entering the chief's presence the utmost precautions must be observed.

More than one instance is on record of men and women who died of fright upon learning they had unwittingly eaten the remains of a chief's meal. Their bodies apparently could not survive so powerful a dosage of *mana*-imbued substance.

There are taboos upon other persons. The same awe with which kings and priests are regarded is easily aroused by other persons in certain circumstances. In many parts of the world, warriors, for example, are taboo before and after battle. Hunters and fishermen are in like case. A taboo is put on those who have had any contact with the dead, and this extends even to the hired mourners. Manslayers are likewise untouchable, until expiation or ceremonial cleansing has taken place and removed the contagion of death and the wrath of the departed spirit. It is generally true among primitive folk that few pass through life without at some time or other becoming taboo. A newly born child, a boy or girl during initiation ceremonies at puberty, a woman in childbed, a husband practicing the curious custom of *couvade* (bringing to bed

* When he is old, his virtue has departed, and he is often put to death.

of the father at the birth of a child), recently widowed women, celebrants in religious ceremonies—all such, in one locality or another, are
temporarily tabooed.

This by no means exhausts the range of taboo. Many different
things, acts, sacred words, names, and places are on the list of the
avoided. Sharp weapons, iron, blood, head and hair (they contain
spirit), cut hair and nails (even when severed from the body they retain
a generous portion of spirit), spittle, certain foods, knots and rings, and
much more, are in this category.

It must be evident that almost anything and everything at one time
or other has been taboo. This holds true not only for primitive peoples
but for people of more advanced cultures as well.*

11. *Purification rites.* Ceremonies of purification and cleansing have
been referred to more than once in the above discussion of taboo. The
reference was inescapable. The existence of taboos means to the primitive not only a very real element of danger in taboo-breaking, because
of the vindictive or retributive action of outraged powers, but also the
guilt and uncleanness of the unfortunate taboo-breaker. This uncleanness
and contamination are such that the whole community may be put in
jeopardy. Until the taboo-breaker is cleansed of his defilement, he is
ostracized, and may even come under the sentence of death.

But taboo-breaking is not the only source of pollution. Birth, death,
bloodshed, blood itself, and contact with tabooed persons, are each
sources of pollution. And there may be a supernatural condition, such as
the presence of an unclean spirit haunting a family or a village, a condition involving as its consequence the need of driving out the objectionable presence.

Purification of ritual pollution is effected in various ways. Common
among the methods are fasting, shaving the hair and cutting the nails,
crawling through cleansing smoke fumes produced during an elaborate
ritual, passing between fires or jumping through fire, washing with water
or blood, and cutting or gashing the body so as to let the evil out with
the rushing blood. If an unclean spirit haunts a community or enters a
man or woman, it may be expelled by introducing a more powerful spirit
whose presence will be cleansing. The modes of purification are numberless, in fact.

12. *Sacrifice.* In an earlier paragraph we traced the relation between anxiety and ritual. The need to act and speak in ways that will
reduce anxiety, so various in its kinds, early issued in sacrifice to the

* For an interesting insight into the college man's *taboos,* see appendix of A. M.
Tozzer, *Social Origins and Social Continuities,* 1925.

spirit-powers involved. This has usually entailed the giving up or destruction (e.g., burning) of something, animate or inanimate, human, animal, or vegetable, in order to cause it to pass from human possession to that of the spirit-powers or gods. The simplest form of sacrifice is always the giving of offerings, gifts of value of many sorts, in the hope of pleasing the spirits. But originally the sacrifices seem to have been more radical than this and to have involved animal and human sacrifice, because the spirits as well as men need the vitality and strength present in life and blood.

When the present day primitive discovers that certain powers behave in an unusual or uncontrollable way, he may offer sacrifices with a view to placating or conciliating the powers he cannot coerce; such sacrifices are *propitiatory*. When he believes he has offended the powers by his actions, he may offer *piacular* sacrifices, intended to expiate or atone for his misdoing. Or he may hope to open the way for the inflow of supernatural power into himself, and then his sacrifice is of a *sacramental* kind. One form of such sacrifice shares something—for example, a sacred meal—with the spirit-powers. All these forms of sacrifice bear the marks of religion; but magic is also generally implicated. It is obvious for one thing that sacrifices may do something to or for the spirit-powers; in particular, they may impart added or needed strength and vigor.* Insofar as the powers are dependent upon man for the vitalizing elements in the sacrifices, the sacrifices gain a magical potency to coerce them. Hence primitives sometimes regard religious rituals as having guaranteed results. They thus anticipate something that occurs explicitly above the primitive level. We shall take note in another chapter that in Vedic times in India a highly sophisticated development converted worship and sacrifice into magic: the priests promised and guaranteed that their rituals would force the gods to do as they directed. This understanding is more implicit than expressed in primitive religion.

A somewhat different development has resemblances to aversive magic. Sacrifices are offered to dreaded powers in mingled fear and confidence that they will stay away or cease to afflict the group with sickness, drought, or other calamity. Sacrifices, because of their momentousness and cost to the givers, carry great weight even with ill-disposed powers.

---

* Survivals of this belief may be found in Homer and among the early Romans. Homer implies that the gods not only lose prestige but power as well when men cease to sacrifice to them. The Romans, we shall find, felt that since their sacrifices increased the *numen* or spiritual power of the gods, the gods owed them a return of favors, which was confidently expected.

If we take our story a little beyond the primitive level, we see in the offering of sacrifices an important element in the origin of what are now called formal religious services. One does not bring offerings and sacrifices without words, words of compliment and conciliation. This is the origin of praise, and along one line of development it resulted in the hymn and psalm. After praise, it is safe to *petition* for favors. Here is the germ of ritual prayer. Again, differentiation in the modes of worship and sacrifice could hardly have taken place without selection of sacred places for the performance of rituals—typically the *sacred grove*. After the passage of centuries, shrines and temples would arise at such places. To perform the sacred ceremonies exactly and effectively there arose the consecrated class of *priests*, set apart to devote their lives to the care of religious property, the preservation and performance of the rituals, and the discovery and declaration of the will of the gods by divination, oracle, and prophecy.

13. *Mythology.* The making of myths is universal among mankind.* Primitives even live by them. Among the Australian aborigines, for example, myths have a vital importance, for they are invoked to explain and give the weight of a supernatural origin and authority to the customs, ceremonials, and beliefs of the tribes. This is a major aspect of mythology. It frequently happens that primitives find themselves following customs and rituals whose precise meaning now eludes them. In this situation it is natural to seek an explanation of the necessity they feel to follow what would otherwise be meaningless rites by saying:

* Because of the vastness of this subject and the tendency of the word "myth" to lose specific meaning when it is made to stretch itself over so many different kinds of tales, some scholars seek to limit the meaning of the word. "True myths," it is said, have the function of corroborating or validating tribal traditions, rituals, and sacred sites. Thus in an article in *Folklore* (December, 1957) E. O. James distinguishes true myths sharply from fantasy, poetry, romance, philosophy, theology, and psychology, because the function of myth is to "validate and justify, conserve and safeguard" established tradition and does not share therefore the interests of several types of lore that are merely speculative or in answer to the promptings of curiosity. This rules out Plato's *mythos* as true myth and excludes the folklore that is an exercise of playful imagination. In the present account, the looser, more inclusive practice of defining myth simply as a story having to do with supernormal (often supernatural) persons, objects, or events is followed. Due acknowledgment is made, it is hoped, of the fact that myths of great anthropological importance have arisen to validate and justify tribal tradition and ritual.

Incidentally, one of the issues much debated by anthropologists is whether myths arise from rituals or rituals from myths. This account follows Clyde Kluckhohn in saying that the facts do not justify an either-or but rather a both-and in this case. Myth and ritual are mutually interdependent and are both causes and effects of each other, depending on circumstances.

"The Fathers taught us to do these things," and then to push back the origins beyond remembered fathers to mythical Progenitors or Culture Heroes at the beginning of the world. Or some "high god" may be cited as the first author of "our tribe and way of life." It will be seen at once that myth here serves the very necessary function of providing sanctions for tribal custom and belief.

In discussing myths, a large place must also be given to cosmogonic or creation myths. It is of course speculative to seek reasons for their being told in such numbers and in such variety. One reason for them is undoubtedly the need to have an explanation of why the earth is so suited to human habitation. Someone—perhaps the High God or a Culture Hero—dove into the waters to bring up the sand with which he made the earth, or brought forth men, animals, and vegetation from an underground cave, or fought with giants for the materials with which he put the world together. Whereas questions like "Was there a First Cause?" would be greeted by primitives with incomprehension, specific questions like "Why are men, bears, and wolves as different as they are?" might stir an individual of imagination to compose and pass on to others a myth drawn from his memories and dreams and particularly from what he thought the old men of his youth might say, were they alive.

Again, many myths are expressions in fantasy-form of subconscious criticism of the injustices and maladjustments of familial and social organizations. Like dreams, they are in this respect full of meaningful symbolism, and when told and retold they afford release to hidden tensions by giving them a disguised but effective voice. This is an important aspect of mythology.

The quasi-historical myth is of another sort. It is the elaboration of an original happening, involving usually a hero or pioneer figure, into a tale of wonder, through all of whose episodes thrills the magic of the hero's name, until his character, looming transfigured through the magico-religious aura in which it is invested, glows with divinity.

14. *Attitudes toward the dead: ancestor-worship.* Here is an important circle of ideas. The notion of the complete extinction of the personality at death is often difficult to reconcile with our daily experience. A man who has been a boon companion for days and years leaves at death a great void in our lives; our habits must be adjusted to his absence; we think of him often; his influence lingers with us; our visual and auditory memories are for some time so vivid that the mere thought of him gives him back to us in living presence; and at night we dream that we see him and talk to him.

These experiences were as vivid, certainly, to our prehistoric ancestors as they are to us. It is not strange that prehistoric man and his modern representatives have felt that the dead not only survive but have the same hungers and needs as in life. But close upon this conviction that the dead have an after-life comes a real uneasiness. The dead, it is realized, have a way of hanging about. This is embarrassing, because they do not play their old part in the round of daily existence.

Very early our primitive forebears developed measures of security against troublous interference by the dead. They raised a heap of stones over the dead body, or tied it up with strong cords, or in some cases even drove a stake through the chest in order to pin the body to the earth. These practices were designed to keep the dead from "walking." At the same time offerings were left at the burial place to keep the dead satisfied and content. Many of these customs still survive. The dead in more than one region of the world are still carried out feet foremost, in order that they may be "pointed away." This procedure is often followed by a zigzag progress on the part of the corpse-bearers, so as to bewilder the dead and make them unable to find their way back. Another custom is the taking of the body out of the house by some other than the ordinary exit, through the window or through a hole made in the wall, which is immediately closed up. Negroes along the Congo strew thorns on the grave and upon the path leading back to the village, to prick the feet of the dead and prevent return. Sometimes magical barriers are erected against the dead, such as fences around the grave, or hedges of twigs to simulate a trackless forest, or deep lines drawn across the path to represent an impassable river.

It seems obvious that such customs presuppose enmity on the part of the dead. This interpretation is, however, not accurate. It is sound only in the case of those who have suffered neglect or who have died dissatisfied or by violence, people cut off in their youth, persons dying in agony from disease and pain, slain by accident, killed in a quarrel, or prematurely brought to their end in childbed. Such spirits have a grudge which they are likely to work off on the living. But not all the dead are going to be inimical. It is well to be wary—and this precaution is always taken—but the dead often are friendly. This is especially true of ancestors. Chinese civilization is founded on the optimistic faith that ancestral spirits are anxious to aid their descendants, and will do so, if only the living pay them proper regard.

Out of the double purpose of conciliating the inimically disposed dead and pleasing the friendly, has arisen the worldwide custom of making offerings at the grave. Food and drink are as much a need of the dead as of the living. The endeavor to placate or to assist the dead begins even before burial, and is especially evident when interment takes place. Weapons, clothing, furniture, every sort of precious object (including sometimes, as in historic Egypt, miniature ovens, wooden loaves, chairs, servants, and the like) are placed in the grave or tomb. Frequently, in times past, wives and servants were "sent along," being either slain upon the grave, burned on a pyre, buried alive, or sealed in tombs. Within living memory, kings' deaths in Africa have been the occasion of the "sending along" of hundreds of men and women.

15. *Totemism.* Our survey of the general characteristics of primitive religions concludes with brief mention of a group of practices rather hard to define. There is, however, a common characteristic present in all the diverse forms of totemism. It is that totemism recognizes the existence of a more or less intimate relationship between certain human groups and particular classes or species of animal, plant, or inanimate object in nature. The recognition of this relationship results in special social groupings (a phenomenon known as social totemism) and also in rituals binding the human groups with their totemic counterparts (cult totemism). The cult rituals are so diverse as to defy generalization. The rituals of the aborigines of Australia are noteworthy in being very closely tied to tribal survival. The tribes there are hard put to it to find enough food to enable them to survive, and totemism has provided what appears to them to be a solution to the problem. Each class of animal, plant, and inanimate object having a place in the food supply has become the totem of a clan within the tribe. The basic realizations here might be put in these terms: "Our food supply depends on there being a plentiful supply of animals, plants, and materials going into the making of food. May these animals, plants, and food materials increase and be abundant! Let therefore each of the tribe's clans have a totem and promote the abundance of the species thus especially sacred to it by practicing magic, offering prayer, and providing constant care and solicitude. The whole community will be benefited. Although those not belonging to the clan may eat of the totem freely, let the totemic clan regard it as taboo, and eat of it sparingly even on the allowed occasion of the sacramental meal at the in-gathering of the species." Undoubtedly the logic of this arrangement was arrived at more by gradual discovery than by reasoning. The Australians have added to these practices the social provision of exogamy, prescribing marriage outside the totemic clan. Other varieties of totemism are found in North and South America, Africa, India (where it exists weakly), and the South Seas. In these areas the particular features of totemism vary, sometimes

widely. Where the food supply is ample, the Australian devices for increasing it are replaced by other interests. In North America, for example, it has been characteristic for Indian tribes to divide into a number of groups that express their individuality by taking their name from some animal, bird, or natural object. In most cases the sense of special relationship with the totem has issued in a myth of descent which derives the members of the clan and their totem from a common ancestor. Sometimes the relationship between the members of the clan and the totem has taken the form of a "mystic affinity." In other cases the rituals seek to propitiate the totem group. Occasionally a tribe's totems are chosen from birds only or exclusively from animals. In Australia and elsewhere single clans have occasionally had two or even more totems. And of course the attendant rituals have varied widely both in importance and complexity.

III SOME ILLUSTRATIVE CASE STUDIES

That the *feel* of primitive religion cannot well be caught from the analysis by categories which we have just pursued must be obvious. Hence it is necessary for more complete understanding to project ourselves in imagination into some particular place and situation and gain thereby a sense of primitive beliefs and practices in the milieu that produced them.

We therefore go first to Australia, to see the interplay of religion, magic, and social custom at a nearly Stone Age level, then to India, to look in upon a little-known jungle tribe, and last to Africa, for an excursion into the life and thought of a more advanced group.

1. *The Dieri of South-East Australia.** Taken as a whole, the Australian aborigines are still at a stage of culture on the border line between upper paleolithic and neolithic. They belong to a very ancient stock therefore. Chocolate brown in color (the white Australians call

---

* One of about 500 tribes circa 1800 A.D., many of which have now disappeared. This account of them is taken from scattered references in A. W. Howitt, *The Native Tribes of South-East Australia* (Macmillan, 1904). This and the two trail-breaking books of Spencer and Gillen—*The Native Tribes of Central Australia* (Macmillan, 1899), and *The Northern Tribes of Central Australia* (Macmillan, 1904)—stand at the beginning of modern research into present-day primitive belief and practice. Anthropologists have moved beyond the categories and theories of these books, but the data contained in them is of great value, because it was gathered before many of the tribes were affected by European settlement in Australia.

them "black fellows"), they have broad noses, deep-set eyes, receding foreheads, and thick skull bones; but unlike the now extinct Tasmanians, whose hair was twisted like the Negro's, their hair is wavy, and the men grow abundant beards. Except in cold weather, when they put on warm kangaroo, wallaby, and opposum skins, they wear only a hip girdle, to which the men attach their weapons. They live in scattered tribes, each occupying a definite territory and speaking a common dialect. Their culture is a food-gathering one, for they are "a people which neither tills nor sows, and which does not breed and pasture animals, but only collects and kills." [7] With them, as was the case with the Tasmanians, the spear is still the most important weapon, but it is provided with a separate hardwood or flaked-stone head, often fitted with barbs; and to hurl it through the air they use a throwing stick. Their knives and axes are of chipped stone. To their credit is the evolution of two kinds of boomerang, one of which is so shaped and twisted that it returns to the sender. Their huts are rude shelters, made of twigs and leaves woven into a half-sphere with a round door at one side. Tribal life, though geographically set apart from that of other settlements, is not completely independent, reciprocity with neighboring tribes being at least as general as hostility; and here totemism plays a powerful role in establishing lines of relatedness crossing and crisscrossing the tribal barriers.

The Dieri were observed by Howitt in the 1860's, when they were still relatively undisturbed in their group beliefs and practices. They inhabited the land to the east and southeast of Lake Eyre in South Australia, a region of minimum rainfall and very high temperatures, with low trees dotting the arid plains. They were divided into two exogamous intermarrying moieties or classes, called *murdus*. The class names were Matteri and Kararu. No Matteri could marry a Matteri, no Kararu a Kararu. The Matteri were subdivided into smaller groups, each having a totem, typical examples of such being the caterpillar, cormorant, emu, eagle hawk, and wild dog. None of these totem groups, of course, could intermarry. The Kararu had as totems such diverse entities as the carpet snake, crow, rat, frog, bat, shrewmouse, red ochre, and rain. Each individual acquired his group-totem from his mother, descent being reckoned through the female line.

Executive power in each division of the tribe resided in the oldest man of the totem group, its *pinnaru* or head. The pinnarus were collectively the headmen of the tribe, and among them one was usually superior to the others. These headmen were of chief importance in the initiation ceremonies to be described later.

From the magico-religious standpoint the outstanding individual in the group was the *kunki* or medicine man. He was credited with the power to communicate directly with supernatural beings called *kutchi* and with the *Mura-muras,* the highly regarded spirits of the legendary heroes (a superhuman race) believed to have preceded the Australians as their prototypes and taught them their rituals. He was thought to have obtained his power from these supernatural beings. By them he interpreted dreams, counteracted evil spells, and drove out evil spirits. It was believed he could project in an invisible manner into his victims substances such as quartz crystals or bones. That meant death, of course. He was also thought to have the power of surreptitiously abstracting from individuals the human fat which he used as a powerful magical infusion; such fat stealing was the *real* cause of the subsequent death of the robbed individuals. A special function of his was to act as a diviner when the relatives of the dead sought the identity of the person or persons who had planned the death. For death was not considered a natural event: it was always due either to magic or the machinations of the kutchi. As to sickness this side of death, if a kutchi had caused anyone to fall ill, the medicine man could drive it out. But sickness was not always due to a kutchi; it might be the result of a "pointing of the bone." That is, some enemy had secured an accomplice and

Australian aborigines engaged in "pointing the bone." Inset shows bone sharpened and wrapped in twine and tassels made from human hair. (Drawing based on photographs)

they had performed a secret ceremony in which they had made magical use of a human shinbone, pointing it at the person they hoped to sicken and then uttering a magic spell. As soon as a person became ill, therefore, his friends consulted the kunki and others to find out if anyone had "given him the bone." If he died, and suspicion of having "pointed the bone" fell on any person, the latter was summarily dealt with by a *pinya*, or party of revenge, which went out at the behest of the older men of the tribe (the tribal council) to track him down and kill him.

Because of the oft-recurring periods of drought, the medicine man acquired great importance as a rain maker and weather changer. The whole tribe united in the ceremony which he and his colleagues conducted. The theory was that the clouds are bodies in which rain is produced by the Mura-muras who live on the elevated plain which is the sky. For the rain making ceremony members of the tribe dug a hole two feet deep, twelve feet long, and from eight to ten feet wide, over which they erected a long hut of twigs and boughs. The hut was occupied by the old men; and during the ceremony their arms were cut by the principal medicine man with a sharp piece of flint and the blood made to flow on the other men sitting around. Then two medicine men, whose arms had previously been lanced, threw handfuls of down in the air. The blood symbolized rain, the down clouds. The ceremony ended when the men, young and old, butted down the hut with their heads. The piercing of the hut symbolized the piercing of the clouds, and the fall of the hut a downpour of rain. Meanwhile, the rainmaking Mura-muras were besought to grant heavy rainfall, in view of the damage caused by the drought and the famine-stricken condition of the people. The significance of the following quotation needs no pointing out:

> Should no clouds appear as soon as expected, the explanation given is that the Mura-mura is angry with them; and should there be no rain for weeks or months, they suppose that some other tribe has stopped their power.[8]

Another and even more important ceremony was designed to exert an influence upon a Mura-mura called Minkani, buried deep in a sandhill, and judged by Howitt, from the description, to be one of the fossil animals or reptiles which are found in the deltas of the rivers emptying into Lake Eyre.* Since the motive of the ceremony, a typically totemic ritual, was to increase the food supply of carpet snakes and lizards in the sandhills, the men who took part in it had these reptiles as their totems.

---

* This is undoubtedly an erroneous inference. It is quite common among Australian aborigines to associate totemic cult-heroes with outcropping rocks which have come to be considered as the latter's remains pushing up from below.

dent—the desire to be at one with and to share the virtue and strength of the deceased.

When the grave was filled in, a large stack of wood was placed over it, the whole group to which the deceased belonged shifted camp, and for fear of offending the dead no one spoke of or referred to him again. Some Dieri groups feared the rising of the dead so much that they tied the toes of the corpse together, bound the thumbs behind its back, swept the ground clean around the grave at dusk, and looked for tracks in the morning. Should tracks appear, the body was reburied elsewhere, on the theory that the first grave was not satisfactory, and the dead person, not lying easy, rose and walked.

Many tribes in southeastern Australia believed in a supernatural being who was not a Mura-mura nor an ancestral spirit, but a high god or old man of the sky who was eternal and uncreated, having existed from the beginning of all things, and was supreme and without equal, a sort of headman of the sky-country; and they believed firmly that he initiated the rites and ceremonies taught them by the Mura-muras and practiced so faithfully in the old days by the Australian tribes. He was known among the tribes by various names, such as Nurrundere, Biamban, Bunjil, Munga-ngama, Nurelli, and the like. Often he was referred to as "Our Father." Some tribes felt that he was not much concerned about the doings of men; others, such as the Kurnai, thought he watched over men constantly. Howitt did not find evidence of belief in such a primitive high god among the Dieri and their neighbors of the Lake Eyre country; but that may have been because he was not told as much as he thought he was. It begins to appear, as further evidence comes in, that practically all of the Australian tribes held a belief in some kind of high god, and the Dieri probably did, too; but we are without knowledge as to this, and so must let the matter remain undetermined.*

We come finally to the fascinating subject of the initiation ceremonies so distinctive of the aborigines all over the Australian continent. Nowhere else among primitive societies do we see so clearly the force which religious sanctions, as brought to bear by old men, can give to the tribal mores.

* More recent findings of anthropologists have introduced some concepts unknown to Howitt. According to Radcliffe-Brown, the Australian cosmology generally begins with chaos, formlessness and unconsciousness. Then comes a Dawn Period, known as the Alcheringa or dream-time, when certain Dawn Beings arose (they were uncreated) and, moving like figures in a dream, gave the earth its present structure, and established the various species and their habits and customs. The High God was one of these Dawn Beings and ascended to the sky-country, while other Dawn Beings established totemic centers on earth.

Whenever a Dieri boy or girl reached puberty, initiatory rites were planned, in order to complete the transformation or rebirth of the boy into a man and the girl into a woman. The ceremonies for boys were especially thorough, and were carried out in different stages over a period of months; all the available tribes-people from miles around gathered for the final ceremonies. It was the principal headman of the tribe who decided when the youths should be initiated. He informed the council of elders who the youths were and when the different ceremonies should take place.

The earliest ceremony had the clear significance that the boys were about to undergo a ritual death in order to rise or be reborn as men. The death symbol was a ceremony by which each boy's two lower middle-front teeth were knocked out by chisel-shaped pieces of wood. The teeth thus dislodged were buried a twelvemonth later eighteen inches underground. At about the same time (as early as in the ninth or tenth year) a ceremony with a similar meaning took place, that of circumcision, at which time each boy's father stooped over him and gave him a new name. Some time later there occurred, suddenly and without warning to the young men, the curious Kulpi rite, or ceremony of sub-incision, after which, and only then, was the youth considered to be a thorough man.

Meanwhile, there took place the rite called the *Wilyaru* ceremony, a rite which definitely cut a youth off from childhood and any former dependence on the womenfolk. It is thus described:

A young man without previous warning is led out of the camp by some older men who are of the relation of *Neyi* (approximately cousin in this case) to him, and not of near, but distant relationship. On the following morning the men, old and young, except his father and elder brothers, surround him, and direct him to close his eyes. One of the old men then binds the arm of another old man tightly with string, and with a sharp piece of flint lances the vein about an inch from the elbow, causing a stream of blood to fall over the young man, until he is covered with it, and the old man is becoming exhausted. Another man takes his place, and so on until the young man becomes quite stiff from the quantity of blood adhering to him. The reason given for this practice is that it infuses courage into the young man, and also shows him that the sight of blood is nothing, so that should he receive a wound in warfare, he may account it a matter of no moment.[10]

The deeper meaning of the rite is that the spirit and wisdom of the older men was transforming the youth into an adult by making him of one blood with them.

In the next stage of the ceremony the blood-covered youth was gashed with a sharp piece of flint on neck and back, so that when the wounds would heal he would bear raised scars as a sign that he was a Wilyaru. At the completion of the rite he was given a bull-roarer, a paddle-shaped slab of wood, fastened to a string made of human hair from ten to twelve feet long. This was his first face-to-face encounter with the actual source of the vibrant roar which had formerly terrified him and the women of the camp when they heard it issuing from the distance of the bush. Even the men, he now learned, considered it to have supernatural effects and to speak with an authoritative voice to all living beings. It was the symbol and the voice of the Mura-muras who had given the tribe its sacred rituals and traditions. Presented now with one which was to be returned to a secret hiding place when not used, he was taught how to whirl it and told never to show it to women or tell them about it.

After this an important psychological experience was required of him: he was sent away alone into the bush, there to be on his own until his wounds were healed and all the blood with which he was covered had been worn off. He was to rehearse in his mind the lessons he had learned.

The young man is never seen by the women, from the time he is made *Wilyaru* till the time when he returns to the camp, after perhaps many months . . . During the time of his absence his near female relatives become very anxious about him, often asking as to his whereabouts. There is great rejoicing in the camp when the *Wilyaru* finally returns to it, and his mother and sisters make much of him.[11]

But he was now a man and did not belong to the women any more.

The Dieri and neighboring tribes united in the remaining ceremony, the *Mindari,* which was a general get-together and dancing of the initiates and the men and women, and was often the occasion for the amicable settlement of any disputes since the last Mindari.

Behind all this there was the running oral commentary of the older men, carefully explaining the origin and meaning of each ceremony, beginning with a retelling of the tribal myths in regard to them. The youths were admonished in their tribal duties and responsibilities. The totemic rules and relationships were defined with exactness. Plainly the laws and customs of the community were sacrosanct and on no consideration to be departed from. The tribal morality thus came to each member of the community with the full weight of religious sanctions behind it. As well rebel against Nature as against it!

2. *The Birhors of Chota Nagpur, India.** This jungle tribe is an

* The details are taken from *The Birhors: A Little-Known Jungle Tribe of Chota Nagpur* by Rai Bahadur Sarat Roy, Ranchi, India, 1925.

interesting one to study, because though its practices remain as primitive as ever, it has allowed its members to entertain ideas taken over from the Hindus around them. The tribe is therefore typical of the changes in culture beginning to overwhelm even the most backward peoples of the world today.

The Birhors are an aboriginal tribe of Dravidian stock who live on a plateau in the jungles of Chota Nagpur in east-central India. The tribe is divided into two groups, *Uthlus* (wanderers) and *Jaghis* (settlers). The latter are few in number; they have settled down near the villages of the Hindus and taken up lands for cultivation. The former, with whom we are here chiefly concerned, live in small migratory bands, always on the move through the jungles, except during the rainy season, when they encamp on the sides of hills, in leaf-huts, in the more inaccessible regions. Sometimes called the "monkey people," because much of their food-supply consists of monkey-meat, they live in a very squalid condition, at a Stone Age level. Their huts, made of leaves and branches pushed together like sheaves of wheat in a field, are placed in a circle, facing an open space in the center, which is swept clean. These primitive wanderers keep no goats, pigs, or cattle themselves, but they have learned, when they need the flesh of these animals for feasts or sacrifices, to overcome their shyness and resort to the jungle edge to barter for them. Otherwise, they live on fowls, rats, and monkeys, and certain leaves and roots of the jungle.

Their social organization presents a two-fold grouping, one an organization for purposes of food-quest, another for purposes of regulating marriage and kinship. By the first grouping the tribe is broken up into bands (or *tandas*) of four to ten families each, led by a headman who is both chief and priest. By the second grouping the tribe is organized into exogamous clans, with some animal, plant, fruit, flower, or other object as the totem.

The principal occupation of the Birhor man is hunting. Since he uses no bows and arrows, a great part of his time and that of his group is consumed in making rope from *chop* fibers and then weaving nets to snare game. The characteristic mode of food-quest—snaring monkeys—is typical of primitive procedures elsewhere, and is described as follows:

On the morning of the appointed day, the *Naya* [the headman] goes to a neighboring stream or spring, and there bathes, fills a jug with water, and brings it home. Then after changing his loincloth, the *Naya*, in company with one or two elders of the *tanda*, proceeds with a handful of rice and the jug of water to the *Jayar* (sacred grove). The *Diguar* [also called

Kotwar, a man appointed to make all the necessary arrangements for the hunt] has carried to the *Jayar* and placed in a heap all the nets of the intending hunters of the *tanda*. Before this heap of nets the *Naya* stands on his left leg with his right heel resting on his left knee, and with his face to the east, and, with arms extended forward, pours a little water three times on the ground and invokes all the spirits by name for success in hunting, as follows: "Here I am making a libation in your names. May blood of game flow like this." The *Naya* then sits down before the nets and puts three vermilion marks on the ground before them, and on these vermilion marks sprinkles a little rice, and addresses the spirits as follows: "Today I am offering this rice to you all. May we have speedy success. May game be caught in our nets as soon as we enter the jungles." Then they return home, leaving the nets at the *Jayar*. After breakfast each intending hunter takes up from the *Jayar* his own net and clubs and bamboo poles for fixing the nets and proceeds to the selected jungle. . . . Arrived there, all sit down together on the ground for a short while in what is called an *awas* or rendezvous.

The *Kotwar* now touches each net with a *tiril* or ebony twig and hands it over to the *Naya*. With this twig, the *Naya* performs what is known as "*bana sana*" in order to neutralize the harmful effects of the evil eye of any of their own women in the *tanda* which may have been directed, even though involuntarily, against the party. With low murmuring voice he says: "Today, I am making *bana sana* in the names of those women who cast their eyes at us while sending us away. May we have success in the hunt as soon as we enter the jungle. May oil of the marking-nut drop in the eyes of those who cast evil eyes on us."

Now some of the party are told off and go in twos in different directions to look for monkeys. . . . When these men return with the desired information, the most suitable position in the jungle is selected where the hunters set up their nets in a line from tree to tree. Two or three men remain squatting in concealment with sticks or clubs in their hands at a distance of about twenty yards straight in front of the line of nets. These men are known as *atawahas*. Two other men are selected as *atomdas* and are stationed further off, one about twenty yards to the right and another about the same distance to the left of the *atawahas*. At about the same distance further off in front of each *atomda* stands a *bajhur*, and still further ahead of them at some distance stands a *babsor*.

Two other men styled *beberas*, one from each side, drive the monkeys toward the *atomdas*. The *atawahas* also come up, and all together drive the monkeys towards the nets and strike them dead with their clubs and sticks. The game bagged, the nets are taken down and the party leave the forest.

When they arrive at a suitable spot near some stream or other water, they light a fire, generally by friction, and scorch the monkeys in it, wash them clean, and cut them up, and take out the brains, heart, lungs, liver, entrails, and flesh of the fore-leg joint, place them in a bag improvised with *gungu* leaves sewn up with reed-needles. These are roasted by placing burning logs of wood above and below. When roasted, the meat is taken out and distributed among the members of the party. But they must not help themselves to it until the *Naya*, who was given a bit of the *ihim* (liver), has by himself roasted it by the same method and standing a little apart from the rest and with this roasted meat in hand, and his back towards them, has offered a little to all the spirits jointly, and promised them similar offerings in future if they always brought them such game.[12]

Among both groups of Birhors it is apparent that the begetting of future hunters (and gardeners) has increased the importance of marriage and child-bearing. Marriage and birth are consequently the occasions of prolonged ceremony, permeated throughout with magic, taboo, and worship of the spirits. The children are very well cared for. Yet, while being carried about on the mother's hip or back, they cannot fail to catch from her the impression that life is difficult, and hostile spirits are everywhere.

So long as a baby is carried in the mother's arms or slung on her back, its mother, while going to some other *tanda* or to some village or market-place, either puts a mark of soot between its eyebrows to protect it from the evil eye or evil spirits, or, while crossing a stream, . . . takes up a little sand, and ties it up at one end of her cloth. On her return journey, when her house is in sight, she takes the sand between the tips of her two fingers and throws it behind her back.[13]

No child can escape the knowledge that evil is ever imminent.

All the ills of life—and life is brimful of ills—are believed to be caused by supernatural agencies—either by spirits hovering about in earth, air, and water, hill and forest, river and spring, or by lesser powers and energies immanent in various animate beings as well as in certain inanimate objects and even in such immaterial things as a spoken word, an expressed wish, a passing thought or emotion, a passing glance, a magic formula or diagram, and certain names and numbers. And the problem of life which has ever presented itself to the tribal mind is how to protect the community and its members and their scanty earthly possessions from the evil attentions of spirits and the harmful influences of other mysterious powers and energies so as to make life worth living.[14]

To the Birhor "everything above, below, and around him is animated either by a spirit or by a spiritual energy or power." [15] The most important spirits are those of the native hills of each Birhor clan, called *Buru-Bongas,* or *Ora-Bongas.* With these are associated the daily-worshipped ancestral spirits (the *Haprom*) and the other deities and spirits recognized by the Birhors. Among the latter are: the supreme god, *Singabonga,* the creator, symbolized by the sun, who ordinarily takes no active part or even interest in human affairs, but must be periodically sacrificed to, and the mother goddesses, *Devi Mai* and *Bushi Mai,* intensely interested in man, and if properly served, bringing him health, progeny, and food.

Many spirits do not ordinarily require regular sacrifices from individuals or families, but at any moment they may begin to do so, very insistently, their way of making their wants known being repeated misfortune visited on some family until they call in a *mati* or ghost-doctor (of whom there are one or two in every *tanda*) and have him divine the spirit's name and wishes. For instance:

A Birhor woman picked up from the road a brass bell which had dropped down unnoticed from the neck of a bullock employed in dragging a country cart, and soon afterwards her daughter fell ill, and a *mati* or spirit-doctor was called in to find out the cause of the illness. The mati discovered by divination that the mother of the girl had picked up something made of metal which carried a spirit called *Banjari-bhut,* and that the child could be cured only if she made a *manita* of that spirit and periodically sacrificed a goat. She did so, and the child was cured. And to this day she along with her husband periodically offers sacrifices to the Banjari-bhut with a brass bell placed before them as the emblem of the spirit. . . . When the mother dies, the spirit, thus acquired by "accident," will pass to one or more of her daughters "by inheritance," so to say.[16]

The Birhors are little given to black magic or any form of witchcraft, but they have developed to some degree the aversive phases of magic; they have procedures for stopping rain, lightning, high winds, and hail storms; driving away bugs, mosquitoes, and snakes; preventing pumpkins from rotting, and so on. The following is an example of the rainmaking magic of the Jaghis, the Birhors who are settlers:

Early in the morning they go up the nearest hill and roll down stones of all sizes which produce a rumbling noise in falling to the ground; and this noise is at the same time intensified by beating a drum so as to produce a low, heavy, continued sound in imitation of the pattering rain on the roof of their huts.[17]

The taboos of the Birhors, a few of which are subjoined, afford an especially clear insight into certain of the mental processes of primitive peoples:

A woman must not step over a hunting net or hunting club. Should she do so, there will be no luck in the chase. The club in such case is thrown away.

A Birhor youth must not eat an egg which emits a sound when shaken; should he do so he will get pus in his ears.

A Birhor must not point with the finger at the rainbow; should he do so, the offending finger will get maimed or curved.

If anyone looks at a Birhor with one eye in the morning, the latter will get no game or *chop* that day. To prevent this, the former is made to look at him again with both eyes open.

A Birhor must not look back when leaving home to join a hunting expedition, as that will bring him ill luck in the chase.

A Birhor family must not leave any metal utensils outside their hut. Should they do so, a thunderbolt will strike the hut.[18]

At the beginning of this sketch it was suggested that the Birhors now exemplify the changes in culture beginning to take place in even the most backward tribes of the world. This has not been very apparent in the facts so far cited. However, the interesting thing about the Birhors is the clear distinction still evident between their primitive and largely unchanged procedures and the Hindu ideas entering their lives at *one* point—through their folk-tales and mythology. The imaginative life of the Birhors has been immensely stimulated by Hindu legend and story. Sita, Rama, Lakshman, Ravana, and Hanuman (the monkey god), all figure in the Birhor version of the great Hindu epic, the *Ramayana*. Brahmins, kings, queens, princesses, warriors, cities, merchants, elephants, palanquins, and palaces form elements in some of their favorite fireside tales.

Meanwhile, in their daily life, the greater proportion of the Birhors stay shyly as far away as possible from the world into which they allow their imagination thus occasionally to take them.

3. *The BaVenda of South Africa.* * The BaVenda are a tribe belonging to the Bantu peoples of South Africa. They live in northern Transvaal, just south of the Limpopo River, in a mountainous district, and number about 150,000 souls. Still showing pastoral skills, they afford an illuminating study of religion at the beginning of the agricultural stage. Physically, the BaVenda show evidences of being a composite people, with a strong Hamitic strain. Socially, they are polite and hospitable, but secretive about personal life and ancestral customs, probably because of memories of exploitation by early European settlers; but they are not inclined to be warlike, as are the other Bantu peoples. They live in cylindrical huts, with conical grass-thatched roofs, the main

* This account, which attempts only to present the religious conceptions and practices of the BaVenda, is drawn from the very inclusive book, *The BaVenda*, by Hugh A. Stayt, Oxford University Press, 1931. Quotations are by permission of the publishers.

structural elements being strong stakes bound together with withes. They keep large herds of cattle, by which they reckon their wealth, but depend for actual livelihood upon agriculture. Their crops include maize, Kaffir corn, millet, beans, pumpkins, watermelons, vegetable marrow, and sweet potatoes, the ground being worked with a hoe, mainly by women. Until the introduction of manufactured products from Europe, the native industries included such arts as weaving, skin-dressing, iron-smelting, hoe-making, and copper-refining.

The social organization shows variety. Each individual is a member of a number of independent groupings. The four mentioned below are the most important. He belongs to his own small family circle. He is a member of a larger group, his patrilineal lineage, through which his descent, succession, and inheritance are reckoned. In addition to this, he has close emotional ties with his whole matrilineal lineage. Lastly, he belongs to a *sib* of totemic character, and is called by the name of some animal, plant, or inanimate object (lion, dove, pig, elephant, goat, water-buffalo, crocodile, etc.) to which he pays special regard as his totem.

The attitude of the BaVenda toward the supernatural is displayed in beliefs and practices that run the whole gamut of religious ideas, from belief in something like *mana,* through animism and ancestor-worship, to belief in a supreme god, mysteriously presiding over his creation.

A fundamental concept is the belief that every object, animate or inanimate, possesses a kinetic power for good or evil. For example, when Stayt inquired about a small piece of wood, worn as a charm around the neck of one of the BaVenda for protection when traveling, he discovered:

It was taken from a bough of a tree overhanging a difficult climb on a well-frequented path. This bough was grasped by every passer-by in order to assist him over the difficult place. In this way the power of that particular bough was inordinately increased . . . , and it became the obvious source from which effective charms for the timid traveller could be obtained. Conversely, the history of some powdered wood, possessing a great deal of power to do evil to the traveller, disclosed the fact that in a well-trodden path a small root caused annoyance to every passer-by, being in a spot where it almost inevitably knocked his toe. This root, unlike the friendly bough, became a source of evil power, and its wood was used for charms to bring harm to the traveller.[19]

From this sort of belief have sprung the magico-religious practices of the BaVenda. The medicine man (*nganga*) and the diviner (*mungoma*) are the most important persons in the BaVenda community.

The former (the *nganga*) has power to cure disease. His rigorous training in his craft has qualified him to be either a specialist in one family of diseases or a general practitioner treating all diseases. By the use of such drugs, emetics, and poisons as are found in plants, he treats a great variety of ailments, such as malaria, rheumatism, pneumonia, insanity, and toothache, often with success. The healing agents are supposed to contain different types of power, and by mixing them in certain ways the nganga directs their energy into the desired channels. It is an important belief, however, that the disease itself is rarely thought to be due to natural causes; it is nearly always attributed to spiritual agencies, either to the adverse influence of offended ancestral spirits or to the much more malevolent operations of the chief obsession of the BaVenda —wizards and witches.

Wizards and witches (sing. *muloi,* pl. *vhaloi*) are universally feared. Vhaloi may be of either sex, but are usually thought to be women. They are of two kinds. Those who consciously and deliberately practice the black art, by themselves or with the aid of a conscienceless nganga, won over by a large fee, compose the first group. The motive that oftenest moves them is hatred, an intense desire to destroy the person or persons disliked.

A very simple way of killing an enemy is for a muloi to obtain from the nganga a death-dealing powder. Looking in the direction of the enemy he blows the powder towards him, saying at the same time, "You must die!" The closer the powder can be brought to the victim the more rapid will be his death.[20]

The other kind of muloi is such unwittingly! The circumstances surrounding cases like this are often tragic. The sense of conscious innocence is no protection from suspicion. It is believed that anyone, at any moment, may become, subconsciously or during sleep, a person possessed by some hideous spirit that has entered him, perhaps from a hyena, crocodile, owl, or snake. During the day, such a muloi, unsuspecting his tragic case, will be an innocuous member of the village community, but during the night a destroyer of health, of property, and of life! It then becomes an urgent matter to ferret out the evil one and exact the extreme penalty. A diviner or a nganga can detect a culprit by occult means, but mere appearances may be enough to fix suspicion, as the following passage proves.

A farmer at Lwamondo shot a crocodile, and to his extreme concern the bullet ricochetted from its hide and severely wounded a boy some distance away; this boy, when he returned to his village, after recovering from the wound, was straightway dubbed a muloi, and he and all his relatives were obliged to leave that part of the country. The people had absolutely no doubt that he was a crocodile, disguised in human form, otherwise the bullet that hit the crocodile could never have hit him as well.[21]

The pathetic fact is that the supposed muloi is usually convinced, to his or her own great horror, of being guilty as charged.

Suspected persons are haled before the diviner or *mungoma*, whose special function it is, in distinction from the nganga, to determine the identity of evil-doers. Since all deaths, save those of very old people, are due to witchcraft, he specializies in detecting those who have caused death. He ostensibly does all his divining by throwing a set of dice, which are read after they come to rest, or by floating seeds in a divining bowl. Woe to the person designated by him as guilty!

The cult of the dead plays a primary role in the religious life of the BaVenda. To them human souls are a combination of breath and shadow, two elements which depart from every living creature at death. The soul after leaving the body at death must find a new place in which to rest. It usually lingers for a while at the grave, but not for long. Soon it will search around for a better abiding place. It may reveal itself to its descendants in dreams, and thus make its needs known. Or it may find another body. There are isolated instances of belief among the BaVenda in reincarnation of souls, especially of ancient chiefs, in lions, leopards, and snakes. But the most desirable state to which the souls of the dead can attain is to be held in the memory of living descendants and to be cherished and cared for by them.

When anyone dies, every relative tries to be present at the death-bed, otherwise suspicion of complicity in the death may fall upon him. The first action after death is to cut off a portion of the garment of the deceased and preserve it for the diviner against the time when the cause of death is to be determined. The relatives keep the place of burial a secret, lest an enemy dig up the remains and practice witchcraft with them. A characteristic bit of ritual is for the eldest son to murmur over the grave of his mother, as he tosses in the first clod of earth, "You can rest in peace, my mother. So do not trouble us; I will give you all that you require." [22] The period of mourning, marked by shaving of the heads of all the relatives, continues until the cause of death has been discovered by the diviner and the death avenged. It is highly important thereafter to keep the ancestral spirit satisfied, for all trouble to the living is caused either by witchcraft or the dissatisfaction of the dead. In order that the ancestral spirits may be focussed or symbolized in something tangible, the ancestors of the father's lineage are collectively represented either by a cow and a sacred black bull, regarded as the embodiments of the patrilineal spirits, or by two large cylindrical, highly polished stones, embedded near the hut of the headman of the

lineage; while the spirits of the mothers are represented by a black female goat. In addition to this, the male members of the lineage are
individually represented by a spear, laid up in the hut of the head of
the lineage with those earlier placed there, and the female members by
an iron or copper ring, or by a miniature hoe fastened to a stick and
carried by a female descendant.

In addition to the ancestral spirits there exists a host of other powers,
less defined in form and character. Some are mountain spirits, the sight
of whom brings death to the traveler, and spirits in streams and pools,
armed with death-dealing bows and arrows. A great many spirits live in
rivers and lakes, some, or perhaps most, of whom are ancestral. But the
greatest and most shadowy of all spirits is the mysterious Supreme
Being, *Raluvhimba.* This elusive, monotheistic deity is associated with
the creation of the world and is thought to live somewhere in the
heavens. "The word *luvhimba,*" says Stayt, "means eagle, the bird that
soars aloft; the BaVenda have a very real idea of this great power
travelling through the sky, using the stars and wind and rain as his
instruments." [23] Raluvhimba is remote and inscrutable, as are the similar
deities of the other Bantu peoples; but the BaVenda are exceptional in
the amount of respect which they pay to him, usually through their
chiefs. They associate him with the rainmaker, Mwari, of the Bantus of
Matebeleland, and seek his favors therefore especially in time of
drought, the bringing on of which is credited to him. Any thunderous
noise is his voice. In 1917 a meteor burst in the middle of the day at
Khalavha, with a loud humming sound and a crash like thunder. The
BaVenda rushed into the open in all their villages, with cries meant to
express joy, clapping their hands and blowing horns, in order to give
a warm welcome to the tremendous god. The same sort of demonstration
follows an earthquake, the people shouting, "Give us rain! Give us
health!" But Raluvhimba is not approached by individuals nor by families in private devotion; he is worshipped either by the whole people
at once or by a representative of the whole people speaking in their
names. Here is an unusually clear instance of a transitional practice by
which an originally aloof high god may become in the higher religions
the one true God to whom, first the group, then individuals, may pray.

SUGGESTIONS FOR FURTHER READING

Ashley-Montague, M. F. *Coming into Being among Australian Aborigines.*
    E. P. Dutton, 1938

Benedict, Ruth. *Patterns of Culture*. Mentor Books, 1952

Breuil, H. *Four Hundred Centuries of Cave Art*. Montignac, 1952

Codrington, R. H. *The Melanesians*. Clarendon Press (Oxford), 1891

Durkheim, Emil. *The Elementary Forms of the Religious Life*. Allen & Unwin, 1915

Elkin, A. P. *The Australian Aborigines: How to Understand Them*. 3rd ed. Angus and Robertson (Sydney), 1954

Evans-Pritchard, E. E. *Nuer Religion*. Clarendon Press (Oxford), 1956

Fortune, R. F. *Sorcerers of Dobu*. Routledge and Sons, 1932

Frazer, James G. *The Golden Bough*. One volume abridgement, Macmillan, 1923

————. *The Fear of the Dead in Primitive Religion*. Macmillan, 1933–36

Goldenweiser, A. A. "Totemism: An Essay on Religion and Society" in V. F. Calverton (ed.), *The Making of Man: An Outline of Anthropology*. Modern Library, 1931

Goode, William J. *Religion among the Primitives*. Free Press (Glencoe, Illinois), 1951

Howells, W. W. *The Heathens: Primitive Man and His Religions*. Doubleday, 1948

James, E. O. *The Beginnings of Religion*. Hutchinson's Library, 1949

————. *Prehistoric Religion*. Harper, 1957

Lessa, W. A. and Vogt, E. Z., eds. *Reader in Comparative Religion: An Anthropological Approach*. Row, Peterson and Co. (Evanston, Illinois), 1958

Lowie, Robert H. *Primitive Religion*. Enl. ed. Liveright, 1948. Available as Universal Lib. pb.

Luquet, G. H. *The Art and Religion of Fossil Man*. Yale, 1930

Malinowski, Bronislaw. *Myth in Primitive Society*. Norton, 1926

————. *Magic, Science, and Religion*. Beacon Press, 1948. (Anchor pb, 1954)

Marett, R. R. *The Threshold of Religion*. Macmillan, 1914

Maringer, J. *The Gods of Prehistoric Man*. Knopf, 1960

Money-Kyrle, R. *The Meaning of Sacrifice*. Hogarth (London), 1930

Murdock, G. P. *Our Primitive Contemporaries*. Macmillan, 1914

————. *Social Structure*. Macmillan, 1949

Otto, Rudolf. *The Idea of the Holy*. Oxford, 1924

Pettazoni, Raffaele. "The Formation of Monotheism," in *Essays on the History Religions*. E. J. Brill, 1954

Radcliffe-Brown, A. R. *The Andaman Islanders*. Cambridge, 1922

————. *Taboo*. Cambridge, 1939

Radin, Paul. *Primitive Religion: Its Nature and Origin*. Viking, 1937. Available as Dover pb

————. *The World of Primitive Man*. Schuman, 1953

Schmidt, Wilhelm. *The Origin and Growth of Religion*. Dial, 1931

Spencer and Gillen. *The Arunta*. Macmillan, 1928

Wallis, W. D. *Religion in Primitive Society*. Crofts, 1939

2 Representative National Religions of the Past

THE CONCLUDING PARAGRAPH OF THE LAST CHAPTER DEALT WITH AN IMportant transition in thought and devotion. It provided us an instance of the emergence of a national idea transcending tribal belief. The national religions which appeared with the rise of states and kingdoms were full of figures like Raluvhimba.

For it is no great step to go from the religion of the BaVenda, with its mysterious, eagle-swift rainmaker and thunderer, its mountain and river spirits and ancestor-worship, to the more highly articulated national religions which came into being when—as happened in Egypt, Mesopotamia, Greece, and Italy—scores of tribes coalesced into nations, and a king, a city, or a confederacy bound many tribes and towns together into one. Marduk, Amon, Zeus, and Jupiter were but Raluvhimba and his associates decked out with the diverse attributes and histories which a more highly developed language, culture, and historical tradition bestowed upon them.

And the later, greater religions never wholly outgrew their origins. They never withdrew their roots from the primitive soil that had first nourished them. Though men regarded with faces upturned in wonder the spreading branches under which they took refuge, they knew, without needing to recognize the fact, that they stood on ancient, hidden roots.

That this is a most interesting area of history to explore needs no argument. Little wonder that so many treatises, monographs, and books, weighty with fact and speculation, have been written on the religions which have perished among the nations, but were the vital agents of transition from primitive animism and polytheism to the higher religions carrying a world message and ministering to the spiritual needs of Everyman. There is profit therefore in doing these two things: in studying the original context from which the primitive elements yet retained in the high religions have been drawn, and in seeing at what point, and with what results, the upsurge to higher levels and a world faith and message began.

This chapter is devoted to the first of these objectives, while the rest of the book is chiefly concerned with the second. There is much to consider. The details, encyclopedic in scope and fullness, intrigue one's curiosity, and beckon eagerly for notice; but though we shall find them crowding around our path, and must indeed look closely at many of them, we hope not to be deflected from pursuing our double aim.*

I   EGYPT

Perhaps Egypt gives us the simplest case of the development from early animism and fetishism to a more or less systematized polytheism and an emerging national ethics. Upper Egypt was comparatively self-contained. It experienced very much less of outside interference than Mesopotamia; and there were long periods of time when there was absolutely none of it. But in the Delta (Lower Egypt) contacts with the outside world were constant; for not only did travelers and traders come in great numbers, bringing with them new ideas and customs from abroad, many of which the Egyptians adopted along the whole Nile, but

* Because of this book's over-all plan, the present chapter is of necessity brief. It may therefore seem to the advanced student oversimplified. Its aim, however, is to sketch in broad lines for the less informed reader the various milieus in which Judaism, Christianity, and Islam rose and spread. The college teacher who might wish to spend more time in this area could ask the students to read one or more of such works (all obtainable in paperback) as: H. Frankfort, *Ancient Egyptian Religion* (Torch) and *Birth of Civilization in the Near East* (Anchor); Gilbert Murray, *The Five Stages of Greek Religion* (Anchor); M. P. Nilsson, *Greek Folk Religion* (Torch); H. J. Rose, *Religion in Greece and Rome* (Torch); T. R. Glover, *Conflict of Religions in the Early Roman Empire* (Beacon).

there were also invasions that wrought forced changes. Nevertheless, taking Egypt as a whole, for longer periods than elsewhere near the Mediterranean, the internal cultural and religious changes went on in a kind of simpleness and singleness of logical development.

The Physical and Social Background of Egyptian Religion

The physical reasons for this comparative self-sufficiency are almost too well-known to rehearse. Cut off from the world by the Mediterranean on the north, and by vast expanses of barren desert rising in the east slowly toward rugged Abyssinia and in the west stretching in "lone and level sands" over more than a thousand miles of Sahara wasteland; fenced off, too, on the south by wild equatorial mountains and the six cataracts falling northward through their gorges, Egypt lay for centuries quiet under the sun, her material needs assured by the annual overflow of the great stream which was veritably her river of life in that rainless land, and the thoughts of her people, perhaps from sheer need of something to do, devoted to their cult of the dead, with its hope of endless life.

The history of Egypt is one of the longest known to us. In the Old Stone Age scattered groups of hunters crept along the mud-strips of the Nile (narrower and thinner even than now), leaving behind them their stone implements, flimsy huts, and buried dead. These wanderers gave way some time during the Neolithic period to the first permanent residents of the Nile valley, a dark-skinned pastoral folk, who, as the centuries advanced, housed themselves in wood, brick, and then stone, organized themselves into communities, and latterly began to employ a distinctive picture-writing (the first Egyptian hieroglyphics) to keep their records and send their messages. Though the wandering tribes of the Stone Age had now vanished, and city-states had appeared, there was no nation of Egyptians as yet. Each community lived out its independent existence as a *nome*, that is, as a group of villages spread across a fertile tract of Nile mud around a larger town that was their county seat. The people of one nome might look across the river at those of another, learn from their neighbors how to regulate and control the overflow of the Nile, but yet have separate customs and gods and be on terms of relative hostility. Then, as cultures grew more attractive, and inter-communication increased, there came amalgamation, usually by way of conquest of one nome by another. For centuries this process went on, until there were but two kingdoms, the Upper Kingdom of inner Egypt and the Lower Kingdom of the Delta. These two kingdoms were finally united into one by Menes (?), the founder of the First Dynasty, about 2900 B.C.*

It is against this background of unification that we must see the history of religion in Egypt. For it too is a story of amalgamations—divine amalgamations that were never quite complete.

Animal-Worship and Animal-headed Gods

The first Egyptian "gods" were, or at least manifested themselves as, animals; and each community had its animal guardian—a sort of urban animal-cult. Thinis and Abydos, for example, worshiped the jackal, Fayum the crocodile. Thebes had its Amon, a ram; Memphis two guardians, Sekhmet, a lioness, and Apis (or Hapi), a bull. At Dendera they paid reverence to Hathor, a cow; at Edfu to the hawk Behudet (later called Horus); and Hierakonpolis honored the vulture Nekhebt. At other places like honors were bestowed on the baboon, hippopotamus, shrew-mouse, ibis, cobra, cat, frog, eel, and other creatures.

But apparently these beasts and birds were not worshiped for their animal qualities alone but also for the human (or super-human) powers and characteristics they possessed, or represented; for, in evident recognition of the belief that divine quality as such could manifest itself in either man or beast and so showed itself in both, they acquired human bodies under their animal heads, and vice versa. For the gods seemed *pictured* best as composite beings. Thus Knummu had a man's body with a ram's head, and was in human fashion skilful in shaping men and beasts on the potter's wheel; Anubis, the guardian of the cemetery and guide of the dead, possessed a jackal's head; while Thoth, the god

---

* The First and Second Dynasties (2900–2600 B.C.), which not only united Egypt but established an ascendancy over Palestine and the coast of Syria, were succeeded by the Old Kingdom (2600–2200 B.C.), so famous for its pyramid builders (often called the Pyramid Age). After an intermediate period of breakdown of central authority (2200–2000 B.C.), the Middle Kingdom was established (*ca.* 1989 B.C.). The Middle Kingdom in turn gave way to the New Empire when the northern conquerors, the Hyksos, who had overrun Egypt, were heroically expelled (*ca.* 1560 B.C.), and Egypt surged on to the reconquest of Palestine and Syria—a bold assertion of an imperialism that only after long centuries and many reverses was to be abandoned, because Egypt herself was to suffer total conquest at the hands successively of Persians, Greeks, and Romans.—For dates see W. F. Albright, *From the Stone Age to Christianity* (Johns Hopkins, 1940), pp. 113–118, 151 f. See also Steindorf and Seele, *When Egypt Ruled the East* (University of Chicago Press, 1942), pp. 274 f.

Knummu with ram's head shaping Pharoah's son on a potter's wheel while ibis-headed Thoth determines the boy's span of life on a scale. (From a papyrus of the Ptolemaic period)

of learning, bore the head of the ibis. The lioness head of Sekhmet and the cat head of Bast surmounted lithe feminine bodies. Most curious was the greyhound form of Set, with an upright tail suggestive of the wart hog, though his legs were human. His great adversary, Horus, had a hawk's head, to signify he is the sun.

Divine Amalgamations

All these were early developments, and reflect political as well as religious change. As we have seen, the original nomes of Egypt—some forty-two in number—were gradually fused by conquest; but each was so closely identified with the animal-like god who was its guardian, that when one nome conquered another, and an over-all guardian deity was sought, the two gods were fused along with their territories, and often bore thereafter a hyphenated name, made from their two names. At times a local deity would be identified with one of the great gods in order to elevate him to a greater and more important role. It was thus that Amon-Re and Ptah-Sokar-Osiris came into being, their separate na-

tures blended so far as possible into one, and their secondary characteristics, if resistant to such a process, separately embodied in accessory
figures or symbols. Thus, on entering the Delta, and merging with Ptah
and Sokar at Memphis, where Apis the bull gave the shape of the godhead, Osiris retained his human form, but adopted the bull as his
associate. Thereafter he was sometimes called Osiris-Apis (whence the
Romans obtained the name Serapis, their term for the immortal bull-
spirit). And when Isis was identified in the Delta with the cow-goddess
Hathor, she sprouted two huge horns curving high above her head.

But in some cases blending was not feasible. In this event two
irreconcilable deities would be set against each other in the dualism of
eternal enmity, or else a triad (or even a larger group) of associates
would be formed, in which the special character of each god and goddess
was preserved. So, when Upper and Lower Egypt were united under
the First Dynasty, Horus, the chief god of the Delta, and Set, dominant
in Upper Egypt, continued their bitter struggle; for since Horus was
now conceived to be the sun, Set became the power of darkness. Even
after their enmity was caught up and made a minor theme in the
dramatic myth of Isis and Osiris, they went on with their feud, Horus
as the son-avenger (he was now the son of Isis by Osiris) and Set,
the brother of Osiris, as the fratricidal uncle, his heart full of murderous
jealousy. But triads and enneads (or groups of nine) were formed also
for other and quite natural reasons. It was, for example, natural to think
that the gods were grouped in families. Thus at Thebes Amon-Re, Mut,
and Khonsu were father, mother, and son. At Memphis Ptah, Sekhmet
and Imhotep were similarly united; while at Heliopolis a family of nine,
in four generations, was worshipped, namely, Atum (the oldest; originally the hill of earth that emerged from the primordial sea; later associated with the evening sun), his children Shu (the air that holds up
the sky) and Tefnut (the latter's female complement), Shu and Tefnut's
children Geb (the earth) and Nut (the sky), and the children in turn
of Geb and Nut: Osiris, Isis, Set, and Nephthys. In other places Osiris
and Isis formed a separate triad with Horus, their son.

The Isis-Osiris-Horus Complex

The Isis-Osiris family group was relatively late in appearing, but its
members stimulated the popular imagination as no other Egyptian gods
did.

Osiris may have had a prehistoric origin. According to one view, he
was initially brought in from Libya, where he was the fructifying water
which produces vegetation even in the desert. But this is by no means

certain; for there is perhaps better reason to think, since he always seems to have been in human form, that he came from Syria, and was originally an agricultural deity. But after he was established in Egypt, and became the son of Geb and Nut, he was more or less identified with the life-giving water of the Nile. His sister Isis, who was also his wife, is perhaps less ancient a figure, but from about 1500 B.C. (during the New Empire) she grew more popular, certainly more adorable, than he. Her appeal was increased by the pathos of her story. According to the Pyramid Texts, which are our earliest sources, Osiris, the good and beneficent king, was killed by his brother Set (by drowning in the inundation of the Nile?). His sisters Isis and Nephthys found his body and wept over it. While Isis was embracing the corpse, it revived for awhile and impregnated her. She later secretly gave birth to Horus, and brought him up in a place in the Delta without discovery. When the child was old enough, she sent him forth to avenge his father. Horus found the corpse of his father still preserved. Before the court of the gods presided over by his grandfather Geb he refuted Set's denial that he had murdered Osiris and won the acclaim of the court as Osiris' successor and king in his place. Set had stolen the third eye of Osiris, fixed in his forehead and betokening his kingship; so Horus now fought Set for it and recovered it, thus becoming king in actuality as well as in name. Horus immediately took the eye to the corpse of his father and his father awoke, stood up, and recovered the control of his limbs. (So might the eye of the kingly sun bring life and resurrection to the grain lying moist in the soil.) But Osiris did not remain above ground; he went to the underworld to become the judge and god of the dead, while Horus became the lord of the upper world, both as the ruler of Egypt (by identification with its kings) and its mighty sun.°

Sun-Worship

But Horus was not the only sun deity. There were others, one of whom (Re) came to eclipse him. From one end of their land to the other, the Egyptians knew of course how much their crops depended on the light and warmth which sped out of the sun into the ground where the seed lay waiting. They were aware of this from the beginning. As has been said:

° This is something of a simplification. There were really three chief Horuses (and others of a minor sort). One, Horus the Elder, was a brother of Osiris and Isis; another was Horus the avenger of his father; and the third was Horus the child (Harpocrates), son of Isis.

The all-enveloping power and glory of the Egyptian sun is the most insistent fact in the Nile valley. . . . The Egyptian saw him in different, doubtless originally local forms.

Probably the oldest notion of him goes back to the days when the pre-historic Egyptians were still leading a hunting life in the Nile marshes, when they pictured the Sun-god as a hunter poling or paddling himself across the reed-grown marshes in a boat made by lashing together two bundles of reeds like a catamaran. Glimpses of this archaic notion are still preserved in the oldest passages of the Pyramid Texts, which often picture the Sun-god ferrying across the celestial marshes in the "double reed-boat". . . .

[Later] the "double reed-boat" was succeeded by a gorgeous royal barge like that of the earthly Pharaoh. In this luminous sun-barque, one for the morning and the other for the evening, it was believed that the Sun-god majestically crossed the celestial ocean as the Pharaoh sailed the Nile.[1]

This was Re (or Ra), the sun conceived in human form, and especially the noontide sun. The rising sun was Kheprer, appearing in the *mandet* boat ascending the morning sky; and the declining sun, going down in the *mesektet* boat to the horizon, was Atum. These were two sun-gods older even than Re.

But the sun was also a bird, and, again, a beetle. As bird he was Horus, the high-flying falcon swiftly spanning the sky. (Indeed, the symbol oftenest used in all Egypt was simply the widespread wings of the mounting falcon, clearest sign of the rising sun.) More unusual was the identification of the sun-god with the scarab or sacred dung-beetle. Here the Egyptian peasant with nimble imagination transferred to the sky his observation of the diligent scarab rolling along the ground the ball of dung in which it was placing its eggs; he thought of the sun as a huge ball rolled along by a mighty sky-beetle, whose name was Kheprer (or Khopri). (It was common in later days for the figure of the scarab to be incised on seals, shown in amulets, or placed on the foreheads of the statues of kings; there was life and protection in it, and by it the power of darkness was held at bay.)

At Heliopolis, in Lower Egypt, the priests of the sun-god Atum coalesced him with Re. This was but the first step. Next, he was co-ordinated and fused with the various Horuses, from the "Horus of the horizon" (Harakhte) on through the other Horuses of the daylight hours. The winged beetle Kheprer was part of him. And not only was he the sun as a natural force; he was also the power in kings that enabled them to overspread and protect their realms.

It is for this reason that the later pharaohs of the Pyramid Age (2600–2200 B.C.) assumed the title of "son of Re" Their obelisks were built, most likely, as massive symbols of the sun's ray; and the pharaohs lying in their long sleep within the mighty pyramids, symbols too of the sun, were one with the sun in death as in life. The sun, their father in life, was now their immortal life in death.

In the time of the New Empire a thousand years later, the queen had become the high-priestess of the sun, and through the pharaohs who impersonated him, the sun was the father of her children, who were gods from birth.

Meanwhile the sun had acquired still another dimension by becoming Amon-Re. Amon was originally the local god of Thebes, in Upper Egypt, and of the temple of Karnak near by, often enlarged and embellished that it might be a thing of utmost magnificence and splendor. When mighty Thebes became by conquest the ruling city of all Egypt (about 2000 B.C.), Amon grew into a god of national stature, and combined with powerful Re as the greatest of the gods. A divine family was placed around him. Mut, the goddess of Thebes, with vulture headdress, was his wife, and the moon-god, Khonsu, was their son. The ram was his representative among the animals. Before him stood the cobra, to signify that he was king of the gods; and above him hung the sun's winged disc.

The Other Gods

There were other gods. In Memphis, for example, the citizens worshipped an abstractly conceived god called Ptah, considering him to be the creator who made the world from primordial mud. He was, strangely enough, always enveloped from head to foot in bandages, exactly like a mummy, as though to suggest that he came from a far past, his special history no longer known. And there was Maat, the goddess of truth, who usually appears in the Egyptian wall-paintings of the judgment, standing at the doorway of the great hall where the heart of the dead is weighed against a feather. Safekht was the goddess of writing, Hu the god of taste, Anubis the jackal-guardian of the cemetery, Neit the goddess of hunting, holding bow and arrows. There were many others. To extend the list would serve little purpose here. Suffice it to say that the names remaining only increase the feeling that the ancient Egyptians were enthusiastic polytheists, to say the least; for not only did they honor the many deities to which Egypt gave birth, but also many foreign importations, like Anaitis, the Anahita of the Zoroastrians, and Qedesh or Ashtarth, the Ishtar or Consecrated Lover of Babylonia and Palestine.°

° A later reaction from this (especially in the Delta) was to identify the foreign with the native gods—a process of amalgamation tending finally toward monotheism.

Doctrines of the Future Life

But however much the Egyptians enjoyed life—and they did—and however devoutly they honored the sun and the Nile that helped them to prolong it, they dwelt in thought more than any other people known to us on something which at first sight seems the opposite of life—the disposal of the dead and the after-life of kings and commoners. At first they thought it was only their kings who were happy in the hereafter. But then the belief began to grow that others could hope for as much—that, either in the West or in the Field of Rushes, there was a chance of blessedness for everyone.

It was not that there had ever been scepticism about an after-life. There was plenty of evidence that the dead did not perish.° The Egyptians were therefore very naturally anxious to secure their immortal satisfactions. Merry in life, they yearned to be joyful after death.

Their beliefs are hard to arrange logically. An early notion convinced them of the existence of the *ba* or animating soul—depicted as a human-headed bird whose seat was the "heart" or "abdomen," but which flew from the body with the last breath. It loved its body, and returned to it after death with longing and hunger, its physical desire for food and drink undiminished; hence, its return was not wholly satisfactory unless the body were somehow preserved, food and drink were provided, and its passage into and from the tomb were made easy by an opening, such as a tiny chimney or air-duct. But there was another

---

° Breasted suggests (in *Development of Religion and Thought in Ancient Egypt*, p. 49) what some of this evidence was. "Experience in the land of Egypt has led me," he wrote, "to believe that [the insistent faith in the hereafter] was greatly favored and influenced by the fact that the conditions of soil and climate resulted in such a remarkable preservation of the human body as may be found under natural conditions nowhere else in the world. In going up to the daily task on some neighboring temple in Nubia, I was not infrequently obliged to pass through the corner of a cemetery, where the feet of a dead man, buried in a shallow grave, were now uncovered and extended directly across my path. They were precisely like the rough and calloused feet of the workmen in our excavations. How old the grave was I do not know, but anyone familiar with the cemeteries of Egypt, ancient and modern, has found numerous bodies or portions of bodies indefinitely old which seemed about as well preserved as those of the living. This must have been a frequent experience of the ancient Egyptian, and like Hamlet with the skull of Yorick in his hands, he must often have pondered deeply as he contemplated these silent witnesses. The surprisingly perfect state of preservation in which he found his ancestors whenever the digging of a new grave disclosed them, must have greatly stimulated his belief in their continued existence, and often aroused his imagination to more detailed pictures of the realm and the life of the mysteriously departed." Reprinted by permission of the publishers.

soul. This was the *ka,* or the mental aspects of personality, the source
of its motives and intuitions, symbolized by two arms outstretched or by
an attendant figure formed as the double of the personality. It was this
soul that after death took up its residence in the lifelike statue of the
deceased placed in the tomb, and saw and enjoyed the pictures and
the models which portrayed its former life. Apparently the *ka* had its
higher and lower counterparts, quite aside from the *ba.* It was sometimes pictured as two outstretched arms with a bird mounting between
them. This bird was the *ikhu* or *"spirit"* (the highest intelligence), which
flew off to heaven at death in the form of a bird. A lower counterpart
was the "shadow" that everywhere accompanies a man walking in the
sunlight, his *khaibit.* (Evidently here as elsewhere the Egyptians had
some power of analysis but little of the ability to reassemble or
synthesize!)

That a happy hereafter was dependent on the preservation of the
body seemed obvious. The Egyptians early set about securing such
preservation.* Eventually they learned the secret of mummification. The
embalming was entrusted to skilled professionals.†

Not only was the body thus preserved for the *ba,* and a statue
besides provided as an abiding place for the *ka,* but the tomb was filled
with all manner of furniture and provisions. The needs of the *ba* were
met by jars of water, wine, grain, dates, cakes, and other foods, such
as portions of beef and fowl that had been dehydrated or reduced to
ashes; while the *ka* was provided with chairs, beds, and even with
chariots, of the usual size, and with hundreds of small models of women-
folk, servants, kitchen utensils and dishes, and many simulated food-
stuffs, down to little wooden loaves and fishes. Combs, hairpins, and

---

* When the idea arose that after three thousand years in the Kingdom of Osiris
(see the next section) the good soul returned to earth to re-enter its old body,
this motivation became still stronger.

† Herodotus tells us how in his time (relatively late, of course) the best embalming was done. The internal organs and the brain having been removed through
incisions, the embalmers, he says, would proceed thus: "They fill the belly with
pure myrrh pounded up with cassia and other spices, except frankincense, and sew
it together again. Having so done they keep it for embalming covered up in natron
for seventy days, but for a longer time than this it is not permitted to embalm it;
and when the seventy days are past, they wash the corpse and roll its whole body
up in fine linen cut into bands, smearing these beneath with gum, which the
Egyptians use generally instead of glue. Then the kinsfolk receive it from them
and have a wooden figure made in the shape of a man, and when they have had
this made they enclose the corpse, and having shut it up within, they store it in
a sepulchral chamber, setting it upright against the wall." ²

ointments were provided for primping, and carriages, boats, and various games for pleasure and pastime. Great treasures were in some cases included. The rich were surrounded in their long sleep with gilded and silver objects of art. Nothing was forgotten.

As to the models of women-folk and servants, a whole chapter of the *Book of the Dead** was devoted to spells for vivifying them into action. They were expected to go to work for the dead in the underworld, and were called *ushebtis* or "answerers." The statuette of a man bearing a bag and a hoe might have a charm written upon his chest: "O statuette, counted for X (name of deceased), . . . thou shalt count thyself for me at all times, to cultivate the fields, water the shores, transport sand of the east to the west, and say 'Here am I.' " [3] This was a spell thought sufficient to effect the desired result.

And what of the history of the soul in the other world? There was no unanimity about that. Many different ideas were current at one time or another. It was early thought that the sky-goddess Nut admitted favored souls (those of kings) to the region of the stars revolving around the Pole, a place high above all change and decay. The worshipers of Re had other expectations. In their tombs fully outfitted boats were placed, so that they might sail across the eastern sea and join the barque of the sun-god. In the mythological development of this idea, all sorts of difficulties were imagined, disagreeably hampering the soul in its initial journey to meet the sun. The eastern sea became Water Lily Lake, and the only way across it was on a ferry operated by a reluctant boatman who had to be coaxed to take a passenger. Sometimes the ferryman could not be persuaded; in which case the soul would have to get itself floated over the lake in a cloud of incense, or take to wing in the form of a bird. On its way it would find everything alive and speaking, nothing inert or dead; even the boat-oars, the boat itself, the objects it would have to pass after landing, had voices. Beyond the lake there would be further perils and delays, locked gates, encounters with hostile animals and serpents, strange wildernesses. When at length the soul would win its way to the sun, it might rest at last; or perhaps it might follow on with the sun to the west and under the earth into the twelve "caverns" of the night, each enclosed by the great gates that mark the hours.

It is an interesting aspect of these conceptions that the dead were often thought to *become* stars or to be *merged* into the sun-god himself, by a kind of multiple incarnation in him.

---

* So-called because it was enclosed in coffins as a complete guide-book, full of directions to the dead and of charms and incantations to make the best happen.

The Kingdom of Osiris

One of the oldest, perhaps *the* oldest conception of the after-life, and one destined to come into great popularity after the Pyramid Age, was that of the kingdom of Osiris. How one got to it differed with period and place. According to one view:

The transit of the soul to the blessed west of Osiris began at Abydos, up the long valley which leads to the Oasis road. The soul is represented setting out sturdily, staff in hand, to begin its long march. The Oasis was the frontier of the unknown. Beyond that lay the end of the world, at the mountains where the sun left the visible world to enter the underworld of stars, the Duat. There the fertile isles would be reached, where the corn grew higher than any on earth.[4]

But some views were that the Osirian fields were in the north (the Delta) or beyond the sea in Syria, or, more remotely, in the Milky Way, the great white Nile of the sky.

Wherever it was, it was a pleasant region. There, upon the fertile land, lush with vegetation, and with grain twelve feet high, the fortunate soul could sit at ease under the shade trees, watching his slaves (the *ushebtis*) plough the black earth with oxen or reap the enormous ears of grain or maize, while he played a leisurely game of draughts with his smiling wife or conversed with his friends.

But since not everyone deserved so blissful a lot, judgment had to

Osiris sitting as judge in the Hall of Truth, with a flail and a crook in his hands. Before him is a lotus supporting his grandchildren, then the Devouress, with the head of a crocodile, the forequarters of a lion, and the hindquarters of a hippopotamus. In the center ibis-headed Thoth serves as a scribe. At the right Anubis with a jackal head weighs a soul against a feather.

be passed before the soul could gain entrance to these enchanted fields. As pictured in the Book of the Dead, the examination of the soul is made in the presence of Osiris himself, and concerns goodness or wickedness. The soul is brought—as we often see in the scenes pictured on the funeral papyri—into the Hall of Truth by the jackal-headed Anubis, guardian of the cemetery, and is made to stand before Osiris, who is enthroned under a canopy and attended on either side by Isis and their sister Nephthys. When the soul beholds the lord of the dead, it immediately begins to justify itself, and does so not by confessing and repenting any sins, but by telling of the evil it has *not* done:

"Hail to thee, great god, lord of Truth . . . Behold, I come to thee, I bring to thee righteousness . . . I knew no wrong. I did no evil thing . . . I did not do that which the god abominates . . . I allowed no one to hunger. I caused no one to weep. I did not murder. I did not command to murder. I caused no man misery. I did not diminish food in the temples . . . I did not take away the food-offerings of the dead . . . I did not commit adultery . . . I did not diminish the grain measure . . . I did not load the weight of the balances. I did not deflect the index of the scales. I did not take milk from the mouth of the child. I did not drive away the cattle from their pasturage . . . I did not dam the running water [and thus divert from others the waters of the irrigation canals at the time of the inundation] . . . I did not interfere with the god in his payments. I am purified four times, I am pure . . ."[5]

After a similar "negative confession" to each of the forty-two judges sitting in a gallery as representatives of the nomes of Egypt, the dead man's heart is balanced by Anubis in the judgment scales against an ostrich feather. If it is a heart made light by goodness, and does not overweigh the scale, the ibis-headed Thoth, who is umpire and scribe, reports the fact to Osiris, and the soul is then allowed to enter the blessed fields of Osiris' realm. But if the scales prove the soul to be evil, retribution overtakes it. According to some conceptions, it is destroyed by a strange creature, "The Devouress," with the head and jaws of a crocodile, the fore-quarters of a lion, and the hind-quarters of a hippopotamus, waiting hungrily nearby, who springs forward and eats it. According to other conceptions it is thrown into a fiery hell, where it is punished severely.

Ikhnaton's Venture in Monotheism

So far, all the conceptions we have examined are polytheistic; but the history of Egyptian religion provides us at one point with a high-minded endeavor to institute a monotheistic reform.

It sprang from the conviction enkindled in a young pharaoh in whose court monotheism had already found voice. Undoubtedly he must have heard the Theban sun-hymn composed by two architects employed by his father Amenhotep II, which celebrated the sun under the appellation *Aton* (Solar Disc), in such words as these:

> O creator of what the earth brings forth, . . .
>   . . . good creator who takes the greatest pains with his
>   innumerable creatures. . . .
> He who reaches the ends of the lands every day and beholds those
>   who walk there . . .
> Every land adores him at his rising every day, in order to praise
>   him.[6]

By such words, and probably in sympathetic response to the urging of monotheistic enthusiasts, he was led to change the name of the national god from Amon to Aton, his own name from Amenhotep ("Amon is satisfied") to Ikhnaton ("Pious to Aton"), and to order Aton to be worshipped as the one and only god, the creator of all things and the sustainer of all creatures. In the temples of Egypt now, the priests who bowed before the exalted lord of creation chanted:

> Thou dawnest beautifully in the horizon of the sky,
> O living Aton who wast the Beginning of life!
> When thou didst rise in the eastern horizon,
> Thou didst fill every land with thy beauty.
> Thou art beautiful, great, glittering, high over every land,
> Thy rays, they encompass the lands, even to the end of all that
>   thou hast made.[7]

In some of the noblest phrases in the literature of Egyptian religion, they proclaimed the excellencies of Aton:

> How manifold are thy works!
> They are hidden before men,
> O sole God, beside whom there is no other.
> Thou didst create the earth according to thy heart.
>
> Thou didst make the distant sky in order to rise therein,
> In order to behold all that thou hast made . . .
> The world subsists in thy hand,
> Even as thou hast made them.
>
> When thou hast risen they live,
> When thou settest they die;
> For thou art length of life of thyself,
> Men live through thee.[8]

The determined young monarch ordered the names and figures of Amon and the other gods expunged from all monuments, temples, and public records. Even Osiris was set aside as one to be forgotten. In order to create an entirely new and helpful atmosphere for his court, Ikhnaton built a splendid new capital further down the Nile from Thebes, and called it Akhetaton ("Horizon of Aton"). Similar cities, meant to serve as centers of the new cult, were projected in Nubia and Syria, then still within the Egyptian Empire.

But the reform of Ikhnaton was not destined to outlive him. His son-in-law, who succeeded him, yielded to the priests of the old Amon party, and changed his name from Tutenkhaton to Tutenkhamon, the name by which he has become so well known today. In the restoration of the older forms of worship, it was Aton's name that was now expunged in every public place.

Amon-Re, Osiris, Isis, and Horus resumed their former reign, not to yield ground again until Christianity, a more formidable foe, overthrew them, beyond hope of restoration.

II   BABYLONIA

Cities, governments, ideographic writing, temples, and priests appeared even earlier in Mesopotamia than in Egypt, but the spirit breathing through them was sterner, more nakedly realistic, brutal, and of this world. The reasons are clear enough. Where Egypt was protected by thinly populated deserts on the east and west, cataracts on the south, and a northern sea, Mesopotamia, lying fertile and flat between the twin rivers that watered her, was open to invasions and attack from every quarter. There was no time to dwell in thought on eternity. The temporal and the changeful were always too present. Nothing remained stable for long; the pleasures of life had to be snatched quickly.

Or let us put the facts in this way: the prehistoric hunters and fishers in the swamps at the conjunction of the Tigris and Euphrates gave place to a culture of villages; and villages, layer on layer,* gave place to cities—Erech, Eridu, Lagash, Ur, Nippur, and others; and cities fought each other until one dominated another; and the Sumerian kingdoms rose, to be followed and absorbed by Semitic empires, and these by the Persian. In the same way also the gods of the fields and

---

* Houses being made of sun-dried bricks crumbled in time and new houses were built on the smoothed-out ruins.

streams, and those of the sky overhead, took to the towns, organized themselves into a super-state, with governing power lodged in a council of the gods, fought, made love, and merged into a vast pantheon with names almost beyond counting.*

The Sumero-Akkadian Pantheon

We hear there were nearly 4000 deities! Many of them, however, had only the status of servants, messengers, and warriors of the greater gods. Every part of nature was represented. Six deities eventually became most important. Each was the deity of a great city. Anu, the god of heaven, was the chief deity of Erech and the "pristine king and ruler" of the gods; Enlil, the air-god, who became the god of the lands beneath and a great warrior, was at Nippur; Sin, the moon-god, reigned at Ur; Babbar (who later took the Semitic name Shamash) was the sun-god at Larsa; Ea (or Enki), the water-god, made his home in Eridu; and Nintud, the mother-goddess, later identified with Ishtar, prevailed at Kish. It was usual for the male deities, major or minor, to have a consort, worshipped in a separate sanctuary built on to his temple. To this rule there were some exceptions. The mother-goddess Nintud was unmarried, and Anu's wife had no importance, her place being taken by her daughter, the virgin heaven-goddess, Innana. The gods were hospitable to one another. No regnant deity excluded other cults from his or her city. Though the chief fane always belonged to the chief god, other deities might have smaller sanctuaries in other parts of the city.

* Though Mesopotamian history before 3000 B.C. was relatively serene, even then the neolithic pottery-makers, who were the earliest villagers, were displaced by the town-building colonists who developed the Halaf culture (before 4500 B.C.) and the el-Obeid culture (*ca.* 4500–3800 B.C.). These were succeeded in the 4th millenium B.C. by the creators of the Uruk culture, probably immigrants from southwestern Iran, who in their turn gave way to still others. The Sumerian kingdoms, dominated by non-Indo-Europeans from highlands southwest of the Caspian Sea, arose and ran their course in the south (from about 2800 to 2360 B.C.). Meanwhile Semites from the Arabian Desert came into the north, to form the Akkadian kingdoms. Thereafter constant war-making on every side brought an end to any hope of security of tenure, whether of property or life, for very long. The great Semitic king Hammurabi of Babylon (1728–1686 B.C.) united north and south into one Sumero-Akkadian kingdom. For dates see Jack Finegan, *Light from the Ancient Past* (Princeton, 1946), pp. 13–39 *passim;* also W. F. Albright, *From the Stone Age to Christianity* (Johns Hopkins, 1957) and Isaac Mendelsohn, ed., *Religions of the Ancient Near East* (Liberal Arts Press, 1955). The last two are currently in paperback.

It was natural that these deities should be grouped into triads. In due course Anu, Enlil, and Ea were believed to divide the physical universe between them as the rulers respectively of heaven above, earth beneath, and the waters on and under the earth. Another (and later) triad had a more agricultural significance. It was composed of Shamash the sun-god, Sin the moon-god, and Ishtar the Semitic goddess of fertility, who, with unequaled ability to keep her name and functions dominant, was identified with the mother-goddesses Ninmah, Nintud, Ninhursag, Aruru, and others, and especially Innana of Erech, the Sumerian queen of heaven and goddess of love and fertility.*

A special group of gods were the Anunnaki, the nether world gods. Their chief was Nergal, originally a sun god but now as the god of pestilence the lord of the world below, the woe-begone Land of No Return. His consort was the dread goddess of death and sterility, Ereshkigal, an elder sister of Ishtar.

Of all these deities Ishtar was to come closest to being universally worshipped. She was the great mother-goddess, and yet had something almost virginal about her. By her attachment to Tammuz, the god of the spring sun and its awakenings, she established herself as a great lover in her own right. As the goddess of fertility, she gave children to women and life to vegetation. As the planet Venus, she was "the queen of the heavens and the stars." Her worship was destined to spread far to the west, to Palestine and to Egypt. Even the Zoroastrians were unable to resist her, and after changing her name to Anahita, "The Spotless One" (and thus purifying her!), they gave to her almost as great prominence as to Ormazd himself. We shall meet her again.

Marduk of Babylon

The greatest rival of Ishtar was Marduk. His prominence may be assigned, curiously enough, to sheer political good fortune. It happened that the sixth king of the first dynasty of Babylon, Hammurabi (2067–2025 B.C.), the same who issued the world-famous law code, made his city the capital of a powerful kingdom stretching from the Persian Gulf to the central provinces embraced between the Tigris and Euphrates. It was an achievement of permanent significance; for Babylon thus became and was to remain through twenty centuries of change one of the great cities of the world. And with the rise to power of Babylon,

---

* Another triad, a variant of this, had a meteorological character, and was composed of Shamash, Sin, and Adad, = the Sun, the Moon, and the Thunderer, a storm-god.

Marduk battling with Tiamat. From wall panel in palace of Ashur-nasir-apal II, 885-860 B. C. (Original in British Museum).

Marduk, its god, rose to greatness too. Not prominent before, he all but absorbed the surrounding gods. Not only did he link to himself Ea of Eridu as his father (whereby he absorbed Ea's earlier son, Ninurta the war-god) and make Nabu of Barsippa, the fire-god, his son, but he absorbed from them some of their functions (the wisdom of Ea and Nabu's power over destiny). The chief attributes of Enlil of Nippur were also transferred to him,* so that he might be acknowledged the lord of the heavens. Finally, the religious literature of Babylon was extensively revised to give him the prominent role his city demanded for him.

The Babylonian Myths and Epics

The Sumerians and Akkadians had fertile imaginations. They loved to tell stories about their gods and heroes. Although it does not serve

* Including Enlil's victory over Tiamat, the dragon of chaos. See the next section.

our purpose to explore the whole of this mythology, the following episodes, in part because of their intrinsic qualities but more because of
the parallels to the stories of the Old Testament which they present,
are of more than usual interest.

A. THE CREATION. According to an old Sumerian legend, the
present world order issued from a primeval conflict between the dragons of darkness and chaos, led by the bird-god Zu (or, in other accounts, by Tiamat) and the gods of light and order, headed by Ninurta,
the war-god. But the Babylonian priests rewrote whatever materials they
inherited, and they made Marduk both the hero of the struggle against
chaos and also the creator of the world and of man. Their story began
with Apsu, the god of fresh water, and Tiamat, the dragon of the
unbounded salt water (chaos). By their intermingling, this pair over a
period of years produced the gods; but the youthful gods were so
lively and boisterous that Apsu could not rest and resolved to destroy
them, against the wish of Tiamat.

> Apsu, opening his mouth,
> Said unto resplendent Tiamat:
> "Their ways are verily loathsome unto me.
> By day I find no relief, nor repose by night.
> I will destroy, I will wreck their ways,
> That quiet may be restored. Let us have rest!"
> As soon as Tiamat heard this,
> She was wroth and called out to her husband.
> She cried out aggrieved, as she raged all alone,
> Injecting woe into her mood:
> "What? Should we destroy that which we have built?
> Their ways indeed are most troublesome, but let us attend kindly!" [9]

But before Apsu could execute his plan, he was destroyed by Ea, who
got wind of it; whereupon Tiamat resolved on avenging him. She created monsters to be her allies, and both Anu and Ea fled before her.
Not until Marduk, assured by the gods that he would be their chief,
came forth to meet her in combat was she halted.

> Then advanced Tiamat and Marduk, counselor of the gods;
> To the combat they marched, they drew nigh to battle,
> The lord spread out his net and caught her,
> The storm wind that was behind him, he let loose in her face.
> When Tiamat opened her mouth to its widest,
> He drove in the evil wind, that she could not close her lips . . .
> He made her powerless, he destroyed her life;
> He cast down her body and stood upon it. [10]

After next subduing the monsters she had arrayed against him, Marduk turned back to Tiamat and split her open like a shellfish into two halves. With one half he made the canopy which holds back the waters that are above the heavens; with the other half he formed the covering which lies above the waters under the earth. He constructed stations for the gods in the heavens. With Ea's help he made man from the blood of the god Kingsu, Tiamat's ally and second husband. Seeing what he had done, the delighted gods bestowed on him many titles as their undisputed leader and king.[11]

B. THE FLOOD. The original Flood Story was Sumerian, and came out of grim experiences with the overflowing of the two rivers. Several of the later versions of the tale, mostly fragmentary, have come down to us. The finest of these forms part of the Gilgamesh epic, into which it was inserted as an interesting interpolation. According to this narrative, the gods decided in anger to punish man's sins by a flood. Their secret decision was revealed to one man. The good god Ea felt kindly toward Utnapishtim, and told him about it. The man proceeded immediately to build an ark:

> 120 cubits high were its sides,
> 140 cubits reached the edge of its roof.[12]

As Utnapishtim later told Gilgamesh (we quote in part):

> "I brought up into the ship my family and household,
> The cattle of the field, the beasts of the field, craftsmen, all of them
>   I brought in.
> A fixed time had Shamash appointed, saying,
> 'When the ruler of darkness sends a heavy rain,
> Then enter into the ship and close the door.'
> The appointed time came near, . . .
> There came up from the horizon a black cloud.
> Adad thundered within it . . .
> Adad's storm reached unto heaven,
> All light was turned into darkness . . .
> The water climbed over the mountains . . .
> The gods feared the deluge,
> They drew back, they climbed up to the heaven of Anu.
> The gods crouched like a dog, they cowered by the wall.
> Ishtar cried like a woman in travail,
> The queen of the gods cried with a loud voice:
> 'The former race is turned to clay.'
>
> When the seventh day drew nigh, the tempest ceased; the deluge,
> Which had fought like an army, ended.

Then rested the sea, the storm fell asleep, the flood ceased . . .
All mankind was turned to clay . . .
I opened the window and the light fell upon my face,
I bowed, I sat down, I wept,
And over my face ran my tears.
I looked upon the world, all was sea.
After twelve days (?) the land emerged.
To the land of Nisir the ship made its way,
The mount of Nisir held it fast, that it moved not . . .
I sent forth a dove and let her go.
The dove flew to and fro,
But there was no resting place and she returned.
I sent forth a swallow and let her go,
The swallow flew to and fro,
But there was no resting place and she returned.
I sent forth a raven and let her go,
The raven flew away, she saw the abatement of the waters,
She drew near, she waded, she croaked, and came not back.
Then I sent everything forth to the four quarters of heaven, I offered
sacrifice,
I made a libation upon the mountain's peak." [13]

The close parallels to the Old Testament are obvious.

C. ISHTAR'S DESCENT TO THE LAND OF THE DEAD.* If the obscure reference to Tammuz at the end of this story is correctly interpreted, Ishtar went down into Hades to recover her dead lover, the personification of the strong sun of spring-time, whose vigor fades away in the autumn. When she came to the door of the Land of No Return, she called imperiously to the porter:

"O gatekeeper, open thy gate,
Open thy gate that I may enter!
If thou openest not the gate so that I cannot enter,
I will smash the door, I will shatter the bolt,
I will smash the doorpost, I will move the doors,
I will raise up the dead, eating the living,
So that the dead will outnumber the living." [14]

Being commanded to do so by the goddess of the dead, the porter admits the queen of heaven; but as she passes through each of the seven gates, he takes an article of clothing from her, until she enters

* This famous Babylonian tale is based on a Sumerian prototype in which Innana and her husband Dumuzi (= Tammuz) are the central figures. The plot differs to this extent: in the Sumerian tale Dumuzi winds up in the Land of No Return in exchange for Innana, while in the Babylonian one Tammuz is already in the Land of No Return and Ishtar seeks his release.

the inner circle of the lower world stark naked. Held there in durance, she goes through much suffering; for the pest-god Namtar afflicts her successively with sixty diseases. Meanwhile, men and animals in the upper world grow listless and dull, unable to reproduce their kind. Love and fertility have left the earth. The gods are distressed.

> Forth went Papsukkal before Sin his father, weeping,
> His tears flowing before Ea, the king:
> "Ishtar has gone down to the nether world, she has not come up." [15]

Ea sends a messenger to Hades, and the goddess of the dead reluctantly orders Namtar to sprinkle Ishtar with "the water of life"; and she, restored to bloom and health, begins her journey back to the upper world, at each gate receiving back the clothing of which she had been divested.

No more poetically satisfying account of the disappearance of the vegetation goddess at the approach of winter and of her return in the spring has ever been conceived.

D. THE JOURNEY OF GILGAMESH. Related in the most finished and literary of the Babylonian epics, this story begins with the tale of the friendship of Gilgamesh, the ruler of the city of Uruk, with the wild man Enkidu, who dies prematurely; it then tells of his journey, through many perils, in search of immortality, to the realm of the departed beyond the western (the Mediterranean?) "waters of death," where his ancestor, Utnapishtim, dwells, and concludes with his disconsolate return to Uruk, after being robbed by a serpent of the herb of immortality which Utnapishtim enabled him to find. The whole story is full of the pathos of human disappointment in the face of death. What can one do about death, except to make this life happy? When Gilgamesh is about to embark on the waters of death in the west, he is addressed by Siduri, a bar-maid dwelling by the sea, who says:

> Gilgamesh, whither hurriest thou?
> The life that thou seekest thou wilt not find.
> When the gods created man,
> They fixed death for mankind.
> Life they took in their own hand.
> Thou, O Gilgamesh, let thy belly be filled!
> Day and night be merry,
> Daily celebrate a feast,
> Day and night dance and make merry!
> Clean be thy clothes,
> Thy head be washed, bathe in water!
> Look joyfully on the child that grasps thy hand,
> Be happy with the wife in thine arms! [16]

Here breathes indeed the spirit of the people of Babylonia. They had no hopes such as the Egyptians had of pleasantness in the world beyond. All joy was in this life.

Sacrifice, Magic, and Astrology

To insure to themselves the blessings of this life, the Babylonians resorted to their priests for sacrifices, incantations, ritual prayers, and the reading of the stars. They listened in rapt attention to the songs for the flute and the songs of prostration which were offered up before the gods. The liturgies were long, but they mellowed the gods. And if the gods would not be kind, there were incantations—powerful and compelling—to which the gods must give heed perforce, and which the evil spirits could not choose but obey. The worshipers paid the priests well to supplicate Ishtar:

> I have cried to thee, suffering, wearied, and distressed, as thy servant.
> See me, O my Lady; accept my prayers . . .
> Forgive my sin, my iniquity, my shameful deeds, and my offense.
> Overlook my shameful deeds; accept my prayer . . .
> Let thy great mercy be upon me.[17]

The priests could do more than pray; they could put a spell upon the evil spirits in the body of the suppliant:

> Out of my body away!
> Out of my body far away!
> Out of my body, for shame!
> My body do not oppress!
> By Shamash, the mighty, be ye exorcised!
> By Ea, the lord of all, be ye exorcised!
> By Marduk, the chief exorciser of the gods, be ye exorcised! [18]

The priests were busy men, well organized for their task, and offering many services to their clientele. They had learned during the centuries, from before 3200 B.C. (!), to act through what must be called in each case the temple corporation, a legal entity often possessed of large land-holdings, and run according to strict business methods, with all receipts and expenditures recorded in written signs on clay tablets. The temple structures administered by the corporations were large buildings, constructed of thick courses of sun-dried brick, and occupying spacious temple compounds, in the center of which often stood man-built mountains, encased in brick, called *ziggurats,* each with a shrine on its top. In these compounds the priests performed their lengthy rituals; here also they conducted schools for the teaching of reading and writing and arithmetic; and here, as well, they practiced divination, in the ambitious endeavor to read the signs of the times and foretell the future.

Divination was in fact one of the main functions of the priesthood. One whole order of priests specialized in the interpretation of dreams and of aberrations in natural events. They devoted much attention especially to the reading of the omens in the sheep's liver; for they thought the will and intentions of the gods were revealed in the creases on the surface and the physical peculiarities inside the liver. But the most important of their divining methods, for us if not for them, was their astrology. The origins of it go back to Sumerian times, and its repute was enormous. In the attempt to establish what might be called scientific method in reading the will of the gods in the disposition of the heavenly bodies, the diviners kept accurate and detailed records of the movements they observed in the heavens, and thus prepared the way for scientific astronomy in our own day. Though each zodiacal constellation was identified with special deities, the astronomical instruments devised for space measurement and time-study of the stars were amazingly precise and accurate.

III GREECE

The last century has seen a thorough revision of earlier ideas of classical Greek religion. Homer is no longer taken at face value. His pantheon, described with his bright and wingéd words, and in conception poetically unsurpassed, was for many centuries accepted in the West as an accurate rendering of early Greek religion. In the light of recent scholarship it is not that at all. We see now that the scholars who read off the characteristics of the Greek gods from the statues of the classic age and the lines of Homer should have paid more attention to "the crude and tangled superstitions of the peasantry of the mainland," [20] half-revealed and half-concealed in the poetry of Hesiod. It is clear from a study of these superstitions that much that was primitive lay at the base of Greek religion. The beauty and balance of the Homeric pantheon was in truth a triumph of unification and sublimation.

In brief, we have here another case of tribal amalgamations accompanied by a mingling and reordering of the gods.

The Gathering of the Gods in Early Hellas

The determinative fact in the formation of early Greek religion is the northern invasions beginning about the 20th century B.C. The invaders were of Aryan or Indo-European speech, and came down from the northern parts of Greece to establish themselves as masters of the earlier, so-called Helladic peoples. Historians are not certain of the origins of all the groups involved; but they are fairly agreed that the earliest true civilizations, those of the Minoans in Crete (who flourished about 2200–1100 B.C.) and of the bronze-age Aegeans of the Greek archipelago and mainland (2500–1100 B.C.), known to the later Greeks as "Pelasgians," were pre-Greek. The Minoan civilization began to decay about 1400 B.C., perhaps as the result of invasions (by Achaeans?) from the mainland. At all events, the Cretan palace of Cnossus fell, and never recovered its earlier glory and wealth. The Cretan culture, however, spread to the Greek mainland, and produced in the northeastern parts of the Peloponnesus and further north the Mycenaean civilization, of which the Homeric (or Achaean) Age was probably a late form.° Finally, about the 12th century B.C. another great wave of northerners— the formidable Dorians and their allies—surged down from the north, and overthrew the Mycenaean civilization, thus causing a widespread displacement which resulted in Greek settlements along the coast of Asia Minor, composed of Ionians, Aeolians, and Dorians too. When everyone had settled down again, the historic Greek city-states came into being, and the patterns of Greek religion, now so familiar to us, began to form.

These new patterns in religion were combinations of many different elements. The Indo-European invaders contributed to the divine *sunoikismos,* or "mingling-together," at least these deities: their chief god Zeus, the sky-father and rain-maker (called Dyaus Pitar by the Indo-Aryans and Jupiter by the Romans); Demeter, the earth-mother; and Hestia (the Vesta of the Romans), virgin goddess of the hearth, sister of Zeus, and a goddess from the far Indo-European past, honored with libations at the beginning and end of every sacrifice. But many of the gods had no such distant origin. Rhea seems to have been Minoan, Athena Mycenaean (at least when we first glimpse her), and Hermes and Hera Aegaean or Helladic; while Apollo appears to be from Ionia, Aphrodite from Cyprus or Cythera, and Dionysus and Ares from Thrace.

° It is likely that the Achaeans—leaders among the long-haired, light-skinned invaders from the north—adopted the Mycenaean culture after mastering its creators, both in Greece and in Crete.

It was as though the gods flocked together to Olympus from all points of the compass.

And this was as true of cities as it was of Greece as a whole.

It proved difficult even in a city like Athens to have gods that would appeal to the loyalty of all Attica. On the Acropolis at Athens there seem originally to have been Athena and some Kouros [Lord] corresponding with her, some Waterer of the earth, like Erechtheus. Then as Attica was united and brought under the lead of the central city, the gods of the outlying districts began to claim places on the Acropolis. Pallas, the thunder-maid of Pallene in the south, came to form a joint personality with Athena. Oinoe, a town in the northeast, on the way from Delos to Delphi, had for its special god a "Pythian Apollo"; when Oinoe became Attic a place for the Pythian Apollo had to be found on the Acropolis. Dionysus came from Eleutherae, Demeter and Korê from Eleusis, Theseus himself perhaps from Marathon or even from Trozên. They were all given official residences on Athena's rock, and Athens in return sent out Athena to new temples built for her in Prasiae and Sunion and various colonies.[21]

But the place of origin of each god or goddess—speculatively interesting though it be to search for it—is not of as great importance for us as the combination of functions which each assumed.

The Complex Functions of the Pre-Homeric Gods

Geographically Greece is a divided land, with small valleys and plains, each hedged in by mountains or straitened between a semi-circle of hills and the "unharvested" sea. Unlike Egypt and Mesopotamia, which threw people together, it separated them. So that before the northern invasions, the primitive or superstitious inhabitants of Helladic Greece worshipped in their isolated territories many nature-spirits, sought the aid of a variety of fertility powers, and engaged in diverse rites connected with magic, taboo, and the cult of the dead. The northerners who came flooding in not only imposed a new language and a certain hearty cheerfulness, but uniformity in the names of the gods; and thenceforth the chief gods and goddesses were identified with the local powers which could in anywise by absorbed by them, taking over their functions, rites, and histories, while also adding their own qualities.

Then, and for a long time later, the chief developments in religion occurred in cities (or city-states), each with its own public cult, provided with its own calendar of religious ceremonies and festivals. The great gods may be said to have come to the towns as "the real thing" and were accepted there as identical with the gods and godlings that had been locally known for many generations under local names. Amalgamation therefore took place within each local tradition.

Zeus is an instructive instance of how an invader's god takes over the duties of local divinities. Because he began as the great sky-father, ruler of the upper air and the giver of rains, as he made his way through Greece he was identified with many mountain-tops. Not only was he Zeus of Olympus, but Zeus Lykaios in Arcadia, Zeus Laphystios in southern Thessaly, and Zeus Kithairon in Boeotia. But he also assumed other, down-to-earth duties. He was the god of fertility in many districts, and in at least three places a deity of the underworld. As Zeus Polieus he was the guardian of several city-states. As Zeus Aphiktor he was the united cry of the suppliants, itself become deity and forcibly beating its way to heaven. At Athens he was Zeus Phratrios, and received on his altar the votes cast by the members of the phratry when a father brought his child for enrollment. At Dodona he spoke oracles through the murmuring leaves of the sanctuary oak. Generally, of course, he was the Cloud-Compeller, the Rain-Maker, carrying his bright thunderbolt, hurled amid earthshaking tremors; but the thunder-bolt sometimes had the judicial use of punishing the wickedness of men. The source of genius, his offspring by goddesses and women was numerous; he fathered a large progeny of heroes, kings, and founders of cities.* Nor was Hera his first wife. When he first arrived in the north at Dodona, he brought with him out of the unknown past a consort called Dione; and in other places he had other wives. But Hera was destined to become his permanent spouse.

Hera is an instance from the other side—the side of the conquered. She brought to her union with Zeus a past of her own. It was at least as respectable as his. Her origins are obscure and dateless. Since the cow plays an important part in early legends about her, she may originally have been a cow-goddess. In Mycenaean times she was the Argive Korê (Maiden), and sported in more than sisterly fashion on the plains of Peloponnesian Argos with Hercules, the strong young hero of that section. But she was also connected, by myth at any rate, with Argos in Thessaly, where, as a matronly friend, she helped Jason, another strong young hero, to launch the ship Argo, when he set out from Pagasae in search of the Golden Fleece. She seems not to have been at that time the goddess of the earth, but a majestic maiden identified with the passage of the year. For her sake Zeus parted with Dione and

---

* Deification of heroes and kings was widespread in the Hellenic world.

became her heavy-browed consort. They had their troubles. In accounting for their early quarrels, Jane Harrison has advanced the interesting theory: "The marriage of Zeus and Hera reflects the subjugation of the indigenous people by incoming Northerners. Only thus can we account for the fact that the divine husband and wife are in constant unseemly conflict. Of course a human motive is alleged; Hera is jealous, Zeus in constant exasperation. But the real reason is racial conflict." [22] Perhaps this explanation will do; or perhaps another: she was the queen of the hinterlands and of backward mountaineers among whom the primitive matrilinear tradition persisted, and Zeus, the lord of the patrilinear northerners, married her to win a footing. However this may be, their marriage was not long unhappy; it was later declared a great success, and became in Greek eyes a "holy union," the very ideal of married existence. Hera became the patroness of married women, their counselor and example.

In the person of Apollo an even greater yoking of diverse functions is seen. He was probably not Hellenic. In the *Iliad* at least, he is not on the side of the Greeks but of the Trojans, an implacable and feared foe of the "bronze-clad" warriors besieging Troy. Perhaps, as the myths suggest, he was originally from the island of Delos, or else from the plains of Asia Minor. His origin cannot be surely traced. Very early he stood for pastoral and agricultural interests. Certainly he was not originally a sun-god. He was a shepherd for Laomedon near Troy and for Admetos in Thessaly. He may once have been a wolf-god, but as shepherd he protected his flocks and herds from the fangs of his lupine brethren. In agricultural areas, groves and trees were under his protection; the laurel was sacred to him. Out of pastoral love of song, he drew to him with his lively playing on the lyre devoted youths and maidens. He heartily believed in youth, and was the sponsor of athletic contests, himself drawing a strong bow. He was Hekatebolos, "the shooter from afar."

> Behind his shoulders hung
> His bow, and ample quiver; at his back
> Rattled the fateful arrows as he mov'd.[23]

His arrows not only drew blood but pierced men with deadly sicknesses. He slew on the slopes of Mt. Parnassus, in Greece, the Python, whom he then displaced at Delphi. (Like Zeus he displaced and absorbed many local spirits.) His exploit at Delphi was an important act, with far-reaching results in the development of Greek religion; for as a consequence of it he became the god of revelation. No other god was the source of such direct oracles except Zeus. In the center of his temple at Delphi was the famous vent in the earth, from which issued from time to time an intoxicating vapor; and when the priestess, called Pythia, sat on the tripod amid the fumes, she muttered words which were universally thought to be from Apollo. It was in this belief that for centuries the famous men of Greece journeyed

> to Delphi, where
> Phoebus, on earth's mid navel o'er the world
> Enthroned, weaveth in eternal song
> The sooth of all that is or is to be.[24]

He was often asked for an oracle before a town was founded, and afterwards became its patron. Not until very late, and then perhaps as the result of Egyptian or other foreign influence, was he identified with Helios, the sun, who drives his golden car from heaven's eastern gates to the dim regions of the night.

The story of the other deities is similar. Artemis, the virginal deity of the wild, ranging through the mountains and forests with her nymphs, in maidenly reserve, but thoroughly at home with the untamed animals of her domain, was also the gentle lover of children, the protectress of men and maidens, and the solicitous friend who sought to ease the pangs of childbirth; and, curiously, in Ionia, where she was a favorite, became the Artemis of Ephesus, a motherly goddess covered with breasts. Hermes, who came from deep in the pre-Hellenic period, outgrew his earliest symbol, a simple cairn of stones such as peasants in the rock-strewn land raised at the edges and corners of fields and associated with their dead;* after he became identified with a square stone pillar, called the *herm*, sometimes surmounted with his head, he was, as it were, pulled up out of the ground, where he had stood immovable, and given wingéd feet; he led the spirits of the dead down

---

* How this came about is thus explained by M. P. Nilsson (*Greek Popular Religion*, Columbia University Press, 1940, p. 8): "If our (Greek) peasant passed a heap of stones, he might lay another stone upon it. If a tall stone was erected on top of the heap, he might place before it a bit of provision as an offering. He performed this act as a result of custom, without knowing the real reason for it, but he knew that a god was embodied in the stone heap and in the tall stone standing on top of it. . . . Our peasant or his forefathers knew that the stone heaps sometimes covered a dead man and that the stone erected on top was a tombstone. Accordingly, the god who dwelt in the stone heap had relations with the dead. . . . Perhaps our peasant wanted to look after his stock, which grazed on the meadows and mountain slopes. The god of the stone heaps was concerned with them, too." An additional fact was that cairns served in mountain tracts and elsewhere as waymarkers, and Hermes was thus thought to guide travelers to their destination.

to Hades, and as the swift messenger between Zeus and the earth below, was clothed in a long belted chiton, and made to wear a cap or a broad-rimmed hat and wingéd boots. Other gods showed a like complexity of function: Poseidon was god of the sea, but was originally a horse-god guarding inland lakes and streams (was he driven into the sea by invaders?); Athena, the wise and virginal warrior-maiden, was originally perhaps an owl goddess (for the owl was sacred to her, and she herself turned on occasion into a bird disappearing upward into the sky); and Demeter, goddess of the fertile soil, was, as mother of slender and beauteous Persephone (the Korê, the Maiden), also connected with the underworld. In all these deities many local gods and spirits were absorbed and sublimated. Even Aphrodite, the goddess of love, a latecomer, perhaps the western form of Ishtar of Babylon, was reborn from the foam of the sea, clear-skinned and delicate and beautiful, still a little a-moral, yet shorn of the accompaniments of temple-prostitution and self-mutilation which attended the worship of her oriental counterparts. Only Dionysus seemed unassimilable and untamed. (Further on, we shall see why.)

The Homeric Pantheon

It is time for us to consider the artful, intellectualized picture of the gods which Homer gives us, and to judge of its character and its effects.

In Homer the gods no longer live in widely separated places. Their common home is the acropolis on high Olympus, more a heavenly region now than the actual mountain top in Thessaly. There Zeus, the Cloud-Compeller, is kind; and white-armed Hera is his "golden-thronéd" queen. The other gods may absent themselves on occasion from their cloud-girt palaces, but usually Zeus must know where they have gone and what they have done. The gods, not without back-talk, submit to his discipline, for he is the father of most of them. His best beloved daughter is grey-eyed Athena, the maiden goddess of wisdom; a favored son is Apollo, the archer-god, he of the flowing golden locks, who both heals and hurts; Artemis, "delighting in wild boars and swift hinds," is the shy daughter who often absents herself in the mountain fastnesses which she prefers; while Ares, "piercer of shields," is the savagely warlike son whom Zeus at times scolds sternly:

> "Come no more to me,
> Thou wav'ring turncoat, with thy whining prayers:
> Of all the Gods who on Olympus dwell

I hate thee most; for thou delight'st in nought
But strife and war; thou hast inherited
Thy mother, Hera's, proud, unbending mood,
Whom I can scarce control." [25]

Aphrodite, the enticing goddess of love, is a daughter of Zeus by Dione, and is married to her half-brother, the lame god of the forge and the fire, Hephaestus, a son of Zeus by Hera; but she is unfaithful to him, and has a notorious amour with Ares. Still another son of Zeus, born of his affair with Semele, is Dionysus, but in Homer he puts in an appearance and no more. Of greater importance is Hermes, the Heavenly Guide, whose birth was the consequence of the love of Zeus and Maia. He is primarily the herald and messenger of the gods, but he is sharp and cunning, and not above consorting with thieves on those occasions when he gets away by himself, as when he departs from Olympus to guide souls to and from Hades. Poseidon, the god of the sea, and Hades (Pluto), the god of the underworld, are full brothers of Zeus, born like him of Kronos and Rhea; and Demeter is his sister by the same parents, but Homer does not have her come up to Olympus.

Here then is the tight-knit family group of the gods of Homer. On the whole they form a very aristocratic company. As gods they are in charge of natural forces, but not any longer such forces *themselves.* They had been such in earlier days, but they are so no longer. Their functions have been both sublimed and simplified. They are no longer primitive. The Minoan fetishes, the deities in animal-form, the mothergoddesses, are gone. The Pelasgian involvements with animal and human fertility, or with vegetation, death, and the underworld have been largely refined out of them. Their personalities are no longer portentous with vague, mysterious force; they have come into the light of day, and are sharply defined, clear-cut, distinct from one another. No two are alike. Indeed they are all but earthy men and women, with thoughts, desires, moods, and passions all too human. Though immortal, they are no longer incalculable and unknown and terrible. Aesthetically, they are attractive, charming, amusing, civilized, better proportioned and more beautiful than humans—they were indeed Homer's priceless gift to the future artists of Greece. In marble and bronze, their stately, poised, and unblemished bodies were in time to rise in market-places and on acropolises, their wondrous heads gazing calmly down from the pediments and pedestals of temples, lordly and aloof, as from another and more perfect world.

And yet the awesome quality, which makes gods bear in their persons a *mysterium tremendum,* had left them!

Zeus, holding thunder-bolt, seated with Athena, armed for war, Hera as goddess of earth, and Aphrodite with dove. Dionysus (or perhaps Ganymede) is pouring wine.

Perhaps the last sentence is a little overstated. The gods in Homer do exert supernatural effects; for when Zeus nods, all Olympus shakes, and once when Poseidon hurried to Olympus in three immense strides,

> Beneath th' immortal feet of Ocean's Lord
> Quak'd the huge mountain and the shadowy wood.[26]

Poseidon's cry—and that of every god—is thunderous.

> As of nine thousand or ten thousand men,
> In deadly combat meeting, is the shout.[27]

The gods also have great power over human lives, whether for bane or blessing. By their will cities fall, men die, and armies fail. Men know they must go through the traditional rituals of sacrifice on every important occasion; or feel the grim wrath of the gods on high. Aeneas, inside Troy, is sure the gods are angry with the Trojans for neglecting their sacrifices; and as for the Greeks, because the builders failed to make the usual sacrifices, the "firm-built" wall they raised to guard their ships before Troy scarcely lasted out their need of it. Zeus watches over men's morals, too. In one lone but significant passage in the *Iliad* he is seen pouring down

> his fiercest storms in wrath to men,
> Who in their courts unrighteous judgments pass,
> And justice yield to lawless violence,
> The wrath of Heav'n despising.[28]

But yet, with all this, the might of the gods is gravely limited. There is something more powerful than Zeus, to which the Cloud-Compeller himself submits. This is Moira or Fate, the relentless force of destiny. It does not stand alone; with it operate vague powers—Blind Folly, Terror, Strife, Turmoil, Rumor, Death. Everything considered, powerful though they are, the gods are contained within the total frame of Nature and History, like men. Though they are superhuman beings, their powers are not boundless.

The Homeric epics had a great influence in guiding the imagination of the Greeks. Recited not only to and for the aristocracy, as was first the case, but also to the masses of the people, at festivals and general assemblies, they became an essential element in the education of Greek youth. And they helped to bring about a sense of unification among the Greeks, culturally and religiously. That is to say, they created a sense among the Greeks that in religion and culture all Hellas was one. And yet Homer was more satisfying for political than for religious reasons. It may be doubted whether in actual local worship, in prayer and sacrifice, the aesthetically pleasing Homeric pantheon won the people even a little away from their ancient loyalties—and interests.

Hesiod's Theogony

Hesiod (8th century B.C.) did no better. In a characteristic effort of Greek rationalism he tried to bring the gods into some semblance of order by raising the question of their origin (theogony).

Influenced perhaps by Near-Eastern attempts in this direction, he declared in his *Theogony* that the pristine Chaos had given room or place to Earth (Gaeus or Ge), Tartarus (the Pit), and Eros (Love). Chaos itself produced Night and Darkness, and they, in turn, by the power of love, mated to bring forth Day and Air. Without a mating, Night gave issue to Sleep, Dream, Death, Old Age, Misery, Friendship, and Discord. Similarly, Discord of herself gave birth to Hunger, Toil, Murder, Battle, and other forms of human strain and struggle, while Earth brought into being unaided Heaven (Ouranos or Uranus), the Mountains, and the Ocean. Mating with Ocean, Earth produced creatures of the sea, and taking as husband Ouranos, conceived the first great gods, but was unable to give birth to them because Ouranos prevented his children from emerging from the mother. With her aid, however, Kronos came forth, stole upon his sleeping father, and castrated him with a sickle. The flowing blood turned into the Furies (Erinyes), the Titans (Giants), and certain nymphs, while from the sea foam forming around the castrated members sprang Aphrodite, the goddess of love. The Triumphant Kronos married his sister Rhea, who had now been born, but fearing overthrow himself, swallowed his children as they were born. Then Rhea, with the help of grandmother Earth, substituted a stone for Zeus, the last born, and Kronos swallowed it unknowing. Zeus was hidden by his grandmother in a cave in Crete and finally emerged to subdue his father and force him to disgorge the young gods and goddesses he had swallowed. Thereafter Zeus began his reign as king of the gods.

This was Hesiod's attempt to bring rational order out of mythological chaos, but while he satisfied the Greeks theologically, he did not alter much the day-to-day practice of religion, which still approached chaos.

The day-to-day observance of religion by the common folk of Greece was mainly a matter of household practices and attendance at public ceremony. The man in the country was concerned with Pan (the Pasturer, a frisky male with horns, pointed ears, a tail, and goat's feet), Demeter the Earth Mother, Hermes ("he of the stone-heap"), *daimons* (spirits full of *mana*, sometimes closer than a brother: Socrates had one), ghosts, omens, taboos, magic (by which to lay ghosts and to promote the fertility of the fields, the live-stock, and womankind), "heroes," the noble dead, and chthonian deities, deep underground, to be appeased in fear. The townsmen had their festivals, which honored the greater gods of the pantheon. To these we turn next.

The Athenian Festivals

We know most, although not enough, about the festivals of Athens, some thirty of them. The very months of the year took their names from centrally important ones.

By and large the Athenians thought of their deities by seasons of the year. Apollo and Athena were honored principally in the summer and fall, Demeter and her daughter in late summer and fall, Dionysus and Artemis in the spring, while Zeus was an exception in receiving public honors all year round.

The official year began in summer with a great sacrifice to Apollo, called the Hecatombaea because a hundred head of cattle were supposed to be offered up. In early summer the Tharpalia honored him with a purification rite in which two filthy men, draped with black and yellow dried figs, were driven as scapegoats from the city. In late summer and early fall three other festivals celebrated his power to promote neighborliness, raise up "helpers," and give aid to agriculture.

Athena, as patroness of the city, received highest honors during the Panathenaea, held to celebrate her "birthday." Performed in mid-summer, it was one of the great festivals of the year. A long procession carried a newly embroidered mantle, mounted like a sail on a ship on wheels, to her image on the Acropolis. There were accompanying sacrifices and games. Earlier in the summer the Kallynteria and Phrynteria purified both her temple and the city, and carried an ancient image of her to the sea to be bathed.

Demeter and her daughter Persephone received honor in late summer and fall at no less than five city festivals. The first in time was the Eleusinia (not to be confused with the Eleusinian mysteries); it was held every two years and with great splendor every fourth year; in the course of its games the prize given to the winning athletes was barley from one of Demeter's holy fields, the Rarian Plain.* The other festivals (the Proerosia, Thesmophoria, Haloa, and Skirophoria) included a magic ploughing, a seeding of the earth with suckling pigs and sacred cakes (a kind of fertility magic), and a magical ritual during which worthy matrons made broad jokes to encourage the fertility powers.

The greatest of the spring festivals, the Diasia, was in honor of Zeus. It included a holocaust, the Greek word for a whole-burnt offering. Hera was celebrated along with him in January during the Gamelia, and there were two other festivals, one in November, another in July.

Artemis' connection with animals received notice at three fertility festivals in the spring. But the great god of the season was Dionysus. In April or May the Great Dionysia took six days to perform. It had, and still has, great literary importance, because it was the occasion for the performance, under the supervision of the priest of Dionysus, of the immortal tragedies of Aeschylus, Sophocles, and Euripides and the comedies of Aristophanes. Religion and art were here memorably combined.

Of the other festivals honoring other gods there is no room to tell. Enough has been said to indicate with what the public ceremonies had to do.† Not only was magic literally involved; there was a finer and higher magic in the poetry and drama of the splendid rituals.

* Games in connection with religious festivals and also at funerals were as old as Homer's Achaeans. There were Pan-hellenic festivals whose games or "meets" are world-famous: the Olympic Games held at Olympia in Elis, the Pythian Games at Delphi, the Isthmian Games at the Isthmus of Corinth, and the Nemean Games at Zeus's shrine at Nemea. The first and last were in honor of Zeus, the second of Apollo, the third of Poseidon.

† Of the ceremonies of the famous Eleusinian mysteries there is more to tell in the next section.

The Mystery Religions

The transitional developments are only dimly known to us; but after the heroic (or Achaean) age had receded into the past, and the Homeric pantheon had been established throughout Greece as the group-standard for conceiving of the appearance and behavior of the gods, an excitingly satisfying way for the Greeks to *feel* the gods within them, and thus to share in their immortal nature, made its appearance. This was the way of the *mysteries*—a way that offered to individuals private and personal religious satisfactions and assurances not provided by the official public sacrifices to the gods.

So ardent indeed became the devotees of these cults that they practiced their rites even when great public crises impended and average citizens were thinking only of the common danger. Herodotus in a famous passage tells of a rapt group which pursued the Eleusinian rites even while Attica was being ravaged by the land army of Xerxes, and the Greeks, hovering off the coast, were debating whether or not to hazard their fleet at Salamis. Witnesses on the Persian side were filled with superstitious dread, Herodotus says, when they saw the procession of the devotees going along the sacred way from Eleusis toward Athens, raising "a cloud of dust such as a host of thirty thousand men might raise," and singing the mystic hymn to Dionysus. One said to another:

"Demaretus, it is certain that some great calamity will fall upon the king's host. For, since Attica is deserted, manifestly it is something more than mortal, coming from Eleusis to avenge the Athenians and their allies. If it descends upon the Peloponnese, there will be peril for the king himself and his land army; but if it turns towards the ships at Salamis, the king will be in danger of losing his fleet. This feast is held by the Athenians every year for the Mother and the Maid, and any Athenian or other Greek who wishes is initiated. The sound you hear is the song of Iacchos° which they sing at this festival."

And Demaretus answered:

"Hold your peace and tell no man of this matter, for if these words should come to the king's ears, you will lose your head, and neither I nor any man living will be able to save you." [29]

The mysteries were so called because they were rites which were kept secret from all except the initiates. Under the guidance of a hierophant ("the revealer of holy things") the candidates underwent: (1) a preparatory purification such as a procession to the sea and washing

° A name of Dionysus.

in it, (2) instruction in mystic knowledge, usually given behind closed doors in a mystic hall, (3) a solemn beholding of sacred objects, followed by (4) the enactment of a divine story, generally in the form of a pageant or play, in which the cult divinities were impersonated, and (5) a crowning or wreathing of each of the candidates as full-fledged initiates. Accompanying these acts, which might spread over a number of days, were processions and sacred revels, including night-long ceremonies, which afforded simultaneously a release of tension and a deepening of the sense of mystic participation in super-sensible realities.

The oldest and most restrained of the mysteries was the Eleusinian. The central figures in the rites were Demeter and her daughter, the Korê. As everyone knew, the Korê had been snatched away to the underworld by Hades (Pluto), that she might be his bride; but her mother, through long days of searching and mourning, had refused to make the corn grow, and at last Zeus bade Hades allow the maiden to return to earth. But the unwary maiden had eaten a pomegranate seed, cunningly given her by Hades; and when, as the hymn which has come to us from the 7th century B.C. relates, her anxious mother asked:

> "Child, hast thou eaten of any food in the world below?
> Tell me; for if not,
> Then mayest thou dwell beside me and Father Zeus,
> Honored among all the Immortals;
> But if thou hast,
> Thou must go back again into the secret places of the earth
> And dwell there a third part of every year,
> And whensoever the earth blossoms with all sweet flowers of spring,
> Then from the misty darkness thou shalt rise and come again,
> A marvel to gods and men," [30]

alas, Persephone had to confess she had done that which required her annual return to the underworld.

The entire story of Demeter and the Maiden was elaborately re-enacted, mostly by women. At some time Dionysus, as Demeter's associate (he being the god of vegetation and the vine), was introduced into the story; it is not clear when. The mystery itself was withheld from public knowledge; but the whole of Athens could see the parade to the sea to bathe the candidates, and any citizen could also witness the procession along the sacred way from Athens to Eleusis bearing along the image of the young Dionysus (Iacchos). The participants hoped to obtain a "better lot," a more glorious immortality in the next world, this, apparently, not as a reward of virtue, but rather by assimilation of the resurrective powers of Demeter, the Korê, and Dionysus.* According to the hymn quoted above:

> Blessed among men upon earth is he who has seen these things;
> But he that is uninitiate in the rites and thus has no part in them
> Has never an equal lot in the cold place of darkness.[31]

The decorous Eleusinian mystery cult was far surpassed in violence and excitement by the Dionysiac and Orphic mysteries. These had a Thraco-Phrygian origin, and construed the intoxication that followed the ritual use of the wine of Dionysus as possession by the god. Added excitement was provided by sacramental communion with the god in the eating of the flesh and the drinking of the blood of a kid or a bull identified with him and actually torn asunder—a rite called *omophagia*. All Greece was familiar with the Dionysiac *maenads* (or Bacchae)—women, maddened by divine possession, "rushing" or "raging" in the frenzy of tearing at the sacred animal; and knew, too, of the sad fate of Orpheus, the inventor of the mysteries of Dionysus, who, become himself the victim of the rite of omophagia, was torn to pieces by the maenads in Thrace, when in grief at his second loss of Eurydice he paid them no heed.

But if the Dionysiac cult remained incurably wild, its Orphic off-shoot, whose conventicles spread throughout the Mediterranean world —or wherever Greeks were—including Southern Italy, Crete, and Cyprus, had this to commend it: by eating the raw flesh of the suffering and dying god (Zagreus-Dionysus), the initiate might strengthen the divine element in him; by following the Orphic rules of purity, wearing white garments, abstaining from all meat (except that of the god in the mystery), avoiding the breaking of taboos against sex-indulgence and pollution, and by being generally ascetic, as Orphism demanded, he might refine the evil out of him, and avoid going to the place of punishment after death. More positively, by being worthy, he might hope to enjoy a better lot in the next world, and at the same time increase his sense of spiritual security in this. Ultimately, he might altogether escape the necessity of rebirth, in which the Orphics believed, and go to the Isles of the Blest.

That these ideas should have had a part in the development of one of the great schools of Greek philosophy may seem at first sight surpris-

---

* That this nonmoral hope shocked even the Greeks is evident in Plutarch's preservation of a comment attributed to Diogenes the Cynic: "Is Pataikion the thief going to have a 'better lot' after death than Epaminondas, just because he was initiated?" (Cornford, *Greek Religious Thought from Homer to the Age of Alexander*, p. 51). Reprinted by permission of J. M. Dent and Sons, publishers.

ing. But it is true that in the philosophic brotherhood which Pythagoras founded, the Orphic coloring was strong. The Pythagorean brothers believed that the major task of one's life is to purify the soul, and by following Orpheus (or perhaps Apollo) they hoped to bring their souls into a state of serenity, understanding, and godlike poise. Their studies in medicine, music, astronomy, mathematics, and pure philosophy were designed to nourish in their souls the divine elements, so that they would not hereafter have to suffer transmigration from earth-body to earth-body but regain a spiritual state of purity and insight.

This was not the only case of the search in Greek thought for higher ground.

Greek Religion and the Tragic Poets

The tragedies of Aeschylus, Sophocles, and Euripedes revolve upon the awful theme that man's disasters are the doom brought upon him by the gods. This is what the myths long had said; but in them it was not always clear whether the gods were impelled by a just purpose, by sheer wilfulness, or by the decrees of an inexorable Fate to which even gods are, willy-nilly, the ministrants. The great dramatists addressed themselves to the human problems which this confusion raises, and in so doing produced passages of moral and religious reflection that have no parallel in ancient literature outside the powerful utterances of the Old Testament prophets.

In the 5th century, Aeschylus and Sophocles more or less followed the poet Pindar in exalting Zeus to the moral height of being the administrator of a cosmic justice. The other deities continue to exist alongside of Zeus, but they yield at once to his will, when he overrules them in the name of the justice he is imposing. No longer is Fate blind. Aeschylus, in general, places Zeus in the superior position of either commanding Fate or being served by it. It is therefore really Zeus who dispatches the avenging Furies who punish the sins of man, ever continuing and multiplying from generation to generation among the wrongdoers. Aeschylus' great trilogy, the *Oresteia*, indeed vigorously declares:

> Zeus, the high god!—whate'er be dim in doubt,
>   This can our thought track out—
> The blow that fells the sinner is of God,
>   And as he wills, the rod
> Of vengeance smiteth sore. . . .
>
> For not forgetful is the high gods' doom
>   Against the sons of carnage: all too long

> Seems the unjust to prosper and be strong,
>   Till the dark Furies come,
> And smite with stern reversal all his home,
>   Down into dim obstruction—he is gone,
> And help and hope, among the lost, is none! [32]

Though in *Prometheus Bound* the tortured titan who is its central figure defies Zeus as unjust, it is evident that Aeschylus thought that Zeus had learned something from this encounter, and was in no doubt that the King of the gods should now be approached with utmost piety as the righteous moral governor of the world.

Sophocles, the wise, tender-hearted, and supremely poised, gave to the character of Zeus some of his own humanity of feeling. Following some hints supplied by Aeschylus, who, however, in general makes Zeus stern and fearsome in his moral fervor, Sophocles softens the great god's judgments with mercy; he makes Polynices, for instance, in *Oedipus at Colonos*, begin his final plea to his royal father by reminding him that Clemency sits by the side of Zeus, sharing his throne and entering into all his decisions, a fact which should influence earthly potentates, and make them more merciful. Yet Sophocles, also, is sure that the favor of Zeus is not easily gained; for one must be pure in word and deed, as Zeus indeed wills from on high, if he is to experience divine clemency.

Euripides, a generation later, filled with doubts that had perhaps been raised in his mind by the Sophists or by such bold minds as Anaxagoras, lifts his voice with less conviction in behalf of obedience to the gods. Although it is a difficult thing for us to decide when Euripides is putting words into the mouths of his characters and when he is speaking his own mind, it seems certain that he had come to question the justice and integrity, if not of Zeus, at least of Apollo, Aphrodite, and others among the gods. Often he pities man, stricken and hurled to earth by the unpitying gods. He makes the proud and pure-hearted Hippolytus cry:

> Ah, pain, pain, pain!
> O unrighteous curse! . . .
> Thou, Zeus, dost see me? Yea, it is I;
> The proud and pure, the server of God,
> The white and shining in sanctity!
> To a visible death, to an open sod,
>   I walk my ways;
> And all the labor of saintly days
>   Lost, lost without meaning! [33]

Meanwhile a maiden of the chorus has already uttered the amazing reproof:

> Ye gods that did snare him,
> Lo, I cast in your faces
> My hate and my scorn! [34]

And the men have chanted in discouragement overwhelming their uncertain faith:

> Surely the thought of the Gods hath balm in it alway, to win me
>   Far from my griefs; and a thought, deep in the dark of my mind,
> Clings to a great Understanding. Yet all the spirit within me
> Faints when I watch men's deeds matched with the guerdon they find.
>   For Good comes in Evil's traces,
>   And the Evil the Good replaces;
>   And Life, 'mid the changing faces,
>   Wandereth weak and blind.[35]

But Euripides was by no means a total disbeliever, it would seem; he was really seeking a notion of God purged of the misconceptions of mythology and tradition. His true voice perhaps comes to us in the groping words:

> Thou deep Base of the World, and thou high Throne
> Above the World, whoe'er thou art, unknown
> And hard of surmise, Chain of Things that be,
> Or Reason of our Reason; God, to thee
> I lift my praise, seeing the silent road
> That bringeth justice ere the end be trod
> To all that breathes and dies.[36]

In this "strange prayer," as the poet himself calls it, the questing spirit of Euripides, like that of his philosophic contemporaries, seems to seek a new theology.

The Philosophers and the Gods

That the philosophers would go far beyond the Homeric point of view was clear from the start. Greek philosophy began as monism: everything in the universe is some form or other of one thing. Thales said this substance was water, Anaximenes that it was air, Heraclitus that it was fire, and Anaximander that it was an indeterminate somewhat. Whatever it was, it was creative or divine, they all agreed. Xenophanes was sure that the creative power was "one god greatest among gods and men, not like mortals in form, nor yet in mind. He sees all over, thinks all over, and hears all over." [37] But men insist on seeing him in their likeness, and so have fallen into the anthropomorphic fallacy:

Homer and Hesiod have ascribed to the gods all things that among men are a shame and a reproach—theft and adultery and deceiving one another.

Mortals think that the gods are begotten, and wear clothes like their own, and have a voice and a form.

If oxen or horses or lions had hands and could draw with them and make works of art as men do, horses would draw the shapes of gods like horses, oxen like oxen; each kind would represent their bodies just like their own forms.

The Ethiopians say their gods are black and flat-nosed; the Thracians, that theirs are blue-eyed and red-haired.[38]

Plato had a different criticism. In the *Republic*, where he considers the education of youth, he fears the moral ill-effects of teaching the Homeric myths in unexpurgated form.

The narrative of Hephaestus binding Hera his mother, or how on another occasion Zeus sent him flying for taking her part when she was being beaten, and all the battles of the gods in Homer—these tales must not be admitted into our State, whether they are supposed to have an allegorical meaning or not. For a young person can not judge what is allegorical and what is literal; anything that he receives into his mind at that age is likely to become indelible and unalterable; and therefore it is most important that the tales which the young hear first should be models of virtuous thoughts.[39]

A similar moral criticism is leveled by Plato against the mystery religions. The trouble with the mysteries is that they do not recommend justice for the sake of justice; they practice virtue for the sake of the rewards it brings, the "shower of benefits which the heavens, as they say, rain upon the pious."

They produce a host of books written by Musaeus and Orpheus, according to which they perform their ritual, and persuade not only individuals, but whole cities, that expiations and atonements for sin may be made by sacrifices and amusements which fill a vacant hour; . . . the latter they call mysteries, and they redeem us from the pains of hell, but if we neglect them no one knows what awaits us.[40]

Plato was far from denying the existence of the gods. But they were, he said, neither as wayward and fallible as Homer pictured them nor as easily swayed from impartial justice as the mysteries implied; they were true to, and dependent in function on, a higher power. There was above them, and behind all other beings and things, a Creator, or Artisan, who had identified himself with the highest of all values, the Good. He it was who in the beginning beheld the realm of ideal forms, which not even he created, and was inspired by them to make a world that participated in their structure and, in mountains, plains, and seas, gods, men, and animals, bodied forth the good, the beautiful, and true in various degrees. As for man, he is a soul in a body, and his soul needs to grow toward the highest Good, that it may no longer have to suffer continued rebirth, but go into that state in which it may, like God, behold and enjoy forever the hierarchy of the ideal forms, in all their truth, beauty, and goodness. The gods, on their part, desire none of the superstitious worships and magical rituals which men have developed in their honor; they desire and expect only that each man shall engage in the proper tendance of his soul and seek the Supreme Good which the high god has set before him. Firm in these beliefs, Plato in old age contended that atheism, or any assertion that God is indifferent to men, or that He can be bought off by gifts or offerings, should be treated as dangerous to society.

Much more could be said both of Plato and his fellow-philosophers. It is of great interest, for example, to see how Aristotle, at least in his earlier period, found no need in his philosophy for the traditional gods of the Greeks but yet, in considering the highest kind of being, had to posit God the Prime Mover, that is, a being causing all the movements of celestial and terrestrial bodies by attraction toward himself while being himself actually without motion. Aristotle, the Stoics, and the Neo-Platonists were as much emancipated as Plato from the confining bonds within which their lesser country men were straining toward a fuller, freer life and greater wisdom.

IV ROME

What we have found true of the religion of Greece is even more true of the religion of Rome: the literature of the classical period is not as it stands a good guide to early religious belief. The writings of the Romans we know best—those who flourished during the days of the late Republic and the early Empire—must be critically analyzed, that the references to the religion of early Rome may be isolated and given their proper value. For if we wish to form a true conception of early Roman religion, we must first lift off, as it were, the accumulated upper layers, representing the borrowings from Greek religion and thought, and the more esoteric importations from Egypt and the Near East, and then proceed to look at the underlying ancient customs and rituals of the Latins.

Like its Greek counterpart, the Italian peninsula was inhabited at first by a non-Indo-European population. At some time early in the second millennium B.C. there occurred invasions from the north by Indo-European (initially Celtic) tribes. Late in this period these tribes crossed the Apennines and settled down along the Tiber and on the hills to the east. They came to be known as the Latins, and their territory as Latium. They were not, however, to be left in undisturbed possession. They were joined in the 8th century B.C. by a kindred people called the Sabines, who came down from the mountains to the east. Shortly before this, the territory to the north—historic Etruria—was settled by ship-borne° invaders from the eastern Mediterranean, the energetic Etruscans, who for so long were the chief enemies of the Romans and for a while dominated them completely. Incursions of foreigners occurred also in the far south, almost too far away at first for the Romans to pay any heed. These were by the Greeks of Magna Graecia, who had come to southern Italy as a result of the Dorian invasions of southern Greece. Thus the Latins found themselves in the 8th century B.C. between the Etruscans on the north and the Greeks on the south, with what effects upon the development of their religious ideas and practices will soon appear.

At first Rome was one of the lesser Latin towns. Its rise to importance dates from the complete merging of its several communities on the famous seven hills and their enclosure in the 6th century B.C. by a long, stout encircling wall. Gradually the surrounding areas came under its control; at last Rome became the mistress of all Italy. By the close of the 3rd century B.C. Carthaginian resistance to Roman dominance was broken, and the Roman imperium thereafter extended itself over the whole Mediterranean world. Thanks to able administration, Roman world-dominion promised to endure indefinitely.

Meanwhile, even as the treasures of the world were being poured into the lap of Rome, so also foreign cults were brought and added to the native deposit of religion. Let us trace out the history of *this* amalgamation or *sunoikismos*.

The Religion of Early Rome

The religion of early Rome had, like the city itself, humble beginnings. The chief holy places were at first outside its territory. Diana was worshipped in the grove of Aricia on Lake Nemi, her temple there

---

° This is still hypothetical. That they were from the eastern Mediterranean seems indicated by their religion and art.

being sacred for the whole Latin federation; and on the Alban hill to the east all Latium united in the festival in honor of Jupiter Latiaris.

In later times the Romans referred to the earliest strata of their religion as "the religion of Numa," as though their traditional law-giver, who could not have invented it, had prescribed it for them. It was a religion very close to magic, precise and scrupulous in its sacerdotalism, with much attention given to charms, taboos, and the reading of omens. Its most general feature was the attention it paid to supernatural forces or potencies called *numina* (sing. *numen*). This word had a meaning similar to that given in the South Seas to *mana* (see again p. 16). Numen meant a kind of potency beyond the ordinary. The gods possess it in abundance and their power and greatness depend on how much of it they have. As the chief of the gods, Jupiter has more than the rest. But numen may be found elsewhere, too, in all sorts of things and places—boundary stones, groves of trees, running rivers, springs. Men also may possess it, particularly in groups or in families. Like the mana of the Pacific, it is transferable and may be conferred by a god upon a man, his house, his field, or his tools and weapons. Or, again, by making appropriate sacrifices men may impart increased numen to their gods—a very desirable outcome indeed if the gods are to have plenty of it to confer in return where it will do men the most good. The means also by which gods and men maintain contact have numen in them, as for instance altars, rituals, and priests.

This attention to numen as of central significance led the early Romans to assign to their gods and spirits a rather vague character. These were lacking in distinct personality, and even sometimes in distinguishable sex. To put it bluntly, "ancient Roman religion knew no mythical histories of personal gods, no genealogies, no marriages or children, no heroic legends, no worship of legendary heroes, no cosmogony, no conceptions of life in the underworld—in a word, nothing of that which Homer and Hesiod had so abundantly supplied for the Greeks." [41] So little of distinct personality had the spirits and powers of the fields and the farm-house, that the early Romans generally regarded them simply as forms or functional expressions of numen to which descriptive or personal names were to be assigned only to distinguish them from each other and little more. Consequently, they made no anthropomorphic images of them, had no pictures of them in their minds that they cared to draw on a wall or paint on a vase. It was only later that they learned from the Etruscans and the Greeks how to visualize and humanize their gods.

Perhaps this failure to personalize their deities was owing to their interest in the diverse *functions* of numen, analyzed out to their logical practical limits. The total logical scheme may well have intrigued the analytical powers of the Romans sufficiently to delay any imaginative attempts to invest the powers bearing these functions with individual characteristics and personal histories. Even when we grant that the priests may have overextended themselves in elaboration and systematization, we still have a unique situation, well worth our review.

A. THE RELIGION OF THE HOME AND THE FARM. The early Romans were mainly engaged in farming, home-making, child-raising, and war. When they desired success in farming, they turned to relevant sources of numen known to and named by them from of old: to Saturnus for sowing, to Ceres for growth of grain, to Consus for harvesting, and to Ops for safe storage of the grain; Tellus was the goddess of the tilled soil; Flora brought blossoms to field and bough, Pomona ripening to the fruit on the bough; Faunus presided over the woods, the Lares over the sown fields, the Pales over the open pasture where the livestock fed. Terminus was the numen of the boundary-stone, Fons of the springs, and Volturnus of the running river. Regnant over all, Jupiter as great sky-father brought rain and sunshine.*

In home-making and child-raising, there was a similar assignment of deity to locus of numen (the process seems not to have been the reverse). Janus was the numen in the door, defending the threshold; and Vesta, equally, if not more, ancient and important, was on the hearth, present, as was Hestia in faraway Greece, in the flame. It was the responsibility of the man of the house, as its priest, to be on good terms with Janus, and of the women to worship Vesta at her place on the hearth and present her with a portion of each meal before anyone ate. The Penates were the numina which presided over the cupboard, preserving its store of food from harm. At first indefinitely conceived, they were in later days identified with whoever was the patron deity of the home—Ceres, Juno, Jupiter, or someone else. More closely con-

---

* As if this was not complete enough: "A much minuter subdivision of functions appears in the pontifical litanies called Indigitamenta. Thus the Flamen Cerealis [the priest of Ceres] invoked no less than twelve [minor] divinities who presided over the successive steps of the husbandman's labors, from the breaking of the ground to the storing of the grain: Vervactor, Redarator, Imporcitor, Insitor, Obarator, Occator, Sarritor, Subruncinator, Messor, Convector, Conditor, Promitor, whose functions are connected respectively with the ploughing of the fallow, second ploughing, running the furrows, sowing, ploughing under, harrowing, hoeing, weeding, reaping, carting home, storing in the granary, and bringing out for use."— George Foot Moore, *History of Religions* (Scribner's, 1913), Vol. I, p. 544. Reprinted by permission of the publishers.

cerned with the history of the family, as a source of numen that exercised watch and ward over the whole household, was the Lar Familiaris. Originally the Lares were guardians of the sown fields and of the crossroads, then more narrowly of the family estate, and finally of the household in particular, receiving from the family regular worship on the Calends, Nones, and Ides of every month. A potency hard to define exactly was the *genius,* the energy and vitality of each male, considered as the essence of his manhood. It was almost a separate being, a guardian and exterior power, resident both in the man and in his marriage-bed. Each male revered and was expectant toward his genius, as was each female toward her corresponding *juno;* but special honor was paid to the Genius Paterfamilias, particularly on the birthday of the family's head. This genius was considered to be somehow symbolized by the house snake, a sort of double of the numen of the head of the house.

It should be emphasized, before we go on, that all these sources of numen were honored and propitiated by a great variety of ceremonies and festivals, whose essence consisted not so much in words as in acts, for in them religion was inextricably bound up with magic and taboo. Where we can recover enough of it for examination, the symbolism in these worshipful performances is usually transparently clear. The Romans wasted no time in vague sentimentality. A marked feature of all their rituals is their severely formal character. We find no suggestion of close person-to-person relationship. Although the word "religion" (from *religio*—binding fast in mutual obligation?) suggests close-knit relations, its practice was singularly free from affection. The ceremonies were matter-of-fact, and markedly legal, a business-like exchange of favors. For, since the character of the Roman was essentially practical:

> His natural mental attitude was that of the lawyer. And so in his relation towards the divine beings whom he worshipped, all must be regulated by clearly understood principles and carried out with formal exactness. . . . Both sides are under obligation to fulfil their part: if the man has fulfilled "his bounden duty and service," the god must make his return: if he does not, either the cause lies in an unconscious failure on the human side to carry out the exact letter of the law, or else, if the god has really broken his contract, he has, as it were, put himself out of court and the man may seek aid elsewhere.[42]

Here lies the reason why in Roman ceremonies the omission or displacement of a single word in the ritual or any deviation in the correct behavior of the participants was believed to make the whole performance of no effect. Hence, too, the need of priests; for they alone could preserve the ceremonies intact from olden times and perform them without error, or if they were not the performers, they alone could coach the lay officiants in the right procedure.

But all this was perhaps not so true of the religion of the farm and the home as it was of the religion of the state.

B. THE RELIGION OF THE EARLY ROMAN STATE. The religion of the early Roman state was in essential respects the domestic cult national-ized. It was very well organized. The chief deities had priests (*flamines*) publicly assigned to them. But the state ceremonies were not always in their charge. In the time of the monarchy, the king was the chief-priest and performed some important ceremonies. In all later periods magistrates frequently did the same, even though religious affairs were supposedly placed in the hands of the pontifices.*

On the publicly prescribed days set down on the state calendar, which came to number 104 days of each year, the priests of the various deities performed a long list of ceremonies and sacrifices. They went

---

* The pontifices formed the higher judicatory of the priesthood (the pontifical college), and were headed by the Pontifex Maximus. This last was an elected office of an executive character, and laymen might fill it. (Julius Caesar, for instance, did.)

Roman priest and priestess conducting sacrifice, with sacrificer carrying axe and presenting animal. (From a Roman frieze)

about their tasks meticulously and drily, whether anyone but themselves was on hand or not. There was really very much to which they must attend.*

The question may well be raised, to what gods were all these state ceremonies dedicated? In some cases no special deities seem to have been involved. We have the list, however, of the state deities who were addressed on the other occasions. This list sounds strange indeed in the ears of those accustomed to think that Greek and Roman religion were like peas in a pod. Alphabetically listed, the deities are: "Anna Perenna, Carmenta, Carna, Ceres, Consus, Diva Angerona, Falacer, Faunus,

---

* This is abundantly clear even in an abbreviated list of the sacred events of the calendar. Near the beginning and end of the old Roman year (which began in March), the Salii, who were the warlike priests of Mars, twice conducted the festival of Equirria, whose main event consisted in races of war-horses; and on the Ides of October they conducted another race, but this time the winning horse (assuredly full of numen) was solemnly sacrificed to Mars. The same priests on March 19 and October 19 performed a purification (lustration) of the arms of the Roman legions by a vigorous dance on the Campus Martius, in which, in an act of war magic, they brandished spears and clashed shields together fiercely, as an accompaniment to their chanting. On the 23rd of March and the 23rd of May they performed a lustration of the war-trumpets. But the greater number of ceremonies was not warlike; they had to do with the concerns of farmer and herdsman. On April 15th, during the Fordicidia, pregnant cows were sacrificed to Tellus, the goddess of the fields, in the hope that good crops might be assured by an increase of numen and that the ashes of the foetus, removed from the womb and buried by the vestal virgins, might prove effective in imparting fertility (numen) to the sheep in the later festival of the Parilia. The Parilia took place on April 21st, and was mainly intended to purify the sheep by making them jump through a ring of burning straw or laurel. Two days before, the Cerealia had been conducted by the priests of Ceres to promote by increase of numen the growth of the grain sown in the fields. A curious ceremony was held on April 25th in a grove five miles from Rome; it was the Robigalia, and during it a red dog was offered up in order to prevent red rust from endangering the grain crops. In May occurred the gloomy Lemuria to quiet the uneasy dead. In June nine days (June 7–15) were devoted to the Vestalia; in that period the women came bare-footed to the temple of Vesta with cakes that the vestal virgins then burned, and the temple and its storehouse were thoroughly cleansed against the day when the new harvest should be brought in. August had no less than six festivals devoted to the various phases of the harvest. There were six also in December, including the famous Saturnalia, when the people rejoiced together in the early winter and exchanged gifts (a pre-Christian sort of Christmas). The two festivals of January were followed by six in February. On February 15th came the Lupercalia, so well known from an incident in the life of Julius Caesar. It began with a sacrifice of goats and a dog, and was concluded when the Luperci, the priests in attendance, after cutting thongs from the skins of the sacrificial victims and thus increasing their numen, ran in two bands around the walls of the old Palatine settlement, striking the women as they went and thus curing any sterility.

Flora, (Fons), Furrina, Janus, Jupiter, Larenta, Lares, (? Lemures),
Liber, Mars, Mater Matuta, Neptunus, Ops, Pales, (Palatua), Pomona,
Portunus, Quirinus, (? Robigus), Saturnus, Tellus, (? Terminus),
Vejovis, Vesta, Volcanus, Volturnus." [43]

The familiar names of Janus, Jupiter, Mars, Vesta, Neptune, and
Vulcan appear, but Juno, Venus, Apollo, Minerva, and Mercury are
absent. Of the names on the list, nothing is known any longer about
Falacer and Furinna, although *flamines* were appointed to serve them.
Others are hardly better known to us. Many altogether dropped from
public notice in later days. Why is anybody's guess. We may note, however, a significant fact: that those that survived to enjoy later prominence were as important to the city as they had been to the country.

Jupiter (Diespiter or Diovis Pater = Father Jove) was of dateless
origin. He is, of course, the Indo-European Dyaus Pitar, or Zeus Pater,
and came over the mountains into Italy in the same manner as he entered Greece. As in Greece, he absorbed the functions of many local
Italian gods. His most exalted title was Optimus Maximus. In consequence of being the god of lightning, thunder, and rain, he acquired the
epithets Fulminator, Tonans, and Pluvius; and because he was the god
of light, he was honored by having the days of the full moon made
sacred to him. He predetermined the course of human affairs and gave
men fore-gleams of coming events by signs in the heavens and the
flight of birds, which the augurs were appointed to read; and hence he
was called Jove Prodigialis, the prodigy-sender. His lightning was often
a judgment, a catastrophic punishment for evil-doing; for he was the
guardian of the laws of the state and of the sanctity of oaths. In Rome
his temple was built on the Capitoline hill; whence he was called
Jupiter Capitolinus. In later days, as the special protector of Rome, he
shared in the imperial glories of that city, and acquired such titles as
Imperator, Invictus, Victor, and Praedator. He received the worship of
the consuls of the Republic when they took up their offices. The celebrated "triumphs" of returning generals were spectacular processions
winding to the shouts of the joyous populace through the city, carrying
booty and captives to his temple.

Mars and Quirinus were the two war-gods. Mars, identified by the
Greeks with Ares, was perhaps originally the protector of the fields and
herds from inimical powers of any kind, animal, human, or superhuman.
He became more and more associated with war as the Roman imperium was extended, and his original character changed. But the
homely, protective nature of his early activity is seen in the description
Cato has left us of the procession of a farmer and his family along his

farm's boundary-line, three times around, accompanied by a pig, sheep, and ox, the victims which were afterwards solemnly sacrificed. During the sacrifice the farmer offered libations to Janus and Jupiter and prayed thus, like a lawyer:

> Father Mars, I pray and beseech thee that thou mayest be propitious and of good will to me, our house and household, for which cause I have ordered the offering of pig, sheep, and ox to be led round my field, my land, and my farm, that thou mightest prevent, ward off and avert diseases, visible and invisible, barrenness and waste, accidents and bad weather; that thou wouldest suffer the crops and fruits of the earth, the vines and shrubs to wax great and prosper, that thou wouldest preserve the shepherds and their flocks in safety, and give prosperity and health to me and our house and household; for all these causes, for the lustration and purification of my farm, land, and field, as I have said, be thou enriched by the sacrifice of this offering of suckling pig, lamb, and calf.[44]

In Rome, where a similar ceremony took place on the Campus Martius around an altar to the god that stood there, Mars' sacred symbols were the lance and shield, his sacred animal the wolf, and his servitors the Salii and the Flamen Martialis.

Of Quirinus we know almost nothing, except that he was the war-god of the community on the Quirinal, while Mars was from the Palatine. Quirinus was served by a *flamen,* and had a festival dedicated to him which took place on February 17th (the Quirinalia). Perhaps he represented defence where Mars stood for offence.

Janus and Vesta were ritualistically linked together as the first and last deities invoked in any ceremony. Janus, as the keeper of the door, was invoked at the opening of almost anything. He was the god of beginnings, and thus of the first hour of the day, of the Calends of every month, and, in the calendar of later days, of the first month of the year (January). His original symbol in Rome was simply a gateway standing at the northeast corner of the Forum. It was under the king's charge, and later was assigned the services of a priest called the Rex Sacrorum, highest in dignity of all the priests. Like Vesta, Janus was not originally personalized; the door, opening and closing, was his only sign, just as the pure flame, guarded by the vestal virgins in the temple of Vesta, sufficed there to show forth the goddess.

Changes Due to Etruscan Influence

Though the facts are not entirely clear, it is certain that Rome came under Etruscan dominance during the whole of the 6th century B.C. There were some significant changes as a consequence. The Etruscans were energetic and commercial-minded. Recognizing the strategic position of Rome, they built a wall around it that enclosed enough space for a population of 200,000. They sought to make residence in the city attractive to plebeians, and therefore favored them as against patricians. And they introduced some entirely new trends in Roman religion.

New deities were brought in, without seriously disturbing, at first, the old entrenched customs. Diana left her grove at Aricia for a temple erected to her on the Aventine. The triumvirate of Jupiter, Mars, and Quirinus was overshadowed by a well-housed triad composed of Jupiter, Juno, and Minerva, established on the Capitoline in a bright new temple of Etruscan workmanship.

The association of Jupiter and Juno, here begun, later led to their being regarded as husband and wife. This was the first clear instance of marriage among the Roman gods. The earlier Roman religion had furnished some instances of the yoking of male and female names; but this had signified so much less than marriage or family connection that scholars find in it only fresh evidence that the early Romans did not unambiguously know what sex their *numina* had: sometimes to be safe they gave them names signifying both sexes. But Juno became Jupiter's consort, and thus took on much more of the aspects of distinct personality than before. Originally she had simply imparted *numen* to women and girls (. . . as men had their *genius*, so women had their *juno*); and in the form of Juno Lucina she had been invoked at the moment of childbirth. Now she attained the characteristics which caused visiting Greeks to identify her with Hera.

Minerva may have been Etruscan. Her character paralleled that of Athena. She was the goddess of wisdom and the patroness of arts and trades. In due time her aid was sought in war; hence she was represented as wearing a helmet and a coat of mail, and she carried a spear and a shield, in the manner of her Greek counterpart.

This visualizing of Minerva as an anthropomorphic deity points to an innovation of the Etruscans which was of the first importance. They set images of the gods in the temples they built. In the temple on the Capitoline, they erected two rows of columns down the center of the sanctuary, and at the northwestern end they placed three images, a statue of Jupiter flanked by one of Juno and another of Minerva. Here was the initial step that led to the imaging and personalizing of all the deities. Even Janus acquired a head—but with two faces, one looking forward and one back. But these changes were not purely Etruscan.

Borrowings from the Greeks

Just as the political power of Rome under the Etruscans was extending southward through Italy, Greek cultural influence began to penetrate northward. Especially impressive to the Romans was Greek ritual. It provided vital elements of warmth and poetry hitherto lacking in Roman religion. The Romans on their part proved ready to adopt many new conceptions offered by the Greeks, without meaning to abandon any of their old ways.

Of far-reaching moment was the introduction into Rome during the 6th century B.C. of a collection of oracles credited to the Cumaean Sibyl—the famous *Sibylline Books.* These books, stored in the basement of the Capitoline temple, were committed to a newly created order of patrician priests, two in number, the *duovi sacris faciundis* (later increased in number to ten, and still later to fifteen). These priests were asked on many grave occasions to consult the oracles; in each case they afterward announced, without revealing the verses consulted, the course of procedure which they said was advised. Since the oracles were of Greek origin, the Duovi usually prescribed as remedies for impending or present disaster, or for public perplexity, resort to deities and ceremonies not before known, except perhaps by report, to the Romans. As a result extensive adoptions into Roman religion took place.

It cannot be said that the Duovi suggested changes without precedent. Castor and Pollux had already been brought to Rome by way of the Latin town of Tusculum, and Hercules had also arrived by way of the town of Tiber. But the Sibylline Books gave impetus to a process which might else have been slow. In 493 B.C. their verses were interpreted to advise the erection of a temple to house Ceres, Liber, and Libera (= Demeter, Dionysus, and Persephone). A temple for Apollo was next prescribed. Similarly, by identifying him with the Roman Neptune, Greek rites in honor of Poseidon were imported. Hermes came to Rome also, but under the name of Mercury, for he was to be the god of commerce (*mercatura*). Later, in much the same way, and with an accompanying Greek ritual, Aphrodite made her appearance as Venus (who had been a minor Italian deity, perhaps of the garden). About the same time, a pestilence led to the advice that Aesculapius, the god of healing, be introduced at once and provided with a temple. These fully personalized deities added an entirely new dimension to Roman religion.

Sometimes the Sibylline advisers suggested a *lectisternium.* Here the Greek ritual called for the introduction of a whole group of gods, appearing as wooden figures, elegantly attired, and reclining on couches around a banquet table, on which was placed a sacramental meal! Livy reports that in 399 B.C., during a severe pestilence, Apollo, Latona, Hercules, Diana, Mercury, and Neptune were together propitiated in this manner. Nor was this the last time this rite was performed. The gods were becoming more human every day.

And as if stirred into original creation by these importations, the Romans added from time to time new deities of their own: Fides to personalize the quality of loyalty celebrated in the title Fidius assigned to Jupiter, and Victoria to do the same for his qualities as Jupiter Victor. A goddess of luck and good fortune appeared also under the name of Fortuna. Each of these newcomers was given a separate temple within the city.

Along with all this came increased interest in the myths and epics of Greece. As a consequence, many of the Greek myths were adapted to the Italian scene and to Roman history, and were reissued in new form, although most were simply taken over with slight change, to become part of the Roman heritage. The life histories of Jupiter, Juno, Minerva, and others, were built up out of the Greek elements into stories ranging over an international scene but with an Italian coloring. At the same time inventive (if not supremely imaginative) minds fell to work on Roman traditions, and elaborated Italian myths about Romulus and Remus, Aeneas, Tiberinus, and others. (The way for Ovid and Vergil was thus prepared.)

Importations from the Orient

So far, the additions to the old Roman beliefs were not out of keeping with the general cultural trends which had appeared in Roman life. But we come now to some which were more esoteric. When Rome was in the process of becoming an international power contending for supremacy in the Mediterranean world, she became conscious of cultures very different from her own. Her people, as they grew entirely away from the agricultural economy of the earlier days toward a completely urban and imperial point of view, became curious about these alien conceptions. Were they perhaps worth investigating? The old Roman religious procedures seemed more and more to fail them, or at least to be inadequate. As increasing numbers of Romans lost their rootage in the soil, and with it the day-filling activities that had once given exercise and discipline to their emotions, they found their lives lacking in the satisfactions which prevent the sense of futility from engulfing the normal feeling that life has meaning and value. Scepticism began to run a race with the search for new faiths.

Mystic cults, promising richer emotional satisfactions, came from the Orient. The first of these was that of the Magna Mater, Cybele, introduced from Phrygia on the advice of the Sibylline oracles. An embassy of five prominent Roman citizens went during the protracted crisis of the Second Punic War (218–201 B.C.) to fetch a sacred stone, dropped from heaven, in which Cybele was thought to be resident.

But the city fathers took a rather sober view, on closer acquaintance with Cybele, of the wildness and fanaticism of her devotees. They passed a law, which was not abrogated until the Empire, forbidding Romans to enter her priesthood; she had to be served by priests brought in from Asia Minor. The people, however, were allowed to, and did, go to her temple to seek her aid, for this life and the next.

Following upon Cybele's arrival came the mystery-religion of Bacchus (Dionysus), with its secret rites. There was swift response to it, not only in Rome but throughout the Italian peninsula. But the upper classes hated secrecy of any kind and were highly suspicious of it; they came to believe the worst of the Bacchanalian orgies. Accordingly, the cult was suppressed by a decree of the Senate in 186 B.C. But it came to life again, and was allowed to continue, under the strict supervision of the state.

In the years that followed, other eastern cults gained a footing and grew in influence. Ma of Cappadocia, Adonis of Syria, Isis and Osiris (Serapis) of Egypt, and Mithras of Persia were all brought to Rome; and each in some measure supplied the religious experience and the hope of immortality which the state religion, fallen now into the hands of agnostic politicians and of priests who also had lost faith, was powerless to call forth or sustain.

The Last Phases

The history of Roman religion during the last century of the Republic (150–49 B.C.) suggests the operation of forces moving in a direction exactly opposite to those of an earlier time; the movement was no longer centripetal, but centrifugal. The state religion had degenerated into pure formalism—the structure was there, but it was empty and void. For one thing, Rome was like a deity herself (Dea Roma), and no longer needed the help of the old gods in the old way. The educated classes, enlightened or disillusioned by Greek philosophy, pursued the atheistic way of the Epicureans, or the pantheistic way of the

Stoics, or else lapsed into indifferentism. The attitude of Cicero was typical: he inclined toward Stoicism, but he was an eclectic, and would commit himself nowhere, because his scepticism prevented him; religion was something to discuss pleasantly over the dinner table or with friends in a moment of leisure, but, apart from its value as a political binding element, it was of no vital concern to a thinking man.

The attempt of Augustus Caesar to bring the world back to normal, after a generation of unnerving civil wars, by reviving the old Roman religious practices, led him to repair the decaying temples of Rome, induce men to enter again the old priesthoods, and build new temples, such as that on the Palatine in honor of Apollo, the patron of his house. But this was not in itself sufficient. It affected Rome only; and even there it aroused only a mild response. He knew already how advantageous it was to him politically to be regarded outside of Italy as a god. The world needed to look to some one power, worship of which might bind it together, and perhaps none might be as useful for this purpose as the ongoing *genius* of the imperial house. To encourage this feeling, Augustus erected a temple in the Forum, furnished with specially appointed priests and dedicated to the honor of Divus Julius (Julius Caesar, his father by adoption), who had already been declared a god by the Roman Senate in 42 B.C. As for himself, he permitted the erection of shrines in which his *genius* was worshipped (though not himself). This marked the beginning of emperor-worship. In the provinces it became mandatory, as a sign of loyalty to the Roman imperium, to pay reverence to the emperor's *genius,* and sometimes to the emperor himself. Although throughout life Augustus steadfastly refused honors to himself in person, it was inevitable that after his death his name should be enrolled with those of the gods, and that a temple should be erected to him, with priests in attendance. Not all the emperors immediately after him were accorded this honor, but in due time consecration of the emperor as a god became part of every imperial funeral. At last the aura of divinity came to attach itself to emperors *before* death; Caligula and Domitian were two who demanded worship while living, and Nero before them is said to have enjoyed being equated with Apollo.

What is significant here is this: to have real unity, the Empire needed more than uniform laws and just government; there had to be also a unifying reverence, a common loyalty to what was central, a commitment to an all highest. When it was apparent that the multiplicity of religions led only to centrifugal scattering, emperor-worship was conceived in an attempt to reverse the flight from the common center. But it was not enough; it just barely served. In a fundamental sense, it was not cosmic enough, not able to link together man, society, and universe under one inclusive meaning or purpose. It failed to rise above the dead level of the multiplying religious faiths of the Mediterranean world. Nor was there vital power in it to stir and change individuals.

But amalgamation of the gods, or any eclecticism on the grand scale, cannot perhaps arrive at a world-faith; the result is too complex. Dynamic qualities are, rather, engendered by simple faiths. At all events, in Rome, as in Egypt, Mesopotamia, and Greece, the national religion, the result of linkages and mergings-together of deities from far and near, proved to be merely provisional; after serving its purpose, it yielded to a greater, simpler, more vitally meaningful faith, which came to take its place.

This was Christianity, a profound and meaningful way of linking together not only man and society, but man, his neighbor, and the universe, under one God. How it triumphed will be told later in this book.

V EUROPE BEYOND THE ALPS

In the early history of Greece and Rome we met bands of southward surging Indo-Europeans; in northern Europe we find them everywhere. (Later in our story we shall meet them also in India, Iran, and Armenia.) One of the great puzzles of history is where these people originated and what sent them on their far-flung journeys, radiating outward like the spokes of a wheel, south, west, north, and southeast. But whatever moved them from their prehistoric homeland (in southern Russia and the Ukraine?), they succeeded not only in subjugating the resident tribes in their path, outnumbered though they were, but in imposing on those they conquered their language and many elements of their magic and religion. The ancient Celts, Teutons, and Slavs developed religious practices and beliefs which, in spite of assimilation of many variant local conceptions and customs, nevertheless illustrate what the original Indo-European world-view might be expected to become when not radically altered by the infusion of foreign ways of behaving and believing.*

The Celts

We turn to the Celts first because we have already met them in

* We are now to see less of amalgamation and syncretism and more of heightening of central themes prior to a final disintegration.

northern Italy. So far as we can determine from the uncertain records, the Celts moved originally from their first homeland to northwestern Germany, where they merged with proto-Nordic and Alpine tribes to form a new amalgam of ethnic groups, marked by tall, green-eyed, red-haired men; then they broke up by migrating southwestward into France (Gaul) and thence into Spain, westward across the Channel to the British Isles, southward into Italy and Greece, and far to the southeast into Asia Minor, where they held on for centuries to the province to which they gave their name (Galatia, the place of the Gauls).

The Celts, according to *The Commentaries* of Julius Caesar, wor-shiped most a god he identifies as Mercury, but he does not give us the Celtic name; he says they also worshipped Apollo, Mars, Jupiter, and Minerva. To this list he adds Dispater, to whom he says the Gauls traced their origin. He is joined by Tacitus, the Elder Pliny, and Lucan in the statement that the Celts were led by their priests (the Druids) in human sacrifice and animal- and tree-worship.*

The Celts were nature-worshippers of a most expansive kind: they revered the sky, mountains, stones, trees, lakes, rivers, springs, sea, and every kind of animal—the boar, the bear, the bull, the horse, the hare,

* When seeking the Gallic and Irish equivalents of the Roman identifications we run into difficulties. Mars, for example, was equated in Roman inscriptions with more than fifty native gods, Mercury with some thirty others, Jupiter with some twenty-five more, Apollo with some twenty, and Minerva with a half-dozen or so. In other words, if the Celts originally had a pantheon—and we cannot say definitely that they had—history and experience had led them to exchange many names for the possible original few.

These difficulties to one side, we can recover many of the names of the Gallic, Irish, and English deities. Prominent among the figures represented in the sur-viving remains is Cernunnos, a horned god shown sometimes with three heads or portrayed pouring out grain to a stag and a bull, evidently as a fertility deity; another god is Sucellos, always carrying a hammer, the symbol of thunder and lightning, but also bearing a cup in one hand, with a gesture of hospitality; Esus, still another, is pictured with an axe cutting branches from a tree; and fertility goddesses, such as Nantosuelta and Epona, are also mentioned. All these are from Gaul. In Ireland we hear of Dagda, "the great father"; of Lug, "inventor of all handicrafts"; of Brigit, also known in Gaul and England, goddess of wisdom and poetry; of Danu and Anu, earth-goddesses, and of others. England and Wales pro-vide us with Andrasta, goddess of victory; Belenos, a sun god; Totatis, god of war; Lyr, god of the sea, and still others, many of them destined to be demoted with the coming of Christianity into legendary kings and queens. It is perhaps a dubious speculation which merges King Arthur, hero of the Brythons of lowland Scotland, with Artor, an English god, possibly of agriculture, or Artaios, a Gallic war god. Perhaps Gwenhwyfar (Guinevere) was first a white fairy, and Myrddin (Merlin) a divine magician; but more likely they were originally as human as Arthur was. We do not know.

the ram, the stag, even the crow, and many female as well as male creatures, the cow, for example. (The snake also received its share of regard; so that when St. Patrick came to Ireland, there grew the legend that he not only drove the ancient gods and goddesses into the hills and glens to serve a lower function as fairies, but also rid Ireland of snakes: in short, he could not tolerate the veneration of them.) Some of the Celtic gods and goddesses were part animal and part human in shape; others resembled Epona, the Gallic fertility goddess, who carried a cornucopia while on horse-back or while seated among horses.

Another certain fact is that the Celts were much concerned with fertility in field, flock, and womankind. There were many fertility powers, male and female, and a number of mother-goddesses; it was common to revere the last in groups of three and to portray them holding in their laps children or baskets of fruit in evidence of their influence on fruitfulness. Among the recurrent festivals and ceremonies of which the Celts were exceedingly fond was the May Day festival. It has survived in a token form as the Maypole dance still observed in Europe and America. The ancient Celtic festival bore all the marks of fertility magic. It was a widespread practice to light bonfires on the hills about May 1st and then do the following things: drive cattle through or between them, have the people dance a sun dance around them, bring new fires from them to the home hearths, and then carry some of the burning brands around the fields like shining suns. It may have been a general practice to sacrifice an animal or a human being in the bonfires, as an invitation to the sun to recover its strength after the long somnolence of winter. There was also a May king and a May queen who symbolized, or were thought of as incarnations of, the vegetation spirits. It is likely that they were given in marriage to each other to stimulate fertility in soil and flock.°

The human sacrifices we have incidentally mentioned shocked the Romans, who took immediate steps to suppress them. We learn that such sacrifices were made not only to promote fertility but more generally to appease, thank, or gain the help of the gods. Though innocent victims were sometimes chosen—wives or children, at times—it was more common to offer up prisoners of war or thieves and other criminals; murderers, for example, were turned over to the Druids for sacrifice to the gods. The Roman authors tell us that the victims were sometimes slain beforehand by arrows or by stakes driven through their temples, but it was common first to build a large effigy of wicker or of wood and

° For particulars see J. A. MacCulloch, *The Celtic and Scandinavian Religions* (Hutchinson's University Library, London, 1948).

straw, then fill it with victims human and animal, and have the Druids set it on fire. It may be assumed that such sacrifices were very special occasions and that ordinarily animal sacrifices were offered, men and dogs joining in the feast after the sacrifice, the dogs, as Arrian tells us of the Galatian Celts, being decked with garlands of flowers. In modified form some of these rites have come down to our own day. Carl Clemen offers us instances from France:

> In the district round Grenoble to this day a goat is slaughtered at harvest-time. Its flesh, with the exception of one piece, which is kept for a year, is eaten by the reapers, and out of its skin the farmer has a coat made, which is believed to have healing virtue. In Pouilly an ox is killed, its skin being kept till the next seedtime. Undoubtedly these animals represent the spirit of vegetation. In former days in Brie on the 23rd of June, and down to the year 1743 in a certain street in Paris on the 3rd of July, a human effigy was burnt, the people fighting for the *debris* . . . Finally, there are certain phrases still current in many districts of France which contain an allusion to the killing of a human being or an animal at harvest-time. When the last sheaf is being garnered or threshed the people say, "We are killing the old woman," or "the hare," "the dog," "the cat," or "the ox." [45]

Frazer's *The Golden Bough* assembles hundreds of similar instances of the survival in Europe of ceremonies from a pre-Christian time.

The worship of the gods was performed with the aid of priests and priestesses both in temples and in homes; but perhaps the more important ceremonies were held in sacred groves under the direction of special class of priests—the Druids. Caesar tells us that the Druids had political as well as religious functions. They played a role in the election of kings, served as ambassadors or legates, and took part in battles. Their teachings were preserved orally only, and could not be learned without a long period of training, lasting sometimes up to twenty years. These teachings, according to Caesar, concerned not only religious and magical matters but also the movements of the stars, the size of the world, and the general constitution of the universe at large.

How true this may be cannot be known, but it does seem probable that the Druids speculated that the world would someday come to an end, that there would be a doomsday overwhelming men and gods, when fire and water would swallow up the earth, the sky would fall, and all men would perish, to make way for a new heaven and earth and a new race of men.

The Teutons

Appearing in history later than the Celts, the Teutons, who were of somewhat purer Indo-European stock, began to press westward from the southern shores of the Baltic as Anglo-Saxons and Jutes, southward as Saxons, Alamanni, Lombards, Frisians and Franks, northward as Scandinavians, and southeastward as Goths and Vandals.

Teutonic tradition comes to us chiefly by way of two Icelandic works, the *Poetic Edda,* an anthology of hymns to the gods and heroic poems, said to have been brought together by Saemundr the Wise (1056–1133), and the *Prose Edda,* the work of Snorri Sturleson, a thirteenth century Christian, scholar and sceptic, who tried to provide a practical manual for young poets who would wish to draw upon the traditional myths of Iceland for their material. Less important as authentic sources are the Norse sagas and scalds (poems), of which eight or ten are especially significant.

From these sources we get a rather crowded picture of a score of gods and goddesses, some ancient, some late, whom we must suppose to have come forward or receded in importance with passing time. It is possible that one of the oldest of the gods was Ziu (Tiu or Tyr), whose name has the same root as Zeus, Jupiter, and the Dyaus Pitar of the Indo-Aryans. (The name appears again in the word "Tuesday.") He was originally the shining sky, but relinquished his high place, perhaps because there was more need of him on earth, to become a god of war. In contrast to him, Donar or Thor, the red-bearded god of thunder (donner) and rain, and therefore of agriculture, grew in importance with the years, becoming the center of a cult that spread throughout the Teutonic world. Carrying his famous hammer, Miollnir, in iron-gloved hands, he rode in a sky chariot drawn by two he-goats. He became the chief god in Norway and Iceland. (We now have his name in Thursday.) If Thor was popular with the common man, Wodan or Odin was exalted by the ruling princes and war chiefs, for he was a god of war who protected heroes and sent his two Valkyries or war maidens to carry warriors fallen in battle to his great hall in the sky, Valhalla. When traveling through the heavens, he galloped upon the eight-legged horse Sleipnir, accompanied by his wolves, Geri and Freki. In heaven he surveyed the world from the windows of Valaskialf, his home, supporting on either shoulder the two ravens, Guggin (Thought) and Muninn (Memory), who whispered in his ear their reports of all that they had seen while in flight. His dreaded spear Gungnir, made by dwarfs, never missed. Knowing and seeing all, he was the source of the wisdom of seers and poets. (We still honor him in our Wednesday.) Snorri of Iceland calls him the chief of the Aesir, the gods in heaven, who dominate the Vanir, the gods beneath. He is called All-father, and he, as we shall see, assisted at the creation.

Three things seem to have concerned the Teutonic peoples greatly —fertility, death, and the end of the world. As to the first, they did not put all their reliance upon the life-quickening rain of Thor. They turned also to Freyr (Frey, Fricco), the "Lord" of fertility in man, animals, and vegetation, and to his sister and wife Freyja (the "Lady"). Freyr and Freyja were quite possibly son and daughter of the god of wealth, Njörd, and the goddess Nerthus, of whom Tacitus had so much to say.°

Freyr and Freyja were the divine May king and May queen whose embrace brought the revival of life in spring. But the cycle of spring, summer, and autumn was symbolized by other gods and goddesses, the most notable of whom is Balder, whose tragic death (autumn?) is recorded in the well-known myth. Balder (the blessed Light) was the kindest, most noble and gentle of the gods. His mother Frigg, consort of Odin and queen of the gods (for whom Friday is named), took oaths from all things not to hurt him, but she neglected to pledge the mistletoe. Thinking Balder to be invulnerable, the gods had great sport throwing every kind of object at him, always without harming him; but Loki, the malicious one among the gods, learned that the mistletoe had not been sworn, and persuaded the blind but powerful Hödr to hurl a sprig of mistletoe at Balder, and he was slain. Balder perforce descended to Hel,† there to await liberation at the end of the world. We shall encounter him again.

Death was a disturbing thought to the Teutons, for it was too often only the beginning of troubles. Until the corpse of a man decayed, it could do harm as a specter or vampire (a belief which the Norse shared with the Chinese on the other side of the world); and the corpse itself was in danger of being torn to pieces by wolves out of hell, by horse-shaped demons, or by swooping eagles, such as the giant wind-demon Hraesvelg. On the other hand, the spirits of the dead, if they had been good in life and were faithfully reverenced after death, could bring good fortune to their descendants.

The convictions concerning the after-life seem confused. In later times, the Teutons believed both that the dead lived on in their burial

---

° Tacitus (*ca.* 100 A.D.) names as the highest of the Teutonic gods Mercury, Mars, and Hercules; and in this case we can identify the Teutonic originals as Wodan (or Odin), Ziu (or Tiu), and Donar (or Thor). The rites in honor of the goddess Nerthus are described by Tacitus in some detail and traced by him to their origin on the shores of the Baltic. This and other information supplied by Tacitus are a valuable confirmation of Teutonic tradition.

† Sometimes in the Eddas the underworld, Hel, is personified by Loki's daughter, Hel, a repulsive and dreadful creature who assigns to all who are sent to her their places in the underworld.

barrows and yet that they traveled nine days and nights by the Hel-way to Hel, the underworld, where they sat in the great hall of Hel on benches and drank beer (mead). But the warriors went to Valhalla, at least those whom Thor favored; and there they feasted on boar's flesh behind the five hundred and forty great doors of the shield-thatched hall, and then rose to fight each other in the courtyard for self-conditioning and for sport.

The reason why the warriors of Valhalla adopted a regimen of self-conditioning lay in their knowledge that Odin would need their services in the cosmic conflict that would take place at the time of the Doom of the Gods (the Götterdämmerung). At this point Teutonic thought reached a certain profundity—or was it no more than a dramatic view of time and history?

According to Snorri (in the *Prose Edda*), the first state of things, the Ginnunga Gap—a yawning gulf or opening suspended between a region of mist and cold, Niflheim, and a region of glowing heat, Muspelheim—generated from its rime and slush a cosmic giant, Ymir. In a similar way there also emerged a cosmic cow, Audumla, whose udders fed Ymir and made it possible for him to generate other beings. Presently from under the hands and feet of Ymir came the frost-giants; the cow Audumla also, while licking the salty ice to the north, de-iced and freed Buri, a giant who became the grandsire, through his son Bor and daughter-in-law Bestla, of Odin, Vili, and Ve. Rising against Ymir, Odin and his brothers slew and dismembered the primal giant, making the earth from his flesh, trees from his hair, mountains from his bones, the earth-encompassing sea from his blood, clouds from his brain, and the bowl of heaven from his hollow skull. (The Hindus and the Chinese have similar stories to tell.) From the sparks out of Muspelheim, the sun, moon, and stars were formed. The three brothers then took the eyebrows of Ymir to make a raised plain, called Midgard, to be the abode of men, and from two trees by the sea they formed the first man and woman, Askr and Embla, the parents of the human race. The three gods also created the dwarfs to live in the ground under the earth and in stones and hills. In the region above the earth, they made Askgard, the abode of the gods, with its great halls and palaces; and between heaven and earth they put a rainbow bridge, guarded against the giants by the god Heimdall. So runs the story of creation in the *Prose Edda,* although other sources, such as the poem *Voluspa* in the *Poetic Edda,* tell the story somewhat differently; but it is not to our purpose to inquire further.

An uneasy world-order was now established: the frost-giants were exiled to the edges of Utgard, the earth-encompassing sea; the gods dwelt in Askgard and men in Midgard; the dead gathered in Hel, its gate in Niflheim guarded by the watchdog Garm. Off in the sea all around the flat earth, lay the huge coil of the dangerous Midgard serpent; and outside the world in Muspelheim, the region of heat, were the ferocious Fenriswolf, bound by a magic chain of the gods, and the giant Sutr, the bold leader of the fire-giants. The gods of Askgard, the rulers of this uneasy world, passed down Bifrost, the rainbow bridge, to stand under the world-tree and pass judgment.

How exactly the world-tree, Yggdrasil, fits into this picture it is difficult to say; but the old tree was "the pillar" between the nine regions of the world. Under its three roots were the three regions where dwelt the dead, men, and the exiled frost-giants; and the regions of the sky were sustained by its branches. (Here is a conception that the Teutons shared with the Celts, Slavs, Mesopotamians, Hindus, and numerous groups in central Asia.)

But the Teutonic peoples knew that the world order would not last forever. In a hall under the world-tree dwelt the three Norns or Fates, who fixed the lot of each man at birth and would someday make known the hour of doomsday. That hour would come when the old tree would groan and tremble; the Fenris-wolf would break his chain and come raging to earth; the giant Sutr would lead the fire-giants in an assault upon the gods; the frost-giants would storm in from the edges of the world; and the Midgard serpent, thrashing heavily in the sea, would toss great tidal waves across the earth. The watch-dog of Hel would set up a howl, and let Loki lead his allies past him up to earth to join in the overthrow of the world order. The invaders would storm Bifrost, only to have that frail bridge break under them. Then the final battle of the world would take place on the plains of earth, with the gods and the heroes of Valhalla going down in defeat; men would suffer apparent extinction, and the earth would be burned up by the victorious forces of fire and chaos.

After a while a new earth would emerge from the sea, and the sons of Odin and Thor, together with Balder and Hödr released from Hel, would establish a new and more promising world order. Human life would begin again from two survivors of the Götterdämmerung and its accompanying world conflagration.

This remarkable conception of time and history links the Teutonic peoples with those of India, who also believed, and still do, in world cycles; it is obvious also that Christianity, when it came, could (and did) profit by the expectation of the death of the old gods and the return of gentle, cruelly slain Balder.

The Slavs

Here we return to interests such as we found among the Celts. Christianity came last to the Teutons, especially to the Scandinavians, and first to the southern Celts and southern Slavs. Consequently, the rich development of ideas concerning death and the end of the world is not so apparent among the Celts and Slavs as among the Teutons, who remained pagan a longer time.*

The Slavs used rather revealing words for their religious realities. *Bogu* (possessor and giver of wealth) was their word for "god," and *besu* (disagreeable, nasty) their word for "demon" or "devil." It is thus apparent that their gods were the source of fertility and prosperity; and that demons interfered with and spoiled what might have turned out well. Another much used term was *duchu* (in its feminine form *dusha*), which meant "spirit" or "breath," and referred to that part of a living person that departed at death to become a spirit. Death and the afterlife deeply concerned and daunted the Slavs. They seemed to think the soul of a dying person fled out of the window or door in the form of some small creature, such as a bird, a mouse, or even an insect. Thereafter, if rightly treated and periodically fed or given gifts, it might come back in ghost-form (as a house-spirit or *domovoj*) to crouch benevolently in the darkness back of the stove and protect the house and barn by night; or, if not well-disposed, it might enter the body of a wolf and as a werewolf bring evil and terror to all. But sooner or later the soul of the departed one would begin a long and difficult journey to a bourne or paradise (*raji*) at the edge of the world, for which it would need food and equipment supplied by or taken from the living.

Demonic beings in general fascinated the Slavic imagination long after the coming of Christianity. There were, for example, malicious female spirits (the *vilen*), beautiful and shapely, who could quickly turn into swans, other birds, or serpents, and do harm to those they disliked or good to those they favored. More forbidding were the *rusalken*, perhaps originally errant souls of the dead, now capable of putting spells upon the living; these demons hid among the growing crops or swung

---

* Historians distinguish between the southern Slavs (the Slavs of the Danube basin and the Balkans) and the northern Slavs (now the Czechs, Slovaks, Poles, and Russians).

Since the pre-Christian Slavs left no literature and no strong oral tradition behind them, we must in part trust to the uncertainly accurate references to them by scornful or hostile Christian writers, and rely still more on philological and cultural survivals that yield us clues to pre-Christian beliefs and practices. It is extremely difficult to determine what the southern Slavs believed; what little we have to say concerns the northern Slavs.

in the treetops and delighted in scoffing at or upsetting with sudden panic the passers-by. The only thing to do was to seek to appease them with gifts of food, wreaths of flowers, or offerings of cloth hung on branches or bushes. If they were lurking in streams or ponds, offerings were thrown to them in the water. Their sadism was an ever-present menace throughout life.

There were also the Fates, to whom offerings of corn, cheese, honey, and bread were due, and who, like the Teutonic Norns and the Greek and Roman Fates, spun the thread of life and fixed its length. Also important were certain female fertility spirits, comparable to Demeter and Ceres, and a vague male figure, Rodu, a god of fruitfulness.

Of greater religious stature were the sun god Dazibogu (Dazbog), and the thunderer Perun, who was the Slavic Thor and was more reverenced even than Svarog, the god of fire. Volos (Viles) was the god of cattle, Stribog the wind god; we need mention no more. These gods, whose worship was conducted by priests with animal sacrifices, libations, and the sprinkling of blood, faded away at the coming of Christianity, apparently without a struggle, leaving only the faintest of traces after the passage of time.

SUGGESTIONS FOR FURTHER READING

EGYPT

Albright, W. F. *From the Stone Age to Christianity.* 2nd ed. with new introduction, Johns Hopkins Press, 1957. Available also as Anchor pb

Breasted, J. H. *The Dawn of Conscience.* Scribner, 1933

————. *Development of Religion and Thought in Ancient Egypt.* Scribner, 1912. Available as Harper Torchbooks pb

Budge, E. A. W. *From Fetish to God in Ancient Egypt.* Oxford, 1934

————. *The Literature of the Ancient Egyptians.* J. M. Dent, 1914

Erman, Adolph. *A Handbook of Egyptian Religion.* Constable, 1907

Frankfort, Henri. *Ancient Egyptian Religion.* Columbia University Press, 1948

Mercer, S. A. B. *Growth of Religious and Moral Ideas in Egypt.* Morehouse (Milwaukee), 1919

Moret, A. *The Nile and Egyptian Civilization.* K. Paul, Trench, Trubner, 1927

Murray, Margaret. *The Spendour That Was Egypt.* Sidgwick & Jackson, 1949

Petri, Sir Flinders. *Religious Life in Ancient Egypt.* Houghton Mifflin, 1924

Shorter, A. H. *An Introduction to Egyptian Religion.* K. Paul, Trench, Trubner, 1932

Steindorff and Seele. *When Egypt Ruled the East.* University of Chicago Press, 1942

BABYLONIA

Chiera, Edward. *They Wrote on Clay.* University of Chicago Press, 1938

Contenau, G. *Everyday Life in Babylon and Assyria.* Edwin Arnold, 1954

Delaporte, L. *Mesopotamia.* K. Paul, Trench, Trubner, 1925

Finegan, Jack. *Light from the Ancient Past.* Princeton, 1946

Frankfort, Henri. *Kingship and the Gods.* University of Chicago Press, 1948 (Deals also with Egypt)

Frankfort, Henri, and others. *The Intellectual Adventure of Ancient Man.* University of Chicago Press, 1946 (Deals with whole Near East) Now available in pb as *Before Philosophy* (Penguin Books)

Heidel, A. *The Gilgamesh Epic and Old Testament Parallels.* 2nd ed. Chicago, 1949

Hocart, A.M. *Kingship.* Oxford, 1927

Jastrow, Morris, Jr. *Aspects of Religious Belief and Practice in Babylonia and Assyria.* Putnam, 1911

Kramer, S. *Sumerian Mythology.* American Philosophical Society, 1944

Langdon, S. *Babylonian Epic of Creation.* Oxford, 1923

Leonard, W. E. translator. *Gilgamesh.* Viking, 1934

Mendelsohn, Isaac, editor. *The Religions of the Ancient Near East: Sumero-Akkadian Religious Texts and Ugaritic Epics.* Lib. Arts Press pb, 1955

Pritchard, James B., ed. *Ancient Near East Texts.* 2nd ed, rev. and enl. Princeton, 1955

GREECE

Adams, James. *The Religious Teachers of Greece.* T. & T. Clark, 1908

Bevan, E. R. *Later Greek Religion.* J. M. Dent, 1927

Cornford, F. M. *Greek Religious Thought from Homer to the Age of Alexander.* J. M. Dent, 1923

Grant, F. C., editor. *Hellenistic Religions.* Liberal Arts Press pb, 1954

Guthrie, W. K. C. *Orpheus and Greek Religion.* Harcourt Brace, 1925

————. *The Greeks and Their Gods.* Beacon, 1950. Available in Beacon pb

Harrison, Jane E. *Prolegomena to the Study of Greek Religion.* Cambridge, 1903. Available as Meridian pb

Jaeger, W. *Paideia: The Ideals of Greek Culture.* 3 vols. Oxford, 1943–1945

Livingstone, Sir Richard W., ed. *The Legacy of Greece.* Oxford, 1928

Moore, C. H. *The Religious Thought of the Greeks.* Harvard University Press, 1916

Murray, Gilbert. *The Five Stages of Greek Religion.* Clarendon Press (Oxford), 1925. Available as an Anchor pb

Nilsson, Martin P. *Greek Popular Religion.* Columbia University Press, 1940

————. *Homer and Mycenae.* Methuen, 1933

Oates and O'Neill, eds. *The Complete Greek Drama.* Random House, 1938

Rhode, Erwin. *Psyche.* Harcourt Brace, 1925

Rose, H. J. *Ancient Greek Religion.* Hutchinson, 1946

Willoughby, H. R. *Pagan Regeneration.* University of Chicago Press, 1929

ROME

Altheim, Franz. *A History of Roman Religion.* Methuen, 1938

Angus, S. *Religious Quests of the Graeco-Roman World.* Scribner, 1929

Bailey, Cyril. *Phases of the Religion of Ancient Rome.* University of California Press, 1932

Carter, J. B. *The Religion of Numa.* Macmillan, 1906

Cumont, F. *The Oriental Religions in Roman Paganism.* Open Court, 1911

Fowler, W. Warde. *The Religious Experience of the Roman People.* Macmillan, 1910

Grant, F. C., ed. *Ancient Roman Religion.* Little Library of Liberal Arts pb, 1953

————. *Roman Ideas of Deity.* Macmillan, 1914

Rose, H. J. *Ancient Roman Religion.* Hutchinson, 1948. Now available along with *Ancient Greek Religion* as Harper Torchbooks pb under title *Religion in Greece and Rome*

Wagenvoort, H. *Roman Dynamism.* Blackwell, 1947

BEYOND THE ALPS

Bellows, H. A., translator. *The Poetic Edda.* Princeton, 1936

Brodem, A. G., translator. *The Prose Edda.* Oxford, 1929

Clemen, Carl, editor. *Religions of the World.* Harcourt Brace, 1931 (Chapters on Celtic, Teutonic, and Slavic religions)

Ellis, Hilda. *The Road to Hel.* Cambridge, 1944

Fowler, Murray on "Old Norse Religion" in *Forgotten Religions,* ed. by Vergilius Ferm. Philosophical Library, 1950

Grönbeck, Vilhelm. *The Culture of the Teutons.* Oxford, 1931

MacCulloch, J. A. *Celtic Mythology* (in *The Mythology of All Races* series, Vol. III). Marshall Jones, 1918

————. *The Celtic and Scandinavian Religions.* Hutchinson, 1948

Machal, Jan. *Slavic Mythology* (in *The Mythology of All Races* series, Vol. III). Marshall Jones, 1918

PART TWO

The
Religions
of
India

Foreword to
PART TWO

THE RELIGIONS OF INDIA ARE INEXHAUSTIVELY FERTILE IN THE SUGGESTIONS they offer for meeting the need man feels for rational and mystical adjustment to life and the world. This suggestiveness is both a present and a past fact. The religions of India can be said to have offered almost every answer to religious need that can be thought of, and to have discarded none; all the answers made in the past are preserved, like bees in amber, along with those offered in the present. One feels in studying the development of Indian religions like an archaeologist digging down through the layers of Near East civilizations and finding the old forever preserved beneath the new.

But, while it is dangerous to generalize when the solutions are so various, it is true to say that there is agreement at one point. If we are to trust the testimony of their religions, the peoples of India, including the Moslems, and even the Zoroastrians, are not easily satisfied with what this world offers in material fare; the physical world is always of secondary or tertiary importance to them; there are realities—those of life, mind and spirit—that matter far more. Many would be more explicit. To most of the leading minds of India's past, but here we should except the Zoroastrians and Moslems, the world of Nature not only presents real difficulties to the fulfillment of the higher potentialities of life, mind and spirit; it must be given the value of an illusional con-

120

struct or else of a deceptive "appearance." The motive of much Hindu, Jaina, and Buddhist thought in India has been *deliverance*—deliverance, as the Jains view it, from the degrading down-drag of gross matter, or deliverance as the Hindus and Buddhists think, from the misleading appearances and experiences of the physical world. Only mental and spiritual realms have an unshakable reality that guarantees eternal satisfactions.

The peculiarly Indian beliefs that have led to the emergence of this point of view will appear early in the story. But let us not exaggerate the pessimism. The pessimism is real, but not absolute. The present and immediate are rejected, but the eternal and the ultimate are sought in hope and expectancy. The religious consciousness of India is disillusioned concerning the near and the physical because it is hungry for the joy that is to be had when the real and the eternal are known and apprehended. The reaction here may be rather superficially compared with that of a man glowering and unhappy because he must listen to the chattering and thumping of a cheap jazz orchestra beating out a primitive rhythm, when he is hungering and thirsting for the musicians to bring him Beethoven, Brahms, or Shostakovich. The point is, that reality and truth are hidden, or at best very inadequately revealed, in the images conjured up by a purely physical experience.

Perhaps it would be useful to add a word more. We shall be concerned with three religions chiefly. They differ in interesting respects, although they may be said to be actually in basic agreement with each other. By and large, philosophical Hinduism (Brahmanism) is based on the conviction that the chief error of man lies in his *thinking*: his miseries are due to fallacies in his conception of things rather than to sin in his living. Jainism, in contrast, puts primary emphasis on *behavior*, how one acts; one must behave so as to avoid contamination by matter, defiling as pitch and destructive of all spirituality of being. Early Buddhism, finally, locates the chief missteps in the area of *feeling*; it is our desires that must be reined in and prevented from flooding us with misery.

Such generalizations should, of course, not be overworked. None of these religions places exclusive emphasis on either thinking, feeling, or action, since these cannot really be divorced. (That this is the case will be evident when we look into the later development of each religion.) But to recognize at the start that in the three religions mentioned, theory is initially concerned with thinking, behaving, and feeling, respectively, is to make it easier to understand their divergences.

3 Early Hinduism: The Passage from Optimistic Polytheism to World Denial

A TYPICAL JUDGMENT OF THE COMMENTATORS ON HINDUISM IS THAT ITS diversity is unlimited. It means so many different things. It attracts so many kinds of minds. It extends a promise of ultimate treasure to so great a variety of seekers of salvation. It is an entire way of life, a total culture. It is not one religion but a family of religions. Certainly if it can be called a single religion, it can claim to have expressed almost every possible variety of religious experience.

So great indeed are the range and complexity of the beliefs and practices denoted by the term Hinduism that a distinction between its "broader" and "narrower" meanings is useful. The broader definition is preferred by many Hindus. To them Hinduism is the whole complex of beliefs and institutions which have appeared from the time when their ancient (and most sacred) scriptures, the Vedas, were composed until now. Western scholars, however, are inclined to prefer the narrower definition, according to which the so-called Vedic and Brahmanistic periods are considered as developments preparatory to Hinduism proper, the latter being identified with the vast social and religious system which has grown up among the peoples of India since about the 3rd century B.C.

Hinduism in the narrower sense is hardly less amazing and diverse than when it is considered in its broader meaning. Orthodox Hindus have an extraordinarily wide selection of beliefs and practices to choose from: they can be pantheists, polytheists, monotheists, agnostics, or even atheists; dualists, pluralists, or monists; they may follow a strict or loose standard of moral conduct, or they may choose instead an amoral emotionalism or mysticism; they may worship regularly at a temple or go not at all. Their only universal obligation, if they are orthodox, is to abide by the rules of their caste and trust that by so doing their next birth will be a happier one.

It seems best in telling the story of this astonishing religion to divide the exposition into two chapters, the one on Early, the other on Later Hinduism. In an attempt to preserve some semblance of historical perspective, these two chapters are separated by three others dealing with Jainism and Buddhism; for the latter religions burst in upon and for a time interrupted the orderly growth and development of Hinduism, so that they should be well studied before Later Hinduism is considered. The present chapter deals with the origins of Hinduism and the progression from optimistic polytheism to world-denying monism which is seen to run its course through the Vedic and Brahmanistic periods.

I   THE RELIGION OF THE VEDIC AGE

Pre-Aryan India

India is an old land filled with old peoples. Before 2000 B.C. its predominant group was the curly-haired ancestors of the still numerous black-skinned Dravidians of the southern half of India. These people were, however, not aboriginal; in their midst were primitive tribes of older, and lower, culture, some of whom yet survive in the jungles of south and central India.* Disputing possession of the land were some Mongoloid tribes holding territories in the northeast. And on the Indus River before 2500 B.C., a people of mixed origin and diverse ethnic composition combined to produce a bronze age civilization with a well-developed art and architecture (brought to light by excavations at Harappa in the Punjab and Mohenjo-dara in Sind), probably matched by an equally advanced religion, containing at least in germ the ideas now embodied in the Hindu doctrines of the Law of Karma and the

* *Vide* the description of the Birhors in Chapter I.

Transmigration of Souls.* Unfortunately no writings have come down from this civilization and we are still much in ignorance about it.

The Coming of the Aryans

Sometime about the middle of the second millennium B.C., there came pouring over the passes of the Hindu Kush mountains in the northwest a people of a different strain, who were eventually to conquer, remake, and be remade by India. They were a tall, light-skinned people, of Indo-European stock, and they called themselves Aryans. They formed five large divisions or peoples, each composed of organized tribes. For a long time they had been moving eastward, looking for a permanent home. At last they issued from the mountains upon the plains of northwest India. They were of the same complex ethnic group to which belonged the powerful tribes that moved south, west, and north in Europe, and with the infusion of their blood and language brought into being the historic Greeks, Latins, Celts, Germans, and Slavs. While the original migrations were still in process, the Indo-Aryans, as we call them, seemingly went south from Europe and then east toward the rising sun. After an unknown number of years spent on the steppes of Bactria and along the Oxus River, they began to migrate again, this time into India. Another large branch of the same ethnic group broke into Iran (ancient Persia). They had been fellow-wanderers with the Indo-Aryans, but at a parting of the ways had turned southward. Time was to see great changes in language, habits, and ideas among both the Iranians and Indo-Aryans, and a difference in religious outlook as wide as that between Hinduism and Zoroastrianism; but the original similarities, both in language and religion, can still be traced without difficulty.†

The Indo-Aryans settled first on the upper branches of the Indus River. They had been a nomadic people; but now they began to live in simple village groups, among their flocks and herds. As they fought their way southeastward along the base of the Himalaya Mountains and began to adjust themselves to the new climate, their life became less pastoral and more agricultural in character. The men seem to have been fully occupied with herding their cattle and waging warfare, while the women carried on the home-making and gardening. The animals which

---

* This is somewhat speculative, for these extraordinary people, who were in touch with but differed markedly from the Sumerians and Akkadians, vanished completely in some unknown catastrophe.

† See Section I in the chapter on Zoroastrianism.

they brought into India with them were those of a pastoral people—cows, horses, sheep, goats, and dogs. Of elephants, monkeys, and tigers they had as yet no knowledge. They clung to their ancient diet of milk and meat; and continued the custom, probably formed centuries before (indeed, the Iranians had an identical practice), of making an intoxicating liquor which they called "soma" (squeezed from a plant whose identity is now uncertain and drunk after it was mixed with milk). They thought their gods enjoyed this potion as much as they, and therefore offered them libations of it whenever they sacrificed.

In the van of the Aryan advance the struggle with the black-skinned Dravidians was continuous; and as successive waves of invaders piled up from the rear, there were inter-tribal clashes which were to be immortalized later in the great Hindu epics, the *Ramayana* and the *Mahabharata*. By the time the whole region of the Five Rivers (the upper branches of the Indus) was occupied, the problem of mastering the new territory had been met by the rise of the first distinct social classes among what had been formerly an undifferentiated nomadic people; these classes, from which the castes of later Hindu society arose, corresponded to a new division of labor among the people.

Each tribe had over it a king or chieftain, called a *rajah* (same root as Lat. *rex*), whose office was generally hereditary. The functions of the king rapidly became complex, as more and more territory came under his sway; until, toward the end of the Vedic period, he was distinguished from other citizens by a large retinue, a palace, and glittering apparel, and was expected not only to maintain a private army for the protection of his people but also to gather around him numbers of priests to aid him in securing divine blessing on his subjects and the gods' approval of his own acts. Far outnumbering the warriors who formed the rajah's private army, and the priests who served both ruler and people, were the farmers and herdsmen, whose home-life was still much like that of their forefathers. The father or *pitar* (same root as Lat. *pater,* Ger. *vater,* Eng. *father,* etc.) was the head of the family, the owner of its property, and, in these early days, still its family priest. Descent was reckoned through him. The wife and mother or *matar* (Lat. *mater,* Ger. *mutter,* etc.) was a comparatively free individual, much less secluded than her descendants in the Ganges valley have been; her authority in the home over the children and black servants was not subject to restraint, except on rare occasions by her husband, who was reckoned the master of the household.

Having been accustomed for centuries to moving toward new horizons and hazards, the Aryans settled down slowly; only one substitute for lost adventure remained to them, and they seized upon it: they continued their wanderings in imagination, when denied them in fact, and surveyed the world about them with nimble wit. They had hardly won a place for themselves in India before they began to develop an extensive oral tradition. Folk-tales and epic stories took shape rapidly. At the same time the hymns and prayers of their priests gave voice to their religious conceptions. Out of these last, together with ancient magic runes and spells, have come Hinduism's earliest sacred writings, four in number, the *Rig-Veda, Sama-Veda, Yajur-Veda,* and *Atharva-Veda.* The Indo-Aryans themselves, no less than their descendants, regarded these works highly. (Veda means "knowledge." The word has the same root as the English words "wit" and "wisdom." *) Virtually all our knowledge of the religion of the Vedic Age is drawn from the study of them. We turn, first, to the most important of the four.

The Rig-Veda

The Rig-Veda (literally, "the Veda of stanzas of praise" †) is an

* Compare also the Greek οἶδα, the Latin *videre,* and the German *wissen.*

† The stanzas are now known as *mantras.*

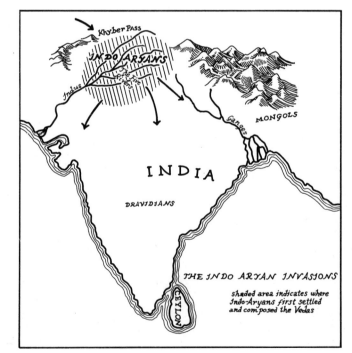

THE INDO ARYAN INVASIONS

shaded area indicates where Indo-Aryans first settled and composed the Vedas anthology of religious poetry in ten books, containing over a thousand hymns and representing the creative efforts of many generations. It was not reduced to writing until about the 8th century B.C.; before that it existed in oral form. The hymns are prayers, addressed to a single, or often to two or more, deities; * and they reveal an interesting form of nature worship.

Many of the deities invoked are obviously of very ancient date. Faith in three of them was shared with the Iranians, the Hittites, the Greeks, and the Romans. They were Dyaus Pitar or Father Sky (whom we have already met as Zeus Pater of the Greeks, Jupiter of the Romans); Prithivi Matar or Mother Broad-Earth (Gaia Mater of the Greeks); and Mitra (the Mithra of the Iranians), a highly moralized god representing faith-keeping and loyalty, but perhaps originally a sungod. In the Rig-Veda, however, these deities are conceived of rather vaguely, and appealed to seldom, being displaced from their earlier pre-eminence by the nature gods and goddesses who reflected more accurately the environment of northwest India.

Prominent among these latter was blustering Indra, the god of storms, especially of the rain storms (monsoons) that end the dry season.† He was the god of war as well. To his worshipers he seemed a gigantic figure, with long flowing hair and a wind-tost beard through which he shouted and roared with a loud voice. Clasping in his hand the enemy-destroying thunderbolt, he took the field as the ally and patron of the Aryans. Small wonder that their enemies fled. In the greatest of his annual feats, he smote the drought dragon, Vritra, which was holding back the waters in the mountain fastnesses. For this dangerous exploit he fortified himself well; hard-fighting, hard-drinking Aryan hero that he was, "in the three Soma-bowls he quaffed the juices." Then with his deadly thunderbolt "he slew the Serpent that rested on the mountains; and quickly flowing, swift to the ocean down sped the waters." [1] His worshipers would chant adoringly:

> In whose command are the horses, the cattle, the villages, and all the chariots; who begot the Sun and the Dawn, who is the leader of the waters— he, O men, is Indra.
> Whom the two battle ranks meeting in conflict invoke, vanguard and rearguard, both the enemies; they utter various invocations—he, O men, is Indra.

* Called *devas* or "heavenly ones," a word identical with the Latin *deus* (whence also comes, of course, the English word *deity*).

† He was an ancient Aryan deity who picked up this special characteristic in India.

Without whom men do not conquer, whom in battle they invoke for help; who is the pattern for all, who is the shaker of the unshaken—he, O men, is Indra. . . .

May we, O Indra, at all times thy friends, with goodly offspring, praise thee in the assembly.[2]

Such laudation must not, of course, be taken as evidence of monotheism, or even of henotheism in the strict sense. The worshipers were prone to flattery that would please; and hence, unlike the ancient Greeks, whom otherwise they resembled in many respects, they did not elevate one deity to permanent Olympic supremacy, but spoke of each of their divinities as supreme—at least during the prayers.[*]

In sharp contrast with Indra was the dread mountain god Rudra, not often addressed, but greatly feared, the fierce author of disastrous storms sweeping down from the snows of the Himalayas, who, in his proper nature, was no ally of the Aryans at all but the destroyer of their goods and persons. Fear and awe accompanied his presence. His worshipers approached him in humility and trembling supplication, beseeching him as "an immortal one" to be "auspicious" (*shiva*) rather than malevolent and to be merciful to their children and grandchildren. They would beseech:

Kill not our great or our small, our growing one or our full-grown man, our father or our mother. Injure not, O Rudra, our dear selves.

Injure us not in our cattle or horses. In thy wrath, O Rudra, slay not our heroes. We invoke thee ever with sacrifices.[3]

But then again Rudra was found to be at times a gentle healer, presiding (in his mountain fastnesses?) over medicinal plants. He had his helpful as well as his destructive side.—This is of some importance historically, for his greatest significance lies in the fact that he is the early form of later Hinduism's great god, Shiva, the Destroyer (and Reviver).

[*] This conclusion might be disputed by those who find in the *Rig Veda* a central myth giving supremacy to Indra. Recent studies suggest that when the demons of whom Vritra was the chief (they were the demons of "bondage") began to worst the good deities led by Varuna (they represented "non-bondage"), Indra offered himself as a champion of the good deities on condition that he would be made chief. This granted, he slew Vritra, released the waters held in bondage, and with them the hidden (unborn) sun. This made it possible to order and regulate air, earth, water, and sun; in other words, to establish creation. See W. Norman Brown's essay "The Mythology of India" in *Mythologies of the Ancient World*, edited by S. N. Kramer (Anchor, 1961). The present writer has not been persuaded of the validity of this reconstruction, in spite of parallels with Mesopotamian myths that can be pointed out.

Surya, the sun god, riding his chariot, his head surrounded by a halo of sun rays and carrying the symbols of his solar might. (After a drawing in Rawlinson, *India, A Short Cultural History*)

The Rig-Veda attains high flights of poetry in the description of these and other nature deities. Vayu, the wind, is the bearer of perfumes. The tempestuous little Maruts or storm spirits are "swift as wind . . . robed in rain . . . the singers of heaven." [4] Ushas, the Dawn (the Greek Eos), is a "young maid in white robes," shining afar in her chariot drawn by red spotted horses.[5] Her male attendants, the Asvins, twin horsemen of the dawn, speed behind her through the sky on a chariot with golden seat, reins of gold, axle and wheels of gold, and with a flight so swift that it exceeds the twinkling of an eye. There are a number of sun-gods, probably representing different phases of light; for example, Surya, mounting up with fleet yellow horses, and causing the constellations, flooded with the radiance of his all-beholding eye, to "pass away, like thieves, together with their beams"; [6] and Savitar, the "golden-haired, bright with sunbeams," who traverses the "ancient dustless pathways well established in the air's midregion"; [7] and Vishnu, the far-striding, who encompasses the extent of earth, atmosphere, and sky in three swift strides, and thus redeems the world from night. Of the last it may be said that, though destined along with Rudra to survive the rest of the Vedic deities and to become a major Hindu god, he is not prominent in the Rig-Veda and has there lost almost all of his solar characteristics.

One of the picturesque figures in the Rig-Veda is Yama, the first man to die, now the god of the dead and the judge and ruler of the departed. Remembering him, the Aryans used to address the spirit of the dead man whose body was being burned on the funeral pyre.

Honor with thine oblations the King, Yama, who gathers men together,
Who travelled to the lofty heights above us, who searches out and shows the path to many.
Yama first found for us a place to dwell in: this pasture never can be taken from us. . . .
Meet Yama, meet the Fathers, meet the merit of free and ordered acts, in highest heaven.
Leave sin and evil, seek anew thy dwelling, and bright with glory wear another body.[8]

Not only do these verses honor Yama and the departing spirit, but in the mention of the Fathers,* they express the veneration the Aryans felt for their ancestors, a very old and important part of their religion. It was their regular practice to set down on the ground a repast of cereal cakes and milk, or milk mingled with soma, or rice-cakes (*pinda*), and then invite the ancestral spirits to draw near and receive nourishment.

Morally far above the other gods stood the awe-compelling deity Varuna, originally the god of the high-arched sky, who was later assigned the inclusive function (analogous to maintaining order among the stars) of directing the forces making everywhere for natural and moral orderliness. His sphere lay in part in the domain of natural laws; for it was he who upheld the physical order of the world against the forces making for its breakdown. In another direction, it was his concern to keep men obedient to the moral law. He was the discloser of sin, the judge of truth and falsehood. His spies were busy finding men out. When men sinned, it was to Varuna that they prayed for forgiveness; so that the acts which were reckoned as sins in those pioneer times appear in the prayers they addressed to him.

If we have sinned against the man who loves us, have ever wronged a brother, friend or comrade,
The neighbor ever with us, or a stranger, O Varuna, remove from us the trespass.

* The *pitaras* (cf. the Latin *patres*).

If we, as gamesters, cheat at play, have cheated, done wrong unwittingly or sinned of purpose,

Cast all these sins away like loosened fetters, and, Varuna, let us be thine own beloved.[9]

Since Varuna's interest lay in maintaining order in the universe, physically and morally, it was natural that he should be associated with Mitra, the god of loyalty and promise-keeping, already mentioned, and also with the mysterious abstract principle called Rita. Rita was conceived to be the indwelling principle in everything in the universe that shows regularity and order of action; in accordance with Rita day succeeds night, summer follows spring, the sun keeps his appointed course, and man goes from birth to death, invisibly guided.

There are still other gods in the Rig-Veda—of a quite novel significance to Western minds—beings who might be called the liturgical gods, because they are chiefly associated with the act of worship itself. They are Agni, the god of fire; Soma, the divine presence in the intoxicating juice of the soma plant; and, not well known to the populace, but very important to the priests, Brahmanaspati (or Brihaspati), the deified power of the sacred prayer-word.

When the Aryans worshipped, they approached the altar joyously and confidently, except, of course, in special cases, as when Rudra was threatening or Varuna angry. They had in those days no temples or sacred precincts, but worshipped under the open sky beside altars erected for the occasion on trimmed and swept grass. A seat on fresh-strewn grass near the altar was reserved for the invisible divine guests who might be present. The offerings might consist of milk, clarified butter (*ghee*), grain, sheep, goats, cows, oxen, or horses, the horse sacrifice being the costliest and hence deemed the most effectual. In time, as the sacrifices lengthened into elaborate ceremonies, priests, each with special functions, took charge. One might be the *adhvaryu* or altar-builder, who also prepared the materials for sacrifice; another was the *hotar*, the invoker of the gods, who would with courteous words call down the gods to enjoy the sacrificial offerings and the soma set out in vessels on the grass:

Thou hast made prayers the means of thine exalting, therefore we wait on thee with hymns, O Indra. . . .

Mark well our sacrificial cake, delighted: Indra, drink Soma and the milk commingled.

Here on the sacrificer's grass be seated. . . .[10]

Another priest might be the *agnidh* or kindler of the sacrificial fire; but as time went on the foremost came to be the *brahmin* or presiding priest, the one who offered the central sacred petition or *brahma* (the prayer).*

No sacrifice was effectual without the presence of Agni (Latin *ignis*), the god of fire in general, celestial or terrestrial, but especially of the altar-fire. Invoked with earnest petition before his coming, which was conceived of always as a new birth (whether on altar or hearth), he was praised and adored with utmost sincerity. (Those who care for historical comparisons will here see a connecting link with the fire-ceremonies of the Zoroastrians.) As fire purifies and cleanses, so Agni removed sin and guilt. He drove away the demons and protected the home whose hearth he occupied. He was light and wisdom, a seer into dark corners, a resolver of mysteries, from whom it was well to have guidance. He consecrated marriage, was a spiritual husband of maidens, a brother of men. He was priest, oblation-bearer, and mediator between gods and men. His worshipers knew their weal depended upon his presence.

The participation of the god Soma (the Haoma of the ancient Persians) was also necessary in the sacrifice. He represented the intoxicating power of the libation. His introduction into the service was a central feature of the ritual. Separate ceremonies were often devoted to the soma-making. The leaves of the soma plant had been gathered by moonlight on the mountains where it could be found, were brought to the place of sacrifice, then crushed between the "pressing-stones," sprinkled with water, strained, and finally offered as a libation and drunk by those who were assembled round the altar. The exhilarating effect was attributed to the presence in the juice of the heady Soma. Both gods and men needed him. Hence, during each ceremony soma-juice was poured into the grass where the gods invisibly sat; and as they too drank, the worshipers chanted:

> We have drunk Soma and become immortal;
> We have attained the light, the gods discovered.
> What can hostility now do against us?
> And what, immortal god, the spite of mortals? [11]

The presence of a third god represented something more subtle. Brahmanaspati (Brihaspati) does not get as much mention in the hymns as Agni and Soma, but he is highly significant of later developments. Glorified for obvious reasons by the brahmins, though regarded perhaps

---

* This word *brahma* was used in different senses. It had the wider meanings of "holy word," "sacred knowledge," and "incantation," with the implication in this last case of the presence of *magic power*. Mystic utterance was *brahma*, too.

with awe and from a distance by the common man, he stood for the holy power in the uttered words of the prayer, able to move the gods and to compel them to grant their favor. Hence, he was sometimes regarded as the deified suppliant-priest interceding with the gods for men.

Sublime Brihaspati, easy of access, granteth his friends most bountiful refreshment . . .

Glorify him, O friends, who merits glory: may he give prayer fair way and easy passage.[12]

It was the doctrine of the priests that Brahmanaspati had to be present along with and in the ritual or it would be but empty sound. If he were indeed active, prayer would have an efficacy so great that it would be compulsive upon gods and men alike; there could be no failure of fulfilment. A moment's consideration will show how much importance this fact gave to the correctly pronounced prayer-word, the *brahma*. It took on the force of an independently existent principle. Equal importance attached to the priest who uttered it, the holy Brahmin.

Little wonder that the priests, as we shall see in the sequel, dwelt in thought on the divine force working in the magically potent prayer.

The Other Vedas

The other Vedas are in many respects dependent upon, even appendages of, the Rig-Veda. The *Yajur-Veda* is mostly in prose, and was meant to supply dedications, prayers, and litanies to accompany the devotional use of the Rig-Veda; while the *Sama-Veda* is a collection of rhythmic chants for the use of the singing priests at the Soma sacrifices, its hymns in great part being borrowed from the Rig-Veda.

The *Atharva-Veda* is more independent. A treasury of charms, incantations, and spells of great antiquity, it afforded expression to aspects of experience left largely inarticulate in the Rig-Veda—fear, passion, anger, hate, physical distress and the human effort to amend it. It abounds in curses and magic blessings. In a manner reminiscent of European magic, it presents remedial charms which were supposed to remove all evil—or bring down the fell strokes of fate on some unlucky hated head.

Away from us may thousand-eyed, immortal evil dwell! Him whom we hate may it strike, and him whom we hate do thou surely smite! [13]

An example of the type of magic spell common in this Veda may be cited. One who wished to promote the growth of his hair might gather the sacred root that prevented baldness and have these words, at various points in the procedure, chanted:

As a goddess upon the goddess earth thou wast born, O plant! We dig thee up, O nitatni, that thou mayest strengthen the growth of the hair.

Strengthen the old hair, beget the new! That which has come forth render more luxurious.

That hair of thine which does drop off, and that which is broken root and all, upon it do I sprinkle here the all-healing herb.[14]

The ancient instructions direct that the patient have his head anointed with the black concoction made from the plant mentioned, and have it applied by a medicine man clothed in black who has eaten black food in the early morning before the rise of the crows (black, too, of course). One cannot fail to see in the symbolism here employed an expression of the hope for the growth of new black hair.

This sort of thing may invite a smile; but it was not altogether foolish, for it was linked up with inquiries of a broader kind that were more nearly scientific.

Several of the sections of the Atharva-Veda (particularly II.3 and X.2) exhibit great interest in the vital organs, body secretions, and bones of the human body, which are separately distinguished and often exactly described. Apparently an anatomically informed medical art was being developed. Indeed, one of the verses in the Atharva-Veda says that there were then hundreds of medical practitioners at work and thousands of herbs in use. The remedial charms were very ancient; but, to some at least, the drugs used suggested a more realistic and more exciting method of attack on disease. The number of diseases known was quite long. But, as might be expected, there was much confusion of exact and inexact knowledge. As Dasgupta says:

Some of the diseases with their troublous symptoms were (poetically) personified, and diseases which often went together were described as being related as brothers and sisters. Diseases due to worms were well-known, in the case of both men and cattle. There were also the diseases due to sorcery, which played a very important part as an offensive measure in Vedic India. Many of the diseases were also known to be hereditary.[15]

Confusion or not, we are adding to the evidence that the Indo-Aryans had brilliant minds. At least they made some good beginnings in inquiries darting in many different directions.

The Close of the Vedic Period

Vedic literature, taken as a whole, illustrates the exuberant culture

which the early Indo-Aryans developed. Very clearly, this vigorous people faced life positively and, in the main, confidently, on many fronts.
In their literary self-expression they gave promise of great things to
come.

One such promise has to be mentioned. Toward the close of the
Vedic period, when the priests were growing in numbers and in power,
and were making religion and the search for knowledge their whole
life-work, the yearning for assurance of unity in the totality of things
began to express itself; and so we have in the later hymns of the Rig-
Veda the sudden emergence of such grand figures as Vishvakarman, "He
Whose Work is the Universe"; Prajapati, "Lord of Creatures," the Creator; and Purusha, the soul of man magnified to cosmic proportions and
regarded as the soul of the universe, giving life to all animated beings,
and indeed bringing the whole world into existence out of himself. Most
arresting is the 129th hymn of the 10th book, addressed to a great un-
named cosmic reality, referred to quite simply as That One Thing, a
neutral principle or activity said to have existed before there was a
universe. This hymn contains an early evolutionary speculation about
the origin of creation, and may be rendered thus:

> Then there was neither being (*Sat*) nor non-being (*Asat*):
> There was no air, nor firmament beyond it.
> Was there a stirring? Where? Beneath what cover?
> Was there a great abyss of unplumbed water?
>
> There was no death nor anything immortal;
> Nor any sign dividing day from night.
> That One Thing, given no breath, was yet self-breathing;
> No second thing existed whatsoever.
>
> Darkness was hidden in a deeper darkness;
> This All was as a sea without dimensions;
> The void still held unformed what was potential,
> Until the power of Warmth produced the sole One.
>
> Then, in that One, Desire stirred into being,
> Desire that was the earliest seed of Spirit.
> (The sages probing in their hearts with wisdom
> Discovered being's kinship in non-being.
>
> Stretching their line across the void, they pondered;
> Was aught above it, or was aught below it?)
> Bestowers of the seed were there; and powers;
> Free energy below; above, swift action.

> Who truly knows, and who can here declare it?
> Whence It was born, and how this world was fashioned?
> The gods came later than the earth's creation:
> Who knows then out of what the world has issued?

> Whether the world was made or whether self-made,
> He knows with full assurance, he alone,
> Who in the highest heaven guards and watches;
> He knows indeed, but then, perhaps, *he* knows not!

From all points of view this is an amazing composition; the last six words are especially striking in their quizzical quality. It is clear that the priests were developing by the end of the Vedic Age considerable philosophical ability; this was their response to their need of determining the origin of the world and of all things. Before the mountains were brought forth, before the gods came into being, before any portion of the visible universe existed, there was a nameless but all-originative ground of being. The priests were excited at the thought. Was there any name they could give it? They wondered. Men had made many attempts heretofore, with less than complete adequacy.

> They call him Indra, Mitra, Varuna, Agni, and he is heavenly noble-winged Garutman.
> To what is One, sages give many a title: they call it Agni, Yama, Matarisvan . . .[16]

The Brahmins were disposed to think further of the matter.

All this time the Aryans were still on the move. They were pressing down the Ganges valley, enslaving or driving before them, eastward and southward, the black-skinned natives. The migration did not halt until the whole of north and central India, to the delta of the Ganges, was in the power and under the active rule of the conquering invaders. The land had gradually changed hands.

Then the invader settled down—and change overtook *him*.

II BRAHMANISM

The Rise of the Caste System

At about the end of the 7th century B.C. the Aryan occupation of the Ganges valley had resulted in the organization of a number of distinct principalities or states, some ruled monarchically by hereditary rajahs, and many still in the form of loose groupings of clans something on the order of republics, with the tribes governed by a central council of chieftains. The Aryans occupied the upper strata of a still fluid social order; below were the dark-skinned non-Aryans, in process of being submerged. And now, though the separation between classes was not hard and fast, there were definitely coming into being four distinct social groups—the *Kshatriyas* or nobles, the *Brahmins* or priests, the *Vaisyas* or Aryan common people* (peasants or artisans), and last the enslaved *Shudras* or non-Aryan blacks. The first three classes were becoming more and more careful to hold themselves aloof from the last. There had now arisen the question of "color"—*varna*, the Hindu word for caste; and not only was marriage across the color barrier forbidden, but also even friendly social intimacies, like drinking from the same cup or sitting down to the same meal, on account of the frequency with which questions regarding purity of blood arose in consequence of such connections. There also existed a struggle for social prestige between the ruling nobles and the Brahmins; each group, in the name either of use and wont, or of religion and supernatural prerogative, claiming final and supreme authority.

The Brahmins had by now developed phenomenal power. The migration down the Ganges provided them with an opportunity which they were not slow to grasp. Religion was still in the making; the nobles were busy fighting and administering new territory, and had to rely upon the priests more and more to carry on the necessary religious functions; meanwhile, the superstitious regard in which all held the *brahma*, or holy power in the sacrificial prayer, resulted in swiftly raising the prestige of those whose function it was to utter it. Indeed the Brahmins finally came to claim a position of more vital importance even than the gods. As we have already seen, the sacred formula, once uttered, was deemed to have a compulsive and magical efficacy; gods as well as men had to obey it. The priests therefore declared they occupied the central place of power; they were the pivotal beings in a vast process reaching into all parts of the universe, hell, earth, and heaven. Through the sacrifices they performed—some of which took weeks and months to complete†—they changed the very course of cosmic events.

---

* Including the Aryo-Dravidians, for there was considerable intermixture in the Ganges plain before a check could be put to it.

† The Asvamedha or Horse Sacrifice, for example, took over a year to complete, and involved in its beginning the gathering and proffering, if not the actual sacrifice, of 609 animals! But the priests assured the rajahs who alone could afford to perform it: "This is the atonement for everything. He who performs the Asvamedha redeems all sin." (*Sacred Books of the East*, XLIV:328.)

By now the names of the gods possessed little more than a ritualistic significance; the sacrifice was the thing of greater moment, and especially the utterance of the sacred prayer formulas in connection with the sacrifices.

The rajahs may have paid little or no heed to all this; they may have laughed at the claim that social supremacy belonged to those who had such supernatural power. The rajahs were in the saddle socially by right of eminent domain, and what they took they could keep. Nevertheless the Brahmins were gaining in popular esteem; in the homes of the people they were treated like gods. They were now making the stout claim that if the sacrifices were performed by them properly, in the manner prescribed by certain treatises, the *Brahmanas,* which they had compiled to be appended to the Vedas, they could procure the desired results as if by necessity.

The Brahmanas

The Brahmanas are a curious and voluminous body of literature. Originally they were probably notes for lectures delivered to candidates for priestly office in the various priests' schools. Written down for the first time during the period turning on 300 B.C., or perhaps even later, and then frequently redacted, they were designed both to give practical directions, in exhaustive detail, for the conduct of all manner of sacrifices, and also to explain the inner meaning of these rites. The Brahmanas were thus the textbooks of the different schools or classes of Brahmins, with a hint here and there of a philosophy of worship. Many passages now seem an endless rigmarole of prolix repetition. No literature affords more detailed instruction for ritual performances.

Mingled with the directions for the sacrifices are expressions of genuine spiritual aspiration and a growing sense of a principle of unity in the universe. Progress toward the conception of such unity is made. The theories of creation suggested in the later hymns of the Rig-Veda are fused here into a monotheistic compromise in which Prajapati, the Lord of Creatures, becomes Brahma Svayanibhu (Brahma Self-existing), the personal creator of the universe. It had occurred to the more speculative of the priests that, if the holy power which worked through the prayer-formula could alter the course of cosmic events, then that power, capable as it was of forcing obedience from gods and men alike, must be an ultimate of some kind. Was it perhaps the true central power in the universe? Could the ultimate reality of the universe be called Brahman?

The authors of the Brahmanas here took a long stride forward, and in a direction along which Indian philosophy was destined to go far.

The Philosophy of the Upanishads

One of the greatest speculative eras in the history of religion now opened. Many alert minds in India pressed on to new and philosophically profound interpretations of the nature of reality. The writings which, over a period of three or four centuries, terminating about 300 B.C., expressed these new ideas, are appendages of the Brahmanas; they form the famous and difficult treatises known as the *Upanishads.*° For the study of the religions of India this is a most important series of speculations. The Upanishads (meaning "sittings near a teacher," in the sense of "intimate sessions for the initiate") are often in the form of dialogues, composed with memorization in view and therefore frequently too repetitious for modern ears; but they are not less profound or subtle for all that. In them Kshatriyas, men of all classes, and even women, are dramatized as taking part in the discussions as readily and ably as, if not sometimes more ably than, the Brahmins themselves. As a matter of fact, the Upanishads were probably not composed entirely by Brahmins; there is more than a little reason to think that non-Brahmins, especially Kshatriyas, composed some of them—probably many of those that reflect the dualistic Sankhya point of view.

It would be impossible here to render the full diversity of view which is to be found in the Upanishads. There is no consensus in them as to the finally correct view of the universe. The dualistic Sankhya philosophy (just referred to, and to be described in more detail in a later chapter) finds its first voice in them. But there is a drift of the Upanishads toward monism, and it is therefore possible to gather from the treatises of the different schools and thinkers what might be called the predominant opinion as to what should be the answer to the questions with which all the treatises are concerned: *What is reality? Of what is the universe the expression? Is it real in itself? Or is it merely an appearance, even an illusion? How did human experience, illusory or real, come to be? What is the meaning of human life?*

After some preliminary analysis, in which various attempts to find a unitary world-ground are made, the Upanishads are, in general, agreed on one fundamental postulate. The ground of all being, whether material or spiritual, whether in the form of men, beasts, or gods, heaven, earth, or hell, is an all-inclusive, unitary reality, beyond sense-apprehension, ultimate in substance, infinite in essence, and self-sufficient; it is the only

---

° Strictly, the older Upanishads for the most part form sections of the Aranyakas or "Forest Books," which in turn form part of the Brahmanas. But the later Upanishads arose independently of the Brahmanas, and even of the Aranyakas.

Rajput conception of Upanishadic scene: a forest-dweller teaching an inquirer. (From an early 19th century Rajput painting, Boston Museum of Fine Arts)

really existent entity. This reality is most commonly called *Brahman*.* No precise definitions are attempted. Descriptions vary. Some of the treatises, for the most part the later ones, conceive of Brahman as a kind of deity endowed with personality.

> Immortal, existing as the Lord,
> Intelligent, omnipresent, the guardian of this world,
> Is He who constantly rules this world . . .[17]

Many passages indiscriminately intermingle impersonal and personal designations for this ultimate reality. In other passages the personal designation seems to be resorted to more from habit or as a concession to the troubled imagination than anything else. The "limitless One" is described as "*He* who awakes the world."

* Neuter. More rarely, *Brahma*. The word has moved out of its Vedic setting. It no longer refers to the holy power of prayer only but applies directly to ultimate reality. In many of the quotations that follow the rarer word *Brahma* is used.

Verily, in the beginning this world was Brahma, the limitless One—limitless to the east, limitless to the north, . . . limitless in every direction. Incomprehensible is that Soul, unlimited, unborn, not to be reasoned about, unthinkable—He whose soul is space! In the dissolution of the world He alone remains awake. From that space, He, assuredly, awakes this world, which is a mass of thought. It is thought by Him, and in Him it disappears. His is that shining form which gives heat in yonder sun and which is the brilliant light in a smokeless fire, as also the fire in the stomach which cooks the food. For thus it has been said: "He who is in the fire, and he who is here in the heart, and he who is yonder in the sun—he is one." [18]

As a rule, though not always, the earlier treatises regularly refer to Brahman as a neuter something, without motion or feeling, the impersonal matrix from which the universe has issued and to which it will in time return. This It, this One Thing, is the substantial substratum of everything.

Verily, this whole world is Brahma. Tranquil let one worship It as that from which he came forth, as that in which he will be dissolved, as that in which he breathes.[19]

It is clear from this that Brahman is *all that is objective,* the whole external world given to us by our senses, all that exists outside of us. In the conversation in the Brihad-Aranyaka Upanishad, between the renowned Brahmin, Gargya Balaki, and the king of Benares, a Kshatriya who is his superior in philosophic understanding, there is a progressive definition of Brahman as the reality within the sun, the moon, lightning, space, wind, fire, water, mirrors, sounds which reverberate, the different quarters of the heavens, shadows and bodies—of all of which it is said, "He is their Real." [20] The other Upanishads have the same general tenor. All things, all creatures, are ultimately phases of That One,—"the priest by the altar, the guest in the house." [21] "Stretched forth below and above, Brahma, indeed, is this whole world, this widest extent." [22]

But this is only half the fact. Brahman is also *all that is subjective,* the whole inward world of feeling and self-consciousness, with which the innermost self is identified. All that goes on in the soul of man, and the soul itself, are phases of That One. The term for the inner self here employed is *atman,* a word used sometimes to denote the empirical individual who is physically seen and felt; but in a deeper sense it refers to the innermost and unseen self of a man as distinct from his body, his sense-organs, and his brain, that is to say, his transcendental self or ego. This is the meaning here. Many of the Upanishads insist that, contrary to the naive popular belief in the absolute individuality of the human soul, *there is an actual identity between Brahman and atman—*

and this is true of any and every form of atman, whether it is found
in man, beast, insect, flower, fish, or any other living thing. "Yajnavalkya,"
cries an eager inquirer in the Brihad-Aranyaka, "explain to me him who
is the Brahma present and not beyond our ken, him who is the soul in
all things." "He is your soul," comes the answer.

"He who, dwelling in the earth . . . in the waters . . . in the fire . . .
the atmosphere . . . the wind . . . the sky . . . the sun . . . the quarters
of heaven . . . the moon and stars . . . space . . . darkness . . . light. . . .
He who, dwelling in all things, yet is other than all things, whom all things do
not know, whose body all things are, who controls all things from within—He
is your soul, the inner Controller, the Immortal . . .

"He who, dwelling in breath . . . in speech . . . the eye . . . the ear
. . . the mind . . . the skin . . . the understanding, yet is other than the
understanding . . . He is the unseen Seer, the unheard Hearer, the un-
thought Thinker, the ununderstood Understander. Other than He there is
no seer. Other than He there is no hearer . . . no thinker . . . no understander . . . He is your soul, the Inner Controller, the Immortal." [23]

Such a passage sufficiently suggests the conclusion to which this
sort of reasoning led. The true self of a man and the world-soul
(*paramatman*: the universal atman) are one; they are identical. This
identity is expressed in the Chandogya Upanishad in the formula *Tat
tvam asi*, which means, "That (or It) art thou!"[24] In other words, the
All-Soul is the very stuff* of which the human soul and its consciousness
are formed, and there is no real distinction between the former and
the latter. We may therefore equate Brahman, the objective All, and
Atman, the subjective or particular self, and call the ultimate reality
henceforth Brahman-Atman, recognizing thereby that the objective and
subjective are one.

It may not be said that this is the unequivocal finding of all the
Upanishads. Some of them do not go so far. None of them quite reach
the later Vedantic doctrine, that since Brahman-Atman alone exists, the
whole universe is either outright illusion or the "sport," "play," or "art"
of the creative All-Soul. There is still a recognition of a sort of derivative
reality of the universe; it is something that has been breathed forth
by Brahman-Atman and pervaded by Its being. And yet perhaps
"breathed forth" and "pervaded by" do not sufficiently suggest the close-
knit unity of being that subsists between the Subjective and the Objective. The Brihad-Aranyaka rather clearly insists that though things and
selves may be spoken of as emanations from, creations of, or constructs

* The Upanishads vary in considering whether this stuff is mental-stuff or
material-stuff.

pervaded by Brahman-Atman, "as a razor would be hidden in a razor-case"; [25] all things ultimately *are* Brahman-Atman without any qualifications.* Says another treatise in phrases of breath-taking sweep:

This soul of mine within the heart is smaller than a grain of rice, or a barleycorn, or a mustard-seed, or a grain of millet, or the kernel of a grain of millet; this soul of mine within the heart is greater than the earth, greater than the atmosphere, greater than the sky, greater than the worlds . . . This soul of mine within the heart, this is Brahma.[26]

The same Upanishad, playing upon the phrase *Tat tvam asi*, tells the story:

Now there was Shvetaketu Aruneya. To him his father said: "That which is the finest essence—this whole world has that as its soul. That is Reality. That is Atman. That art thou, Shvetaketu."

"Do you, Sir, cause me to understand even more."

"So be it, my dear," said he . . . "Bring hither a fig."

"Here it is, Sir."

"Divide it."

"It is divided, Sir."

"What do you see there?"

"Those rather fine seeds, Sir."

"Of these, please divide one."

"It is divided, Sir."

"What do you see there?"

"Nothing at all, Sir."

Then said he to him: "Verily, my dear, that finest essence which you do not perceive—verily, my dear, from that finest essence this great Nyagrodha (sacred fig) tree thus arises. Believe me, my dear," said he, "that which is the finest essence—this whole world has that as its soul. That is Reality. That is Atman. *That art thou*, Shvetaketu." [27]

The thinkers of the Upanishads did not stop here. They took a step which carried their philosophy over into mysticism. They called it *entering Nirvana*. This step was made by recognizing that, when the human soul *knows* its complete identity with Brahman, it celebrates this knowledge with a feeling of unity approaching ecstasy. The experience of such assured knowledge was pronounced so beatific as to be indescribable, a blissfulness

> Wherefrom words turn back,
> Together with the mind, not having attained.[28]

Undoubtedly most of the writers of the Upanishads knew of, if they did not themselves practice, the technique of such realization of identity

---

* The point is that Brahman is both razor and razor-case.

with or complete absorption into Brahman. In this technique, the prospective Brahman-knower would sit meditating in profound quiet of mind, seeking to know, verily *know*, not have an opinion or a mere belief, but be spiritually certain, that he and the world of sense about him had alike the same ground of being; that he and the tree near him were one, because they were both phases of the One; in short, *were* Brahman-Atman and not any other. The certitude of such unity came to him when he was more in a nonconscious than a conscious state.° In seeking analogies for it, the later Upanishadic thinkers declared that there are three mental states which may be usefully compared with it: the state of waking consciousness, the state of dreaming sleep, and the state of deep, dreamless sleep. As modes of experience of truth and reality, all three were found defective; especially the first two, because in them there is a persistence of the consciousness of a duality of subject and object, self and not-self, ego and non-ego. Deep, dreamless sleep is nearest to affording an analogy for the state of union with Brahman because it represents a sinking back into a type of nonconsciousness in which subject and object are no longer distinguished. But this state is also defective, on account of the negativity and lack of meaning and value which characterize it. Real union with Brahman (called *turiya* or *caturtha*) is considered to be the highest of all states of mind, because it represents the purest *being* of soul, when the soul is sleeplessly intent and when subject and object are indistinguishable in the purity of being. A modern interpreter from India identifies it as "pure intuitional consciousness, where there is no knowledge of objects internal or external." [29] The Mandukya Upanishad contains an interesting definition of it.

The fourth state is not that which is conscious of the subjective, nor that which is conscious of the objective, nor that which is conscious of both, nor that which is simple consciousness, nor that which is an all-sentient mass, nor that which is all darkness. It is unseen, transcendent, the sole essence of the consciousness of self, the completion of the world.[30]

In the turiya state the world and the self are not obliterated as they would be in deep, dreamless sleep, but both the self and the world are seen together in their pure essences, stripped of all distortion and illusion, and recognized as being united with the being of Brahman-Atman, where their reality is found to subsist.

One doctrine evolved during this period does, however, provide for a periodical obliteration of all souls and of the entire world in

° Strictly speaking, he would be neither conscious nor nonconscious. Cf. being in an ecstasy.

Brahman. This is the famous theory of the cyclic destruction and re-creation of the world. According to this theory, the world dissolves away at the end of every *kalpa* or period of created being, and all the souls in the universe depart from their bodies into a state of suspended being. After a period of absolute nullity and repose, called a *pralaya*, the world comes again into being, and the long-quiescent souls take up a new embodiment in vegetables, animals, men, gods, and demons. The castes are re-formed, the Vedas re-composed, and another *kalpa* proceeds to its inevitable end, with history generally repeating itself over again.

Such conceptions contain the germs of much future philosophizing. The six great systems of Hindu philosophy were to develop from these first-fruits of speculation. The Indian mind had indeed launched out into the deep.

First Appearance in Indian Thought of
Reincarnation and Karma

It was in this same period that a new color was given to Indo-Aryan thought by the adoption of two doctrines that were to become permanent elements in the outlook of India. Both make their first definite appearance in Indian literature in the Upanishads, but they were very probably not inventions of the time. They may have been taken over from Dravidian beliefs. In any case they are not in the earlier Aryan spirit; they derive their relevance, rather, from India itself, considered as the thought-evoking background of human living.

One of these doctrines, the belief in the *transmigration of souls* or *reincarnation* (known in India as *samsara*), is not, as any student knows, peculiar to India. It has been held rather widely throughout the world, both among primitives and peoples of higher cultural development. In its Indo-Aryan form it runs like this: the soul of a man who dies does not, except in the single case of one who at death returns into indistinguishable oneness with Brahman, pass into a permanent state of being in heaven or hell or elsewhere; the soul, rather, is reborn into another existence which will terminate in due time and necessitate yet another birth. Rebirth follows rebirth, with the one exception named, in an endless chain. The successive births are not likely to be on the same plane of being. Rebirth may occur for a finite period of time in any of the series of heavens or hells, or upon earth in any of the forms of life, vegetable, animal, or human; it may thus be either higher or lower than the present or any past existence. A man of low social status now may be reborn as a rajah or a Brahmin; or, which is more likely, as a scavenger, or even as a beetle, worm, vegetable, or soul in hell.

But what determines the nature of the next birth? What causes it to enter a higher or lower state of existence? The second of the new doctrines, and the one that is peculiar to India, provides the answer. One's future existence is determined by the *Law of Karma* (*karma* meaning "deeds" or "works"), the law that one's thoughts, words, and deeds have an ethical consequence fixing one's lot in future existences.

The earliest statements of this important law are among the clearest. "Those who are of pleasant conduct here—the prospect is, indeed," so runs the Chandogya Upanishad, "that they will enter a pleasant womb, either the womb of a Brahmin, or the womb of a Kshatriya, or the womb of a Vaisya. But those who are of stinking conduct here—the prospect is, indeed, that they will enter either the womb of a dog, or the womb of a swine, or the womb of an outcast." [31]

Though it is here much more moderately stated than it was later, this is not quite the doctrine that character makes destiny, that a man of good character when life ends is reborn good in the next existence, or that one who is evil at the moment of death is reborn in evil case. The Law of Karma gradually assumed a more terrible aspect than this. In its more literal interpretation, it implies that everything a man does, each separate deed of his life, weighed along with every other deed, determines destiny. Single acts have each their inevitable consequence which must be worked out to the uttermost, whether for good or evil. This is the extreme view. Many Hindus, who construe the Law as being less rigorous in its weighing of the consequences of each separate act, say it is simply the law that a man reaps what he sows; or to put the fact in terms of another metaphor, his deeds shape not only his character but his soul, so that in his next incarnation his soul, as having a definite shape, "can find re-embodiment only in a form into which that shape can squeeze." [32] In any case, the law operates like a law of nature. The process is quite impersonal. "There is no judge and no judgment; no punishment, no repentance or amends, no remission of sins by divine clemency . . . just the inexorable causal nexus of the eternal universe itself." [33]

In a somewhat later time than the one we are here considering, the exact recompense of one's deeds was thus precisely estimated:

In consequence of many sinful acts committed with his body, a man becomes in the next birth something inanimate, in consequence of sins committed by speech, a bird, and in consequence of mental sins he is reborn in a low caste . . . Those who committed mortal sins, having passed during large numbers of years through dreadful hells, obtain, after the expiration of that term of punishment, the following births. The slayer of a Brahmin enters the womb of a dog, a pig, an ass, a camel, a cow, a goat, a sheep, a deer, a bird, a Kandala, and a Pukhasa . . . A Brahmin who steals the gold of a Brahmin shall pass a thousand times through the bodies of spiders, snakes, lizards, of aquatic animals and of destructive Pukhasas . . . Men who delight in doing hurt become carnivorous animals; those who eat forbidden food, worms; thieves, creatures consuming their own kind . . . For stealing grain a man becomes a rat; . . . for stealing a horse, a tiger; for stealing fruits and roots, a monkey; for stealing a woman, a bear; for stealing cattle, a he-goat.[34]

The discouragement which this kind of prospect evoked is well expressed in the Maitri Upanishad: "In this sort of cycle of existence (samsara) what is the good of enjoyment of desires, when after a man has fed on them there is seen repeatedly his return here to earth? Be pleased to deliver me. In this cycle of existence I am like a frog in a waterless well." [35] The unhappiness which characterized the emotional revulsion from the Law of Karma is here very clearly expressed. Even the enjoyment of desires is brought into question by the man of sense and reason who contemplates the effects of his acts upon his future.[°] The prospect did indeed suggest unpleasant possibilities. And yet into all this the newly established caste system fitted perfectly.

The Place of Caste in the
Religious Dogma

During the period turning on 500 B.C. the caste system, so distinctive of Hindu social life, was gradually establishing itself in its final form. The order of rank was now as follows: first, the *Brahmins;* then the *Kshatriyas;* below these, the dependent *Vaisyas* or "vassals"; and, last, the *Shudras* or servants. Outside the caste system altogether—"beyond the pale"—were the outcastes, including a group that was "untouchable." The outcastes constituted the dregs of society, unclean and without the hope of ever rising in the social scale, unless they happened to be in the small group out-casted temporarily for infraction of caste rules and awaiting reinstatement after expiation of their offences. The stratification of society proceeded further. Not only between, but within each caste, hard and fast lines were being drawn. The main castes

---

[°] That this was a widespread feeling of the time is evident in early Buddhism, which gave even more prominence to the Law of Karma than did the thinkers of the Upanishads and their followers. See below, Chapter V.

fissured into scores, even hundreds, of subcastes, each forbidding intermarriage into other subcastes and otherwise restricting freedom of association.*

But our interest here is not in the social extension of the caste system, but rather in its place within the religious dogma evolved by the Brahmins. When the caste system was linked up with the Law of Karma, the inequalities of life had at once a simple and comprehensive explanation. The existence of caste in the social structure immediately acquired a kind of moral justification. If a man was born a Shudra, it was because he had sinned in previous existences, and deserved no better lot. A Brahmin, on the other hand, had every right to exalt his position and prerogatives; by good deeds in previous existences he had merited his present high station. And here, too, the ranking of the castes with the Brahmins at the top, the Kshatriyas next, the Vaisyas third, and the Shudras last, seemed justified by a spiritual sliding scale, as it were; the class in society with the best record of spiritual attainment should be at the top. (So, at least, the Brahmins argued; and in spite of die-hard resistance, the Kshatriyas, with no notion of contradicting the fact of transmigration and the consequences of karma in determining destiny, and thus deprived of any weighty counterargument to offer, had to be content at length with second place—after fostering some stout heresies in a last rebellious stand, as will be seen.†)

The social consequence of the moral justification of caste was apparent in another direction. Any attempt to level up the inequalities of society and lay a broader basis for social justice and reward now became either impious or morally wrong-headed. To question the operations of the Law of Karma, as fixing the just retribution for deeds in former lives, became the rankest of heresies.

The Rise of Indian Pessimism
or World Denial

The Aryans who came into India were a robust and optimistic people, but this confident frame of mind persisted only so long as the mood expressed in the Vedas did. With the rise of the caste system, the introduction of the doctrines of Transmigration and the Law of Karma, and the development of a world-denying philosophical idealism, disaffection with the world grew in the mind of ancient India. This turning

---

* Today there are more than 2,000 such castes.

† The reference here is to Jainism and Buddhism.

away from life had other causes, too. There were undoubtedly physical and psychological conditions making for it. Up to the time of their descent into the Ganges valley the Aryans had not finally given up their nomadic habit of life; the world still appealed to them as a sphere of action and adventure; obstacles and difficult endeavors still called out their aggressive qualities; the "native hue of resolution" being not yet "sicklied o'er with the pale cast of thought," they were activistic, joyous, and practical. But after they had descended the Ganges river plain and ended their wanderings, their life in that hot and enervating climate became recessive, and the energies of their bodies waned. Keen minds will not cease from thinking under such conditions; thought may substitute for legs, and provide the intellectualist, sensualist, or lover of romantic dreams with vicarious adventure—that of the mind and imagination; and yet, unless the fundamental outlook on life remains joyous, the spirit tends to grow heavy and thought to rest more and more in negations.

The negativist tendency in this instance was vastly increased by the new convictions the Aryans adopted. The widely held doctrine that complete reality can be experienced only by one's becoming absorbed in Brahman-Atman led inevitably to a devaluation of the more ordinary modes of consciousness. At first blush, the belief that all is Brahman carried with it the promise of eventually entering the realm of absolute reality—something that any truth-seeking mind might wish for. With this was bound up the hope of ecstatic experiences of union with Brahman. Nor were these the only promising considerations. On the whole the Upanishads reflect the happy feeling that if all is Brahman all is right. Again, if one's soul *is* Brahman can it possibly be of no worth? Moreover, a certain moral release offered itself here: if one realizes he is identical with the truly Real, is he not elevated to a plane of being where moral distinctions no longer hold? As an early thinker put it, "Such a one, verily, the thought does not torment: 'Why have I not done good? Why have I done evil?' He who knows this, saves himself from these thoughts." [36]

On the other hand, however, there were serious drawbacks in this view of reality. The conclusion that, if all is Brahman or some phase of Brahman, there is no true individuality, made the vigorous soul, upon further reflection, feel weak and faint; it overbore and crushed him with a sense of the unreality of all his previous thought about himself; it persuaded him, in fact, of the ultimate wrongness of the struggle of the ego, away, as it were, from Brahman, toward self-fulfilment; it robbed of conviction and resolution any human attack on the objective world in the spirit of practical enterprise. The result was either lethargy of mind, feeling, and will, or a definite renunciation of the world. Though "there was enough faith in life to support all genuine search for truth," [37] there was little left to allure one to the venture of making one's self at home in the world.

When we turn to the effects on the Indian spirit of the belief in Transmigration and the Law of Karma, we see the tendency toward world-withdrawal sharply accentuated. The masses of the people were not adversely affected, either in that day or in this, except in the few instances when the Brahmins attempted to explain to them the causes of their general misery; but more highly reflective and sensitive minds were profoundly depressed. When these contemplated the apparently endless series of rebirths which the doctrine of transmigration conjured up to their imagination, they felt acute distress. Hindus have come to speak of the process of rebirth as "The Wheel." They look upon it with despair. Beholding it eternally revolving, their hearts have failed them at the prospect of a possible thousand million rebirths stretching out their length before them.

The inexorable character of the operations of the Law of Karma added to this distressing consideration feelings of fear that daunted the stoutest heart. Few can await retribution with complacency. Even the prospect of being reborn in the next life on the human plane offered little consolation—for it was but too likely to be on a lower level.

Hence, the whole complex of developing beliefs, in that hot climate, amid the disease, the poverty, and the degradation of the lower classes, filled most sensitive Indian souls with a sense of terrifying need: *"Oh, would that I could be delivered from the power of my karma over me! Would that I could find my way into a state of being where misery would be at an end and only joy remain!"*

In this cry of the heart, we reach the central concern of all Indian religion.

The Need of a Way of Release

To this point the ideas which we have been examining have been steadily tending. The further history of Indian religion, orthodox or heterodox, is essentially that of a search for the solution of the problem, how may one reach a state of experience or being which ends life's imperfections? Specifically, since rebirth is seen to supply a network of suffering extended over great stretches of time and space, how may one achieve release from the round of rebirths?

Barely four centuries passed after the Aryans invaded the Ganges plain before this problem became both clear and urgent. The mind of India has been at work on it ever since.

It now becomes our task to consider the chief solutions, heretical and orthodox, that have been offered.

SUGGESTIONS FOR FURTHER READING

Dasgupta, S. *Hindu Mysticism.* Open Court, 1927. Available as Ungar pb

Deussen, Paul. *The Philosophy of the Upanishads.* T. & T. Clark, 1906

Eliot, Sir Charles. *Hinduism and Buddhism.* 3 vols. Routledge and Kegar Paul, 1954. Earlier ed., Edward Arnold, London, 1921

Farquhar, J. N. *An Outline of the Religious Literature of India.* Oxford, 1920

Griffith, R. T. H., trans. *The Hymns of the Rig Veda.* 2 vols. E. J. Lazarus and Co., Benares, 1895

Griswold, H. D. *The Religion of the Rig Veda.* Oxford, 1923

Hume, R. E., trans. *The Thirteen Principal Upanishads.* Oxford, 1934

Keith, A. B. *The Religion and Philosophy of the Veda and the Upanishads.* Harvard University Press, 1920

Macnicol, N., ed. *Hindu Scriptures.* Everyman Library. J. M. Dent

Morgan, Kenneth W., ed. *The Religion of the Hindus.* Ronald Press, 1953

Piggott, S. *Prehistoric India.* Penguin pb, 1950

Prabhavananda and Manchester, trans. *The Upanishads.* Mentor pb, 1957

Radhakrishnan, S. *The Philosophy of the Upanishads.* Allen and Unwin, 1924

———— (ed.). *History of Philosophy, Eastern and Western.* Allen and Unwin, 1952–53

Renou, L. *Religions of Ancient India.* Oxford, 1953

4 Jainism: A Study in Asceticism

TWO HERESIES* SPRANG UP TO VEX THE COURSE OF HINDUISM WITH THEIR answers to that central problem of Indian life, how to find release from Karma and the ever-lengthening round of rebirths entailed by it. Hardly had this problem issued its challenge to the mind of India and begun to bear down upon the human spirit with weight and force, before the two heresies appeared. One of them—Jainism—was destined to win adherents in India only, but to survive every assault upon it; so that, even though it never became a religion with a great and elemental appeal, it has continued to exist in India to this day. The other heresy—Buddhism—spread rapidly over the whole of India and overflowed its boundaries to the south, east, and north, winning a permanent footing in Ceylon, Burma, Cambodia, Siam, and the larger countries to the north, China, Korea, Japan, Tibet, and Mongolia, and supplying these regions with some profoundly satisfactory answers to universal human needs; but it was destined at length to die out in India itself, except upon the fringes of that amazing land. For a thousand years Hinduism was almost overborne by the two heresies it had mothered, and its eventual return to dominance over the field of religion is something of a marvel.

The reasons for the strong appeal which both Jainism and Buddhism

* Heresies is perhaps a strong word here, especially if it is taken out of the Western context and used here. "Opposition parties" might be a better term, if the political connotations are removed. However, the Brahmins did call their rivals *pasanda*, heretics, at times.

possessed for the people of later India seem to have been their ethical strength and their doctrinal clarity. They gave unconfused solutions for India's central religious perplexity; or, to put the fact from a slightly different angle, the roads to freedom which they proposed were, originally at least, straight and clearly marked.

When we turn to see what Jainism had to offer, our Occidental minds receive an initial shock. To anyone schooled in the attitudes of the West, Jainism may seem at first glance an adjustment to life and world as rigorous as any the history of religions affords. But the raising of Western eyebrows at its uncompromising devotion to self-discipline is identified by the people of India as just another instance of the naive absorption in material values that characterizes Europe and America. In India, at any rate, Jainism is not a queer kind of behavior at all, and does not stand alone in adopting asceticism as the highest way of salvation.

Like the greater faith Buddhism, which arose a generation after it, Jainism was, at the time it came into being, a reaction to, and in some part against, the tendencies set in motion by the Brahmins. At that time (the 6th century B.C.), the caste system was still in the making, and when the priestly class put forward their broad claims to spiritual and social ascendancy, many in the ranks of the nobility, of whose caste Mahavira was a member, resisted these claims actively by expressing their independent points of view. The Brahmins offended them deeply, for one thing, by professing that the possibility was unlikely that anyone but a Brahmin could successfully complete the preparatory steps leading to Nirvana. The Kshatriyas were at that time active and able in philosophic discussion, as the Upanishads bear witness; and many of them found in Brahmanism a system of thought which at a number of points gave them pause. Sturdy minds among them found unacceptable the monistic idealism which resolved the substantial world of everyday into one thing, and there were honest souls, practical and realistic in their outlook, who roundly declared that it was not the physical world (rather it was this much-spoken of Brahman) that was unreal. To their commonsense eyes each living thing, and all manner of other entities, were as real as they appeared to be; men and men's souls, stones, trees, and hills, footed and flying creatures, and fishes of the sea, all entered experience as realities that were independently and in their own right existent. The struggle against the monistic idealism of the Brahmins frequently took the form of denying the reality of all hypothetical world-souls, however defined or named—whether supreme persons or all-inclusive neutral somethings—and maintaining stoutly a position that was ultimately atheistic.

To the group which took this latter stand Mahavira belonged. But he belonged to it primarily not for intellectual or social reasons, but from motives grounded in personal need—the intense desire for salvation.

I *MAHAVIRA'S MANNER OF LIFE*

Mahavira is the accepted name for the founder of Jainism. Anyone familiar with Latin and allied tongues will see at once that it is an honorific title meaning "Great Man" or "Hero." It has quite superseded Nataputta Vardhamana, the name by which he was originally known. He is said to have been born near Vaisali (in modern Bihar) in 599 B.C. and to have died in 527.* His father, it is claimed, was a rajah. Mahavira was not the oldest son—a circumstance which made his renunciation of the princely life, later on, easier.

It is hard to recover the truth, of course, because of the uncertain state of the records, but the data given below, lifted out of the legends, probably contain it. It is the picture of Mahavira presented by one of the two main Jaina sects, the Shvetambaras.† The story is at heart a very simple one, and, whether true *in toto* or not, it is representative of all Indian asceticism.

That Mahavira was reared in the luxury of the ancient courts of India may be gathered from the assertion that he was attended by five nurses: "a wet-nurse, a nurse to bathe him, one to dress him, one to play with him, and one to carry him"; and that, "transferred from the lap of one nurse to that of another, he grew up," living "in the enjoyment of the allowed, noble, five-fold joys and pleasures, consisting in sound, touch, taste, color, and smell," [1]—the pleasures of sense which he was later to renounce.‡ He married and had a daughter. But he was not content with a prince's life. Outside of the town, in a park, which he must often have visited, dwelt a body of monks who followed the rule of the ascetic Parshva, who had lived a century or two earlier and founded a monastic order which took his name. Mahavira was much attracted to their mode of life. However, out of respect for his parents

---

* These are the traditional dates set by the Shvetambara sect.

† The canon of this sect is probably the oldest, but this is a debatable point. The writers of this canon admit themselves that they are writing 980 years after the death of Mahavira! (See *Sacred Books of the East*, Vol. XXII, p. 270.)

‡ India is tolerant of the sensuous pleasures, if they be renounced in time. See p. 255.

he decided: "It will not behoove me, during the life of my parents, to enter the state of houselessness." [2] As soon as his parents did die (the legend has it that they died by careful prearrangement, in accordance with the strictest religious usage: "On a bed of kusa-grass they rejected all food, and their bodies dried up by the last mortification of the flesh" [3]), Mahavira prepared to give up the princely life. He was now thirty years of age, but he had to ask his brother's consent; and, on condition that he would remain in the palace one more year (thinking it over?), that consent was obtained. But he used the time to give up "his gold and silver, his troops and chariots"; he "distributed, portioned out and gave away his valuable treasures." [4]

Then in the first month of winter, he "retired from the world." He joined the body of monks in their cells outside the town. As part of his initiation into their order, he took off all his ornaments and finery, and retained only one garment, a robe with "a flamingo pattern." Next, he "plucked out with his right and left hands on the right and left sides of his head his hair in five handfuls." He took the required pledge: "I shall neglect my body and abandon the care of it; I shall with equanimity bear, undergo, and suffer all calamities arising from divine powers, men, or animals." [5]

Some months after joining the order of Parshva, Mahavira struck out for himself. Throwing off his robe, and thenceforth going completely naked, he began a long wandering through the villages and plains of central India in quest of release from the cycle of birth, death, and rebirth. His two convictions were: (1) that saving one's soul from evil (that is, purging contaminating matter from the soul) is impossible without practicing the severest asceticism, and (2) that maintaining the purity and integrity of one's own soul involves practicing *ahimsa* or noninjury to any and all living beings. Neither of these convictions was new, for Mahavira took them from his predecessors in the tradition of thought with which his name is now associated; but the faithfulness and sincerity with which he lived by them were remarkable.

In moving about, he never stayed more than one night in a village or more than five in a town. He was determined to form no attachments to any place or people that might bind him to the world and its pleasures. Only during the four months of the rainy season did he remain in the same place, because then the roads and paths were teeming with life, and the principle of *ahimsa* required his remaining quiescent.

The following passages from the oldest Jaina documents are worthy of close study. Every phrase counts. They constitute a unique record of consistency to principle.

The first group of passages illustrates with great vividness the un-usual precautions Mahavira took not to injure any living thing, directly or indirectly.

Thoroughly knowing the earth-bodies and water-bodies and fire-bodies and wind-bodies, the lichens, seeds, and sprouts, he comprehended that they are, if narrowly inspected, imbued with life, and avoided to injure them.

Walking, he meditated with his eyes fixed on a square space before him of the length of a man . . . Looking a little sideward, looking a little behind, attentively looking on his path, [he walked so as not to step on any living thing].

Many sorts of living beings gathered on his body, crawled about it and caused pain there. [But he exercised self-control so as not to scratch himself.]

Without ceasing in his reflections, the Venerable One slowly wandered about, and, killing no creatures, he begged for his food.[6]

Other passages condense into this picture: Mahavira apparently made it his practice, when walking, to carry a soft broom for sweeping the path wherever it might be covered with insects. Out of doors, he cleared the ground before lying down to rest or sleep; and within doors, he examined his bed to be sure it was free from eggs and living beings. He refused all raw food of any kind and took into his begging bowl only food prepared originally for someone else and left over (for if he allowed anyone to take the life out of something expressly for him, he must hold himself accountable for being the cause of the killing of a living being). He carried a cloth for straining water before drinking it;* and always went carefully through a bowl of food to see if any of it was affected by eggs, sprouts, worms, mildew, cobwebs, or any living thing, and if it was so affected, he removed the portions containing them before "circumspectly" eating the rest.

As to the strictness with which he practiced asceticism, the next group of passages is a sufficient testimony.

This is the rule followed by the Venerable One: When the cold season has halfway advanced, the houseless one, leaving off his robe and stretching out his arms, should wander about, not leaning against a tree-trunk.

When a cold wind blows, in which some feel pain, then some houseless monks in the cold rain seek a place sheltered from the wind. "We shall put on more clothes; kindling wood, or well covered, we shall be able to bear the very painful influence of the cold." But the Venerable One desired nothing of the kind; strong in control, he suffered, despising all shelter.

Sometimes in the cold season the Venerable One was meditating in the shade. In summer he [exposed] himself to the heat, he [sat] squatting in the sun.

* And for holding before his mouth when speaking, lest insects fly into it.

The Venerable One did not seek sleep for the sake of pleasure; he waked up himself, and slept only a little.

Purgatives and emetics, anointing of the body and bathing, shampooing, and cleansing of the teeth do not behoove him.[7]

Fearful of forming agreeable personal attachments, he refrained from speaking to or greeting anyone. This procured him a good deal of ill-will from inquisitive villagers, but he bore all affronts with determined indifference.

For some it is not easy to do what he did, not to answer those who salute; he was beaten with sticks, and struck by sinful people.

Giving up the company of all householders whomsoever, he meditated. Asked, he gave no answer.

Disregarding slights difficult to bear, the Sage wandered about, not attracted by story-tellers, pantomimes, songs, fights at the quarter-staff, and boxing matches.

The dogs bit him, ran at him. Few people kept off the attacking, biting dogs. Striking the monk, they cried "Khukkhu," and made the dogs bite him.

When he once sat without moving his body, they cut his flesh, tore his hair, covered him with dust. Throwing him up, they let him fall, or disturbed him in his religious postures; abandoning the care of his body, the Venerable One humbled himself.[8]

On another occasion, it is related (though it puts a strain on credulity to believe it) that sportive villagers, seeing him sitting naked and motionless in a field, lit a fire between his feet, to see if he would move, and drove "nails" into his ears; but the Venerable One remained oblivious to them, masterly in self-control. He was determined to maintain a meditative calm unaffected by the discomforts of the body.

Keeping steadfastly to this invincible self-discipline, Mahavira wandered about for twelve years, hopeful of *moksha,* deliverance. The crowning experience which he sought was not withheld; it came at last. The Jaina record tells of the event with great particularity.

During the thirteenth year, in the second month of summer, in the fourth fortnight . . . when the shadow had turned toward the east, . . . outside the town Grimbhikagrama, on the northern bank of the river Rigupalika, in the field of the householder Samaga, in a northeastern direction from an old temple, not far from a sal tree, in a squatting position, with knees high and head low, in deep meditation, in the midst of abstract meditation, he reached Nirvana, the complete and full . . . called Kevala.[9]

He thus became the Jina (the Conqueror), and all his followers Jains, for he had achieved a complete "victory" over his body and the desires that bind one to this world of matter and sin.

Having attained the experience he had been twelve years in winning, Mahavira began to seek people out and teach them. Conversions to his way of life followed. And after thirty years of successful teaching and organizing, at the age of seventy-two, he "cut asunder the ties of birth, old age, and death" and was "finally liberated, freed from all pains." [10] He is now, according to all the Jaina sects, enjoying supreme bliss in a place of reward called Isatpragbhara, in a state no longer subject to rebirth.

II PHILOSOPHY AND ETHICS OF JAINISM

The story of Mahavira has been told in the previous section in the simplest way, with the smallest use of Jaina technical terms, in order that the essential passion for release or escape exhibited in it might stand out clearly. But the followers of Mahavira—and he himself, though doubtless to a less degree—thought of his course of life as operating within a philosophical and ethical context requiring for its description Jaina technical terms and distinctions. Karma, soul, matter, salvation—all had meanings reflecting a world-view distinct from that either of Brahmanism or Buddhism.

The Jains have never questioned the belief that man is gravely conditioned in his progress toward salvation by the Law of Karma; indeed the disquieting implications of this law have loomed very large in their view. They interpret the doctrine of Karma strictly, in accordance with their idea that the consequences of one's deeds are literally deposited in and on the soul. Various kinds of karmas are accumulated during this and previous births like layers or incrustations of foreign substance that may form as many as five sheaths around the soul and must be worn off by the process of living; or, as the predecessors of Mahavira, going back to the ascetic Parshva, taught, it is like a rarefied material, poisonous and alien, that penetrates the soul and must be thrown off by the soul's activity.

This Jaina idea is based on a very interesting view of the relation between matter and mind. Matter ranges in density from solidity to the thinnest sort of being beyond the reach of the senses; in the former case it is heavy and gross, in the latter light and volatile. Matter is eternal, and consists of atoms which may cluster together into any shape or quality, such as earth, water, wind, sounds, colors, and sentient bodies of all sorts, including in the last case their senses and sensations. The subtlest mode of matter is *karma*-matter. It forms in the soul in the following way: whenever moved by bad desire or passion, the soul becomes, as it were, sticky, and gets itself covered with matter or permeated by it. Such adhesions and infiltrations of matter affect the course of transmigration; for the soul at the end of each period of existence carries the matter which vitiates its purity along with it; and if it is *full* of matter, it sinks lower in the scale of existence, perhaps into hell; and if it has only a little matter in it, it will be light enough to rise, perhaps into the heavens, and find its embodiment there in the body of some god, or rise higher still and become an eternally "liberated" being.

In scrutinizing the nature of Karma, the Jains have distinguished at least eight kinds of it,° depending on the effects produced. One form of it fixes the length of an individual's life, another his physical and mental characteristics, a third his nationality and caste, a fourth his power of resolution, a fifth his intelligence and degree of knowledge, a sixth his intuitiveness, a seventh his capacity for pleasure and pain, and an eighth his attitudes whether of faith or doubt, purity or passion, and the like. Singly and in combination these kinds of karmas fix one's lot in each existence and effect the whole course of life.

The soul's chief problem, that of managing to throw off or expel karma-matter from itself, is in part automatically taken care of, simply by the karmas exerting their effects and passing off. But the ethical activity of the soul annihilates the old karmas more swiftly, and at the same time (since *any* action creates a new karma) produces only those new karmas that have the briefest effects and are quickly dissipated or neutralized.

The major fact of life which emerges from all this is the inherent opposition (or opposite tendency) of soul and flesh, matter and mind. Mahavira and his followers were pluralists, but they roughly grouped all things into two distinct categories: (1) the *ajiva* or lifeless things in the universe, composing the realm of thick, dead matter, and (2) the *jiva* or living beings in the universe, to be defined more precisely as the infinite multitude of individual souls composing the realm of spirit (or thin, lively matter). The *ajiva* is eternal yet evil; but the *jiva*, also eternal, is of an infinite value, and contains all good; for souls are indestructible and infinitely precious. Souls are classed according to the number of senses they have. Those having five senses—gods, men, animals, and hell-beings—are in the highest group. Next are the four-sensed beings, for example, the larger insects, such as bees, flies, and butterflies. Without sight and hearing, the third group includes moths and the smaller insects. The group of two-sensed beings, possessing touch and

° And 148 subdivisions!

taste, includes worms, shell-fish, leeches, and minute creatures. A final group with only the sense of touch is often referred to in Jaina writings; it includes vegetables, trees, seeds, lichens, earth-bodies, wind-bodies, water-bodies, and fire-bodies.

In their pure state, when entirely freed from matter, all souls are perfect, possessing infinite perception, infinite knowledge, infinite power, and infinite bliss. When liberated from matter, they rise straight to the top of the universe, where they join the souls in Isatpragbhara that have been liberated before them.

Incidentally, the souls that have entered Isatpragbhara are not reduced to nothingness, for though they may be described as being without qualities or relations of any sort, there is no cessation of consciousness in them. "The liberated," so runs a Jaina text, "is not long nor small . . . neither heavy nor light; he is without body, without resurrection, without contact with matter; he is not feminine, nor masculine, nor neuter; he perceives, he knows, but there is no analogy (whereby to know the nature of the liberated soul)." [11] And there, without further ado, the text lets the matter rest, as well it might!

Being indestructible and absolutely independent, souls are not phases of nor emanations thrown out by something else. The Jains from the beginning have held that there is no Brahman-Atman, such as the Brahmins describe. No unity of substance or being holds the universe together. There is no Supreme Ruler of the world, such as the devout look to. There are numerous higher beings, who might be called "gods," and who exist on the various levels of the celestial regions; but they are finite beings, subject like men to rebirth. No help, Mahavira taught, could be expected from such beings, themselves in need of redemption. Therefore human souls caught in the predicament of existence in the physical world, and needing to find a way of escape from karma through *moksha* or release, must realize that salvation is self-attained. Praying to the gods is of no avail.

A monk or nun should not say, "The god of the sky! The god of the thunderstorm! The god of lightning! The god who begins to rain! . . . May rain fall, or may it not fall! May the crops grow! May the sun rise!" They should not use such speech. But, knowing the nature of things, he should say, "The air; a cloud has gathered, or come down; the cloud has rained." [12]

Nor does it avail to turn to other men, nor to the words of others, as having inherent efficacy to save. The priests are of no special authority. The Vedas are not especially sacred, and cannot be used as miraculous agencies of release from rebirth. Rather than trust to these external aids, let each man realize that salvation lies within himself. "Man," runs one of Mahavira's most emphatic utterances, "thou art thine own friend. Why wishest thou for a friend beyond thyself?" [13]

The surest and swiftest way to reach liberation or *moksha* is the practice of asceticism or austerities (*tapas*). What Mahavira meant by asceticism may be seen from his own practice of it. His followers have added fasting according to certain rules, and types of meditation leading to a trance-state marked by complete dissociation from the outward world and transcendence of one's own physical being. This trance-state is supposed to be like the one which Mahavira entered in the thirteenth year of his seeking and which assured him of his final deliverance. One cannot reach such a state, the Jains hold, without severe control of the mind and passions, for acts cannot be controlled, and karmas be prevented thereby from accumulating, unless the mind is so controlled as to be purified of all love of or dependence upon the world and its objects, animate and inanimate.

Mahavira's ascetic practice was (probably not by himself) summed up in the "Five Great Vows" for monks. These vows were later written out in very full form. In these fuller statements[14] there are some interesting definitions of what Mahavira meant by ahimsa and the breaking off of every attachment to the world and its objects. Ahimsa is the subject of the first vow.

1. The first great vow, Sir, runs thus: I renounce all killing of living beings, whether movable or immovable. Nor shall I myself kill living beings nor cause others to do it, nor consent to it. As long as I live I confess, and blame, and exempt myself of these sins, in mind, speech, and body.

There are five clauses:

A Nirgrantha [ascetic; literally, the undraped one] is careful in his walk, not careless.

A Nirgrantha searches into his mind. If his mind is sinful, acting on impulse, produces quarrels, pains, he should not employ such a mind.

A Nirgrantha searches into his speech. If his speech is sinful, produces quarrels, pains, he should not utter such speech.

A Nirgrantha is careful in laying down his utensils of begging.

A Nirgrantha eats and drinks after inspecting his food and drink. If a Nirgrantha would eat and drink without inspecting his food and drink, he might hurt and displace or injure or kill all sorts of living beings.

The second vow concerns truth speaking.

2. I renounce all vices of lying speech arising from anger or greed or fear or mirth. I shall neither myself speak lies, nor cause others to speak lies, nor consent to the speaking of lies by others.

There are five clauses subjoined to this vow also, and they provide that a Nirgrantha should speak only after deliberation, so as to be sure his words are true; should never be angry, greedy, nor fearful, lest these emotions betray him into falsehood; and should not be given to mirth-making, or, as we should say, "joking" or "kidding," because these forms of diversion are based on departures from fact.

3. The third great vow runs thus: I renounce all taking of anything not given, either in a village or a town or a wood, either of little or much, of great or small, of living or lifeless things. I shall neither take myself what is not given, nor cause others to take it, nor consent to their taking it.

Again there are five clauses, enjoining severe self-restraint upon every form of greed.

4. The fourth great vow runs thus: I renounce all sexual pleasure. I shall not give way to sensuality, nor cause others to do so, nor consent to it in others.

The five clauses under this vow explain how a Nirgrantha does not allow himself, even in the remotest way, to feel the allure of sex.

5. The fifth vow runs thus: I renounce all attachments, whether to little or much, small or great, living or lifeless things; neither shall I myself form such attachments, nor cause others to do so, nor consent to their doing so.

The five clauses of this startlingly comprehensive vow may be condensed as follows:

If a creature with ears hears agreeable and disagreeable sounds, it should not be attached to, nor delighted with, nor disturbed by the sounds. If it is impossible not to hear sounds which reach the ear, the mendicant should avoid love or hate originated by them.

If a creature with eyes sees forms, if a creature with an organ of smell smells smells, if a creature with a tongue tastes tastes, if a creature with an organ of feeling feels agreeable or disagreeable touches, it should not be attached to them, (and) should avoid love or hate originated by them.

Of these vows the most radically ascetic is the last. The vows concerning ahimsa and the renunciation of all sexual pleasures are important, of course. The renunciation of sex-interests was stressed by Mahavira, who is quoted as saying: "The greatest temptation in the world are women . . . Men forsooth say, 'These are the vessels of happiness.' But this leads them to pain, to delusion, to death, to hell, to birth as hell-beings or brute beasts." [15] The language is sufficiently strong. Nevertheless, the fifth vow is more inclusive, and by implication contains all the rest. It does in fact make sure that, though the monk may be in the world, he is, if he practices the fifth vow, emphatically not of it.

It was obvious from the beginning that the Five Great Vows could be only for Jaina ascetics. For the lay-folk, to whom the way of life prescribed in the severer code is impossible, the Jaina leaders have laid down a much modified rule of life. The lay adherents are to make twelve vows: (1) never knowingly to take the life of a sentient creature (hence, never to till the soil, nor engage in butchering, fishing, brewing, or any occupation involving the taking of life); (2) never to lie; (3) never to steal, or take what is not given; (4) never to be unchaste (or, to put it positively, always to be faithful to husband, or wife, and be pure in thought and word); (5) to check greed, by placing a limit upon one's wealth and giving away any excess; (6) to avoid temptation to sin by, for example, refraining from unnecessary travel; (7) to limit the number of things in daily use; (8) to be on guard against evils that can be avoided; (9) to keep stated periods for meditation; (10) to observe special periods of self-denial; (11) to spend occasional days as a monk; and (12) to give alms, especially in support of ascetics. Of these vows the first is undoubtedly the most important in its social effect. It constituted a limitation that must have seemed serious to the early followers of Mahavira; but at long last it actually proved to have economic as well as religious worth, for the Jains found they could make higher profits when they turned from occupations involving direct harm to living creatures to careers in business as bankers, lawyers, merchants, and proprietors of land. The other moral restrictions of their creed, which prohibited gambling, eating meat, drinking wine, adultery, hunting, thieving, and debauchery, earned them social respect, and thus contributed to their survival in the social scene.

III MAHAVIRA'S FOLLOWERS

So great was the impression that Mahavira made upon his followers that legend grew rapidly about him. While his followers were dividing ("in proper protestant fashion" [16]), they were busy elaborating their stories of the divine origin and attributes of Mahavira.

His birth was regarded as supernatural. He was declared to be the last of a long series of savior beings called Tirthankaras. He descended from heaven to enter the womb of a woman. When the gods discovered that this woman was Brahmin merely(!), they transferred the embryo to the womb of a woman of the Kshatriya caste instead. He grew up

Great head-annointing ceremony of Jains, occurring at Mysore every twelve years, during which over a thousand pots of milk, curds, and sandal paste are poured upon the head of the 57-foot monolithic statue of Gomatesvara, one of the Tirthankaras. (From a photograph)

sinless ("whatever is sinful, the Venerable One left that undone"[17]), and was omniscient ("he knew and saw all conditions of all living beings in the world"[18]).

Yet as time passed, the eminence of Mahavira was a little obscured by the veneration accorded to the twenty-three Tirthankaras who were thought to have preceded him. Parshva, his immediate predecessor, and hence the twenty-third "ford-finder" (which is what Tirthankara means), had a great temple erected in his honor on Mt. Parasnath, bearing his name, two hundred miles northwest of Calcutta; and Nemi, the twenty-second, had another erected to him upon the cliff under Mt. Girnar, far in western India on the peninsula of Kathiawar. Two very holy shrines, one on Mt. Satrunjaya near Palitana, in Kathiawar, and another on the plateau of Mt. Abu in the Aravalli Hills, have been built to honor Rishabha, the first of the Tirthankaras. Although the only cultus that accords with Jainist theory is "a kind of memorial service in honor of the teacher of the way of salvation," [19] these temples are of very elaborate and distinguished design. Jainism has come, in fact, to hold a prominent place in the architectural history of India. Other temples besides those mentioned—like the ones at Ahmedebad and Ajinere in western India and a monolithic shrine of exquisite beauty at Kaligamalai in south India—have become show-places of Indian architecture.

Early in the history of the faith the Jains divided on the question of wearing clothes. The Shvetambaras or "the white-clad" were the liberals who took their stand on wearing at least one garment, while the stricter and more conservative Digambaras got their name from their insistence on going about, whenever religious duty demanded it, "clad in atmosphere." Mahavira did not wear clothes, these latter pointed out; so why, when there is a religious reason for not wearing clothes,* should they? The Shvetambraras were in the north and yielded a bit both to the cold winds and to the social and cultural influences of the Ganges River plain. The Digambaras, not looked at askance by the Dravidian residents of their southland, have more easily maintained the earlier, sterner attitudes down the years. Another difference exists in the fact that, whereas the Shvetambaras admit women to their monastic order and assume that they have a chance to enter Nirvana, the Digambaras cling to Mahavira's reputed verdict that women are "the greatest temptation in the world" and "the cause of all sinful acts," and are therefore not to be admitted to their temples or to monastic life. Women, in this latter view, cannot win salvation until they have been reborn as men. That is their only hope.

Still another Jaina sect, the Sthanakvasis, tolerate no idols and have no temples. They worship "everywhere," mainly through meditation and introspection.

Meanwhile, Jainist philosophy has had some effect on the thought of India at large, especially in the realm of logic. The effect has been that of curbing any tendency to overstatement. Jainist logic considers all knowledge relative and transient. To every question one may answer with both yes and no. No proposition is either absolutely true or false. The Jains are fond of their ancient illustration of the logical fallacy inherent in all human thought—the story of the six blind men who put their hands on different parts of an elephant, and concluded, each to his own satisfaction, that the elephant was exactly "like a fan," "like a wall," "like a snake," "like a rope," and so on. It is only the free and purified soul, gone to the Jainist heaven, that possesses perfect knowledge.

Today the Jains number approximately 2,000,000, most being in the Bombay area, where in early life Mahatma Gandhi felt their influence

---

* I.e., while being a monk, when on pilgrimage, or during religious fasts and rituals. The Digambaras say that any monk who owns property or wears clothes cannot reach Nirvana.

on his own outlook. The paradox of their present status is, as already indicated, that their essentially world-renouncing religion has, in the devious course of events, secured their economic advantage among the struggling masses of India.

SUGGESTIONS FOR FURTHER READING

Barodia, U. D. *History and Literature of Jainism.* Bombay, 1909
Hastings, *Encyclopaedia of Religion and Ethics.* Articles "Ajivakas" and "Jainism"
Jacobi, Hermann, trans. *The Gaina Sutras* (in the Sacred Books of the East series). Oxford, 1884
Jaini, J. *Outlines of Jainism.* Cambridge, 1916
Pratt, J. B. *India and Its Faiths* (chapter XIII). Houghton Mifflin, 1915
Stevenson, Mrs. Sinclair. *The Heart of Jainism.* Oxford, 1915

5 Buddhism in its First Phase: Common Sense in World Denial

THOUGH IT AROSE A GENERATION LATER, IN THE LENGTHENING PERSPECTIVE of time Buddhism seems contemporaneous with Jainism; moreover, it shares with Jainism some of its deepest motives. Like Jainism it was a world-denying movement looking toward liberation of the true self. It was also a step toward independence of thought and action, springing from the Kshatriya caste and appealing to all classes and conditions of men. Like Mahavira, the monk Gautama found the philosophy of the Brahmins unacceptable and their claims unsubstantiated; he too came to deny the doctrine of the saving efficacy of the Vedas and of the ritual observances based upon them, and he challenged the claim of the Brahmin priesthood to prescriptive rights in showing the way to salvation.

But though Buddhism's similarities with Jainism are in some respects close, the differences in other respects are wide. Where one faith fixed its whole hope on an uncompromising and extreme asceticism, the other found deliverance in a moderate and common-sense "middle way." To the Buddha, extreme asceticism was not common sense, any more than sensuality was. Coolly and objectively, he tested every way of salvation offered by the teachers and spiritual leaders of his time, and refusing to be swept away into any vagary of religious behavior, however logically self-consistent, he stood at last firmly by the conviction supplied him by his common sense, that one's salvation must come through a disinterested clearheadedness about what one should seek. The keynote of Buddhism in its first phase is the calm pronouncement of its founder in an age when everything was in transition: "There is a Middle Path."

I   LIFE OF THE FOUNDER

Youth

There is a kind of parallelism between the lives of Mahavira and the Buddha which led some early scholars to regard the two men as identical. Both were, for instance, if we are to accept the traditional accounts,* born to high station as members of prominent Kshatriya families; both experienced dissatisfaction with their lot, and though married and having one child, abandoned their homes and became wandering mendicant monks; both rejected the monistic idealism of the Brahmins; both founded orders for monks and nuns which ruled out caste distinctions; and both were nonconformists from the Hindu point of view because they denied the special sacredness of the Vedas. But it is now evident that they differed more pronouncedly than they agreed; that insofar as they were alike in careers and in beliefs, it was due partly

---

* As in the case of Mahavira (and we shall find the same precaution advisable in other cases that shall come before us), the reader must be on guard not to believe the traditional biographies *in toto*. The historical personages who founded the great religions have been lovingly and reverently handled by their followers, who have had a very human need to visualize them clearly, and have therefore unconsciously added to the accounts handed down to them the details that did this for them. It will be well if the reader says to himself: "Here is the story that millions have taken for truth, *and they have also lived by it; but* the historians are very doubtful of its accuracy."

It may not be out of place here to emphasize the fact that historical criticism of the Oriental religions has been only recently begun, and in the interval before there is something like completion of the critical analysis of the records of these religions, it will be necessary to remain in a state of sceptical suspense.

As to India, the probability is that this suspense will always have to continue to some degree; for since the peoples of India have been more idea-centered than history-minded, the difficulty of distilling historical truth from tradition is increased.

For some of the problems involved in the study of Buddhist origins, see Mrs. Rhys Davids, *Sakya or Buddhist Origins* (London, 1931); A. B. Keith, *Buddhist Philosophy in India and Ceylon* (Oxford, 1923); Sir Charles Eliot, *Hinduism and Buddhism*, Vol. I, pp. 129–176, 275–301 (Edward Arnold, 1921).

to the similarity imposed upon them by their times and environment,°
and partly to sheer coincidence.

Siddhartha was the given, and Gautama the family name of the
founder of Buddhism. He was born in 560 B.C. in northern India, some
one hundred miles from Benares, in a fertile tract of country among
the foothills of the Himalayas. His father was a petty chieftain of the
Sakya clan, the various families of which held their territory in joint
control.

Legend has been prolifically at work on the scanty facts concerning
the childhood of Gautama. Tradition insists that the father hoped his
son would become "a universal monarch," the emperor of all India. But
if this was in actual fact his expectation, it was doomed to disappointment. The young Gautama was possessed of a mordantly clear mind
and sensitive spirit. He was destined to become more and more a
stranger in the house of his father. The traditions undoubtedly exaggerate the luxury that surrounded him; but there is probably some truth
in the stock phrases with which Gautama was afterwards credited: "I
wore garments of silk and my attendants held a white umbrella over
me." [1] It is hardly true, as later tradition asserts, that his father was a
"king." The facts are more truly suggested in the statement of Kenneth
Saunders that life at the house of Gautama's father was "not unlike
that at a Scottish castle in the Middle Ages." [2] Even marriage offered
no lasting balm to his inner dispeace. At sixteen, or as some accounts
say, at nineteen, he married a neighboring "princess." Legend declares
she was "majestic as a queen of heaven, constant ever, cheerful night
and day, full of dignity and exceeding grace," [3]—a paragon of wifely
devotion. But Gautama became more and more unhappy inwardly.
Sometime during his twenties he seems secretly to have made up his
mind to "go out from the household life into the homeless state" of the
religious mendicant; and when, in his late twenties, his wife bore
him a son, he felt free to follow his secret inclination.

This determination to renounce the household life has presented
an interesting problem to Buddhist believers. Why, they have asked, did
the fortunate prince, with so devoted a wife and father, and so young
a son, resolve nevertheless to renounce life under the same roof with
them? With true psychological insight, they have looked for the cause
not only in the spiritual reaction of the young prince to his immediate

° This similarity lay in the fact that they both came from districts north of the
Ganges where Aryan dominance was still being resisted and where Brahmanism
was questioned. It is significant that in each case their followers set down their
doctrines initially, not in Sanskrit, the language of the Aryans, but in local dialects,
Ardhamagadhin in the case of Jainism, Pali in the case of Buddhism.

surroundings, which were of the pleasantest, but to life itself as every man must live it, whether prince or pauper. They have developed the famous legend of "The Four Passing Sights." The essence of the many variants of this story° runs something like this: Gautama's father was forewarned by soothsayers at the time of the prince's birth, that his son might give up the household life, and become a houseless monk; but that on the other hand, should he be kept from taking such a step, he might become the emperor of all India ("a universal monarch"). So the father saw to it that the young prince should never experience the severities and sorrows of life, nor know the sad fact which turns so many to religion, the fact, namely, that human life is cut short by old age, disease, and death. Gautama was surrounded by young attendants. His father built him three palaces, "and in the enjoyment of great magnificence he lived, as the seasons changed, in each of these palaces." [4] So successful was the father in keeping out of sight the aged and the sick, so thoroughly did he clear from the highways all but youths and maidens when the prince went riding, that the latter grew up in ignorance of the common fate of men, the constant imminence of old age, disease, and death. The gods, therefore, looking down from the heavens and knowing that they must take a hand in the affair, sent one of their number down to earth to assume the shapes that should awaken the young prince to his true destiny. The god appeared suddenly by the wayside one day in the form of a very feeble and decrepit old man. The prince ordered the charioteer to tell him what it was they saw, and learned for the first time of the miserable close of every man's life. On another day the prince saw the second apparition, that of a loathsomely diseased man, and knew for the first time how physical misery may attend man all the days of his life. The third sight was that of a dead man being carried along on a bier, and the prince knew of the dreadful fact of death. These three awful sights robbed him of all peace of mind. (It is a fact, and perhaps the legend is based upon it, that in one of the oldest passages in the Buddhist writings he is reported as saying: "I also am subject to decay and am not free from the power of old age, sickness and death. Is it right that I should feel horror, repulsion and disgust when I see another in such plight? And when I reflected thus, my disciples, all the joy of life which there is in life died within me." [5]) Alarmed at the depression of spirit under which the prince labored, his father sought to cheer him with elaborate entertainment, but in vain. The prince remained distraught until he beheld the fourth sight, that of a calm ascetic, in a yellow robe, walking

° The best known account is in the *Jataka* tales.

toward him as he sat under a tree by the roadside. From this person, who had gained true peace of soul, he learned how freedom from the miseries of old age, disease and death may be won. Then, it is said, the prince made the resolve to go out from the household life into the homeless state.

The Great Renunciation

"In all the beauty of my early prime," an early passage runs, "with a wealth of coal-black hair untouched by grey—despite the wishes of my parents, who wept and lamented—I cut off my hair and beard, donned the yellow robes and went forth from home to homelessness." [6] The Buddhist legends tell in loving detail of the struggle by which the decision to renounce his high place in the world was reached; how his father ordered dancing girls to entertain the brooding prince, but all in vain; for the prince sat silently on the couch until all the dancing girls had fallen exhausted to the floor and passed into deep slumber; how the prince then rose and stepped with inward disgust over the sprawling forms of the sleepers, and made his way to his wife's apartment. There, gazing silently down on the sleeping mother with the infant Rahula at her side, he bade an unspoken farewell, then went out to leap on his great white horse and ride away, with his charioteer pacing at his side, to a far place, beyond a river. Having shaved off hair and beard, and exchanged his rich garments for the coarse yellow robe, he sent back his charioteer and plunged into the forest, one of the great anonymous group of mendicants vowed to the religious life.

Thus began a six-year period of intensive struggle for realization of salvation.

The Six Years of Quest

The legends say he was anxious not to reject the Brahmin philosophy until he had tested it, and went first to Rajagaha, the royal city of the province of Magadha, and became the disciple in turn of two ascetic Brahmin philosophers living in hillside caves. He explored speculative Brahmanism with them, and evidently practiced various Yoga disciplines. The first teacher, the ascetic Alara Kalama, taught him of "the realm of nothingness" to which a man might attain if he followed "the stages of meditation." But Gautama was disappointed; the temper of his mind was too objective and practical; so he went on to the second teacher, the ascetic Uddaka Ramaputta, who discoursed of "the state of neither-perception-nor-nonperception," with no better results.[7] In the end, convinced that the technique and substance of Brahmanism would not conduct him to the true way of enlightenment, he withdrew, and resolved, with the same objectivity, to test the extreme bodily asceticism which Jainism, among other sects, was then advocating.

After a short period of wandering, he entered a grove at Uruvela, past which flowed a clear river, with, "hard by, a village for sustenance." [8] There, sitting under the trees, he undertook for five years such rigid self-discipline that life itself almost left him, and he became mere skin and bone. His theory, according to the earliest accounts, was that the mind becomes clearer as the body becomes more disciplined; for, thought he, "It is just as if there were a green sappy stick in the water, and a man came along with his drill-stick, set on lighting a fire and making a blaze. Do you think he could succeed by rubbing with his drill-stick that green sappy stick from the water? Toil and moil as he may, he couldn't. It is just the same with all recluses or brahmins whose life is not lived aloof from pleasures of sense in the matter of their bodies." [9] On the other hand, he reasoned, Brahmins whose life is lived aloof from pleasures of sense in the matter of their bodies find that the dry light of understanding may flame up in them at last.

Undoubtedly ample allowance must be made for historical exaggeration, but it is said Gautama now sat with set teeth and tongue pressed against his palate seeking "by sheer force of mind" to "restrain, coerce, and dominate" his heart, until "the sweat streamed" from his armpits.[10] He practiced restraint of breath until he heard a roaring in his head and felt as if a sword were boring into his skull; violent pain almost drove him senseless; and still no insight came. He lived for periods on all sorts of nauseous foods, dressed in chafing and irritating garments, stood for days in one posture, or having squatted, moved asquat; he sat on a couch of thorns, lay in the cemetery on charred bones among rotting bodies, let dirt and filth accumulate on his body till it dropped off of itself, and even ate his own excrement in the extremity of self-discipline. He reduced his diet to "only one hemp grain" or "a single grain of rice" or "one jujube fruit" a day. He became excessively thin. The *Majjhima Nikaya* credits him with these vivid words of self-description: "When I was living on a single fruit a day, my body grew emaciated in the extreme; [my limbs became] like the knotted joints of withered creepers; like a buffalo's hoof were my shrunken buttocks; like the twists in a rope were my spinal vertebrae; like the rafters of a tumble-down roof were my gaunt ribs; like the starry gleams on water deep down in the depths of a well, so shone my gleaming eyes deep down in the depths of their sockets; and as the rind of a cut gourd shrinks and shrivels in the heat, so shrank and shrivelled the scalp of my head. . . . If I sought to feel my belly, it was my backbone which I found in my grasp." [11]

Such extraordinary self-mortification should have produced results, if the theory was sound that meditation pursued diligently in a rigorously disciplined body brought one to the goal; but to Gautama's great distress of mind he was as far from enlightenment as ever. According to the source from which we have already quoted, he thought to himself: "With all these severe austerities, I fail to transcend ordinary human limits and to rise to the heights of noblest understanding and vision. Could there be another path to Enlightenment?" [12] He had returned to common sense! Meanwhile five other ascetics had joined him, hoping that he would share his knowledge with them. While they watched, he rose one day from his seat to go down to the stream, and fainted dead away. The five ascetics gathered round his motionless body and thought: "He will die. The ascetic Gautama will die." They wondered if he had now

Gautama Buddha in an emaciated state after practicing austerities at Uruvela, some time before his enlightenment. (From an image at Peshawar)

entered Nirvana. But he came to, and after lying in the shallow water near the bank of the stream, he was sufficiently refreshed in mind and body to begin life anew. With the objectivity of view which marked him all his life, he now concluded: "This way of mortification has utterly failed. My body cannot support my intellect. I will eat and drink and strengthen it." [13] Accordingly he took his begging bowl in hand and resumed the life of a parrib-bajaker (wandering mendicant). The five ascetics were outraged. With indignant words they departed for Benares, saying that luxuriousness had reclaimed him, and that, in abandoning the struggle, he had become a backslider into self-indulgence.

But though he had returned to common sense, Gautama could not rejoice. Six years of search along the two most widely recognized roads to salvation known to India, philosophic meditation and bodily asceticism, had yielded no results. But he did not give up the struggle. His thinking now became much more profound and meaningful.

The Great Enlightenment

He turned aside at a place now called Budhgaya, into a grove, and sat down at the foot of a tree (a tree which came to be known as the Knowledge- or Bodhi-tree, or more simply the Bo-tree); and there he entered upon a process of meditation that was to affect the thinking of millions of men after him. The Buddhist books insist that he set his teeth and said to himself determinedly: "Though skin, nerves, and bone shall waste away, and life-blood itself be dried up, here sit I till I attain Enlightenment." [14] In all probability the fact was far otherwise; psychology probably can suggest a truer version of the real course of Gautama's enlightenment: he had tried too hard altogether, so that his very determination stood between him and the state of consciousness which he desired; but now, in the face of self-defeat, his will relaxed, he let his mind wander back over his previous experience. Some such questions as these must have arisen in his mind: What was he to think of his life and his search for salvation until now? Why had he failed?

And suddenly the answer came. The stumbling-block to his own salvation, and the cause of all human misery, he reasoned, was *desire*—too intense desire (*tanha,* "thirst," "craving,")—desire for the wrong things, arising out of the carnal will-to-live-and-have. The intensity of his own desire had defeated him. If he could get rid of that desire! If he could, he would know what peace was, the peace the Brahmins sought, the peace of high Nirvana. As this insight, with all its implications, grew upon him, Gautama realized that *he was, now, without*

Gautama under the Bo-tree. (From a frieze depicting the temptation of the Buddha by Mara, the devil, at Borobudur, Java)

desire; he felt no sensual yearnings, was purged of "wrong states of mind." The Buddhist books say he then passed into an ecstasy having four phases, culminating in "the state that, knowing neither satisfaction nor dissatisfaction, is the consummate purity of poised equanimity and mindfulness." [15] It seemed to him "ignorance was destroyed, knowledge had arisen, darkness was destroyed, light had arisen," as he sat there "earnest, strenuous, resolute." [16] Also he was convinced that "Rebirth is no more; I have lived the highest life; my task is done; and now for me there is no more of what I have been." [17] He thus experienced the earthly foretaste of Nirvana. From now on he was the Buddha, the Enlightened One.

After the ecstasy had passed, he was immediately confronted with a problem, a temptation. This is one of the best attested facts in the Buddhist books. He had attained to a Doctrine that was "profound, recondite, hard to comprehend." [18] Were he to preach the Doctrine, and were others not to understand it, that would be labor and annoyance to him. After some struggle with himself, whether he should remain a Buddha for his own sake or become a Buddha for all, a teaching Buddha, he rose and went back into the world to communicate to others his saving truth.

He sought out the five ascetics who had deserted him at Uruvela. He found them in the Deer Park at Benares, and there experienced a great personal triumph. At first, when they saw him coming toward them among the trees, they said bitterly: "Here comes the ascetic Gautama, he who eats rich food and lives in self-indulgence. Let us show him no respect, nor rise to meet him. Yet let us put out a seat; he can sit on it if he wants to." [19] But the Buddha radiated such calm and self-possession that they could not withhold their gaze nor refrain from receiving him. They rose; one came forward to relieve him of his bowl and robes; another indicated his seat; another brought water to wash his feet. Then a discussion, which lasted for several days, began. To their accusation that he had forfeited the possibility of enlightenment by abandoning asceticism and reverting to self-indulgence, he replied in the words of what is known as the Sermon in the Deer Park at Benares: "There are two extremes, O Almsmen, which he who has given up the world ought to avoid. What are those two extremes?—A life given to pleasures, devoted to pleasures and lusts; this is degrading, sensual, vulgar, ignoble and profitless. And a life given to mortifications; this is painful, ignoble, and profitless. By avoiding these two extremes the Truthfinder [the Tathagata: the Buddha's designation for himself] has gained the knowledge of the Middle Path which leads to insight, which leads to wisdom, which conduces to calm, to knowledge, to Enlightenment, to Nirvana." [20] He opened to them his own experience, and challenged them to believe his testimony, to admit that he was an "arahat" (a monk who had experienced enlightenment), and to try the "middle way" which he now advocated. The five ascetics were converted; and thus the Sangha (the Buddhist monastic order) came into being.

The Buddha then energetically entered upon his itinerant ministry in North India.

The Establishment of the Buddhist Order

As the Buddha wandered about preaching, other conversions, especially from his own, the Kshatriya caste, followed, until the number of disciples rose to sixty. Then the monks multiplied rapidly. Not only Kshatriyas and members of the lower castes, but many Brahmins joined the group of inquirers and disciples. Among these was one who became a leader among his disciples, the Brahmin Sariputta. Others came of his own class, like his cousin Ananda. Caste distinctions were then not so sharply defined in society at large as later, and in any case caste ceased to apply to individuals who joined the Buddhist Order. At first all candidates for ordination into the Order were brought by disciples to the Buddha; but when in course of time converts came from a distance and in increasing numbers, he authorized ordained monks to confer ordination themselves, following certain simple rules. In fact, as the converts grew in number it became expedient to inaugurate a program and draw up rules for behavior. During the dry season the Buddha annually sent his disciples out to preach, himself setting the example. During the three months of the rainy season he and the monks gathered together, some here, some there, and lived a monastic life of self-discipline, instruction, and mutual service.

So in a very natural way rose a great Order, the Sangha, governed by definite rules and schedules. The essential rules, perhaps developed after the Buddha's own time, were simple: the wearing of the yellow robe, the adoption of the shaven head, the carrying of the begging bowl, the habit of daily meditation, and subscription to the initiate's confession: "I take refuge in the Buddha, I take refuge in the Dharma (the Law or Truth), I take refuge in the Sangha (the Order)." All undertook also to obey the Ten Precepts, which may be simplified thus:

1. Refrain from destroying life (the principle of ahimsa).
2. Do not take what is not given.
3. Abstain from unchastity.
4. Do not lie or deceive.
5. Abstain from intoxicants.
6. Eat moderately and not after noon.
7. Do not look on at dancing, singing, or dramatic spectacles.
8. Do not affect the use of garlands, scents, unguents, or ornaments.
9. Do not use high or broad beds.
10. Do not accept gold or silver.[21]

The first four of these precepts are the same as the first four vows undertaken by the Jaina monks, but instead of the extremely comprehensive fifth vow of the Jains there appears the precept against the use of intoxicants. It may be said that the Precepts illustrate the Middle Way between asceticism and self-indulgence in a specially concrete way; on the one hand self-indulgence in the pleasures of life is explicitly disavowed, and on the other the more extreme ascetic practices are not enjoined. Faithfulness in carrying out the Precepts was expected. If any monk broke any of them, he made public confession of his sin before the assembly of his chapter on the bi-monthly fast-days.

The first five of these injunctions (known as the Five Precepts) were prescribed for all lay-associates of the Order. The Buddha recognized that there were those who for one reason or another could not "give up the household life" but who were so sympathetic with the ideals of the Order that they should be brought into active association with it. He therefore made provision for the attachment of thousands of lay-associates to the Order, on the condition that they undertook to obey the Five Precepts, and evinced the spirit of helpfulness in promoting the growth and progress of the Order. It was largely through the lay-membership that the Order acquired its extensive property holdings. High-born laymen of the Kshatriya caste enthusiastically donated groves, parks, and monasteries to the Order.

Women clamored for admission, and the Buddha had at last, it is said, to overcome his reluctance to forming an order of nuns; but he is reported to have made the dry remark in private: "If, Ananda, women had not received permission to enter the Order, the pure religion would have lasted long, the good law would have stood fast a thousand years. But since they have received permission, it will now stand fast for only five hundred years." [22]

It seems well-attested that a fairly large group of relatives became monks and nuns. The Buddha's cousin, Ananda, stands out among all his followers as the perfect type of devoted disciple, ministering with untiring love to his teacher's personal needs and in constant attendance upon him. Another cousin, Devadatta, so utterly identified himself with the Order that he became guilty of an attempted schism, in the interest of greater strictness.

Forty-five years passed in the work of preaching, teaching, and constructive planning. At last, on a journey to an obscure town, by the name of Kusinara, northeast of Benares, in his eightieth year, he came to his end. He took his mid-day meal in the house of Chunda, a goldsmith. The pork he ate (or, as some would have it, the dish of truffles)

Gautama Buddha passing into Nirvana at death; Ananda mourning at the right. (From Coomaraswami, *History of Indian and Indonesian Art*)

brought on an attack of mortal illness. He had not gone the full distance toward Kusinara when death claimed him as he lay down upon the ground between two sal trees.

II   THE TEACHINGS OF THE BUDDHA

Philosophical Conceptions

Paradoxically enough, one must begin study of the Buddha's philosophical conceptions with the observation that he rejected philosophical speculation ("the way of knowledge": *jnana marga*) as the way of salvation. Purely metaphysical issues were to him of little moment. He had an intensely practical outlook, and such issues offended his common sense. He was not interested in speculative philosophy as long as so many humanly vital issues were at stake; his interest lay in another direction, in the realm now considered the province of psychology. The Buddhist records transmit his plain-spoken repudiation of certain then current problems in philosophy:

"Bear always in mind what it is that I have not elucidated, and what it is that I have elucidated. And what have I not elucidated? I have not elucidated that the world is eternal; I have not elucidated that the world is not eternal; I have not elucidated that the world is finite; I have not elucidated that the world is infinite; I have not elucidated that the soul and the body are identical; I have not elucidated that the monk who has attained (the arahat) exists after death; I have not elucidated that the arahat does not exist after death; I have not elucidated that the arahat both exists and does not exist after death; I have not elucidated that the arahat neither exists nor does not exist after death.° And why have I not elucidated this? Because this profits not, nor has to do with the fundamentals of religion; therefore I have not elucidated this."

The Buddha's psychological interest is expressed in the next sentences attributed to him:

"And what have I elucidated? Misery have I elucidated; the origin of misery have I elucidated; the cessation of misery have I elucidated; and the path leading to the cessation of misery have I elucidated. And why have I elucidated this? Because this does profit, has to do with the fundamentals of religion, and tends to absence of passion, to knowledge, supreme wisdom, and Nirvana." [23]

° The Buddha here refers to what has been called the Indian *tetralemma*: after death, does the arahat exist, or not exist, or both exist and not exist, or neither exist nor not exist?

In other words, the basic difficulty of man is not so much in the way he philosophizes, as in the way he feels. What thinking he does he ought to devote to understanding and controlling his desires; in them is where the chief danger lurks.

The Buddha also rejected religious devotion (*bhakti*) as a way of salvation. His position was the sort of atheism we have already noted in Mahavira. He believed that the universe abounded in gods, goddesses, demons, and other nonhuman powers and agencies; but all were without exception finite, subject to death and rebirth. In the absence, then, of some transcendent, eternal Being, older than the Creation, and the Maker of heaven and earth, who could direct men's destinies and hear and grant human wishes, prayer, to the Buddha, was of no avail; he at least did not resort to it. For similar reasons he did not put any reliance on the Vedas, or on practice of their nature worship, or on the performance of their rituals as a way of redemption; nor would he countenance going to the Brahmins as priests. (These are among the chief reasons why Buddhism is a heresy to the devout Hindu.) Like Mahavira, the Buddha showed each disciple how to rely for salvation upon himself, on his own powers, focussed upon redemption by psychological self-culture.

Here was the strictest sort of humanism in religion.

But while the Buddha uprooted from his world-view most of what is commonly regarded as distinctive of religion as such, he held to two major Hindu doctrines that have religious implications; he believed in the Law of Karma and in the transmigration of souls. He modified both of these doctrines, however.

He gave the Law of Karma more flexibility than most later philosophers were wont to do. In his view a man of any caste or class could experience so complete a change of heart or disposition as to escape the full consequence of sins committed in previous existences; the Law of Karma operated remorselessly and without remission of one jot or tittle of the full recompense upon all who go on in the old way—the way of unchecked desire; but it could not lay hold upon a man completely changed, who had achieved arahatship, "the state of him that is worthy." The arahats "who by steadfast mind have become exempt from evil desire" may feel assured that "their old karma is exhausted; no new karma is being produced; their hearts are free from the longing after a future life; the cause of their existence being destroyed, and no new longing springing up within them, they, the wise, are extinguished at death like a lamp": [24] there will be no rebirth for them.

It is those who are not emancipated from "the will-to-live-and-have" (tanha) who will be reborn.

The Buddha held firmly to the doctrine of rebirth, but the form which he gave to that doctrine has puzzled men ever since. It seems he held that rebirth takes place without any actual soul-substance passing over from one existence to another. Later formulators of this doctrine declared, that after analysis of the human person one must conclude: "There is no ego here to be found." [25] This is one of the obscurest and profoundest points in the Buddha's system of thought. Over this doctrine his expositors have agonized and quarreled for centuries.*

Instead of the age-old faith that an imperishable and substantial soul goes over from one existence to another, its direction and status absolutely determined from stage to stage by the inexorable causal nexus of the Law of Karma, the Buddha maintained a doctrine that seems surprisingly objective and modern. (One might point out some analogies to Behaviorism in psychology.) His reflection upon his own personality led him to deny that any of its elements had any permanence. What men have called the continuing entity of the immortal soul is really to be resolved back into an impermanent aggregation or composite of constantly changing states of being or *skandhas*. These skandhas are five in number: (1) the body, (2) sense-perception, (3) the feelings, (4) the *sankharas* (hard to translate; literally, "predispositions"; the nearest modern equivalent would be a lumping together of "the instincts and the subconscious"), and (5) reason. It is the union of these that constitutes the individual. As long as they are held together the individual functions as a single being, lives, and has a history. But each component is in perpetual flux. The body changes from day to day only a little less obviously than the mental states. At death the union is dissolved and the skandhas disperse.

What is known to us as the ego is therefore but an appearance, merely the name we give to the functional unity which subsists when the five changing skandhas set up that complex interplay which constitutes the personal life of the individual. Only the ceaseless flow of Being itself, of which these changing states are signs, has reality.

With this view of the nature of the human individual, how could the Buddha hold to the doctrine of transmigration of souls, as in fact he did? He could not contend that any substantial entity ("soul" or "psyche") passed over from one existence to another; that theory was

---

* There is perhaps good reason to think that Buddha did not teach so negative a view with regard to the existence of soul-substance as the later formulators of his teachings supposed. See Mrs. Rhys Davids' *A Manual of Buddhism* and H. G. Jennings' *The Vedantic Buddhism of the Buddha* for a defence of this thesis. The following account assumes that this thesis is not sufficiently proved.

precluded by his analysis. He taught, therefore, that all that passes over to the next life is the karma-laden character structure going on from one life to the next. It is as though, for example, a seal were pressed upon wax. What, in such case, passes from the former to the latter? Only the characters engraved on the seal and retained by the wax. Nothing substantial. So in respect to rebirth, at the end of one existence an individual will possess definite characteristics hardened into a kind of rigidity; but at the moment of dissolution these characteristics are passed over to the soft wax of a new existence in another womb. Nothing substantial passes over, yet there is a definite connection between one complex of elements and the next. Buddhist lore abounds in similes which aid in clarifying the point. Several hundred years after the Buddha the matter was regarded thus:

Said the king [King Milinda]: "Bhante Nagasena, does rebirth take place without anything transmigrating?"

"Yes, your majesty, rebirth takes place without anything transmigrating."

"How, bhante Nagasena, does rebirth take place without anything transmigrating? Give an illustration."

"Suppose, your majesty, a man were to light a light from another light; pray, would the one light have passed over to the other light?"

"Nay, verily, bhante."

"In exactly the same way, your majesty, does rebirth take place without anything transmigrating."

"Give another illustration."

"Do you remember, your majesty, having learnt, when you were a boy, some verse or other from your professor of poetry?"

"Yes, bhante."

"Pray, your majesty, did the verse pass over (transmigrate) to you from your teacher?"

"Nay, verily, bhante."

"In exactly the same way, your majesty, does rebirth take place without anything transmigrating."

"You are an able man, bhante Nagasena." [26]

In other words, as one process leads to another, from cause to effect, so human personality in one existence is the direct cause of the type of individuality which appears in the next. One text explains it thus:

This consciousness being in its series inclined toward the object by desire, and impelled toward it by karma, like a man who swings himself over a ditch by means of a rope hanging from a tree on the hither bank, quits its first resting place and continues (in the next existence) to subsist in dependence on objects of sense and other things. . . . Here the former consciousness, from its passing out of existence, is called passing away, and the latter, from its being reborn into a new existence, is called rebirth. But it is understood that this latter consciousness did not come to the present existence from the previous one, and also that it is only to causes contained in the old existence,—namely to karma called the predispositions, to inclination, an object, etc.—that its present appearance is due. . . . As illustrations of how consciousness does not come over from the last existence into the present, and how it springs up by means of causes belonging to the former existence here may serve echoes, light, the impressions of a seal, and reflections in a mirror. For as echoes, light, the impressions of a seal, and shadows have sound, etc., for their causes, and exist without having come from elsewhere, just so it is with this mind.[27]

This does not mean, the Buddha said, that he who is born is different from the preceding person who has passed his karma on at death to him; nor does it mean that he is the same. Such an issue is as meaningless as to say that the body is different from the self or that the self and body are the same. Since there is no permanent ego-entity, and everything is composite and in flux, discussions as to whether the successive personalities in a continuous series of rebirths are the same or different lack point; it is better simply to know that a kind of inner necessity leads to the origination of one life as the total result of the having-been-ness of another, and that the connection is as close as that of cause and effect, or as the transfer of flame from one wick to another. It is difficult to construe, but the fundamental fact remains—that what a man does and thinks now carries over into tomorrow and tomorrow and tomorrow.

Interesting as this astute discrimination of distinctions is, the implications for the Buddha's larger conceptions of life and destiny are more important. The conclusions involved seem to be these: Wherever we observe it, the living world, whether about us or within ourselves, is constantly in flux, in a state of endless becoming; there is no central, planning world-self, no sovereign Person in the heavens holding all together in unity; there is only the ultimate impersonal unity of Being itself, whose peace enfolds the individual self when it ceases to call itself "I" and dissolves in the featureless purity of Nirvana, as a drop of spray is merged in its mother sea. The permanency of the world is an illusion, and this also holds true of the empirical ego; there remain for human experience only processes of change and decay, of becoming and passing away, of appearing and disappearing.

The Buddha is said to have talked about all this in his Sermon at the Deer Park in Benares, when he spoke of the *turning of the Wheel*.*

---

* He himself also started a wheel turning—the wheel of the doctrine (*dharma*), and consequently his sermon is commonly called "The Setting in Motion of the Wheel of the Doctrine."

His followers called the symbol to which he was referring the Kalacakra ("the Wheel of Time"). Taking their clues from his teaching, later followers portrayed it (see end paper) as having at its hub the three causes of pain, the serpent of ill-will or hatred, the pig of ignorance with its snout forever searching the ground, and the dove (or cock-bird) of lust or uncontrolled desire. The segments of the Wheel divide off the six states of rebirth: existence as a warring demi-god, as an animal, as a dweller in hell, as a human being, as a god in heaven, and as a happy soul in a Buddhist paradise. The whole is held in the grip of the Demon of Change and Impermanence. Probably neither the Buddha nor his early disciples were thus explicit; but the Wheel represents the unceasing becoming and passing away of the states of existence to which the Buddha was so sensitive.

It is likely that the Buddha spoke much more explicitly and in detail about the causes operating in the turning of the wheel. The Buddhist books call this the *Chain of Causation* or *Dependent Origination*. The reasoning goes like this: the first and most fundamental of the causes of the turning of the wheel is ignorance, especially taking

Gautama Buddha preaching to his disciples and turning the Wheel of the Law—the Dharma, symbolized at lower left. (From *Archives Photographiques*)

at face value the reality of the self and the permanence of the world. From this basic fault arises the original set or bent of the personality, the predispositions (sankharas). Thus predisposed, the personality becomes conscious of or cognizes the world and itself. This in turn determines the distinctive traits one has ("name and form"; the individuality one is known by). Individuality expresses itself causally in a particular exercise of the five senses and the mind. These in turn make contact with other selves and with things. Thence arises feeling. Feeling originates desire (*tanha* or craving). From craving comes clinging to existence. Clinging to existence entails the process of becoming. Becoming brings on a new state of being not like the one preceding it (a new birth of being during life as well as at death). Finally, such a new birth inevitably entails its own "old age, disease, and death."

These convictions were not encouraging. The Buddha discerned in them his basic reasons for withdrawal from the world. As he seems to have taught, all "composite beings" able to reason suffer from these three flaws vexing their existence: transitoriness (*anicca*), the ultimate unreality of the self or soul (*anatta*), and sorrow (*dukkha*). The third aspect seemed to follow remorselessly upon the other two. The impermanence in everything that appears to exist, the ceaseless change, the endless becoming that is never quite being, filled him with weariness, a real misery; he longed for peace, the cessation of desire, for some state of consciousness with enough permanence to guarantee deliverance from "the Wheel" of perpetual and painful becoming. This, of course, is all over again the immemorial desire of India; here, however, the thought process moves through obscure feeling states. It is *painful*, the Buddha felt, to experience continuance in a stream of consciousness made up mostly of states of incompletion.

"Now pleasant sensations, unpleasant sensations, indifferent sensations, Ananda, are transitory, are due to causes, originate by dependence, and are subject to decay, disappearance, effacement, and cessation. While this person is experiencing a pleasant sensation, he thinks, 'This is my Ego.' And after the cessation of this same pleasant sensation, he thinks, 'My Ego has passed away.' While he is experiencing an unpleasant sensation, he thinks, 'This is my Ego.' And after the cessation of this same unpleasant sensation, he thinks, 'My Ego has passed away.' And while he is experiencing an indifferent sensation, he thinks, 'This is my Ego.' And after the cessation of this same indifferent sensation, he thinks, 'My Ego has passed away.' " [28]

So the Buddha seems to have felt that it was human, no doubt, but it was foolish, it was stupid and ignorant, to cling with longing, as most people do, to sentient life and its pitifully few pleasures, when all through life the pain of change is so predominant. This will-to-live-and-have, this "thirst," this "clinging" to the world and its objects, was, it seemed, far and away the most striking of the characteristics that pass from one existence to the next; and if it could be made to die away, the chief cause of rebirth would be removed. *If it could be made to die away, it should be made to do so!*

To this conclusion the Buddha's profound psychological analysis of life and personality conducted him. In his ethical teaching he sought to show men how to answer the questions raised by it.

Ethics

The fundamental ethical problem to which the Buddha addressed himself was: In what way ought one to live so as to obtain surcease of pain and suffering, bring to an end the unwise will-to-live-and-have, and finally attain the fullness of the joy of liberation?

The answer to this problem he compressed into the Four Noble Truths. In the official report of his first sermon—in the Deer Park at Benares to the five ascetics—they are given thus:

"This, O Bhikkhus, is the Noble Truth of Suffering: Birth is suffering; decay is suffering; illness is suffering; death is suffering. Presence of objects we hate is suffering; separation from objects we love is suffering; not to obtain what we desire is suffering. Briefly, the fivefold clinging to existence [by means of the five *skandhas*] is suffering.

"This, O Bhikkhus, is the Noble Truth of the Cause of Suffering: Thirst, that leads to rebirth, accompanied by pleasure and lust, finding its delight here and there. (This thirst is threefold) namely, thirst for pleasure, thirst for existence, thirst for prosperity.

"This, O Bhikkhus, is the Noble Truth of the Cessation of Suffering: (it ceases with) the complete cessation of this thirst—a cessation which consists in the absence of every passion,—with the abandoning of this thirst, with the doing away with it, with the deliverance from it, with the destruction of desire.

"This, O Bhikkhus, is the Noble Truth of the Path which leads to the cessation of suffering: that holy eightfold Path, that is to say, Right Belief, Right Aspiration, Right Speech, Right Conduct, Right Means of Livelihood, Right Endeavor, Right Mindfulness, Right Meditation." [29]

Analysis of these words discloses two facts: that the Buddha's ethical system balances its stress on the life of negation with more positive counsels, and that it is not nearly so pessimistic as Western thought has been accustomed to construe it to be.° It seems, in fact, that the Buddha does not condemn *all* desire, does not say that *all* existence is misery. There are good values in desire, if we may put it so, as well as bad values; and the wise man knows (has overcome ignorance to a sufficient degree to know) how to discriminate between them.

1. The first, and negative, principle in the Buddha's ethics requires *strict non-indulgence of the desires known to cause suffering.* But how will one know they are desires of this sort? The first three of the Four Noble Truths furnish the criterion. Reduced to the simplest form, they produce this formula: Where life becomes miserable, the misery is always found to spring from indulgence of some form of desire; hence *such* desire is to be abandoned, done away with, uprooted. Or, in one sentence, any form of desire whose indulgence entails misery is to be overcome.

So put, the ethical thought of the Buddha strikes a note of clear common sense. It is not from this *principle* that Western minds can intelligently dissent, it is from the *application* of this principle in the further reaches of Buddhist ethics. For in such application the Buddha goes far in a negative direction. Some of his ethical judgments are common enough in most ethical systems. There is widespread agreement among the ethical philosophers, for example, that pursuit of the sensuously pleasant as an end in itself is misery-producing. But while the Buddha agrees with this common enough observation, he advises far more than the abandonment of sensuous desires. Ownership of houses and lands, love of parents, wives, children, or friends—these are also ultimately woe-bringing, he taught. There is constant worry and unsatisfied desire in each case. If one loves his wife, then death, separation, the life of poverty, sickness, hundreds of situations are painful; the very intensity of love itself is painful. So it is with children, aged parents, and even with friends. "Let therefore no man love anything; loss of the beloved is evil. Those who love nothing and hate nothing have no fetters." [30]

The Buddha's attitude is best presented through illustration. The legend runs that one day a grandmother appeared before him in tears. She had just lost a very dear grandchild. The Buddha looked at her gravely. "How many people are there in this city of Savatthi?" he asked, with apparent irrelevance. Upon receiving her reply, he came to the point: "Would you like to have as many children and grandchildren as

---

° That the Buddha's negativism had a positive goal—the attainment of "blessedness" or spiritual happiness—is now recognized. See Mrs. Rhys Davids, *op. cit. passim.*

there are people in Savatthi?" The old lady, still weeping, cried out yes, yes. "But," the Buddha gently remonstrated, "if you had as many children and grandchildren as there are people in Savatthi, you would have to weep every day, for people die daily there." The old lady thought a moment; he was right! As she prepared to go away comforted, she carried with her the Buddha's saying: "Those who have a hundred dear ones have a hundred woes; those who have ninety dear ones have ninety woes; . . . those who have one dear one have one woe; those who hold nothing dear have no woe." [31]

If this story be true, then the Buddha would have approved, had he been alive to hear the story, of the young monk who, after being gone from home a long while, returned to his birthplace, to occupy a cell built by his father for passing monks, and to beg food daily at his mother's door. His mother did not recognize him in his monk's garb and emaciated condition. For three months he took food from her hands without announcing himself, and then quietly departed. When his mother heard afterwards who he was, she worshipped, saying: "Methinks, the Blessed One must have had in mind a body of priests like my son . . . This man ate for three months in the house of the mother who bore him, and never said, 'I am thy son, and thou art my mother.' O the wonderful man!" And the Buddhist account concludes: "For such a one, mother and father are no hindrances." [32]

The consistent Buddhist will exercise restraint even over his attachment to the Blessed One, the Buddha himself.

The venerable Sariputta said this: "As I was meditating in seclusion there arose the consideration: Is there now anything in the whole world wherein a change would give rise in me to grief, lamenting, despair? And methought, No, there is no such thing." Then the venerable Ananda said to the venerable Sariputta: "But the Master—would not the loss of him give rise in you to grief, lamenting, despair?" "Not even the loss of him, Friend Ananda. Nevertheless, I should feel thus: O may not the mighty one, O may not the Master so gifted, so wonderful, be taken from us!" [33]

Also, of course, all self-regard, all emotional bias in behalf of the empirical self, must be entirely overcome. The self-defensive and self-assertive attitudes are especially ruinous to peace.*

* Among the qualities of the monk are those which Kassapa exhibited, when, making his rounds for alms about the streets, he met a leper, and, in order to let the leper acquire merit by almsgiving, gave him the opportunity to cast a morsel into his own outstretched bowl. Though in the process "a finger, mortifying, broke and fell," Kassapa felt no disgust, but, in his cell once more, ate with undisturbed equanimity the food that lay beside the leprous finger in the bowl. [34]

Like the Jains, the Buddhists determined to renounce all attachments disturbing to absolute peace of mind and soul. To them salvation, here and hereafter, meant just this, a state of perfectly painless peace and joy, a psychologically achieved freedom from misery of any kind.

This explains why Buddhist literature makes so many lists of things to be avoided, desires to be given up, bonds to be broken: "The Three Intoxications," "The Five Hindrances," "The Ten Fetters: by which beings are bound to the wheel of existence," etc. That these lists are rather exhaustive is evident in the analysis of the Ten Fetters, as follows: (1) belief in the existence of the self, (2) doubt, (3) trust in ceremonies of good works, (4) lust, (5) anger, (6) desire for rebirth in worlds of form, (7) desire for rebirth in formless worlds, (8) pride, (9) self-righteousness, and (10) ignorance.[35] This list, it will be seen, covers much ground.

2. But freedom from "fetters" obviously cannot be attained by negative means only. *It is by living toward the attainment of the right or truly joy-bringing desires that one completely transcends and erases from consciousness the kinds of desire that produce suffering.*

Consider in this connection the fourth of the Four Noble Truths. The principle expressed is this: desires whose indulgence will not result in increase of misery but rather in a decrease of it (or in entire doing away of misery) are desires which conduct steadily to salvation, the ultimate state in which *all* desires are swallowed up in the utter peace of no-desire.

It was in applying this principle that the Buddha formulated the *Noble Eightfold Path,* "the path that leads to no-desire."

The first step in the Eightfold Path is *right belief;* that is, belief in the Four Noble Truths and the view of life implied in them. The next step, *right aspiration or purpose,* is reached by resolving to overcome sensuality, have the right love of others, harm no living being, and suppress all misery-producing desires generally. The third and fourth steps, *right speech* and *right conduct,* are defined as non-indulgence in loose or hurtful talk or in ill-will; one must love all creatures with the right sort of love in word and deed. *Right means of livelihood,* the fifth step, means choosing the proper occupation of one's time and energies, obtaining one's livelihood in ways consistent with Buddhist principles. The sixth step, *right effort,* implies untiring and unremitting intellectual alertness in discriminating between wise and unwise desires and attachments; while *right mindfulness,* the seventh step, is made possible by well-disciplined thought habits during long hours spent in attention to helpful topics. Lastly, *right meditation* or *absorption* refers to the climax of all the other processes, the final attainment of the trance states that are the advanced stages on the road to arahatship (sainthood) and the assurance of passage at death into Nirvana, the state of quiescence, all karma consumed, and rebirth at an end forever.

Two things ought to be noted about the steps in the Eightfold Path: first, that they fall under three headings—understanding, morals, and concentration; secondly, that they are so planned as to lead progressively to arahatship and thus finally to Nirvana. Of the three groups into which the steps of the Path fall, the first two groups are natural enough. Understanding of the theory, and practice of the ethic, of Buddhism are certainly necessary, if the Buddhist believer is to justify his faith at all. But the third group leads onto a different level. Here Buddhism is most akin to Brahmanism. The goal of these steps is the pure ecstasy that follows on meditative exercises. By them one turns away in aversion from the unhappy world to spiritual realities beyond sense. In early Buddhism, part of this mental discipline consisted in certain processes of thought which the Buddha himself recommended: for example, deepening one's aversion to life by thinking concentratedly of the perishableness of the body and of the body's loathsome features, or by analyzing the disgusting changes wrought by death in the most beautiful human body, and then in grateful relief turning to the thought of the permanent and the eternal. When this kind of thinking failed, some of the early Buddhists turned to *yoga* methods, in the hope of bringing on ecstasy psychologically. They breathed in certain ways, stared at bright objects, repeated certain formulas, and so on. The Buddha condemned giving too high a value to such technical means to ecstasy. Arahatship, he held, could be reached without resort to any special practices of the more technical sort. It was heretical, in fact, to seek entrance into Nirvana by the cultivation of ecstasy alone. The way to "bliss" was not the way of merely formalistic procedure, it was the way of ethical self-culture, the moral reconstitution of personality. Here the Buddha took a common-sense position, once more, which differentiates him clearly from many of his own later followers.

The steps of the Path, we have said, lead to *arahatship*. This is the state of "him who is worthy," of him "who has reached the end of the Eightfold Path." The *arahat* is the Buddhist saint. He has conquered "the three intoxications"—sensuality, ignorance, and the "thirst" leading to rebirth; and he enjoys the "higher insight" (*sambodhi*) with its mingling of joy, energy, calm, benevolence, and concentration. His joy is deep, because he has already had a foretaste of Nirvana in the trance of his enlightenment, and for the balance of his days he will know the bliss of liberation from misery-bringing desires. He has reached self-fulfillment—that is, of the higher self. His energy is purely spiritual. He no longer feels suffering, and takes no pleasure in earthly joys; he is able to say, "I do not wish for death, I do not wish for life." In this state he awaits with calm contentment and without apprehension the "putting out of his lamp of life"—the entrance into final Nirvana at death. Just what this final state will be, he does not greatly care. He is now no longer unhappy. As previously noted, the Buddha refused to give any decision as to whether an arahat either exists after death, or does not exist. Nirvana seems a completely negative conception. It means the end, "the blowing out," of existence, so that there will be no more transmigration; and since the *skandhas* of the last earthly existence are dispersed and there is no ego remaining over, it would seem that Nirvana is "annihilation." But the Buddha would not say that. He did not know whether that was true. All he knew, and all he cared to know, was that Nirvana was the end of painful becoming; it was the final peace; it was an eternal state of being. And so, though our Western minds, trained to logic and analytic thinking, boggle at it, he declared that Nirvana was so much more than merely a negative condition that it was a state of happiness, "bliss."

But we have not completed our description of the arahat. One of his outstanding qualities is benevolence. He is the Buddhist ideal of what one may become and ought to be. He is magnanimous; he overflows with good will. To grasp this is very important for our understanding of the later history of Buddhism. Although fundamentally, the Buddhist seeker is bent on *his own* self-culture, *his own* blessedness, and is often encouraged, in the words of the Buddha himself, to "wander alone like a rhinoceros," [36] forsaking houses and lands and kindred because they hinder him, nevertheless, he is charged to love all mankind without exception.* That the Buddha himself possessed the quality of compassion for all men is evident in a life devoted to preaching and teaching. Though he strove to sunder every personal tie to particular individuals based on emotion, on the ground, as we have seen, that any such tie is misery-producing, he charged his disciples to love all mankind with a mother's love.

"As a mother, even at the risk of her own life, protects her son, her only son, so let him cultivate love without measure toward all beings. Let him cultivate towards the whole world—above, below, around—a heart of love unstinted, unmixed with the sense of differing or opposing interests." [37]

* This account assumes that J. G. Jennings' suggestion in *The Vedantic Buddhism of the Buddha* (Oxford, 1948) that Buddha's egolessness included the utter abandonment of self in altruism is a one-sided reading of the early texts.

It became a part of the Buddhist self-schooling to sit quietly in a concentrated effort to call forth from the depths of the heart a love so comprehensive that it embraced every living being in the universe and at the same time so intense that it was unlimited. It was by such loving thought that the Buddhist monk prepared himself for his evangelistic task.

But here we are brought to a pause. Is this warmth of redemptive love consistent with the cloister-seeking motive that is so primary in the life of the monk yearning for Nirvana? How can love issue from anyone engrossed in his own salvation? The question is a serious one. That there is at least a practical inconsistency here was recognized early in the history of Buddhism. In fact, it led eventually, as we shall see, to the fundamental division within Buddhism between the Mahayana and the Hinayana. But benevolence had a place in the full theory of the Buddha. What he evidently meant was that the love which his disciples should cultivate for all mankind should be general or universal in character, the love of men as Man. This love of men (one may put it, the love of everyone, but not the love of any *one*) can be the source only of high and disinterested joy. It is not like the love of one individual for another, which is a relation of dependence and passionate attachment, and therefore fraught with the miseries attendant upon unhappy chance and change; it is the love of Man, and its benevolent ministry to individuals *as representatives of mankind* can be unstinted and even maternal in quality. Kept on a high, impersonal level, it can bring no pain; rather, it may remain pure and unalloyed through every circumstance; nothing can check it, and no sorrow can enter it. Bestowed on good and evil alike without discrimination, it need not suffer a change in its warmth and saintly quality by any knowledge of good or evil. And it is not affected by the response it meets; through every rebuff, it remains inalienable.

The secret of this patience and good will is thus explained in some of the opening sentences of the *Dhammapada*:

> If a man speaks or acts with a pure thought, happiness follows him, like a shadow that never leaves him. "He abused me, he beat me, he defeated me, he robbed me"—in those who harbor such thoughts hatred will never cease,—in those who do not harbor such thoughts hatred will cease. For hatred does not cease by hatred at any time; hatred ceases by love, this is an old rule.[38]

And in the *Majjhima Nikaya* occur these words, expressive of the same lofty and inalterable good will:

If some one curses you, you must repress all resentment, and make the firm determination, "My mind shall not be disturbed, no angry word shall escape my lips, I shall remain kind and friendly, with loving thoughts and no secret spite." If then you are attacked with fists, with stones, with sticks, with swords, you must still repress all resentment and preserve a loving mind with no secret spite.[39]

The right kind of love as the Buddha himself conceived of it is best illustrated in a story. One of his most promising disciples wished to preach, it is said, among a certain wild jungle folk. The Buddha, seeking to test him, held with him this conversation:

"But, O Punna, the men of that country are violent, cruel and savage. When they become angry at you and do you harm, what will you think then?"

"I shall think them truly good and kind folk, for whilst they speak angry and insolent words, they refrain from striking or stoning me."

"They are very violent folk, Punna. What if they strike or stone you?"

"I shall think them kind and good not to smite me with staff and sword." . . .

"And what if they kill you?"

"I shall think them kind and good indeed who free me from this vile body with so little pain."

"Well said, Punna, well said. With your great gift of patience, you may indeed essay this task. Go, Punna, yourself saved, save others." [40]

Though one must grant a fine ethical quality to this inalienable magnanimity, the difficulty for Westerners, and for the Buddhists themselves from the first, has been this: such love is the product of an almost infinite withdrawal from everyday life. It is not a love whose chief mark is selfless self-identification with others. This was to come later. Rather, it is impartial good will on the part of one who has saved himself and wishes to teach others how to save themselves too.

That this love was so guarded and withdrawn was its historic weakness. In Buddhism's aftermath, life and the compassion it arouses were to prove too strong for the bridle of prudential control which the Buddha devised for their restraint.

But to let the matter rest here would be to do an injustice to the founder of a great faith. We should be giving less than full credit to the true humanity of the man, and that of his followers, unless we observed, as we do here, and with admiration, that his, and their, *practice* was so much more generous than their cautious world-denying theory. How true this was of the followers we are about to see.

SUGGESTIONS FOR FURTHER READING

Arnold, Sir Edwin. *The Light of Asia.* Any edition

Babbit, Irving. *The Dhammapada—with an Essay on Buddha and the Occident.* Oxford, 1936

Brewster, E. H. *Life of Gotama the Buddha* (compiled from the Pali canon). K. Paul, Trench, Trubner, 1926

Burtt, E. A., ed. *The Teachings of the Compassionate Buddha.* Mentor pb, 1955

Carus, Paul. *The Gospel of the Buddha.* Compiled from ancient records. Open Court, 1917

Lord Chalmers, trans. *Further Dialogues of the Buddha.* Oxford, 1926

Conze, Edward, trans. *Buddhist Scriptures.* Penguin pb, 1959

Coomaraswamy, A. K. *Buddha and the Gospel of Buddhism.* Putnam, 1916

Coomaraswamy, A. K. and Horner, I. B. *The Living Thoughts of Gotama the Buddha.* Cassell, 1949

Cowell, E. B., trans. *The Jataka.* Cambridge, 1895–1907

Davids, T. W. Rhys, trans. *Dialogues of the Buddha.* Oxford, 1899–1921

Davids, Mrs. T. W. Rhys. *Buddhism, A Study of the Buddhist Norm.* Henry Holt, 1912

————. *A Manual of Buddhism.* Macmillan, 1932

————. *Psalms of the Brethren.* Oxford, 1909

————. *Psalms of the Sisters.* Oxford, 1913

Hamilton, C. H., ed. *Buddhism, a Religion of Infinite Compassion.* Selections from Buddhist literature. Liberal Arts Press pb, 1952

Jennings, J. G. *The Vedantic Buddhism of the Buddha.* Oxford, 1948

Oldenburg, Hermann. *Buddha: His Life, His Doctrine, His Order.* Trans. Wm. Hoey. Williams and Norgate, 1882

Pratt, J. B. *The Pilgrimage of Buddhism* (chapters I–V). Macmillan, 1928

Saunders, Kenneth J. *Gotama Buddha.* A biography based on the canonical books of the Theravadin. Association Press, 1920

Thomas, E. J. *History of Buddhist Thought.* K. Paul, Trench, Trubner, 1931

————. *The Life of Buddha as Legend and History.* K. Paul, Trench, Trubner, 1931

Valée Poussin, L. de la. *The Way to Nirvana.* Cambridge, 1917

Warren, Henry Clarke. *Buddhism in Translation.* Harvard University Press, 1922

6 The Religious Development of Buddhism: The Return to Optimism

THE FOLLOWERS OF THE BUDDHA HAD WHAT HE OF COURSE COULD NOT have: they had a keen-minded, great-hearted founder to believe in and follow. It was natural that they should magnify his religious meaning for them, as indeed they did. They endowed him with a supernatural origin and intention that made him one of the world's grandest religious figures, and they surrounded him with a great company of supporting supernatural beings equally concerned as he was for human redemption from selfishness and pain.

Whether the Buddha's outlook was religious in the strict sense is certainly debatable. His chief concern, some commentators say, was with measures to solve the problems of the self rather than with measures to secure favorable conditions in the world outside. Religion in the sense of a hopeful appeal to the gods to alter one's circumstances was irrelevant. Heinrich Hackmann has pointed out that in original Buddhism the gods are virtually dethroned; their heavenly seats become merely transitory places of reward; no deity, in the complete sense of the word, exists; worship seems an absurdity; prayer has no place; to know or not to know becomes the only primary concern; and true knowledge can be found only in the narrow circle of monks or anchorites. "The great world outside is excluded. It must be left behind. The path to salvation leads not into the world and through the world, but

195

away from it. In a life of seclusion each individual must take upon himself the heavy task of working out his own salvation by self-discipline, self-purification, study, thought, meditation, and concentration." And, though the philosophical and abstract character of original Buddhism commended it to superior minds far beyond the bounds of India, "it would seem as if a special temperament were necessary to appreciate its profound appeal. Buddhism, in its original form, found no response among the masses." [1]

But the masses became interested—secondarily in the teaching, primarily in *the man*. Original Buddhism would not have had so great an effect on the history of religion in the Orient, if the coolly rational philosophy of the sage of the Sakyas had not been mediated through a warm and friendly personality that could be adored. Fortunately for the future of Buddhism, its founder balanced the arahat ideal of self-salvation with the ideal of compassionate good will toward all living beings, and practiced that compassion himself. Thus there grew up after him a cult that took refuge in *him*, the compassionate as well as enlightened one, even more than it did in his teaching, so difficult to understand and practice.

When the masses became interested, they would not be denied. Original Buddhism came to them as a philosophy, but they turned it into a religion to meet their need. By a process such as we have seen in Jainism, and will see at work in other great religions, the common people laid hold of the man behind the teaching, saw divinity in him, felt a redemptive intention in his coming among men, and adoringly surrendered themselves to him. In India, and beyond India, the common people who espoused Buddhism let the intellectuals, with their unusual mental gifts, go on constructing their profound and abstruse theories, and very generally admired them for their gifts, but they themselves engaged in something much more to their liking, and much more satisfying to their deepest needs, the religious development of Buddhism.

This is a simplification of the matter, of course. The process was historically complex, and was aided throughout, very materially, by the intellectuals who shared the feeling of the masses.

The rather odd fact is that there ultimately developed within Buddhism so many forms of religious organization, cultus, and belief, that it is difficult at times to know where the Buddhist element is. One must agree with the comment that such great changes even in the fundamentals of religion have been introduced, that Buddhism as a whole is really, like Hinduism, a family of religions rather than a single religion. But families have a likeness; and if anything can be called the family likeness in these later developments, it is optimism restored, in one sense or another, to the heart of what was originally a way of liberation dominated by a sense of radical human misery.

I THE SPREAD OF BUDDHISM IN INDIA AND SOUTH-EAST ASIA

The First Two Centuries in India

During the first two centuries after the Buddha's death his doctrines found wide acceptance within the basin of the Ganges. Not only did the body of monks grow, but the lay adherents increased even more rapidly, and included in their number many members of the ruling classes.

The tradition has it that immediately after the Buddha's death five hundred arahats, under the leadership of Kassapa, gathered to spend the rainy season at Rajagaha, and there recited and chanted together the precepts now found in the *Tripitaka*. Whether this be so or not, the teachings of the Buddha were early fixed in the repetitious forms of oral tradition.

When were they reduced to writing? The tradition is certainly untrue in maintaining that the monks of the First Council recited the present contents of the *Tripitaka*. (For example, that Ananda, the Buddha's cousin and loving attendant, recited the whole of the *Sutta Pitaka*, and Upali, another prominent disciple, the *Vinaya Pitaka*.) Probably several centuries passed before the oral tradition took form as the books of the Pali canon.° When finally reduced to writing, they were divided into "three baskets" (which is what Tripitaka means), namely, the *Vinaya Pitaka*, or Monastic Rules, the *Sutta* (Sanskrit Sutra) *Pitaka* or Discourses, and, last to be composed, the *Abhidamma* (Sanskrit Abhidharma) *Pitaka* or Supplement to the Doctrines. The second is the most important, because the principal voice heard in the discourses is that of the Buddha himself. It is subdivided into the *Digha Nikaya* (The Longer Discourses), the *Majjhima Nikaya* (The Shorter Discourses), the *Samyutta Nikaya* (The Connected Teachings), the *Anguttara Nikaya* (The Graduated Teachings), and the *Khuddaka Nikaya* (The Small

° Let us note again that it was part of the Buddhist rejection of Brahmanism that the early books were written in the Pali dialect instead of in the Brahmins' Sanskrit.

Book Collection). The last is a sort of miscellany which includes the very important moral treatise, the *Dhammapada* (Verses on the Law), the *Buddha Vamsa* giving the life of Gautama and his twenty-four predecessors, the *Theragatha* and the *Therigatha* (Hymns of the Elder Monks and Nuns), and the *Jataka,* a collection of some five hundred story-poems which are said to be recollections by the Buddha of his former lives while he was still a *bodhisattva* or future buddha.* The importance of the *Digha Nikaya* and *Majjhima Nikaya* is indicated by the number of times we have quoted them heretofore; for nowhere else do we get so clear an indication of the interests and character of the historical Buddha.

A century after the First Council, according to tradition, the Second Council met at Vesali and fought over the question of moderating the severity of the early Buddhist discipline. Many monks wished to be allowed a private, instead of the accustomed public, bi-monthly confession before the assembled chapter; and they also held out for comfortable beds, a second meal after midday, fermented liquors, and the individual possession of gold and silver; or so it is said. The result was a schism, the minority who wanted easier rules seceding to form a new order of their own, calling itself by the ambitious name the *Mahasanghikas* or "Members of the Great Sangha." The more orthodox monks were called the *Sthaviravadins* (Pali, Theravadins) or "Adherents of the Teaching of the Elders." It was the latter who survived to give their name to the older Buddhism, the Theravada (or Hinayana) Buddhism.

The process of inner division, once set going, produced no less than sixteen sects during the next three centuries, and might have brought disaster to the cause had not a major accession to the Buddhist faith given it India-wide prominence.

Asoka

In 273 B.C. there came to the throne of Magadha, which then dominated the whole of India, one of the greatest emperors in Indian history. His name was Asoka. He was the grandson of the famous Chandra-

---

* These books were soon made the basis of commentary. In the 5th century A.D. the learned Buddhaghosa of Ceylon compiled (or is said to have compiled) them into the *Vissuddhimagga* (The Way of Purification); he added a prose commentary on the poems of the *Jataka,* giving their complete setting in story form. An important treatise in supplementation of the *Tripitaka* is the *Milindapanha* (Questions of King Menander), quoted from in the last chapter.

gupta who, after overrunning the Macedonian garrisons left in India in 325 B.C. by Alexander the Great, went on to conquer most of the rest of India for himself. Asoka on his own part added to the great domain he inherited a fiercely resistant kingdom along the Bay of Bengal; but the bloodshed and suffering which he brought on the conquered people pricked a conscience already quickened by Buddhist teachers. He publicly embraced Buddhism as his faith, and became intensely interested in its propagation.

To express his "profound sorrow and regret" for the suffering he had caused by his warfare, he issued an edict, engraved upon enduring rock, for all to see, declaring that His Sacred Majesty felt remorse for the death and dislocation of so many hundreds of thousands of folk, and that thenceforth "if the hundredth part or the thousandth part" of all the people who were then slain, done to death, or carried away captive "were now to suffer the same fate, it would be a matter of regret to His Sacred Majesty." [2] His Sacred Majesty would henceforth practice gentleness, and bear all wrongs done to himself with all possible meekness and patience.

Realizing that the slaughter of animals for the imperial table was inconsistent with his Buddhism, Asoka cut down the palace consumption to two peacocks and one antelope daily, and then forbade even this amount. He had already abolished the royal hunt. In 259 B.C. he issued decrees regulating throughout the empire the slaughter of animals, and prohibiting entirely the killing of many classes of living creatures.

Even more important were his royal exhortations to his people to live peaceably, without violence, and to practice all the Buddhist pieties. In 256 B.C. he issued a series of edicts, incised on rocks in seven widely scattered places (the "Fourteen Rock Edicts"), so that they could be read and reread by his people. These were followed by the "Seven Pillar Inscriptions," the two "Kalinga Edicts," the three "Cave Inscriptions," the four "Minor Pillar Edicts," and others. Totaling thirty-five in all, these edicts told how he wished his people to live.

Thus saith His Sacred Majesty:—"Father and mother must be hearkened to; similarly, respect for living creatures must be firmly established; truth must be spoken. These are the virtues of the Law which must be practiced. Similarly, the teacher must be reverenced by the pupil, and fitting courtesy must be shown to relations." This is the ancient nature of things—this leads to length of days, and according to this men must act.

People perform various ceremonies. In sickness, at the weddings of sons, the weddings of daughters, the birth of children, departure on journeys—on those and other similar occasions people perform many ceremonies, . . . although that kind bears little fruit . . . On the other hand, the Ceremonial of Piety bears great fruit. In it are included proper treatment of slaves and servants, honor to teachers, gentleness toward living creatures, and liberality toward ascetics and Brahmins . . . Even if this Ceremonial of Piety fails to attain the desired end in this world, it certainly produces endless merit in the world beyond.[3]

This is a layman's idealistic but practical creed. There is no reference here, nor elsewhere in the edicts, to the Four Noble Truths, or to Nirvana, the goal of the arahat. What Asoka was interested in was that his people should practice the glorious ethic of the Dharma, or piety, and store up merit toward rebirth in a paradise hereafter. With this prospect he was more than satisfied; for he was no monk, and could not reach Nirvana without becoming one.*

In order to give effect to the moral exhortations contained in his inscriptions, Asoka required that the officials of the government, from the least to the greatest, give oral expositions of the Dharma to the people, and appointed Censors of the Law of Piety to supervise the populace in general and Censors of Women to supervise female morals in particular. These special officers were sent out to every part of the empire, even to the most backward and remote districts.

Asoka was also much interested in Buddhism as an organized religion. To show his devotion to the memory of the Buddha, he made pious pilgrimages to spots sacred to the Blessed One. Realizing, too, the divided and weakened condition of Buddhism in its home territory, he called together, so old tradition relates, the Third Council, which reorganized and reformed the Order.

Most important, he boldly conceived of Buddhism as a world religion, and may justly be called its second founder, because he gave it a world-vision. It was he who persuaded it to transcend its localized status as a minor Indian sect. He sent missionaries and ambassadors of Buddhism to lands far and near. His emissaries reached Syria, Egypt, Cyrene, and Greece! His own brother (or son?) headed a missionary band, as we shall soon see, to Ceylon. All this was the beginning of an extraordinary expansion, the full extent of which Asoka could not himself have foreseen.

---

* Nirvana was for the arahats. The great mass of the people had to rest content with the prospect of accumulating enough merit to enter Swarga, Heaven. In some far-off rebirth they might be monks and attain Nirvana; meanwhile the bliss of paradise awaited and invited. It was enough.—Still, tradition says Asoka prepared himself for monkhood by accepting ordination into the Sangha and retiring to a monastery after forty years of rule.

Ceylon

In an exchange of gifts and compliments Asoka first broached the subject of sending teachers of the Buddhist doctrine to this island. Subsequently, he sent Mahinda, said by some to be his son, by others his brother, at the head of a band of missionaries. From that time the civilization of Ceylon may be dated. Buddhist shrines and monasteries rose to perpetuate the Buddhist doctrine. For that perpetuation the rest of the Buddhist world came to be very grateful. For since Ceylon was for centuries unaffected by the sometimes catastrophic changes that went on in India itself, the Buddhist doctrine remained through the years true to the tenets of early Buddhism, with little or no change. It was, therefore, the historic destiny of the Buddhist monks of Ceylon to conserve for posterity the oldest Buddhist texts.

The story is this. Mahinda apparently brought no written records with him to Ceylon, but he and his associates are said to have held in memory the whole of what constitutes today the older Pali texts. Whether this be true or not, the original scriptures were all rendered into the Singhalese dialect, and for a time were the only complete collection of ancient texts in the whole Buddhist world. In the 5th century A.D., the great Buddhist scholar, Buddhaghosa, went to Ceylon, learned the Singhalese tongue, and began the task of retranslating the old texts back into Pali. Other scholars from India eventually brought the task to completion.

The devotional zeal of the Buddhists of Ceylon has been nourished through the years by the relics brought over from India. These include what the devout believe are the begging-bowl, the left canine tooth, and a collar-bone of the Buddha. Impressive shrines—now of great age—house these treasures.

The Singhalese are to this day predominantly of the older (Hinayana*) Buddhist school.

Burma and Southeast Asia

Burma and the countries of southeast Asia are also predominantly Hinayanist. All at one time or other felt the influence of Hinduism, and each, at least in the northern parts and wherever the Chinese have

* The origin and meaning of this term will be explained in Section II, p. 205 n. infra. The term is here used because of its wide currency. Modern Southern Buddhists now prefer to call their faith Theravada Buddhism. Another term, much like it in meaning, is also coming into use: The Old School of Wisdom.

settled, has come under Mahayana (later) Buddhist influences; but in the main the more conservative Hinayanist tendencies have prevailed. What has this meant? The reader may well wonder; so we shall pause to see.

The General Character of the Hinayana

In the Hinayanist areas, the monk is, as he always has been, the central figure. His scriptures are the comparatively few but ancient Pali texts. He professes (sometimes because the scriptures say so, not always because the understanding assents or comprehends) that there is no ego, that the world is transient and the scene of sorrow, and Nirvana is the goal. The monastic discipline is that of early Buddhism. The ideal of the individual monk is the attainment of arahatship. Hence, in all the Hinayana monasteries solitary meditation is the rule. The monks go forth in the morning to beg, clad in yellow robes and with shaven heads, just as in Gautama's day, and they follow the same daily schedule as of old. The whole emphasis of life is on acquiring merit toward one's salvation.

If one asks the Hinayanist monk whether the Buddha exists or not, the correct answer is always that the Buddha entered Nirvana and is therefore no longer exercising an active personal influence as a living self; he is at peace, and knows nothing any more of becoming and ceasing to be.

It is still taught that everything in the universe, including gods, men, and beasts, is in a state of constant flux. To abide in flux means suffering. To experience liberation from "the scene of sorrow" requires concentration (*dhyana*), and this in turn demands *prajna* or the highest wisdom, that is, transcendental insight penetrating beyond phenomena to final truth; in short, enlightenment (*bodhi*).

But while all this is in strict conformity with Gautama's original teaching, even the Hinayana doctrine has developed in the direction of religion. For one thing, all Hinayanists take a reverent attitude toward the relics of the Buddha, and have made images of him of every size, from the minute to the colossal.

Even the Pali texts depart at a number of points from Gautama's own views of life and reality, and contain in germ many of the ideas elaborated later in the Mahayana. For example, they declare (what Gautama himself *may* have said, though it is doubtful) that the Sage of the Sakyas was not the only Buddha to appear in the world; he had predecessors in other ages—to the number of six, say the earlier texts,

Spires of the Shwe Dagon Temple at Rangoon, Burma, which the pious cover with gold leaf as an act of merit. The temple is erected over a supposed footprint of the Buddha in the solid rock.

or of twenty-four, says a later. They also affirm that the Buddha was a divine being, omniscient and sinless; that through countless incarnations he lived so perfectly that he became through sheer merit a divine being who lived in the Tusita heaven. From thence he came to earth, entered his mother's womb, and was born as a man. His divine nature became manifest in his enlightenment and life of pure example and teaching. His way of life is the true one for all; there is no other way out of misery into peace. He himself is at peace—perfect peace. The *next* Buddha—now a Bodhisattva, that is, a Buddha-in-the-making—will be Maitreya. He is waiting for the proper time to come to earth, where he will reach enlightenment and do for men in his age what Gautama has done for this one.

The religion implicit in this view of things becomes evident to any observer of the typical Hinayana religious establishment of today. In Thailand, where conditions are typical, such an establishment is called a *wat*. This is a cluster of buildings within a walled enclosure. The entrance is from the east, and is guarded by grotesque animal or human figures, a carry-over from the animism of pre-Buddhist days, when tutelary demons were thought essential to a well-guarded gateway. The main building in the enclosure is known as the *bot*. It usually has a curious three-fold roof, one roof close upon another, with finials of a horn-shape curving upward and said to represent snake heads. Inside, the building is designed as a hall for worship and preaching. Near the middle of the floor there may be a high seat for the leader of the preaching services, and on the floor around mats for the congregation— laity and monks. At the end of the hall farthest from the door is a Buddha-image, resplendent on a seat above the altar, with perhaps smaller standing or seated images, of the same great being, arranged about it, and, on either side, images of the two famous disciples of the Buddha, Moggalana and Sariputta, looking up worshipfully. The altar is covered with offerings of the devout, incense-burners, expensive candlesticks with their candles in place, flowers in costly vases, solid gold or plated images—and Western clocks! * These are all precious gifts to the Founder of the Faith, and increase the merit of the givers.

In addition to the *bot*, there may be several other halls, one perhaps to house images in serried rows, and another to cover perhaps a reputed footprint of the Buddha in the solid rock. Also, distributed picturesquely through the compound there may be a number of stupas (*dagobas* or *phras* to the Thais), tower-like structures of tapering designs, usually ending in a sharp-pointed pinnacle. These are built by the laity as an act of special merit. (Indeed, the highest ambition of the devout layman is to build one during his lifetime.)

Adjoining the other buildings, or outside the walls of the *wat*, the monasteries may be found. They are simple in structure, partitioned into cells, and very barely furnished. Here the monks live out their simple life, devoted to meditation and the duties of the *wat* and to lay-education under government patronage. In Thailand, and in Burma, it is the general custom for every male, at the age of twenty, to live in a monastery for not less than two months—less time would not be respectable. This period is supposed to be spent in intensive study and cultivation of Hinayana principles.

One question may be raised. It has to do with the services in the central hall of the *wat*. What is the attitude of the Hinayanist toward the great Buddha-image on its throne above the flower- and gift-laden altar? The answer is that the attitude of the *average* Hinayanist of Asia is undoubtedly religious. In the image he sees the representation of a

* Some kept running, others allowed to stand unwound. So reports J. B. Pratt in his *Pilgrimage of Buddhism* (Macmillan, 1928), p. 153.

living, responsive, supernatural personality, who is able to hear and answer prayers, if the need be great. It is only the more learned of the monks who know better what the true doctrine is. They know that prayer increases merit, especially if it consists of the repetition of sacred words and verses; but there is no *answer*.

II THE RISE OF THE MAHAYANA IN INDIA

The Locus: Northwest India

After Asoka, Buddhism enjoyed great prestige, throughout India, for eight hundred years. And yet forty years after his death, when Asoka's dynasty fell from power, influences hostile to Buddhism—like those of the empire of the Guptas—rose to ascendancy in central India.

But then Buddhism simply transferred its center of gravity westward. In northwestern India it began to flourish and take on new forms. In the 2nd and 1st centuries B.C., Syrians, Greeks, and Scythians poured into the Punjab, and having made themselves its masters, became the leading spirits in a buoyant Greco-Bactrian culture. The conversion of their king Menander (King Milinda on native tongues) brought the new kingdom within the reach of Buddhist influence. Then in the 1st century A.D. the Kushans, a tribe of central Asian nomads akin to the Turks, overran Afghanistan and northwestern India, and absorbed the arts and culture of the Greco-Bactrians. Their greatest king, Kanishka, had his capital in Peshawar, and inquired into many religions, Zoroastrianism among them, before he adopted Buddhism. The Buddhist world had subsequent cause to be thankful that he gave his royal approval and patronage to the new and beautiful Greco-Buddhist sculpture and architecture, art-forms which resulted when interested Greeks turned their talents to the adornment of Buddhist themes. The curly-headed Buddhas, which they created, were destined to dominate the aesthetic consciousness of all later Buddhism, as far away as Japan.

It was here in northwest India that Mahayana Buddhism first came to flower.*

---

* When the Mahayanists took their name (*Mahayana* means "the Great Vehicle"), the conservative, older Buddhism had to reconcile itself to being called the *Hinayana* ("the Lesser Vehicle"). Vehicle (*yana*) here refers to a means of transportation, such as a raft, a ferry, or a carriage. If the crossing of the river analogy is used for Buddhist salvation, then Mahayana is the Great Ferry or Raft and Hinayana the Lesser Ferry or Raft.

Sometime between the 3rd century B.C., the age of Asoka, whose inscriptions give us no reason to think the religious development of Buddhism had proceeded very far, and the 1st century A.D., when Kanishka ruled northwest India, the doctrines later embodied in the Mahayana, the most elaborately developed form of Buddhism, began to take shape, though they were then known only to a few. It was a momentous new development—more effective in making Buddhism a world-religion than even Asoka's well-laid plans. For it turned the negativistic philosophy of early Buddhism into a religion that offered eternal rewards to the optimists.

The First Step: The Glorification of Gautama

This religious transformation of the original deposit of Buddhist tradition began to develop rapidly after Kanishka's conversion (whether with his encouragement or not is a matter of debate), and became public property. It is impossible now to determine precisely in just what order the various ideas arose; but the process expanded and developed

Gautama Buddha in the style of the Greco-Buddhist sculpture of the Ghandhara School, Mathura, 5th century A.D.

Queen Mahamaya conceiving the Buddha. (From railing medallion at Bharhut Museum, Calcutta)

certain intimations in the Hinayana, and seems to have pursued some such course as this:—

First, Gautama Buddha was adored and worshipped as a divine being who came to earth out of compassion for suffering humanity. He desired to teach man the way out of misery. A complete mythology, recorded in the *Jataka*, explains how through many existences the great being who became the Buddha lived according to all "the perfections" and finally reached a place in the Tusita heaven from which he came to earth. These assertions about him were a logical consequence of certain primary assumptions: (1) that the Buddha was a person of superhuman qualities, and (2) that when we inquire about his previous incarnation, we must believe, according to the principle of the fitness of things which marks the operations of the Law of Karma, that he could not have come from hell nor from the animal and human levels, but must have come from heaven, and without doubt from the Tusita heaven, for it is a place specifically meant for highly meritorious contemplatives. The logic here runs as follows: what should or must have happened did, in the absence of evidence to the contrary, actually happen. Much else that the *Jataka* relates—how the gods went to the Tusita heaven to ask the great being to go to earth; how he assented after making five observations as to the rightness of the time and as to where and to whom he should be born; how he took the form of a white elephant, descended from heaven, and entered the womb of his mother while she lay sleeping in a Himalayan palace to which angels bore her for his immaculate conception; how she gave birth to him while in a sacred grove with angels in attendance,—all this can be understood as being logically what must have happened and therefore did happen.* To the question concerning his name before his descent to earth, the answer was, "He was a Bodhisattva." This word occurs in rather early texts, but is there purely descriptive; it merely recites a fact that was perfectly obvious, namely, that before Gautama was enlightened he was a person destined to be enlightened. But in the growth of the Mahayana doctrine, this word was to make religious history; it became a term of great importance.

The Next Step: Discovering Other Buddhas and Bodhisattvas

Possibly the next step followed as the result of the indirect influence of Brahmanism, which insists on a Reality behind all phenomena displaying itself over and over in recurring events; or perhaps the doctrine of the avatars of Vishnu† had an influence. For whatever reason, the Mahayanists heavily emphasized a belief which the more conservative (the Hinayanists) also, with less prominence, set forth, that Gautama was not the only Buddha, that there had been many Buddhas before him. Some had come to earth; and some had remained in the heavens; and some were in the making, the Buddhas of the future, the Bodhisattvas.

The myth-making process was rounded out to some sort of completion, when, in a manner far surpassing the modest earlier achievements in this respect, the Mahayanists recovered the names and histories of these other Buddhas and of the Buddhas-to-be! (The reader is doubtless puzzled. How could the names and histories of these beings be recovered without the proper documents and other historical traces? In Oriental lands, those who give full credence to intuitions, revelations, and insight into past and future through trance-visions would regard such a question as barrenly sceptical.) The literature of the Mahayana,

---

* It may be noted that this "logic of faith" has been invoked in other religions; for example, in Jainism to tell how Mahavira had two mothers; in Zoroastrianism to explain how his fifteen-year-old mother came to conceive Zoroaster; in Roman Catholicism to provide for the Virgin's immaculate conception by her parents and for her bodily assumption to heaven. Duns Scotus put the logic of the doctrinal development thus: "It could be; it ought to be; therefore it is."

† The doctrine that Vishnu has made "descents" (*avataras*) to earth by incarnating himself in men and animals will be discussed in Section V of the next chapter.

in Sanskrit manuscript after manuscript, thus added immense stores of knowledge to the devout. Before their eyes immeasurable vistas opened up. The universe became radiant to its outer limits with compassionate beings who could and wanted to aid them. Their imaginations had now much to feed on. Furthermore, prayers were now again possible. A rich and luxuriant cultus sprang into being. The devout were furnished with wall-paintings and sculptures as aids to devotion. Salvation was no longer something to be achieved only by self-effort. Divine beings with vast stores of merit were eager to share with the faithful.

Much was to flow from this. Not only was the whole aspect of Buddhism changed for the believer, but its fortunes abroad improved at once. Countries which responded slowly to the appeal of the Hinayana doctrines now took up the Mahayana with eagerness. And because the Mahayana was by nature expansive, it changed as it moved; the peoples among which it made its way contributed to its development.

For this reason it is well to see where it thus made its way before we summarize its full tenets at the height of its development.

III THE SPREAD OF BUDDHISM IN NORTHERN LANDS

China

This is a story very difficult to compress into a few paragraphs. Only its broadest outlines can be touched on here.

At a very early period—perhaps as early as the 3rd century B.C.— China and India were in contact. Military and commercial activity found both a way over the sea and a route through central Asia; but the length and difficulty of the journey tended to make the contacts few and brief. Just how much more than the name of the Buddha, in travelers' accounts of him and his teachings, was known in China before the time of the Emperor Ming Ti (58–75 A.D.), of the Later Han dynasty, is difficult to determine. Perhaps the knowledge was considerable. Chinese historians of the past have related that some half dozen years after Ming Ti began to reign this emperor became actively interested in Buddhism, because he had seen in a dream the golden image of the Buddha flying into his room, with head glowing like the sun. According to the ancient tale, which is very likely pure legend, he sent twelve special envoys to India to bring back more exact knowledge of the teachings of the Blessed One. The envoys brought with them on their return a library of holy books, statues of the Buddha, and, what was of more importance, two Buddhist monks, full of gentle missionary zeal. The monks, it was said, unloaded their holy books from the back of their horse, entered the monastery which the emperor erected for them, and began the work of translating their sacred literature into Chinese. Incidents *like* this occurred, but perhaps not at this time nor at an emperor's insistence. We are on sounder ground in believing that Ming Ti, in 65 A.D., permitted a statue of the Buddha to be erected and the Buddhist cult to spread, without himself being an adherent of the Blessed One.

But Buddhism made little progress in China then. It seemed in its Hinayana version to be alien to the Chinese temperament and tradition. Monasticism could not easily be reconciled either with the Chinese ideal of devotion to family life or with their love of life and optimism. Moreover, the Chinese were a self-sufficient, practical, even a materialistic people, and the speculative and mystical temper of Buddhism had to prove its kinship to native Chinese mysticism (Taoism), before it

The Spread of Buddhism
  ▥ scene of Gautama's activities
  ▤ area of rise of Mahayana

held any lure for them; they had first to be shown the life-value of the doctrines of the transitory nature of the world, the unreality of worldly activity, the non-existence of the ego, and the need of salvation from the misery of existence. It is a well-founded tradition that during the two Han dynasties (206 B.C.–8 A.D. and 23–220 A.D.) family opposition to monkhood was such that a public ban lay upon the entrance of Chinese boys into monasteries.

But this attitude of coolness broke down, and for a number of reasons. During the period of the Hans, China was united, and could devote itself to building upon earth an ideal feudal or Confucian society; but at last the Later Han dynasty dissolved in the turmoil which produced the Three Kingdoms (220–280 A.D.), and, during the three centuries that followed, the nomad tribes of central Asia, waiting beyond the Great Wall, broke into China in great numbers, producing thereby a vast disunion and misery. The scholars and intellectuals looked in vain for signs of public return to the old Chinese will to make this world a happy dwelling-place for an orderly and harmonious human family. In their great discouragement, many of them turned from the optimistic humanism of the Confucians to the mystic consolations and back-to-nature quietude of Taoism. An un-Chinese contempt for the world possessed them. They became ripe for Buddhism. Indeed, there is evidence that even in the time of the Hans, the Taoists had already shown an interest in Buddhism, because it seemed to them to have resemblances to their own outlook. And many others felt the same interest, because the world as they knew it reduced them to hopelessness, if not actual despair.

But the common people were also being readied for Buddhism. Among the nomads who broke into China through the breaches of the fabulous Great Wall were Mahayanists. They brought a gospel for the masses. From the south, too, the Mahayanist missionaries pressed in, directly from India. Their flexible creed enabled them to recognize the validity of Chinese needs and modes of thought. The emphasis on filial piety which is to be found within Buddhism itself enabled them now to rank this virtue alongside of guarding the sanctity of animal life, abstaining from intoxicants, and the rest of the Five Precepts of the Buddhist Order; indeed, they began to say that to fulfil the duty of filial piety, sons should add to their traditional rites Buddhist masses for the dead, as a means of making the lot of their ancestors happier. Here the vivid imagery of the Buddhist monks, who drew freely from Indian conceptions of the after-life, began to tell. There had been lacking in the life and thought of China a really satisfying conception of

the future life. Chinese hopes had had little to offer in the way of comfort, except the bare fact that one would join his ancestors at death
and be dependent forever thereafter on the filial piety and remembrance of one's descendants. It was in part just because Mahayana
Buddhism, as it came to flower, far surpassed either Taoism or Confucianism in presenting attractive pictures of the after-life that it began
by the 4th century to exercise a wider popular appeal.

North China, where the racial stock was now largely intermixed
with the blood of "barbarian" invaders, and where the ancient Chinese
culture was most disturbed and shaken, was the first to respond generally. South China was slower to yield. Here Confucianism still had
staying power, and even the Taoists were cool. Nationalistic pride was
stronger in them there. But eventually, all over the land, monasteries
sprang up; temples filled with images of the various Buddhas of the
Mahayana faith multiplied; and the intellectuals divided into many
schools of Buddhist thought, worthy of our examination later.

The number of adherents to the various Buddhist groups was large,
and remained large, while dynasties rose and fell. Sometimes a sternly
Confucian or vigorously Taoist emperor would institute widespread persecution; one such—it was Wu Tsung of the T'ang dynasty—in 845 A.D.
destroyed 45,000 Buddhist buildings, melted down tens of thousands of
Buddha images, and sent over 400,000 monks, nuns, and temple servitors
back into the world; but tolerant emperors always followed the anti-
Buddhist ones, and at least the physical damage was repaired.

That is the essence of the story of a thousand years.*

Korea

The introduction of Buddhism into Korea followed soon on the 4th
century spread of that religion in China. At the time, Korea was divided
into three independent states, none of which had a culture much above
primitive animism. When a Buddhist monk, by the name of Sundo,
encouraged by the Buddhist ruler of a little state in north China, crossed

---

* Spiritual damage is another matter. Eclipse of Buddhism in the rise of Neo-
Confucianism during and after the Sung dynasty led to a loss of creative influence
and spiritual decline. Today, although the nominal adherents of Buddhism in China
(people who resort to Buddhist shrines or priests at least occasionally) number
perhaps 250,000,000 souls, and a Buddhist revival has had some effect in middle
China, Chinese Buddhism has lost the force it once possessed; and unless it re-
acquires pertinence to rapidly changing Chinese needs, it will not long maintain
even its present diminishing strength. It is damaging that the Communists are
ideologically opposed to it.

into Korea with Buddha images, sacred books, and missionary ardor, in a remarkably short time the three Korean states took up the new religion and its accompanying culture. By the middle of the 6th century the king of the southwestern state was sending missionaries, images, and books to the emperor of Japan.

Japan

It was in the year 552 A.D. that Kimmei, the emperor of Japan, received from his Korean correspondent a gold-plated image of a Buddha, some sacred writings, some flags and umbrellas, and a letter concerning the excellent but difficult Buddhist doctrine, which should, it was claimed, produce illimitable and immeasurable good fortune—or painful retribution—and which could transform a man into a Buddha (i.e. a person possessed of *bodhi*). This claim probably did not impress the emperor as much as the further statement that from farthest India, through all China, even to Korea, the doctrine had found reverent acceptance. That did impress the emperor. Perhaps, he thought, there was a great deal more to the religion which a Chinese monk at Yamato had been quietly practicing in his self-built temple these thirty years, than appeared on the surface. At any rate the emperor, the ancient story tells, took up the matter with his councilors. Some were as impressed but as cautious as himself; others were in outright opposition to the new religion, in the devout belief that the *Kami*, the native gods of Japan, would be angered; and a few followed the prime minister, chief of the Soga clan, in suggesting favorable action. The emperor took the part of prudence, and passed the golden Buddha-image on to the head of the Soga clan to try it out on his family, to see if the Kami would object. When a pestilence broke out among the people it was thought the Kami did object, so the golden image was thrown into a canal, and Buddhism fell irretrievably out of the emperor's favor.

In due course the emperor died, and the Korean monarch sent another embassy, which included, besides the priests and two hundred sacred texts, a nun, an image-maker, and a temple architect. In the spirit of courtesy, the embassy was allowed to construct a temple for its own use; and once more the Soga clan supported the view that the new religion should be given a fair trial. Again, however, a pestilence broke out, and, if we are to believe the ancient tale, again the Buddha images found a resting-place at the bottom of a canal; all looked dark for Buddhism. But presently a perplexity arose. The pestilence continued! So the head of the Soga clan advanced the thought-provoking argument that it was not the Kami who were angered, else the pestilence would have ended, but it was the Buddhas who resented the coldness of their reception. The cautious authorities decided to let matters drift.

By the time the next emperor reached the throne Buddhism had made actual progress; in fact the emperor, in spite of military and priestly opposition, viewed it with favor. With new Buddhist missionaries ever arriving, the tide began to turn. In 588 A.D., when the empress Suiko ascended the throne, her nephew, Shotoku Taishi, an ardent Buddhist, became regent. He sent groups of scholars to China to bring back as complete knowledge as possible both of Buddhism and the Chinese system of government. He built the first public Buddhist temple in Japan, and organized the first monastic school. To exemplify the humanitarianism of the Mahayana, he erected a hospital, a dispensary, and a house of refuge. Other Buddhist leaders donated on their part alms-houses, irrigation canals, orchards, harbors, ferries, reservoirs, and good roads. The new religion was demonstrated to be good not only for the individual, but also for society as a whole.

Having won the adherence of the court, Buddhism began slowly to reach down to the common people. In time, as in China, various schools or sects sprang up, largely under Chinese tutelage. The whole population eventually became at least partially Buddhist. The native religion, Shinto, had offered some difficulty at first, but when the Kami, the ancient gods, were taken into the Buddhist pantheon as Buddhas and Bodhisattvas, the difficulties were largely removed. In fact, it was the common practice, for centuries, for a man to be a good Buddhist, a good Shintoist, and a good Confucianist all at the same time.*

Buddhism long was the dominant religion of Japan and reached some of its finest and noblest forms there. However, during the first century of the Tokogawa Shoguns (the 17th century), Shintoism was revived in an anti-Buddhist form and became a rival of Buddhism in seeking the adherence of the Japanese people. Buddhism suffered a further set-back with the coming during the 19th century of the Christian missionaries. For a while even the government frowned on it. At present, the restrictions of World War II at an end, it is actively engaged in modernizing its methods of appeal to win back its old popular support. How far this will succeed in the face of changing Japanese needs is for the future to tell.

---

* Shintoism expressed gratitude for and loyalty to the national and family heritage; Confucianism provided a social ethic for the present; and Buddhism took care of the future (the next life).

The Daibutsu at Kamakura, Japan; a bronze image 49 feet high.

Tibet and Mongolia

Buddhism was late in coming to these regions. It established itself in a form so different from the Hinayana and Mahayana, as these are usually known, that it is called by other names. It is sometimes given the name of Lamaism, because of the prominence of the *lamas* in it; but this is misleading. Other names refer to its practices or doctrines. Thus it may be called the Mantrayana ("the Vehicle of Mantras"; which emphasizes its magical character), or the Tantrayana (which points out its relation to Tantric Hinduism), or, better still, the Vajrayana ("the Vehicle of the Thunderbolt"; which reflects its bold theology). Because of its belated coming, strange history, and stranger doctrines, it will be described separately in the next to last section of this chapter.

The Decline of Buddhism in India

Strangely enough, the up-curve of the Mahayana in China and Japan is matched by a swift down-curve in India. This is perhaps as good a place as any to note a startling fact: Buddhism declined and almost disappeared in India after the 7th century A.D. We do not know precisely why. The Chinese pilgrim Fa Hien, who visited India from 405–

411 A.D., noted with joy the flourishing condition of both the Hinayana and Mahayana; but when his countryman, Hsüan Chuang, came two centuries later (629–645 A.D.), decline had set in apace. When we ask the reasons, part of the decline may be assigned to the ferocious invasions of the White Huns in northern India during the 6th century A.D., incursions which resulted in the raiding and destruction of the Buddhist monasteries and the disorganization of the Buddhist leadership. Then, too, it was a serious threat to Buddhism as a separate movement when the followers of Vishnu, who were very vigorous at this time, adopted the Buddha as the ninth incarnation of Vishnu. More serious was the decline of creative intellectual energy within Buddhism itself. A final blow came in the 12th century. In 1193 A.D. the Moslems, who had entered India over a century before, invaded the last of the Buddhist strongholds. What was left of the debased Buddhism in Maghada was roughly stamped out. Only a few followers of the Blessed One obscurely hung on to the faith. Except for the believers in the foothills of the Himalayas, they remain comparatively few in India to this day.

IV THE GOSPEL OF THE FULL MAHAYANA

What was the secret of the success of the Mahayana outside India? The answer is perhaps not hard to find.

The Divine Authors of Salvation

To the common people, the Mahayana offered the good news of the existence of multitudes of saviors, real and potential, whose chief desire was the cure or the amelioration of the sufferings of men. This was glad tidings. The pure benevolence of these saviors was the best of all assurances. Even the intellectuals were interested. After all, they too preferred to believe that the universe was friendly.

Of course, when the learned examined this assurance, they saw that the tenets of original Buddhism were caught up and almost lost in it, like palely colored threads in a vivid tapestry. In the discourses of the Mahayana texts Gautama, as the golden-voiced Sakyamuni, lectured to his disciples through hundreds of pages; yet the message he brought but faintly echoed the tenor of his discourses in the Hinayana texts—

it is Mahayana religion and philosophy that he is expounding. A similar recession of the themes of original Buddhism appeared in the worship and cultus of the Mahayana.*

But the Mahayanists claimed that the Buddha *privately* taught that a man does not have to save himself; he can get help.

In the Mahayana, the authors of salvation are of three kinds, falling naturally into order. They are the Manushi Buddhas, the Bodhisattvas, and the Dhyani Buddhas.

Manushi Buddhas are saviors who, like Gautama, have appeared on earth in the past as human beings, attained enlightenment, instructed men in the true way of life, and then, their duty done, entered Nirvana. They are primarily teachers. Prayers cannot now reach them.

Bodhisattvas would never have become vital concepts if it had not been for the historical Buddhas, like Gautama; but in the Mahayana, if anything, they are more important, and have a greater religious reality. The Hinayana scriptures recognize but two beings of the kind, Gautama before his enlightenment and Maitreya. But in the full form of the Mahayana the Bodhisattvas are a great, even an innumerable, company of supernatural beings, who hear prayers and come actively to men's aid. The prevalent popular view of Bodhisattvas, especially in China and Japan, is that they are beings who have made a vow many existences ago to become Buddhas, and have lived ever since in such a way as to acquire almost exhaustless stores of merit. This merit is so great that they could readily achieve the full status of Buddhas and pass into Nirvana; but they are compassionate beings; out of love and pity for suffering humanity, they postpone their entrance into Nirvana and transfer their merit, as need arises, to those who call upon them in prayer or give devotional thought to them. They sit enthroned in the heavens, looking down on the needy world, and sometimes, in redemptive pity, they descend in the guise of ministering angels, to perform deeds of mercy.

* In the Chinese temples, for instance, the arahats are indeed remembered and honored, but more because they belong to the pageantry of Buddhism than because they have any vital religious function to perform. Eighteen of these early saints of Buddhism are given a place in Chinese temples under the name of the *Lohan* (which is as near as the Chinese, with their tendency to pronounce r's like l's, have come to pronouncing arahat). They often are seated, on either hand, along the side walls of the temples, their images rendered almost grotesque by the realistic touches added to their appearance by the temple artists. Plainly, they are men and not gods; and the worshipers do not regard them as saviors. They are there because they are a part of Sakyamuni's original company, and because the Chinese believe that somewhere in the inaccessible fastnesses of the mountains they still sit in immortal, serene, and mindful meditation.

Avalokita kneeling on lotus; a Chinese conception.

We have space here only for brief mention of the most widely popular among them. *Maitreya,* the next Buddha (known in China as Milo-fu), has already been mentioned; he was honored first in India and then all over the Mahayana world; numerous images of him show the high respect in which he has always been held, but, strange to say, the worship never has been so ardent as in the case of some other Bodhisattvas. Perhaps the faith that he is going to be the next Buddha has made for a feeling that he is, or should be, saving his merit for his earthly career and cannot give it away. The people turned to others, like *Manjusri* (Chinese Wen-yu) and *Avalokitesvara* (Kwan-Yin). The former is one of the earliest of the Mahayana creations. He is the Bodhisattva who assists those who wish to know and follow the Buddhist Law. So he is represented as a princely figure, carrying in addition to his sword (logic) a book (the Buddhist Law or Truth). Near his image there often appears that of another Bodhisattva, *Samantabhadra* (Pu-hien), who brings happiness to his following and fosters in them his own universal kindness. But the most popular by far, in himself and

Kwan Yin. Avalokita in a female form. (After a white enamel figure from Puchien, 18th century)

in his metamorphoses, is *Avalokitesvara*, or Lord Avalokita. As his Indian name implies (it means "the Lord Who Appears to This Age"*), he has a special interest in the people of the current time. The personification of divine compassion, he watches over all who inhabit the world, and is said to have come to earth over three hundred times in human form, and once as a miraculous horse, in order to save those in peril who have called upon him. He not only averts moral catastrophes, such as rage, folly, and lust, but physical pains and disasters as well, such as shipwreck, robbery, or violent death. He grants to women the children they implore. His image usually represents him as in the garb of a great prince, with high headdress, carrying in his left hand a red lotus (one of his aliases is Padmapani, the Lotus-handed), and extending his right hand with a gracious gesture. Frequently he is shown seated on a large lotus, and called, with poetic devotion, "The Jewel in the Lotus." Sometimes he is given four, or many more, arms—all laden with gifts to men. Sometimes he kneels; his postures are many.

We shall see that in Tibet Avalokita is accompanied by a spouse,

* This is an awkward phrase, but it is expected to say that Avalokitesvara is *the eternal contemporary* of each generation.

one of the Taras; but in China, by a metamorphosis whose history is obscure, he changed his sex and became the enormously popular *Kwan Yin*, the Goddess of Mercy, whose place in the esteem of the Chinese and Japanese is analogous to that of the Virgin Mary in Roman Catholicism. Her attitudes are exactly those of Avalokita in India, with the addition of the warmth of a madonna-like maternal feeling. Her images, upon which sculptors have lavished their highest art, show her in every variety of gracious and winsome posture. They are to be found all over China, Korea (where she is called Koan-Eum), and Japan (where her name has been further modified into Kwannon). Like her Indian alter ego, she is often shown seated on a lotus or standing on one; or, she rides upon a cloud or glides on a wave of the sea. In her arms she often bears a child, for it is such she gives to her women adorers; and on her head she may wear a crown set with an image in miniature of Amitabha Buddha, the Lord of the Western Paradise, to whom she takes those faithful to her. Again, she may be shown without ornament.

Of the other Bodhisattvas one more should be mentioned. He is *Kshitigarbha*. In China, under the name of Ti-Tsang, and in Japan as Jizo, he ranks high in popular regard, chiefly because, at the instance of grieving relatives and friends, he descends into the hells, delivers its sufferers, and transports them to heaven. In previous incarnations he was twice a woman, which explains his untiring kindness and tender mercy, and his interest in helping women in the pangs of child-birth. As if to credit him with the endeavor to be in many places at once and thus multiply his power to aid, the Chinese declared there were six of him, one for each of the six life-levels of the universe. In Japan, in the character of a single being, Jizo was identified with the Shinto war-god, Hachiman; represented as riding on horseback, wearing a war-helmet, he became the favorite of the Japanese soldiery; but he was also the beloved friend of little children, in which relation he appeared to them in the guise of a simple, honest monk.

The third class of savior-beings is composed of *Dhyani Buddhas*. These "blessed ones" differ from Bodhisattvas in having fully achieved their Buddhahood; but they stand in a different category also from the Manushi Buddhas, in not having achieved their Buddhahood in human form. They dwell in the heavens, and in the indefinite interval between the present time and their compassionately postponed final entrance into Nirvana, they actively minister to men's needs, as did Gautama between his enlightenment and death. Their name implies that they are Buddhas of contemplation (*dhyana*), and their images convey the impression of deep meditation and calm. Whereas the Bodhisattvas are usually princely in aspect, and wear rich clothes, studded with gold and jewels, the Dhyani Buddhas sit or stand in the simple garments of the monk, their hands held in front of them or folded in their laps in the five established *mudras* or positions, their eyes turned downward, and a quiet smile lighting up their otherwise grave and composed countenances.

Taking the whole of the Mahayanist world into account, we find the three principle Dhyani Buddhas to be *Vairocana, Bhaisajyaguru,* and *Amitabha.* They are but a few among many. The first is a solar Buddha, whose functions link him with the Persian Mithra, the Vedic Savitar, and the Mediterranean Apollo. He is a Buddha of first importance in Java; and in Japan the sun-goddess Amaterasu has been called his manifestation. The second is the Buddha of Healing, and has a great following in Tibet, China, and Japan. But *Amitabha* (known to the Chinese as *O-mi-to* and the Koreans and Japanese as *Amida*) is one of the great gods of Asia. Once he was a monk, took the vow to become a bodhisattva, rose to his present rank, and now presides over the Western Paradise, called Sukhavati, or the Land of Bliss, generally known as "the Pure Land." Since he is the kindly lord of this happy heaven of the western quarter, and freely admits all who beseech him in faith, he has surpassed in the estimation of the masses in China and Japan even Sakyamuni, the deified Gautama. The core of the matter is this:—whereas the Bodhisattvas serve present need, Amitabha assures future bliss. The hopeful devotee, unable to emulate Sakayamuni in helpfulness or to acquire the merit stored up by arahats and Bodhisattvas, turns to Amitabha, and has merit transferred to him from the great being's store. Some sects among the Chinese and Japanese believe that the grace of O-mi-to is granted in fulness to anyone who merely repeats with devotion his sacred name. A Mahayana treatise widely read in China and Japan, *A Description of the Land of Bliss* (the *Lesser Sukhavati-vyuha*), says distinctly that faith in Amitabha, quite apart from meritorious works and deeds, is alone sufficient unto salvation. It declares:

Beings are not born in that Buddha country as a reward and result of good works performed in this present life. No, all men or women who hear and bear in mind for one, two, three, four, five, six, or seven nights the name of Amitayus,* when they come to die, Amitayus will stand before them in the hour of death, they will depart this life with quiet minds, and after death they will be born in Paradise.[4]

* The active forth-going or emanation of the unmoving Amitabha.

In this conception original Buddhism is completely transcended.

But this is no less true of the whole of the Mahayana scheme of salvation. No one will deny that Gautama taught and practiced good-will and compassion for all, but these expressions of love were to a certain degree impersonalized, as his philosophy of life demanded; so far as possible, love was made, as we have observed before, a love for everyone, not of any *one*; and at no time was the acquiring of merit forgotten—at least in theory. But in its conception of the character of the Bodhisattvas and Dhyani Buddhas, Mahayana Buddhism exalts pure altruism to supremacy in the moral sphere; and by insisting on its expression in supernatural beings who answer prayers, it has moved directly counter to Gautama's teaching that one should not pray, but should devote his energies to something really effective—saving oneself.

The Mahayanists frankly recognize this departure from early Buddhist teaching, but they have the belief that Gautama taught several kinds of doctrine, depending on the nature of the hearers: to the weak and selfish he outlined the eightfold arahat path; to those of greater understanding and strength of character he imparted the ideal of the compassionate and altruistic Bodhisattva. This version of Gautama's teaching has enabled the Mahayanists vigorously to attack the selfish-ness of the Hinayanists, who are accused of abandoning the world to its fate while they seek their own salvation individually, each "wandering alone like a rhinoceros."

The Ethics of the Mahayana

The line of thought just outlined led, in actual fact, to perhaps the most inspiring of all Buddhist teachings. It may be rather awkwardly stated thus: just as the Bodhisattvas, who are now divine but once were human, vowed in a distant past to become Buddhas and then from pure altruism postponed their entrance into Nirvana by making their merit over to others in order to help the needy, so any human being of the present, man or woman, can, if he or she wishes, make a similar vow with regard to the future. Everyone is potentially a Buddha, and should now take the vow to be a Bodhisattva. The length of time necessary to fulfil the destiny thus undertaken may be almost beyond reckoning, but true benevolence needs no urging and waits for nothing. The time to begin is now.

As the Mahayana doctrines developed into their fuller forms, this ideal was more clearly articulated, and was linked up, as will shortly appear, with a vast metaphysical background. Various stages in the career of a Bodhisattva were distinguished, and a body of literature emerged to convey instructions on how to enter the initiatory stages. According to a 7th century manual, called the *Bodhicaryavatara*, the initial stages can be entered upon by anyone who feels joy in the good actions of all living beings, and who wishes to spend himself in the increase of such good. A person of this temperament may then pray to the Buddhas to aid him in acquiring enlightenment—not that he may pass into Nirvana, but rather that he may secure the good of all living beings. To this end he requests the Buddhas to postpone his entrance into Nirvana until he has aided all living beings within range or until the last blade of grass shall have been set free!

In the Far East, the Buddhist monks pass through successive degrees of ordination which culminate in that of a Bodhisattva. The degree that immediately precedes the last, is, significantly, that of an arahat; and this order of the degrees clearly shows how the Mahayana feels it has transcended the ethical ideals of the Hinayana.

V   THE MAHAYANA PHILOSOPHIES OF RELIGION

What to the people was a message of salvation was to the intellectuals and mystics a philosophy, profound and subtle. It was so all-explanatory that it intrigued the minds that believed it no less than it rejoiced them.

The Schools

Most of the Buddhist philosophizing was done in India. There the two main schools thought out their characteristic views in the 2nd, 3rd, and 4th centuries A.D., and were greatly influenced by, and in turn influenced, the philosophizing being done by Hindu and Jaina thinkers, during what was in fact the great systematizing era in Indian thought.

In the 2nd century A.D. Nagarjuna organized the *Madhyamika* (or *Intermediate*) *School*, founded on earlier speculations. It took its point of departure from the teaching of Gautama that there is no such thing as an ego, but instead merely a loose grouping of ever-changing *skandhas*. Early followers of the Buddha had reasoned that this analysis of

the human personality holds good of all objects or existents whatsoever: anything at all is a loose collection of pulsating, transitory "elements." Nagarjuna now took the step of saying that these elements
(*dharmas*), when closely examined, are no more than mental phenomena or phantasms; they are "empty," and do not really exist as
experienced; they are but the fictions of ignorance-clouded minds. If
one sees an object, say a man, or even the Buddha, walking down the
street, one really experiences seeing such an object; the experience
means something in one's mental history; but the object is nevertheless
not the solid, material object one initially senses it to be. The sub-
stantiality of the external world is thus denied. "Everything is void
(*sunya*)." Things are not what they seem. *In reality* they are empty of
the characteristics assigned to them.

In this void there is no form, no perception, no name, no concepts,
no knowledge. There is no eye, ear, body, mind; no taste, touch, objects; no knowledge, no ignorance, no destruction of ignorance, no decay, no death, no Four Noble Truths, no obtaining of Nirvana.[5]

However, certain important qualifications may be noted as being
inherent in this view. What has just been argued is the transcendental
truth (paramartha-satya). Only minds that have shed "ignorance" can
apprehend it. So long as minds and consciousnesses continue to function
in the ordinary or usual way, they experience everyday or relative
truth (samvriti-satya). In the light of everyday truth things seem not to
be void but to have relations that give them existence and reality for
experience. This is the realm of the imperfect and impure, in which
men are born and reborn.

To a mind heretofore struggling with relative truth, the thing that
happens when enlightenment comes to it is a perception of the vacuity
of things in the light of absolute truth (paramartha-satya).[*] This does
not mean that nothing exists whatever. Properly interpreted, the thought
runs thus: the mind liberated from the notions of everyday experience

[*] For instance, in any mental act of everyday experience dealing with description, the object described, the description, and the person doing the describing are
all devoid of any verifiably real attributes if viewed in the light of absolute truth;
they are not really existent in the- way they are conceived to exist. But the
phantasms have reality as phantasms. The same reasoning holds true of rest and
motion, transmigration, Karma, the Buddha himself, or anything whatever to which
the everyday consciousness ascribes attributes.

The reason why this view is called "intermediate" is because it is a qualified
realism, intermediate between the realism of early Buddhism, which grants outright reality to *dharmas* in the sense given above, and the idealism next to be
described as characterizing the Yogacara School.

knows that things are void of *the attributes assigned to them,** and indeed are not to be given any attributes at all, because they are in themselves unknowable and unknown. The reality which must be behind the appearances known to our consciousnesses as the Buddha, the world of bondage, Karma, and transmigration is ineffable. (Here the thought resembles Immanuel Kant's transcendental idealism and the epistemology of other Western philosophers.) Since Reality cannot be assigned any attributes, in it there is "neither production, nor destruction, nor annihilation, nor persistence, nor unity, nor plurality, nor coming in, nor going out." [6] Furthermore, entrance into Nirvana is entering a void, because it means stripping the attributes from everything and passing into vacuity and silence.

In the 5th century the *Yogacara* (or *Idealist*) *School,* founded in India by the brothers Asanga and Vasubandhu, began where the Madhyamika left off. In this view the mentalism or idealism is complete. Only mind exists, and the objects of its thought are ideas only. But how then, it may be asked, does the mind always perceive what other minds do and not just what it pleases to perceive; that is, how does it share the everyday world with other minds? How does it learn about the Buddha and seek Nirvana? (This same kind of problem arises in the West for philosophers like Berkeley and Hume.) The answer is simply that there is a reservoir or store of perceptions on which all minds draw, namely, "the consciousness that holds all" or "the receptacle consciousness" (*Alaya-vijnana*). This "consciousness" is the storehouse of all ideas. It is a cosmic all-mind. It is like an ocean; it carries on its surface the tossing and evanescent waves that are the phenomenal world apprehended by the seven illusion-making levels of consciousness,—namely, sight, hearing, smell, taste, touch, discrimination between the various phenomena of the universe, and distinguishing between subject and object. In contrast to these seven deceptive forms of consciousness, the "receptacle consciousness" itself (the eighth type of consciousness) is complete and ultimate. To identify oneself with it is to be in Nirvana.

Earlier, in the famous treatise *The Awakening of Faith* (very uncertainly ascribed to Ashvaghosa ca., 100 A.D.) the ultimate consciousness had been named the Absolute Suchness (the *Bhutatathata,* "that which is such as it is"); and it was said that when a mind hampered

---

* I.e., by the everyday consciousness. Dr. Chan Wing-Tsit puts the fact thus: "Reality is [presumed to be] Void in the sense of 'devoid' of any specific character." (Article, "Chinese Philosophy" in *Dictionary of Philosophy,* Philosophical Library, New York, 1942.)

by ignorance attempts to comprehend it, the illusion which constitutes the seeming multiplicity of the phenomenal world is produced; but in itself the Absolute Suchness is pure and at rest, the "oneness of the totality of things." This way of putting the matter was destined to have great influence on later Buddhist thought.

The Wisdom That Has Gone Beyond
(Prajna-paramita)

By now the language of Buddhist scholarship was no longer Pali but a variant of Sanskrit, the classical language of India. From the beginning of the Christian era and through the next five hundred years a vast literature in Sanskrit began to appear. Early examples of this literature were the *Mahavastu* and the *Lalita-Vistara*, two versions of the life of the Buddha filled with miracles and wonders. Next came the *Buddha-Carita* of Ashvaghosa (ca. 100 A.D.), a famous biography of the Buddha in the noblest verse form; there followed the *Lotus of the Good Law* (the *Saddharma-Pundarika*), which is the most beloved of all Mahayanist scriptures, filled, as it is, with supposed discourses of the Buddha on Vulture Peak near Gaya; the *Sukhavati-Vyuha,* a favorite description of Amitabha's Pure Land and how to get there; and a large group of sutras, a hundred or more in number, dealing with problems of philosophy of religion. Of these last the *Lankavatara* and *Surangama* sutras have been the most influential.

A special category of this literature, of which the popular *Diamond-Cutter* (the *Vajracchedika*) is typical, goes by the name of the *Prajna-paramita Sutras,* so called because they are "Discourses on the Wisdom That Has Gone Beyond" (a close translation), that is to say, teachings concerning transcendental wisdom (*prajna*).

It is in this last group of treatises that we come upon a wonderful metaphor that perfectly suggests what prajna-paramita means. It is the metaphor of crossing a river by raft or ferry to get to the farther shore (Nirvana). In the light of this metaphor, prajna-paramita may be translated as "the Wisdom gone to the Other Shore." * The nearer bank of the river is this world, known to the senses since childhood. From it one cannot imagine at all what the Other Shore, far away, is like. But the ferry arrives, piloted by the Buddha, and when one boards it (i.e., adopts Buddhism as his faith) and begins the crossing, the re-

---

* No one has written of this more forcefully and beautifully than Heinrich Zimmer in *Philosophies of India* (p. 475 ff., paperback edition). The student is recommended to read for his own enjoyment this full and fascinating description.

ceding nearer bank gradually loses reality and the far shore begins to take shape. At length only the far shore seems real, and when one arrives there and leaves behind him the river and the ferry, they too lose all reality, because one has now gained final release in the Great Beyond, which alone is utterly real. Here the former bank, the river, the ferry, the Buddha, and even the human goal which had been all along "The Far Shore" or Nirvana, are equally and completely void. As concepts they had once been the useful means of attaining *prajna* or transcendental wisdom, but they are empty now and useless forever.

This reasoning, we find, is based on a famous passage in the Pali *Majjhima Nikaya,* where the Buddha asks his monks:

"What would be your opinion of this man, would he be a clever man, if, out of gratitude for the raft that had carried him across the stream to safety, he, having reached the other shore, should cling to it, take it on his back, and walk about with the weight of it? . . . Would not the clever man be the one who left the raft (of no use to him any longer) to the current of the stream, and walked ahead without turning back to look at it? Is it not simply a tool to be cast away and forsaken once it has served the purpose for which it was made? . . . In the same way the vehicle of the doctrine is to be cast away and forsaken, once the other shore of Enlightenment (Nirvana) has been attained." [7]

One more point needs to be added. Not only is every human concept of reality discarded in Nirvana; the empirical self, as one thinks of it in life, is discarded too. The *Astasahasrika Prajnaparamita* says this with great subtlety:

The Enlightened One sets forth in the Great Ferryboat; but there is nothing from which he sets forth. He starts from the universe; but in truth he starts from nowhere. His boat is manned with all the perfections; and is manned by no one. It will . . . find its support on the state of all-knowing, which will serve it as a non-support. Moreover, no one has ever set forth in the Great Ferryboat; no one will ever set forth in it, and no one is setting forth in it now. And why is this? Because neither the one setting forth nor the goal for which he sets forth is to be found. [8]

The Trikaya or Triple Body

In the doctrines of the Bhutatathata and the Receptacle Consciousness the reader will find no difficulty in seeing a similarity with Vedantic speculation. We have here an Absolute that resembles in many respects the Brahman-Atman of Hindu monism. But there is a difference that must ultimately be ascribed to the influence of the career and personality of Gautama Buddha upon Mahayana speculation. Whereas in Vedantic thought Brahman-Atman remains the Absolute of strictly neutral being, in Mahayana Buddhism the Absolute Essence or Suchness is identified with a sort of Love-behind-things that produces Buddhas—a Buddha-essence at the heart of the universe. The importance of this conclusion for religion is surely evident. For here the Buddhas become the expression of the Absolute within phenomena or that which is Being-Itself—and not merely an indifferent or unfeeling expression of it, something wholly nonpersonal, but an expression of redemptive love (*karuna*), drawing ignorance-clouded minds along the Bodhisattva way of love back to itself.

Halting though the logic, if we go into it, seems at many points, this conclusion of the Mahayana schools reaches a great height of religious thought. Christian theology and Buddhist metaphysics here share something of a common ground. This becomes still more evident in a further phase of the thought of the Mahayana schools. In trying to relate the Absolute Suchness with the appearances of the Buddhas and other holy beings and saviors in the phenomenal world, the Mahayana systematizers evolved the doctrine of the "triple Body" (the *Trikaya*), a doctrine with some resemblances, at certain points, to Christian theories of the position of Christ in the Trinity. There are three "bodies" in the totality that is the universe, first "the Body of Essence and Being" (the *Dharmakaya*), second, "the Body of Spiritual Bliss" (the *Sambhogakaya*), and third "The Body of Forms (literally, Transformations)" or the *Nirmanakaya*. The first indicates the eternal reality that is the ground or source of the forms (*dharmas*) that compose the universe known to the senses; it is identical in different contexts with the Absolute Suchness, the Void, the Alaya-vijnana, prajna, and Nirvana. The Body of Spiritual Bliss is the heavenly manifestation of the Dharmakaya, particularly in the Buddhas and Bodhisattvas, and generally in spiritual reality or force capable of redemptively entering history and taking name and form. The Body of Forms is the manifestation of the Body of Spiritual Bliss in earthly appearances, the prime example being the historical buddha, Gautama. The first is undifferentiated and impersonal, the second differentiated and personal, and the third an earthly manifestation of the second. Applied to Gautama Buddha, this doctrine of the Triple Body led to the following formulation of the faith concerning him: the Absolute Suchness or Void is the ground of being from which emanates the Body of Spiritual Bliss manifested in such heavenly powers as Amitabha, Avalokitesvara, *and* the bodhisattva who once dwelt in the Tusita heaven and who compassionately came down to earth to be the historical Gautama Buddha. When his earthly mission was accomplished, Gautama Buddha returned to the source of all being, the Dharmakaya (= Nirvana).

Applied to the common man, these philosophical positions of the Mahayana led to the view that, since the Absolute Suchness or Buddha-essence is manifest in all things, the Buddha-nature is in every man. Anyone may take up the career of a Buddha-to-be without having to be reborn. Throughout the Far East the influence of this belief penetrated, and its optimistic implications thrilled the aspiring natures of the devout with a new zeal and a great hope.

VI MAHAYANA SCHOOLS OF THOUGHT IN CHINA AND JAPAN

Our study of the religious development of Buddhism would be far from complete either in scope or interest if we did not, briefly at least, consider the leading Mahayana schools and sects in China and Japan. In general the picture is this: what the Buddhist speculative theologians of India put forward by way of suggestion and outreach, the Chinese took up and developed as the logical basis of their differentiations; and the Japanese, eager to learn, came forward to put the finishing touches on the Chinese developments, always adding something of their own in the process.

The formation of differing schools of thought was in some instances due to Indian teachers coming to China; but for the most part the Chinese were influenced toward variation in point of view chiefly by the Mahayana literature they read and discussed. This literature came to them in the form of translations from the Sanskrit originals or as literary works produced by the Chinese themselves. The first influential Mahayana text was the *Diamond-Cutter Sutra,* translated in the 4th century A.D. Next came translations of the *Pure Land Sutras,* the *Lotus of the Good Law,* and the *Awakening of Faith.* Other important influences streamed from the lengthy Sanskrit works known as the *Avatamsaka Sutra* and the *Lankavatara Sutra,* which were in whole or in part translated into Chinese. The Chinese themselves seem to have composed the *Sutra of Brahma's Net,* the most widely used manual on the monastic life. Different schools of thought also justified their positions by issuing treatises like the *Practice of Dhyana for Beginners,* and the *Sutra of the Sixth Patriarch,* and others.

It would be tedious for the ordinary reader, were we to attempt to trace out individually the manifold differences between the schools and sects of China and Japan; such a study would be as detailed and difficult to follow as an inquiry, say, into the differences between Protestant sects in Europe and America. Fortunately, we may pursue another course. The main trends among the Buddhist schools are clearly distinguishable, and may be comprehensively considered under five heads.

1. *The Pure Land Sects.* Here the motive is one that appeals to the common man, that of getting to heaven. The chief interest and ultimate goal of the Pure Land Buddhists is the Western Paradise of Amitabha Buddha. By concentration of attention solely on this aspect of Buddhist belief an extraordinary simplification is achieved. The strenuous life of "works" is rendered unnecessary. The whole emphasis is on faith, and faith is believed to be sufficient for salvation; in fact, the practical-minded Chinese have called the Pure Land way the "short cut," and such it appears to be. Unquestioning faith in Amitabha, and the devout repetition of his name, especially by the use of the formula *Namu Omito Fo* ("Hail, Amitabha Buddha!"), are so all-sufficient in admitting one to Paradise that intellectual exertions and moral effort are virtually superfluous.

In China the *Ching-t'u* (Pure Land) school represents this point of view. Its founder, a converted Taoist, appeared in the 4th century A.D. In Japan the chief representatives of Amidism have been the *Jodo* and *Shin* sects. The Jodo sect was founded in the 12th century by a Japanese scholar named Genku (later known as Honen Shonin or "Saint Honen"). As a young man he had sought vainly for peace by means of the three Buddhist disciplines ("precepts, meditation, and knowledge"), and had then found enlightenment in a library when he read in a Chinese Amidist commentary the comforting words: "Only repeat the name of Amitabha with all your heart, whether walking or standing, whether sitting or lying: never cease the practice for a moment. This is the very work which unfailingly issues in salvation." [9] He thereupon accepted salvation as coming solely by grace through faith. The Shin sect, founded by his disciple Shinran Shonin, has introduced some radical Japanese innovations, hardly paralleled in Buddhism elsewhere, and is now the most powerful of the Japanese sects, having the greatest number of temples, monks, and teachers. It has taken the confident position that simple faith in Amida, without even the repetition of the Amidist formula (telescoped in Japan to *Nembutsu*), secures the full grace of that Buddha; indeed Amida seeks and saves without human good works being at all required; faith alone is needed, *and Amida engenders that,* for faith is Amida's gift, not man's achievement. Freed from celibacy, Shin priests are allowed to marry, eat meat, and live in the world like lay persons. As in the case of Christian churches, its institutions depend, not on endowments, but on voluntary contributions. Because the priests can marry, an innovation something like that in Tibet has occurred: the abbots are hereditary. In the past, by acquiring political and even military power, these abbots "were even more like barons than the celibate prelates" [10] of the older, semi-militarized sects of the feudal era. The cheerful, world-accepting nature of the Shin sect has had a natural result: emotional and religiously easy-going persons have found it a highly attractive faith.

2. *The Intuitive Sects: Ch'an and Zen.* The goal here is immediate insight, enlightenment such as Gautama achieved under the Bo-tree. The method of salvation is *dhyana* or contemplation. To this way of thinking, scholarly research, the reading of books, the doing of good works, the performance of rituals, and so on, are not only of little merit in themselves, but often a hindrance to true insight into the Buddha reality. One must find salvation by an inward look into one's heart.

In attempting to pronounce the Sanskrit word *dhyana,* the Chinese elicited their name for this way of faith, namely, the Ch'an school. The founder was said to have been an Indian scholar and teacher by the name of Bodhidharma. Now no more than a dim legendary figure, he may have come to China in the 6th century A.D. at the time when the growing influence of Buddhism had claimed an imperial convert, the Emperor Wu Ti of the Liang dynasty. The interesting old tale, which is to be viewed with historical scepticism, says that when Bodhidharma came to North China and established himself there, the emperor sent for him. In the course of the interview the renowned teacher was asked how much merit flowed from making imperial donations to the Buddhist order and continuing the translations of sacred books. "No merit at all!" the gruff monk replied, and went on to say to his shocked hearer that knowledge gleaned from reading is worthless; no merit flows from good works; only meditation that admits one to direct insight into the Buddha reality, only truth revealed to one's thought when one turns inward to see the Buddha in one's heart, is of any value. To demonstrate to the uncomprehending monarch what he meant, Bodhidharma is said next to have retired to Mt. Su and to have sat meditating with his face to a wall for nine years.

Whatever the circumstances of its origin, the Ch'an school began at first with just simple living and stern self-discipline as the preparation for meditation and the inward vision. It disdained all scriptures, and was at first rigidly individualistic, iconoclastic, and averse to regarding the ultimate Buddha principle as in any sense definable. Gradually, however, the old aids to the religious life were reinstated and in a moderate way made use of. Nevertheless, it was realized that such aids cannot substitute for meditation, even though differences developed as to the nature of the meditation itself. There are different kinds of it. The question arose: should one "sit still" in meditation, carefully eliminating false views, without any specific aims or problems in mind, waiting and hoping for *bodhi* (a gradual enlightenment); or should one focus upon a tough problem with intensity, hoping to wear down the intellect to the point where it gives up and "sudden enlightenment" (intuition) takes place? Ultimately, of the seven Ch'an sects two survived: the *Lin-Chi* and the *Ts'ao-tung*, the first devoted to abrupt procedures and stiff problems leading to sudden enlightenment and the second to a broad development of the understanding through book learning and instruction leading to gradual enlightenment. In either case,

Bodhidharma meditating for nine years before a rock wall. (Detail from a painting by Sesshu, 15th century A.D.)

the ability to meditate properly was required, and one did not need to be learned in history or philosophy nor expert in the traditional rites and ceremonies to attain it. Profundity of insight into one's own "heart" was all that was required. By way of illustration, the following auto-biographical passage from a Ch'an text is worth quoting, since it shows how an illiterate country boy became, on account of his intuitive qualities, the renowned Sixth Patriarch, Hui-neng:

I was selling firewood in the market (of Canton) one day when one of my customers ordered some to be sent to his shop. Upon delivery and payment for the same as I went outside I found a man reciting a Sutra. No sooner had I heard the text of this Sutra than my mind became at once enlightened. I asked the man the name of the book he was reciting and was told it was the Diamond Sutra. I asked where he came from and why he recited this particular Sutra. He replied that he came from the Tung-tsan Monastery in Wongmui; that the Abbot in charge was Hwang-yan who was the Fifth Patriarch and had about a thousand disciples under him. . . .

It must be due to my good karma accumulated from past lives that I heard about this and that later on I was given ten taels for the maintenance of my mother by a man who advised me to go to Wongmui to interview the Fifth Patriarch. After arrangements had been made for my mother's support, I left for Wongmui, which it took me about thirty days to reach.

I paid homage to the Patriarch and was asked where I came from and what I expected to get from him. I replied that I was a commoner from Sun-chow in Kwang-tung and said, "I ask for nothing but Buddhahood."

The Patriarch replied: "So you are a native of Kwang-tung, are you? You evidently belong to the aborigines; how can you expect to become a Buddha?"

I replied: "Although there are Northern men and Southern men, North or South makes no difference in their Buddha-Nature. An aborigine is different from your Eminence physically but there is no difference in our Buddha-nature." [11]

This reply of the untrained country lad revealed his high capacity for understanding and insight to the Fifth Patriarch. The Patriarch subsequently expounded the *Diamond-Cutter* (usually just called the *Diamond Sutra*) to him, and though the younger man could neither read nor write, he became so thoroughly enlightened that he was made the Sixth Patriarch.

Such individuals, however, are rare, and it was recognized that most beginners need careful guidance. Hence reading of the basic sutras or texts, assigned problems for concentrated reflection, and practical suggestions as to posture and breathing during meditation have been a feature of Ch'an sects almost from the beginning. Theoretically intuitive insight was alone necessary, but practically a definite degree of preparatory learning was needed.

In Japan the Ch'an school goes by the name of *Zen* (for thus the Chinese word was pronounced there). Three branches of Zen were established in the 12th, 13th, and 17th centuries, and have had a far-reaching, if quiet, influence on the whole of Japanese religion. The two Zen sects that are now most active are derived from the two most durable Chinese sects: the *Rinzai* (so named from the Japanese pronunciation of Lin-Chi) and the *Sōtō* (from the Chinese Ts'ao-tung). In the chapter on Shinto, the native Japanese religion, we shall have occasion to mention its attraction for the grim, taciturn army men of Japan, resolved as they have been upon self-sacrificial and single-minded devotion to emperor and country. Beyond this circle, the stress laid by both branches of Zen upon the intuitional search for the essential in life has had a determinative effect upon Japanese art, household furnishings, architecture, and the forms of social etiquette, especially in introducing reticence and restraint as the marks of good taste. The unexcelled Japanese art of flower-arrangement is a Zen by-product.

Let us see how this could be so.°

Zen is primarily an attempt to experience the unitary character of reality. "I" and "not-I" are one; both are aspects of Buddha-reality. This becomes clear when one "sees into one's own nature," in a moment of intuition. Deliberative reason will not succeed here. One cannot *think* oneself into the realization that there is no duality of oneself and the world, and that "I" and "not-I" are, in the last analysis, indistinguishably one. Such a realization must come suddenly by an intuitive flash of insight, something that the Japanese call *satori*. There are two ways of dealing with Nature. One is to distinguish, describe, analyze, and, in pursuit of practical ends, manipulate its objects from the outside; this is to deal in concepts and acts that are disjunctive and misleading. The other way is to contemplate Nature, much as the Taoist of China does, from the position of one who is indistinguishably at one with it; this is to pass into the One, the Void (*sunyata*), the Dharmakaya, concerning which "one must be silent," since to say anything about it is to frame misleading concepts of it. Within oneself there is an

---

° What follows is for the most part according to the point of view of Rinzai Zen, since this seems to be the more notable of the two sects, although the Sōtō sect has more members. Rinzai Zen's most vigorous advocate is the world-famous Prof. D. T. Suzuki. A useful selection from his many works has been put into paperback under the title *Zen Buddhism* (edited by William Barrett; Anchor Books).

illusion-making ability which is exercised to the full by all those who dwell in the world of the senses as if it were the whole of reality; but this is to submit to ignorance; truth lies in another direction. Deep within everyone there is a Buddha-nature (a nature capable of *bodhi*), by identifying oneself with which one ceases to reason ignorantly and acquires instead *prajna-paramita,* the wisdom that has gone beyond—to the beyond that is within.

Zen masters here lean heavily on their Ch'an predecessors, who worked out in practice various ways of awaking novices from their dogmatic slumbers, that is, from their reasoning in a dualistic strain concerning the Buddha *and* I, the essence of Buddhism for *me,* the basic challenge of Buddha *to* me, etc. Since all things are part of the Buddha-nature, the learners must stop distinguishing, defining, analyzing, describing; they must stop asking questions, for these are essentially dualistic and to such questions there are no answers; they must instead

Zen novices meditating in monastery at Kamakura, Japan. Monk with rod watches to rap on the shoulder of any novice caught napping. (After Cartier-Bresson photograph)

await the mighty surge of "realization" that overpowers all thought. If the learner persists in trying to reason things out and keeps asking questions, the Master may slap him, kick him, or throw him out into the hall; perhaps this will make him realize that his questions are nonsensical and cause him to be enlightened then and there. Another tactic of the Master may be to answer the question more or less nonsensically and then ask the learner to make sense of it, knowing that he will be baffled and have to give up. (In Japanese terminology, this is to give him a *koan* to think over.) Again, the Master may recount to the learner a puzzling dialogue (which the Japanese call a *mondo*). The point is that he must realize that discursive reason misleads; that when the ferry reaches the Far Shore, he who is about to be enfolded in Oneness (Nirvana) will only be distracted by further attention to the ferry (Buddhism) or to the ferryman (the Buddha).

Consider the following famous *koans* as, in effect, saying: "Stop asking dualistic questions and give yourself up to the undifferentiated One."

A monk asked Tung-shan, "Who is the Buddha?" and received the reply: "Three measures of flax."

When asked by a monk, "Is there a Buddha-nature in a dog?" Chao-chou barked, "Wu!" ("No!")

A monk asked Hui-neng to reveal the secret of Zen and was asked in turn: "What did your face look like before your parents begot you?"

The great Japanese monk Hakuin replied to an inquirer by clapping both hands and then asking, "What sound does one hand make?"

Here is a *mondo*:

A monk who saw Yao-shan meditating asked: "In this motionless position what are you thinking?"

"Thinking that which is beyond thinking."

"How do you go about thinking that which is beyond thinking?"

"By an act of not-thinking."

What is *distinctive* about Japanese Zen? Several things. First, it is a fundamental point that in Japanese Zen man and Nature are not seen to be in opposition, since man is part of Nature or part of the Buddha-reality. To see a frog leaping into a pond is to feel at one with it in its diving, to be for the moment a frog also. The Buddhist monk Basho set the conditions for experiencing this in his famous *haiku* (seventeen syllable poem) for which it is so hard to find an English equivalent.

An old pond, mirror-still.
A quick frog, slanting waterward.
A liquid *plop!*

Here one merges self with pond, then frog, and finally water sound. The Japanese contemplate beautiful things—cherry blossoms, pine branches, field-flowers—in a meditative way that allows the object to absorb and possess the perceiver. This is Zen. Or to take an example from such a sport as archery, one does not "master" the handsome bow and shoot the arrow; the arrow shoots itself from the bow. In the tea ceremony, one performs the beautiful ritual as in an aesthetic dream having the dimensions of eternity. Zen, with its sense of cosmic unity and its immediate aesthetic response to reality, fortifies these attitudes.

Another thing is that the Japanese sects have worked out a technique of meditation that is highly disciplined; it is called *zazen*, and calls for stated periods of meditation in a hall designed for the purpose. The monks sit on two long platforms facing each other for eighteen hour stretches day after day. Their meditations are tied in with *sanzen* or consultation with a "master" to whom the monk regularly reports. This plan for mental self-discipline appeals strongly to many serious-minded Orientals, not to speak of influential intellectuals of the west, who turn to it hopefully as a means of insight.

3. *The Rationalist Sects.* But the intuitionist's thorough purging of the mind in the hope of enlightenment is so obviously anti-intellectualist, and moreover so fundamentally grounded in feeling-states rather than in reason, that one can easily understand the rise of the rationalist sects. In China, where they are known as the *T'ien-T'ai* sects, they rose out of, but grew away from, the Meditation school. The basic issue that led to their rise was the one between some hoped-for "sudden enlightenment" after the mind is emptied of all empirical content and "gradual attainment" through study of the scriptures and a philosophically mature practice of contemplation. In the 6th century A.D., a monk in one of the Ch'an monasteries in eastern China whose name was Chih-K'ai (or Chih-I) took a stand for an inclusive point of view. Buddhism or the True Faith was, he said, greater than any of its schools, and one should open his mind to insight from more than one source. Meditation (*dhyana*) was necessary but not all-sufficient for insight. He believed that the gathering of knowledge from teachers and scriptures, the performance of ceremonials and rituals, and the regular discipline of the monastery were all very valuable in the preparation for the ecstatic vision. Because he wished to find room for every major point of view expressed by Buddhism up to his time, Chih-K'ai evolved the doctrine

that the Buddha (Gautama) taught differently at different stages of his life, according to the understanding of his hearers: at first he taught the doctrines of the Hinayana sutras, and at later periods he revealed, in progressively profounder versions, the Mahayana doctrines. The fullest revelation of the eternal truth was made near the end of Buddha's life, and is contained in the *Lotus of the Good Law*,—the favorite text of the T'ien-T'ai school.

In accordance with the teaching of its founder, the T'ien-T'ai school has tried to reconcile the Hinayana and the Mahayana by subsuming both under the philosophical idealism of Nagarjuna (the Madhayamika school of India). Three levels of truth—one for the simple-minded who believe in the reality and value of the material world, another for those who seek confusedly to live a spiritual life in the material world, and a third for the seekers of intuitive insight through meditation—are discerned in Buddhist teaching. The recognition and consideration of all three levels of truth have made for tolerance and breadth of learning among T'ien-T'ai scholars.

The genetic relation between Ch'an and T'ien-T'ai in China was reversed in Japan. There, under the name of *Tendai*, the rationalist school of thought came first to Japan (as early as the 8th century, A.D.) and Zen followed later as its intuitionist outgrowth. Tendai was founded by a Japanese noble, Saicho, later known as Dengyo Daishi ("Priest Dengyo"). Many important monasteries, with their attendant temples, have flourished under the knowledge-fostering Tendai sect. Its influence in Japan is pervasive and powerful still, though its lay membership is not so great as is that of some of the other Buddhist sects.

4. *The Mystery or True Word Sects.* In every religion the power of the saving name or true word has at some time been stressed. The beneficial effects are sought by a kind of holy magic, performed against a background of rational belief—a pantheon or a cosmogony of impressive character. The tendency to make use of wonder-working formulas and gestures issued in China during the 8th century A.D. in the rise of the *Chen Yen* or True Word school. The chief features of this school were derived from Indian and Tibetan Tantrism.* The school was strongly supernaturalistic. It placed its chief reliance upon a large pantheon of Buddhist savior beings, both male and female, whose good offices were solicited through "efficacious" formulas, gestures, invocations, and liturgies, which were believed to bring infallibly good results. The devotees performed their mystery rites to the accompaniment of music and bursting fire-crackers, in the confident expectation of thereby

---

* For this form of Buddhism, sometimes called the Vajrayana, see infra, p. 241 ff.

curing sickness, rescuing the dead from hell, controlling the weather, insuring health and good fortune, and the like. The school still exists in China, under the government's frown, and finds its main support among the uneducated.

In Japan the True Word school took form as the powerful *Shingon* sect. But the Japanese adherents widened its outlook and subdued its magical features by assimilating to it the rational and eclectic interests of the Tendai sect. The Shingon has thus turned out to be even more comprehensive and many-sided than the Tendai. Its popular appeal has been great. It was founded in the 9th century A.D. by one of Japan's great men, Kobo Daishi. This eager and forceful person went to China to study the doctrines of the True Word school and returned to Japan to teach that a "true" or "secret" word, apprehensible only by immediate, sudden intuition, provides the universal truth underlying all the varieties of religious faith. The common man can understand something, but only something, of the Faith, for it is but partially conveyed to him in the allegory and symbol of ritual and ceremony; let him, however, be encouraged (as Gautama is supposed to have taught) in his love of temples and worship. But more discerning minds, and pre-eminently the highly trained priests of the Shingon sect, can know the truth directly and fully through a secret word of life, a word intuitively apprehended from magical picture-charts, efficacious formulas, or mysterious enlightening syllables constantly repeated. Kobo taught that the great Dhyani Buddha, Vairocana, the Great Sun (known in Japan as Dainichi), is the ultimate Buddha-reality. The other Buddhas and the Bodhisattvas are his emanations, phases of his "indestructible" energy at work in the universe. Gautama Buddha was his historical earthly manifestation. In schematically presenting this synthesis of Buddhist theology, the Shingon sect has drawn up two picture-charts or mandalas, each in the form of two or more concentric circles; on one (called the Diamond Mandala), Vairocana is shown seated on a white lotus in profound meditation, while widening rings of Buddhas and Bodhisattvas wheel round him; on the other (the Womb Mandala), the six material elements of the world appear in the form of a central ring of deities, with room for the Shinto gods on the outer rim; for Kobo held that, prior to the advent of Buddhism, the Japanese people dimly understood the true scheme of things and embodied their insight in the gods of Shinto mythology,* who are therefore to be equated with the more precisely and truly conceived Buddhist savior beings. This was the Shingon sect's contribution to the formation of the Ryobu or mixed

---

* Especially the sun-goddess Amaterasu.

Shinto described in the chapter on Shinto (Chapter XI). Largely through the efforts of Shingon (and Tendai), the two religions, Buddhism and Shinto, were practiced as a single faith in Japan for a thousand years.

Because it presented a doctrinal and ritual synthesis, Shingon appealed strongly both to the aristocracy and to the masses. The latter had great faith in the performances of the proficient Shingon priests, whose solemn masses for the dead and elaborate temple ceremonies, of a high-church character, fascinated and consoled them with hopes of supernatural aid. The nobility were no less delighted; for they liked especially the teaching that, just as the eternal Buddhas do not rest forever in spiritual contemplation but manifest themselves in the realm of material appearances, so a man may emerge from monastic training and show his spirituality in activities in the secular sphere. This made it possible for numbers of young nobles to retire to Shingon monasteries for their education and then re-enter the world to pursue active careers as soldiers or statesmen.

5. *The Socio-political Sect.* This sect, the Nichiren, is an expression solely of Japanese Buddhism, and reflects a social and political orientation characteristically Japanese. It was founded during the tumultuous 13th century, when the emperor was vainly struggling with the lords (*daimyos*) of the provinces for control of the nation and needed more religious support than he was receiving. Help came from an unexpected quarter. A monk, who thereafter took the name Nichiren ("Sun-Lotus"), experienced on a mountain top, while looking at the rising sun, a sense of identity between the Buddha-reality in the sun and the truth revealed in the *Lotus of the Good Law*. Previously he had studied both the Shingon and Tendai doctrines, but now he found both these systems unorthodox, along with the teachings of the Pure Land and Zen sects; so he set out to restore original Buddhism, as he thought, by launching a sect based exclusively on the doctrines of the Lotus sutra. He spoke with uncompromising forthrightness, believing that he was the incarnation of the Bodhisattva whose coming is foretold in the later sections of the Lotus sutra. In violent language, he rejected as mythical and fictitious the pantheon of great Buddhas and Bodhisattvas "invented" after the time of the Lotus sutra. The Amidists and their imaginary Western Paradise were the objects of his special attack. It seemed to him a mark of a degenerate age, when men neglected the concerns of this world for the happiness of the next. He spoke with the boldness and wrath of an Old Testament prophet against the evils of his age, especially the political corruption following in the wake of the over-

throw of the emperor's power by the provincial daimyos or lords. Once he aroused great anger by predicting that a foreign invader would destroy Japan for its sins. He was banished for his temerity. But the nearly successful Mongol descent upon the south coast which occurred shortly afterwards seemed so clearly a verification of his prophecy that he was recalled to help avert any further danger to the nation. To this day the welfare of Japan and the spirit of nationalism are of central importance in the Nichiren sect. The three vows of the sect are: "I will be the Pillar of Japan; I will be Eyes to Japan; I will be a great Ship for Japan. Inviolable shall remain these vows." Thus nationalism has made its appearance even in Buddhist guise.

VII BUDDHISM IN TIBET °

As was said earlier, Buddhism was late in coming to Tibet. Long after the countries to the south and east of that high plateau had yielded to the gospel pleas of the Buddhist missionaries, Tibet remained unaffected. At last, about 630 A.D., a Tibetan prince, Srong Tsan Gam Po, who established a well-organized state centered in Lhasa, its capital, sent emissaries to northern India, in part with the purpose of securing the introduction of Buddhism into his realm. This sudden interest may have been due, as tradition relates, to the fact that his two wives, princesses from China and Nepal respectively, acquainted him with their own faith and desired to practice it.

Yet Srong's introduction of Buddhism into Tibet was not very successful. The native demonolatry was too strong for it; and, besides, the Tibetans found it hard to understand. A century passed before anything effective was accomplished, and then the true founder of Buddhism in Tibet came up from Bengal. He was Padma-Sambhava, a vigorous teacher of the corrupt Buddhism of 8th century northern India. Through his influence the Buddhism of Bengal, with its Tantric infusion of sex symbolism, took root, and ultimately, after various vicissitudes and "reforms," became the religion of Tibet, and subsequently also of Mongolia, to which it spread in the 13th and 14th centuries.

° The Chinese occupation of Tibet since 1951 has so radically altered the situation there that the past tense is used hereafter, even up to the last paragraph in this section. It should be said also that the fact that this section is lengthier than that on, say, the Buddhism of Burma, Thailand, Laos, and Cambodia should not be construed to indicate greater comparative importance, for the fuller treatment is only a concession to general curiosity about an extraordinary land marked by equally extraordinary religious beliefs and practices.

It is not possible now to know just what Padma-Sambhava believed and taught, but the fact that he introduced a Tantric Buddhism gives us a clue. *Tantrism* is a form of devotion to natural energy (*shakti*).*
It was (and is) based on manuals (*tantras*) having a distinctly magical and spell-making character and inculcating a psychological doctrine, the practice of which, its adherents admit, is "as difficult as walking on the edge of a sword or holding a tiger," [12] namely, the doctrine that passion can be exhausted by passion (the craving for food, drink, or sexual indulgence can best be overcome by rising above it while it is being satisfied). But this is not all. Contemplation of Nature, Tantrists say, reveals that all the great natural forces, when closely inspected, are a union of male and female elements. This is true of deity as well. Gods are in the nature of the case quiescent (i.e., profound) and aloof,

* We shall hear more of it in the next chapter.

The five Tibetan Dhyani Buddhas that have emanated from the Buddha. In the center: Vairocana. Clockwise from top right: Amog-hasiddhi, Amitabha, Ashobhya, and Ratna-Sambhava. (After a Tibetan mandala)

but each has a complement in the form of an active spouse (a shakti); and the god's highest power is attained from union with her, for she rouses and draws it forth. Still another belief is entwined with this: in sexual union non-duality and, still more profoundly, the Void itself are momentarily experienced; there is an erasure of the distinction between male and female. The kind of Buddhism which finally took root in Tibet transformed original Buddhism by assimilating these Tantric doctrines to it.

The new and strange faith which resulted has some striking features. In the first place, the various Buddhas and Bodhisattvas were provided with spouses or consorts. These were the *taras* or savioresses who were the active aspects of each buddha-being. In the second place, a new genealogy of the gods was now made possible. It was said that there were five celestial Dhyani Buddhas, namely, Amitabha in the west, Ashobhya in the east, Amogha-siddhi in the north, Ratna-sambhava in the south, and Vairocana at the zenith, all of whom were supposedly fathered by the Adi-Buddha, the originative Buddha-essence, pictured as a kind of far-off god, wielding a magic thunderbolt. The five Dhyani Buddhas in their turn gave rise to the great Bodhisattvas, and these, stirred by their taras, produced and sent down males and females to earth. Thus Avalokita, who was an issue of Amitabha, was paired with a tara by whom he was aroused to bring into existence Gautama Buddha on earth.

The human devotee meanwhile was believed able to identify himself with any of the celestial Buddhas or their consorts by a period of fasting and prayer, climaxed by the utterance of powerful mystic syllables, full of magic, and the visual evocation of the divine personage, followed by a merging of identities. This was a Tibetan version of entering Nirvana. Some further doctrines were involved: that the human being is the universe in microcosm; that just as nature is pervaded by hidden energy (shakti), so the human being has secret stores of energy coiled up in him (at the base of the spine, it was said); and that certain sounds and the display of groups of letters and images, accompanied by movements of the body and hands, aroused as if by a thunder clap the shakti of the body and put the devotee on a level with the divine power he was approaching.°

° One may now see why this system of religion, usually called Lamaism, has been named the *Vajrayana* ("The Vehicle of the Thunderbolt") to distinguish it from the Hinayana and Mahayana. Another translation of this name is "Vehicle of the Diamond." The diamond flashes miniature lightning, and may be said to carry it as the thunderbolt does. Both are associated with *bodhi* or enlightenment, which comes like a lightning flash. Magic is obviously involved.

The public ceremonies which were gradually evolved appealed most strongly to the common people of Tibet. Four ritual components came to be characteristic of a complete ceremony: the *mandala* or frame, in picture form or described in the air and imagined, in which the gods were placed; the *mantras* or verses uttered; the *puja* or offering of one or more of the following: prayers, confessions of sin, sacrifices of flowers, lights, incense, perfumes, and ointments; and the *mudras* or hand positions, which were believed to establish "actual contact with the gods." [13] These *mudras* were directed to thirty-five or more Tantric deities, great and minor, and ran in sequences which often required thirty to fifty hand patterns in each sequence. They not only attracted the presence of the benevolent powers but also drove off the evil ones. By describing with the hands certain cabalistic patterns on the air and uttering at the same time the proper Sanskrit formulas it was believed that goblins and demons (those of the mountains, desert plateaus, cemeteries, roads, air, courtyards, dwellings, hearths, wells, and fields) could be exorcised; and by the same means ferocious animals, robbers, madmen, souls of the unburied or of enemies, demons of the storm, spirits of bad dreams, or devils of disease and nervous ailments could be kept away.

The native and ineradicable demonophobia of the Tibetans* predisposed them to accept a religion so well calculated to meet their needs. The measures taken to secure the protective presence of the Buddhas promised security at last. Their hard life on the windy plateaus of Tibet, ten thousand feet above sea-level, surrounded by mountains down whose slopes whistling blasts of icy air would at any moment rush upon them, made them fear at every turn the demonic in nature. They craved supernatural protection.

The demonic in Nature colored even their conception of benevolent divine beings. Not only had they pictured in imagination numerous evil powers with distorted and hideous faces; they portrayed even the mild and beneficent Buddhas and Bodhisattvas as though they were in a towering rage. The Buddha images seemed designed to frighten the wits out of the devout who approached them. But the fearsome visage had after all this good effect: it scared off the evil demons, while it merely chastened the worshiper.

The quest for protection led in more than one direction. The

---

* Expressed in the sub-surface indigenous religion called P'ön-po, or Bon, which dealt in animal-sacrifice, devil-dancing, skull-caps, skull-drums, and thigh-bone trumpets. It was never completely suppressed. Much of it in fact crept into Buddhist ceremonies; devil-dancing, for example.

prayer-wheel (or mill) is an instance of the union of magic and religion. Whether the Tibetans invented it or not is a moot question, but they made a universal use of it. Not strictly wheel-like, it is to be described as a barrel revolving on an axis and containing within written prayers and books of sacred writing. What the Communists allow now is difficult to say; but Tibetans used to carry miniature prayer-wheels about with them everywhere. (The temples had big ones, in a long line, which were whirled about one after another upon entering.) To turn the crank of the portable prayer-wheel and toss the prayers about was an act of devotion which assured. the Buddhas one's heart was in the right place. Some prayer-wheels had paddles attached to them so that the blades could be dipped into a running stream and the prayers revolved automatically from one year's end to another, to the great merit of the owner.

Another protective device was the repeated utterance of the sacred Sanskrit phrase, *Om mani padme hum* ("Om! the jewel is in the lotus,

Tibetan prayer wheel, its cylinder covered with yak hide and gilded symbols, its interior filled with prayers on parchment and sacred texts. (After *National Geographic* photograph)

hum!"). This phrase was both an expression of religious faith and a powerful spell. Repeated up the mountain and down the valley, inscribed on walls and rocks, churned about endlessly in prayer-wheels, and displayed on banners and streamers, it stood for a central element in the national consciousness. Few who repeated it knew its significance; for that matter, even Western scholars are divided on whether it refers to Avalokita, as Tibetan monks have said, or to the shaktis or Taras. (In the latter case it would have a sexual meaning.) The formula was all but a Tibetan obsession.

The priests had among other things also a protective function. The people looked to them for the performance of rites and the utterance of prayers to the Buddhas that would secure long life and protection against the power of death. And when the great monasteries held their festivals, pilgrims came from all parts, supplied with quantities of butter and cloth for the monks, their priestly protectors; for days they looked on at exciting processions, masked dances, and pageants of the monks, as if their lives depended upon it. In the intervals they turned aside to honor the mythological and historical personages depicted in sculpturesque show-pieces wrought in butter and put on display; there was not only art but magic in them. Finally they went home comforted by the blessing of the head lama and the assurance of the continued favor of the Buddhas.

The clergy of Tibet have had an absorbingly interesting history. They early acquired the name of *lamas,* a term of respect meaning "one who is superior." For a thousand years they lived in thick-walled monasteries. These were originally of the unmilitary Indian model, but finally developed into fortresses of a distinctively Tibetan style, with massive walls rising firmly from the foundation rocks to overhanging roofs far above. The climate, with its extreme cold and its long winters, made necessary the building of walled structures with plenty of room in them for winter stores. In the early days, the life that went on there was more like that of princely magicians than of monks. The tantric Buddhism which was practiced encouraged the lamas to take spouses. Celibacy, at least among the higher clergy, became a rarity. The monasteries therefore often had hereditary heads, the abbots passing their offices on to their sons. In the 9th century the power of the monasteries was greatly increased when the king of Tibet made them grants of land and acknowledged their right to collect tithes thereon. By giving the lamas so much temporal power, the king unwittingly disintegrated his kingdom. He became a nonentity. Several centuries of civil turmoil followed. Kings disappeared from Tibet. In the 13th and 14th centuries the head lama of the Sakya monastery (apparently by appointment from Peking) ruled Tibet politically as well as religiously, though there were rival monasteries that did not submit to his authority.

With the fall of the Mongol empire in China, in the second half of the 14th century, the conditions were created for the final "reform" of Lamaism by the great Tibetan monk Tsong-kha-pa. He organized the so-called Yellow Church, whose executive head is the Dalai Lama. Its monks are popularly known as Yellow Hats, for their hats and girdles are yellow—an evidence of Tsong's attempt to purify Lamaism and take it back in theory and practice toward early Buddhism.* (Yet he re-emphasized the tantric theological doctrine of the Adi-Buddha and saw in Chenregi, which is the Tibetan name for Avalokita, that Buddha's supreme manifestation.) Tsong's reform was in part an imposition of a stricter monastic discipline: there was to be less alcohol and more praying; but what counted most and had the greatest future consequences was the reintroduction of celibacy. The practice of celibacy had the obvious and immediate effect of ending hereditary rule in the Yellow Hat monasteries; the abbots had no sons. But another result ultimately followed (about a century later) which gave the Yellow Church its world-famous theory of the reincarnation of the head lamas in their successors. The principle of unbroken succession has been very strong in the Orient (witness the familial organization in China and emperor-worship in Japan). But the unique thing about Yellow Hat Lamaism is that it applied this principle, not to the family (as in China) nor to the state (as in Japan) but to the ecclesiastical organization (here paralleling Roman Catholicism). When celibacy broke up the old type of succession, the Yellow Hats drew out of their strong Tibetan sense of the continuity and self-perpetuating character of the ecclesiastical organization the theory that the Grand Lamas are the incarnations of the souls of their predecessors, who in turn were Buddhas incarnate. Thus the Grand Lama at Lhasa was considered to be an incarnation of Avalokita, and the abbot of Tashilunpo, the Panchen Lama, was thought to be an incarnation of Amitabha. This idea was extended to the other Yellow Hat monasteries, and spread later to the branch establishments in Mongolia and Peking.

The search for the new living Buddha when a head lama died was often prolonged, and has been known to take years. The object of the search was some child, born in the period after the head lama died, who showed familiarity with his predecessor's belongings, met the test

* The monasteries that resisted reform continued the use of red and constitute the "Red" sects.

of esoteric markings on his body, and was attended otherwise by signs such as the ghostly appearance of the symbols of the deceased lama on the walls of his home. An elaborate series of divination ceremonies was carried through. Among other things a prophetic lake was consulted.

The Grand Lama at Lhasa acquired the name Dalai Lama in the 16th century, when, in response to an invitation from a powerful Mongol chieftain, the Lama journeyed to Mongolia in the guise of Avalokita incarnate, and revived Buddhism there by setting up a revised pantheon, a corrected system of festivals, and a new hierarchy. The grateful Mongol chieftain bestowed upon him the title Dalai, which means "the sea" (i.e., the measureless and profound). This visit extended the operating range and power of the Yellow Church; for it resulted in the spread of Lamaism throughout Mongolia and the establishment of a line of prelates at Urga who were believed to be incarnations of the soul of the famous Indian historian Taranatha, who traveled in Mongolia and was taken by the Mongols to be a very great man.

The success of the Yellow Church in Mongolia furnished the basis for its further spread in China, Siberia, Russia, and along the borders of India.

That Lamaism was vital in the lives of the people of the Snow Land until the Communists came is evident in the fact that one-fifth of the total population resided in the lamaseries. It was a popular ambition to have at least one son out of every family enter the priesthood. The lamaseries were not only religious establishments of venerable age, but centers of political influence and seats of learning. In the Yellow Church, the Dalai Lama had supreme political significance, while the Panchen Lama, of the Tashilunpo monastery, had commanding spiritual prestige.

VIII BUDDHISM TODAY

For centuries all forms of Buddhism, except the Vajrayana, seemed to be in decline. Early Christian missionaries found the temples in decay and the priests somnolent. In some areas the revival of other faiths had dealt a blow, as when Shinto revived in Japan in the 17th century. Today two mighty blows have been dealt Buddhism in China and Tibet, where its future is even in doubt.

But a strong Buddhist revival has occurred in recent years in southern Asia and in Japan. This revival has had mixed causes. One cause is the arrival from the West of a religion whose purpose was to supplant the native religions, but whose missionaries in the very course of seeking more conversions provided the stimulus instead for revival. It happened in this way. In seeking to find points of contact with non-Christians through a more thorough understanding of the native religions, the missionary scholars—and also Westerners who became independently interested—translated, and supplied commentaries to, hundreds of native classics, Hindu, Buddhist, Taoist, and Confucian; and thus, in the very attempt more fully to inform themselves, opened the eyes of educated Asians to the riches of their own cultures.

Another and more widespread cause of revival has been the rise of Asian nationalisms, whose early phases combined anti-colonialism with disillusionment concerning the culture and religions of the West that have proved so prone to wars. Furthermore, the social revolution that has accompanied the growing industrialization of Asia, with its inevitable adoption of many techniques and attitudes of the West, has brought new aims into view—social equality, economic justice, and political self-determination. Concrete measures toward social progress through human action have replaced resignation to fate (Karma). Humanism and secularism have appeared as rivals of the old religions. But the old religions have risen to these challenges and shown new strength.

Theravada (or Hinayana) Buddhism is self-consciously stronger and more alive today in Ceylon, Burma, and Thailand, where it is now the established national faith. There are about 40,000 Theravada monks in Cambodia, and it is said that 90 per cent of the population of Vietnam is Buddhist. A great proportion of these last are Mahayanists, as are the Buddhists of Malaya and particularly of Singapore, where there are many overseas Chinese. Japanese Buddhists are also Mahayanist, with some three hundred sects existing at present as self-supporting units.

In spite of the broad historical differences between Mahayana and Hinayana Buddhism, theoretical and practical efforts are being made to bring about unity. Scholars of the Buddhist world now stress the complementary nature of the two divisions of Buddhism and say that the doctrinal divergences are natural and logical and presuppose a common deposit of faith. The practical measures have taken the form of such relatively international group movements as the Maha Bodhi Society for Theravada Buddhism (founded over fifty years ago), the Young East Association for Mahayana Buddhism, and the Y.M.B.A. (the Young Men's Buddhist Association). These have had a pronounced missionary character. The first has long issued publications for world distribution.

But a more recent movement has projected an even wider outreach; it is the World Fellowship of Buddhists for World Buddhism. Its aim, to bring all branches of Buddhism together, was shown when it held its first Buddhist World Congress in Ceylon and its second in Japan.

The whole Buddhist world was stirred by the Sixth Buddhist Council * held near Rangoon from May 1954 to May 1956 in the newly built World Peace Pagoda. It celebrated the 2500th aniversary of Gautama Buddha's birth. Here the delegates went carefully through the world message of early Buddhism and laid plans for the conversion of the world.

The missionary efforts of Buddhism now encircle the globe. There are active Buddhist missionaries, for example, in the United States. The Shin sect of Japanese Buddhism alone lists over a hundred missionaries at work in the United States and Canada.

It is significant, finally, that Buddhist missionaries have returned to India. In 1953 the Indian government formally handed over to Buddhist care Budhgaya, the site of the Bo-tree under which Gautama experienced enlightenment. There is rising hope in the hearts of many Buddhists that the whole world will someday come at last to the feet of the Enlightened One.

SUGGESTIONS FOR FURTHER READING

ON THE BUDDHIST WORLD AS A WHOLE

Conze, Edward. *Buddhism, Its Essence and Development.* Philosophical Library, 1954. Available as Harper Torchbooks pb

————, trans. *Buddhist Scriptures.* Penguin Classics pb, 1959

Coomaraswamy, Ananda. *Hinduism and Buddhism.* Philosophical Library, 1943. Available as Wisdom Lib. pb

Daval, Har. *The Bodhisattva Doctrine in Buddhist Sanskrit Literature.* K. Paul, Trench, Trubner, 1932

Eliot, Sir Charles. *Hinduism and Buddhism.* 3 vols. Routledge and Kegar Paul, 1954. Earlier edition, Edward Arnold, 1921

Goddard, Dwight, editor. *A Buddhist Bible.* 2nd ed., rev. and enl. An anthology of late texts. Dwight Goddard Estate, Thetford, Vermont, 1938

Grousset, René. *In the Footsteps of the Buddha.* Trans. M. Leon. Routledge, 1932

* The first, second, and third took place, Buddhists say, in the three centuries after the Buddha's death, the fourth and fifth in Burma in the 19th century.

Hackmann, Heinrich. *Buddhism as a Religion.* Probsthain, 1910

Hamilton, C. H. *Buddhism, a Religion of Infinite Compassion.* Selections from Buddhist literature. Liberal Arts Press pb, 1952

Moore, Charles A., ed. *Philosophy—East and West.* Princeton University Press, 1944. Especially chapters IV & V

Morgan, Kenneth W., ed. *The Path of the Buddha.* Ronald Press, 1956

Percheron, Maurice. *Buddha and Buddhism.* Harper, Men of Wisdom pb, 1957

Pratt, J. B. *The Pilgrimage of Buddhism.* Macmillan, 1928

Schayer, S. *Mahayana Doctrines of Salvation.* Probsthain, 1923

Soothill, W. E., trans. *The Lotus of the Wonderful Law.* Oxford, 1920

Suzuki, Beatrice (Lane). *Mahayana Buddhism.* 2nd ed. enl., Marlowe, 1948

Suzuki, D. T. *Outlines of Mahayana Buddhism.* Luzac, 1907

Takakusu, J. *Essentials of Buddhist Philosophy.* 2d ed., University of Hawaii Press, 1949

Thomas, Edward J. *The History of Buddhist Thought.* Knopf, 1933

Winternitz, Moriz. *A History of Indian Literature.* Vol. II, treating of Buddhist literature. University of Calcutta Press, 1933

ON INDIAN BUDDHISM

Burlingame, E. W., ed. *Buddhist Parables,* translated from the Pali. Yale University Press, 1922

Horner, I. *Women under Primitive Buddhism.* Routledge, 1930

Jones, J. J. *The Mahavastu,* a translation from the Sanskrit. Luzac, 1949

Keith, A. B. *Buddhist Philosophy in India and Ceylon.* Oxford, 1923

Smith, Vincent A. *Asoka, the Buddhist Emperor of India.* Oxford, 1920

Vasubandhu. *The Treatise in Twenty Stanzas on Representation—Only.* Trans. C. H. Hamilton from Chinese version of Sanskrit original. American Oriental Society, 1938

Zimmer, Heinrich. *Philosophies of India.* Pantheon, 1951. Available as Meridian pb

ON BUDDHISM IN SOUTHEAST ASIA

Landon, K. P. *Southeast Asia, Crossroad of Religions.* University of Chicago Press, 1949

Saunders, Kenneth J. *Buddhism and Buddhists in Southern Asia.* Macmillan, 1923

ON CHINESE BUDDHISM

Chan, Wing-tsit. *Religious Trends in Modern China.* Columbia University Press, 1953

Johnston, Sir R. F. *Buddhist China.* Dutton, 1913

Lee, Shao Chang. *Popular Buddhism in China.* Shanghai, 1939

Reichelt, K. L. *Truth and Tradition in Chinese Buddhism.* Shanghai, 1927

————. *Religion in Chinese Garment.* Philosophical Library, 1952

ON JAPANESE BUDDHISM

Anesaki, M. A. *A History of Japanese Religion.* K. Paul, Trench, Trubner, 1930

Briggs, William A., ed. *Anthology of Zen.* Grove Press Evergreen pb, 1961

Eliot, Sir Charles. *Japanese Buddhism.* Edward Arnold, 1935

Reischauer, A. K. *Studies in Japanese Buddhism.* Macmillan, 1917

Steinilber-Oberlin, Emile. *The Buddhist Sects of Japan;* their history, philosophical doctrines and sanctuaries. Allen and Unwin, 1938

Suzuki, D. T. *Essays in Zen Buddhism.* Luzac, 1928–1934

————. *Zen Buddhism.* Selected writings edited by William Barrett. Anchor pb, 1956

Watts, Alan W. *The Way of Zen.* Pantheon, 1957. Now available as a Mentor pb, 1959

ON TIBETAN BUDDHISM

Bell, Charles. *The Religion of Tibet.* Oxford, 1931

Evans-Wentz, W. Y. *Tibetan Yoga and Secret Doctrines.* Oxford, 1935

Waddell, L. A. *The Buddhism of Tibet.* 2nd ed., Cambridge, 1939

7 Later Hinduism: Religion as the Basis of the Social Structure

THE RELIGIOUS AWAKENING THAT OCCURRED IN INDIA IN THE SIXTH CENTURY
B.C. manifested itself first in the great heresies, Jainism and Buddhism,
which we have just considered. The urgency of the need to which
these heresies were an answer had been such as to drive men to seek
near-at-hand *practical* modes of escape from their growing sense of
misery rather than to turn for remedy or solace to philosophical speculation or to priestly sacrifices that did not immediately help the individual where he hurt most. So Brahmanism had been rejected as
ineffectual for souls inwardly pained. Such rejection did not require as
much intellectual temerity in the 6th century B.C. as in later periods of
India's history, for Brahmanism had not yet been shaped into system
and logical clarity, and so it was still relatively easy to challenge its
positions as being without relevance. There was in those days just the
beginning of orthodoxy and heterodoxy—no more.

We have seen that Brahmanism had hardly been formulated before vigorous dissent appeared. The Kshatriyas were particularly
aroused to dissent. They did not like either the social or the religious
implications of Brahmanism. The Kshatriyas, some of whom were of
non-Aryan background, possessed among their ranks many brilliant
minds, and these were not slow to detect encroachment on the ruling
caste's domain. The costly sacrifices which the Brahmins prescribed
might ease the anxieties of those who feared or hoped in the gods,

but they did not satisfy the doubtful. Goodness had in it something more than ceremonial zeal and the offering of sacrifices. Moreover, as might be expected, the idealistic monism toward which the Upanishads and their expositors tended struck many of the realistically inclined members of the ruling class as philosophically absurd. Jainism expressed, in part, their commonsense revolt against a world-view that devaluated the individual and turned the evil of the world into illusion. On the other hand it seemed to the ethically minded, that Brahmanism's solution of the problem of human misery was utterly beside the point—not only a waste of precious time but misleading. This was particularly the position taken by early Buddhism.

In the turmoil and clash of opinion that reigned, Brahmanism changed perforce its early character. Thàt it ultimately rose victorious over its rival systems is due to its self-adaptation to changing conditions. The Brahmins never organized under a central authority, never adopted any concerted tactics either of defence or attack upon the heretical systems. They ultimately prevailed, not by being intolerant and defiant toward these other creeds, but precisely by being tolerant toward them. Instead of totally outlawing the distinctive Jainist and Buddhist religious and philosophical views, they pronounced many of them good, and adopted them. Thus the Hindus came to accept as of central importance the Jainist principle of *ahimsa* or non-injury to living beings, until gradually the more strict among them abandoned meat-eating and became vegetarian. From Buddhism the Hindus took over the doctrine of the moral desirability of quenching desire and in this way preparing for final entrance into Nirvana.* They seemed endlessly hospitable to good ideas, however derived or labeled.

The inclusiveness and tolerance of the Brahmins was demonstrated as time went on in other ways. It took centuries to formulate the final positions that were taken, but all along a quiet development of doctrines and laws took place. We shall take note here of two of the more inclusive sets of judgments, one that endorsed four permissible goals in life, and another that recognized not just one but three ways of salvation.

The Four Permissible Goals in Life

With great realism, Hinduism has recognized that men naturally and therefore legitimately seek, in the course of many rebirths, four

---

* This they could do with good grace, because the Vedic literature at certain points anticipated both Jainism and Buddhism.

aims in life. The first two follow the path of desire, the last two that of renunciation.

1. *Kama* or pleasure, especially through love, is the first. So great a place does pleasure occupy in human life that some Hindus have deified it as the god Kama, carrying a flowery bow armed with five flower-arrows that pierce the heart and fill it with desire. Not only is pleasure a permissible human goal, but pleasure seekers need not go unguided. Those who are awkward in love or unskilled in the pleasure-bringing arts of poetry and drama may find instruction either in Vatsyayana's *Kamasutra* (if they seek knowledge of the art of love) or in the *Natyasastras* (if their interest is in the literary arts and skills). Should a man openly choose to make pleasure his aim, he is not criticized, provided he stays within the bounds set by general social rules; he may even be commended for vitality and a sense of direction; but it is thoroughly understood, nevertheless, that in this or some future existence he will come to realize that pleasure is not enough, and that he really wants something more deeply satisfying.

2. *Artha* or power and substance—immediately, things, material possessions; ultimately, high social position or success—is the second permissible goal. A man who is able and alert may quite naturally wish for great possessions and the power and influence that may be obtained through them. This is understood to be a legitimate aspiration, but it requires ruthlessness and toughness. "The big fish eat the little ones." Machiavelli was anticipated in more than one piece of Indian literature. In the *Arthasatras* (by Kautiliya, Kamandaki, and others) or in the beast fables of the *Panchatantra* one may find both sober and humorous instruction in the ruthless competition involved in this way of life. No special blame rests upon the seeker of wealth and power; but it is recognized once again that, if he is allowed to learn for himself, either in this or some future existence, he will discover that he has not sought the highest goal. He will learn that deeper satisfaction comes from following the path of renunciation.

3. *Dharma,* or religious and moral law, sets the standards for a far worthier and more deeply satisfying life. He who follows *dharma* devotes his life to doing his duty by his family, his caste, and his community. He guides himself by the *Code of Manu* and other law books (*dharmasastras*). He renounces his egoistic desire for personal pleasure and social success, and seeks instead the good of all. Profound joy attends this obedience to ethical principles, as the really good man

discovers. But, once more, the joy, however great, is not ultimate. There is of course only one ultimate satisfaction.

4. *Moksha*, salvation or liberation, is the highest and only truly satisfying goal. Negatively, this goal means release from the round of rebirths and all the miseries of human existence, physical and spiritual; positively, it means liberation into fullness of being in Nirvana, for description of which no human words are adequate.

The Three Ways of Salvation

The essential vigor of the older faith was demonstrated further by the fact that the three ways of release or liberation now recognized by orthodox Hinduism were clearly worked out and described.

The first of these is what has come to be known as the *Karma Marga* or Way of Works.

I   THE WAY OF WORKS

This was a very old way. Though held in least esteem by the philosophers, it was followed by the overwhelming majority of the people. It had the triple advantage of being practical, of being understandable and of enjoying the sanctity of age-old custom. It was the plodder's way of salvation. Not markedly emotional, and still less intellectual, it was just a methodical and hopeful carrying out of rites, ceremonies, and duties that added to one's merit (favorable Karma). Many a Hindu has believed that by sacrificing to the gods and his ancestors, revering the rising sun, keeping the sacred hearth fire alight, and performing meticulously the rites and ceremonies that are appropriate at a birth, a death, a marriage, or a harvest, he can acquire enough merit to pass at death into one of the heavens or be reborn as a Brahmin with a real predisposition toward achieving final union with Brahman, the Absolute.

The Way of Works is defined for the first time in the *Brahmanas*, where there occurs a list of "man's debts" in the way of good works. The list is simple and severe. Each man owes to the gods sacrifices, which are good works *par excellence*; in addition, he owes to his seers and teachers the study of the Vedas, to the ancestral spirits offspring, and to his fellowmen hospitality. If he discharges these debts faithfully he has done his whole duty, and by him "all is obtained, all is won." [1] But the simplicity of this conception, with its heavy emphasis on sacrifices, was modified during the passage of the years; and gradually various codes sprang into existence, combining old and new customs into authoritative systems. Typical of these law-books (the famous *dharma-shastras*) is the *Code of Manu*, composed as a collection of rules of life by legalistically minded priests about 200 B.C.

All the lawbooks, beginning with the Code of Manu, lay heavy stress on the ceremonies which should surround the life of each individual and accompany him from birth to death and beyond. Not only must a man observe all the rules of his caste—never marrying outside of it and breaking none of the strict dietary laws and social regulations laid down for it—but he must be faithful in performing for himself and others many religious rites and ceremonies. The Code of Manu prescribes for each individual a long list of sacramental rites for each significant episode of life—for example, at birth, at name-giving, at the first taking out to see the sun, the first feeding with boiled rice, the first hair-cutting, at initiation into manhood, at marriage, and so on. And then there are the honors owing to the tutelary deities of the household. The head of the house must see to it that they are properly worshipped each day and that before each meal they are presented with portions of prepared food, fresh from the hands of the lady of the house. No one may eat until this has been done.

Among the most important of all rites are those following death and directed toward ministering to the ancestral spirits. These are called the *shraddha* rites. To most Hindus it would appear true that without these ceremonies the after-life of the soul *as ancestor* would be cut short, and the soul would have at once to resume the course of rebirth in accordance with the Law of Karma. The shraddha rites, consisting as they do of periodical offerings of memorial prayers and food substances, are thought to be necessary to the very being of the ancestral spirits; without these attentions their strength would completely fail and they would be swept away into the unknown. The most important elements in the food offerings are the *pinda* (food-balls, usually of cooked rice pressed into a firm cake), and these are commonly supposed to provide the dead with a kind of corporeal substance, a "new body." According to one view:

On the first day the dead man gains his head; on the second his ears, eyes, and nose; on the third his hands, breast, and neck; on the fourth his middle parts; on the fifth his legs and feet; on the sixth his vital organs; on the seventh his bones, marrow, veins, and arteries; on the eighth his nails, hair, and teeth; on the ninth all the remaining limbs and organs and his manly strength. The rites of the tenth day are usually specially devoted to the task of removing the sensations of hunger and thirst which the new body then begins to experience.[2]

Pinda are offered to father and mother, to relatives on the father's and mother's side, and to those who have died away from home without rites and who are therefore especially in need of strengthening attentions. (The immature, however—girls who die unmarried and boys who have not reached the age of initiation—have no shraddha rites performed for them.) The pinda must be offered by a male descendant; hence, one must have sons or cease to exist with the same identity after death! Most spirits are considered amply provided for by the obsequy rites immediately following death, but the leading males receive further attentions, once a month for the first year, and then yearly thereafter on the anniversary of death.

There is a Way of Works for women. It is easily stated: their duty is to serve meekly their men. The Code of Manu lays down the Asiatic principle:

In childhood a female must be subject to her father, in youth to her husband, when her lord is dead to her sons; a woman must never be independent.[3]

In line with her dependent status, she should occupy herself with household duties, yielding unquestioning obedience to the old lady at the head of the female side of the family, and worshipping her men. As a faithful wife aspiring to dwell with her husband in the next existence, she should honor and obey him in this, and never displease him, even though he be destitute of virtue, unfaithful, or devoid of good qualities. "A husband must be constantly worshipped as a god by a faithful wife."[4] * After his death she may not marry again; she may

---

* In certain quarters, usually high in the social scale, the wife is taught to show honor to her husband by prostrating herself and touching her head to his feet; or, again, she may adore the big toe of his right foot when he is about to rise in the morning, bathing it as one would an idol, and even offering incense to it and waving lights before it, as though it belonged to a great god.

In the *Padmapurana* the wife's rule of life is put in these uncompromising terms: "There is no other god on earth for a woman than her husband. The most excellent of all good works that she can do is to seek to please him by manifesting perfect obedience to him. Therein should lie her sole rule of life.

"Be her husband deformed, aged, infirm, offensive in his manner; let him be choleric, debauched, immoral, a drunkard, a gambler; let him frequent places of "never even mention the name of another man," but must keep watch over herself, lest she entice one such to evil; and until death remain quiet, patient, and chaste, striving to fulfil "that most excellent duty which is prescribed for wives who have one husband only." [5] The widow "who, from a desire to have offspring, violates her duty to her deceased husband, brings on herself disgrace in this world," and instead of joining her husband in the next existence will "enter the womb of a jackal." [6]

From their superior position men are required, however, to honor women. Their own welfare and happiness, as well as the blessing of offspring, depend thereon. Special gifts of ornaments, clothes, and dainty foods are enjoined on holidays and festivals. But this is the honor bestowed by superiors upon those who serve them well. The superiority of the male must not be lost sight of. A Brahmin, therefore, may not eat in the company of his wife, nor look at her while she eats; and it is prohibited for him to watch her while she dresses herself and applies collyrium to her eyes. So, at least, runs the theoretical statement of what is right and proper. It is, of course, to be borne in mind that all rules like this are never observed without exception, even in the most orthodox circles; and that modern conditions have produced changes in old manners.

Many other rules might be mentioned as part of the orthodox Hindu code down to the present day. On the whole, they prescribe a dry, legalistic, Brahmin-ridden way of life. And yet, the faithful would not say so. The Way of Works is to them a way of true salvation, a means to future freedom and joy.

By all those who studied the matter, however, the Way of Works was considered inferior to another and more philosophic road to salvation, the *Jnana Marga* or Way of Knowledge.

---

ill-repute, live in open sin with other women, have no affection for his home; let him rave like a lunatic; let him live without honor; let him be blind, deaf, dumb, or crippled; in a word, let his defects be what they may, a wife must always look upon him as her god, should lavish him with all her affection and care, paying no heed whatsoever to his character and giving him no cause whatsoever for disapproval.

"A wife must eat only after her husband has had his fill. If the latter fasts, she shall fast, too; if he touch not food, she also shall not touch it; if he be in affliction, she shall be so, too; if he be cheerful, she shall share his joy. She must on the death of her husband allow herself to be burnt alive on the same funeral pyre; then everybody will praise her virtue."

The last part of this quotation refers, of course, to the well-known custom of *suttee*, once widely practiced in India, now forbidden by law, though isolated instances of self-immolation by widows still occur in spite of every precaution of the police.

II THE WAY OF KNOWLEDGE

This solution of the problem of life is based on the reasoning in the Upanishads. Only those who shared the philosophic passion of the Upanishads could follow it.

At the threshold of the Way of Knowledge is the premise that the cause of human misery and evil is Ignorance (*Avidya*). Man in general is so darkly ignorant about his own nature that all his actions have the wrong orientation. Not moral transgression, then, but mental error is the root of human misery and evil.

All the Hindu philosophical systems agree in this presupposition. It is distinctive of the Hindu point of view.

And yet these same philosophical systems do not agree on the propositions to be erected on its basis. There is a good deal of difference of conception as to just what convictions constitute the mental error in the primal Ignorance. For ignorance also has its presuppositions.

It would be interesting here to go into the rival views, but space forbids. We confine ourselves therefore (for the sake of convenience and simplicity) to the best known form of Hindu teaching about Ignorance and its cure, namely, the teaching based on the monistic philosophical position which we have already found in the Upanishads.

According to the monistic view, the evil of man's situation lies in this: he persists in thinking himself a real and separate self, when such is not the fact; for since Brahman-Atman is the sole real being, in whose unity there exists no duality, man is in reality Brahman-Atman and not another. It is hard to realize such a truth, the monistic philosophers admit; too often, "in this Brahma-wheel the soul flutters about, thinking that itself and the Actuator are different." [7] But persistence in the ignorance-fostered illusion that the individual self and the world it knows exist apart from, and are other than, the All-Soul is the cause of the world-entangled life of men and of their incessant births into one existence after another. So long as man continues ignorant and lives on in the illusion of separate selfhood, so long he is bound to the ever-turning Wheel.

In seeking to clarify and illustrate this idea the monists, from the time of the Upanishads, have often resorted to analogies. They say that the relation between the individual and Brahman-Atman is similar to that between rivers and the ocean within which they disappear.

> As the flowing rivers in the ocean
> Disappear, quitting name and form,
> So the knower, being liberated from
> name and form,

> Goes into the heavenly Person, higher
> than the high.[8]

The individual is also said to be like a wave rising from and sinking again in the sea, or like a drop of spray, which momentarily flies above the sea. A brief amplification of this last analogy will further bring out the meaning. A drop of brine beheld apart from the ocean, flying, let us say, across the face of the sea, may be viewed under two aspects; under the first, it appears to be an individual drop of a certain size and consistency, with a particular location in time and space differentiating it from any other drop or any other entity whatever; under the second view, however, this is a misleading description of the case, for the drop is in reality *only the ocean in the air*, it is after all only *apparently* a thing by itself, a pure individual. This second view of the nature of the drop is that supported by Hindu thought. By analogies such as this the belief is driven home that all created things, all the "appearances"which commonsense realism accepts as being exactly as they seem, are in reality Brahman-Atman and not what they seem. They all have reality, but it is the reality of being Brahman-Atman.

For man, then, salvation comes with right understanding, and then

> The knot of the heart is loosened,
> All doubts are cut off,
> And one's deeds (karma) cease.[9]

There remains this point to make clear: how does one *know* "the knot of the heart is loosened"? When does faith in union become knowledge of union?

Here all the intellectual systems agree that knowledge of union is not merely a matter of accepting good doctrine. There are varieties of acceptable doctrine, and the adoption of any one variety comes short of salvation itself. Salvation itself—the saving knowledge that one has reached a state of consciousness which admits him into the realm of reality where karma ceases to exert its effects and rebirth reaches an end—comes by an ecstatic flash of certitude in the midst of deep meditation.

This flash of certitude is the ultimate goal of the Way of Knowledge. To reach it requires long preparation and self-discipline.

The classical conception of the life-preparation required to reach this last step in the Way of Knowledge is given in the *Code of Manu*. The ideal career of the pious Brahmin is there outlined for all India to admire, and for Brahmins, sometimes, to emulate. There are four stages or *ashramas* in the ideal life-plan. Under one exacting program, the Way of Works and the Way of Knowledge are interfused. The stages are: (1) that of student of religion, (2) that of married man and householder, (3) that of hermit, and (4) that of *sannyasin* or mendicant "holy man."

It was proposed that when the young Brahmin had passed through the sacramental rites surrounding early childhood (at birth, name-giving, the first taking out to see the sun, the first feeding with boiled rice, the first hair-cutting, and so on), he should enter upon the initial stage of his conscious journey to salvation, that of *student of religion.* This was to begin with ceremonial investiture with the badge of caste, the sacred cord, during which solemnity, while tending the sacred fire and going through holy rites of purification, he would experience his second or spiritual birth. He was then to be conducted to the home of a teacher to study the Vedas, the purificatory and sacrificial rites, and the duties of his caste. His residence at the house of his teacher was to last for an indefinite period, perhaps until his twenty-fifth year, depending on the number of Vedic treatises he wished to study. His teacher meanwhile was not to supply him with food; that was to be obtained by the student himself, by going from house to house, begging-bowl in hand.

When he reached the end of his period of study, he was to leave his teacher and enter upon the second stage of his life. He was now to rejoin his family, marry, and take up the duties of *householder.* This was thought very necessary. No Brahmin, however deep his religious preoccupation, was considered worthy or wise unless he left a son to carry out the periodical obsequy rites for the ancestors and to leave children in his turn. The stage of householder was to be closely regulated by ancient religious rules and filled with ceremonies, all of which he was to perform with utmost diligence. He was to be well aware that every householder of necessity injures living things, especially in cooking.

A householder has five slaughter-houses as it were, viz., the hearth, the grinding-stone, the broom, the pestle and mortar, and the water-vessel, by using which he is bound with the fetters of sin. In order successively to expiate the offences committed by means of all these five, the great sages have prescribed for householders the daily performance of the five great sacrifices. Teaching and studying is the sacrifice offered to Brahma, the offerings of water and food called Tarpana the sacrifice to the ancestors, the burnt oblation the sacrifice offered to the gods, the Bali offering that offered to the Bhutas [good and evil spirits of many sorts], and the hospitable reception of guests the offering to men.[10]

He was to be extremely careful in his diet. He was never to break any caste rules. At length, sometimes after many years, when he saw his "skin wrinkled, and his hair white, and the sons of his sons," [11] he was to enter upon the third stage of his career.

As a *hermit* he was not expected to live an easy life. His whole thought was to be concentered on developing a complete indifference toward everything in the world to which he had been previously attached.

> Abandoning all food raised by cultivation, and all his belongings, he may depart into the forest, either committing his wife to his sons, or accompanied by her. Taking with him the sacred fire and the implements required for domestic sacrifices, he may reside there. Let him offer those five great sacrifices according to the rule. Let him wear a (deer-) skin or a tattered garment . . . be always industrious in privately reciting the Veda . . . never a receiver of gifts . . . compassionate toward all living creatures . . . Let him not eat anything grown on ploughed land or in a village . . . In order to obtain complete union with the supreme Soul, he must study the various sacred texts contained in the Upanishads . . . abandoning all attachments to worldly objects.[12]

When he had become wholly and purely spiritual, he was released from any further offering of sacrifices to gods and ancestors, and free therefore to let his sacred fire die out, for it was now "reposited in his mind." If she were still with him, his wife would see he had reached liberation from all earthly ties and would depart, leaving him alone in the forest. Thus would be ushered in the fourth and last stage of his existence.

In this last stage—that of *holy man*—he was to seek attainment of the final goal of the Way of Knowledge: the trance of union with the Infinite. Death might overtake him before he had completely realized absorption in the eternal Brahman, but the *summum bonum* was to have the experience before death. Such an experience would come, as he knew, only in the midst of deep meditation. "All depends on meditation," says the *Code of Manu*, "for he who is not proficient in the knowledge of that which refers to the supreme Soul reaps not the full reward."[13] The Code gives us a vivid description of the final situation:

> Let him always wander alone, without any companion . . . He shall possess neither a fire nor a dwelling . . . Let him go to beg once a day . . . When no smoke ascends from the kitchen, when the pestle lies motionless, when the embers have been extinguished, when the people have finished their meal, when the remnants in the dishes have been removed, let the ascetic beg. . . . The roots of trees for a dwelling, coarse worn-out garments, life in solitude and indifference towards everything, are the marks of one

who has obtained liberation. Let him not desire to die, let him not desire to live, let him wait for his appointed time, as a servant waits for the payment of his wages . . . By deep meditation let him recognize the subtle nature of the supreme Soul, and its presence in all organisms . . . He who has in this manner gradually given up all attachments reposes in Brahman alone . . . He attains the eternal Brahman . . .[14]

Down to the present day this final state of absorption in the Ultimate (called *samadhi*) is the goal toward which all who take the Way of Knowledge aspire. But it is not easy to attain it by purely intellectual processes. From the very first it was felt that the body had to assist the mind in suspending, in part at least, its normal functions. The Upanishads contain the first hints about a method, called *Yoga*, beginning with "restraint of the breath, withdrawal of the senses from objects" and ending with "contemplation" and "absorption."[15] There is reference also to the mystic syllable OM, which is to be repeated over and over again, until the devotee reaches ecstasy. Of Yoga and yogis we shall hear later; for we shall appreciate their importance better in another connection. But we may note now that the followers of the Yoga disciplines gave great support to the Way of Knowledge as a primarily important method of release from the burdensomeness of life betrayed into ignorance of mind by the seductions of the senses.

III THE WAY OF DEVOTION

Perhaps the greatest single element in the successful resistance of Hinduism to absorption by Buddhism was the attitude of the common people of India. Through the long years of the crisis and slow recovery of Hinduism, the common people, not greatly affected by the intellectual excitement of the upper classes, calmly went on being religious in their own way. The Brahmins felt this ground swell, and helped to save Hinduism by yielding to it. While the more sophisticated minds of the time discoursed philosophy, the people insisted on getting help from gods and goddesses. The *Code of Manu*, in fact, contains more than one intimation of the presence of a new factor in the religious outlook, and with it the rise of a third way of salvation or release, rivaling the Way of Works and the Way of Knowledge. It mentions temples and temple priests for the first time in Hindu literature. *Bhakti Marga* (the Way of Devotion) had come into being.

Bhakti may be defined as ardent and hopeful devotion to a particular deity in grateful recognition of aid received or promised. It often assumes the form of a passionate love of the deity, whether god or goddess. Its marks are surrender of self to the divine being and acts of devotion in temple worship and in private life and thought.

Bhakti emerged at a comparatively late period, but it brought with it the savor of ancient faith. That it did emerge prompts the reflection that the needs of the common man can never for long be gainsaid. From primitive times he has sought the favor of gods and goddesses, and he cannot be made to believe that devotion to deities does not bring salvation. His experience has been that the world is filled with powers greater than himself from whom saving help may come. The common man never could follow the philosophers and meditative intellects down the Way of Knowledge; he was not capable of long and close introspection into the obscure movements of his own soul. Not that he held the findings of the intellectual classes to be untrue; on the contrary, he regarded with respect the opinions of the intelligentsia, much as the man of the masses today applauds, without understanding, the incomprehensible theories of an Einstein. But such acknowledgement of the rightfulness in their own sphere of the reasoning of pundits does not now, and never did in India, affect the daily course of life. The common man thinks: "The philosopher's way may be all right for him; but I must follow my lights as best I can." *

In popular Hinduism the far-reaching effect of bhakti on the external forms of religion has been incalculable. Many different sects seek salvation through devotion. No denial of the efficacy of the Way of Knowledge and of the Way of Works is implied; it is even admitted that these may have a superior efficacy; but the positive claim is made, that devotion to deity is a true way of salvation in itself, whether or not one interweaves with it, as one may, certain aspects of the other two ways.

The first important literary recognition of Bhakti Marga as a true way of salvation was made in the famed *Bhagavad Gita* or *Song of the Blessed Lord*, one of the great classics of religious literature. To it we must devote special attention, for it has very greatly influenced Hinduism for over a thousand years.

This poem occurs in its present form as an episode in the enormous epic, the *Mahabharata*, which was composed over a period of eight hundred years (400 B.C. to 400 A.D.), contains 100,000 couplets, and deals in the main with the exploits of Kshatriya clans, specifically with the fall of the Kuru (Kaurava) princes at the hands of their relatives, the Pandavas, directed by the hero-god Krishna. The Bhagavad Gita

---

* In India he may add: "In some future existence I'll be a philosopher."

was interpolated into the Mahabharata about the 1st century A.D. In every respect a remarkable poem, it has been more admired and more used for devotional and intellectual needs than any other Hindu work— this in spite of its eclectic character, philosophically and otherwise.*
Its verve and emotional power have won many converts to its doctrines.

The Gita's greatest historical significance lies in its endorsement of bhakti as a true way of salvation and release. This endorsement comes in the course of a story dramatically conceived and told. Arjuna, the great warrior of the family of Pandavas, hesitates suddenly when on the point of leading his brothers and their allies into battle against the Kuru princes, sons of his uncle, the blind Dhritirashtra, and thus his close relatives. The hero-god Krishna is his charioteer, and stands at his side poised for instant action. But it is not Arjuna who acts; it is the Kuru leader, his uncle, who orders the conch-shell to be blown as the signal for battle.

> Then at the signal of the aged king.
> With blare to wake the blood, rolling around
> Like to a lion's roar, the trumpeter
> Blew the great Conch; and, at the noise of it,
> Trumpets and drums, cymbals and gongs and horns,
> Burst into sudden clamor; as the blasts
> Of loosened tempest, such the tumult seemed!
>
> Then 'twas—
> Beholding Dhritirashtra's battle set,
> Weapons unsheathing, bows drawn forth, the war
> Instant to break—Arjuna spake this thing
> To Krishna the Divine his charioteer:
> "Drive, Dauntless One! to yonder open ground
> Betwixt the armies; I would see more nigh
> Those who will fight with us, those we must slay
> Today!" [16]

But when Krishna drives the chariot, with its milk-white steeds, between the lines, Arjuna marks on each hand

* It makes the eclectic attempt, for example, to interweave into one way of life *all three* ways of release—knowledge, works, and devotion. It grants that knowledge leads to unconditioned release, and that the doing of good works is not to be scorned. But it agrees with those who protest against the performance of the prescribed works merely out of desire for the rewards that accrue, and says that such working for rewards secures only certain transient blessings in the next existence. It goes on, however, to take a position far in advance of the common Brahmin opinion when it declares that the performance of works, if carried out without any desire for reward, but only for the god, or for righteousness' sake, can win release on the basis of such works alone.

the kinsmen of his house,
Grandsires and sires, uncles and brothers and sons,
Cousins and sons-in-law and nephews, mixed
With friends and honored elders; some this side,
Some that side ranged.[17]

At this sight his heart melts with sudden compunction. He addresses his charioteer in tones of anguish:

"Krishna! as I behold, come here to shed
Their common blood, yon concourse of our kin,
My members fail, my tongue dries in my mouth,
A shudder thrills my body, and my hair
Bristles with horror; hardly may I stand.

. . . What rich spoils
Could profit; what rule recompense; what span
Of life seem sweet, bought with such blood?
Seeing that these stand here, ready to die,
For whose sake life was fair, and pleasure pleased,
And power grew precious:—grandsires, sires, and sons,
Brothers, and fathers-in-law, and sons-in-law,
Elders and friends!"

So speaking, in the face of those two hosts,
Arjuna sank upon his chariot-seat,
And let fall bow and arrows, sick at heart.[18]

When Krishna tries to stir the conscience-stricken warrior with the charge: "Cast off the coward-fit! Wake! Be thyself! Arise, Scourge of thy foes!" Arjuna's only reply is to reiterate his doubts and ask Krishna's counsel. Krishna's answer is made in the course of a long dialogue, whose design, in the first instance, is to exalt caste-duty above every other consideration, no matter what is entailed and without thought of reward. Arjuna is told that his duty as a Kshatriya is to fight, when just war is joined, whether in doing so he kills his relatives or not. If he shuns the honorable field—he, a Kshatriya—if, knowing his duty and his task, he lets duty and task go by,—that would be sin! If he fights and is killed, he will enter the Swarga-heaven; while if he is victorious, he will mount a king's throne. As to those he may slay, grief for them would be lacking in reflection. The soul cannot be slain.

"Thou grievest where no grief should be! thou speak'st
Words lacking wisdom! for the wise in heart
Mourn not for those that live, nor those that die.
Nor I, nor thou, nor any one of these,
Ever was not, nor ever will not be.

All, that doth live, lives always! . . .
                . . . Indestructible,
Learn thou! the Life is, spreading life through all . . .
But for these fleeting frames which it informs
With spirit deathless, endless, infinite,
They perish. Let them perish, Prince! and fight!
He who shall say, 'Lo! I have slain a man!'
He who shall think, 'Lo! I am slain!' those both
Know naught! Life cannot slay. Life is not slain!" [19]

Having thus looked philosophically at the immediate difficulties, Krishna proceeds to tell the still emotionally disturbed warrior that there are two ways of exerting oneself—one is the way of action and the other the way of meditation—and that the way of meditation or wisdom, leading as it does to insight and self-identification with the Ultimate Reality, is of the first importance if one is to have the right attitude in action. But these paths, as it were, cross. For "no one can ever rest (in meditation) even for an instant without performing action," [20] and, what is more important for Arjuna, no one can act rightly unless he acts in accordance with the insights given in meditation.

To begin with, meditation discloses that the way to act rightly is to act without thought of fruit (rewards) and from duty alone.

            "Let right deeds be
Thy motive, not the fruit which comes from them.
And live in action! Labor! Make thine acts
Thy piety, casting all self aside,
Contemning gain and merit. . . .
            "Therefore, thy task prescribed
With spirit unattached gladly perform,
Since in performance of plain duty man
Mounts to his highest bliss. . . .
            "For My sake, then,
With meditation centered inwardly,
Seeking no profit, satisfied, serene,
Heedless of issue—fight!" [21]

Arjuna is gently urged to grasp the fact that men who have attained the calm which comes with the vision of Ultimate Reality do what is prescribed for them by birth and station, not for their own sakes, but for the sake of the All, the eternal Brahman.

And now Krishna, who is the incarnation of Vishnu and so no less than the Supreme God come to earth in human form, points out to Arjuna the spiritual benefits of action-illuminating Yoga. By Yoga Arjuna may see all things—all actions—in their proper perspective, as the work of the eternal World-Spirit, Brahman, the ruling Soul of all things.

But Brahman is not here given a purely impersonal connotation. Krishna is Vishnu, and Vishnu is Brahman, the One Subject in which all-that-is is gathered up into one. He who attaches himself to Vishnu may therefore experience the reality of union with Brahman. The yogin whose greatest desire is to enjoy the ecstasy of perfect release by absorption into the Ultimate, may find such release through meditative absorption in a Person—that of Vishnu, if he considers the deity on high; or that of Krishna, if the incarnation in the gallant charioteer attracts his trust.

> Sequestered should he sit,
> Steadfastly meditating, solitary,
> His thoughts controlled, his passions laid away,
> Quit of belongings. In a fair, still spot
> Having his fixed abode,—not too much raised,
> Nor yet too low,—let him abide, his goods
> A cloth, a deerskin, and the Kusa-grass.
> There, setting hard his mind upon The One,
> Restraining heart and senses, silent, calm,
> Let him accomplish Yoga, and achieve
> Pureness of soul, holding immovable
> Body and neck and head, his gaze absorbed
> Upon his nose-end, rapt from all around,
> Tranquil in spirit, free of fear, intent
> Upon his Brahmacharya vow, devout,
> Musing on Me, lost in the thought of Me.
> That Yojin, so devoted, so controlled,
> Comes to the peace beyond,—My peace, the peace
> Of high Nirvana! . . .
> He who thus vows
> His soul to the Supreme Soul, quitting sin,
> Passes unhindered to the endless bliss
> Of unity with Brahma. He so vowed,
> So blended, sees the Life-Soul resident
> In all things living, and all living things
> In that Life-Soul contained. And whoso thus
> Discerneth Me in all, and all in Me,
> I never let him go; nor looseneth he
> Hold upon Me; but dwell he where he may,
> Whate'er his life, in Me he dwells and lives.[22]

In this remarkable passage the Gita seeks to assimilate the doctrines of the Upanishads to its partial theism. (The theism is only partial, because it has so pronounced a pantheistic side.) With the same purpose, in later passages Krishna declares, "I Brahma am! the one eternal God!" Hence:

"I am the Sacrifice! I am the Prayer!
I am the Funeral-cake set for the dead!
I am—of all this boundless Universe—
The Father, Mother, Ancestor and Guard!
The end of Learning! That which purifies
In lustral water! I am OM! I am
Rig-Veda, Sama-Veda, Yajur-Ved;
The Way, the Fosterer, the Lord, the Judge,
The Witness; the Abode, the Refuge-House,
The Friend, the Fountain and the Sea of Life
Which sends and swallows up! Seed and Seed-sower,
Whence endless harvests spring! . . .
Death am I, and Immortal Life I am,
Arjuna! SAT and ASAT, Visible Life
And Life Invisible!" [23]

And then, as Arjuna looks on with wonder, Krishna is transfigured before him into Vishnu, the eternal Brahman in god-form, displaying to the astounded warrior his true reality, endowed with numberless mouths, countless eyes, "all-regarding" faces turned in every direction, and clothed in ornaments, wreaths, and divine apparel scented with heavenly fragrance.

If there should rise
Suddenly within the skies
Sunburst of a thousand suns
Flooding earth with rays undeemed-of,
Then might be that Holy One's
Majesty and glory dreamed of! [24]

At this sight, which makes his every hair bristle with awe, Arjuna gives voice to his adoration, and then prays that the too sublime vision be removed and the god return to the kindly disguise of Krishna, the Charioteer. The god accedes to this request, and then proceeds to deliver the heart of the Gita's message; he demands the uttermost surrender of perfect faith in himself—unconditioned *bhakti*—as the way to full and final release.

"Cling thou to Me!
Clasp Me with heart and mind! so shalt thou dwell
Surely with Me on high. But if thy thought
Droops from such height; if thou be'st weak to set

Body and soul upon Me constantly,
Despair not! give Me lower service! seek
To read Me, worshipping with steadfast will;
And, if thou canst not worship steadfastly,
Work for Me, toil in works pleasing to Me!
For he that laboreth right for love of Me
Shall finally attain! But, if in this
Thy faint heart fails, bring Me thy failure! find
Refuge in Me! let fruits of labor go,
Renouncing all for Me, with lowliest heart,
So shalt thou come; for, though to know is more
Then diligence, yet worship better is
Than knowing, and renouncing better still.
Near to renunciation—very near—
Dwelleth eternal Peace! . . .

"Take my last word, my utmost meaning have!
Give Me thy heart! adore Me! serve Me! cling
In faith and love and reverence to Me!
So shalt thou come to Me! I promise true.
Make Me thy single refuge! I will free
Thy soul from all its sins! Be of good cheer!" [25]

These passages have had historic importance, not only because of their beauty, but also because of their influence on the intimate life of thousands of Hindu leaders and holy men, down to Mahatma Gandhi in the present day. Though philosophically the Bhagavad Gita's whole conception of reality and of the meaning of life is shot through with unresolved inconsistencies, its practical effect has been to stimulate and deepen Hinduism on its religious side, and to make the Bhakti Marga of popular Hinduism intellectually respectable. It must be quite evident at this point that neither the Way of Knowledge, which is so highly intellectual and self-disciplinary, nor the Way of Works, which is so largely moral and practical, can satisfy fully the religious need of the average man as can the Way of Devotion. The Bhagavad Gita, therefore, has won for itself a unique place in the esteem of all Hindus; and though the followers of Vishnu lay first claim to it as their most blessed scripture, educated Hindus of all sects honor it as a worthy expression of the emotional factor in religion.

There is yet another reason why the Bhagavad Gita is so appreciated in India. In it Krishna throws wide open the gate of the Way of Devotion and invites all wayfarers, whatever their sex or caste, to enter.

"Be certain none can perish, trusting Me!
O Pritha's Son! whoso will turn to Me,

> Though they be born from the very womb of Sin,
> Woman or man; sprung of the Vaisya caste
> Or lowly disregarded Sudra,—all
> Plant foot upon the highest path; how then
> The holy Brahmins and My Royal Saints? . . .
> Fix heart and thought on Me! Adore Me! Bring
> Offerings to Me! Make me prostrations! Make
> Me your supremest joy! and, undivided,
> Unto My rest your spirits shall be guided." [26]

Nothing could be more suited to meet the profound and unspoken need of millions in India for a ray of hope in their troubled bondage to social and religious restrictions.

IV THE SIX SYSTEMS OF ORTHODOX HINDU PHILOSOPHY

During the millenium from 500 B.C. to 500 A.D. the orthodox systems of Hindu philosophy took shape. In another thousand years they were refined into final fixed form. Their number is far greater than six, but Hindus themselves have singled out that many as the most significant, because between them they cover the whole ground gone over by all the orthodox philosophical views. These six make the one assumption that is considered necessary by Hindus to meet the conditions of orthodoxy, namely, that the Vedas are the inspired and final rule of faith. It is usually understood that in this case the Vedas include the early commentaries and interpretations (the Brahmanas and Upanishads) which are appended to the original four books.

We shall not follow the Hindu savants in considering each of the six orthodox philosophics in order; we are chiefly interested in those that have had the greatest effect on religion. (The rest will be treated briefly in footnotes.*)

* Hindu scholars have arranged the six philosophies in their logical rather than their chronological order, beginning first with the philosophy that is most concerned with logic and epistemological method. This is the *Nyaya System,* based upon a text ascribed to a philosopher bearing the same name as the founder of Buddhism, i.e. Gautama. A complete analysis of correct reasoning is attempted. True knowledge is said to follow upon four processes of knowing: sense-perception, inference, comparison of fact, and trustworthy testimony. Emphasis is placed on testing knowledge by the findings of the five senses, whose report of the reality of the external world, for example, is accepted as correct. A major conclusion is, that all misery follows from false notions, for such notions give rise to activities having bad consequences in successive rebirths. Hence, emancipation depends on sound knowledge.

The Sankhya System

This important system of thought was in the first instance a reaction from the monism expressed in the Upanishads. It is almost as old as the first Upanishadic speculations and finds expression itself in some of the later Upanishads. Its founder is said to have been one Kapila, born at Kapilavastu, a century before Gautama Buddha was born there. The Sankhya system derived from him profoundly influenced both Jainism and Buddhism. It is staunchly dualistic and atheistic, maintaining that there are two eternal categories of being: (1) Matter or the phenomenal world (*prakriti,* nature) and (2) Soul (*purusha*). The former, or the world of Nature, is made up of twenty-three kinds of entities or substances (*tattvas*), including higher intellect (*buddhi*), mind (*manas*) and ego (*ahankara*), and each of these is characterized by three dispositions or *gunas* ("strands"): a light, happy, open one called *sattva* (purity or goodness), an active, driving, passionate one called *rajas* (passion, energy), and a brooding, stupid, moody one called *tamas* (darkness). These concepts have had great influence on Hindu psychology. As for the realm of soul (*purusha*), it is not constituted of a single All-Soul, like the Brahman-Atman of the monists, but of an infinite number of individual souls, each independent and eternal. The souls entangled in nature have fallen into misery and suffering through ignorance (*avidya*) of the distinction between soul and matter, an ignorance which has led directly to the fettering of the soul to bodily processes and to nature (*prakriti*), and this causes the soul to be reborn again and again. Salvation from the recurring cycle of existences comes, not through knowledge of identity with any All-Soul (declared non-existent), but through knowledge of *the soul's existential diversity from matter,* followed by final passage into a state of eternal but unconscious individuality, in the purity of the spirit. Here, too, salvation is sought by the Way of Knowledge.

The Yoga System

This system of mental discipline has been greatly developed since it was first mentioned in the Upanishads, and it has won an important place in the practice of the Way of Knowledge. It became a highly refined technique in the hands of Patanjali (2nd century A.D.), a yogin who derived most of his ideas from the Sankhya system, though he differed from it in accepting theism as a part of his world-view. The philosophical basis of Yoga is, however, not as important historically as the practical measures, the technique of meditation and concentration,

developed in connection with it. These practical measures are a psychologically sophisticated modification of the purely metaphysical way to
"release and liberation." It was as apparent then as now, that the Way
of Knowledge, as at first formulated, required an intellectual effort most
difficult to attain, because concentration of pure thought to the proper
degree is beyond the capacity of all but the clearest minds and strongest
wills. Hence, when a modification of its intellectual rigors, leading in
the end to the same experience, was found, it was eagerly taken up.
Yoga's greatest appeal lies in its physiological and psychological measures to assist the mind in the effort to concentrate. It consists largely of
special postures, methods of breathing, and rhythmical repetition of the
proper thought-formulas. The typical procedure, that of the classic *Raja
Yoga* of Patanjali, has eight steps:

1. Performing the five desire-killing vows, or Yama; a step by which the
yoga-aspirant abstains from harming living things (that is, he practices
ahimsa), from deceit, stealing, unchastity (he takes the brahmacharya vow),
and from acquisitiveness.

2. Observance (Niyama) of self-disciplinary rules—cleanliness, calm,
mortification, study, and prayer.

3. Sitting in the proper posture (Asana); for example, with the right
foot upon the left thigh, the left foot upon the right thigh, the hands crossed,
and the eyes focused on the tip of the nose.

4. Regulation of the breath or Pranayama; where the aim is to reduce
the whole of being alive to one or two simple and rhythmic processes, all the
muscles, voluntary and involuntary, and the nerve-currents, being brought
under control. The aspirant is advised to sit upright, with head, neck, and
chest in a straight line, and to breathe in and out rhythmically, while, perhaps, inwardly repeating the sacred word AUM. (Later refinements of this
step suggested breathing up the left nostril, then out of the right, holding
the breath between times, in order to allow nerve-currents to descend the
spinal column, strike forcefully the reserves of nervous energy at the base of
the spine and release them!)

5. Withdrawal of the senses from all sense objects, or Pratyahara, much
as a tortoise retreats under his shell by drawing in its head and limbs. This
step shuts out the outside world.

6. Concentration, or Dharana, during which the mind is held steadily to
the contemplation of a single idea or object until it is emptied of all else.

7. Meditation, or Dhyana, a half unconscious condition affording a transition to the last step.

8. Samadhi, a trance in which the mind, now emptied of all content and
no longer aware of either object or subject, is absorbed into the Ultimate,
and is one with the One.

The central feature of Yoga practice, whether in this or its other forms, is the use of the mind to suppress its own conscious movements, the whole body being so disciplined as to aid in the gradual suspension of consciousness and the bringing on of a state of pure ecstasy that is without thought and without sensation. The result is felt to be a complete freeing of the true self from the external world and natural causation. Extraordinary claims of psychic power are made by those who accept the intuitions which precede or follow this state: for example, that the' yogin actually achieves levitation, can transcend the limits of space and time and be in several places or times at once, or can acquire the powers and qualities of anything upon which he chooses to concentrate. But, of course, the chief aim of Yoga is none of these things; it is, rather, the experience of utter and complete freedom of the self from earthly bonds.

The Vedanta System

The name of this system is derived from the source of its leading doctrines, the Upanishads, which were commonly called the Vedanta— that is, "the concluding portions of the Vedas." An exciting basis for future speculation was contained in the Upanishads, especially in the treatises which tended toward philosophical monism or pantheism. The conservatives, following the lead of literalists like Jaimini,* might refuse to budge from their fundamentalist positions; the mediationalists, like

---

* Founder of the *Purva-Mimansa System*, listed by scholars as the fifth of the orthodox systems. This is the least philosophical of the six systems. It clings with unique consistency and simplicity to its doctrine of the literal inspiration of the four Vedas. Jaimini scorned to philosophize in the manner of the Upanishads; his thought ran, rather, in the moulds provided by the Brahmanas. So highly did he regard the truth of the Vedas that he asserted they never had an author, but were themselves uncreated and eternal. Hence, he felt under no necessity to postulate a Supreme Being as the source of the revelation contained in them. He did not know whether there was such a being. It was enough to know that the Vedas and Brahmanas contained the whole Dharma or duty of man, and that by determining their literal meaning and carrying out the rites and ceremonies described in them liberation could be attained. When so much eternal and absolute truth was at hand, it seemed a monstrous impiety for men to want to spin their vain-glorious speculation about the universe out of their own desire-filled heads. ("Mere rationalizations!" he would perhaps have said had he been a modern.) Jaimini's position in this matter was not essentially altered by his later followers, even though they became theists who declared that the Dharma, still considered literally true in every part, should be studied and practiced as an offering to a supreme God, who waited to redeem them as a reward for their faithfulness.

Kanada* and Kapila, might continue in their commonsense way to affirm the reality both of the world and of individual souls; but the liberals and the radicals, who were sure that intuition superseded and transcended common sense, rushed on with speculative enthusiasm to propound the doctrine that the external world and human consciousness are alike Maya or Illusion, and claimed the authority of the Upanishads for it. Advanced Indian thought has usually sided with them.

The first attempt to set forth the monistic teachings of the Upanishads in a consistent philosophic system is contained in the difficult aphorisms of the *Vedanta Sutra*. These are said to have been prepared by Badarayana, a noted teacher who lived, it seems probable, during the 1st century before the Christian era. His aphorisms were meant to be committed to memory and were so pithy as to be ambiguous and confusing in effect. Even during his lifetime his own oral commentary was necessary to render them intelligible. During the centuries that followed, such oral interpretation, often rather dubiously supported by the original text, was continued, and resulted finally in the rise of three different systems of Vedanta philosophy—those founded by Sankara, Ramanuja, and Madhva.

Sankara's system of thought—"illusionist monism"—is called "non-dualism" (*advaita*), because it holds that the world and Brahman do not really exist separately; in reality nothing but the impersonal and indescribable Brahman exists; all else is illusion (*Maya*). The physical universe, the individuality of the soul, rebirth itself, are all illusions—such illusions or phantasmagoria as one meets in dreams or at the hands of the conjurer. The source of this view is traced back to the later Upanishads, where, for example, in the *Shvetasvatara Upanishad*, it is said:

> Sacred poetry, the sacrifices, the ceremonies, the ordinances,
> The past, the future, and what the Vedas declare—
> This whole world the illusion-maker projects out of this Brahman,

* Founder of the *Vaisheshika System*, the second of the orthodox systems. His school of thought applied logical methods (specifically, seven "categories") to the study of the external world. In accordance with the postulates of an atomic theory resembling in its initial (but not final) positions the philosophy of the western philosopher Democritus, the external world is declared to be a self-existent reality, formed of eternal and indivisible atoms combining and recombining eternally. Later thinkers of the school say that this process is not purely mechanistic, for it takes place by the power of Advishta ("the unseen force" of deity). Thus, alongside the eternal atoms is an eternal Soul, the source of all transmigrating souls. The cosmos thus conceived will, it is argued, never be destroyed, for both atoms and souls will abide indestructible forever.

And in it by illusion the individual soul is confined.
Now, one should know that Nature is illusion,
And that Mighty Lord is the illusion-maker.[27]

But the illusion is not said to be absolute. Sankara was true to the
spirit of Indian philosophy in treating this point with great subtlety.
The word "illusion" had about the same meaning for him that the word
"appearance" had for Immanuel Kant. The apposition in Kant's thought
between the phenomenal and the noumenal worlds is matched in Sankara's thought by the apposition between the world of Maya and the
world of Brahman. The human soul, according to Sankara, can apprehend only the deceptive appearance of things when he relies on his
senses for knowledge. The sensible world in which his everyday experience takes place is the subjective spatio-temporal frame of reference
through which his ignorance (*avidya*: non-knowledge) self-deceivingly
perceives the Real. The notion that the objects of sense-experience are
"realities" is the work of this ignorance. Ignorance is, indeed, the active
force that creates the everyday world by a process just the same as
that by which the piece of rope lying by the roadside is seen in the
twilight as a snake, or the distant post as a man. To believe that one
has seen a snake or a man in such circumstances is to submit uncritically to Maya, the illusion-making power that has produced the
phenomenal world as its "sport" or "play."

Therefore, to believe in the reality of the individual soul, as is the
common experience, is to move in the world of Maya, and to have only
the lower kind of knowledge; but to know that our separate selves are
identical with the one Self, Brahman-Atman, is to apprehend reality
and have the higher knowledge. Similarly, to credit the world of sense-
experienced objects in space and time, if one accepts their reality, to
the work of the Creator, Ishvara, the living god-principle, worshipped
and sacrificed to by the people under such names as Vishnu, Shiva,
and Rama, is to apprehend the absolute truth through the appearances
created by ignorance. All this belongs to the world of Maya. In reality,
there is only Brahman-Atman, solely existent, spaceless, timeless, and
eternal. The Upanishads have rightly said: *Tat tvam asi!* (That art
thou!) Emancipation from the long-drawn-out nightmare of the cycle
of rebirth comes only with the lifting of the veil of ignorance which
prevents one from knowing that the soul is and always has been identical with Brahman.

This, it may be seen, is the logical culmination of the monistic
speculations of the Upanishads.

Sankara wrote out his commentary on the Vedanta Sutra about

800 A.D.; three hundred years later Ramanuja, the most renowned of Vishnuite scholars, undertook to reinterpret the Upanishads so as to justify belief in Vishnu as the sole *real* being. He took a monistic position, but with qualifications (whence the name of his system: "qualified non-dualism"). He asserted that the physical world, individual souls, and the ultimate Reality or Supreme Being are each real and yet one; for the first two make up the "body" of the last; they are the "forms" through which God manifests himself. The ultimate Reality is a personal and not an impersonal being. His name is Vishnu. In short, *Vishnu is Brahman.* He lives in a glorious heavenly city and manifests himself in the created world generally, and particularly through his avatars or incarnations in the earthly forms of men and animals, through which in times of crisis he displays his redemptive power and goodness. The best goal of man—and the happy lot of those who render Vishnu proper devotion (bhakti)—is not extinction in an impersonal Absolute but a going to heaven to enjoy Vishnu's presence in full consciousness.

The third version of the Vedanta, that of Madhva (13th century A.D.), has been called the "Duality School." Madhva maintained that the individual soul is not one with nor to be identified, here or hereafter, with an Absolute or Supreme Soul. His view is monotheistic, for he believed that the souls that are saved will enjoy bliss in the presence of the Supreme Soul (God); others are doomed to spend eternity either in the hells or in endless transmigration. How does salvation come? It comes, Madhva said, through Vayu, the wind god, the son of Vishnu; he is the vehicle of the grace of God, and a sort of Holy Spirit who breathes his life-giving power into those whom he saves. This version of the Vedanta contains more than an echo of Islam and Christianity, which were by Madhva's time known in India; it has had, like Ramanuja's version, an immense influence not only on the followers of Vishnu but on all India. Many modern liberal thought movements credit their general attitude, if not the substance of their beliefs, to Ramanuja or Madhva or both.

V   POPULAR HINDUISM

The Hindu masses may not be said to have ever had a clear conception of any of these matters which we have just discussed. They go about being religious in the manner which has been traditional in their localities, practicing all sorts of beliefs: animism, fetishism, shamanism,

demonolatry, animal-worship, and devotion to village ⸱pirits and godlings—all these with or without the more respected and higher worship
of the great deities of the Hindu pantheon. In the past, British officials
have often expressed in their state papers and reports judgments like
this:

> The ordinary villager, who in his everyday life takes no thought for the
> morrow of a subsequent existence, is content to worship the village godlings
> to whom he looks for rain, bountiful harvests, and escape from plague,
> cholera, and small-pox. . . . There are, as it were, two religions: a work-a-
> day religion to meet the requirements of everyday existence and a higher
> religion, known only to the Brahmin, . . . which the ordinary man does not
> attempt to understand.[28]

In some regions Hinduism may hardly be said to exist; a primitive
animism takes its place. This sub-Hinduism is common among the forty
million "untouchables." But it is not so usual outside of the outcaste
group. Most people in India practice orthodox Hinduism conjointly with
the primitive forms of religion common in their locality. In the same
village, shrines for the worship of the great gods of Hinduism, with
Brahmins in attendance to perform the ritual properly, exist side by
side with wayside stones, trees, or small shrines sacred to village godlings and spirits. To these last the villagers resort for worship "without
benefit of clergy." The need which impels them is that of the common
man all over the world; and few in India would attempt to check them.
The Brahmins tolerate the practice but keep more or less aloof.

The Great Triad of Gods

In the more universal forms of Hinduism a triad of great gods appears. These beings—Brahmā * the Creator, Shiva the Destroyer, and
Vishnu the Preserver—are recognized by the Brahmins as undoubtedly
standing for realities within the frame of the universe; in any event, they
command the believing trust and devotion of millions of the common
people of India. In the course of years these three great deities have
between them gradually absorbed the functions of scores and hundreds
of local aboriginal gods. Their existence is rationalized by the Brahmins
in the following way: they say that Brahman-Atman, the impersonal
ultimate reality, achieves a religiously significant threefold manifestation
or *trimurti* through the three personal deities who represent the divine
functions of creation, destruction, and preservation respectively.

* Masculine. The terminal ā here receives an accent to distinguish it from the
neuter Brahman (unaccented), the name for the Absolute (Brahman-Atman).

This idea was first developed in the *Mahabharata*. Subsequently a considerable literature sprang up to develop it further in one direction or another. These writings are the numerous *Puranas* ("Ancient Stories") and *Tantras* ("Threads"; "Basic Teachings"). Although originally the three members of the Great Triad were thought to be of equal importance and complementary to each other, later on the rivalries and antagonisms which sprang up between the followers of one or the other were expressed in the Puranas, eighteen of which are generally held to be authoritative. Neatly divided into three groups of six each, they exalt, as the case may be, Brahmā, Vishnu, or Shiva above the rest. Taken together, the Puranas are an inexhaustible treasury of folklore and myth, some of it extraordinarily rich in symbols.* When the female counterparts or *shaktis* of these deities occupy the center of attention, we have the numerous *Tantras,* the manuals or textbooks which are the basis of the Tantrism already discussed in the last chapter (p. 242 ff.).

Brahmā

Of the three great gods, Brahmā, the Creator, is the least widely worshipped. Scarcely half a dozen temples are now dedicated to him. He may be compared with the "high god" of primitive peoples, no longer active on earth, after having finished the work of creation. Yet he is deeply respected. In art he is depicted as a kingly personage, with four heads, severely reading the Vedas, and is shown riding a white wild goose, symbolic of his aloofness.

Shiva

Shiva is one of the great gods of Asia. His followers have given him the title *Mahadeva,* "the great god," and he measures up to the name. His character is most complex, and has some fascinating aspects. As the later form of the dread god Rudra of Vedic days, he still is (in an important aspect) the Destroyer. In the words of the *Yajur Veda,* he is "the threatener, the slayer, the vexer, and the afflicter." His presence is felt "in the fall of the leaf," and he is the bringer of disease and death, and, hence, a "man-slayer." His presence is felt at the funeral-pyre, and he should be honored there. But he is not purely evil. His name shows that he is, or can be made, "auspicious" (*shiva*).

---

* See Heinrich Zimmer's *Myth and Symbol in Indian Art and Civilization* for a fascinating taste of this literature.

Shiva as Nataraja (Lord of the Dance) performing the dance of life on the body of the demon Muyalaka, who is holding a cobra. (After a drawing in Rawlinson, *India, A Short Cultural History*)

It is of some interest to speculate about the giving of this name to him. At the end of the Vedic Age Rudra seems to have been so feared that his name was never mentioned; this was all in the spirit of the European proverb, "Speak of the devil, and he is sure to appear." Like the peasants of Europe in similar circumstances, the Indo-Aryans spoke of him preferably through descriptive titles. At length the title *shiva*, at first applied to other deities also, came to stand for him alone. Not only *could* he be auspicious, if he would; but perhaps a flattering reference to him as such would *make* him so?

Moreover, there were reasons for believing he had a constructive and helpful aspect. Originally, he was a mountain god given to destructive and punitive raids on the plains; but those who penetrated to his mountain fastnesses discovered that under his kindly care grew medicinal herbs for the healing of men. Could it be that his sole interest was destruction? Was not his coming often "a blessing in disguise"? Gradually it came to be felt that Shiva destroyed in order to make room for new creation. No doubt he was "in the fall of the leaf"; yet he was primarily concerned with fulfilling the hope so well expressed by Shelley:

Kali, with a necklace of skulls, a girdle of human arms, and protruding tongue, treading on the body of Shiva. (From a modern popular print)

If winter comes, can spring be far behind?

After all, pure destructiveness achieves no lasting results in tropical countries; the death and decay of vegetation is but the prelude to the rise of new forms of life, all the more vigorous for having humus to feed on. Besides, in a land where reincarnation is an accepted belief, death means almost instantaneous release into new life. By suggestions flowing from realizations such as this, the functions of Shiva received a meaningful enlargement.

He became identified with the processes of reproduction in every realm of life—vegetable, animal, and human. The sex-energy which was identified with him was represented to the eyes of his worshipers by symbols. Chief among these representations have been the *lingam* and *yoni,* conventional emblems of the male and female organs of generation. With a naive but wholly reverent sense of the mystery of divine and human creative force, Shiva's worshipers, in their homes as well as in their temples, approach these symbols in devout worship.

By a further development of this association of ideas, Shiva stands for Life itself, as pure energy or force. He is often shown dancing on the squirming body of the demon of delusion, with his four arms gracefully waving in the air, one hand holding a small drum, another a flame or fire-pot. Poised on one leg, his whole figure shows a tremendous vitality, and it is felt that the dance is speeding the cycles of birth and death. Further evidences of vitality are suggested by endowing Shiva with a third eye placed vertically in the middle of the forehead and picturing him as having a blue body and a dark throat encircled by a necklace of serpents. Some of his images display him with five or six faces varying in expression, all of which, taken together, suggest his multiple attributes and energies.

At first view it may come as a surprise that Shiva is also the patron of ascetics and holy men. He is often represented as being himself deep in meditation, his naked body smeared with ashes and his hair braided after the fashion of an ascetic. The rationale of the ascription to him of ascetic interests seems to be something like this: the ascetic "destroys" his lower self to allow his higher or spiritual self to come to expression; the body must be curbed to free the soul; all worldly affections and lusts must be rooted out. The result will be a great access of power. But such regeneration is just what Shiva most desires to further. He is therefore on the side of the ascetics.

Sir Charles Eliot justly observes:

> As an idea, as a philosophy, Shivaism possesses truth and force. It gives the best picture . . . of the force which rules the Universe as it is, which reproduces and destroys, and in performing one of these acts necessarily performs the other, seeing that both are but aspects of change. . . . The Creator is also the Destroyer, not in anger but by the very nature of his activity. . . . The egg is destroyed when the chicken is hatched: the embryo ceases to exist when the child is born; when the man comes into being, the child is no more.[29]

Shiva's Consorts and Associates

That Shiva has come to represent life-energy in all its aspects is amply attested by the character of his various consorts and associates. His divine spouse is many persons in one, and bears different names in the various regions of India. As Parbati, "the mountaineer," or Uma, "light," she is gracious and kind. As Durga, "the unapproachable," Chandi, "the wild," or Kali, "the black," she is helpful and baleful and terrible at once; a spreader of disease, thereby awaking men's terror, yet an implacable enemy of the demons, thereby filling them with gratitude; kindly to her favored ones, yet accustomed to devour men and animals. Durga, the unapproachable, has been the patroness of the robber caste bearing the name of Thugs. Kali, the black, wears round her dark neck a necklace of skulls, and uses her four strong arms as flails to demolish her victims before she fills her mouth with their flesh; but she is infinitely generous and kind to those whom she loves and who love her in return. In Bengal she is adored as the great Mother; mystics and seers like Ramakrishna and Vivekananda have devoted themselves to her with the most intense kind of passionate attachment (bhakti).

Associated with Shiva also are Ganesha, the elephant-headed god, and Nandi, the white bull. Ganesha is Shiva's son by Parbati, his mountaineer consort. The elephant head, found everywhere in Shiva's temples, symbolizes Ganesha's cunning and his elephant-like ability to remove obstacles by great strength. Nandi, whose milk-white or black bull-image reclines in Shiva's temples, and whose representative, the live white bull, wanders in the temple courts and down the streets of towns and villages in inviolable freedom from all let or hindrance, is Shiva's temple chamberlain and the guardian of quadrupeds.

Shaktism

As a general rule the worship of Shiva's consorts, conceived as forms of his *shakti* or active power displayed in female energy, constitutes a minor theme in the adoration addressed primarily to himself. But a distinct sub-division of Hinduism concerns itself with the worship of Shiva's spouse or spouses, and in northeastern India particularly, it almost attains the status of a separate religion. As such, it is a form of Tantrism; but since, as we have seen in the previous chapter, there is a Buddhist Tantrism, this worship is more precisely called *shaktism*. As practiced, it has what have been called its "right-hand" and "left-hand" forms. Right-hand shaktism has a refined and philosophic aspect; it centers attention on the white or benignant side of shakti; that is, the benevolent phases of the energy of nature, considered under the symbol of a mother-goddess, "combining in one shape life and death." Recent Bengali poets and swamis, like Tagore and Ramakrishna, have made much of this aspect of the mystery and reality of the universe; they identify Shakti with Maya, the illusion-creating power that has produced the beautiful and terrible phenomenal world. Thus Ramakrishna, in adoring the black goddess Kali as the fitting symbol of Reality truly and justly understood, could exclaim:

"When I think of the Supreme Being as inactive, neither creating, nor preserving, nor destroying, I call him *Brahman* or *Purusha,* the impersonal God. When I think of him as active, creating, preserving, destroying, I call him *Shakti* or *Maya* . . . the personal god. But the distinction between them does not mean a difference. The personal and the impersonal are the same Being, in the same way as are milk and its whiteness, or the diamond and its lustre, or the serpent and its undulations. It is impossible to conceive of the one without the other. The Divine Mother (Kali) and *Brahman* are one." [30]

"Kali is none other than He whom you call *Brahman.* Kali is Primitive Energy (Shakti) . . . To accept Kali is to accept *Brahman* . . . *Brahman* and his Power are identical." [31]

Left-hand shaktism is both primitive and highly sophisticated. Its rites are essentially magical and esoteric. Our earlier discussion of Vajrayana Buddhism (p. 241 ff.) indicates its general outlook. Here, in the Hindu setting, Durga and Kali, as representatives of the black and violent side of shakti, are the favorite manifestations of divine energy. Being identified with them means being swept into conventionally forbidden expressions of natural impulse. In secret rites, the details of which are not fully known, the carefully screened adherents meet in "circle worship" marked by dances of naked women, drinking of wine and blood, and ritualistic sex acts. The five M's, ordinarily forbidden, are indulged in, namely, wine (*madya*), meat (*mansa*), fish (*matsya*), parched grain (*mudra*), and sexual union (*maithuna*). It is understood to be highly dangerous to the participant's welfare (karmic position), if pleasure is sought. Rightly the aim is to have such tight control of the senses as to rise entirely above pleasure to a complete self-identification ("nondualistic union") with holy natural force, ultimately with the purpose of riding the back of this "tiger" into Nirvana.

Vishnu

This member of the great Hindu triad is called the Preserver. He is always benevolent, primarily the conservator of values and an active agent in their realization. Unlike the complex Shiva, he is the perfect and patient exemplar of winsome divine Love. He watches from the skies; and whenever he sees values threatened or the good in peril, he exerts all his preservative influence in their behalf. He therefore rivals Shiva in popularity among the masses. The stories of his divine activity attract a growing following. He is usually represented with four arms, in two hands holding the symbols of his royal power, the mace and the discus, and in two others the emblems of his magic power and stainless purity, the conch and the lotus respectively. His head is surmounted by a high crown and diadem, his feet are blue, his vesture yellow; and he has the lotus eyes so much admired by Hindus. When reclining, he is shown resting on the world-serpent, Shesha or Ananta; his vehicle is the bird Garuda; and a fish is his symbol. His shakti or spouse is the lovely goddess of fortune and beauty, Lakshmi.

Vishnu's rise to high popular favor is in part due to Vedic mythology. In the Vedas, as we have seen, he is a solar deity. Taking their cue from the fact that the sun redeems the earth from darkness in his passage between earth and sky, the Vedic people developed the myth relating how, when the demon-king, Bali, seized control of the earth, Vishnu appeared in the form of a dwarf and meekly asked and ob-

Vishnu reclining on the world serpent Shesha while Brahmā, suspended on a lotus and reading the Vedas, emerges from his navel and Lakshmi, his spouse, the goddess of beauty and fortune, strokes his feet in wifely devotion. (From a drawing in Rawlinson, *India, A Short Cultural History*)

tained from the amused giant the promise of as much ground as he could traverse in three steps; the bargain concluded, Vishnu at once returned to his own shape, and restored heaven and earth to gods and men by encompassing them in two swift strides. By not taking a third stride across hell, he left it in the demon's possession. This myth provided the intimation concerning the character of Vishnu's interests and activity which has led to his rise in popular esteem. It was seen that he "comes to earth" in *avataras* or "descents" when needed. He has not come down once only, his devotees have urged. Besides descending as a dwarf, he was incarnate in Rama, the Galahad-like hero of the *Ramayana,* and in Krishna, the warrior-hero and pastoral Don Juan of the *Mahabharata* and folk-lore; indeed, a fast developing mythology went on to relate that he has had animal as well as human avatars.

The Avatars of Vishnu

The avatars of Vishnu have been traditionally set at ten, though popular belief has much enlarged the number. Of the traditional list, nine avatars are said to have already occurred, while the tenth is yet to come. We have already mentioned three of them. In the other avatars Vishnu became in turn:—a fish, which rescued the first man, Manu, being swept away in a world-flood; a tortoise, which swam under Mt. Mandara and assisted the gods in using it to churn the nectar of immortality and other valuable products from the ocean of milk; a boar, which, with its tusks, lifted the sunken earth above the depths of the sea into which it had been plunged; a man-lion, who tore to pieces a demon-father attempting the life of his son because he prayed to Vishnu; a Brahmin warrior-hero, who twenty-one times utterly defeated the Kshatriya caste and finally established Brahmin supremacy; and Gautama, the founder of Buddhism. The tenth avatar is to be that of Kalki, a messiah with a sword of flame, riding on a white horse,* who shall come to save the righteous and destroy the wicked at the end of the fourth and depraved world period.

It is interesting to find the Buddha in the list. One suspects the name of the great founder of Buddhism was added to Vishnu's avatars as a tactical maneuver, designed, and successfully too, to reconcile Buddhism and Hinduism; how well it served to facilitate Indian Buddhism's return to the mother-fold of Hinduism has already been seen on p. 216, in the chapter on the Religious Development of Buddhism.

* To some the horse is so prominent, that they name this avatar the *Ashvatara* (the "Horse Avatar").

Incomparably the most popular of the avatars are those of Rama and Krishna. Rama is the ideal man of the Hindu epics, and his wife is the ideal woman. As the *Ramayana* relates, Rama's happy marriage to Sita, a beauteous princess of the royal house of Mithila, was followed by great trouble. The demon-king of Ceylon, Ravana, treacherously seized Sita and carried her off to his island home. In great distress, Rama enlisted the aid of Hanuman, the monkey-king (the earliest detective in world literature, by the way, and now a Hindu god in his own right). The monkey-king was able to conduct an extensive search from the vantage point of the tree-tops, and Sita was finally found. Rama fought and slew Ravana, and Sita, after successfully passing through an ordeal of fire to prove her chastity, rejoined her mate. Because of the currency in all parts of India of the various versions of the Ramayana, Rama is widely revered; millions make him the object of their prayers, and his image is often worshiped in a manner to suggest that he is no mere savior-hero but the all-god. There are, in fact, two phases of Rama-worship: (1) reverential respect for Rama as a hero who was an avatar of Vishnu, and (2) theistic worship of Rama, which gives him exclusive devotion as the supreme deity.

It would be interesting to explore, as we cannot here, the theological doctrines evolved as a result of the theistic attitude to Rama. Yet one doctrinal issue calls for mention. It has to do with the famous controversy as to whether Rama saves by the "monkey-hold" or the "cat-hold"—that is, with man's cooperation or without it. One group of Rama-devotees contends that Rama saves only through the free cooperation of the believer with him; the believer must cling to the god as a baby monkey clings to its mother when the latter is swinging off to safety through the trees. The other group believes that salvation is of God only, and that Rama saves his chosen ones by carrying them off as a cat carries a kitten by the scruff of the neck.

Highly regarded though Rama is, Krishna is even more popular, both as an avatar and as a god. His character is more complex than Rama's, presenting two distinct aspects not a little difficult to reconcile. The *Mahabharata* shows him in one phase, pastoral poetry and folklore in another. In the Mahabharata he is serious and severe, a resourceful war-hero. Throughout the strenuous episodes of the epic he seems primarily anxious to direct man's attention to Vishnu, the god-form of the Absolute, of whom he is the incarnation. In this connection (as we have already noted in our summary of the episode called the *Bhagavard Gita*) he asks for the unconditioned devotion of true bhakti toward himself as the earthly form of Vishnu, the supreme Lord of the World.

The other Krishna is a gay youth, the pivot-figure in a vast folklore. Hindu imagination has dwelt lovingly on his childhood as a pantry-haunting "butter-thief" and fat little play-fellow. Thousands of Hindu women daily worship him in this phase, gazing upon his chubby infant-images with as much devotion as Italian women regard their beloved Bambino, the child Jesus. But this Krishna is more representatively portrayed as an enchanting pastoral figure; in most of the folk-tales he is a sprightly and amorous cowherd, a melodious flute at his lips, piping as he moves among the cattle the ravishing airs which win him the love of the *gopis* or milk-maids, with whom he dallies in dark-eyed passion. He unites himself with hundreds* of these adoring ones, but values above all the beautiful Radha, his favorite mistress. The erotic literature which has sprung up to describe this phase of the god's activity bears some resemblance in general tone to the literature of Shaktism, though it prefers expression in story to the latter's philosophy and tantrism.

* One Purana says 16,000!

Krishna playing on a flute and charming the *gopis* or milk-maids. (Detail from Rajput painting, ca. 1790. Mehta Collection, Bombay)

The sects which give Krishna a more or less exclusive devotion rank him as high as the Rama-worshipers do their paragon. In Bengal one sect sets Radha beside Krishna as his eternal consort, and directs worshipers to seek the favor of both diligently, in the hope of being transported at death to the pleasure groves of the Brindaban heaven, where Krishna and Radha make love forever, in ever-young delight. It is not unexpected that the excesses of left-hand Shaktism occur in some Krishna cults; yet virtually all the devotees of Krishna stress love of the god as a spiritual rather than a carnal passion. The infatuation of the *gopis* for the divinely adorable cowherd is given a symbolic meaning; even their transports of love, the thrilling sensation at the roots of the hair, the choking emotion, and the swooning, are said to give a true picture in sensuous imagery of the exaltation produced in the worshiper who is looking upon the image of Krishna and thinking of his love.

The Common Man's Worship at Home and Abroad

The common man of India is uncritically and perhaps limitlessly polytheistic. Even though experience usually leads him to adopt one particular god or goddess as a patron or tutelary deity, whose image or symbol he enshrines in his house and whose name he repeats with special devotion at dawn and dusk, he honors nevertheless all supernatural beings whatever. The number of these is uncountable. Hindus are accustomed to saying their deities number some 33 crores; that is, some 330 millions. With so polytheistic an outlook, the average villager goes from shrine to shrine as need arises. If he wishes to have obstacles to some undertaking removed, he worships Ganesha, the elephant-headed son of Shiva; if he wishes to have greater bodily strength for some heavy work, he prays to Hanuman, the monkey-god; if his father is dying, he offers his anguished supplications to Rama; while his hopes for immunity from smallpox or cholera, or for safety on a journey, or for the enjoyment of good fortune, or plenty of children, or the health of his cattle, take him to still other deities. His reverence is expressed not only at the shrines or before images; he may worship anywhere, recognizing in round stones lifted from the river-bed to the roadside symbols of Shiva, in trees decorated with vermillion paint the divine fertility force in nature, and in dark caves suggestions of Yama, the god of the dead, and so on.

In his life of devotion, the common man feels not only his personal need to express his religious consciousness but also the necessity of worship going on in his behalf all the time. Worship in his own locality takes three different forms simultaneously: first, he himself worships as need arises either at home or in a temple or elsewhere through his own devotional acts; second, a priest or someone in the family (one of the women or it may be his father or brother—or himself) conducts the simple domestic rites in behalf of the family before an image or symbol of the household god; third, in his and the whole community's behalf, the local priests conduct several times daily a ceremony of homage—a *puja*—at the local temple or shrine.

But the common man's need is not fully met even by all this. He craves to go to some holy place of pilgrimage where he may receive a special blessing. It would not be wide of the mark to say that millions of Hindus derive their chief religious satisfaction from the pilgrimages they make and the temple festivals they attend; by these activities not only do they give testimony and expression to their faith, but they enjoy themselves hugely in an earthly as well as spiritual sense. What Pratt says of the Magh Mela celebration at Allahabad is true of Hindu fore-gatherings elsewhere: "It would be hard to compare the scene to anything in America; but if you should put together a county fair, a circus, a campmeeting, and a fancy dress lawn party, you would get a mixture distantly approaching it." [32]

Given a religion as polytheistic as Hinduism, it is to be expected that sacred places should multiply during the years. Indeed, from the Hindu point of view India may be said to be growing in sanctity all the time, owing to the slowly increasing number of sacred places to be found in it. Sacred places are of two general types: (1) sacred places as such, whose holiness made inevitable the rise of temples and shrines there, and (2) places that have become sacred *after* temples or shrines were erected on them. It is sometimes difficult, however, to know in which group to put the oldest sacred places.

Sacred places of the first type may come into being at almost any spot on mountain or plain where a cavern, strangely formed rock, fissure in the ground, hot spring or natural wonder has given rise to a tale of spirit-visitation or of miracle; but in most cases they are along the great rivers. Hindus have long regarded their mightiest streams as holy from source to mouth. The *Puranas* have glorified almost every bend and every tributary with stories of some theophany—a visit of Shiva or one of his shaktis, an exploit of Rama, Krishna, or some other divine being who came to the spot to consecrate it by a significant conversation or wondrous deed. Consequently it is a work of great merit to follow the course of a holy river from its source to its mouth and back along the other bank to the source again, stopping always at every sacred spot to read or hear again the sacred legends, visit the holy shrines, and engage in pious devotions there. But pilgrims do not often take this long and arduous journey: it is enough for them if they can go to one or more of the many temples that line the holy stream's banks, throw flowers on the river's sacred surface, bathe in the purifying flood, and carry its water home in small containers for last offices to the dying and other ministrations.

The holiest river of all—the Ganges—is known throughout India as "Mother Ganga." Its sacredness is explained by the myth that it issues from the feet of Vishnu in heaven, and falls far below upon Shiva's head and flows out of his hair. One of the most sacred spots along its entire course is the place where it issues, strong and clear, from the Himalayas; that is the site of the famous pilgrim-center, Hardwar, with its long lines of steps going down into the river and its crowds of bathers seeking purification in the icy water. Equally sacred is the juncture of the Jumna River with the Ganges, at which spot a third river, the holy Saraswati, is supposed to rise to the surface. Here lies Allahabad, the city that attracts millions of pilgrims to its *melas* or religious fairs. The mouths of the Ganges, emptying through a great delta into the Bay of Bengal, are also holy, and particularly is this true of Saugor Island, which lies within the delta and is the site of a sacred bathing festival at the beginning of the year.

But it is to Benares that most pilgrims go to wash away their sins. The pilgrims who enter on its hallowed territory are often so overcome with joy at the sight of its temple towers in the distance that they prostrate themselves and pour the dust of the ground on their heads as a sign of their spiritual submission. They proceed joyfully to the bathing *ghats* along the river and are purified by immersion in the cleansing waters of sacred Mother Ganga. And when they finally turn homeward, it is with the joyous conviction that all past sins have been atoned for and the future made secure. Had any pilgrim been seized by a mortal illness while within the sacred territory, all would still have been well; whoever dies upon that sacred soil, especially if his feet be immersed in the sacred river, goes to Shiva's heaven of unending delight.

Cow Protection

Scholars who readily appreciate the importance of the idea of reincarnation have sometimes failed to give like recognition to an equally widespread feature of Hindu religious life—the veneration of the cow. Perhaps there is less disposition to overlook this unique feature of Hindu religious practice since Katherine Mayo's *Mother India* made it a factor in an acrimonious controversy spreading over three continents. Hindus, said Miss Mayo, hold the cow in *such* honor that they let her wander in inviolate loneliness, suffering and starving along the parched roads of India! There was an immediate reaction from India, all of it indignant. No less an advocate than Mahatma Gandhi led in the defence of "cow-protection," as he liked to call it; he even named it "the central fact of Hinduism, the one concrete belief common to all Hindus," and justified it in the memorable words:

> Cow-protection is to me one of the most wonderful phenomena in human evolution. It takes the human being beyond his species. The cow to me means the entire sub-human world. Man through the cow is enjoined to realize his identity with all that lives . . . She is the mother to millions of Indian mankind. The cow is a poem of pity. Protection of the cow means protection of the whole dumb creation of God.[33]

The sincerity of the feeling here is beyond question. Certainly something can be said for the symbolism. Hindus are not without a case in saying that the exaltation of the cow is morally far above that of the eagle or the lion. But the Hindu attitude is rather more unreserved than the words of Gandhi just quoted would indicate. Ancient India came to *worship* the cow. In the words of Monier-Williams, who has written what is often quoted as the classic summary of Hindu cow-worship:

> The cow is of all animals the most sacred. Every part of its body is inhabited by some deity or other. Every hair on its body is inviolable. All its excreta are hallowed. Not a particle ought to be thrown away as impure. On the contrary, the water it ejects ought to be preserved as the best of all holy waters—a sin-destroying liquid which sanctifies everything it touches, while nothing purifies like cow-dung. Any spot which a cow has condescended to honor with the sacred deposit of her excrement is forever afterwards consecrated ground, and the filthiest place plastered with it is at once cleansed and freed from pollution, while the ashes produced by burning this hallowed substance are of such a holy nature, that they not only make clean all material things, however previously unclean, but have only to be sprinkled over a sinner to convert him into a saint.[34]

The merit of the cow has in some degree been passed on to the ox and the bull. To free oxen dedicated to Shiva so that they may wander through the streets is a work of high merit, and when done in the name of one recently deceased is of great benefit to him in his next life.

The killing of cows has in times past been visited with capital punishment; men are still outcasted for it. It has been a major source of conflict between Moslems and Hindus that, on the day annually commemorating Abraham's offering up of Isaac, the former sacrifice the gentle creature that spends its life in the selfless giving of its nourishment to others.° Since the partition of India into Hindu and Moslem states, the Hindu areas have attempted to suppress this practice.

In many parts of India cows receive at certain seasons of the year the honor given to deities. Garlands are placed around their necks, oil is poured on their foreheads and water at their feet; while tears of affection and gratitude start into the eyes of bystanders.

Cow-dung is today used in most of the villages of Hindu India in many ways: as a fuel; as a disinfectant element dissolved in the water used to wash floors, thresholds, and walls; as an ingredient in clay-mortar and mud-plaster; and as a medicine. In some rural regions, when a man is dying and wishes to assure himself a safe passage from this life into the next, he grasps the tail of a cow backed up to his bedside, or should the room be inaccessible to the animal, he holds a rope fastened to a cow's tail outside the room.

One observer, after a year's residence in a remote northern village, says with evident justice:

The charge that India is consciously cruel or indifferent to cattle is certainly not substantiated by anything I saw in my village. As a rule, out of self-interest, if for no higher reason, the villagers give the cattle the best care they can provide. If they go half-starved, so do their owners.[35]

The Holiness of Brahmins

Holiness as a potent element in human personality has fascinated India in the past, and still does. Although men of other castes may be recognized as holy (witness Gandhi, and the title given him), Brahmins have had sanctity above all others. The *Code of Manu* long since made this clear. It placed the Brahmin in the position of "the lord of this whole creation," whose birth is "an eternal incarnation of the sacred law." [36] As priest, or as *guru* (teacher), or in any occupation, the Brahmin is "the highest on earth"; and "whatever exists in the world is his property"; on account of the excellence of his origin he is entitled to all.

° The British ran into trouble during the Indian Mutiny in 1857, when both Hindu and Moslem recruits refused any longer to oil their guns with grease obtained from cows and pigs.

A Brahmin, be he ignorant or learned, is a great divinity, just as the fire is a great divinity. The brilliant fire is not contaminated even in burial places, and, when presented with oblations of butter at sacrifices, it again increases mightily. Thus, though Brahmins employ themselves in all sorts of mean occupations, they must be honored in every way; for each of them is a very great deity.[37]

Today the mysterious quality of his person can only with difficulty be preserved, but it is being preserved. No matter what his manner of life may be, to kill or to maltreat him is always a heinous sin. Yet it would be erroneous to conclude that each individual Brahmin is necessarily revered. He is indeed theoretically a great lord among men, whatever his occupation; but then one may regard the person of a king as sacred and still despise his spirit or mock at his acts. Today, when Brahmins engage in all sorts of occupations, it is perhaps natural that in some cases they should be ridiculed, as were the monks of medieval Europe, for their petty vices, especially if they belie even while they adopt an air of ultra-respectability. But even those who laugh at a Brahmin may wish themselves in his place, and hope after death to become a Brahmin in the next life.

Among the most highly honored Brahmins in India are the *gurus*. As a group, they exhibit Hinduism's conscious effort in the direction of religious education. Their function is to teach Hindus those tenets of their religion most directly bearing upon home-life and household ceremony. The wealthy often permanently retain a guru in their homes as a family tutor and religious mentor; but in most cases he serves a number of families and goes the rounds among them. He is usually a high-minded, conscientious person who is an effective force for good. His special function is to train boys in religious knowledge and the duties of caste, and to initiate them into manhood (in the case of the three upper castes) by ceremonially investing them with the sacred cord.

We must not overlook the "holy men," the *sadhus, sannyasis,* and *yogis,* who are so distinctive of India. Some slight differences distinguish them. The yogis are, as their name implies, those who hope that their practice of Yoga will someday give them the insight and status of sannyasis and sadhus. Sannyasis are today usually ash-smeared followers of Shiva imitating the great god's ascetic ardors; but in the classical Hindu conception, they win their status by reaching the fourth stage of the ideal life career. The sadhu is so called because he is acknowledged to be a person of great sanctity, one who has "attained" or "arrived" at his goal of spiritual unity with whatever he considers to be ultimate reality; he has probably enjoyed more than one experience of samadhi or trance, and is now truly holy. Of this kind there are thousands in India today. Most live fully clothed among their fellow-men, and exercise a great influence over them; a few, in the zeal of concentrated effort, go half-clothed or naked, smeared with ashes, or frozen in unbroken silence; some are half mad or even quite insane. The sacred places of India are like a lodestone to the more fanatic among them. During festivals these eccentric sadhus—a special sect—march along naked, hundreds strong; and after they have passed, the people run to scoop up the dust made sacred by their footprints, that they may rub it on themselves or carry it away.

The West is familiar with pictures of Hindu holy men displaying their self-mastery by reclining on beds of spikes, sitting between fires or hanging with head down in the smoke, wearing feathered barbs set in their flesh, holding one or both arms (or legs) in the same position until atrophy renders them useless, looking at the sun with undeviating gaze until the eyes go blind, wearing heavy clanking chains wrapped around the legs and body, and so on. In these positions, or cumbered with these hampering weights, they remain for hours, days, weeks, or years together. The Western observer is filled with amazement at the mere thought of so much self-imposed suffering and such indomitable patience and endurance. But it would be too much to expect equal sincerity and devotion in every instance. The more philosophic holy man bears his self-inflicted torment in the silence and solitude of his forest or mountain retreat, perfecting himself in the quietude of his own thought; others crave the presence of the multitudes and live by the

Sadhu at Benares sitting on bed of spikes. (After photograph by Herbert G. Ponting)

offerings of the pious. All this is not without its logic. It may seem a strange sort of reasoning that leads to such maltreatment of the body, but the earnest basic purpose is there—to control the flesh for the sake of freedom of the spirit.

VI ISSUES AND PROBLEMS OF
THE PRESENT

The story of Hinduism as we have so far told it suggests something that ought to be stated clearly. It is this: the originality and diversity of thought in this complex culture defy a simple setting forth. It would be quite impossible even in a long book—not to mention a single chapter like this—to give due consideration to the astonishing variety of opinion and range of disagreement that have accompanied the unfolding of Hinduism. Few Hindu doctrines have ever stood for long without being challenged; this is true even of what might be called the essentials of Hinduism—the beliefs, namely, that the doctrines in the Vedas and Upanishads, properly interpreted, are true, and that the caste system represents what is right and just, according to the Law of Karma. The heretical views in Jainism, Buddhism, and Sikhism only partially suggest the conflict of view shown by men of original minds and reforming zeal. In the space remaining to us it seems best to look into this interesting matter by raising and discussing some of the issues and problems of recent Hinduism, especially those that have made for change.

A. THE REACTION TO WESTERN RELIGION AND SCIENCE. Hinduism is paradoxically both one of the most liberal and one of the most conservative of religions. Its liberalism flows from the intellectual freedom granted to its adherents, a freedom whereby they may even deny the inspiration of the Vedas, the holiness of Brahmins, or the orthodox conceptions of the caste system, and yet remain Hindu—*provided* that they do not break completely with the accepted moral practices of their localities or the code of social regulations to which they have been bred, especially the dietary restrictions, prohibitions against inter-dining or taking a cup of water from the hands of a person of lower caste, rigid marriage laws, and cow-veneration; in short, provided that they seek to reform Hinduism *from within* and are not complete rebels.

In the course of the centuries a large number of Hindu sects were allowed to adopt with little change the leading doctrines of heretical or foreign religions. The Brahmins complained and objected at times,

but there was no marked disturbance of the religious peace, unless some
sect broke utterly with caste law, or, as occasionally happened under
Moslem influence, ate the flesh of the cow.

During the 19th century a new type of liberalism made its appearance. It was the direct result of the favorable impressions created by
the teaching of Christian missionaries and by education in Western
history and science in schools established under European auspices.
When this liberal movement got under way, other movements followed,
some reactionary, some radical, some latitudinarian. They may be briefly
described under the following four heads.

1. *The Brahmo Samaj,* or the liberal movement of rapprochement
with the West. The Brahmo Samaj is an important movement within
modern Hinduism, not so much because of the number of its members
as because of its influence. It was founded in Calcutta in 1828 by Ram
Mohan Rai, a Brahmin of brilliant mind, whose religious heritage contained strong Vishnuite and Shivaite influences, from which he was
partially weaned away by an education which brought him in touch with
Buddhism, Zoroastrianism, Islam, and Christianity. He found in all the
religions he learned to know a similar spiritual core, and was therefore
led to organize a religious society devoted to the essence that seemed
to him to be central in every religious faith. His own creed grew out
of the conviction that the truth underlying all religions is the unity,
personality, and spirituality of God, "the Eternal, Unsearchable and Im-
mutable Being who is the Author and Preserver of the Universe."
Accordingly he denounced all forms of polytheism and idolatry and
advocated purging Hindu ceremonies of these elements. He welcomed
any witness to the unity and personality of God. The precepts of Jesus
were from his point of view, he said, "the Guide to Peace and Happiness." In seeking to formulate a universal religion he gave up many of
the general beliefs of Hinduism, such as the doctrine of the transmigration of souls and the theory that the soul is destined to be eventually
absorbed into the World-Soul.

From the beginning no pictures or images and no animal sacrifices
were permitted in the religious services of the Brahmo Samaj. The
worship was conducted (for the first time by Hindus) congregationally,
as in European Protestantism, with hymns, sermons, and scripture readings. Social reforms, such as abolition of suttee (to the official outlawing
of which Ram Mohan Rai contributed not a little), and prohibition of
child-marriage and polygamy were urged but not actively sought. Agitation rather than action was the objective. The reason for this moderation
lay in part in the fact that Ram Mohan Rai remained true to the social

restrictions of his own caste and never ceased to wear the sacred cord
of the Brahmin. He did not wish to break off communion with his fellow
Hindus. He was thus able to win gifted aristocrats to his movement.
The grandfather, and later the father, of the famous Bengali poet,
Rabindranath Tagore, became leaders in the Brahmo Samaj.

The Brahmo Samaj split in two in the 1860's, when the socially-
minded Keshab Chandra Sen, who was brought up in an English school
and had learned to love the figure of Christ as a divine social reformer,
began to attack the caste system root and branch, and pled for a radical
sweeping away of caste restrictions, including those placed upon inter-
caste marriages. A rupture between the radicals and conservatives followed. Keshab's adherents followed him in organizing a new society,
called the Brahmo Samaj of India, to distinguish it from the Adi (or
Original) Brahmo Samaj, which was the name given to the old society.
Later, most of his followers left him to form the Sadharan (or General)
Brahmo Samaj. Keshab renamed his diminished society the Nava Bidhana Samaj or Church of the New Dispensation. During the few years
of life that remained to him he came to feel more and more that he
was continuing the work of Christ on earth. After his death, this startling
phase of his thought was played down as much as possible by his
followers.

Today the Adi Brahmo Samaj and the Nava Bidhana Samaj are
less influential than the Sadharan Brahmo Samaj; but all three groups
continue to stand for a universal religion based on the Fatherhood of
God and the Brotherhood of Man.

2. *The Arya Samaj*, or the movement "back to the Vedas." Here
is an effort to establish a universal religion which has had some success
in India. Its anti-Christian and anti-Western bias appeals to national
pride. It was founded in 1875 by Swami Dayanand, a Brahmin who
had had the interesting religious experience of revolting in boyhood
from the worship of Shiva and then of passing as an ascetic through a
period of belief in the monism of the Upanishads into a period of belief
in the dualism of the Sankhya philosophy. He finally arrived at the conviction that the religion of the Vedas is the oldest and purest of all
religions. He found it to be untainted by superstition, idolatry, or erroneous conceptions like the doctrine of avatars, and free from the objectionable features of the caste system. The Vedas, he taught, were a
direct revelation from the one God, and, properly understood, do not
teach either polytheism or pantheism. Not only do they furnish the one
true key to the past, but they anticipate all future developments of
thought. They have forecast all the recent discoveries of science,

including the steam engines, railways, busses, ocean liners, and electric lights of today! In them are set forth the basic principles of such sciences as physics and chemistry. The Vedas are therefore the ideal charts or blueprints of Nature; there is an exact correspondence between them and the structure of the world.

Two branches of the Arya Samaj now exist. One is liberal, the other conservative. Both engage in educational and philanthropic work throughout North India. In their schools modern science, "based on the Vedas," is taught. Their adherents number perhaps a half million.*

3. *The Ramakrishna Movement,* or the response of tolerance and inclusion. The broadminded acceptance of the essence of the Western religious tradition and its inclusion in the teachings of Hinduism may be seen very clearly in the life and opinions of perhaps the outstanding Hindu saint and seer of the 19th century, called Ramakrishna.† Born a Brahmin in Bengal, he followed the family tradition in becoming one of the priests of a Kali temple near Calcutta. With a spiritual hunger that was not appeased by the performance of his priestly functions, he longed for an immediate experience of the divine. He concentrated on the image of Kali, the Divine Mother. In gazing at her image he experienced trance (samadhi) not once but many times and with increasing intensity, often seeing her move and come to him. He understood from the first that this was but one way of knowing God. He set out to try all the other ways. In a twelve year period he meditated like a yogi, worshipped like a bhakta, practiced Jainism, Buddhism,

* A related but unclassifiable modern religious movement is *Theosophy.* Though this movement was founded in New York City, its headquarters since 1878 have been in India, where its real inspiration lies. The realization of its aim—the establishment of a real brotherhood amongst all peoples—is held to be dependent on an esoteric, ancient wisdom, expressed in the Vedanta, and transmitted through "masters" or "Mahatmas" who appear from age to age. These "great souls" have occult powers which give them unique control over their own bodies and over natural forces. Under their guidance, humanity, bound to the ever-turning wheel of reincarnation by the Law of Karma, will someday gain happiness—in a world which will drink as one from the one wonderful Fountain of Wisdom from which all religions have drawn their hitherto partial truths. Two women have been outstanding in the leadership of the Theosophical Society, Madam Blavatsky, its co-founder (along with Colonel Olcott), and its English president, Mrs. Annie Besant. Dreamy, fanciful, and tolerant, the Theosophists have defended prophecy, second sight, Hindu idol worship, and caste, with little critical discrimination between ideas. The Society has done some useful educational work in India, Mrs. Besant being the founder of Benares Hindu University. Today it lends its support to Indian nationalism; this is natural enough, for Theosophy is, in spite of its professed hospitality to all religions, Hindu at heart.

† This was his title; his original name was Gadadhar Chatterji.

and shaktism, and experienced the reality both of Brahman without attributes (the impersonal Brahman) and Brahman with attributes (i.e., the personal God). Dressed like a Moslem, he prayed until he knew God as Allah. He turned to Christianity and found God in Christ. God also became real to him as Rama, as Krishna, as Sita, as Muhammad. All religions were to him different ways to God, and all creatures were God in so many different forms. He made friends with the members of the Brahmo Samaj; Keshab Chandra Sen particularly befriended him. He once told the latter, in a typical expression of conviction:

"Everything is in the mind. Bondage and freedom are in the mind. You can dye the mind with any color you wish. It is like a piece of clean white linen: dip it in red and it will be red, in blue it will be blue, in green it will be green, or any other color. Do you not see that if you study English, English words will come readily to you? Again, if a pandit studies Sanskrit, he will readily quote verse from Sacred Books. If you keep your mind in evil company, your thoughts, ideas, and words will be colored with evil; but keep in the company of Bhaktas, then your thoughts, ideas and words will be of God. The mind is everything." [38]

A revealing bit of reminiscence is the following:

One day I went to the Zoological Garden in Calcutta. I desired to see the lion, but when I beheld him, I lost all sense-consciousness and went into samadhi. Those who were with me wished to show me the other animals, but I replied: "I saw everything when I saw the king of beasts. Take me home." The strength of the lion had aroused in me the consciousness of the omnipotence of God and had lifted me above the world of phenomena.

Another day I went to the parade ground to see the ascension of a balloon. Suddenly my eyes fell upon a young English boy leaning against a tree. The very posture of his body brought before me the vision of the form of Krishna and I went into samadhi.

Again I saw a woman wearing a blue garment under a tree. She was a harlot. As I looked at her, instantly the ideal of Sita appeared before me! . . . For a long time I remained motionless. I worshiped all women as representatives of the Divine Mother.[39]

An organized group of disciples gathered round him during the last six years of his life, led by a young student of the law who became his successor, under the name of Swami Vivekananda. A brilliant speaker and ardent apologist for the Vedanta, Vivekananda, after Ramakrishna's death, founded the Ramakrishna Movement and spread it all over the world. He was the spokesman for Hinduism at the Parliament of Religions in Chicago in 1893, where he made a great impression that electrified India. He was instrumental in founding Vedanta societies in New York and other American cities. He also founded Ramakrishna centers in Europe, on the Ganges, and in the Himalayas. A marked result of his success in interpreting Hinduism to the world was a revival of interest in the Vedanta in India itself, an interest which has continued to the present time.

4. *The Rise of Secularism* or the acceptance of science and technology and the rejection of all religion. While most Hindus exult in the "spirituality" of India, there has been in the last century an "ominous drift" toward materialism and secularism. This has caused great concern among the thoughtful people of India. Under the influence of modern trends of thought, some intellectuals are showing less and less interest in organized religion. They view it coldly as a mass of superstition built around an antiquated view of life and the world. They condemn its pessimistic tone, its world-denying attitude. Observing religion and religious men with more detachment and critical judgment than has ever before been possible in India, thousands have ceased to believe in the old Hindu Dharma and its ceremonies. And yet in many cases, even though religious convictions have been given up, the attitude of belief has been maintained for family and social reasons.

Of late, Western humanism and new departures in ideology like Marxism have increased the process of religious dissolution. In some circles, especially where Communism has penetrated, a new attitude of defiant atheism has been voiced. However prepared one may be to hear it, one is nevertheless startled by the knowledge that young Hindus have written for publication: "Of all the people in the world it is we Indians that require more and more materialism. We have had too much religion."[40]

B. SOCIAL REFORMS. Not only have there been changes in intellectual outlook; the past century has also seen, as our sketch of the Brahmo Samaj must have indicated, vigorous advocacy of far-reaching social changes. This has been especially true of proposed changes in caste and marriage laws, regulations which from their beginnings have constituted major sources of social and religious difficulty.

1. *Caste problems.* In ancient India the rigidity of the caste system was predicated upon the presumed finality of the economic structure, then relatively simple; but the social order could not be kept simple, it became more and more complex. Accordingly the castes of ancient times virtually broke up, and the many so-called functional castes in reality superseded them. As one authority tells us:

There is a separate caste, or group of castes, for every one of the occupations that were followed in earlier times before the introduction of machinery . . . They include numerous groups of ordinary cultivators; . . . of artisans such as . . . potters, goldsmiths, blacksmiths, workers in brass and bell-metal, tailors, cloth-printers and dyers, etc.; of village servants, such as cowherds, barbers, washermen, watchmen, and scavengers; and various other occupations, such as . . . boatmen, fishermen, cattle-breeders, musicians, actors, salt- and earth-workers, rice-huskers, hunters, fowlers, etc.[41]

As can well be imagined, industrialization, to the degree that it has been introduced, has produced still further variations in caste structure.

Besides these functional castes there are race-castes (tribal and national groups taken into the Hindu fold), sectarian castes (originating from sects which, ironically enough, rejected the caste system and withdrew from it, only to become yet another caste), and castes formed by invasion, by migration, or by crossing.

The lowest castes have been separated into the "clean" and the "unclean." The clean may be generally grouped under the ancient name of Shudra. They do not follow degrading occupations, are in some sense orthodox in their social and religious practices, and are able, at least on occasion, to engage reputable Brahmins as their priests. The unclean are in general those engaged in a degrading occupation, one involving, say, defiling contacts with dead bodies, human or animal, or entailing sweeping up the dirt and refuse of the streets. The unclean castes include the leather-cutters and shoemakers, the sweepers or scavengers, the cane-chair makers, and the Kulis (coolies) or unskilled day-laborers.

The members of these unclean and degraded castes have long been regarded by the higher castes as "out-castes" and "untouchables." * Technically, there are more than fifty million of them in India today. In the past their plight was pitiable. Like the despised Chandala of the *Code of Manu*, who was ranked with the village pig and homeless dog, the untouchable was an object of contempt, despised by all. Not his touch only but even his shadow polluted a person of high caste. In some parts of India therefore he was required loudly to announce his presence as he came down the street, in order that those who might be defiled by him might draw their skirts away or move out of reach. Passage through certain public roads and bazaars was forbidden to him. He was not permitted to come within so many feet of certain temples.

* Technically speaking, the out-castes are of no caste. They are "pariahs," or un-organized, casteless people, "outside the pale." This was quite true of them in ancient times. But the out-castes in course of time organized themselves along caste lines. A score of such "castes" now exists, as our quotation on functional castes indicates.

He was not allowed to draw water from the public wells but had to go to those used only by his own group. If a Brahmin neared, he had to get off the road into a field. Did he approach the Brahmin too closely, the latter bathed, renewed his sacred cord, and underwent other purification. In some places an out-caste could not take purchases out of the hand of the merchant, but waited until the latter deposited them on the ground and walked away, or tossed them to him. It would seem to have been the object of the higher castes to reduce the untouchable to such a beaten, abject creature that he would never so much as attempt to better his lot. *

It is easy to see why Hinduism has witnessed one attempt after another, by persons who have gained fresh insight, to get around untouchability and other restrictions imposed by the caste system, or to get rid of the caste system altogether. These attempts have been mainly of two sorts.

The earliest attempts to deal with caste restrictions were made by heretical thinkers with a large following. Converts were invited to give up their caste positions, retire from the world, and join a new religious fellowship, a brotherhood of monks in which caste distinctions were erased. Jainism and Buddhism furnish the best instances of this attempt to deal with caste by saying "Come ye out from among them." And yet, those who remained outside the inner circle of monks continued to live under the old caste regulations. Not only did no real reform of the caste system result, but the lay-members married and gave in marriage according to the old caste laws, and this led to the intrenchment of caste rather than to its opposite, except only among those who actually retired from the world to monasteries. More pronounced social effects occurred when a religious leader, inspired by a revelation, formed a new sect in which all converts, as equals in the sight of God, no matter what their previous caste affiliations had been, were free to eat, visit, and intermarry with other members of the new sect. But because they could not marry outside the sect, either because they did not desire to do so or could not arrange it, the new sect in time became to all intents and purposes just another caste. The Shiva-worshiping Lingayats of Bombay and southern India, numbering nearly three million members, and the Baishtams of Bengal furnish excellent examples of this type of protest against the Brahmin-dominated caste system.†

* It will be remembered that the higher castes invoked the Law of Karma to justify this morally; the untouchable was suffering retribution for past sins.

† The above description applies to the *beginnings* of a religious movement, not to its whole history. The Lingayats began as a casteless community, but now have their own castelike subdivisions.

A second type of assault on the caste system sought its reform from within. This is a comparatively recent type of reform, and is usually motivated by a high social idealism, directly or indirectly influenced by Christianity and studies of Western social organization. One liberal proposal, with which Mahatma Gandhi was identified, may be summed up thus: let occupations be hereditary (on a kind of guild principle) but let the other restrictions be done away. *Especially should Untouchability be abolished.*

Since his death, Mahatma Gandhi has finally prevailed. Hindu India's Constituent Assembly, late in 1948, abolished untouchability and forbade its practice "in any form." What is on the statute books, however, will probably be a long time in being adhered to, for as the United States can bear witness, integration is a slow social process.

What has come to pass is that the political leaders of India are reacting constructively to the commonsense realization that the old order is disintegrating under modern industrialized and mechanized conditions of society. The old-time exclusiveness of the castes is crumbling away. The unavoidable mixing of high and low caste people in the trains and at railroad stations has made it a modern convention that a man of high caste may relax his observance of the old rules while on a journey, provided he is unbendingly strict when he is in his own village. While traveling he may sit beside persons whose nearness would defile him at home. In a big hotel he is not required to be as particular as he once had to be about the food and drink served to him; for he cannot demand that every dish be prepared only by ritualistically clean hands.

The masses of the people are meanwhile being shaken out of the grooves in which their lives have run for so many generations. Great changes in village life are following upon the growth of modern trade and the increasing industrialization of the country. Century-old village crafts are no longer being pursued, because mills, mines, and factories are driving them out of business. People are deserting their traditional occupations for new and more profitable vocations. A man's caste now less certainly suggests his occupation. Thus change has entered the very heart of the caste system.

2. *Child-marriage and widowhood.* Child-marriage has existed in India for many centuries. It is usually traced to a family-law, going back to the 5th century B.C., which required the marriage of all girls before puberty. This law (only imperfectly observed until eight or nine hundred years ago) may have originated out of a desire to forestall romantic attachments between young people of different castes; but there were other factors in the situation. For one thing, the old caste-law

prohibiting marriages outside of one's caste made it urgent that fathers search out eligible girls for their sons as soon as possible, lest there be none left; so parents took to betrothing their children when they were but a few months old, and marriage was frequently celebrated when bride and groom were only seven or eight years old. Another factor— ultimately important—was the great practical usefulness of child-marriage to the family-system, insofar as it helped to keep the family group united. Daughters-in-law coming into the family in the late teens were comparatively hard to assimilate to a family's fixed habits; but a bride of eight could easily be molded and fitted into the family routine so as to become an integral part of it. From this point of view child-marriage became a demand of the patriarchal family system. To this day, as a result, many Hindu wives hardly remember having lived anywhere else than with the family of their husbands.

A tragic consequence of the very early marriages has been the widowhood, through the death of boy-husbands, of many virgin child-wives, who, according to the *Code of Manu*, may never remarry, and therefore must spend long years of unhappy subjection to the members of the husband's family, with no hope of being regarded as anything but a burden on the family and no prospect of being given a higher status than that of a servant obliged to work if she wishes to eat.*

Widowers are not so unfortunate. They may remarry, if they can find a suitable bride. But this has often led to unequal marriages between middle-aged men and child-wives, it being impossible for the men to contract themselves to widows or to find unmarried women of their own age.

Until recently this situation has been shrugged off as inevitable and unavoidable; but, largely through the criticisms of Christian missionaries, the protests of Hindu reformers, and the adverse reports of medical authorities, an acute consciousness of the problem has been aroused among Hindus. The government, after an experimental trial with laws progressively lifting the age of consent, passed in 1930 the Child Marriage Restraint Bill, which made marriage of girls under fourteen and of boys under eighteen illegal; but the law was confined to British India. Today the whole of Hindu India is feeling the pressure, and rising opinion favors at least the revival of the ancient practice of postponing the full consummation of any marriage until after puberty.

---

* There are more than 500,000 child widows under fifteen years of age in India. It should be said, however, that the (unorthodox) lower classes have not always followed the higher castes in forbidding the re-marriage of widows, and so the situation described in this and the following paragraphs does not universally exist.

C. RECENT CHANGE

1. *Religious liberalism and reaction.* In recent decades two Hindus have earnestly sought an integration of "Eastern Religions and Western Thought" (the title of a book by one of them).* One, the late Aurobindo Ghose, a Bengali Brahmin, abandoned nationalistic politics for philosophy, in order to urge the possibility that "integral yoga," as he called it, may enable man to become a superman. In the eternal *shakti* he saw the downward movement of Reality (i.e., of the infinite, all-inclusive Brahman) in "descents, eruptions, messages or revelations." After this has had its spiritual effect on the human mind, there can be an "ascent" from the ordinary human to the superman level of being.

Dr. Sarvepalli Radhakrishnan, now president of India, is an internationally known scholar and lecturer, whose cordiality to Western religion and philosophy is accompanied by consistent stress on mysticism as the very heart of religion; consequently, Hinduism emerges in his numerous writings as the greatest of the religions. He defends Hinduism against the criticism that it is "non-ethical" (a criticism made by Albert Schweitzer) by emphasizing the moral growth that is the necessary preparation for mystic union with the ultimately real and by pointing to the duty of applying the spiritual lessons of religion in social and political activity.

Opposing this cordiality to the West are such groups supporting orthodox Hinduism as the *Mahasabha* and the *Rashtriya Swayamasevak Sangh* (the "National Service Organization"), which advocate making India officially a Hindu state. It was a member of the second group that assassinated Mahatma Gandhi.

Traditionally Hindus have been tolerant of other faiths, but while this is still the case, paradoxically the prevailing view throughout India now is that conversion from one religion to another should be discouraged.† One's native religion is always the best. But efforts to embody this principle in the law have not succeeded at this date (1962).

---

* It is by S. Radhakrishnan (and available to the student in paperback).

† Conversion is viewed as an effect of proselytization or as a "migration" which as its social consequence leaves the convert culturally alien and displaced, breaks up homes, separates kinsfolk, and unsettles the social and national order. Memories of Moslem pressures toward conversion and of British favor toward missionaries, who, as an extreme view puts it, "invaded" India and other Asiatic countries as "an integral part of the domination of the white races over Asia," have reinforced the nationalist desire to preserve Indian unity and prevent "religious nationalism" from developing among minority religious groups, e.g., the Sikhs and aboriginal peoples under the influence of Lutheran and Roman Catholic missions. When

(Footnote concluded on page 308.)

2. *Political change.* To pursue this topic in detail would take us far beyond the scope of this volume; yet not to pursue it at all would, on the other hand, narrow our study unduly; for it is not possible to divorce Indian politics from religion.

In the generation-long, organized struggle of the peoples of India for self-determination, three factors have been of supreme importance. The first is the well-founded feeling of the leading minds of India that in the intellectual sphere they have established their competence to engage in the life of reason on at least an equality with the world's greatest. Why then should they be kept in the role of a subject people?

The second factor is the personality and leadership of Mahatma Gandhi. With great patience, and a moral imagination not matched by any other individual in our time, he planned and led the political struggle for national self-determination. He fought with Hindu weapons —non-violent resistance, soul-force, a baffling use of tolerance and inclusive good will when confronted with strong opposition, but firm insistence on *swadeshi* (loyalty to one's own inherited religion and way of life). With astonishing practicality as to means but unyielding idealism in matters of principle, he completely controlled the diverse elements in the Congress Party up to and beyond the agreement with the British Raj which established national self-determination for Hindu India.

The third factor has been the mounting sense of deep difference between Hindu and Moslem. At first the Hindus refused to believe that such difference existed; but the highly organized Pakistan movement proved at last convincing, and the Hindus consented to the formation of the separate Moslem state. It is hardly necessary to add that there was tragedy in this not only for Gandhi and Nehru, the leaders of the nationalist cause in India, but for millions of Moslems, Sikhs, and Hindus, who suffered death and displacement when partition came in 1947. Gandhi himself was assassinated in the aftermath.

But one may be permitted to reflect, in conclusion, that, so far as Hinduism is concerned, incalculable consequences were bound to flow from so startling a circumstance as this: a great religion of escape has produced leaders in this latter day who have not sought Nirvana in

---

(Footnote continued from page 307.)

Hindus turn from these objective considerations to the subjective factors in conversion, they tend to make a distinction between yielding to the improper outside pressures of proselytization and the experience of genuine conversion, which they are inclined to view sympathetically. Conversion, they think, if it is from inward conviction, is not so likely to alienate the convert from his Hindu heritage, since, subjectively considered, all religions are essentially the same.[42]

the solitude of the forests, but have rather come forth into the world, to engage realistically and practically in the task of human betterment by social action. The leaders of the other great religions of the world cannot fail to see how great is the portent of this *volte-face* of the most influential recent leaders of the Hindu world.

SUGGESTIONS FOR FURTHER READING

Arnold, Sir Edwin. *The Song Celestial* (The Bhavagad Gita). Any edition
Sri Aurobindo. *The Synthesis of Yoga.* Aurobindo Library, 1950
Bouquet, A. C. *Hinduism.* Hutchinson's Library, 1949
Bühler, G., trans. *The Code of Manu.* Sacred Books of the East. Oxford, 1886
Crooke, W. N. *Religion and Folklore in Northern India.* Oxford, 1926
Dasgupta, S. *A History of Indian Philosophy.* 3 vols. Cambridge, 1922–1932
Dutt, R. C., trans. *Mahabharata and Ramayana.* Any edition
Eliot, Sir Charles. *Hinduism and Buddhism.* 3 vols. Routledge and Kegar Paul, 1954. Earlier edition, Edward Arnold, 1921
Emerson, Gertrude. *Voiceless India.* Doubleday, Doran, 1931
Farquhar, J. N. *An Outline of the Religious Literature of India.* Oxford, 1920
Griswold, H. D. *Insights into Modern Hinduism.* Henry Holt, 1934
Hiriyanna, M. *Essentials of Indian Philosophy.* Allen and Unwin, 1949
McKenzie, J. *Hindu Ethics.* Oxford, 1922
Monier-Williams, M. *Brahmanism and Hinduism.* Macmillan, 1891
Morgan, K. W., editor. *Religion of the Hindus.* Ronald Press, 1953
Nehru, Jawharlal. *Toward Freedom.* John Day, 1941
Nikhilananda, Swami, trans. *Prophet of New India.* Abridged from the *Gospel of Ramakrishna.* Harper, 1948
O'Malley, L. S. S. *Popular Hinduism.* Macmillan, 1935
Prabhavananda, S. and Christopher Isherwood, trans. *The Song of God: Bhagavad Gita.* Mentor Books pb, 1954
Pratt, J. B. *India and Its Faiths.* Houghton Mifflin, 1915
Radhakrishnan, S. *Indian Philosophy.* 2 vols, Allen and Unwin, 1923, 1927
Stevenson, Mrs. S. *The Hindu View of Life.* Macmillan, 1927
———. *Rites of the Twice-born.* Oxford, 1920
Wood, James H., trans. *The Yoga Sutras of Patanjali.* Harvard University Press, 1913
Woodruffe, Sir John. *Shakti and Shakta.* Luzac, 1929
Zimmer, H. *Myth and Symbol in Indian Art and Civilization.* Pantheon, 1946
———. *Philosophies of India.* Pantheon, 1951. Available as a Meridian Books pb

8 Sikhism: A Study in Syncretism

SIKHISM IS A LITTLE KNOWN RELIGION IN EUROPE AND AMERICA. IT WAS for a long time known to few save British colonial administrators and army officers, who thought it a useful set of beliefs because its adherents were neither Hindu nor Moslem, but were a little of both, and thus stood apart from the realm of violent prejudice dividing the two major religious groups. Colonial administrators were gratified at the combination of qualities that made Sikhs ideal police recruits: they were a stalwart, meat-eating people, of exceptionally fine physique, trained to meet the hazards of war and violence with fierce courage, and at the same time not religiously abhorrent to Hindus or Moslems.

Another reason for Sikhism's obscure fame is that it is one of the world's youngest faiths. Its foundation dates only from the 15th century.

It is not in any absolute sense new. Its basic conviction—monotheism—is drawn from Islamic sources; most of the other doctrines it professes are taken, with little if any change, directly from Hinduism. Indeed, Sikhism is an outstanding example of conscious syncretism—one of the few that have ever been successful.

On the other hand, Sikhism is not simply two old religions made one; it is, rather, a genuinely fresh start. Its followers believe it to have been authenticated by a new divine revelation to the founder, Nanak. It is therefore felt by its adherents to be the opposite of an intellectual reconstruction of faith arrived at after an academic examination of the articles of older religions. God—"The True Name"—appeared to Nanak and charged him with a redemptive mission to a lost world. It is thus

310

evident that the religion of the Sikhs is not to be confused with the rationalistic syncretisms whose adherents have been engaged in a re-working of philosophy rather than in a revival of religion, properly conceived.

I   THE LIFE AND WORK OF NANAK

The Historical Antecedents of Nanak

Before Nanak appeared on the historical scene the ground was pre-pared for him by men who had no thought of founding a new religion, but who saw a need of cleansing and purifying what seemed to them a decadent Hinduism. Their recurrent efforts of reform were the in-direct effects of the severe and militant monotheism of the Moslems, who had reached India in the 10th century A.D. and wielded an enor-mous power. By the 11th century the Moslems firmly dominated the whole of northwest India, and then, with remorseless pressure, extended their suzerainty over most of India. As early as in the 12th century a Hindu reformer-poet, called Jaidev, used the phrase that was to be the key-word of Sikhism at a later date; he taught that the practice of religious ceremonials and austerities was of no value compared with "the pious repetition of God's name." This is an Islamic teaching adapted to Hindu use. Two centuries later another reformer, by the name of Ramananda, established a Vishnuite sect which sought to purge itself of certain Hindu beliefs and practices; he excited great discussion by "liberating" himself and his disciples both from accepted Hindu re-strictions of social contacts between castes and from prohibitions against meat-eating. But his chief claim to fame today rests upon the fact that he had a follower greater than himself, who in turn nourished the soul of the founder of Sikhism. This disciple—Kabir (1440–1518)—has given his name to sects still flourishing in India, the Kabir-panthis (those who follow the path of Kabir). Kabir caught from the Moslems their hatred of idols, and, like the Hindu poet Namdev a generation before him, he scorned to believe that God can dwell in an image of stone or find satisfaction in the external forms of religion—rituals, scriptures, pilgrim-ages, asceticism, bathing in the Ganges and such like—if these are un-accompanied by inward sincerity or morality of life. As a monotheist, he declared that the love of God was sufficient to free anyone of any class or race from the Law of Karma. In other words, the all-sufficient means of bringing an end to reincarnation is the simple, complete love of God which absorbs the soul into the Absolute. He denied the special authority of the Hindu Vedas; wrote in the vernacular, not in Sanskrit; attacked both Brahmins and Moslems for their barren ritualism; and set up in place of their standards of belief the person of the inspired spiritual leader and teacher (the *guru*), apart from whom, he held, the right life-attitudes cannot be gained. Clearly, a combination of Hindu and Moslem elements appears in Kabir's teaching.

Upon this foundation of ethical monotheism Nanak was to rear his own doctrinal position. He was often to appeal back to Kabir as an authority.

Nanak's Life and Work

As nearly as the facts can be ascertained, Nanak was born in 1469 A.D. at the village of Talwandi, about thirty miles from Lahore, the capital of the Punjab. His parents were Hindus belonging to a mercantile caste locally called Khati (descended from the ancient Kshatriya caste), but they were comparatively low in the economic scale, his father being a village accountant and farmer. His mother, a pious woman, was very devoted to her husband and son. The town of Talwandi, at the time of the birth of Nanak, was governed by a petty noble, named Rai Bular, who was of Hindu stock but had been converted to the Moslem faith. He maintained, however, a tolerant attitude toward the adherents of the old faith, and encouraged attempts to reconcile the two creeds. Nanak was in due time to excite his friendly interest.

The stories of Nanak's youth are typical examples of historical fact transmuted into wonder-tales. It is said that he was a precocious youth, a poet by nature, and so much given to meditation and religious speculation as to be worthless in the capacity of herdsman or store-keeper, two occupations chosen for him by his solicitous parents. He was also a failure as a husband, we are told. His father agreed with some relief to his acceptance of a brother-in-law's offer of a government job in Sultanpur. Nanak left his wife and two children with his parents, and set out for the district capital. During business hours he worked, it is claimed, hard and capably; but he spent the evenings singing hymns to his Creator. His friend, the minstrel Mardana, a Moslem who was to have an important part to play in his career, came on from Talwandi to join him. Gradually they became the center of a small group of seekers.

The inward religious excitement of Nanak was meanwhile approaching a crisis. Suddenly there came a decisive experience.

One day after bathing in the river Nanak disappeared in the forest, and was taken in a vision to God's presence. He was offered a cup of nectar, which he gratefully accepted. God said to him, "I am with thee. I have made thee happy, and also those who shall take thy name. Go and repeat Mine, and cause others to do likewise. Abide uncontaminated by the world. Practice the repetition of My name, charity, ablutions, worship, and meditation. I have given thee this cup of nectar, a pledge of My regard." [1]

Under the stress of his feelings Nanak is said to have then uttered the preamble of the *Japji*, the composition which is silently repeated as a morning devotional rite by every devout Sikh to this day.

"There is but one God whose name is True, the Creator, devoid of fear and enmity, immortal, unborn, self-existent, great and bountiful.

"The True One was in the beginning, the True One was in the primal age.

"The True One is, was, O Nanak,* and the True One also shall be." [2]

After three days Nanak emerged from the forest.

He remained silent for one day, and the next he uttered the pregnant announcement, "There is no Hindu and no Musalman." [3]

This was the opening statement of what was to become a campaign of evangelism that had as its object the conversion of all India, Persia, and Arabia to the religion of the True Name.

Setting out on an extended tour of north and west India, which lengthened into years of wandering, he took as his sole companion his friend, the minstrel Mardana, who, while Nanak was singing his evangelistic hymns, played an accompaniment upon a small stringed instrument called a rebeck. The far-traveling pair visited the chief places of Hindu pilgrimage, including Hardwar, Delhi, Benares, the Temple of Jaganath, and holy places in the Himalaya Mountains. Undaunted by the rebuffs and hostility of religious authorities, Nanak sang and preached in market-places, open squares, and on street corners, pausing only to make a few converts before proceeding on his way, apparently in faith that God, the True Name, would cause the seed he broadcast to spring up and bear fruit of itself. He devised for his own wear a motley garb that at sight proclaimed his attempt to combine the two great faiths:

He put on a mango-colored jacket, over which he threw a white safa or sheet. On his head he carried the hat of a Musalman Qalander,† while he

---

* It was the custom of Persian and Indian poets to address themselves by name at the end of their compositions—a kind of oral signature.

† A Moslem anchorite corresponding to the Hindu sannyasi; usually called a dervish.

wore a necklace of bones, and imprinted a saffron mark on his forehead in the style of the Hindus.[4]

But it was not until they reached the Punjab that they had any marked success. There groups of *Sikhs* (literally, *Disciples*) began to form.

Late in life he took Mardana with him, it is said, but the account may be pure legend, into the heart of the Arab world. In the blue dress of the Moslem pilgrims, staff in hand, and carrying cups for their ablutions and carpets for prayer, they eventually reached Mecca, after many months. According to tradition (but the same story is told—more credibly—of his spiritual predecessor Kabir):

When the Guru arrived, weary and footsore, he went and sat in the great mosque where pilgrims were engaged in their devotions. His disregard of Moslem customs soon involved him in difficulties. When he lay down to sleep at night he turned his feet toward the Kaaba. An Arab priest kicked him and said, "Who is this sleeping infidel? Why hast thou, O sinner, turned thy feet towards God?" The Guru replied, "Turn my feet in the direction in which God is not." Upon this the priest seized the Guru's feet and dragged them in the opposite direction.[5]

He turned home to India. At Kartarpur, Mardana fell ill and died. He had grown old and was wearied out with wandering. Nanak, now sixty-nine years old, did not long survive him. Knowing his end was drawing near, and with his eye upon the future growth of his following of Sikhs, he made a decision which was to have far-reaching consequences. He determined to appoint a successor. His own sons were not available for choice; they had not obeyed him. So he appointed his disciple, Angad, to be his successor.

In October, 1538, he laid him down to die. The tradition says that Sikhs, Hindus, and Moslems gathered round him, mourning together. The Moslem converts, so runs the tale, said they would bury him after his death; the Sikhs of Hindu extraction said they would cremate him. When they referred the matter to the Guru, he said: "Let the Hindus place flowers on my right, and the Musalmans on my left. They whose flowers are found fresh in the morning may have the disposal of my body." So saying, he drew the sheet over his head and became still. When the sheet was removed the next morning, "there was nothing found beneath it. The flowers on both sides were in bloom."[6]

Thus, even in death, Nanak reconciled Hindu and Moslem! So the pious legend tells us.

II NANAK'S TEACHING

The doctrinal position of Nanak has a surprisingly simple form, in spite of its attempt to combine the insights of two widely differing faiths. The consistency is due to adherence to a single central concept— the sovereignty of the one God, the Creator.

Nanak called his god the True Name, because he meant to avoid any delimiting name for Him, like Allah, Rama, Shiva, or Ganesha. He taught that the True Name is manifest in manifold ways and in manifold places, and is known by manifold names; but He is eternally one, the sovereign and omnipotent God. If any name is to be used, let it be *Hari* (the Kindly), for that is a good description of His character. At the same time God inscrutably predestinates all creatures, and ordains that the highest of the creatures, man, be served by the lower creation. (This removed the Hindu taboo against meat-eating.) In these articles of Nanak's creed the strong Moslem element is evident.

On the other hand, Nanak subscribed to the Hindu doctrine of Maya or Illusion as unquestioningly as did his Brahmin opponents. God, he held, created matter by drawing a veil of illusion over Himself—an illusion producing by its mystic power all the diverse forms of the creation: the finite gods, Brahmā, Vishnu, and Shiva; the heavens, the hells, the earth; men, animals, and plants. In the words of the *Japji*, the summary of the doctrines of the Guru:

One Maya in union with God gave birth to three acceptable children.
One of them is the creator [Brahmā], the second the provider [Vishnu],
   the third performeth the functions of destroyer [Shiva]. . . .
He beholdeth them, but is not seen by them. This is very marvellous.[7]

Such, however, is not Nanak's usual way of speaking. Finite creative agents, themselves created, are after all mere instruments, and Nanak's customary attitude was that of adoring the True Name as Himself the Creator.

God Himself created the world and Himself gave names to things.
He made Maya by His power.[8]

The world is, then, ultimately unreal. "The world is very transient, like a flash of lightning," [9] Nanak sang, and did not shrink from the parallel thought that man is in like case. Retaining the Hindu doctrine of the transmigration of souls, together with its usual corollary, the Law of Karma, Nanak warned his hearers not to prolong the round of their births by living apart from God and accumulating Karma. Let them think only of God, endlessly repeat his name, and be absorbed into

Him; in such absorption alone lies the bliss of Nirvana. For salvation is not going to Paradise after a last judgment, but absorption—individuality-extinguishing absorption—in God, the True Name.

Nanak swung away from the firm Moslem emphasis on divine transcendence to a Hindu insistence that God pervades the world and is in man's heart.

Search not for the True One afar off; He is in every heart, and is known by the Guru's instruction.[10]

With almost a Quaker's distrust of ritual and ceremonial, he denounced Hindus and Moslems for going through the forms of worship without really thinking about God. In fact, he felt that ritual was a positive distraction; it turned the current of men's thoughts away from God to mere forms and motions of worship. On every hand he found illustrations of his thesis. In the first Moslem religious service that he attended after his call to be the Guru of God, he is said to have laughed aloud. The Moslems could scarcely wait till the service was over before pouncing on him for an explanation.

The Guru replied that immediately before prayer the Qazi had unloosed a new-born filly. While he ostensibly performed divine service, he remembered there was a well in the enclosure, and his mind was filled with apprehension lest the filly should fall into it.[11]

Therefore the Qazi's prayer was not accepted of God, Nanak said.

He felt a similar distrust of Hindu rites, going on pilgrimages, asceticism of the extreme type, and idolatry of any sort. In the last case he not only thought that idols distracted men's thoughts from God's reality, but, as he declared with all but Moslem fervor, God could not be contained in an image of wood or stone. As for pilgrimages, merely repeating the True Name is equal to bathing at the sixty-eight places of pilgrimage. In regard to the ascetic retreat from the world, "Why go searching for God in the forest? I have found Him at home," Nanak cried.[12]

Religion consisteth not in a patched coat, or in a Yogi's staff, or in ashes smeared over the body;
Religion consisteth not in earrings worn, or a shaven head, or in the blowing of horns. . . .
Religion consisteth not in wanderings to tombs or places of cremation, or sitting in attitudes of contemplation.
Religion consisteth not in wandering in foreign countries, or in bathing at places of pilgrimage.[13]

The good man and the good Sikh is pure in motive and in act, serves the virtuous and those superior to him in intelligence, honors those who can teach him, craves the Guru's word and all divine knowledge as a man craves food; loves his wife and renounces all other women; avoids quarrelsome topics, is not arrogant, does not trample on others, and forsakes evil company, associating instead only with the holy.

Nanak's creed and practice were distinctly quietistic; and yet it was the singular fate of the religion he established to change with the years into a vigorously activist political faith. Various influences were to provide a notable modification of this code of philanthropy, honesty, and holiness, and introduce in full strength a military ardor, a self-dedication to the arbitrament of the sword. That is a unique and in some respects distressing story.

III THE POLITICAL HISTORY OF SIKHISM

Nine gurus, as official heads of the Sikh religion, succeeded Nanak; and the body of believers grew.

Of the first four, Guru Amar Das (1552–1574) is typical. He was noted for his humility and freedom from pride of class, saying: "Let no one be proud of his caste. . . . The world is all made out of one clay." [14] The quietism of the older Sikh religion was evident in all he did. The Sikhs of his time lived by the truly pacifist rule: "If anyone treat you ill, bear it. If you bear it three times, God Himself will fight for you the fourth time." [15]

But the fifth guru, Guru Arjan (1581–1606), marks a period of transition to something more militant. This was due partly to a changed attitude on the part of the Moslem authorities, and partly within Sikhism itself to the vigor and leadership of the handsome Arjan. In addition to completing the ambitious project of his predecessors—the artificial lake of Amritsar and the Golden Temple on its island—Arjan did two things of lasting significance. First, he compiled the *Granth*, the Sikh Bible. Realizing that the devotional hymns used by the Sikhs in their worship were in danger of being lost, he brought them together into one collection. He was himself a talented poet, and half of the collection consisted of hymns of his own composition; the rest were mostly by Nanak, with a number by the second, third, and fourth gurus, and by Jaidev, Namdev, Kabir, and others. This compilation was at once recognized as notable by persons both within and outside the ranks of the

Sikh following. The Moslem emperor Akbar was told of it by his advisers, who considered it a dangerous infidel work; but Akbar was a tolerant monarch, and after examining the Granth, declared he discovered no dangerous ideas in it. He even paid Arjan a respectful visit and thus indicated his general approval. But the liberal-minded Akbar was succeeded by his cruel and fanatical son, Jahangir, who, on the charge of political conspiracy, seized Guru Arjan and tortured him to death. Before he died, however, Arjan did the second thing whose significance was to be lasting: he left the injunction to his son, Har Govind, to "sit fully armed on his throne, and maintain an army to the best of his ability." [16]

Guru Har Govind (1606–1645) obeyed the last injunction of his father. At his installation he refused to wear, as too suggestive of quietism, the turban and necklace which had come down from his predecessors. His intention was clearly expressed: "My *seli* [necklace] shall be a swordbelt, and my turban shall be adorned with a royal aigrette." [17] He lost no time in suiting his actions to his words. He surrounded himself with an armed bodyguard, built the first Sikh stronghold, and in due time drew to his standard thousands of Sikhs eager for military service. He was able to provide rations and clothing, as well as weapons, out of the moneys in the treasury of the Golden Temple. The Moslem world around him had been getting more and more hostile as the Sikhs, provided now with a capital city and a rich and beautiful temple, began to develop a national feeling. The Sikhs were no longer, from the Moslem point of view, an inconveniently closeknit yet otherwise harmless sect; they were a political and social reality that menaced the balance of power in northwest India. So the Moslems began to bestir themselves. And the Sikhs were ready for them. What with their strain of Hindu mysticism on the one hand and their rugged Moslem-like staunchness on the other, they found in themselves the qualities of fighting men. Things did not go too well at first, however. Guru Har Govind fought and was imprisoned by the same Jahangir who had put his father to death; but this time the payment of a fine released him—to fight again.

The rather unequal struggle continued until the time of the tenth guru, Govind Singh (1675–1708). On his accession this guru was called Govind Rai, but he is better known as Govind Singh, Govind the Lion. He found the Sikhs aroused for a major struggle. They were eager to establish an autonomous military state, independent of Moslem control. Govind was militant, but prudent. While he waited for a favorable opportunity to risk a clash of arms, he fortified the spirits of his followers by writing hymns, after the manner of the first gurus, but in a very martial style. For example:

I bow to Him who holdeth the arrow in His hand; I bow to the Fearless One;
I bow to the God of gods who is in the present and the future.
I bow to the Scimitar, the two-edged Sword, the Falchion, and the Dagger. . . .
I bow to the Holder of the Mace. . . .
I bow to the Arrow and the Cannon. . . .[18]

These words are prefaced with the startling invocation:

Hail, hail to the Creator of the world, the Savior of creation, my Cherisher, hail to Thee, O Sword!

These hymns were later compiled into *The Granth of the Tenth Guru,* and made an authoritative supplement to the First (or Adi) Granth. One tradition says this was done after Govind Singh's death, in his honor; another credits the "Lion" Guru with the deliberate intention to compose a new scripture.

The Guru discovered that, from reading the original Granth, the Sikhs became very feeble-hearted. He therefore determined himself to compose such a Granth that, from reading it, his disciples should become fit for fighting.[19]

There can be no question of the fact that Govind Singh was thoroughly convinced of his divine authority. When the inspiration came to him to institute his greatest innovation, the *Khanda di-Pahul* or Baptism of the Sword, he felt it was of God. One day after adequately testing the sincerity of five followers, he poured water into an iron basin and stirred it with a sharp sword, mixing in an Indian sweetmeat the while. He then gave each of the group five palmsful of the sweetened water to drink, and sprinkled the water five times on each one's hair and eyes. Thus baptized into a new order of life, they were made to repeat what became the war-cry of the Sikhs, "*Sri wahguru ji ka Kahalso, Sri wahguru ji ki fatah*"—"The Pure are of God, and the victory is to God." These men formed the group of the Khalsa or Pure; and they bore the name of Singhs or Lions. They were charged to wear ever after the five Ks: (1) the *Kes,* or long hair on head and chin, (2) the *Kangha* or comb, (3) the *Kachk* or short drawers,* (4) the *Kara* or steel bracelet, and (5) the *Khanda* or steel dagger. Beyond this, they pledged

* The origin of Khaki drawers, the forerunners of present day shorts.

themselves to worship the one invisible God, honor the gurus, and reverence one visible object, the holy Granth. They gave up all stimulants, especially alcoholic liquors, and eschewed tobacco. They were encouraged to begin the eating of meat, if they had not already done so. The Guru Govind himself became a Singh, by obliging the first five neophytes, after he had initiated them, to baptize him in turn. Then he threw the new cult open to men of very class, regardless of caste. To the open distress of the higher castes, many individuals from the lower classes, and even pariahs, flocked to join the Guru's organization, and, thrilled by the baptism of the sword, were transformed from shrinking untouchables and timid low-caste men into free and fearless soldiers, equal to the best. Clean living, and the all-round diet, gave them strong physiques; the enthusiasm of a confident faith gave them courage in battle; and confident and independent leaders gave them direction.

Not all Sikhs became Singhs. Some remained Nanakpanthis ("Followers of Nanak"), displaying various shades of quietism and remaining dubious of war-making.

The struggles of Govind Singh with the resourceful Moslem ruler Aurangzeb were without advantage to the Sikhs. While Aurangzeb lived they could get nowhere. The Guru lost his two sons on whom his hopes of succession depended, and the Sikh army was routed. After the doughty emperor died, Govind Singh was on friendly terms with his successor, Bahadur Shah; only to be himself the next to fall—by the knife of a Moslem assassin in 1708. He had provided, however, for such an event, and told his Sikhs, disappointed as he was in his hopes of succession, that after his death they were to regard the Granth as their Guru; there was no need of other leadership than the teaching of the holy book.

The Sikhs were obedient. They have had no Guru since then; instead, they have worshipped the Granth as their one divine authority. At the Golden Temple in Amritsar the Granth receives the honors of divinity. "Every morning it is dressed out in costly brocade, and reverently placed on a low throne under a jewelled canopy. Every evening it is made to repose for the night in a golden bed within a sacred chamber, railed off and protected from all profane intrusion by bolts and bars." [22] But, though its words, as read from a duplicate copy, resound daily in the temple, it is written in so many languages and archaic dialects, that the people, even while reverencing it, do not understand it.

The political history of Sikhism since Govind Singh's day has been one of great military renown. The Sikhs won many battles, and in due time dominated the whole Punjab. When the British came to subdue them in 1845 and 1848, they put up an exciting struggle. In 1849 the last Sikh ruler, Maharajah Dhulip Singh, surrendered to the victorious British arms, and as a sign of submission and a pledge of loyalty gave over to Queen Victoria the world-renowned Koh-i-nur diamond. After that the Sikhs came to feel respect for their conquerors, and never went back on their word to them. When the Indian Mutiny broke out, the Singhs of the Khalsa rushed to the British colors, and helped save India for the British crown. The crown rewarded them. All over the East they were the favorite constabulary of the British colonial power. They could be seen in Hongkong and Shanghai as well as in the nearer areas of Singapore and Burma.

Today, their fortunes have again worsened. In the partition of India in 1947 their home territory was divided between Pakistan and Hindu India, with Amritsar assigned to the latter dominion. Aggrieved and terrified, thousands of them joined in organized assault on Hindu and Moslem alike. Once more, but in the uglier sense, they became the "lions of the Punjab," fighting as they said for their social and religious rights. They have since been assured by both Hindus and Moslems of religious freedom and social justice, promises which it remains for the future to see carried out. So far their pleas for "home rule" have not been granted.

SUGGESTIONS FOR FURTHER READING

Archer, J. C. *The Sikhs.* Princeton University Press, 1946
Field, Dorothy. *The Religion of the Sikhs.* In the Wisdom of the East series. John Murray, 1911
Gupta, H. R. *History of the Sikhs.* Dawson, 1950
MacAuliffe, M. A. *The Sikh Religion: Its Gurus, Sacred Writings, and Anthems.* Oxford, 1909
Trumpp, Ernest, trans. *The Adi Granth or Holy Scriptures of the Sikhs.* Trubner, 1877

PART THREE

The Religions of the Far East

Foreword to
PART THREE

THE CHARACTERISTIC OF PRESERVING THE OLD WITH THE NEW WHICH WE noted in the religions of India is clearly present in the religions of the Far East. Perhaps no religion can entirely transcend its past; even in the cases of those religions which at their inception consciously rejected the older faiths they sought to replace, much of the old re-entered the new at a later date. But rejection of the past is a rather unusual procedure. In India and the Far East, indeed, the old is seldom cast away, even when it is left behind in an advance, because it is felt that there is truth still there.

However, despite this and other likenesses, the general religious attitude in the Far East differs from that of India in important respects. India tends to give the value of an illusion to Nature, or at least yearns to triumph over it in thought as a thing of secondary or tertiary value. The Chinese and Japanese do not do this easily. In general they have cultivated an aesthetic appreciation of Nature, which, apart from Buddhist and Taoist influences, has reached such heights of satisfaction as to make the Far Easterner want to prolong life in this world as long as possible. Nature is not the ultimate reality, but it has a valuable role to play in the life of man; it is a real and not deceptive structure of forms and forces, and it displays sublime order and beauty in both action and being. The only dissenting opinion here might be that of the Taoists, who, especially in the case of the witty Chuang-tzu, have considered Nature to be of value chiefly in signifying the operational presence of the only wholly real entity in the universe—the mysterious and wonderful Tao. But even here Chuang-tzu has been an inspiration to Chinese artists and poets; for he has helped them to treat the forms and forces of Nature either as passively beautiful exteriorizations, or as aesthetically effective dynamic expressions, of the Tao. The Japanese, without any such philosophy to go by, have come to love the trees, flowers, and scenic glories of their land as surpassingly beautiful in form and structure, and not only lovely when committed in their essential lines by brush to paper, but also worthy of being graphically suggested in the objectively descriptive phrases of the world's briefest poems, the Japanese *haiku*. Consider this characteristically Oriental episode in the life of Prince Taira no Tadanori, fleeing for his life into the mountains of the western provinces. In the gravest peril though he was, he waited as twilight fell around him to write down in the required seventeen syllables the serene reflection:

> Twilight upon my path tonight,
> And for mine inn tonight
> The shadow of a tree,
> And for mine host a flower.*

Nature and the life of the Spirit are but the obverse and converse of the same reality. In the opinion of F. S. C. Northrop:

The Orientals are an exceedingly concrete, practical, and realistic people; and their religion is best thought of by Westerners as something nearer to what the West regards as aesthetics than it is to what the West has regarded as religion . . . But in saying this care must be taken. For . . . the aesthetic must be conceived in its Oriental sense as the aesthetically immediate for its own sake and not in its Western sense as the handmaid of commonsense beliefs in external, three-dimensional objects, or of more sophisticated . . . scientific, philosophical, or theological objects. In short, the Oriental uses the purely aesthetic to constitute the nature of the divine . . . As Chiang Yee has written of Chinese painting—

"Perhaps the most important mental process in it is that movement of the sympathies where the onlooker loses his own identity and becomes one with the 'observed' and eventually with the Great Spirit of the Universe, which informs everything that has life." †

There is a further aspect of the Far Eastern religious consciousness

---

* *An Anthology of Japanese Poems*, trans. Miyamori Asataro, p. 174. (This *haiku* translated by James A. B. Scherer.) Tokyo, 1938. Quoted by permission.

† F. S. C. Northrop, *The Meeting of East and West*, pp. 403-404. Copyright 1946 by the Macmillan Co. Reprinted by permission of the publishers.

which needs to be noted. Not to see it is to fail seriously in understanding. Man and Nature are organically, not externally or accidentally, related. The basic concepts of Chinese religion may be cited in illustration. It is the central belief of the ancient Chinese that Heaven, Earth, and men are so sensitively related to each other that any untoward development affects them all; the misbehavior of men, or even of the emperor alone, throws the whole of Nature off stride, and Heaven is disturbed; the pleasure of Heaven and Earth in the obedience of men to the law of Nature's being (the *Tao*) causes a universal harmony to obtain: the crops will thrive and men will be at peace and prosperous. The various parts of the universe therefore are not externally related to each other as are the parts of a mechanism; they are mutually sensitive to each other as are the elements within an organism. Something of this same feeling has long been present among the Japanese. It is common among those who still live under the influence of the old traditions to consider that the emperor, his people, the mountains of Japan, and the heavens above, form an interrelated community, in which all the vital forces are acutely sensitive to each other.

There is a hidden pantheism here, or shall we call it the spiritual conception of things?

9 Chinese Religion and the Taoists

THE ANCIENT CHINESE SCHOLARS LIVING IN THE TIMES OF LAO-TZU AND Confucius believed they were enjoying the ripe results of a nearly two-thousand-year-old culture. Their backward look, if they were right, traversed a stretch of time so long that to experience anything comparable we should have to think of the landing of the Pilgrims as having taken place, not in 1620, but at the time of Augustus Caesar. They were perhaps looking back too far; recent historical and archaeological investigation throws considerable doubt on the traditional dates; but they were not wrong in the main, in assuming that their culture was both old and thoroughly Chinese.

The Chinese have embodied their recognition of this fact in their popular traditions. In many myths concerning the beginnings of their history, they have told of the clever Yu Ch'ao, who taught the ancient Chinese to build "nests" (the first houses); of the ingenious Sui Jen, who made fire by twirling one dry stick upon another; of the great hunter, Fu Hsi, emperor and originator extraordinary, who taught the early men of China how to domesticate animals, use iron in making hunting and fishing implements, fish with nets, write with pictograms, forecast with the Eight Trigrams, and play upon the musical instruments which he invented; of Shen Nung, the Divine Farmer, who while emperor invented ox-drawn carts and instructed men in the arts of agriculture and medicine; and of the Yellow Emperor, Huang Ti, most famous of all in after-times, who invented bricks, vessels of wood and clay, the calendar, and money, and whose principal wife introduced the people to silkworm culture. These great personages, the myths relate, were by no means the first to appear in China. Long ages lay behind them. In the distant past, but badly jumbled together by the confusing accounts, there reigned through ten great epochs, totaling two million years (!), groups of human, half-human, and animal-like sovereigns, who often occupied the throne for periods lasting up to eighteen thousand years. Yet even these sovereigns did not go back to the absolute beginnings of things. Before the first of the Celestial Sovereigns there lived and labored, more than two million years ago,* P'an Ku, the first man, four times the size of ordinary men to begin with, and destined to grow larger with his toil. He came when the world was still in chaos, and with hammer and chisel, during a period of epic labor lasting eighteen thousand years, he separated heaven and earth, hewed out places in the heavens for the sun, moon, and stars, dug out the valleys on the surface of the earth, piled high the mountains, and finally enriched the scene of his labors by his own self-distribution. "When he died his remains fell apart and formed the Five Sacred Mountains of China. His head became T'ai Mountain in the East; his body Sung Mountain in the center; his right arm Heng Mountain in the North and his left Heng Mountain in the South; his two feet Hua Mountain in the West." [1] His breath became "winds and clouds, his voice thunder, his flesh the fields; his beard was turned into stars, his bones into metals; his dropping sweat increased to rain, and lastly the insects which stuck to his body were transformed into people." [2]

These fanciful stories accent the Chinese belief in the great age of their native culture. But of course no great culture anywhere is entirely indigenous. The Chinese undoubtedly learned much from others. Certain production techniques, like the baking of pottery and the making and casting of bronze, seem to have come in from Central Asia. It is uncertain now whether these borrowings were the results of contacts made through trade or whether they followed upon the immigration or invasion of moving peoples. It is not to our purpose to speculate further on this point. So impossible is it now to untangle the complex pattern of the indigenous and borrowed elements of Chinese culture that we may well leave the matter to the archaeologists to solve, if they can.

Turning then from this problem, let us consider the religious conceptions which the common people of China have held. They are old, too.

---

* Ninety-six million years ago, says another account!

I   THE BASIC ELEMENTS OF CHINESE RELIGION

The religions of China are a blend of many elements, native and foreign, sophisticated and naive, rational and superstitious. Since we have already glanced at Buddhism in China and are about to consider separately Taoism and Confucianism, our present topic is limited to those elements of popular religion which serve as background and foil to the more highly developed systems of thought and faith just mentioned. But even this limited topic is hard to discuss within a brief compass; so many of the old and superseded beliefs and practices of China must be considered along with the beliefs and practices that have supplanted them. Moreover, since the triumph of the Communists in 1949 and the lowering of the Bamboo Curtain, present changes cannot be observed; no doubt they are incalculable and are probably accelerating. However, not even the most radical revolution can be total. Some of the old beliefs and habits undoubtedly still remain.

First, let us ask what the cosmology of Old China was.

The Cosmology of Ancient China

About the time that the monistic idealism of the Upanishads was being formulated in India, there arose in China an attempt to *order* the spirits, to see in all the processes of heaven and earth a display of fundamental regularity and harmony of operation.

As have many other peoples, the ancient Chinese believed that the earth is a flat, motionless disc with bowed heavens above. To their mind, China occupied the central place on the earth's surface. It was "The Middle Kingdom." The farther one went from the heart of China, which was where the emperor's palace and the imperial altars to heaven and earth stood, the less cultured and respectable one found the people.

When they looked up into the heavens, with the "natural piety" with which agricultural peoples view the dome of heaven by day and by night, they were impressed by the order and harmony of the celestial movements. Each heavenly body followed its appointed order and course, from year to year the same. If Heaven in anger summoned meteors and thunderbolts to crash to earth in pursuance of the ends of justice and order, that would be because it had been disturbed out of its wonted equilibrium by some occurrence on earth, perhaps some human crime.

Earth also showed a like, if less apparent, obedience to law. There was order in the unvarying succession of the seasons, the growth of plants, the upward leap of flame, the down-flowing of water, and in thousands of instances of natural process. Here, too, demonic powers, or Heaven's punishing will, caused disturbance, delay, or miscarriage. Floods, tornadoes, earthquakes, drought, and unseasonable cold were not uncommon. And yet, where Earth was left to work out her processes without molestation, there was order and harmonious functioning everywhere.

The Yang and the Yin

As they pondered this matter, some early, now unknown Chinese philosophers, several centuries before Confucius, perhaps even as early as 1000 B.C., distinguished within every natural object two interacting energy-modes, the *yang* and the *yin*. Everything that is in existence, they and their successors, amplifying upon them,* said, is constituted by the interplay of these two modes of energy, and therefore has the characteristics of each. The *yang* is described as masculine in character —active, warm, dry, bright, procreative, positive. It is seen in the sun, in anything that is brilliant, the south side of a hill, the north side of a river, male properties of all kinds, fire. The *yin* is an energy mode in a lower and slower key; it is fertile and breeding, dark, cold, wet, mysterious, secret; the female or negative principle in nature. It is seen in shadows, quiescent things, the north side of a hill, the shadowed south bank of a river. A single object may at one moment show *yin* characteristics and at another become a *yang* object aflame with energy. Thus a dried-out log is to all appearance wholly *yin* in character, but if put in the fire it will prove to have *yang* qualities in abundance. This is not because its substance has altered, but because its inner activity has changed from one mode to another. The like is true of anything else, although there may be things in which either the *yin* or the *yang* remains a deeply dormant mode of being. Examples of objects in which one or the other mode is dominant are the ever-fiery sun, Earth as a whole (predominantly *yin* in character), and Heaven (which is full of *yang* energy-modes). That this way of regarding the compound objects of nature is not unlike the theories of modern physical science is an inference one might draw from the following description:

* A whole school of Chinese philosophers devoted themselves to Yin-Yang inter-actionism in the 2nd century B.C. Outstanding among them were Huai-nan-tzu, and the Confucians Tung Chung-shu and Wang Ch'ung. (See Fung, *A History of Chinese Philosophy,* Chapters III and VII. See also infra pp. 413 and 418 ff.)

The Chinese physical world is a world of action . . . Things are differentiated, not by the stuff of which they are composed, but by the way they act. Stuffs pass from a state of having one sort of properties to a state of having another; in the latter state they have a different name, but the only difference is one of activity. . . . To say the same thing otherwise, the Chinese seem to have lacked a conception of substance, matter, as such, since this can only exist over against that which is not material. To the ancient Chinese thinker, the differences between things consist in degree of density (itself a kind of activity) and nature of activity.[3]

Men and women are, not less than inanimate things, the product of the interaction in varying degrees of the *yang* and the *yin*; they show differing proportions of the qualities of each activity-mode, men being celestial (that is, predominantly *yang*) and of great worth, while women are earthy (predominantly *yin*) and of little account on the whole!

Looking in another direction, one sees that the *shen* (or good spirits) are *yang* in character, the *kwei* (or evil spirits) are *yin*.

In still another direction, the "five elements," viz. metal, wood, water, fire, and earth, are the result of the interaction in the cosmic sphere of *yang* and *yin*, earth being a kind of sedimentary deposit, while the others are more volatile.

Finally, *events* reveal *yin* and *yang* influences in the alternation of success and failure, rise and fall, fluorescence and decay in all things.

The Conception of the Tao

But the ancient Chinese thinkers were not content with framing a neat theory to account for becoming, being, and passing away of single objects; they wished also to account for the evident harmony and order in nature as a whole. To what was *this* due?

The concept at which they arrived by way of answer was the Tao. The harmony and orderliness displayed in Heaven and Earth were, they said, the result of the cosmic energy of the Tao. Literally, the Tao means "a way" or "a road." Sometimes it denotes the "channel" of a river. In general, it means "the way to go." It refers to the standard procedure of things, the correct method of their operation or behavior.

This Tao of the universe is conceived to be eternal. It would seem that the ancient Chinese distinguished between the mechanism of the universe and the powerful *way* in which, as if by inner necessity, it ran. To their minds it seemed that the way in which the universe runs must have existed before the universe itself did. First, the preordained Plan, the proper Way-to-Go; then, the physical universe going that way.

The next step was to see that this way of nature's functioning was a way of perfection. It was a pre-established pattern into which all things ought to fall if they are to be in their proper place and do their proper work. The Tao is emphatically a way of harmony, integration, and cooperation. Its natural tendency is toward peace, prosperity, and health. If it were not for the perverse men and demonic beings that refuse to adjust themselves to it, this would quickly become evident. In fact, if the Tao were ever to be followed everywhere, heaven, mankind, and earth would form a single, harmonious unit, in every part cooperating toward universal well-being.

This state of perfection, the Chinese dreamed, did obtain in the Golden Age, when the good emperors Yao and Shun ruled their subjects by knowing and following the Tao. That was a time of universal felicity; men then lived in an earthly paradise. Such a state of perfection could return to earth, if the conditions for its restoration were met. The possibility appeared to lie largely with the emperor. If he lived according to the Tao, he became, as we learn under the next topic, the earthly instrument of a cosmic power making for peace and harmony among men, animals, and natural forces, and so prosperity existed throughout his realm.

The Ancient Chinese Theory of History

The casual reader of Chinese history and folklore might too easily conclude that imperial authority in times past was absolute and uncontrolled, and that the emperor had no wishes to consult save his own. But this impression, however well supported by tales of imperial extravagance and arbitrary rule, would be wide of the mark. Chinese emperors schooled in the old imperial tradition carried a heavy load of responsibility, such as few monarchs in other parts of the world have had to bear. When an emperor regularly worshipped the spirits and lived in conscientious regard for the welfare of his people, he was highly revered for fulfilling the duty of a Son of Heaven, who had been set upon the throne by its holy decree; but he was never entirely comfortable; he lived in the uneasy knowledge that his people held him strictly accountable for any failure to live by the celestial mandate, since if he did less he endangered the prosperity of the realm. If he failed to carry out the divine mandate and became licentious, lazy, and careless, calamity befell the nation as a sign of celestial displeasure, and the people had the right to revolt and depose their ruler. In such case Heaven guided some rebel to the throne who was more amenable to its will.*

Among the most pathetic scenes in history are those in which we see Chinese emperors going before Heaven to plead for mercy for their people—and some light on what they themselves had wrought amiss! What had they done? They wished they knew! Let Heaven inform them, they prayed. One of the emperors of the Chou dynasty is pictured by the *Book of Poetry* as having been in this predicament.

> Grand shone the Milky Way on high,
> With brilliant sun athwart the sky,
>   Nor promise gave of rain.
> King Seuen long gazed; then from him broke,
>
> In anguished tones the words he spoke . . .
> "The drought consumes us. Nor do I
> To fix the blame on others try . . .
> Why upon me has come this drought?
> Vainly I try to search it out,
>   Vainly, with quest severe.
> God in great heaven, be just, be kind!
> My cry, ye wisest spirits, hear!
>   Why do I this endure?" [4]

By the 2nd century B.C. this idea had reached so formidable an elaboration as this:

> If the king and his ministers do not practice the ritual courtesies; if there be no majesty (on the one hand) and no reverence (on the other), then the trees will not grow (as they should), and in summer there will be an excess of high winds . . .
>
> If the king's mind fail to be penetrating, then the sowing and reaping will not be completed, so that in autumn there will be an excess of rumbling thunder. [5]

Earth-Worship

The religion of ancient China faithfully mirrored the agricultural character of early Chinese civilization. It made much of a mound of earth symbolizing the fertility of the soil, called the *she*, which was raised in every village, surmounted sometimes by a tree or placed in a sacred grove. This mound was the center of an agricultural cult, whose rites

---

* For many centuries war-lords justified themselves by this theory. The Communists have discarded the theory, but have at the same time appealed to the tradition that poor rule should be overthrown by revolution.

in honor of the local gods of the soil sought to insure increase of the fertility of the ground and the growth of crops. In the spring a festival celebrated before the *she* included dancing and ceremonial songs, in general character resembling the European May-pole festival. The *she* also provided in the early autumn the scene of a Chinese harvest-home. When China became a feudal empire, the land became dotted with larger mounds, one in each provincial or state capital, symbolizing the territory of the feudal lord, while one at the imperial capital, composed of earth of five different colors, represented the earth-emperor himself, during the summer solstice, ploughed a furrow and principle (or soil-spirit) of the whole realm. At the last mound the conducted a ceremony of earth-worship in behalf of the empire as a whole, a practice which was continued down to modern times.

Worship of Heaven

With the passage of time the worship of Earth lessened, while the worship of Heaven steadily increased. In the time of the Shangs, a deity by the name of Ti or Shang Ti was worshiped. Shang means "upper" and Ti is usually translated as "ruler" or "emperor." This deity was, then, the god of the upper regions or the heavens. The Shangs asked him for rain and believed he had oversight over the whole earth. Before they went into battle they bade their diviners find out whether Shang Ti approved. When the Chous began their rule, another name appeared and alternated with Shang Ti. It was the word T'ien—Heaven. This was in general use a rather impersonal designation. Originally it meant "the abode of the Great Spirits," that is the heavens, or the sky.

The Chou and subsequent emperors, because of their reputed close relation to Heaven, bore the title T'ien Tzu or "Son of Heaven." They worshipped Heaven in the people's behalf at regular annual ceremonies. In later centuries at Peking, the Chinese emperors used to perform during the winter solstice a solemn sacrifice to Imperial Heaven on the beautiful marble terraces of the Altar of Heaven south of the city (across the city from the Altar of Earth). After the Spirit of Heaven had been invited to come down and take up its abode in a large tablet inscribed "Imperial Heaven, Supreme Ruler," the emperor offered during the various stages of the ceremony incense, jade, silk, broth, and rice wine, and pressed his forehead nine times to the pavement while statutory prayers were recited by an official in a loud voice. Without this ceremony and its attendant appeals to the imperial ancestors it was felt that the harmony between earth and heaven would be disrupted.

The Worship of Localized Spirits

The Chinese believed that all Nature is alive with spirits of many different kinds. Heaven throngs with spirits, and so does Earth. On the second terrace of the Altar of Heaven stood tablets for the spirits of the sun, moon, the five planets, the seven stars of the Great Bear, the twenty-eight principal constellations, the stars considered collectively, the winds, the clouds, rain, and thunder. The spirits were of course not all in the sky. They were in hills and streams and even in roads and cultivated fields. The Yellow River and the principle mountains of China were from time immemorial the objects of special official worship.

Not all spirits have been considered beneficent. From the earliest times it has been a prevailing belief that devils and demons of many sorts and kinds throng about every human dwelling, haunt lonely spots, and infest all roads, especially when at night-fall travelers thin out along the way and are few and far between; they lurk, too, in the shadows of forests and mountains. The different species of demons make a long list, for there are demons in water, soil, and air, all varieties of animal

Chinese Demons. (After a drawing in Bacot, *La Vie du Bouddha*)

demons (were-tigers, -wolves, -foxes, -dogs, and domestic animals that are demons in disguise), bird-demons, fish-demons, and snake-demons. So extensive is the list that it includes plant-demons and demons in inanimate things. Very terrible are the man-eating specters, the vampires, ghouls, and gigantic devils with horned foreheads, long fangs, and a complete covering of fuzzy red hair.

After a long period of confusion of thought, all these spirits were finally* regarded as falling into two classes: (1) the *shen,* good, and (2) the *kwei,* bad or unpredictable. Both kinds of spirits were considered to be almost infinite in number, crowding the universe in all its parts. The *shen* were believed to animate heaven, the arable earth, sun, moon, stars, winds, clouds, rain, thunder, fire, mountains, rivers, seas, trees, springs, stones, and plants. Ancestors, too, were *shen.*

The *kwei* or untrustworthy powers of the universe were ubiquitous, affecting human fate in manifold ways and making night and darkness everywhere terrorsome—unless one had a lantern.

Perhaps no people have gone to such lengths to keep the good spirits on their side as the Chinese, because no people have been more afraid of demons. The sun was supposed to be the chief dispeller of devils; and since the cock by his crowing announces the sunrise, he was held to have power over the *kwei.* Earthenware cocks were thought to have special power to ward off demons and were placed on housetops and over gateways. The triumphant march of the season of spring (so full of *shen* potencies) was seen in peach blossoms. Therefore from the oldest times branches of peach trees, peach boards with mottoes drawn from the sayings of the sages inscribed on them, sheets of red paper in imitation of peach blossoms, and similar objects, were nailed to doors and gates on New Year's Day. Bonfires, torches, candles, lanterns, and firecrackers scared off the *kwei* effectually, and were used during popular festivals, especially on New Year's Day, when a general housecleaning of evil spirits was effected by their means.

Ancestor-Worship

We have already seen in our study of the attitudes to the dead of contemporary primitives how natural it is for the living to be vividly aware of the continued being of persons who have recently died, especially if such persons have filled a large place in the lives of the survivors. Just the thought of them is enough to evoke their presence; one

---

* Perhaps in the time of the first Han dynasty (206 B.C.–8 A.D.).

feels it not unnatural to want to talk to them; but if one should do so, they would not speak, they would merely be vaguely approving or disapproving. It is clear that faith may build upon such experiences and subsequently convince itself of the reasonableness of its assumptions.

The Chinese always have tied their belief in survival after death to their tremendous sense of family solidarity. When they spoke of "the family," they did not mean merely father, mother, and children, they meant all that would be comprehended in an American family reunion, *and more*. For, included in the family group were the ancestors, conceived as living and powerful spirits, all vitally concerned about the welfare of their living descendants, but capable of punitive anger if displeased. The relationship of the living and the dead was markedly one of inter-dependence. On the one hand, the dead were dependent upon the living for the maintenance of the strong bond tying them to the living; which bond was renewed every time prayers or sacrifices were offered to them. Prayers kept their memory alive, and sacrifices provided them with the food they needed. Not that they actually ate the meat and drink proffered them, for when the sacrifice was placed before them it did not disappear; what they availed themselves of, obviously, was its essence, which they inhaled, not its substance, the latter remaining for the priests and sacrificers to eat after a proper interval. On the other hand, the living were just as dependent upon the dead. Ancestors, if themselves properly provided for, actively promoted the prosperity of the family. Any favor done to the family, was one done to them, any injury their injury; a fact of which the friends or the enemies of a powerful family were very well aware.

In the past, burials were momentous and expensive occasions. In ancient China, ancestors of wealthy families were buried with bronze vessels and hunting weapons, and sometimes also with dogs, horses, and human attendants. Some Shang kings, according to surviving bone inscriptions, were buried with anywhere from a hundred to three hundred human victims, who were to be his attendants in the next world. (This practice links ancient China with Egypt, Africa, Japan, and other places, where similar sacrifices were made.)

In 621 B.C. Duke Mu of the state of Ch'in died with the request that three of his ablest subjects be sent after him. An ode in the *Book of Poetry* (Bk. XI, Ode 6) recounts the events of the sacrifice which took place by the grave of the noble lord. Consider the touching and natural reaction of one of the doomed men:

> Who followed Duke Mu to the grave?
> Tzu-ch'e Chen-hu.

And this Chen-hu
Could withstand a hundred men.
But when he came to the grave,
He looked terrified and trembled.[6]

This poem, full as it is of considerate human feeling, anticipates coming changes. Though human sacrifice continued late into Chou times, it was gradually discontinued as barbarous; and first pottery and then later on paper substitutes, not only for the human but also the animal victims, were evolved.*

If any single place in the home could be selected as the center of family life it was the ancestral shrine. In the homes of the humble this shrine occupied an alcove specially built for it and contained wooden tablets inscribed with the names of the ancestors. Local clan organizations maintained family temples, often elaborately furnished. In front of the domestic shrine or inside the ancestral temple, food sacrifices were offered and other ceremonies took place; here in the presence of the ancestors proposals of marriage were received by a girl's father; here the bridegroom's father asked approval of his marriage plans; here the bride, by joining in the family ceremonies, became a full member of the new family; here announcements were made to the ancestors when a journey or an important business venture was undertaken; here all sorts of decisions were referred to the ancestors for endorsement.

In G. E. Simon's *La Cité Chinoise* occurs an interesting and vivid description of the ancestor worship of a few generations ago as he observed it being performed by Chinese families of high standing. A part of it is here quoted:

At the back of the room, standing against the wall and taking up almost the whole length of it, a long table of varnished wood forms the altar. On this altar are stands holding small lacquered tablets, chronologically arranged, on which the names of the ancestors are inscribed. Hanging at the very top of the wall is the sign of deity [T'ien]; and in front of the tablets are lights and incense burners. Lastly, at some distance from the altar, there is a common square table with chairs round it, and in the middle of the table a register with books on each side of it.

Everybody has put on his best clothes and is waiting. The father and mother, who in preparation for the ceremony have been abstinent from the evening before last, enter, followed by two acolytes, and take their places in front of the altar. They address a short invocation to Heaven, and those present chaunt the ancestral hymn . . . A variety of things are offered

* The manufacture of these paper substitutes and of paper money to be burned at the grave for the use of the dead has been a major industry in China.

. . . : a pigeon or a chicken, fruits, wine and grain, either rice or wheat, whichever is grown in the district. Or wine alone, with rice or wheat, may be offered. The two acolytes go to fetch these offerings, the wife takes them from their hands and gives them to her husband, who lifts them above his head, his wife standing beside him, and places them on the altar in sign of thanksgiving. The father then reads the names of the ancestors inscribed on the tablets, and recalling them more particularly to the memory of the family, he speaks in their name and makes them as it were arise from the grave. The corn and wine that he has just consecrated to them, which are a symbol of the efforts made and the progress realized, he now returns, on behalf of the ancestors to those present, in token of their indissoluble union. Lastly, the officiator exhorts the family to meditate on the meaning of this true communion, on the engagements that it implies, which all present swear to carry out: and then, after a last prayer, a meal is served, in which the consecrated offerings are included.[7]

Here we have ancestor worship at its best. But this was only the first part of the ceremony which Simon saw. In the next or second part (the third part was a solemn family council) the father read from the

Chinese ancestor worship; the father lifting an offering, accompanied by his wife and two acolytes. (Adapted from old print)

family register the record of recent events, that the whole family, and the ancestors, too, might be fully informed; and then he read the biography of one of the ancestors.

He makes comments on it, emphasizing the claims of the said ancestor to be remembered by his descendants, and exhorts everyone to follow the example he gave.—A new biography is read in this way at every meeting* till the whole series is finished, after which they go back to the first, the second, and so on until everyone knows them all by heart, and none at least of the worthier ancestors remains unknown.[8]

An important part of ancestor worship was and probably still is the family pilgrimage in spring and autumn to the graves of ancestors, in order to make sacrifices and leave offerings there. The spring visit usually includes the sweeping and rebuilding of the grave mounds; and in the autumn, sheets of paper with pictures of warm blankets and clothing are burned at the grave in order to provide the dead with protection against the coming cold.

It cannot be surprising that in the past anyone who was believed to have abandoned or betrayed his family was regarded as an outcast,

* Twice a month.

despised by men and pursued by the vengeance of his ancestral spirits. When such a person died, he became luckless ever, a hungry ghost, unhonored and unsung, without any family to sustain his lonely spirit with their sacrifices and their affection. Though Confucius made it his life-mission to restore the rightful authority of the state over its citizens, he is thought not to have approved of the implications in the statement of the Duke of She: "Among us there are those who may be styled upright in their conduct; if their father have stolen a sheep, they will bear witness to the fact"; for he countered with the reply: "Amongst us, in our part of the country, those who are upright are different from this. The father conceals the misconduct of the son, and the son conceals the misconduct of the father. Uprightness is to be found in this." [9] Significantly, China accepted the principle formulated by Confucius, although since 1912 the sense of duty to the nation has grown stronger. The Communists, of course, demand the highest priority for such a sense, and they consider the Confucian principle criminal.

The Grading of Social and Religious Functions in the Ancient Feudal Era

It is an interesting fact that the feudal system of ancient China, which Confucius was so anxious to conserve, was a graded hierarchy of an exceedingly thorough-going sort. In the heyday of the Chou dynasty China was divided into several hundred vassal states,* whose ruling princes were lieges of the emperor and directly responsible to him. These states were again divided into prefectures or districts, ruled by governors and other officers. In well-regulated states each district was as nearly as possible divided into approximately square areas, which were, in the standard cases, subdivided again into eight outer and one central field (the well-field system), the outer ones cultivated by single families for their own use and the central one cultivated in common by all eight families for the overlord. The villages of China were therefore surrounded by neatly divided areas, so parceled out that groups of families cultivated a public field whose produce and cattle were destined for the overlord. Almost as neat was the grading of the population. The emperor, as liege lord, had under him the vassal lords holding their offices in hereditary perpetuity, in four descending ranks (dukes, marquises, earls, viscounts and barons); the vassal lords had under them the governors of the prefectures; the governors of the prefectures had under them officers, the officers subalterns, the subalterns petty officers,

* Each was small, and their total area did not much exceed the region lying north and south of the Yellow River.

the petty officers assistants, the assistants employees, the employees menials, the menials helpers! * Emperors, nobles, officials, and common people were subject to detailed rules of conduct governing all their inter-relations and duties.

Nor was this by any means the whole story. Long before the time of Confucius there was a general recognition of the impropriety of ordinary men or even lesser officials sacrificing to the major cosmic or earth spirits. No prince was allowed to perform any of the sacrifices which were the emperor's function, and no ordinary man could take over a prince's religious duties. The mountains and rivers were not to be addressed by unauthorized individuals, lest their spirit-forces be offended, or else induced to act in a way not consonant with the general welfare. In later China, therefore, from about the 2nd century B.C. on, it became the settled practice for the common man to worship only his ancestors and such household and personal spirits as the guardians of the door and of the stove and the gods of health and luck; he let the feudal lords or their officers worship the hills and streams of the province for him, as well as certain roads and cultivated fields; for they could do this acceptably, and he could not. The emperor, on his part, made a tour of the empire every seven years to perform sacrifices near or on the chief rivers and mountains of the land. And of course the emperor alone addressed Shang Ti, or sublime T'ien, in the ceremonies at the Altar of Heaven outside the capital of the empire.

The Decay of the Feudal System and the Rise of the Schools

The period from 722 to 221 B.C.—a period of five hundred years— saw the gradual decay of the feudal system which we have just outlined and its replacement by a less rigid organization of society, which allowed men of lowly rank—farmers and merchants—to climb to positions of political importance and thus break up the aristocracy of hereditary vassal lords. On the one hand, many of the old noble families were impoverished by conflicts with upstart usurpers within their realms. On the other hand, the inability of the Chou emperors to protect their domain from invasion by Tartar hordes, pushing in from the northwest, led to the rise of powerful nobles, each fortified for his own protection with private armies and virtually supreme in his own territory. In due time these great lords thrust the emperor to one side and sprang at each other. At the same time the agricultural serfs began to shake

* Or, under another nomenclature, the officials were classified thus: chief ministers, great officers, upper scholars, middle scholars, and low scholars.

themselves free from the land system which denied them possession of property and confined them to small areas; they became the owners of their own fields, and some of them by joining field to field rose to power as landed proprietors. Merchants appeared in the villages and attained wealth. Some aristocratic families now found themselves so stripped of their power and brought down to the level of common people, that they were obliged to take positions and earn their livelihood by their own labor. (Confucius came, it would seem, of a noble family, and found himself so obliged.) The decay of the feudal system finally culminated in a two hundred year period of violent civil disorders, called the Warring States Period. The smaller states disappeared, and the seven larger states that remained fought savagely for supremacy. The emperor by this time was an impotent figurehead, the puppet of the strongest feudal prince. Finally, in 221 B.C. Duke Cheng of the State of Ch'in conquered all his rivals and, as the great emperor Shih Huang-ti, completely unified China under his arbitrary rule. The royal families of all the states were brought tumbling down into the ranks of the common people, and the feudal system was dealt a blow from which it never recovered.

In the period of the dissolution of the old order, and while the new was struggling to establish itself, a number of differing schools of thought arose to lay claim to the assent of thinking men—as always happens during a period of transition and change. Some of these schools of thought attacked the feudal system and wished it done away; these were the Legalists. Others wanted the feudal system to be restored, in a rationalized and idealized form; and among these were the Confucians. Still others would have nothing to do with any political system requiring a high degree of centralization; the Taoists took this point of view. A few, like the Mohists, advocated, from the standpoint of utility and common sense, a return to the old-time religion and the cultivation of a universal benevolence that would seek the welfare of all men together.*

* Lin Mousheng, in his interesting *Men and Ideas* (John Day, New York, 1942), p. 9, puts the situation thus: "The Confucian school apparently was the school of gentlemen—princes and dukes. The Taoist school was made up of disillusioned intellectuals. The Mocian school represented the lower middle class—free artisans and free farmers. The Legalist school stood for the interests of the upper middle class—plutocrats and landlords." Chinese scholars are, however, in no agreement on this. Many contend that the various schools sprang, not from classes of the population, but from localities. For example, Confucianism issued from the Yellow River region, dominated by the Chou culture, Taoism from the Yang-tse, where lived the less feudalistic suppressed people of Yin, who were in opposition to Chou culture; and so on. See in this connection Francis C. M. Wei, *The Spirit of Chinese Culture* (Scribner's, 1947).—Quotation above by permission of the publisher.

It shall be our task to examine some of these proposals for social change or restoration, and to see what religious consequences they had during the long history of Chinese religion to the present day.

II TAOISM

Taoism is an ambiguous term signifying either the thought system which in ancient times gave the Tao centrality in all thinking and living, or a mixture of magic and religion dating from the two Han dynasties (206 B.C.–221 A.D.). Under either aspect it has been the vehicle of beliefs and practices which, during a long emergence from the soil of popular faith and superstition, have expressed the philosophical and mystical aspects of Chinese thought and life.

The Legendary Lao-tsu

It all began, we have been told, with Lao-tzu or Lao Tan, a legendary scholar or seer of whom so little can be learned, even on the hypothesis that he lived, that it has been common for some authorities in the matter to be sceptical about his ever having lived at all! He was born, the old tradition relates, in the State of Ch'u in 604 B.C.,* and obtained the important post of curator of the imperial archives at Loh-yang, the capital city. But he began to question the wisdom of having any sort of government; he thought the search for knowledge itself was vain, since it led only to a perversion of the simplicity in which men are meant to live. So, having found his position as an official a false one, he resigned from it and returned to "his own house." The rest of the story is even more questionable. Driven, it is said, by an unceasing desire for escape into the unknown, fed by his aversion to curious visitors,

---

* Even on the assumption that the Lao-tzu of the traditions is historical, this date is in dispute. Some scholars think the records do not bear it out, and find on fresh computations that the date 570 B.C. is preferable. This would bring Lao-tzu much closer to Confucius in time. But many Chinese and Western scholars distinguish between Lao Tan, a legendary person, and Li Erh, presumably nicknamed Lao-tzu, who lived in the 4th century B.C., long after Confucius. Others even say the traditional Lao-tzu is a fictitious character invented by Taoists in order to establish their historical priority to Confucianism. See Arthur Waley, *The Way and Its Power;* Y. L. Fung, *The History of Chinese Philosophy,* I, chapter VIII; Homer H. Dubs, "The Date and Circumstances of the Philosopher Lao-dz," *Journal of the American Oriental Society,* Vol. LXI, No. 4, Dec. 1941, pp. 215 f. But Hu Shih continues to think the evidence for the tradition is sufficient. See his "A Criticism of Some Recent Methods Used in Dating Lao Tsu," in *The Harvard Journal of Asiatic Studies,* Vol. II, Nos. 3 and 4, Dec. 1937.

Confucius among them, the aged philosopher decided upon flight into the West. In a two-wheeled carriage drawn by black oxen, he set out, prepared to leave the world of deluded, society-corrupted men behind him. But the keeper of the gate at the western pass, his friend Yin-hsi, persuaded him to write down his philosophy. Lao-tzu thereupon lingered in the gatehouse long enough to compose the treatise which has come to be called the *Tao Te Ching* or *Treatise of the Tao and Its Power*. In short crisp sentences, some of them obscure and cryptic, he expounded his views; and then he departed over the pass, to be heard of no more.

That even in the Warring States Period this romantic story was not firmly established in tradition is all too apparent from the fact that the 4th century scholar Chuang-tzu makes the Old Master die in his bed!

The legendary Lao-tzu may have lived; that possibility exists; * but authoritative scholarship is convinced that, even if such a person actually fathered the Taoist philosophy in the period prior to Confucius, he did not write the Tao Te Ching. That great classic of religious thought had a later origin. Of its dating, this must be said: the Tao Te Ching expresses an attitude toward life and nature which presupposes a rather advanced disintegration of the feudal order; moreover, its conceptions had the freshness of a new idea for a number of brilliant minds in the Warring States Period. It may be supposed it was they who gave to Taoism the permanently significant form of the Tao Te Ching. And this was a great achievement. Their thinking was in part an aroused and determined effort, in sorry times, to come to grips with unchanging reality, and in part an expression of temperamental revulsion from the ritual-minded Confucian school which came into being about the same time.

Since it was the destiny of Taoism to pass through three periods or phases, it will be convenient to consider in turn: (A) the philosophical or formative phase, characterized by strong mystical interests; (B) the magical phase; and (C) the phase of intermittent recognition by the Chinese government as the official religion of the empire.

A. The Formative Philosophical Phase of Taoism

The philosophical formulation of Taoism took place during the 5th and 4th centuries B.C.

---

* So this writer feels. There is a strong Confucian tradition for his existence. But the writer agrees that we know nothing certainly about him, if he did exist.

Some contributory developments came first. There were forerunners (let us assume that a Lao Tan, an obscure originative figure,
moved among them) who prepared the way. Already in the 6th century, Confucius seems to have met some nameless representatives of a
pre-Taoist school. They were recluses who rejected "civilization." After
his time other forerunners, more clearly seen by us now, appeared. Some
of them were critics of human ways and institutions resembling the
Sceptics and Cynics even then stirring up the Greeks.* Few more interesting, and engagingly impudent, persons have ever pressed their
opinions on their fellows. They spoke with wit and pungency; and a
certain unconventionality in their point of view made their sayings all
the more intriguing.

This unconventionality is well illustrated by *Yang Chu*, who lived
at the end of the 5th and the beginning of the 4th century. Seeing that
China was in a chaotic state beyond all help that he could devise, he
seems to have concluded that turning his back on society and cultivating
his own personal life was the only true good. Unabashed by the consequences of this reasoning, he said quite smartly, "Each one for himself!";
and shocked the Confucians by asserting that, even if all he had to
do to be given the whole world would be to pluck a single hair from
his shank, he would not do so. This was because he valued his own
life above even the sum of all external things. "Not allowing outside
things to entangle one's person" [10] was his cardinal principle.

Even more unconventional were *P'eng Meng* and his followers,
T'ien P'ien and *Shen Tao*. They resolved to discard knowledge, be impartial and non-partisan, adopt an easy-going and unobtrusive manner,
have no anxiety for the morrow, and let events just take their course
without interfering. Perhaps the later Taoist Chuang-tzu was thinking
of them when he made Tzuyü, a Confucian (!), say in carefree acceptance of fate: "If my left arm should be transformed into a cock, I
would mark with it the time of night. If my right arm should be transformed into a crossbow, I would look for a bird to bring down and
roast. If my rump-bone should be transformed into a wheel, and my
spirit into a horse, I would mount and would have no need of any
other steed." [11] It was their opinion that the wise man who has acquired
the secret of the good life "follows the inevitable," and "simply moves
with things." Of one of them we read:

Shen Tao discarded knowledge, abandoned self, followed the inevitable,
and was indifferent to things . . . He said: "Knowledge is not to know."

* From them, and the exponents of divers other viewpoints, sprang the "Hundred Schools" so often referred to in later times.

He was one who despised knowledge and would destroy it. Stupid and irresponsible, he ridiculed the world's way of preferring the virtuous; careless and impractical, he condemned the world's great Sages; shifting and slippery, he changed about with circumstances; disregarding right and wrong, he was only concerned with avoiding trouble; learning nothing with knowledge and thinking, paying no attention to past or future, he stood loftily indifferent to everything.

He went where he was pushed and followed where he was led, like a whirling gale, like a feather tossed in the wind, like a turning mill-stone. He was complete without defects; in action or at rest he was free from mistakes and never offended others. How could this be? Because creatures without knowledge are freed from the trouble of self-assertion and the entanglements of knowledge; in motion or at rest they do not depart from the principles of nature . . . Therefore, he said: "Let us be like creatures without knowledge. That will be sufficient . . . For a clod of earth does not miss the Way [Tao]." [12]

While Yang Chu and Shen Tao were thus venturing their own persons, so to speak, in an attempt to find the course (Tao) which Nature prescribes for those who wish to be right, superior, and happy, other and more profound, more discriminating minds were assembling the Tao Te Ching and the essays of Chuang-tzu.

THE PHILOSOPHY AND ETHICS OF THE TAO TE CHING. As it stands, the Tao Te Ching is hardly the product of one mind. Interpolations and repeated editing have altered its original form. But doubtless most of the present version comes from the 4th century B.C.

The Tao Te Ching accepts unquestioningly the theory that when things are allowed to take their natural course they move with a wonderful perfection and harmony. This is because, in such case, the Tao (the eternal Way of the universe) is not hindered in its smooth operation.

What is the Tao? Its definition is acknowledged to be difficult. The opening sentences of the Tao Te Ching say it is impossible. The Tao that can be expressed in words is not the eternal Tao; the name that can be named is not the real, the absolute name. The Tao is wrapped in cosmic mystery, and reaching for it is grasping through mystery into deeper mystery. Yet it is the sole source of the active power (*Te*) in existent things.

The mightiest manifestations of active force flow solely from the Tao.

The Tao in itself is vague, impalpable,—how impalpable, how vague! Yet within it there is Form. How vague, how impalpable! Yet within it there is Substance. How profound, how obscure! Yet within it there is a Vital Principle.[13]

Inquiry concerning the Tao takes us into the realm of pre-existence and *non-being,* yet we cannot prevent the question from arising: how does the Tao operate in the realm of *being*? This is for the Tao Te Ching the central question, really, for it considers that the chief aim of human existence must be to attain *fulness of life by present harmony with the Tao.*

How important a matter this is for the Taoist may readily be seen. For just as Heaven and Earth attain complete harmony and order only by letting the Tao take its course, and even as the emperors of the Golden Age brought health and prosperity to themselves and their people by attuning themselves to the Tao, so any man can attain the highest well-being only by arriving at thorough conformity with it. Man has the power, and he has used his power, to choose his own way and build up his social habits after his own plan rather than after the eternal plan of the great Tao; but thence have sprung all the ills and pains of man, in the midst of the strange, queer "civilization" he has formed. He has chosen to move contrariwise to the eternal Tao, and it has been like swimming against the current: Nature is fighting him by flowing the other way. Perhaps he thinks he is big enough to overcome Nature. But he is not. Men have the power to think and feel and act as they like, and the Tao allows, or rather does not disallow them. But not to the extent of ceasing to be itself!

Nature is not benevolent; with ruthless indifference she makes all things serve their purposes, like the straw dogs we use at sacrifices.[14]

What is contrary to the Tao soon perishes.[15]

He who is self-approving does not shine. He who exalts himself does not rise high. Judged according to the Tao, he is like remnants of food or a tumour on the body—an object of universal disgust.[16]

The Tao is quiet, so quiet that its presence cannot be detected, save by intuition.

The Way of Heaven is not to contend and yet to be able to conquer,
Not to declare its will and yet to get a response,
Not to summon but have things come spontaneously.[17]

Tao produces all things; . . .
It produces them without holding possession of them.
It acts without depending upon them, and raises without lording it
  over them.[18]

Therefore Heaven and Earth—and men, too, if only they would—may safely resign themselves to it, and experience complete fulfillment of being.

> The Tao is ever inactive,
> And yet there is nothing that it does not do.[19]

People who do not follow the Tao-way may meet with temporary success; but let them beware! For there is an invariable law in things, that if any movement goes to its extreme of development, it necessarily has to execute a "return" or "reversion."

> All things come into existence,
> And thence we see them return.
> Look at the things that have been flourishing;
> Each goes back to its origin.[20]
>
> Returning is the motion of the Tao.[21]
>
> Stretch a bow to the full,
> And you will wish you had stopped in time;
> Temper a sword-edge to its very sharpest,
> And you will find it soon grows dull.
> When bronze and jade fill your hall
> It can no longer be guarded.
> Wealth and place breed insolence
> That brings ruin in its train.
> When your work is done, then withdraw! [22]

The man "who moves on the even Tao (Path) seems to go up and down"! [23]

So universal and constant in all things is the process of reversion and return, that all natural process is marked by sameness; all things go back to their common origin; ultimately they all blend into one. The Tao at work in each of the "ten thousand things under heaven" is the same Tao, obscure but originative, hidden but all-encompassing.

> Because the eye gazes but can catch no glimpse of it,
> It is called elusive.
> Because the ear listens but cannot hear it,
> It is called rarefied.
> Because the hand feels for it but cannot find it,
> It is called the infinitesimal.
> These three, because they cannot be further scrutinized,
> Blend into one.[24]

Tao begets One; one begets two; two begets three; three begets all things.[25]

> Therefore the Sage embraces the One.[26]

The sage knows that he is himself one with all things in the One. He himself, and all the distinguishable phenomena of Nature, the events in space and time which make their appearance to the senses, are at heart indistinguishable; they are the same in their rise and fall, their growth and decay, but above all in the derivation of their being from original non-being and their return to non-being. All this is the Way of Nature, and is the destiny of all things.

The sage therefore yields himself to Nature (the Tao), and does not struggle to assert himself aggressively nor strive for a sharply distinguishable being of his own.

> The ancient saying "Be humble and you shall remain entire"—
> Can this be regarded as mere empty words? [27]

> Nature does not have to insist,
> Can blow for only half a morning,
> Rain for only half a day,
> And what are these winds and these rains but natural?
> If nature does not have to insist,
> Why should man? [28]

Leave all things to take their natural course, and do not interfere.[29]

It may be objected that there is little of religion here. For one thing, it may be urged, the Tao is impersonal; and although persons are its expressions in some areas, it is itself without form and void. Therefore one meditates on the Tao but does not engage in formal worship of it. The Tao is not aware of nor does it make a compassionate response to persons; it is but the cosmic mode of action by which Non-being becomes Being. Yet religion may breathe in this rare air—a one-sidedly intellectual and intuitional type of religion no doubt, but something more than bare philosophy. For the Tao determines destiny; may even be said to be a ruling Force; and conformity to it is a species of religious mysticism. The study of the Tao begins in philosophy: what is the ultimate reality? and concludes as religion: how may I be in complete accord with this reality?

We turn now to the Tao Te Ching's *ethics*. What we have said has already suggested it.

The central consideration may be expressed in two sentences—one positive, the other negative. Positively stated, the principle is: one must exhibit within himself the nature of the Tao, and be characterized by its quietude of power, its production without possession, action without self-assertion, development without domination. Negatively, the principle runs: do not meddle with the smooth course of Nature going on her blessed way. As the Tao Te Ching puts it, it is wise to practice *wu-wei*

Lao-Tzu on ox, with disciple. Riding the ox is traditionally symbolic of unity with Nature and its processes. (From an old Chinese painting)

(quietism, non-aggression, non-meddlesome action). It is possible to achieve without doing.

Therefore, the sage carries on his business without action, and gives his teaching without words.[30]

The sage exhibits a retiring, not to say a stay-at-home disposition. He says to himself:

> Without going out of the door
> One can know the whole world;
> Without peeping out of the window
> One can see the Tao of heaven.
> The further one travels
> The less one knows.
> Therefore the sage knows everything without traveling;
> He names everything without seeing it;
> He accomplishes everything without doing it.[31]

Such a one will appear "stupid" or "out of this world." Other people are wideawake, knowing; he alone appears dull, confused, even uncomprehending, like a baby who is as yet unable to smile.

This seems negative indeed; but not so, says the Tao Te Ching; there is affirmative power in the quietism of *wu-wei*; its attendant virtues in human life are kindness, sincerity, and humility; if one does not meddle with others, human relations will fall as the Tao brings them to pass, naturally and simply; there will be a spontaneous birth of true love, real kindness, simplicity, and contentment in the lives and relationships of men. Just the restraint of self from anger, ambition, and meddlesome action is never merely negative in its consequences; power is in it, power for good.

To those who are good to me I am good; and to those who are not good to me, I am also good;—and thus all get to be good. To those who are sincere with me, I am sincere; and to those who are not sincere with me, I am also sincere;—and thus all get to be sincere.° 32

Oft-repeated is the conviction that in the presence of natural kindness the strong become harmless, while by its means the weak become irresistible.

There is nothing in the world more soft and weak than water, yet for attacking things that are hard and strong there is nothing that surpasses it . . . The soft overcomes the hard; the weak overcomes the strong.34

The highest goodness is like water . . . It stays in places which others despise. Therefore it is near to Tao.35

In developing the implications of this doctrine the Tao Te Ching went so far as to suggest that the Taoist sage possessed, through being in accord with the Tao, a magical power, more passive than active, which made him invulnerable to the attack of fierce beasts or violent men, and immune to the assaults of death itself. It seems to be implied that when a man is possessed of the Tao he lives long, and during life he is exempt from decay. In one passage this idea is put forward with a modest "I have heard"; but it came later to have great significance:

I have heard that he who possesses the secret of life, when traveling abroad, will not flee from rhinoceros or tiger; when entering a hostile camp, he will not equip himself with sword or buckler. The rhinoceros finds in him no place to insert its horn; the tiger has nowhere to fasten its claw; the soldier has nowhere to thrust his blade. And why? Because he has no spot where death can enter.36

Elsewhere it is said:

He who is endowed with ample virtue may be compared to an infant.
No venomous insects sting him;
Nor fierce beasts seize;
Nor birds of prey strike him.37
He who attains Tao is everlasting.
Though his body may decay he never perishes.38

We shall see presently where pursuit of this conviction led the later Taoists.

Meanwhile, a word on the Tao Te Ching's distinctive theory of government.

° The obverse of this is given in another section of the Tao Te Ching:

"It is by not believing in people that you turn them into liars." 33

It will readily be seen that the only political principle consistent with the Tao Te Ching's philosophy of life is laissez faire. Non-interference by government in the lives of citizens is the one way to peace and freedom.

Tao is eternally inactive, and yet it leaves nothing undone. If kings and princes could but hold fast to this principle, all things would work out their own reformation.[39]

Now this is how I know what I lay down:—

As restrictions and prohibitions are multiplied in the Empire, the people grow poorer and poorer. When the people are subjected to overmuch government, the land is thrown into confusion . . . The greater the number of laws and enactments, the more thieves and robbers there will be. Therefore the Sage says: "So long as I do nothing, the people will work out their own reformation. So long as I love calm, the people will right themselves. If only I keep from meddling, the people will grow rich. If only I am free from desire, the people will come naturally back to simplicity." [40]

An interesting passage gives us the Tao Te Ching's picture of the ideal community—a small village-state, quiet, self-contained, and always keeping at home within its tiny boundaries.

Take a small country with a small population. It might well be that there were machines which saved labor ten times or a hundred times, and yet the people would not use them . . . They would not emigrate to distant countries. Although there might be carriages and boats, no one would ride in them. Although there might be weapons of war, no one would issue them. It might well be that people would go back to using knotted cords.*

Make the people's food sweet, their clothes beautiful, their houses comfortable, their daily life a source of pleasure. Then the people will look at the country over the border, will hear the cocks crowing and the dogs barking there, but right down to old age and the day of their death, they will not trouble to go there [and see what it is like].[41]

Of course there was no room in this scheme of things for war, and we find the Tao Te Ching very firm on the point that "weapons, however beautiful, are instruments of ill omen, hateful to all creatures. Therefore he who has Tao will have nothing to do with them." [42] But we are hardly prepared for the breath-taking insight:

Therefore, if a great kingdom humbles itself before a small kingdom, it shall make that small kingdom its prize. And if a small kingdom humbles itself before a great kingdom, it shall win over that great kingdom. Thus the one humbles itself in order to attain, the other attains because it is humble.

* In keeping records.

If the great kingdom has no further desire than to bring men together and to nourish them, the small kingdom will have no further desire than to enter the service of the other. But in order that both may have their desire, the great one must learn humility.[43]

We may not, perhaps, be in sympathy with the Tao Te Ching's political and social obscurantism, but this is an amazing vision of international altruism which is still too high for us. Ironically enough, China *in the past* has not been unmindful of the possibilities suggested in it.

THE ESSAYS OF CHUANG-TZU. Chuang-tzu (or Chuang Chou) is, except for the legendary Lao-tzu himself, the most famous of the philosophical Taoists. He lived during the 4th century B.C., and skilfully popularized the teachings of his presumed master, performing for him in this respect the same service that Mencius, Chuang-tzu's contemporary, performed for Confucius. Thirty-three essays, which may be considered to contain large amounts of material from his own hand, have come down to us. They are brilliantly written, with many a witty anecdote, entertaining allegory, and imaginary conversation to enhance their literary charm. He especially enjoyed tilting at the ideas expressed by contemporary Confucianism.*

Chuang-tzu was true to Taoist teaching in giving the Tao centrality. But he went beyond the Tao Te Ching in elaborating a doctrine of "transformations of the Tao" which resembles at some points the fluxionist speculations of Western philosophers. Objects originate in a whirl of being and becoming, out of preceding states of existence. Times succeed each other circularly; the seasons mutually produce and destroy each other, without end. The *yin* and *yang*, springing from the Tao, produce each other, influence each other, and destroy each other in a neverceasing process. In the moral realm, he said, we have attractions and repulsions, loves and hates, distinctions of the sexes and their union for reproduction, but no lasting state either of peace or its opposite. Adversity and prosperity, security and danger succeed each other according to a law of reciprocal causality.

> For there is (the process of) reverse evolution (uniting opposites) . . . The succession of growth and decay, of increase and diminution, goes in a cycle, each end becoming a new beginning. In this sense only may we discuss the ways of truth and the principles of the universe. The life of things passes by like a rushing, galloping horse, changing at every turn, at

---

* He seems to have used the ironic propaganda device of making Confucius repudiate his love of learning and duty to society, talk like a Taoist, *but not quite be one!* This will appear in some of our quotations later on.

every hour. What should one do, or what should one not do? Let the (cycle of) changes go on by themselves! [44]

What seemed to Chuang-tzu to justify the Taoist do-nothingism was the fact that in such a world of perfectly natural change, absolute truth and absolute good are unknowable. All things are equal. Whatever Nature (Tao) brings to pass is at least as good and necessary as anything else it brings to pass before or after. As to man, he may well ask: When is anything just right, or not just right? There is no means of knowing.

If a man sleeps in a damp place, he gets lumbago and dies. But how about an eel? And living up in a tree is precarious and trying to the nerves;— but how about monkeys? Of the man, the eel, and the monkey, whose habitat is the right one, absolutely? Human beings feed on flesh, deer on grass, centipedes on snakes, owls and crows on mice. Of these four, whose is the right taste, absolutely? [45]

In regard to man's desires or interests, if we say that anything is either good or bad according to our individual (subjective) standards, then there is nothing which is not good, nothing which is not bad.[46]

This point of view led Chuang-tzu to make the unconventional statement about the Three Dynasties:

Those who came at the wrong time and went against the tide are called usurpers. Those who came at the right time and fitted in with their age are called defenders of Right. . . . How can you know the distinctions of high and low and of the houses of the great and small? [47]

Chuang-tzu likened the confusions of men to the puzzlement which would surely reign in the non-human world, if the creatures could make comparisons of excellencies and defects.

The walrus envies the centipede; the centepede envies the snake; the snake envies the wind; the wind envies the eye; the eye envies the mind.

The walrus said to the centipede, "I hop about on one leg, but not very successfully. How do you manage all the legs you have?"

"I don't manage them," replied the centipede. "Have you never seen saliva? When it is ejected, the big drops are the size of pearls, the small ones like mist. They fall promiscuously on the ground and cannot be counted. And so it is that my mechanism works naturally, without my being conscious of the fact."

The centipede said to the snake, "With all my legs I do not move as fast as you with none. How is that?"

"One's natural mechanism," replied the snake, "is not a thing to be changed. What need have I for legs?"

The snake said to the wind, "I can manage to wriggle along, but I have a form. Now you come blustering down from the north sea to bluster away to the south sea, and you seem to be without form. How is that?"

" 'Tis true," replied the wind, "that I bluster as you say; but any one who can kick at me, excels me. On the other hand, I can break huge trees and destroy large buildings. That is my strong point." [48]

The wind was wise. It did not weaken itself by false value-judgments issuing in envy. It realized that though, on an intellectual analysis of its differences from other things, it was relatively weak ("anyone who can kick at me, excels me"), whenever it let itself go as Nature intended it should, it was mighty and strong. Using similar logic, Chuang-tzu contends that a man should not argue about large and small, high and low, right and wrong, but let happen what will according to the transformations of the Tao. In so doing he will join the wind, the snake, and the centipede in the economy of Nature.

Take no heed of time, nor of right or wrong. But passing into the realm of the Infinite, take your final rest therein. [49]

This is the way of the Sage, the truly natural man, who can seat himself by the sun and moon, and hold the universe in his grasp, because:

He blends everything into one harmonious whole, rejecting the confusion of this and that. Rank and precedence, which the vulgar prize, the sage stolidly ignores. The revolutions of ten thousand years leave his unity unscathed. [50]

The wise man does not wear out his senses trying to know individually and in detail the changing objects and beings of the material world; he dwells in the generality of a comprehensive view of all things; he makes his spiritual home in the Tao, in which all things lose their distinctions and merge into one.

The experience here referred to is not attainable by the searchings of reason; the reason is too actively concerned with the discrimination of particulars. Real knowing is passive, receptive.

Hear not with your ears, but with your mind; not with your mind, but with your spirit. Let your hearing stop with the ears, and let your mind stop with its images. Let your spirit, however, be like a blank, passively responsive to externals. In such open receptivity only can Tao abide. [51]

The final goal is the ecstasy of absorption into the quietude and ultimate truth of the Tao. One cannot push his way into this ecstasy; *it must come of itself, in utter spontaneity.* But when it comes, it changes the one who has experienced it. The "artificial and illusory self" has now been eliminated and the "heavenly" has taken "full possession." [52]

Thereafter the Sage cultivates an air of stupidity to keep people from rousing him out of his aloofness from the "ten thousand things" of which the world is composed. His mind is cool and tranquil under the realization that thoughts and dreams have little importance, for they are subjective phenomena. In a world of rapidly shifting and changing appearances, he knows it is best to be calm and not active, to accept life and not take it seriously. He is like Mr. Mengsun.

Mr. Mengsun knows not whence we come in life nor whither we go in death. He knows not which to put first and which to put last. He is ready to be transformed into other things without caring into what he may be transformed. [53]

True to this conviction, Chuang-tzu, if we are to trust the anecdotes supplied by his followers, lived without worry or fret. It is said that when his wife died, his friend Hui-tzu, the logician, went to condole with him, according to custom, and found him seated on the ground, singing and beating time on a metal bowl, which he held between his legs. Shocked at this sight, Hui-tzu said to him: "To live with your wife, and see your eldest son grow up to be a man, and then not to shed a tear over her corpse—this would be bad enough. But to drum on a bowl, and sing; surely this is going too far." "Not at all," replied Chuang-tzu. "When she first died, how could I help being affected? But then on examining the matter, I saw that in the Beginning she had originally been lifeless. And not only lifeless, but she had originally been formless. And not only formless, but she had originally lacked all substance. During this first state of confused chaos, there came a change which resulted in substance. This substance changed to assume form. The form changed and became alive. And now it has changed again to reach death. In this it has been like the passing of the four seasons, spring, autumn, winter, and summer. And while she is thus lying asleep in the Great House (i.e., the Universe), for me to go about weeping and wailing, would be to show myself ignorant of Fate. Therefore I refrain." [54]

Another tale illustrates Chuang-tzu's philosophic pride. While he was walking along the road in a coarse patched robe and with shoes fastened to his feet with strings, he met the marquis of Wei. "Master," said the marquis, "what distress is this that I see you in?" "Pardon," replied Chuang-tzu; "poverty, not distress. The scholar who possesses knowledge of the Principle [Tao] and its action is never in distress!" [55]

But the most famous story about Chuang-tzu is the one concerning the offer of office made to him while he was fishing with line and float on the bank of the river P'u. The marquis of Ch'u sent two of his officials to offer Chuang-tzu the post of minister. Chuang-tzu went on fishing without turning his head, and said, "I have heard that in Ch'u there is a sacred tortoise which has been dead now some three thousand years. And that the prince keeps this tortoise carefully enclosed in a chest on the altar of his ancestral temple. Now would this tortoise rather be dead and have its remains venerated, or be alive and wagging its tail in the mud?" "It would rather be alive," replied the two officials together. "Then," cried Chuang-tzu, "begone! I too will wag my tail in the mud." [56]

The indictment which Chuang-tzu brought against his age was powerful. He idealized the past, as both his Taoist predecessors and the Confucians did; but he saw it from a point of view quite different from the Confucians', whose moralism he criticized as a forced matter which badly confused the true issues of life: under it men could not be simple and natural.* As he viewed it:

In the days when natural instincts prevailed, men moved quietly and gazed steadily. At that time, there were no roads over mountains, nor boats, nor bridges over water. All things were produced, each for its own proper sphere. Birds and beasts multiplied; trees and shrubs grew up. The former might be led by the hand; you could climb up and peep into the raven's nest. For then men dwelt with birds and beasts, and all creation was one. There were no distinctions of good and bad men. Being all equally without knowledge, their virtue could not go astray. Being all equally without evil desires, they were in a state of natural integrity, the perfection of human existence.

But when sages appeared, tripping people over charity and fettering with duty to one's neighbor, doubt found its way into the world. And then with their gushing over music and fussing over ceremony, the empire became divided against itself. [57]

In this primitivism of his, Chuang-tzu went much further than the Tao Te Ching. His thesis plainly is that none of the forms and institutions of social life under the Chou culture did anything but confuse men about their natural equality and thus corrupt their native integrity. With social institutions, he said violently, "gangsters appeared. Overthrow the Sages and set the gangsters free, and then the empire will be in order." [58]

His animus against all social institutions died away when he turned his admiring eye toward Nature. He taught Chinese artists in which

---

* For more of this criticism see Section III of the next chapter.

Man contemplating waterfall in Taoist tradition. (After painting by Morikage, ca. 1700)

direction to look for truth in their art. Since his time Nature has been their first love; and, we are told, "he still is today the main fountain of [their] inspiration and imagination." [59]

And yet Chuang-tzu must not be supposed to have led artists to look merely at the outward forms of Nature; for how much reality is there in forms taken by themselves? His inspiration for them has been in enabling them to look at the eternal Way *within* Nature; that is, at the reality of which every form the poet or painter beholds is an expression, just as the poet or painter himself is. In one piquant illustration he posed for artists—and for philosophers—one of the knottiest problems of human knowledge: how to assess the reality of forms within the mind.

Once upon a time, I, Chuang-tzu, dreamt I was a butterfly, fluttering hither and thither, to all intents and purposes a butterfly . . . suddenly, I awaked . . . Now I do not know whether I was then a man dreaming I was a butterfly, or whether I am now a butterfly dreaming I am a man. [60]

But Taoism was not going to continue for long in this intriguing vein, philosophically defining the nature of things and the meaning of life; it was going to be turned into a species of magical theory and practice, and Chuang-tzu, as we shall see, was to share the responsibility for giving it an impetus in this direction.

B. *The Magical Phase of Taoism*

The problem of how to prolong life by mastering one's body and preventing the processes of natural decay from setting in has always interested the Chinese. No people have looked forward more than they have to old age—the period of patriarchal ease and leisure.

But there has been also a strong interest in "eternal life." And Taoism seemed to promise help. The Tao Te Ching, we have seen, suggested that anyone who possesses the secret of the Tao becomes immune to the attack of armed men and wild animals; he who is endowed with the ample virtue which the Tao engenders may be compared to an infant whom no venomous reptiles sting, no birds of prey strike.[*] Furthermore: "He who attains Tao is everlasting." Chuang-tzu (along with others, probably) added his speculations by way of further development. The mythical emperor Fu Hsi, he said, obtained Tao, "and was able to steal the secrets of eternal principles." "The Yellow Emperor obtained it, and soared upon the clouds of heaven . . . The Western (Fairy) Queen Mother obtained it, and settled at Shao Kuang, since when and until when, no one knows." [61]

It is, of course, possible that Chuang-tzu was not entirely in earnest about all this; yet he brought this discussion, which had been confined to very ancient worthies, down to his own period, in this lively dialogue:

Nanpo Tzek'uei said to Nü Yü (or Female Yü), "You are of a high age, and yet you have a child's complexion. How is this?"

Nü Yü replied, "I have learnt Tao."

"Could I get Tao by studying it?" asked the other.

"No! How can you?" said Nü Yü. "You are not the type of person. There was Puliang I. He had all the mental talents of a sage, but not Tao of the sage. Now I had Tao, though not those talents . . . I had to wait patiently to reveal it to him. In three days, he could transcend this mundane world.

---

[*] It may be remarked that this doctrine had at least a slight justification psychologically. Infants, aged people, and innocents are notoriously safe among violent men. As a rule animals, reptiles, and the larger insects are known to do no harm to people unafraid and gentle in movement. It may well have been that the complete Taoist sage enjoyed a comparatively high degree of personal safety in town and field. But such immunity from death and harm could be easily misconstrued as evidence of superhuman or magical potencies.

Again I waited for seven days more, then he could transcend all material existence. After he could transcend all material existence, I waited for another nine days, after which he could transcend all life. After he could transcend all life, then he had the clear vision of the morning, and after that, was able to see the Solitary (One). After seeing the Solitary, he could abolish the distinctions of past and present. After abolishing the past and present, he was able to enter there where life and death are no more.[62]

Down this road of mysticism and magic Taoist speculation and experimentation turned. In the 2nd century B.C. the emperor Wu Ti of the Han dynasty was, in spite of his patronage of Confucianism, attracted to Taoism by the empress dowager and her associates. Ssu-ma Ch'ien, the famous Chinese historian of the 1st century B.C., records the tradition, whether true or not, that the geomancer Li Shao-Chin urged the emperor to apply himself to the alchemy furnace, for thus he would gain the good graces of the spirits and learn from them the formula for converting cinnabar into gold; after which he could have eating and drinking vessels made of the gold produced from the cinnabar and acquire longevity from the food and drink served in them. (Somehow the Chinese had come to connect "eatable gold" with immortality—if such gold could be had.) The geomancer further advised the emperor that, if he performed on the sacred mountain T'ai Shan the ceremony known as *feng-shan* (in honor of Heaven or the Sovereign on High), he would not die anymore. It was thus, said the geomancer, that the emperor Huang-ti had obtained immortality. From that time on, we are told, Wu Ti surrounded himself with Taoists and at their suggestion introduced many innovations into the practice of Chinese religion, against the wishes of the Confucians.*

By the 1st century A.D. the magical emphasis in Taoism had become supreme. At that time a certain Chang-ling, better known as Chang Tao-ling, migrated from eastern to western China, and founded a secret society devoted primarily to alchemy and the cultivation of the Taoist meditative trance, but availing itself also of ideas probably borrowed from Zoroastrian circles in western China. Since all who joined his society had to pay him with five pecks of rice, his sect was tauntingly called the Wu Tou Mi Tao, "The Five Pecks of Rice Way." On the foundation thus laid his son and grandson built an organization that attracted the superstitious adherence of many followers and through vigorous military activity acquired great political power. In course of time Chang Tao-ling was apotheosized as a "Celestial Teacher"; for he was said to have been personally ordained by Lao-tzu, who appeared to

---

* But in due time he was thoroughly disillusioned.

him out of the spirit world. In addition he was said to have discovered the formula for the potion of immortality, a powerful elixir of life; and to have ascended alive to heaven from the top of Mount Lung-hu (Dragon-Tiger Mountain) in Kiangsi, on the back of a tiger, after having prolonged his life by the use of his elixir to the ripe age of one hundred and twenty-two years.

His influence proved to be lasting, for in the course of centuries his successors became a line of high priests or "popes," living on Dragon-Tiger Mountain. Each pope was thought to be a reincarnation of Chang Tao-ling, and for some centuries flourished on the endowment provided for his see's expenses by the Sung emperor Chen Tsung (998–1023 A.D.). But at length serious decay of power and inner vitality set in. In the turmoil of recent years the popes have been driven from their mountain, probably never to return.

Another of the Taoist sects, the Yellow Turbans, headed by a Chang-Chüeh and his two brothers, numbered hundreds of thousands of adepts, and in an attempted rising in the 2nd century A.D., held for a time the whole of the Yellow River. In spite of the subsequent decline and failure of this and similar movements, the Taoists always hoped someday to make a serious bid for power.

Meanwhile Taoist magic continued to develop. The scholar Ko Hung of the 4th century A.D., who wrote a famous book on magical matters and himself spent the last years of his life on Lo-fu Mountain experimenting with the pill of immortality,* has described in detail the breathing exercises (a technique clearly taken over from Indian mysticism), dietetics, alchemy, and magic of the time; so that a dip into his storehouse of facts is illuminating. The object of the breathing exercises was to increase the spiritual powers of the body and mind, and of the dietetics to prolong life and particularly to enable one to live exclusively on air and dew, in a state immune to illness, though death from old age could not be prevented by this method alone. The alchemy had as its object the discovery of liquid or eatable gold, a commodity

---

* While most of his influence is due to his book, *Pao P'u-tzu*, much of his popular fame comes from the story that when he was eighty-one years old a friend whom he had invited to visit him found only his empty clothes—proof enough that he had disappeared among the Immortals! But he was not the only one thus to achieve immortality. He himself told the story that the author of another book on occult matters succeeded in preparing pills of immortality, and gave one to a dog, only to see it drop dead; but he had so much faith in his pill that he took one himself, and fell to the ground. His elder brother, faith unshaken, took the pill with the same result. A younger brother was about to bury them, when they came back to life. They were Immortals!

which should confer immortality on those who would swallow it.° This amalgam had to be other than one based on mercury, which is a *yin* substance and produces death. Cinnabar was thought to be the proper substance; but the alchemists never quite succeeded in attaining the results they desired, in spite of instances cited by Ko Hung of individuals who passed on into the immortal state, but who, alas! took the secret of their formulas with them! As to the magic, it could do all sorts of things in establishing control over natural processes. Ko Hung describes certain charms, which, if swallowed, or worn on the person, rendered one invulnerable to warlike weapons, though immunity could be gained only from the weapons specifically named in the charms. Care should therefore be taken to name every weapon by which one might ever conceivably be injured; for otherwise one might be caught like the magician "who being proof against every pointed or edged weapon, was killed by a blow from a cudgel, a common weapon he had not foreseen."[63] Other charms are mentioned for making oneself invisible, for changing one's shape at will, for freeing oneself from all bonds, and for raising and transporting oneself through space. And then there was the little pill making one able to walk on water. It was only necessary to take "seven, three times a day, for three years, without forgetting a single time." In another place Ko Hung describes a magical seal, which, "impressed on the dust or mud, prevents ferocious beasts or malignant goblins from passing. The same, placed on the doors of storages and stables, protects the provisions and the animals." [63]

In these last sentences, of which many parallels could be cited, there is to be seen the reason for the power of the Taoist priests among the common people of China down to this day. They were notable geomancers and doctors of thaumaturgy. But to attain this power over the common people these wonder-workers had to have all the sanctions of religion. And Taoism became a religion.

C. Taoism as a Religion

The third phase of Taoism was prefigured in 165 A.D. by the act of the Emperor Huan of the second Han dynasty in ordering for the first time official offerings to Lao-tzu and the building of a temple in his honor. But what was thus anticipated did not get under way until the 7th century when Li Shih-min, who established the great T'ang dynasty, gave Taoism imperial recognition as an organized religion.

° Salt, says Ko Hung, preserves dead meat; it must be possible to find some preservative for *live flesh!*

By this time Buddhism had made its appearance as a great and significant factor in Chinese religious life. Confucianism, the rather stiff and formal mode of thought and behavior known chiefly to the literati and officials, and Taoism, still the preoccupation either of intellectuals on the one hand or of students of the esoteric and the occult on the other, were neither of them wholly satisfactory to the unlearned and lowly masses. Hinayana Buddhism was no better in the eyes of these unlettered but spiritually hungry souls; but the Mahayana was another matter. The beneficent bodhisattvas who gave aid in daily life, and the dhyani buddhas who admitted one to paradise, were soon being plied with gifts and prayers by millions.

As Buddhism swept across China and into Korea, the Taoists, struck with amazement and yet sure that China had her own resources, so to speak, in the ways of gods and spirits, began to look into their own heritage; and having found much to go on, they began to ape the powerful faith brought in from India. One cannot be too positive that the effort was a sustained and self-conscious process, but what actually happened was that Chinese history was searched for personages that might compare in popular appeal with the Buddhas. Lao-tzu was formally apotheosized, with the title "Emperor of Mysterious Origin," and he was provided with heavenly associates, in imitation of Buddha and the Lohans; the Taoist writings were united into a canon; temples were erected; and groups of ascetics were called together in close copying of the Buddhist models. But this as yet was not sufficient to give Taoism the status among the populace of a satisfactory religion. It was still not clearly theistic. So the Taoist gods and spirits were brought together into a systematized pantheon. The motivation may well have been as sincere as it was nationalistic: why resort to foreign gods, when the Chinese had long had on their own soil beings who were near at hand and able to help them with a proven sympathetic response to their immediate needs? *

But the Taoists' reconstruction of Chinese religion was not utterly sincere. There was some outright fabrication. One of the most amazing incidents in all religion-making took place when the Emperor Chen Tsung, of the Sung dynasty, effected by fraud the final step in the transformation of Taoism into a complete theism. His ulterior purpose was the recovery of his own prestige, which needed bolstering badly.

---

* This would not necessarily, and did not, mean that Buddhist beings were to be denied value as efficacious helpers *in their own sphere*—i.e., release from suffering and admission to heaven of persons who would rather go to a Buddhist than a Taoist paradise.

At the turn of the year 1005 A.D. the emperor "lost face" because, being unable to drive back the nomad invaders from the northwest, the dreaded Kitan Tartars, who were pouring into China across the Great Wall, he had been forced to make a disgraceful peace by which he ceded away large portions of north China. He consulted the Taoist sooth-sayers and geomancers for advice. How could he reinstate himself in the favor of his people? The tradition has it that his minister, the wiley Wang Ch'in-jo, surprised the emperor by advising a fabricated revelation from Heaven, and when the emperor protested, said brazenly: "Bah! the Ancients had no such scruples. Each time the need was felt the Sages caused Heaven and the spirits to intervene in order to bring their policy into popular favor. It is precisely in this that their wisdom consisted." [64] The emperor, much impressed, visited the imperial library and consulted the scholars there. In 1008 A.D. he called his ministers together and told them he had been informed in a dream that Heaven was about to send him a letter, and that the governor of the capital had just reported seeing a yellow scarf hanging from one of the cornices of the Gate of Heaven. The emperor then went on foot to watch the scarf being lowered. It proved to contain a letter, ostensibly from a celestial being writing in the style of Lao-tzu. Officers were dispatched throughout the empire to make known the news. Another revelation followed in six months. And then in 1012 A.D. it was disclosed that the celestial being thus communicating with the emperor was Yü Huang. This being had not been heard of in China before the 9th century, but he was now raised to supremacy, and by succeeding emperors declared to be the Pure and Great One, Author of the visible heaven and of physical laws, the controller of Time and of the processes making divination valid, and the embodiment of Good and the Way (Tao). It was said finally that the celestial sovereign whom the ancients had called Imperial Ruler on High (Shang-ti) was and always had been none other than Yü Huang, the Jade Emperor!

There was a widespread popular response. The people were ap-parently well-pleased to have so many of their favorite folklore gods given imperial recognition, and they soon became accustomed to think-ing of Shang-ti and the Jade Emperor as one and the same being. The stories which began to circulate, giving the latter's history, entered the body of popular tradition without difficulty.

The popular satisfaction was increased by another sort of invention. Heaven and Hell were added to the scheme. Paradise was found in various places but most delightfully in the Three Isles of the Blessed (*San Hsien Shan*), long held in Chinese folklore to be located some-

where in the Eastern Sea (between the Chinese and Japanese main-
lands, but nobody who had gone there had come back). Hell was given
every appurtenance of torture and punishment, becoming a place full
of ogres and goblins of every malevolent and horrifying kind. It became
a major concern of the living to procure release of relatives from this
terrifying place.

Whether the final product of Taoist religion-making should be called
Taoist in any proper sense of that word is a question; but the Taoist
priests had no hesitations, assured that since the common people shared
in the decision as to which of the deities and spirits, old and new,
should be the most important to them, there was no need to hold back.
While as a matter of course the Jade Emperor was granted the highest
place, and was commonly associated with Lao-tzu and a third being,
Ling Pao, marshal of the supernatural beings, the three together forming
the official Taoist Trinity (the Three Purities), more interest and affection were shown toward adoptions from popular, originally non-Taoist,
religion: the Eight Immortals, the God of the Hearth, the Guardians
of the Door, and the City God. To these therefore we turn for a brief
description.

The Eight Immortals have long been beloved figures of folklore.
They are wholly and delightfully Chinese. Their abode is usually
thought to be either somewhere in the mountains or on the Three Isles
of the Blessed. They are supposed to have been (and most of them
probably originally were) human beings, but they are also thought to
have been ascetics to such good purpose that they achieved immortality
and now live on in their old bodies with minds and spirits ever young.
Four of them are often represented together as seated under a pine
tree, two of them sipping the wine heated for them by a third, while
a fourth pipes upon a flute in entertainment. The others are usually
portrayed singly. The "Maiden Immortal," Ho Hsien Ku, was long ago a
mortal of course, but while at home with her shop-keeping parents, she
lived on a diet of powdered mother-of-pearl and moonbeams and thus
became immortal. She has often appeared to men floating on the clouds,
carrying in her hand a lotus blossom or, at times, the peach of immortality. Because they are Fairies, the Eight Immortals belong to a larger
group, whose presiding spirits are, for the females, the very popular
Fairy Queen Mother, who is the subject of countless tales, and for the
males, Tung Wang Kung, a less well-known being.

The God of the Hearth, Tsao Shen (not exclusively Taoist; once
the spirit of the alchemy-furnace honored by the Han emperor, Wu Ti,
in the 2nd century B.C.), has been honored throughout China as the

kitchen spirit who sits in the chimney corner viewlessly watching all that the family does. His presence used to be constantly recalled to the remembrance of naughty children. On the twenty-fourth day of the twelfth moon, food and wine offerings were presented to his paper image; and when this image and the paper money, horses, and chariots accompanying it were burned together below the chimney, he ascended up the flue to heaven to make his annual report on the behavior of the family.

At New Year, invocations used to be offered to two Guardians of the Door, the Men Shen, both spirits of great antiquity; and their paper images, in military garb and carrying swords or spears, were attached to the two halves of the front door to ward off evil spirits during the coming year.

The City God, Cheng Huang, was worshipped in almost every Chinese city, for five centuries officially. He was first adopted by the religion-makers of the T'ang dynasty, but it was not until the 14th century that his worship was made an official requirement. Today he belongs to the past.

Of all the other spirits honored by the Taoists there is no space here to tell. They were many. One could linger, not only with the river, soil, mountain, and star spirits and with the patron deities of all the trades and occupations, but also with the apotheosized national heroes, the gods of health and luck, and the many animal and vegetable spirits, the dragons and phoenixes and unicorns; but these must be found described in some other place.

Taoism has for many years been in decline. According to the latest reports, as a religion it is now dead. The government frowns upon it, and is determined to suppress it. But many still cling to it as magic, no matter how secret they must be about it nor how carefully they must try to elude the vigilant eye of the Communist district leaders.

SUGGESTIONS FOR FURTHER READING

Blakney, R. B. *The Way of Life: Lao Tzu.* Mentor pb, 1955
Carus, Paul. *The Canon of Reason and Virtue.* Open Court, 1913. Available in pb
Chan, Wing-tsit. *Religious Trends in Modern China.* Columbia University Press, 1953
Creel, H. G. *The Birth of China.* John Day, 1937

————. *Sinism.* Open Court, 1928

Dubbs, H. H. Chapter on "Taoism" in *China,* ed. H. F. MacNair. University of Chicago Press, 1946

Fung, Y. L. *A History of Chinese Philosophy.* Trans. Derk Bodde. 2 vols. Princeton University Press, 1952

Giles, H. A. *Chuang Tzu—Mystic, Moralist and Social Reformer.* Kelly and Walsh, Shanghai, 1926

Giles, Lionel. *The Sayings of Lao Tzu.* In the Wisdom of the East series. John Murray, 1905

Goodrich, L. C. *A Short History of the Chinese People.* Harper, 1943

Grousset, René. *The Rise and Splendour of the Chinese Empire.* 1st Amer. ed., University of California Press, 1953

Hodous, L. *Folkways in China.* Probsthain, London, 1929

Hughes, E. R. *Chinese Philosophy in Classical Times.* Everyman's Library. J. M. Dent, 1941

Lang, Olga. *The Chinese Family and Society.* Yale University Press, 1950

Latourette, K. S. *The Chinese, Their History and Culture.* Macmillan, 1934

Legge, James, trans. *The Texts of Taoism.* In the Sacred Books of the East series. Oxford, 1891

Lin Yutang. *The Wisdom of China and India.* An anthology. Random House, 1942. Includes new translation of *Tao Te Ching*

————, trans. and ed. *The Wisdom of Laotse.* Modern Library, 1948

Tsui Chi. *A Short History of Chinese Civilization.* Putnam, 1943

Wang Gung-hsing. *The Chinese Mind.* John Day, 1946

Waley, Arthur, trans. *The Book of Songs.* Allen and Unwin, 1937

————. *The Way and Its Power, a Study of the Tao Te Ching.* Allen and Unwin, 1934

————. *Three Ways of Thought in Ancient China.* Allen and Unwin, 1939. Available as Anchor pb

Wei, Francis C. M. *The Spirit of Chinese Culture.* Scribner, 1947

Welch, Holmes. *The Parting of the Way: Lao Tzu and the Taoist Movement.* Beacon, 1957

10 Confucius and Confucianism: A Study in Optimistic Humanism

WE ARE FORTUNATE IN THE CASE OF CONFUCIUS IN HAVING FAIRLY RELIABLE information about his attitudes and his opinions. His disciples made attempts to preserve his teachings from the first, and the descriptions they left of his personal habits are detailed and probably accurate. We cannot say as much for the accuracy of the later, traditional biographies; for they present us with much questionable history, containing many obviously legendary incidents. But even these doubtful accounts have value: they incorporate authentic material left by Confucius' disciples, and thus manage to present us with what seems on the whole a dependable portrait of the man.

That after all is the important thing. The kind of man Confucius was is of major importance. That the Chinese have eagerly studied and followed his teachings in the past, and have founded not only their educational procedure, but much of their governmental practice, until very recently, on the principles he was understood to lay down is due in large part to the fact that they have had such confidence in his character, shining nobly through the traditions of his life and permeating his teachings. He was not only a wise man or a clever one, they have said; he was an incorruptible man, a human-hearted man. He was a model gentleman.

But there is something more. The character of Confucius has seemed

369

to exemplify the principles of order and harmony for which he stood in his teachings. During most of their history the Chinese have felt that their land would be well off indeed if the application of his principles could produce more men with his character. Not only would there then be better order in men's personal lives, but a superior order as well in the family and in the state, and harmony between Earth and Heaven. The moral influence of truly Confucian men would make this a certainty.

It is not strange that Confucius rather than the Taoists should have laid the foundation for traditional Chinese education. The Taoists turned for the secret of life to Nature and her laws, but Confucius was a humanist; he found the secret of life in men and their better relationships.

Let us see first of all what kind of man Confucius was, and what his beliefs were; and then we shall be prepared to trace out the effects of his character and teaching on the rich development of Chinese thought.

I   THE MAN CONFUCIUS

The best source of information on Confucius is the *Analects*, the famous collection of his sayings by his disciples; but the biographical matter in it is scant. Later Confucian tradition therefore busied itself with supplying an abundance of biographical detail, from birth to old age. As we have already observed, much of this later material is of doubtful historical value. Is then one to credit none of it, and to stand firm on the Analects alone? Or is it better to go part of the way with Ssu-ma Ch'ien (China's famous ancient historian, who died about 80 B.C.), and consider the body of tradition sound where it is not actually incredible? * Neither course is satisfactory. The former does not sufficiently account for the clearcut political aims of the Confucian school; the latter is apt to go too far in its acceptance of tradition.

If we pursue the moderate course of accepting just so much of the tradition as is needed to account for the eagerness of Confucius' disciples to take office and to set up a school of thought devoted to the training of officials and teachers, something like this brief biography results:

Confucius came of a poor but respected family in the ancient province of Lu, at the base of the Shantung Peninsula. His ancestors were

---

* The radical procedure of going on the Analects alone is sketched out for us in Arthur Waley's *Analects of Confucius*, p. 14; on the other hand, Carl Crow in *Master K'ung* accepts nearly all of the tradition.

reputed to have been aristocratic refugees who fled from the state of Sung to Lu when a revolution overthrew the ducal house. Shortly after his birth (probably in 551 B.C.), his father died, and he and his young mother were left in straitened circumstances. According to the Analects (IX. 6), Confucius said later that he was a poor man's son and could therefore do many menial things that are done by the common man— things that the princely (or superior) man does not have to do. Perhaps reflection on these early struggles led him to observe in after days, "It is hard not to chafe at poverty." [1]

In spite of their straitened circumstances Confucius was provided by his self-sacrificing mother with the proper intellectual training to be a gentleman. He apparently studied under a village tutor, and became a lifelong student of the poetry and historical tradition of ancient China. He also developed a consuming interest in the several varieties of Chinese classical music (now lost to us), which he performed on the lute, often singing the old songs to this accompaniment. According to the famous autobiographical summary in the Analects, at fifteen he began to be seriously interested in these studies; that is, he determined to be a scholar.

But the same source of information indicates that he did not spend all his time at his books. He did a good deal of hunting and fishing, but always with an aristocratic sense of sportsmanship; for his disciples noted: "The Master angled, but did not fish with a net; he shot, but not at birds sitting." [2] He enjoyed chariot- and carriage-driving; and was well aware of the high sportsmanship demanded in archery: "A gentleman has no rivalries—except perhaps in archery; and then, as, bowing, he joins the winners or steps down to see the loser drink, throughout the struggle he is still a gentleman." [3]

In his late teens he accepted a minor government post as a collector of grain and livestock due as taxes to the Duke of Lu, and also contracted a not too successful marriage, which, however, realized one major objective, the bringing of a son into the world to carry on the family line. In his middle twenties, his mother died. To Confucius this was a great personal tragedy. He at once retired from public life for twenty-seven months—a period reckoned in Chinese funerary tradition to be equivalent to three full years. Tradition insists that he more than fulfilled the conventions; at the end of the mourning period, he took up his lute, but he played haltingly, and was unable to sing to the notes for another five days, thus furnishing China with a classic instance of filial piety.

He now set himself up as a teacher, offering instruction in history, poetry, government, propriety, music, and divination (the traditional

"Six Disciplines"). Disciples joined him, some remaining with him for years. But though his reputation was great, and the scions of the best families in Lu were sent to him, he kept saying that his principles could be made effective in improving the now decadent social system only if he and his disciples took office in the higher echelons of government.

Tradition, not verifiable on the evidence of the Analects, insists that he took office in the cabinet of the Duke of Lu when fifty years of age, and that he ascended through the offices of Minister of Public Works and Minister of Justice to the position of Prime Minister; but that, through intrigue occasioned by his highly successful and upright administration, he was placed in a position where he "lost face" and resigned.

Whether this is true or not, at the age of fifty-five, he left Lu, accompanied by three of his disciples, and wandered for thirteen years from state to state, seeking a post under some government; and all in vain. The great feudal lords entertained him courteously, tongue in cheek. Some thought him a very wise and great man, yet even in this event his idea of governing by the sheer force of moral example aroused

Confucius telling disciples, "A river, like truth, will flow on forever and have no end." (From engraving on stone tablet in great Confucian Temple in Shantung, ca. 700 A.D. After drawing in Carl Crow, *Master Kung*)

no response. But if the feudal lords listened to him with respect, the officials intrigued to get rid of him. In some districts he was met with open suspicion, at the town of K'uang mobbed and imprisoned, at P'u surrounded and forced to accept armed protection, and in Sung, the state whence (perhaps) his ancestors had come, obliged to escape on foot into Cheng. In this last instance, his disciples, knowing that a certain military officer called Huan T'uei was close on their heels, kept urging him to hurry, but he replied: "Heaven begat the power (*te*) that is in me. What have I to fear from such a one as Huan T'uei?" [4] Although he was fundamentally a serious man, he was not above regarding his plight humorously.[*] In passing through Tahsiang, a man taunted him, "Great indeed is Confucius! He knows about everything and has made no name in anything!" Confucius turned to his disciples in mock dismay. "Now what shall I take up? Shall I take up charioteering? Shall I take up archery?" [6]

Through the good offices of one of his disciples who held a high official appointment in Lu, a cordial invitation to return was extended to Confucius by Duke Ai, in 484 B.C., and Confucius, now sixty-seven years old, came home. Sometimes called into consultation by the duke, he otherwise passed his last years in retirement. Late Confucian tradition gave rise to the belief that he spent his time compiling the materials he used in his teaching into the famous Confucian Classics, the *Shu Ching* or Book of History, the *Shih Ching* or Book of Poetry, the *Li Chi* or Book of Rites, the *I Ching* or Book of Changes, and the *Ch'un Ch'iu* or Annals of Spring and Autumn, the first four being anthologies of older source material, the last his own composition.[†] But all this is, as we shall see in a moment, highly doubtful. Just before his death in 479 B.C. he expressed discouragement about his own career, yet left his disciples more determined than ever to carry out his political and social aims.

---

[*] According to Ssu-ma Ch'ien, his lightheartedness offended the members of his party on one occasion, when between Ch'en and Ts'ai they were surrounded by a guard of hostile soldiers, who were instructed not to let them escape into the state of Ch'u. Food supplies ran short; some of the party fell sick and were confined to bed; but Confucius kept on reading and singing, accompanying himself with his lute. Only Yen Huei, his favorite disciple, understood his mood. He said to Confucius: "What do you care if [your ideas] are not accepted? The very fact that they are not accepted shows that you are a true gentleman [with ideas too great to be accepted by the people]." And Confucius was pleased with this flattery. "Is that so? Oh, son of Yen, if you were a rich man, I would be your butler!" [5]

[†] He is also said to have compiled a sixth book, the *Yüeh* or Book of Music, of which only a portion has survived (in Chapter X of the Li Chi).

II   THE TEACHING OF CONFUCIUS

Present Estimate of the Sources

A discussion of our sources of the teaching of Confucius is important, first of all, because it is generally agreed upon today that the Five Classics are at least not wholly from Confucius' hands—if they have come from his hands at all. For one thing, his disciples edited, altered, and amplified the materials they inherited. Thus Ssu-ma Ch'ien says that Mencius, over a hundred years after Confucius, "put the Shih and Shu in order." [7] It is especially true of the Li Chi that it cannot possibly be called, as it now stands, the product of Confucius' editorial work, but seems rather to date from the early years of the Han dynasty (2nd century B.C.).

But there is a more fundamental point to make: a careful scholarship must recognize it as a possibility that Confucius used, rather than first assembled, the materials of the earlier editions of the Classics; and that these collections were already in existence, and may have been in use by teachers before his time.*

If we assume that Confucius adopted the Classics as already-known and valued anthologies, then his chief purpose was to *point out the lessons* contained in them. As a matter of fact, the Analects is full of evidence of this. It was in this that we may see his originality. It is possible that he may have done some editing while he was about it, editing that had decisive effects. But even when we assume such editing, we cannot know where or on what materials he did it.†

* This is the contention of Dr. Y. L. Fung in *A History of Chinese Philosophy* (Henri Vetch, Peiping, 1937), pp. 46–47. He says: "The *Kuo Yü* informs us concerning a crown prince of Ch'u, son of King Chuan of Ch'u (613–591 B.C.), that the prince was given instruction in such works as the 'Odes,' 'Rites,' 'Music,' 'Spring and Autumn,' and 'Old Records.' Both the *Kuo Yü* and *Tso Chuan* record numerous conversations between important personages, in which the 'Odes' and 'History' are frequently mentioned; while the 'Rites' (*Li*) were used in diplomatic relations, and the 'Changes' (*I*) in divination. This indicates that an education of this sort was acquired by a portion, at least, of the nobility of that time. Confucius was the first man, however, to use the Six Disciplines for teaching the common people." It must be granted, this Chinese authority says also, that Confucius had a special connection with the Six Disciplines, for both the New Text School in its claim that Confucius organized the Six Disciplines himself and the Old Text School in its contention that he was merely their transmitter, agree that he was very closely connected with them.

† Present critical opinion concerning the Five Classics comes to something like this:—

Another fact should be made clear. The possibility that Confucius made changes in the Five Classics cannot be ruled out; but if he did so, he behaved as an editor should: he did not intrude his private convictions into these collections; he conceived his function to be merely that of a "transmitter," and that is actually what he said he was. The Analects records two sayings of his which testify to his great respect for the learning of the "ancients": "I am a transmitter and not a creator. I believe in and have a passion for the Ancients," [8] "I'm not born a wise man. I'm merely one in love with ancient studies and work very hard to learn them." [9] The Classics, then, are not a source of Confucius' original ideas; his private views and interpretations can be judged uncertainly, or at best to a limited degree only, from his textbook materials.

This might seem at first glance a serious difficulty, but actually little exists, for we have other sources of his teaching which are far more revealing. When he was using or studying the Classics, he offered his comments and interpretations to bystanders freely and in ample

---

The *Shih Ching* or Book of Poetry is authentically old, a valuable treasure-trove of information about Chou times. Its archaic language and simple grammar mark it as a genuine survival from the Chou dynasty's heyday (1000–600 B.C.).

The *Shu Ching* or Book of History contains some later forgeries and has lost a good deal of its once great historical authority; but the greater bulk of it may be judged from its archaic style to have been composed, in some part during early Chou times (but not earlier), and in other parts during late Chou and Early Han times (600–50 B.C.).

The *Ch'un Ch'iu* or Annals of Spring and Autumn is in two parts: the original extremely concise year-by-year annals of the state of Lu; and a commentary, the Tso Chuan, traditionally ascribed to Tso Chiu-Ming, a personal disciple of Confucius. The first part probably antedates Confucius; the second part seems to have been composed not earlier than the 4th century B.C., if not later.

The *I Ching* or Book of Changes is also in two main parts. The original sixty-four hexagrams, with a list of very brief oracles to accompany each line in them, probably dates from somewhere around 1000–800 B.C.; but the number of explanatory appendices, called the Shih I or Ten Wings, assigned by tradition to Confucius, seem rather to have been written by Confucians some time after him, perhaps during the early years of the Han dynasty, when the original I Ching (mysterious even to Confucius) needed to have the proper interpretations supplied from the oral tradition preserved by the Confucian school.

As it stands the *Li Chi* or Book of Rites, as has been noted, is very late. Its sixty-four chapters may contain earlier material but are in their present form a compilation not earlier than Early Han times.

For the student, the most easily accessible brief discussions of these matters may be found in *A History of Chinese Philosophy* by Fung Yu-Lan, Vol. I, translated by Derk Bodde (see the bibliography and index at the end of the volume); and in the brief introductions written for each part of *Chinese Philosophy in Classical Times*, edited and translated by E. R. Hughes (No. 973 in the Everyman's Library).

detail. He went further, and developed his own conception of what men must do to preserve, and live by, the best insights contained in the literature he so highly valued. These comments and discussions seemed so important to those who heard them, that they wrote them down on slips of bamboo, at first fragmentarily, then more fully by way of interpretation and paraphrase. The details of Confucius' own teaching have thus come to us through his disciples and owe much to their phrasing. Their recollections and interpretations are found in the Four Books, which are:

1. The *Analects* (the Lun Yü); this is a collection of the sayings of Confucius and of some of his disciples, and might be called the salient points of his and their conversations removed from the context and condensed. Although it is of very composite origin, and though "not much more than half [of it] can be really trusted even as good second-hand evidence," as one estimate puts it; [10] nevertheless, in spite of its inaccuracies, Confucius vividly and in his own person speaks to us through it. It is our most important source of material on him.

2. The *Great Learning* (Ta Hsüeh); this was originally chapter 39 of the Li Chi, but since Chu Hsi's time* it has been removed for separate use. We cannot consider it to be from Confucius; rather it seems to be dependent for its point of view upon Hsün-tzu (298–238 B.C.). Obviously a treatise in itself, it was initially designed to serve as the basis of the education of gentlemen in general, princes in particular. In classical Chinese education it was the first text studied by school boys.

3. The *Doctrine of the Mean* (Chung Yung); this also was a part of the Li Chi (as chapter 28). It is an excellent exposition of the philosophical presuppositions of Confucian thought, dealing particularly with the relation of human nature to the underlying moral order of the universe. Its contents have been traditionally attributed to Confucius' grandson, Tzu Ssu; but this is now regarded as subject to serious qualification. For one thing, it is apparently composed of two parts, one later than the other. The earlier, central part *may* have come from Tzu Ssu, but the later portion appears to have been written after the time of Mencius, perhaps in the 2nd century B.C.

4. The *Book of Mencius*, dating from the 3rd century B.C. This is a collection of the writings and sayings of the most original of the earlier Confucian thinkers, and constitutes the first attempt to reach a rounded and systematic exposition of Confucian philosophy.

* The 12th century A.D. For Chu Hsi, see the section later in this chapter in which he is discussed (p. 417 ff.).

It would be foolish to say the Four Books have removed all our difficulties. Though perhaps hardly anyone ever lived who succeeded as well as Confucius in reshaping the minds of his disciples into accurate reflections of his own, it has to be recognized that the Four Books changed with the passage of time through the editing of later hands, as must be evident from the descriptions of them just given, and therefore any competent exposition of Confucius' teachings must take these changes into account, wherever they can be detected.

One final difficulty remains. It can be said to have arisen historically and been largely settled for us historically. The long history of the Five Classics and the Four Books is punctuated at one point with a great threat to their survival. The first real emperor of all China, and perhaps its greatest, was Duke Cheng of Ch'in, the founder of the short-lived Ch'in dynasty, who conquered and in 221 B.C. forcibly unified the provinces of China as that had never been done before, and who accordingly took the proud title Shih Huang-ti or the First Emperor. We have referred to him on a previous page. An administrative and military genius, he established a new imperial capital; abolished the old feudal system; concentrated authority in himself; redivided the empire into thirty-six new administrative districts; built the Great Wall; introduced a new currency; instituted reforms among the officials, many of whom lost their jobs; substituted silk, painted with a soft hair brush, for the old bamboo records incised with a metal stylus; and encouraged the simplification of the writing of Chinese characters which followed, and which resulted in a new script. He found amidst all these changes that his attempts to establish a new order were obstructed by traditionalists and conservatives, chief among whom were the Confucian-trained schoolmasters and officials, who clung on to the feudal traditions of the first three dynasties (the Hsia, the Shang, and the Chou), and openly resisted his innovations as destructive of public order and morality. On the advice of his prime minister, Li Ssu, who was an advocate of the doctrines of the Legalists,* the Emperor in 213 B.C. ordered the famous "Burning of the Books" for which Chinese scholarship has since so execrated him. His purpose was to standardize the thinking of the common people, and therefore he wished to destroy every privately owned copy of the writings which preserved the knowledge of past ways of conducting public affairs, except such books as the I Ching (useful in divination) and manuals on agriculture and medicine. Special wrath was vented on the Book of Poetry and the Book of History. He decreed that any persons who failed to deliver up to the prefects their copies

---

* Opponents or rivals of the Confucians discussed in Section III of this chapter.

of the proscribed books should be branded with hot iron and compelled to work for four years at hard labor on the Great Wall. Some four hundred and sixty scholars, many of them Confucian, were buried alive for treason in the years that followed.

But three years after he issued his decree Shih Huang-ti died, and all his animus against the past came at last to nothing. To do him justice, he had "merely burned the books which existed among the people, but did not burn those in the official archives." [11] And during the Han dynasty which succeeded his within five years after his death, the Confucian classics were restored to public use, with, if anything, a heightened renown.

Were they the worse for their misadventure? Curiously enough, not as the result of their suppression, but as the result of their recopying; for they were recopied in the New Script! This seems to have resulted in something like this: the scholars now wrote rapidly on long pieces of silk instead of slowly on short pieces of bamboo, and they began to *fill out* the bare bones of the Old Texts with the interpretative glosses which they had learned in the schools. Without any conscious wish to make grave alterations, they practically rewrote the Li Chi, and added to the Shu Ching, to the I Ching, and to the Chung Yung. Included in these additions were certain ascriptions of divinity to Confucius, the tradition that he was the first to compile the Five Classics, and stories of his miraculous birth. Then gradually there was a recovery of some writings, composed in the Old Script, which contradicted the New Script writings in matters of fact, and at once the Old Text school was born. The battle between the Old Text and the New Text schools was to continue intermittently for nearly two thousand years; but it had this good result: as a consequence of the enormous amount of textual criticism which was done down the centuries, and especially by the Ch'ing scholars of the 17th to 19th centuries, forgeries (largely Old Text) have been located, variant readings reduced, and conflicting passages clearly defined.

And now, after this long excursus, let us proceed to the most careful statement of Confucius' own teaching that we can achieve in the light of present knowledge.

The Ethical Principles of Confucius

The ethical thought of Confucius sprang from a double realization: first, that the China of his day was disturbingly corrupt; but secondly, that the moral condition of the country was not beyond redemption.

The situation was bad, but not hopeless. Man's practices had grown corrupt, but man himself had not yet become corrupt; he was still as apt to good as to evil. But why had man's practices grown corrupt? Confucius answered this question quite simply: men had failed from moral causes to live by *li* as those of their ancestors who were devoted to the common good had lived by it.

This word *li* is one of the most important words used by Confucius to formulate his program for the recovery of China. It is a difficult word to translate, for it means different things in different contexts. In one connection or another it means "propriety" (the usual translation, but not always adequate), "courtesy," "reverence," "rites and ceremonies," "the correct forms of social ceremony," "ritual," "ritual and music," "the due order of public ceremony," "the ideal standard of social and religious conduct," "the religious and moral way of life." Put into its historical perspective, it means in the words of Lin Yutang, "an ideal social order with everything in its place, and particularly a rationalized feudal order, [like that] which was breaking down in Confucius' days." [12]

In the Li Chi (the Confucian classic on the subject) comprehensive and illuminating discussions of the meaning of *li* are attempted. The following passages are particularly worthy of study: *

Duke Ai asked Confucius, "What is this great *li?* Why is it that you talk about *li* as though it were such an important thing?"

Confucius replied, "Your humble servant is really not worthy to understand *li*."

"But you do constantly speak about it," said Duke Ai.

Confucius: "What I have learned is this, that of all the things that people live by, *li* is the greatest. Without *li*, we do not know how to conduct a proper worship of the spirits of the universe; or how to establish the proper status of the king and the ministers, the ruler and the ruled, and the elders and the juniors; or how to establish the moral relationships between the sexes; between parents and children, and between brothers; or how to distinguish the different degrees of relationships in the family. That is why a gentleman holds *li* in such high regard." [13]

Confucius said [in conversation with Tsuyu]: "The principles of *li* and righteousness serve as the principles of social discipline. By means of these principles, people try to maintain the official status of rulers and subjects, to teach the parents and children and elder brothers and younger brothers and husbands and wives to live in harmony, to establish social institutions, and to live in groups of hamlets . . ."

* These passages show the influence of later Confucian thought, particularly that of Hsün-tzu; but with due caution in their use we may get from them authentic glimpses into the mind of Confucius.

"Is *li* so very important as all that?" asked Tsuyu again.

"This *li*," replied Confucius, "is the principle by which the ancient kings embodied the laws of heaven and regulated the expressions of human nature. Therefore he who has attained *li* lives, and he who has lost it, dies . . . *Li* is based on heaven, patterned on earth, deals with the worship of the spirits and is extended to the rites and ceremonies of funerals, sacrifices to ancestors, archery, carriage driving, 'capping,' * marriage, and court audience or exchange of diplomatic visits. Therefore the Sage shows the people this principle of a rationalized social order (*li*) and through it everything becomes right in the family, the state, and the world." 14

These passages reveal, upon examination, certain basic Confucian principles.

1. *Li* is of vital importance in ordering and regulating the principal human relationships. These relationships are five in number. They are the relationships between ruler and subject, father and son, husband and wife, the oldest son and his younger brothers, and elders and juniors (or friends). Besides these five relationships others are incidentally mentioned, such as the relationships between men and the spirits of the universe, between rulers and their ministers, and between diplomats; but the five relationships given above are the "great" ones, because they are judged fundamental to the social order.

2. By the practice of *li* the principal relationships in society can be so regulated and set straight, that complete harmony may reign in every home, in every village, and throughout the empire. Ultimately—*and here Confucius and his school proved themselves to be true to the deepest feelings of the Chinese people about the ultimate nature of the universe* —the goal is to obtain a cosmic harmony between men, Earth and Heaven, and thus put into actual operation among men the Tao or the will of Heaven.

3. The forms of social ceremony which best exemplify the practice of *li* are observable in the manners of those ancients who sought the common welfare and exhibited a humane spirit of mutual respect and courtesy.

The last of these principles deserves more than passing notice. The ancients lived harmoniously and courteously together in a social order that was profoundly just, Confucius believed. Superiors and inferiors knew their places, and behaved politely according to their several stations. So he reverently studied and tried to embody in his own conduct the ceremonial procedures of the olden time. He wished to be instrumental in getting all China to do the same. This won him the mocking

---

* The ceremony of putting a cap on a boy when he reaches maturity.

criticism of the Taoists, who raged at his formalism as being unnatural and futile. But Confucius believed he stood for "the crystallization of what is right" * [15] in terms of formal behavior. *For the sake of giving his conduct the force of a moral example, he acted out his principles with obvious symbolism.* This accounts for his supposed meticulous behavior in the ducal court of Lu, described in Book X of the Analects. Consider this description of his conduct.†

When the duke bade him receive guests, his face seemed to change, his knees to bend. He bowed left and right to those beside him, straightened his robes in front and behind, and sped forward, his elbows spread like wings. When the guest had left, he always reported: "The guest has ceased to look back."

Entering the palace gate he stooped, as though it were too low for him. He did not stand in the middle of the gate, nor step on the threshold.

Passing the throne, his face seemed to change, his knees to bend, he spake with bated breath.

Mounting the dais, he lifted his robes, bowed his back and masked his breathing, till it seemed to stop.

Coming down, his face relaxed below the first step, and bore a pleased look. From the foot of the steps he sped forward, his elbows spread like wings; and when again in his seat he looked intent and solemn as before.

When bearing the sceptre, his back bent, as under too heavy a burden. He held his hands not higher than in bowing, nor lower than in giving a present. He wore an awed look and dragged his feet, as though they were fettered.

On the duke coming to see him in sickness, he turned his face to the east and had his court dress spread across him, with the girdle over it.

When summoned by the duke, he walked, without waiting for his carriage.

In mounting his chariot he stood straight and grasped the cord. When in his chariot he did not look round, speak fast, or point. [16]

This description, whether it describes Confucius himself or merely an imagined ideal Confucian official, raises the question: Was Confucius just a narrow formalist, or was he a social philosopher to be taken seriously? The answer would seem to depend on whether he lived by purely formal rules or by a deeper principle.

That Confucius found in the practices of the ancients a profound

---

* One of the definitions of *li* in the Li Chi.

† There is serious doubt as to whether this is an authentic description. Arthur Waley, for example, considers it simply a collection of traditional ritual maxims altered so as to apply to Confucius. This may be the fact. But even so Confucius would have endorsed in another the behavior here attributed to him.

principle which provided him with a key to ideal relationships among men is more than once indicated in the Analects and elsewhere.

Tzu-kung asked, saying, "Is there one word which may serve as a rule of practice for all one's life?" The Master said, "Is not Reciprocity (*shu*) such a word? What you do not want done to yourself, do not do to others." [17]

In these words Confucius formulated a law of human relationships identical with the Golden Rule of the New Testament. He happened to define reciprocity (*shu*) negatively (and hence won from some Western scholars the grudging judgment that he had given China the "Silver Rule"), but the word means "fellow-feeling" or "mutual consideration," and its definition need not have been put negatively. In the Doctrine of the Mean Confucius is in fact quoted as having explained this central ethical principle in positive terms making it quite comparable with Jesus' Golden Rule. He is there found saying:

"There are four things in the moral life of man, not one of which I have been able to carry out in my life. To serve my father as I would expect my son to serve me: that I have not been able to do. To serve my sovereign as I would expect a minister under me to serve me: that I have not been able to do. To act towards my elder brother as I would expect my younger brother to act towards me: that I have not been able to do.* To be the first to behave towards friends as I would expect them to behave towards me: that I have not been able to do." [18]

However, it is true that Confucius did not go as far as Jesus (or, for that matter, the Taoists of his own land) in defining the scope of the application of this ideal of ethical conduct. He made a significant reservation when confronted with the Taoist rule of returning good for evil. Someone asked him: "What do you think of repaying evil with kindness?" He replied, "Then what are you going to repay kindness with? . . . Repay kindness with kindness, but repay evil with justice." [19] It would seem that Confucius limited the operation of the law of reciprocity, in its complete sense, to the circle of the good, because evil persons were judged unworthy of the mutual consideration prompted by fellow-feeling.

It cannot be emphasized too strongly, however, that Confucius' primary purpose was to persuade all men to cooperate in securing the general good. True virtue, he taught, lay in the expression of *jen* or human-heartedness. This consisted essentially in two things: the recog-

* Here, of course, he is being made to speak by one who lived after his time—by his grandson perhaps; and we note that he is using the word "brother" in the most general sense.

nition of the worth of any human being of any rank or station, and kindly behavior toward one's fellows as a consequence of this recognition. Many instances could be cited of Confucius' insistence that government should be directed toward the welfare of the whole people; that families must safeguard the good of each of their members and bring harmony into the interrelationships of old and young; and that in society at large, men, knowing that all who live within the four seas are brothers, should display to each other in action their real humane and kindly character (their *jen*).

Confucius was not aware (did not live in a culture that permitted him to know) that government may be based on the democratic process of election to office by ballot; but he did demand that government be for if not by the people, and that feudal lords be responsive to the needs of the people at large.*

The Five Great Relationships

The Li Chi presents the following scheme as growing out of Confucius' study of *shu* as applied to the Five Relationships: †

Kindness in the father, filial piety in the son

Gentility in the eldest brother, humility and respect in the younger

Righteous behavior in the husband, obedience in the wife

Humane consideration in elders, deference in juniors

Benevolence in rulers, loyalty in ministers and subjects

If these ten attitudes (known as the ten *I* or appropriate attitudes) are generally present in society, then the highest propriety (*li*) will be actualized, and perfect harmony will reign between all individuals. Then people will show their real human character (*jen*). No quarrels, no disturbance, no injustices, will exist. There will be happiness among friends, harmony in the home, peace in the state. The Doctrine of the Mean quotes approvingly from the Book of Poetry:

* See for a strong treatment of the "democratic" aspect of Confucius' teaching H. G. Creel, *Confucius, Man and Myth* (John Day, 1949) and *Chinese Thought from Confucius to Mao T-* (University of Chicago Press, 1953). If Prof. Creel's thesis is ᵃ ⸗, ᴛne word "democratic" must be used in a rather broad ᶜ⸗

⸗ ıs very doubtful whether Confucius developed so schematic a treatment of this matter, but it follows logically from his teaching.

> "When wives and children and their sires are one,
> 'Tis like the harp and lute in unison.
> When brothers live in concord and at peace
> The strain of harmony shall never cease.
> The lamp of happy union lights the home,
> And bright days follow when the children come." [20]

And the Great Learning (Chapter VII) quotes from the same source lines which may be translated:

> A prince by courteous carriage may create
> Concord at court and order in the state.

To see that Confucius was a practical sort of philosopher and did not lose himself in vague contemplation of an ideal that was conceived only in general terms, let us turn now to the subjects concerning which he oftenest spoke when amplifying upon what he meant by practicing *li*: the relationship of fathers and sons, the relationship of rulers and subjects, and the nature of the superior man.

Filial Piety

Confucius did not, of course, bring into being the fact that the whole of Chinese culture has rested upon the basis of the family. Yet what he said has helped to make the interests of the family the first consideration of the Chinese. Nothing has stood higher. In China, loyalty to the family has been one's first loyalty. No lad in China ever comes of age, in the Western sense of the phrase; his whole service is expected to be devoted to the family until death; and he is expected to obey his father, and when his father dies, his eldest brother, with a perfect compliance.* This has meant in the past that every father has a great and grave responsibility to fulfil toward his family. He must seek to produce virtue in his sons by being himself the best example of it.

Confucius considered this so self-evident a proposition that he laid far heavier stress on the filial piety without which the father's goodness would remain ineffective. Here he touched a chord that has had the

---

* This statement presumes that the old order in China has not been entirely swept away by the Communist regime. However, it is being said by escapees from behind the Bamboo Curtain that the present Chinese state is determined to make itself "the father and elder brother" by breaking up the old family system, through the institution of "communes" in its place, and, above all, by claiming the first loyalty (or filial piety) of every citizen. The last paragraph on this topic shows how they are able to explain this.

most resounding response in the Chinese consciousness since his time. It struck home. Consider a few of the many important utterances of Confucius on the subject (and thereby glimpse an essential aspect of the folk-mind of China):

The Master said, "Whilst thy father lives look for his purpose; when he is gone, look how he walked. To change nothing in thy father's way for three years may be called pious." [21]

Meng Wu asked the duty of a son.

The Master said, "He shall not grieve his father and mother by anything but illness." [22]

Tsu-yu asked the duty of a son.

The Master said, "He that can feed his parents is now called a good son. But both dogs and horses are fed, and unless we honor our parents, what is the difference?" [23]

The Master said, "Whilst thy father and mother are living, do not wander afar. If thou must travel, hold a set course." [24]

The Doctrine of the Mean lays down these very influential precepts:

Confucius remarked: "The Emperor Wu and his brother, Duke Chou, were indeed eminently pious men . . .

"In spring and autumn they repaired and put in order the ancestral temple, arranged the sacrificial vessels, exhibited the regalia and heirlooms of the family, and presented the appropriate offerings of the season . . .

"To gather in the same places where our fathers before us have gathered; to perform the same ceremonies which they before us have performed; to play the same music which they before us have played; to pay respect to those whom they have honored; to love those who were dear to them—in fact, to serve those now dead as if they were living, and now departed as if they were still with us: this is the highest achievement of true filial piety." [25]

Confucius may not have been as firm about it, but the majority of his followers concluded that the duty of a son is to obey his father in all things while he lives and to honor and still obey him in all things after he is dead. Indeed the filial relationship has been made since Confucius' time the type and symbol of all life-enriching and wisdom-conserving subordination to the leadership of the old and wise. "By the principle of filial piety the whole world can be made happy and all calamities and dangers can be averted" [26] is one of the claims made for treating not only one's father as a father should be treated, but also such superior spirits as one's ancestors, one's elders, noted scholars, and one's emperor or prince as they should be treated. The attitude of filial piety can thus be almost indefinitely extended.

Political Philosophy

But Confucius was equally emphatic about the importance of the relationship between rulers and their subjects. Here he merged ethics and politics. He told everyone who would listen to him that if rulers adopt and act upon the highest principles and laws of social propriety, then the spiritual climate of a whole state may be changed, and all the people from the higher officials on down to the poorest and least of citizens may be led to live more virtuously in their several stations. The reform of society begins at the top, among the rulers, and thence reaches down to the lower orders of society.*

On one occasion the head of the Chi clan in Lu, Baron Chi K'ang Tsu, a person of importance, asked Confucius how to rule. The Sage replied: "To govern is to keep straight. If you, Sir, lead the people straight, which of your subjects will venture to fall out of line?" [27] The same baron in another conversation asked: "Ought not I to cut off the lawless in order to establish law and order? What do you think?" To this crucial question Confucius made the sort of reply that won him profound respect as the enunciator of ultimate ethical principles, but that made the legalistic smile in derision: "Sir, what need is there of the death-penalty in your system of government? If you showed a sincere desire to be good, your people would likewise be good. The virtue of the prince is like unto wind; that of the people like unto grass. For it is the nature of grass to bend when the wind blows upon it." [28]

For an understanding of his point of view, too much stress can hardly be laid upon this fundamental conviction of Confucius. People, he held, being at heart good, are responsive to good in those above them to whom they look for leadership. "If a country," he insisted, "had none but good rulers for a hundred years, crime might be stamped out and the death-penalty abolished. How true this saying is!" [29]

One of the main conclusions which Confucius' followers, thinking in his spirit, drew from his study of history is contained in this curious piece of close-linked, circular logic which is to be found in the Great Learning:

The ancients [i.e., the ancient kings] who wished to cause their virtue to shine forth first ordered well their own states. Wishing to order well their states, they first regulated their families. Wishing to regulate their families, they first cultivated their persons. Wishing to cultivate their persons, they first rectified their hearts. Wishing to rectify their hearts, they first sought to be sincere in their thoughts. Wishing to be sincere in their thoughts, they

* The communists can make good use of this, too.

first extended to the utmost their knowledge. Such extension of knowledge lay in the investigation of things. Things being investigated, their knowledge became complete. Their knowledge being complete, their thoughts were sincere. Their thoughts being sincere, their hearts were then rectified. Their hearts being rectified, their persons were cultivated. Their persons being cultivated, their families were regulated. Their families being regulated, their states were rightly governed. Their states being rightly governed, the whole kingdom was made tranquil and happy.[30]

In this, perhaps the most famous of all Confucian paragraphs, and in the previous quotations, it is apparent that according to Confucian teaching the good life is a spiritual rather than a legal attainment. A good example may prevent crime, but statutory law breeds it. A well-ordered state cannot be legislated into existence; it grows out of a contagious spirit of good will and earnestness in well-doing. Love or cooperative good will makes law unnecessary. When propriety is cultivated by a prince whose heart is rectified and whose thoughts are sincere, his family falls in line (is "regulated") and his State is happy under officials who are like their prince (is then "rightly governed").

The Doctrine of the Mean quotes Confucius as saying to the Duke of Lu: "When the men are there, good government will flourish, when the men are gone, good government decays and becomes extinct. . . . The conduct of government, therefore, depends upon the men. The right men are obtained by the ruler's personal character. To cultivate his personal character, the ruler must use the moral law (Tao). To cultivate the moral law, the ruler must use the moral sense [*jen*, or the principles of true manhood]." [31] In the words of the Book of Poetry concerning the good emperor Shun:

> That great and noble Prince displayed
> The sense of right in all he wrought;
> The spirit of his wisdom swayed
> Peasant and peer; the crowd, the court.[32]

Since Confucius believed in government by moral example, he took no interest in written laws. In fact, he is quoted as saying: "Guide the people by law, keep them in line by punishment, and they may shun crime, but they will be shameless. Guide them by mind, keep them in line by courtesy, and they will learn shame and grow good." [33] A high hope!

He used to admit the truth of the old saying, "To be a good king is difficult." But he went on to say: "He who realizes the difficulty of being a good king—has he not almost succeeded in making his country prosper?" [34] What he meant was, obviously, that when a king pauses to think long enough about being a good king, he will feel within him the strong native tendencies toward virtue, and the result will be a virtuous and prosperous people. No one has defined more clearly the best hopes for a paternalistic state.

The Rectification of Names

A place was made for logic. (It was a sort of semantics.) Moral and political reorganization had a side which was to be called "the rectification of names." We must consider this concept, if Confucius discussed it,* his chief contribution to straight thinking in politics and morals. The crucial passage is in the Analects.

Tsu-lu said: "The prince of Wei is awaiting you, Sir, to take control of his administration. What will you undertake first, Sir?" The Master replied: "The one thing needed is the rectification of names." [35]

The disciple then says in bewilderment, "That is far-fetched, Sir! Why rectify them?" Confucius rebukes him for showing lack of logical acuteness, and proceeds to explain that if names are incorrect, words will be misused; and when words are misused, nothing can be on a sound footing; *li* and music will languish, law and punishments will not be just, and people will not know where to place hand or foot; this is why one cannot be too careful about words and names.

In another conversation Confucius declared that only when the ruler is ruler, the minister is minister, the father is father, and the son is son, can there be good government. He meant to say that only when men know what names stand for, and then act as the definitions indicate, can there be true social order. Morality cannot exist apart from precision of thought and speech. To quote one eminent modern Chinese scholar: "Confucius considered [there was] an inseparable connection between intellectual disorder and moral perversity." Hu Shih, whose statement this is, explains Confucius' point of view further, thus:

The rectification of names consists in making real relationships and duties and institutions conform as far as possible to their *ideal* meanings . . . When this intellectual reorganization is at last effected, the ideal social order will come as night follows day,—a social order where, just as a circle is a

---

* He may not have done so, although, as we shall see in a moment, eminent authorities believe he did. For the view that the whole so-called "language crisis" must be dated not earlier than the 4th century B.C., see Arthur Waley, *The Analects of Confucius*, pp. 22 f.

circle and a square a square, so every prince is princely, every official is faithful, every father is fatherly, and every child is filially pious.[36]

The principle then is, that everyone must act in life in accordance with the highest, that is, the socially-agreed-upon ideal of his true place and function in society.

The Superior Man

The kind of man Confucius most firmly believed in, and was always talking about, was the man whose mind was perfectly clear about names and duties, and who moreover acted with an altruistic uprightness (*jen*) and good taste (*li*). He called him the Higher Type of Man, or the Superior Man, one who is truly a *chün-tzu* (literally, a superior person, a prince). One must take seriously Confucius' description of this true gentleman, who as a son is always filial, as a father just and kind, as an official loyal and faithful, as a husband righteous and judicious, as a friend sincere and tactful. It is this ideal which constitutes Confucius' greatest claim to distinction as a moral philosopher.

The Superior Man, he said, displays the Five Constant Virtues; for "moral virtue simply consists," he asserted, "in being able, anywhere and everywhere, to exercise five particular qualities: self-respect, magnanimity, sincerity, earnestness, and benevolence," [37]—the qualities of the Superior Man.

This list of virtues suggests that, though Confucius loved the order which punctilious observance of rules and ceremonies brings, he saw the fallacy of a merely legalistic formalism. The harmony which he sought could issue only from inward uprightness, a sincere and basic *feeling* of mutuality with others; he had no use for the insincere politeness that comes from mere etiquette. He emphatically rejected "the glib talker," "the smoothie," "the goody-goody." Mencius quotes him as saying: "I hate things that resemble the real things but are not the real things . . . I hate the ingratiating fellows, because they get mixed up with the good men. I hate the glib talkers because they confuse us about honest people . . . I hate goody-goodys because they confuse us about virtuous people." [38] In the Analects we hear him saying: "Your goody-goody people are the thieves of virtue." [39] In another connection he remarked: "If a man is not a true man, what is the use of rituals? If a man is not a true man, what is the use of music?" [40] This touches on the very heart of Confucius' philosophy of life.

The Superior Man *feels* like practicing *li*, because he is realizing his own uprightness (*jen*) through it. This is an important moral point, and Dr. Y. L. Fung suggests it in these words:

The *li* are imposed on man from outside. But besides this outer mould, we each still have within us something which we may take as a model for our conduct. If we "can find in ourselves a rule for the similar treatment of others"; if we do to others what we wish for ourselves, and "do not do to others what we do not like ourselves," then the outpourings of our nature will of themselves be in accord with what is proper. Hence while there are still occasions on which one's own natural uprightness (*chih*) cannot be followed, there is none upon which *jen* (which is one's own uprightness conforming to what is proper) may not be acted upon. This is why *jen* is the "all pervading" principle of Confucius' teaching, and the center of his philosophy.[41]

Because of the perfect adjustment which he has achieved between his manners and his motives, the Superior Man embodies in his conduct a golden mean, something that Confucius said was rare among men. To the Superior Man decorum is as natural as breathing. He has a compelling sense of duty, but no difficulty in carrying it out. "In his progress through the world he has neither narrow predilections nor obstinate antipathies."[42] His uprightness never takes the form of rudeness, because he controls its expression by the rules of good taste. He is modest. He is catholic-minded. He is simple, honest, and a lover of justice. "He weighs men's words and observes the expression on their faces";[43] then his response is tactful but conscientious and truthful. In trying to establish his own character, he also tries to establish the character of others. "The higher type of man makes a sense of duty the groundwork of his character, blends with it in action a sense of harmonious proportion, manifests it in a spirit of unselfishness, and perfects it by the addition of sincerity and truth."[44] Surely a noble ideal of manhood—whether attainable or not on the basis of Confucius' ethics! And this noble man never forgets himself. He obeys the inner law of self-control. He keeps his head, and with it his equilibrium and his virtue. "Not even whilst he eats his meal will the superior man forget what he owes to his fellowmen. Even in his hurried leave-takings, even in moments of frantic confusion, he keeps true to his virtue."[45] He is a real gentleman because he lives by a superior law—a law of proportion and equilibrium in acting on his inner motives, and of mutuality and fellow-feeling as regards others.

It was left to the Confucian school to develop the "Doctrine of the Golden Mean." Confucius spoke of it, apparently, only suggestively and in passing:

"Since I cannot find people who follow the Golden Mean to teach, I suppose I will have to work with those who are brilliant or erratic (*k'uang*) and those who are a little dull but careful (*chuan*). The brilliant but erratic persons are always ready to go forward (or are too active), and the dull but careful persons always hold themselves back (or are not active enough)." [46]

One of his sayings had the ambiguous but profoundly suggestive character that always excites speculation and leads to further development of thought. It has been both narrowly and broadly translated, as the following two English versions show. The succinct, less explanatory rendering is:

"That virtue is perfect which adheres to a constant mean." [47]

In the more philosophically phrased translation this becomes:

"The use of the moral sentiment, well balanced and kept in perfect equilibrium,—that is the true state of human perfection." [48]

Perhaps Confucius (if he used the word at all) meant by *chungyung* (the word in dispute) something like the Middle Way of early Buddhism, even then being worked out in India; and, if we sense his meaning aright, he was as well touching upon a theme which the Greeks, in the person of Aristotle, far away "across the roof of the world," were soon to place at the center of their ethics.

There is no doubt, whatever suggestions he may have made along this line, that Confucius himself was a good example of "the higher type of man" who walks the middle way and does nothing in excess. He had true decorum. He himself was modest about his achievements. "In three ways I fall short of a gentleman. Love is never vexed; wisdom has no doubts; courage is without fear." [49] But he knew he possessed one qualification of the superior type of man; he had a compelling sense of duty. "To divine wisdom and perfect virtue," he said, "I can lay no claim. All that can be said of me is that I never falter in the course which I pursue and am unwearying in my instruction of others —this and nothing more." [50] "There are men, I daresay, who act rightly without knowing the reason why, but I am not one of them. Having heard much, I sift out the good and practice it; having seen much I retain it in my memory. This is the second order of wisdom." [51] "I am a transmitter and not an originator, and as one who believes in and loves the ancients, venture to compare myself with our old P'ang" [52]— an ancient sage of the 11th (?) century B.C. who was said to have disappeared, as Lao-tzu was said to have done years later, into the West. There is little boasting here; and yet in his old age, he is quoted as saying calmly, as from a great height: "At fifteen I had my mind bent on learning. At thirty I stood firm. At forty I had no doubts. At fifty I knew the decrees of Heaven. At sixty my ear was an obedient organ for the reception of truth. At seventy I could do what my heart desired without transgressing what was right." [53]

Religious Teaching

It may be granted that Confucius was primarily a teacher of ethics. Some would say that little more need be added; he was no more than that. But this is a contention that cannot be maintained. In private belief and in public practice he exhibited faith in religious reality. So carefully, moreover, did he adhere to the established religious ceremonies of his time that he set an example which was, until a generation ago, officially considered to be the Chinese ideal.

However, his attitude in religion was critical and discriminating, even marked by an evident restraint; for he was rationalistic and decidedly humanistic in his outlook. Only in the milder sense of the word can he be called mystical or supernaturalistic. His position in matters of faith was this: whatever seemed contrary to common sense in popular tradition, *and whatever did not serve any discoverable social purpose,* he regarded coldly. In his teaching, he avoided discussing such subjects as prodigies, feats of strength, crime, and the supernatural, apparently because he did not wish to spend time discussing perturbing exceptions to human and natural law. "Absorption in the study of the supernatural is most harmful," he said,[54] not that he disbelieved in the supernatural, but that it would not do to let the pressing concerns of human welfare suffer neglect. It is from this point of view that we should weigh two sayings of his that have perhaps received overmuch attention. His disciple Tsu-yu asked him about one's duty to the spirits of the dead. He replied: "Before we are able to do our duty by the living, how can we do it by the spirits of the dead?" [55] He defined what he believed was the proper attitude with great exactness thus: "To devote oneself earnestly to one's duty to humanity, and, while respecting the spirits, to keep aloof from them, may be called wisdom." [56]

Yet the effect of his desire to support whatever made for unity in the state and harmony in the home was that he went as far as he could in observing the rites and ceremonies of his time. One might even hazard the opinion with Dr. Lin Yutang, that "Confucius would undoubtedly have been a High Churchman," could he have been a Christian.[57] Perhaps his interest in the stabilizing moral effect of the old inherited rituals was strengthened by his own aesthetic satisfaction in them. At any rate, at the village exorcisms he put on court dress and stood on the east steps. He took seriously the ceremonial bath before religious worship. When one of his disciples (Tzu Kung) suggested doing away with the sheep offering at the new moon, he disagreed, saying: "Tzu, you love the sheep; I love the ceremony!" [58] On going into the Great Temple he asked about everything. This once brought from a bystander the criticism that he knew shockingly little about the rites; but when he heard this, he said that asking about everything was part of the rite. In offering sacrifices to ancestors, he behaved as if they were physically present; and this was also his attitude toward the other spirits to whom sacrifices were made. He felt it his duty to participate in the sacrifice actively, saying: "For me, to take no part in the sacrifice is the same as not sacrificing." [59] Asked the meaning of the Grand Sacrifice to the Imperial Ancestors, he said: "I do not know. He who knew its meaning would find it as easy to govern the Empire as to look upon this"—pointing to his palm.[60]

His endorsement of ancestor worship seems to have been unreserved. In a quotation from the Doctrine of the Mean, given on an earlier page, we were assured that he judged the Emperor Wu and his brother, the Duke of Chou, to be eminently pious men, because they repaired and put in order the ancestral temple each spring and autumn, carefully arranging the sacrificial vessels, the regalia, and the heirlooms of the family, and presenting appropriate sacrifices at the same time. He is said to have thought that the great emperors of the past were fortunate indeed; after their deaths their descendants continued to sacrifice to them for many generations.

What, in view of all this, was Confucius' own philosophy of religion? Was he teasing his disciples, when, while he was seriously ill, and Tsu-Yu asked to be allowed to say prayers for him, he parried with "Are such available?" "Yes," said Tsu-Yu; "and the Manual of Prayers says, 'Pray to the spirits above and to those here below!'" Thereupon Confucius said: "My praying has been going on a long while." [61] The exact meaning of this remark is difficult to determine, of course; and so we must turn elsewhere for further evidence.

The clue to his own belief is contained in the conviction that when a man practices the moral law he does the will of Heaven. The writer of the Doctrine of the Mean (reputed, but probably apocryphally, to be Confucius' grandson) says that Confucius made it evident that the truths handed down from the ancient emperors Yao and Shun "harmonize with the divine order which governs the revolutions of the seasons in the Heaven above and . . . fit in with the moral design which is to be seen in physical nature upon the Earth below." [62] This seems to be a pretty accurate statement of Confucius' real, though perhaps never expressed, intent. One can hardly call such an attitude supernaturalistic or monotheistic. It is vaguely mystical, and at the same time aloof from the concerns of popular religion. An inquirer once asked, "Why do people say it is better to be on good terms with the kitchen god than with the god of the southwestern corner of the house?" (two deities popularly believed to dwell in every house and to intercede for those under their protection); whereupon Confucius replied sharply: "Nonsense; if you have committed sins against Heaven, you haven't got a god to pray to." [63]

The basic fact is that, for himself, he felt that he had the backing of Heaven. He must indeed be ranged with the other religious leaders whom we have studied. He had a prophetic consciousness, all his own. Once, in the city of K'uang, he was surrounded by a threatening crowd, and his disciples feared for his life; but he said: "Since King Wen [the founder of the Chou feudal order] died, is not the tradition of King Wen in my keeping or possession? If it be the will of Heaven that this moral tradition should be lost, posterity shall never again share in the knowledge of this tradition. But if it be the will of Heaven that this tradition shall not be lost, what can the people of K'uang do to me?" *[64] We have heard him on another occasion exclaiming "Heaven begat the power (*te*) that is in me. What have I to fear from such a one as Huan T'uei?" † There were thus moments when he felt clearly that his message to his times was one that carried eternal significances, because it had its origin in the moral order of the world. His teachings seemed to him to be firmly grounded in the ultimate nature of things. It was a conviction to which we cannot justly deny the adjective religious.

III THE CONFUCIAN SCHOOL—ITS RIVALS AND CHAMPIONS

The Formation of the Confucian School

In a famous passage, Mencius gives the tradition concerning the mourning of Confucius' disciples:

* There is a play on words here which may be suggested by a similar pun in English: "The Great Wan is dead, but is not *this one* preserving his Way?"

† See supra, p. 373.

When Confucius died, after three years had elapsed, his disciples collected their baggage, and prepared to return to their several homes. But on entering to take their leave of Tzu Kung, as they looked toward one another, they wailed, till they all lost their voices. After this they returned to their homes, but Tzu Kung went back, and built a house for himself on the altar-ground, where he lived alone three years, before he returned home.[65]

This was, presumably, the beginning of the Confucian school. Most of its members—said to have numbered seventy in all—scattered, and offered their services to the feudal lords. "The important ones," says Ssu-ma Ch'ien, "became teachers and ministers (of the feudal lords). The lesser ones became friends and teachers of the officials or went into retirement and were no longer seen." [66] Some started schools devoted to spreading the teachings of the Master. All helped during the next generation to gather the material which was ultimately fashioned into the Analects. Gradually during a period of three or four centuries the Confucian school produced the Great Learning, the Doctrine of the Mean, the Book of Filial Piety (the *Hsiao Ching*, destined to become a great favorite but not to be listed in the canon of the Four Books), the present Book of Rites, and the commentaries on the Book of Changes and on the Annals of Spring and Autumn. Some other writings, which have not survived, came from their hands. Among the leaders of the school in the second generation was Tzu Ssu, the scholarly grandson of Confucius, who like his grandfather devoted himself to teaching.

The spread of Confucian thought was impeded, however, by two factors, the rapid decay of the Chou feudal system during the Warring States Period (403–221 B.C.), and the rise in this period of the many different schools of thought which proposed moral and political solutions for the perplexities of the times. Only the princes descended from the old feudal families, and the usurpers who wished to keep their positions by a prolongation of the feudal order, listened readily to the Confucian scholars. But though many of the feudal princes would have liked to see Confucianism make headway, they thought it had no chance. The world was changing. And furthermore in the community at large there was widespread scorn of the highbrow *ju chiao* (the "scholar—or literatus —school") and its advocates.

We can understand this better if we look briefly now at some of the rival schools of thought.

Rival Views: (1) *The Taoists*

The compilers of the Tao Te Ching were not gentle toward the

Confucians. The scorn they felt toward all advocates of social discipline
or managed economy was directed especially at the Confucians (although Mohists and Legalists were just as abhorrent to them). Consider
the implications of these verses:

> The man of superior virtue never acts,
> 　　Nor ever (does so) with an ulterior motive.
> The man of inferior virtue acts,
> 　　And (does so) with an ulterior motive . . .
> (When) the man of superior *li* acts and finds no response,
> He rolls up his sleeves to force it on others.
>
> Therefore:
> After Tao is lost, then (arises the doctrine of) kindness,
> After kindness is lost, then (arises the doctrine of) justice.
> After justice is lost, then (arises the doctrine of) *li.*
> Now *li* is the thinning out of loyalty and honesty of heart.
> And the beginning of chaos.[67]

Or of these, which seem directly aimed at Confucians:

> On the decline of the great Tao,
> 　　The doctrines of "love" and "justice" arose.
> When knowledge and cleverness appeared,
> 　　Great hypocrisy followed in its wake.
>
> When the six relationships no longer lived at peace,
> 　　There was (praise of) "kind parents" and "filial sons."
> When the country fell into chaos and misrule,
> 　　There was (praise of) "loyal ministers." [68]

Though Chuang-tzu writes at greater length, and with equal scorn,
he does not achieve a more rapier-like thrust than this, even when he
says:

Of old the Yellow Emperor first interfered with the natural goodness of
the heart of man, by means of charity and duty. In consequence, Yao and
Shun . . . tortured the people's internal economy in order to conform to
charity and duty. They exhausted the people's energies to live in accordance
with the laws and statutes. Even then they did not succeed . . . By and by,
the Confucianists and the Motseanists* arose; and then came confusion between joy and anger, fraud between the simple and the cunning, recrimina-
tion between the virtuous and the evil-minded, slander between the honest
and the liars, and the world order collapsed . . .

Then, when dead men lay about pillowed on each other's corpses, when
. . . criminals were seen everywhere, then the Confucianists and the

* Or Mohists. See next page.

Motseanists bustled about and rolled up their sleeves in the midst of gyves and fetters! Alas, they know not shame, nor what it is to blush! [69]

But sometimes Chuang-tzu preferred to laugh at Confucius by making him say Taoist things, as in this delicious bit of mockery:

> Yen Huei spoke to Chungni (Confucius), "I am getting on."
> "How so?" asked the latter.
> "I have got rid of charity and duty," replied the former.
> "Very good," replied Chungni, "but not quite perfect."
> Another day, Yen Huei met Chungni and said, "I am getting on."
> "How so?"
> "I can forget myself while sitting," replied Yen Huei.
> "What do you mean by that?" said Chungni, changing his countenance.
> "I have freed myself from my body," answered Yen Huei. "I have discarded my reasoning powers. And by thus getting rid of my body and mind, I have become One with the Infinite. This is what I mean by forgetting myself while sitting."
> "If you have become One," said Chungni, "there can be no room for bias. If you have lost yourself, there can be no more hindrance. Perhaps you are really a wise one. I trust to be allowed to follow in your steps." [70]

Rival Views: (2) The Mohists

Another sort of rivalry was expressed by the philosopher Mo-tzu or Mo Ti (ca. 468–390 B.C.). He was an earnest, humane sort of man, who thought that the government should operate strictly under religious sanctions, always insist on simplicity and thrift everywhere, and do away with all Chou institutions, in order to build up a community of workers generally alike in station and filled with homely good will and brotherly kindness toward each other and all men. In some ways he was a proto-Communist.

Even though his school of thought died out and his name was for two thousand years known only to Chinese scholars, Mo-tzu was an important figure in his time, and remains so in any history of Chinese philosophy and religion. He lived at the height of the dislocations of the Warring States Period, for he was born not long after the death of Confucius, probably in Lu. He seems to have spent his early life under Confucian influence and for a short time became an official in Sung and then an envoy from Sung to Wei. He broke away from Confucianism and adopted a less formal, more broadly democratic attitude, perhaps as a result of living in Sung, where the Chou culture was apparently regarded by the inhabitants as an oppressive system.

Mo-tzu was motivated by two major aims. The first was to unite all his fellowmen in a working brotherhood altruistically devoted to the common good, and the second was to have all men do the will of Heaven and the spirits, Heaven being conceived as the Sovereign on High (Shang-ti), from whom a universal love or benevolence is flowing out to all creatures.

In pursuing the first aim, Mo-tzu combined love of mankind with a hard-headed utilitarian logic:

> Mutual attacks among states, mutual usurpation among houses, mutual injuries among individuals; the lack of grace and loyalty between ruler and ruled, the lack of affection and filial piety between father and son, the lack of harmony between elder and younger brothers—these are the major calamities in the world.
>
> But whence did these calamities arise? . . .
>
> They arise out of want of mutual love. At present feudal lords have learned only to love their own states and not those of others. Therefore they do not scruple about attacking other states. The heads of houses have learned only to love their own houses and not those of others. Therefore they do not scruple about usurping other houses. And individuals have learned only to love themselves and not others. Therefore they do not scruple about injuring others . . . Therefore all the calamities, strifes, complaints, and hatred in the world have arisen out of want of mutual love . . .
>
> How can we have the condition altered?
>
> It is to be altered by the way of universal love and mutual aid.
>
> But what is the way of universal love and mutual aid?
>
> It is to regard the state of others as one's own, the houses of others as one's own, the persons of others as one's self. When feudal lords love one another there will be no more war; when heads of houses love one another there will be no more mutual usurpation; when individuals love one another there will be no more mutual injury. When ruler and ruled love each other they will be gracious and loyal; when father and son love each other they will be affectionate and filial; when elder and younger brothers love each other they will be harmonious. When all the people in the world love one another, then the strong will not overpower the weak, the many will not oppress the few, the wealthy will not mock the poor, the honored will not disdain the humble, and the cunning will not deceive the simple. And it is all due to mutual love that calamities, strifes, complaints, and hatred are prevented from arising. Therefore the benevolent exalt it.[71]

Lest anyone should think that this is all impractical idealism, Mo-tzu asserts: "If it were not useful then even I would disapprove of it. But how can there be anything that is good but not useful?" [72]

The essence of his thesis is that the principle of universal love and mutual aid "pays off," as we say today. "Whoever loves others is loved by others; whoever benefits others is benefited by others; whoever hates others is hated by others; whoever injures others is injured by others." [73] Love pays all around, while hate never works. Unfortunately, "the gentlemen of the world" fail to see that this is so.

Within the state there should be no waste of wealth nor of the time of the laboring man that means wealth. Time-consuming and expensive rituals, ceremonies with long passages of music, and the like, were to be pared down to a minimum. It was not that they were evil in themselves, but they took too much time and were useless in promoting increase of wealth and of population. He condemned for like reasons the economic waste of the funerals so beloved of the Confucians; funerals and mourning periods should be simplified and shortened, he insisted. All pious and cultural embroideries on life should be minimized until the common welfare was better served. Even recreation was out of the question.

This reasoning brought down on Mo-tzu the wrath of Confucians and Taoists alike. They said he sacrificed culture and the amenities that make life pleasant for bare economic benefit. In words of condemnation that were to carry great weight in the future and help to keep the tide running against Mo-tzu, the Confucian scholar, Mencius, whom we shall soon be meeting, said:

The words of Yang Chu° and Mo Ti fill the empire. If you listen to people's discourses throughout it, you will find that they have adopted the views of the one or the other. Now, Yang's principle is—"Each for himself"—which does not acknowledge the claims of the sovereign. Mo's principle is—"To love all equally"—which does not acknowledge the peculiar affection due to a father. To acknowledge neither king nor father is to be in the state of a beast.[74]

But Mo-tzu, who never lived to hear but actually anticipated these criticisms, found justification for his way of life in the sanctions of Heaven. He was sure of two things: first, that Heaven *wanted* men to love each other equally, and secondly, that this belief had a high utility. It is a great incentive to universal love if men just believe that Heaven is the source and sanction of it. He severely condemned his contemporaries for scepticism with regard to the spirit-worship which the ancient sage-kings of the Hsia dynasty practiced, and he taught with religious fervor that Heaven above and Earth below are spheres in which a universal love is operating.

° See the previous chapter, p. 346.

I know Heaven loves men dearly . . . Heaven ordered the sun, the moon, and the stars . . . the four seasons . . . sent down snow, frost, rain, and dew . . . established the hills and rivers, ravines and valleys . . . appointed dukes and lords to reward the virtuous and punish the wicked . . . This has been taking place from antiquity to the present . . . Heaven loves the whole world universally. Everything is prepared for the good of man.[75]

Now, what does Heaven desire and what does it abominate? Heaven desires righteousness and abominates unrighteousness . . . For, with righteousness the world lives and without it the world dies; with it the world becomes rich and without it the world becomes poor; with it the world becomes orderly and without it the world becomes chaotic. And Heaven likes to have the world live and dislikes to have it die, likes to have it rich and dislikes to have it poor, and likes to have it orderly and dislikes to have it disorderly. Therefore we know Heaven desires righteousness and abominates unrighteousness.[76]

Mo-tzu was very well aware, it seems, that "the gentlemen of the world" would reject his proposals as impractical and revolutionary. Hence it is touching to hear him say:

The gentlemen of the world would say: "So far so good. It is of course very excellent when love becomes universal. But it is only a difficult and distant ideal." . . . This is simply because the gentlemen of the world do not recognize what is to the benefit of the world, or understand what is its calamity.[77]

Rival Views: (3) The Legalists

But of greater force at the time than Mo-tzu's attack upon the Confucians was the opposition of the so-called *School of Law*. This loosely associated group was composed of thinkers of a wide variety of views who agreed on one thing—that the disjointed and easy-going feudal system must give place to a social order held together by a tough, all-embracing law in all the states. The Confucian ideal of government by moral example and polite ideal behavior seemed impracticable to these hard-headed realists. Many of them laid down rules which startlingly anticipate present-day fascist totalitarianism; others took a position closely resembling Machiavelli's; the prince should, they said, make and unmake laws and alliances according to expediency and immediate advantage, *or* according to the changing drift of the Tao! Above all, since man is a creature to be ruled for his own good by playing upon his desire for material rewards and his fear of suffering and punishment, the laws must be made clear and strong, so that he will know what will bring rewards and what punishment. From the standpoint of the prince, men taken in the mass are like a flock of geese or a herd of deer; they need the discipline of strong laws to make them into one homogeneous whole, obedient to the prince, in peace and war.

The Legalists were powerful in the councils of the various states during the two closing centuries of the Warring States Period (from approximately 425-225 B.C.) and left a permanent impress on Chinese political and ethical theory. One of their earliest representatives was the ultra-realistic Shang Yang (Lord Shang), who served for some time as minister in the far western state of Ch'in, but finally became involved in a bloody intrigue, which led to his falling in battle and having his body crushed by chariots (338 B.C.). He advised his prince to confine his people to two activities only, farming and fighting.

> That through which the country is important and that through which the ruler is honored is force . . . Bring about a condition where people find it bitter not to till the soil, and where they find it dangerous not to fight.[78]

Among the Legalists, he was held to be the leader of those who emphasized strict administration of the law (*fa*). Another group, headed by the Shen Tao whom we met on pages 346 ff., emphasized princely power or authority (*shih*), alleging: "The reason why . . . subjects do not dare to deceive their ruler, is not because they love him, but because they fear his awe-inspiring power (*shih*)."[79] A third group emphasized *shu* or statescraft in the handling of men and affairs. Their leader was Han Fei.

Han Fei (d. 233 B.C.) was, like Shang Yang, an official in the state of Ch'in. He was, however, a more brilliant man and served under a more brilliant prince—the same who conquered and unified China not long after Han Fei's tragic death, the totalitarian emperor Shih Huang-ti. Along the way Han Fei acquired a deep admiration for the Tao Te Ching. He studied, too, under the Confucian scholar Hsün-tzu. These influences appear in his writings (the *Han-fei-tzu*) and give them a richness and depth not found in other Legalist treatises. Unfortunately, Han Fei fell a victim to intrigue, and while in prison was either poisoned or, as one story has it, committed suicide on the secret advice of his jealous erstwhile friend Li Ssu.

Han Fei believed that every man is naturally selfish and materialistic. His religion, his obedience to the ruler, his relations to parents, wife, and children, and his dealings with his fellowmen are all permeated by his desire for advantage.

That people love each other Han Fei did not deny; but such love, he maintained, was secondary to the desire for advantage.

There is nothing like the warm feelings between sons and fathers; and anyone who wants to act on the basis of public morality and issue prohibitions to those under his jurisdiction must needs take into account the intimacy of the flesh-and-blood relation. But there is something more [than love] in the relationship of fathers and mothers with their sons. If a son is born, then they congratulate each other. If a daughter is born, they (may) kill it. Both these have come out of the mother's womb, and when it is a boy, congratulations, when it is a girl, death! The parents are thinking of convenience later on. They calculate on longterm profit. Thus it is that even fathers and mothers in their relation to their children have calculating minds and treat them accordingly.[80]

He makes a better case of his thesis when he turns to the farm:

When a man sells his services as a farm hand, the master will give him good food at the expense of his own family, and pay him money and cloth. This is not because he loves the farm hand, but he says: "In this way, his ploughing of the ground will go deeper and his sowing of seeds be more active." The farm hand, on the other hand, exerts his strength and works busily at tilling and weeding. He exerts all his skill cultivating the fields. This is not because he loves his master, but he says: "In this way I shall have good soup, and money and cloth will come easily." Thus he expends his strength as if between them there were a bond of love such as that of father and son. Yet their hearts are centered on utility, and they both harbor the idea of serving themselves.[81]

Han Fei was impressed by certain lessons he had learned from a study of the Tao Te Ching. Men are as they are because of the Tao. The prince should emulate the Tao and be not too active nor too deeply involved in arranging every matter himself.

Be too great to be measured, too profound to be surveyed . . . Hence the saying, "The ruler must not reveal his wants; for if he reveals his wants, the ministers will polish their manners accordingly . . . If the likes and dislikes of the ruler be concealed, the true hearts of the ministers will be revealed." . . . Accordingly the ruler, wise though he may be, should not bother but let everything find its proper place.[82]

Han Fei warns his prince that statescraft and *wu-wei* have a close connection; he draws a clear and deadly picture of the perils that surround a prince, if he fails to be properly aloof and Tao-like.

Ministers, in relation to the ruler, have no tie of kinship, but serve him solely because constrained by the force of circumstances. Therefore those who minister to a ruler always watch the mental condition of their master without stopping even for a moment; whereas the lord of men remains idle and arrogant over them . . .

If the lord of men has much confidence in his son, then wicked ministers will utilize his son to accomplish their selfish purposes . . . If the lord of men has much confidence in his wife, then wicked ministers will utilize her . . .

The physician sucks patients' cuts and holds their blood in his mouth, not because he is intimate with them like a blood relation, but because he expects profit from them. Likewise, when the cartwright finishes making carriages, he wants people to be rich and noble; when the carpenter finishes making coffins, he wants people to die early. Not that the cartwright is benevolent and the carpenter is cruel, but that unless people are noble, the carriages will not sell, and unless people die, the coffins will not be bought. Thus the carpenter's motive is not hatred for anybody, but his profits which are due to people's death. For the same reason, when the clique of the queen, the princess, the concubine, or the crown prince is formed, they want the ruler to die early; for, unless the ruler die, their positions will not be powerful. Their motive is not hatred for the ruler, but their profits are dependent on the ruler's death.

The hard, realist conclusion is then drawn:

Therefore the lord of men must specially mind those who will profit by his death.[83]

It was these thinkers of the School of Law who, as we have previously noted, prepared the ground for the ruthless and autocratic Shih Huang-ti, the "First Emperor." But we have run a little ahead of our story. Han Fei and his associates (but not Lord Shang) came after Mencius and Hsün-tzu, the great Confucian champions. They came at the end of the two-century movement which culminated in the political triumph of their conceptions. Meanwhile the Confucians had been struggling without much success for influence and power. Fortunately for their long-term prospects, a series of brilliant variations on the Confucian theme appeared from the pens of Mencius and Hsün-tzu, and Confucianism took on added significance.

Mencius: The "Orthodox" Champion

Born a little over a hundred years after the death of Confucius, this greatest writer of the Confucian school magnified and gave studied emphasis to the Master's belief in the innate goodness of man and the adequacy of the feudal system to develop and maintain that goodness. Mencius (or Meng K'o) was a native of T'sou, a small state near Lu, and early came under Confucian influence. The way in which his love of learning was aroused is told in a delightful tradition which caused later Chinese to regard his mother as an ideal parent. According to this apocryphal tale, his father died young, and his mother lived alone with her small son near a cemetery. After a while she began to worry, because she noticed that he was playing constantly at the etiquette of attending funerals; so she moved with him to a house near a market-place; whereupon the boy, influenced again by his environment, began to play at buying and selling. She liked this so little that she made haste to take a house near a school, in the expectation—which was fulfilled —that he would pattern his behavior after the pupils and teachers whom he observed.* In time he became a scholar in his own right, in a school which was, it is likely, conducted by disciples of Tsu Ssu, Confucius' grandson. Later, he sought office under the Duke of Ch'i, but the duke proving beyond "reform" (in the Confucian sense, of course), he departed, and like his Master, wandered from state to state, exhorting rulers to follow the Confucian way, but always in vain; so he found it expedient to retire to T'sou, his native place, to spend the rest of his days—until his death in 289 B.C., at the age of eighty-one—teaching and writing in the graceful, if somewhat academic style that won favor for the doctrines of Confucius among the intelligentsia of the time.

The mellow flavor and genial atmosphere of Mencius' writings are evident in almost any quotation from him.

He believed wholeheartedly in the innate goodness of human nature. Here are two famous passages in exposition of this theme:

> The tendency of man's nature to good is like the tendency of water to flow downwards. There are none but have this tendency to good, just as all water flows downwards.[84]
> If men become evil, that is not the fault of their original endowment. The sense of mercy is found in all men; the sense of shame is found in all men; the sense of respect is found in all men; the sense of right and wrong is found in all men. The sense of mercy is what we call· benevolence or charity. The sense of shame is what we call righteousness. The sense of respect is what we call propriety. The sense of right and wrong is what we call wisdom, or moral consciousness. Charity, righteousness, propriety and moral consciousness are not something that is drilled into us; we have got them originally with us.[85]

All men possess these fundamental qualities as "tender shoots"[86] within them, ready to grow. Sometimes they ripen into the fullness of the virtue that is seen in the moral nature of a Sage. No man is born without them. Oft-quoted by the Chinese themselves is this argument:

* This story, incidentally, neatly illustrates Mencius' teaching that surroundings so greatly influence human beings that all they need is the right kind.

All men have the sense of compassion for others . . . What I mean by all men having a sense of compassion is that if, for instance, a child is suddenly seen to be on the point of falling into a well, everybody without exception will have a sense of distress. It is not by reason of any close intimacy with the parents of the child, nor by reason of a desire for the praise of neighbors and friends, nor by reason of disliking to be known as the kind of man (who is not moved by compassion). From this point of view we observe that it is inhuman to have no sense of compassion, inhuman to have no sense of shame over wickedness, inhuman to have no sense of modesty and the need for yielding place to a better man, inhuman not to distinguish right and wrong.[87]

And yet all men, though morally equal in the sense that they are all alike essentially good, or good at heart, are not equal in moral achievement. Some use their minds; others do not. This creates distinctions between them which alter their status in a properly constituted society.

There is a saying, "Some labor with their minds, and some labor with their strength. Those who labor with their minds govern others; those who labor with their strength are governed by others. Those who are governed by others support them; those who govern others are supported by others." This is a principle universally recognized.[88]

This fact is so puzzling to one of Mencius' disciples that he asks: "All are equally men, but some are great men, and some are little men;

Mencius, according to an old print.

—how is this?" Mencius replies: "Those who follow that part of themselves which is great are great men; those who follow that part which is
little are little men." [89]

But why are not more great men in evidence? Mencius would seem
to suggest that environment and circumstances have a great deal to do
with the extent to which different men fulfil their natural powers.

In good years the children of the people are most of them good, while
in bad years the most of them abandon themselves to evil. It is not owing
to their natural powers conferred by heaven that they are thus different.
The abandonment is owing to the circumstances through which they allow
their minds to be ensnarled and drowned in evil.[90]

The best environment and the most encouraging circumstances for
the flowering out of men's essential goodness are found under a paternalistic feudal system, *provided the latter is administered for the benefit,
not of the aristocrats, but of the people.* It is recorded that when
Mencius went to see King Hsüan of Ch'i, the king, who had ambitions
to become the emperor of China, asked what virtues a man must display
to gain imperial sway. Mencius answered, "The love and protection of
the people."

The king asked again, "Is such a one as I competent to love and protect the people?" Mencius said, "Yes . . .

"Treat with the reverence due to age the elders in your own family,
so that the elders in the families of others shall be similarly treated; treat
with the kindness due to youth the young in your family, so that the young
in the families of others shall be similarly treated:—do this, and the empire
may be made to go round in your palm . . .

"Now, if your Majesty will institute a government whose action shall be
all benevolent, this will cause all the officers in the empire to wish to stand
in your Majesty's court, and the farmers all to wish to plough in your
Majesty's fields, and the merchants, both travelling and stationary, all to wish
to store their goods in your Majesty's market-places." [91]

It may thus be seen that, though Mencius is conservative so far as
the *form* of his ideal society is concerned—it is the old feudal system—
yet he makes a strong point of it that:

The people are the most important element in the state . . . Therefore
to gain the peasantry is the way to become Emperor.[92]

He hit hard at the Machiavellian councilors who made common cause
with Shang Yang and later Legalists.

Those who nowadays serve their sovereigns say, "We can for our sovereign enlarge the limits of the cultivated ground, and fill his treasuries and

arsenals." Such persons are nowadays called "Good ministers," but anciently they were called "Robbers of the people." [93]

Mencius realized full well from studying his times that war destroyed the possibility of attaining his ideals of government, and so he constantly inveighed against it. War-makers are also "Robbers of the people." But he had some over-beliefs in this connection. War not only harms the state but it signifies Heaven's punishment for offences against its dispensations. When a kingdom is badly governed, Heaven lets the strong triumph over the weak, until corruption is unbounded. Then the righteous, thoroughly aroused, unite in rebellion, and, with Heaven's sanction, drive the hopelessly corrupt ruler from his throne.

This brings us to Mencius' religious views, a type of mysticism. He believed like Confucius in a guiding will or appointment of Heaven. Heaven sees and hears; and "there is an appointment for everything." [94] One who exercises his mind to the utmost, and studies his own nature, knows Heaven, and Heaven's will. It is Heaven that creates the inner disposition.

What belongs by his nature to the superior man cannot be increased by the largeness of his sphere of action, nor diminished by his dwelling in poverty and retirement;—for this reason, that it is determinately apportioned to him by Heaven.[95]

To look with sincerity into this inner disposition is to know Heaven through it. In contradistinction to the Taoists, Mencius believed that the predispositions toward moral order are complete within us; so, as Dr. Chan Wing-tsit puts it, "instead of looking to nature in order to know ourselves, we look within ourselves in order to know nature." [96] It is thus that we may fulfil our destiny as Heaven prepares it for us.

At this point Mencius made a suggestion which was to have great influence, over a thousand years later, on the Neo-Confucians. He believed that within each person there is a "vast-flowing vital energy"; [97] he called it *ch'i*, a sort of *élan vital*. Anyone who lives rightly removes within himself the obstructions to the free flow of this spiritual force. It will not do to try to help its growth, he said; it is already there as a great potential of force; and all it needs is to have the channels cleared for it by uprightness, and then it will flow. The spiritual man thus gains a power which projects his influence far and wide.

Such is the nature of this energy that it is immensely great and immensely strong, and if it be nourished by uprightness and so sustain no injury, then it pervades the whole space between the heavens and the earth.[98]

To make a perhaps over-sharp distinction between Mencius' point of view and that of the Taoists, we may say that the latter found the Tao in Nature outside them, where he found it flowing deep within himself.

Later generations were to play down Mencius' confidence in the goodness of man; but his optimism, gentleness, love of wisdom, and pacifism were eventually to increase his influence among the literati, so that he ultimately took rank next to Confucius in Confucian eyes.

Hsün-tzu: The "Heterodox" Champion

Born a little before the death of Mencius, Hsün-tzu had greater immediate influence. This was in part due to his many-sidedness. He came to some extent under the influence both of the Taoists, on the one hand, and of the Legalists on the other. Like the latter he exalted the functions and prerogatives of the state, and was brutally realistic about the weaknesses of human nature.

Hsün-tzu or Hsün Ch'ing (ca. 298–238 B.C.) was a native of Chao, but much of his life was spent in Ch'i, where he was one of the "great officers" of the court and an active member of a group of scholars and teachers at the capital. He taught Han Fei and Li Ssu, who became leaders in Legalist circles. On being the victim of slander, he went to Ch'u, where he spent his declining years as a magistrate at Lan-ling.

In developing his philosophy Hsün-tzu rejected the two cardinal principles of Mencius, that man's nature is innately good, and that Heaven watches over earth with something of a personal concern. He held that "man is by nature bad; his goodness is only acquired training." [99] Though he is capable, under proper conditions, of indefinite improvement, left to himself he grows crooked, like some sapling that must be tied into position before it will grow straight. The restraints which force improvement on his unruly nature are the rules of propriety and the laws compelling respect for property and the personal rights of others. Education of the right kind helps to subdue the bad in human nature and develop the good.

These views led Hsün-tzu to emphasize, even more than Confucius did, the importance of *li*, the ceremonies and rules of proper conduct which are the legacy left by the great sage-kings to after-times. The state should undertake to enforce education in *li* upon disorderly humanity.

The nature of man is evil . . . Therefore to give rein to man's original nature, to follow man's feelings, inevitably results in strife and rapacity . . .

Crooked wood needs to undergo steaming and bending to conform to the carpenter's rule; then only is it straight. Blunt metal needs to undergo grinding and whetting; then only is it sharp. The original nature of man is evil, so he needs to undergo the instruction of teachers and laws, then only will he be upright.[100]

Against the Mencian view that, even though the rules of proper conduct are just the accumulation of acquired training, after all the sage-kings *could* bring them forth, and thus they are from or out of man's nature anyway, Hsün-tzu argued:

The relation of the Sage to the rules of proper conduct (Li) and justice (Yi) and accumulated acquired training is the same as that of the potter and the clay: he brings the pottery into being [by pounding and molding the clay].[101]

The sage-kings knew that man's nature is evil, corrupt, rebellious, and disorderly; hence they set forth clearly the rules of proper conduct to reform him; they were aware that:

If a man is without a teacher or precepts, then if he is intelligent, he will certainly become a robber; if he is brave, he will certainly become a murderer; if he has ability, he will certainly cause disorder; if he is a dialectician, he will certainly go far from the truth. [But] if he has a teacher and precepts, then if he is intelligent, he will quickly become learned; if he is brave, he will quickly become awe-inspiring; if he has ability, he will quickly become perfect; if he is a dialectician, he will quickly be able to determine the truth or falsity of things.[102]

In his attitude toward Heaven (T'ien), Hsün-tzu leaned far over in the direction of the Taoists' impersonal, naturalistic Way (Tao). Heaven is not to be anthropomorphically viewed, for it is just our name for the law of compensation operating within cosmic events; and one cannot ever expect it to respond to prayer.

One ought not to grumble at Heaven that things happen according to its Way (Tao). . . . When stars fall or the sacred tree groans, the people of the whole state are afraid. They ask, "Why is it?" I answer: There is no reason. This is due to a modification of Heaven and Earth, to the mutation of *Yin* and *Yang*. . . . If people pray for rain and get rain, why is that? I answer: There is no reason for it. If people do not pray for rain, it will nevertheless rain.[103]

Heaven will not abolish winter just because mankind does not like cold weather. Nor will Earth shrink because we object to long distance . . .

As long as we practice thriftiness and enrich the sources of our wealth, Heaven is powerless to make us poor. Likewise, Heaven can hardly make us sick if we nourish ourselves well, take proper care, and exercise regularly. . . .

The way to do things is neither the way of Heaven nor that of Earth but that of Man.[104]

All natural events, then, come to pass according to natural law. There are no supernatural agencies anywhere. So sure was Hsün-tzu of this that he took the radical step of denying the existence of spirits: neither the popular gods nor the demons nor even the ancestral spirits exist. Divination may have some uncertain bearing on the future; but when the knowing decide an important affair after divination, this is not because they think in this way they will get what they seek, but only to "gloss over the matter"!

The people think it is supernatural. He who thinks it is glossing over the matter is fortunate; he who thinks it is supernatural is unfortunate.[105]

Hsün-tzu was obliged in the light of these naturalistic views to reevaluate the funeral and sacrificial ceremonies inherited from the great sage-kings. He took a down-to-earth view of the matter. Rites and ceremonies are good for people. Nothing supernatural occurs during them; but they have a valuable subjective effect in allowing the expression and catharsis of human feeling, while also introducing beauty into human life, and cultivating the sense of propriety.

Hence I say: Sacrifice is because of the emotions produced by memories, ideas, thoughts, and longings; it is the extreme of loyalty, faithfulness, love and reverence; it is the greatest thing of the rites and of beautiful actions. If there were no Sages, no one could have understood this. The Sage plainly understands it; the official observes it; among the people it becomes an established custom. Among superior men it is considered to be a human practice; among the common people it is considered to be serving the spirits.[106]

The aesthetic value of ceremony appealed especially to Hsün-tzu.

All rites, if for the service of the living, are to beautify joy; or if to send off the dead, they are to beautify sorrow; or if for sacrifice, they are to beautify reverence; or if they are military, they are to beautify majesty.[107]

On the whole, Hsün-tzu was unwilling to go beyond what was required to guide the living. In funerals, for example, the living properly desire to "send off" the dead as if they were still living and to beautify their departure. Therefore the living perform the traditional rituals with thoroughness and care. The carriages, and all the other articles traditionally sent along with the dead, are duly burned or buried, but—

The horses are sent away and informed that they are not to be buried . . . The metal rein-ends, the reins, the horse-collars do not go into the grave . . . Things for the dead are showy, but not useful.[108]

This may be called a strictly *rational* propriety, expressing and yet reining in the emotions, lest they lead to extravagance, an unreasoning waste. The emotions have their place; but they are not to be allowed too much scope. There should be balance here as elsewhere. Each age should judge for itself what is useful in its traditions.

The rules of proper conduct (Li) cut off that which is too long and stretch out that which is too short; they diminish that which is too much and increase that which is insufficient; they attain to the beauty of love and reverence, and they strengthen the excellence of character and right moral feeling . . . They provide for weeping and sorrow, but do not go so far as an undue degree of distress and self-injury. This is the middle path of the rites (Li) . . . Anything beyond this is evil.[109]

Hsün-tzu was no narrow Confucian. He found such values in the Taoist point of view that he was led to equate Li with the Tao, the latter being in his conception the cosmological principle "whereby Heaven and Earth unite, whereby the sun and moon are bright, whereby the four seasons are ordered, whereby the stars move in their courses," and "whereby joy and anger keep their proper place." [110] He also showed the extent of Taoist influence upon him in holding that meditative reflection confirms the faith that the universe at large tends steadily toward perfection and in its impersonal way is on the side of the righteous.

The Triumph of the Confucians under the Early Han

The Legalists scored their greatest victory in the reign of Shih Huang-ti, but with the fall of his dynasty their school gradually disintegrated. Only those Legalist doctrines which were taken up by the Confucians ultimately entered the accepted body of Chinese political thought; for China had not taken kindly to the arbitrariness of the regime of Shih Huang-ti and his attempted complete reordering of their lives and thinking. During the first years of the Early Han dynasty the nation breathed a sigh of relief and relaxed into a Taoist-like quietude, as though worn out by the late disturbances. The first Han emperors encouraged this psychological reaction. Taoism met with their approval. The people turned from fighting to dreaming. The Taoist geomancers were able to attract widespread attention to their alchemy and experimentation with the pill of immortality. But the Confucians were also busy. Gradually they were repossessing themselves of copies—in the New Script—of the books which Shih Huang-ti had taken from them and burned. They had not liked the regimentation of life under Shih Huang-ti, but they liked anarchistic drifting and disorganization less; so they appealed to the Han emperors to reinstitute order and proper procedure in official life.

Not, however, until the reign of the great Han emperor Wu Ti, to whom we have already referred, were their pleas heeded. It was probably in 136 B.C., in the fourth year of that reign, that the Confucian scholar Tung Chung-shu (179?–104 B.C.) presented his famous memorial to the emperor. Knowing the emperor to be desirous of greater national unity, he reminded that monarch that general unification would not come so long as the teachers and philosophic schools of the day had such diverse standards. The people did not know what to cling to, and the government statutes were in a state of confusion. The only way out, said Tung Chung-shu, was a return to the Six Disciplines of Confucius. All other standards should be "cut short" and not allowed to progress further. Only thus could the government statutes be made consistent and the people know what to follow. He accompanied this firm and unequivocal proposal with the suggestion that the emperor found an imperial academy or college for the training of officials in the uniform procedures which the Confucians had worked out on the basis of the best experience of the past. The emperor was impressed. He adopted Tung Chung-shu's suggestions. The Confucians were put in charge of a government-sponsored system of education, designed to train officials.

Thereupon Confucianism began a two-thousand year career as the predominant intellectual discipline used in the training of the governing class. It was not the Confucianism of earlier times which triumphed, however; it was Confucianism (1) modified by a tendency to magnify Confucius into a more than human being, (2) infused with Legalist ideas as to the nature of the enlarged bureaucracy which was needed to cope with the problems of an empire grown so vast as to lie on the borders of India, stretch into central Asia, and penetrate Korea, and (3) tempered with Mo-tzu's conviction that a government that was to win and hold the common people must have back of it the sanctions of religion—the approval of Heaven above and the spirits below.

Confucian Scholasticism and Rationalism

From the intellectual standpoint, Confucianism reached the end of its formative period when the Later Han dynasty (23–220 A.D.) began. In fact, it would be correct to say, with Dr. Y. L. Fung, that this was true even earlier; for "with the putting into practice of Tung Chung-shu's suggestion, the Period of the Philosophers came to an end, and that of the Study of the Classics commenced." [111] The shift was from formative thinking to textual criticism, systematization, and syncretism.

This appears in the writings of Tung Chung-shu himself. Self-consciously more a scholar than an imperial counsellor, he followed Hsün-tzu rather than Mencius, and sought to absorb into Confucianism the truth elements, as he saw them, in Taoist *yin-yang* interactionism and in the Five Forces theories. His pure scholasticism may be seen in a sentence or two from his treatises.

> Heaven has Five Forces, first Wood, second Fire, third Soil, fourth Metal, fifth Water. . . .
> These Five Forces correspond to the actions of filial sons and loyal ministers . . . Thus, as a son welcomes the completion of his years (of nurture), so Fire delights in Wood; and, as (the time comes when) the son buries his father, so (the time comes when) Water conquers Metal. Also the service of one's sovereign is like the reverent service Soil renders to Heaven. Thus we may well say that there are Force men, and that there are both Five Forces, each keeping its right turn, and Five-Force officials, each doing his utmost.[112]

And so forth. This sort of scholasticism was to absorb the Confucians for centuries.

But the systematizers were not to have it all their own way. Realizing perhaps that scholasticism already had or would become "a matter of intellectual sport, a game of puzzles, and finally a superstition," [113] Wang Ch'ung (ca. 27–100 A.D.), a left-wing rationalist of the Confucian school, strove for a less theoretical, and a more empirical, viewpoint. He attacked the superstition and supernaturalism he found in religion. He was a thorough-going naturalist and humanist, armed with all the vigor and clarity of style characteristic of so many of the Chinese writers whom we have quoted. It would be too bad not to quote him. The following passages speak for themselves:

> The Scholars at the present day have a passion for believing that what their teachers say is (genuinely) old, and they regard the words of worthies and sages as all of the very essence of truth. In expounding and learning these words off by heart, they do not realize that there are any difficulties requiring explanation.[114]
> The common idea is that the dead become ghosts, have knowledge, and can injure people . . . (I maintain that) the dead do not become ghosts, have no consciousness, and cannot injure people. How do I prove my position? By means of other beings. Man is a being and other creatures also are beings. When they die, they do not become ghosts: why then should man alone when he dies be able to become a ghost? [115]

At the height of summer, thunder and lightning come with tremendous force, splitting trees, demolishing houses, and from time to time killing people. The common idea is that this splitting of trees and demolishing of houses is Heaven setting a dragon to work. And when the thunder and lightning rush on people and kill them, this is described as due to hidden faults, for example, people eating unclean things, and so Heaven in its anger striking them and killing them. The roar of the thunder is the voice of Heaven's anger, like men gasping with rage . . . This is all nonsense.[116]

Wang Ch'ung tried also to reverse the tendency to convert the fallible man Confucius into some kind of infallible authority touched with the qualities of divinity. In his treatment of the sayings in the Analects, he examined the teachings of Confucius as casually and critically as though he were looking into the opinions of a person who had to establish his authority like anyone else—by winning the assent of the reason.

Confucianism and Buddhism

The coming of Buddhism to China put Confucianism to a severe test. Taoism felt far less antipathy to the new religion when it first appeared, and was aroused to resistance only by jealousy. But all orthodox Confucians remained stiff in opposition. Buddhism seemed to them too other-worldly and nihilistic; they did not like the concentration of attention on transmigration, birth, and death; above all they condemned the Buddhists, as they already had the Taoists, for diverting men from the service of society to self-salvation. Yet two factors operated to make their protests without much effect: the novelty and freshness of Buddhism, and the formal and lifeless character of their own scholasticism and of the official ritualism and ceremony practiced in the court and at the Confucian temples which by this time had appeared.* Moreover, the Later Han dynasty had collapsed in the turmoil in which the Three Kingdoms (A.D. 220–280) rose up to divide China. For three hundred and fifty years China was to suffer inroads by "barbarians" from the north, and to know disunion and misery. Many brilliant minds, distracted by the chaos, were unable to embrace Buddhism, yet were equally repelled by Confucian formalism and "ineptitude."

Caught between the scoffing Taoists on the one hand, and the Buddhists, on the other, riding high on the success of the spectacular and glamorous Mahayana, the Confucians weakened. Except for a few stern

---

* See the final section of this chapter for an explanation of how these temples appeared.

Old Text die-hards who would not yield, they began to add semi-Buddhist touches to their Confucian temples, and warmed up their beliefs about Confucius with stories of miracles and signs in heaven and on earth. Original Confucianism had been singularly free from legend and miracle; but now that even the Taoists attributed miracles to Confucius, the Confucians insensibly veered from their orthodox course toward meeting the Buddhist and Taoist challenges. They adopted stories of the appearance of a unicorn before Confucius' birth, saying his mother even tied a ribbon on its horn. On the night of his birth two dragons appeared, and the five planets drew near in the shapes of interested old men. Heavenly harmonies sounded, and a voice said: "Divine harmony strikes the ear, because Heaven has caused a saint to be born. His doctrine will be the law of the world." [117] Other stories, circulated perhaps by the Taoists before the Confucianists themselves believed them, told how when Confucius was dying a meteor descended and turned into an inscribed jade tablet; and how when Shih Huang-ti ordered his soldiers to open Confucius' tomb, they found within it a written prophecy of this very event and a prediction of the death of the First Emperor, which was later exactly verified.

One should not, probably, lay all this entirely to the influence of Taoism and Buddhism; it might have happened anyway.

What could not have occurred, however, without the presence of rival faiths was the rise of scholars who attempted a syncretism of the *San Chiao* ("The Three Religions").* On the Taoist side there was T'an Ch'iao (probably 6th century) who held that the Tao is the central or underlying principle of all three religions. The Buddhists on their part proved not averse to this type of thinking, for they quoted favorably Li Shih-ch'ien (ca. 590 A.D.), who said Buddhism was the sun, Taoism the moon, and Confucianism the five planets; while later on a Buddhist monk founded a cult which had official sanction for a long time and which placed the images of Confucius, Lao-tzu, and Buddha side by side on the altar. Among the Confucians there was Wang T'ung (583–616 A.D.), who held that the doctrine of the mean or middle way is the common ground between the three religions.

But Confucianism was able nevertheless to maintain its distinctive character. It had a steadying factor to keep it on a straight course—the curriculum of its school. So long as the imperial academy and the lesser schools drilled their students in the Analects and the Five Classics—

---

* We have already seen in the chapter on The Religious Development of Buddhism how Buddhism combined with Chinese thought to produce such varieties of Buddhism as the Ch'an (or Zen) sects.

particularly the Li Chi and the Ch'un Ch'iu—Confucianism was safe from the temptation to stray too far from its historic basis. Indeed its hard, resistant core finally gave rise to a Confucian revival.

Neo-Confucianism

The first sign that such a revival would eventually come about was the famous protest made by the scholar Han Yü to the thirteenth emperor of the T'ang dynasty, Hsien Tsung, concerning the Bone of the Buddha. Han Yü (or Han T'ui-chih, 767–824 A.D.) was a valiant champion of the Mencian point of view in Confucianism. His protest was made in 820 A.D., when the emperor made a great pageant of receiving from the Buddhist priests, marching to him in public procession, a bone that was reputed to be a relic of the Buddha. Han Yü addressed a vigorous memorial to the emperor, reminding him that the founder of the T'ang dynasty had contemplated exterminating Buddhism, because its founder was a foreigner who could not speak Chinese, wore outlandish clothes such as a barbarian would wear, and had no conception of the sacred ties that bind ruler and subject, or father and son. At that time, he went on, Kao Tsu had unfortunately been prevented from carrying out his intention by his foolish ministers. But now, Han Yü begged, let the present emperor give the noxious, putrid bone to the public executioner so that he might throw it in the water or burn it in a fire—and, if the Buddha became angered at such action, let the blame be upon him, Han Yü, as alone responsible!

For these spirited words the audacious scholar was banished to an official post in the far south, where he languished in virtual exile.

The Confucian revival foreshadowed by Han Yü came two centuries later during a period of distressing social change. The Sung dynasty (960–1279 A.D.) which, after an interval of civil wars, succeeded the brilliant T'ang dynasty, was perhaps equally great in the things of the spirit, but was dogged by disastrous military and political failures. Whereas the T'angs had come to grips with and mastered the "barbarian" tribes that surrounded China, and had extended the domain of their empire from Korea in the northeast to Afghanistan on the west, the Sungs, made inept and weak by internal corruption, failed to prevent the resurgence of the border tribes. First the Kitans, then the Chins, and finally the Mongols, fiercer yet, poured across the Yellow River and down to the Yangtse, the Mongols finally being able, under Kublai Khan, to wipe out the dynasty altogether by conquering the regions south of the Yangtse and even rolling on into Indo-China and Burma.

It was natural that the Chinese should from the very beginning of these events react to conquest by withdrawing into themselves until their conquerors should once more be absorbed and made over by Chinese culture. In particular there was a return to the older Confucianism. Han Yü had been a very early voice presaging this, but the true Neo-Confucian revival did not begin until it was evident that the Sung dynasty was to fall on evil days. The two figures within the movement whom we shall consider are only the most celebrated of a large group of scholars expressing the related views which these two ably brought together and systematized. Some of the names are worth rehearsing: Hu Yüan (993–1059), who started the movement, Chou Tun-i (1017–1073), Shao Yung (1011–1077), Chang Tsai (1020–1076), and the inimitable Cheng brothers (Hao, 1032–1086, and Yi, 1033–1107), who between them gave rise to two divergent schools among the Neo-Confucians, although this was not realized at the time. The younger brother, Yi, initiated the School of Laws and Principles which Chu Hsi systematized, while Hao, the elder brother, started a trend which led to the rise of the School of Mind championed by Wang Yang-ming. What the Neo-Confucians professed to do was to get back to pure Confucianism, before there had been any manifest borrowing from Taoist and Buddhist sources.

Chu Hsi (1130–1200) was a scholar of the first rank, whose commentaries on the Confucian classics were immediately recognized as the final words on the subject. In his distress at the invasions of the Chin tribes, he said such bitter things about the official appeasement policy that he incurred imperial displeasure. But his lectures at the White Deer Grotto drew distinguished audiences of scholars. Of his austere personal habits we learn from a Chinese biographer:

> Rising at dawn, he clothed himself decently and paid homage to his ancestors and to Confucius. Then he went to his study and attended to his daily work. Sitting or sleeping he held himself erect; working or resting he behaved according to the model of behavior prescribed by Confucius in his Classics. Everything in his home was permanently in good order, and in this way he lived from youth to old age.[118]

To Chu Hsi fell the lot of determining finally the question of Hsün-tzu's orthodoxy. He pronounced the earlier thinker a heretic for departing from Confucius' belief in the original goodness of human nature. This proved enough to set up Mencius, Hsün-tzu's rival, as the orthodox interpreter of Confucius' thought. But it was only one of Chu Hsi's services to Confucianism that he thus distinguished between the "sound" and "unsound" interpretations. His chief contribution to the Confucian

School lay in his clarifying the orthodox attitude toward the themes appearing in Taoism and Buddhism. In other words, he led the Neo-Confucians in their attempt to discuss the philosophical concepts of the rival religions, and to adapt what was sound in them.

The way in which Chu Hsi went about his task was to take key passages from the Confucian texts and use them as touchstones of truth and error. To cite one (the chief) instance, he selected the passage from the Great Learning in which appears the sentence, "To extend their knowledge to the utmost they [the ancients] investigated things." Chu Hsi interpreted this to mean that the ancients examined the world about them objectively, in order to increase their grasp of general truth. He concluded, in short, that the ancients thought Nature, quite apart from human nature, embodied laws or principles independent of the human mind.

In his objective examination of the cosmos, Chu Hsi, speaking for his fellow-Confucians as well as himself, was, he said, led to the view that all things are brought into being by the following two elements mentioned by Confucius and Mencius: vital (or physical) force (*ch'i*), and law or rational principle (*li*). The latter in its cosmic operations, where it may be called the *T'ai Chi* or Great Ultimate, impels the vital force to generate movement and change within matter; and thereby are produced the two energy-modes (*yang* and *yin*) and the five elements (fire, water, wood, metal, and earth). Every object in Nature exhibits some aspect of the rational law (*li*) or Great Ultimate that works within it. In the words of his summary:

With reference to the entire universe, there is in it one Great Ultimate. With reference to the myriad things, there is a Great Ultimate in each of them.[119]

This is true of man also. What we call his soul or nature is the supreme regulative principle of the universe working in him as mind or spirit. This law of his being works toward good; so man's nature is fundamentally good, whatever evil habits he may display.

The rational principle and the vital force interact in mutual dependence.

There is no Reason independent of the vital force, and there is no vital force independent of Reason . . .

The Great Ultimate is Reason, whereas activity and tranquility are the vital force. The two are mutually dependent and never separated. The Great Ultimate may be compared to a man, the activity and tranquility may be compared to a horse. The horse carries the man and the man rides on the horse. As the horse comes and goes, so does the man.[120]

Though the description so far might suggest it, this was not conceived to be a purely nonphysical process, for it results in the creation of matter. The Great Ultimate or Reason, constituting the metaphysical principle, "rides on" the activating or physical principle, *ch'i*; and when the pace is swift, the *yang* energy-mode is generated; when the pace slows down, the *yin* mode is produced. Once brought into being, the *yang* and *yin*, by their eternal interaction and alternation of dominance over each other, give rise to the energy-structures which are the Five Elements or the physical constituents of the "myriad things" of the material world.

Chu Hsi found in the concept of the Great Ultimate what he felt to be the truth element in Taoism; for the law or reason of any entity was its "right way to go" or *tao*. But he did not regard his T'ai Chi, as the Taoists did their Tao, as something "still and silent," nor did he think it operated to reduce all things ultimately to equality and indistinguishability; by its cooperation with vital energy it exhibits itself as a differentiating principle which may at any moment produce something new. At this point also, Chu Hsi disagreed with Buddhism. He could not conceive of reality as a Void (a something devoid of any assignable attributes), nor did he expect the universe to return again to the Void. There is a central harmony, but it is not a static nor a qualityless harmony; it is a dynamic harmony. The Great Ultimate never ceases to act, and therefore it is not to be identified with the Buddhist Ultimate within which the universe forms, flowers, deteriorates, and is finally swallowed up again. To use an American phrase, "there is always something doing."

Though he had gone pretty far toward rendering the older terminology no longer usable, Chu Hsi tried to make some concessions to the ancient conception of Heaven. He refused to be anthropomorphic, and indeed spoke of Heaven in such abstract language that he encouraged the agnostic tendency in Confucianism, but because his Great Ultimate is reason, he sensed behind the cosmos something like an ordering will. In a passage in which he summed up the opinion of the Classics, he wrote:

"These passages indicate that there is a man, *as it were*, in the heavens ruling all." [121]

In other respects he gave religion in its traditional forms little place. Worship of spirits and offerings to images even excited his contempt; and although he granted to ancestor-worship the slight basis which is found in biological and social immortality, he denied that the souls of ancestors exist: ancestor worship has the appropriateness and value which are derived from gratitude to forebears piously felt and expressed.

In his personal practice Chu Hsi found his spiritual and moral development best served by devoting a certain portion of each day to solitary meditation—something he called "silent sitting." It resembled the Buddhist *dhyana* or meditation. He wrote:

> Introspection is most effective when employed quietly. One should with eternal vigilance constantly examine himself. If he finds himself too talkative, he should quiet down. If he is careless, he should learn to be prudent. If he is too fresh and shallow, he should balance this with dignity and dependability.[122]

But he denied that this "self-correction through introspection" [123] was actually the Buddhist *dhyana* (or *Ch'an-ting*).

> Silent-sitting is not the Buddhist type of *Ch'an-ting* which requires the cessation of all processes of thinking. Mine is to help aim our mind so that it will not be distracted by conflicting streams of thought. When our mind is calm and undisturbed, concentration is a matter of course.[124]

As a matter of fact, for Chu Hsi meditation, as was natural in a Confucian, had more a moral than a metaphysical or mystical bearing. Feeling that "centrality is the order of the universe and harmony is its unalterable law," [125] he wished to get himself into the equable state that enabled him to apprehend this order and harmony, and to feel at one with the Reason in it. When he succeeded in doing so, he found that "all people are brothers and sisters, and all things are my companions." [126]

Because of his combination of manysidedness with practicality, Chu Hsi became, as we have little difficulty in being able to understand, the almost infallible interpreter of Confucianism from his time on. (He has been called the Thomas Aquinas of Confucianism.)

Yet he did not dominate the scene so completely that no other interpretations were countenanced. He perhaps carried the majority with him; but there were many Neo-Confucians, more under the spell of Buddhism and Taoism, who thought that the clue to the reason in things is to be found, not so much in the investigation of the reason in Nature as within the mind or consciousness of man. They therefore gave chief emphasis to an examination of the mental content disclosed in introspection. The greatest name of this group is that of Wang Yang-ming (1473–1529 A.D.), a scholar appearing two and a half centuries after Chu Hsi, when both the Sung and the Yüan (or Mongol) dynasties had passed into history and the Ming dynasty (1368–1644 A.D.) had for more than a hundred years demonstrated, in spite of licentiousness and corruption, its staying power. For offending a corrupt eunuch who had acquired great power in the imperial court, Wang Yang-ming was exiled for a time to a distant province, but he was able to summon up sufficient interior resources to spend the time in developing his philosophy. His reflections led him to say that objects are not independent of the mind, for the mind shapes them within itself. This emphasis on the part mind plays in constituting objects as they are known in experience may have been due to an experiment Wang Yang-ming performed when he was twenty-one. It seems he took seriously Chu Hsi's suggestion that to know the Reason in things one must investigate to the utmost all sorts of external objects. He chose his father's bamboo grove for a test of this method. For three days and nights, it is said, he sat among the bamboos, to see what they would teach him, and caught a bad cold without arriving at any satisfactory results. He concluded that, since objects do not put reason into the mind, the mind must put reason into them. In a modern interpreter's words:

> In the case of bamboo, for instance, . . . if one views it as a plant which is humble enough to be hollow inside, hardy enough to stay green the year round, plain enough to adorn itself with slender leaves instead of luxurious blossoms, and dignified enough to stand straight and erect, then one perceives a number of reasons in its worth as a garden companion.[127]

Our own minds, then, are the source of reasonableness in things.

All this had for Wang Yang-ming important moral bearings. The reason in us is a moral reason, and is not only intelligent but good. It is an inner light, an innate goodness. Knowledge of the good is not imparted to us from without, but is inborn; and if the inborn knowledge is clouded over, then all that is necessary is to have the reflective surface of the mind polished by teaching and experience.

> The mind may be compared to a mirror. . . . When, after effort has been made to polish the mirror, it is bright, the power of reflecting has not been lost.[128]

> The mind has the native ability to know. If one follows his (pure) mind, he naturally is able to know (what is morally good). When he sees his parents, he naturally knows what filial piety is; . . . when he sees a child fall into a well, he naturally knows what commiseration is. This is inborn knowledge of the good, without any necessity of going beyond the mind itself.[129]

In a further point that Wang Yang-ming makes we perceive resemblances to a central belief of Socrates. Knowledge of the good leads immediately to practice of the good. ("Knowledge," said Socrates, as we know, "*is* virtue.") Wang Yang-ming put it thus:

There has been no one who really has knowledge and yet fails to practice it . . . As soon as one perceives a bad odor, one already hates it.[130]

It is important, then, to keep the mirror of one's mind clear by eliminating the selfish desires that cloud it. This may be done only by practicing a "tranquil repose" resembling the meditative self-discipline of Ch'an (Zen) Buddhism, by which one may be purged of such desires.

This is not all of the story of the Confucian School. (We could go on to tell of the Neo-Confucians of the Ch'ing period.) But what has been told must surely exhibit Confucianism in its true light as a highly evolved philosophy of religion with a complexity and competence comparable to those which we have already examined elsewhere in the world.

IV THE STATE CULT OF CONFUCIUS

All this while a state cult honoring the spirit of Confucius had been in existence. It had developed slowly. The reason for this tardiness of growth is not far to seek. Confucius was in his own time unsuccessful as a public figure. Mencius, like his Master, was also unable to make a great mark in public affairs. For several hundred years after the Master's death no Confucian came anywhere to power long enough to make permanent changes in the official outlook on problems of government. But then, suddenly, when the ways and works of Shih Huang-ti, the First Emperor, had been swept away, and the Confucian Classics had been recovered, the Emperor Wu Ti of the Han dynasty (who, it will be remembered, reigned 141–87 B.C.) took up Confucianism, and made its teaching the policy of the state. For officialdom, this was a momentous decision, for from this time on, even when Taoist or Buddhist emperors sat on the throne, Confucius was honored by the state as a great sage and was periodically advanced in official status.

The progressive elevation of Confucius to higher and higher official rank makes an interesting story. At first only the K'ung family, and perhaps Confucius' immediate disciples, rendered to his spirit a regular worship. Later on, sacrifices were made at the grave of Confucius by politically minded sovereigns, anxious to conciliate local feelings. The first of these to do so was the Han Emperor Kao Tsu. Though himself inclined toward Taoism, he sacrificed three victims—an ox, a sheep, and a pig—when in 195 B.C. he passed through Lu on a tour of the empire and stopped at the grave of Confucius. Thereafter other emperors with an eye to political effect stopped off at the sage's grave to render tribute. In the year 1 A.D. the Emperor P'ing of the Han dynasty ordered the repair of the nearby temple of Confucius and elevated the sage to the rank of Duke. By this time readings, prayers, and gifts of money and silk were added to the sacrifices made at the grave. The habit of bestowing posthumous titles grew. At intervals during succeeding centuries various emperors bestowed upon Confucius honorific titles, such as "The Venerable, the Accomplished Sage," "The Sage of Former Times," and the like. He acquired a long string of such titles. His descendants also were elevated to nobility and made the recipients of state honors.

Another step in the development of the state cult came in 630 A.D. when the T'ang Emperor T'ai Tsung issued a decree obliging every prefecture of China to erect a state temple to Confucius, in which regular sacrifices to him were ordered. The same emperor converted these temples into national halls of fame, by placing tablets to distinguished scholars and literary men alongside that of Confucius, thus honoring both him and them. In the 8th century, and under the influence of Buddhism, a T'ang emperor adopted and carried out the suggestion that images of Confucius be placed in the Great Hall of the state temples and pictures of his chief followers be painted on the walls. For the next eight centuries Confucian temples had little to distinguish them from their Buddhist models.

The sacrifices offered to the spirit of Confucius became progressively more elaborate. The T'ang emperors came with great pomp, in spring and autumn, to the state temple at the capital, to add the dignity of their presence to the celebrations. It was customary that a bull, a pig, and a sheep be offered to Confucius' image, while dances and pantomimes were performed to stately music, and prayers were solemnly presented. By the time of the Mongol rulers the ritual of the sacrifices became still more impressive. Incense was freely used, and much formal kow-towing took place before the image of Confucius and the various altars. Hundreds of bronze, wood, and porcelain vessels were required for the ceremonies; two kinds of wine were offered; and an ox, five sheep, and five pigs, as well as much food, were presented. It was the opinion of the time, that the music and rites used in this worship of Confucius were those of an emperor, though the actual title of emperor (*Ti*) was withheld, because it was not deemed consistent with the practices of antiquity, and particularly not in accord with Confucius' teaching condemning bestowal of this title on men of less than imperial rank. However, there were those who said it would not have been too much if Confucius had been regarded as equal to Heaven.

In 1530 a remarkable reform in the cult of Confucius was effected, and proved permanent. The Ming emperor Chia Ching, on the advice of a learned Confucian scholar, revoked the lengthy and cumbrous titles borne by Confucius, and called him simply "Master K'ung, the Perfectly Holy Teacher of Antiquity." The temples to Confucius were ordered restored to their historic simplicity; the ceremonies were revised in accordance with the practices of antiquity; and the images of Confucius were replaced by tablets in the antique style, or by plain wood panels with written characters inscribed on them.

At the beginning of the present century, when the Manchus were vainly seeking to recover the good opinion of the Chinese, an edict was issued abolishing the old classical examination system in favor of more modern educational training. To make good whatever disrespect to the memory of Confucius was involved in this significant change, another edict was issued in 1906 making the sacrifices to Confucius equal with those offered to Heaven and Earth; but this signal honor to the Great Sage came too late to save the Manchus from the revolution that brought into being the Republic.

After 1911 the state cult of Confucius languished. With no emperor to participate in the worship of Heaven at the altar in Peking, the famous marble terraces fell into such neglect that sometimes grass grew in their crevasses. Only the Temple of Heaven near by was kept in order. Elsewhere, except for the temple at Confucius' birthplace, the state temples fell into disuse, many of them even becoming dilapidated in their utter abandonment.

V   RECENT CHANGES

In intermittent attempts after the Revolution of 1911 to recover itself, Confucianism had some bad moments. After the Republic had written into its constitution a grant of religious liberty to all, the attempt of the scholars who formed the Confucian Society to have Confucianism made the state religion failed. But the situation was not without some hopeful signs, from the Confucian point of view. Although the Kuomintang, or Nationalist Party, in forming for political action, committed itself to no particular religious views, its motto was nevertheless a reassertion of the eight Confucian virtues: loyalty, filial piety, benevolence, human heartedness, fidelity, just attitudes, harmony, and peace. And when in 1934 Chiang Kai-shek inaugurated the New Life Movement, it proved to have a distinctly Confucian coloring. (Even after he was baptized a Christian, he still saw China's problems through Confucian eyes.) The Movement was announced as having "four binding principles": *Li* or courtesy and good manners, *I* or justice and uprightness, *Lien* or integrity, and *Ch'ih* or modesty and self-respect.

At the same time it should be said that the New Life Movement was never officially affiliated with Confucianism; it was meant to be principally a movement of moral regeneration, and it found the traditional ethical concepts expressive. More indicative of national goals was the temple which the government erected in 1937 at Nanking. This imposing structure was intended as a national shrine. In the highest place was the tablet of Confucius and just below it a marble bust of Dr. Sun Yat-sen, "the father of modern China." On surrounding pillars were portraits of great Western "sages": Newton, Pasteur, Lavoisier, Galileo, James Watt, Lord Kelvin, Dalton, and Benjamin Franklin! The meaning seemed to be, that the China of the future would make a synthesis of the old and the new, combining the best of its philosophy and ethics with the best of the science and culture of the West.

But now all this is in doubt. Chinese Communism has gained the strength to remake China. Not only is it the present government's intention to alter permanently the economic and social structures of China; the mental outlook is to be thoroughly reoriented to a "materialistic" point of view. The entire history of Chinese philosophy and religion is being rewritten. A government sponsored text, issued for international distribution and published in Peking in 1959 under the title *A Short History of Chinese Philosophy*, says the chief issue in the development of Chinese thought is one between "the feudal, bourgeois, reactionary culture and the democratic, socialist revolutionary culture"; ideologically, this is the issue between "the idealist, metaphysical theory and the dialectical, materialist theory." Confucius in this perspective becomes a metaphysical idealist who tried to preserve the interests of the declining clan aristocracy, his one "progressive" achievement being his innovations in private education. Mo Ti represented on the other hand the interests of the rising class of freemen, and pitted his materialistic theory against the idealism of the Confucians. Lao-tzu was on the whole an idealist and mystic who considered the Tao a transcendental absolute, but he was progressive in two respects: in discussing natural laws (*teh*) he accepted some elements of materialism, and in seeing an opposition of *yin* and *yang* he developed the rudiments of dialectics. In his quietist political theory he reflected the feeling of the peasants and their naive attitude of non-resistance. Chuang-tzu was so much of an idealist and mystic that he settled for relativism, pessimism, and "philistinism" (i.e., opposition to the true trend of historical forces). Yang Chu as a rebellious egoist was in some sense progressive in reflecting the desire of the freemen of the time to seek personal interest. As for Mencius, in turning for knowledge of right and wrong from objective reality to an innate power to distinguish them, he used an idealist logic that savors of sophistry. Hsün-tzu on the other hand was against idealism; he was materialistic and atheistic, and said that man should conquer and exploit nature by using his mind so as to give him power over the objective world. He was a true progressive; and so was Han Fei of the Legalist School. Han Fei represented the interests of the freemen in stressing that human nature is selfish and society is a battleground of calculating minds. All this time materialism was taking a firm hold on the Chinese mind, and so was a gradually emerging vision of a Great Togetherness, a cosmopolitan society in which all men are brothers and there exists a world community. This vision was as yet idealist (Confucian in name) and seemed but a dream so transcendent that it could not be realized; but it laid the groundwork for future more realistic and materialistic planning and action. In combating Confucian scholasticism, Wang Ch'ung, who came of a poor family and was a true democrat, is a "glorious example" of rationalism, materialism, and rebellious struggle against idealist authoritarianism. There were others like him, before and after, who spoke for the true nature of historical forces. Meanwhile Buddhism, "a foreign religion," with a mistaken theory of transmigration and retributive justice, lured men into fancying that they could, by conscious effort, free themselves from the world of reality and attain a mysterious, spiritual world of eternal bliss. Buddhism emasculated the will of the people to free themselves from the existing feudal order. It influenced the socially conservative Neo-Confucians to support methods of thinking that led to unrealistic objective and subjective idealisms. Yet all the same, strains of materialism and atheism appeared also in Chinese thought then and later. At long last, from the 16th century onward there came the beginnings of enlightenment and a brilliant development of materialism and atheism that prepared the way for a culmination of the wisdom of the Chinese people in the philosophy of Mao Tse-tung. So reads the government sponsored text.

It remains only to ask, is the Confucian element in Chinese culture ineradicable enough to modify the Communists' will-to-change and to add one more culture-saving compromise to those of China's long past? Or will the Communist opposition to Confucianism prevail?

SUGGESTIONS FOR FURTHER READING

Bruce, J. P. *Chu Hsi and His Masters*. Probsthain, 1923
Chan Wing-tsit. *Religious Trends in Modern China*. Columbia University Press, 1953
Creel, H. G. *Confucius, The Man and The Myth*. John Day, 1949
————. *Chinese Thought from Confucius to Mao Tse-tung*. University of Chicago Press, 1953. Available as Mentor pb, 1960
Dubs, H. H. *Hsüntze, the Moulder of Ancient Confucianism*. Probsthain, 1927
————. *The Works of Hsüntze*. Probsthain, 1928
Giles, Lionel, trans. *The Sayings of Confucius*. In the Wisdom of the East series. John Murray, 1917
Fung, Y. L. *A History of Chinese Philosophy*. Trans. Derk Bodde. 2 vols. Princeton University Press, 1952
————. *A Short History of Chinese Philosophy*. Ed. Derk Bodde. Macmillan, 1948. Macmillan pb ed., 1960
Henke, F. G. *The Philosophy of Wang Yang-ming*. Open Court, 1916
Hughes, E. R. *Chinese Philosophy in Classical Times*. An anthology. Everyman's Library. J. M. Dent, 1941
————. *The Religion of China*. Hutchinson, 1950
Johnston, R. F. *Confucianism and Modern China*. Appleton-Century, 1935
Ku Hung Ming. *The Conduct of Life*. A translation of The Doctrine of the Mean. Wisdom of the East series. John Murray, 1906
Legge, James. *The Works of Mencius*. Clarendon Press, Oxford, 1895
Lin Mousheng. *Men and Ideas*. John Day, 1943
Lin Yutang. *The Wisdom of Confucius*. The Modern Library. Random House, 1938
Liu, Wu-Chi. *A Short History of Confucian Philosophy*. Penguin Books, 1955
Lyall, L. A., trans. *Mencius*. Longmans, Green, 1932
Mei Yi Pao. *The Ethical and Political Works of Motse*. Probsthain, 1930
————. *Motse, the Neglected Rival of Confucius*. Probsthain, 1934
Moore, Charles A., editor. *Philosophy—East and West*. Princeton University Press, 1944
Shryock, John. *The Origin and Development of the State Cult of Confucius*. Century, 1932
Waley, Arthur. *The Analects of Confucius*. Allen and Unwin, 1938
————. *Three Ways of Thought in Ancient China*. Allen and Unwin, 1939. Available as Anchor pb, 1956
Ware, J. R. *The Sayings of Confucius*. Mentor pb, 1955
Yang, Y. C. *China's Religious Heritage*. Abingdon, 1943
Wei, Francis C. M. *The Spirit of Chinese Culture*. Scribner's, 1947
Wilhelm, Richard. *Confucius and Confucianism*. Harcourt, Brace, 1931

11 Shinto:
The Religion
of Japanese Patriotism

THIS, THE NATIVE RELIGION OF JAPAN, IS NOT FUNDAMENTALLY A SYSTEM of doctrines, though it has taken on doctrines; it is basically a reverent loyalty to familiar ways of life and familiar places. The rank and file of any country do not, unless they are submitted to a process of indoctrination, readily express themselves through a dialectic or an ideology built on premises and logical inferences. At least it is true to say that for the masses in Japan patriotism is a matter of the heart, first, and of doctrinal substance, second. From a deep love of their land, they have unquestioningly assumed that the best way to express that love is to do what the emperor expects them to do. This has sufficed to supply them with a motive for living. Around the emperor and their country they have accordingly developed an emotional loyalty of an intense kind. They have found no difficulty in being faithful to *kokutai*, a rather special word, which may be translated as "the national organization" or "the solidarity of the nation."

The Japanese love their land with great constancy. It is a love of the country as a whole, and of each part of it, existing less in abstract idea than in an aesthetic love of things and places. Every hill and lake, all their mountains and rivers are dear to them, so dear that they can with difficulty think of parting from them. Their cherry trees, their shrines, their scenic resorts seem indispensable to a full enjoyment of life. Among these scenes their fathers lived and died. Here, with the

428

ancestral spirits looking on, their families abide and have their complex being. Moreover, their country has always been their own. Until 1945, no invaders ever crossed their shores. It is unthinkable to them that any but Japanese should live where they live, and to most Japanese it is unthinkable that they should live anywhere but where they do. It goes without saying that, when their country is in peril, they gladly die for it.

There is nothing doctrinaire about this; this is emotional disposition or feeling, so bred in the bone that psychologists of an earlier generation would have called it innate or even instinctive. It is the sort of feeling that readily expresses itself in myth. And so it did express itself in Japan —in myth first, in nationalistic ideology afterwards.

It is pleasant to reflect that the poetry and playfulness of myth came first—many centuries first. The Japanese came early to the belief that their land was divine, but late to the dogma that no other land is divine, that the divinity of Japan is so special and unique, so absent elsewhere, as to make Japan "the center of this phenomenal world."

I THE MYTH OF SHINTO

Shinto means "The Way of the Gods." * The word expresses religious faith about the past of Japan. That this is true may be gauged from the interesting and fabulous story of the origin of Japan, its people, and its imperial family contained in the *Kojiki* or Chronicle of Ancient Events, a work dating from the 8th century A.D. The story runs as follows: [1]

The Japanese islands are a special creation of the gods. After the primal chaos had in the course of events separated into heaven and ocean, various gods appeared in the heavenly drift-mist, only to disappear without event, until finally there came upon the scene the two deities who produced the Japanese islands and their inhabitants. These were the primal male and female, Izanagi, the Male-Who-Invites, and Izanami, the Female-Who-Invites. Their heavenly associates commanded them to "make, consolidate, and give birth to" the Japanese islands. These two beings descended the Floating Bridge of Heaven (a rainbow?); and when they reached its lower end, Izanagi pushed down his jeweled spear into the muddy brine and stirred it until the fluid below them became "thick and glutinous"; and then he drew the spear up; whereupon "the brine that dripped down from the end of the spear

---

* The name is, ironically enough, derived from the Chinese "shen-tao." Cultured Japanese in ancient times often borrowed Chinese words, as being more distinguished. In pure Japanese, the word is Kami-no-michi, which has the same meaning.

Izanagi and Izanami descending from heaven to create and people the Japanese islands. (After drawing in Museum of Fine Arts, Boston)

was piled up and became an island." Stepping down on the island, they came together, and Izanami bore from her womb the eight great islands of Japan. After that they brought into being a populace of thirty-five deities, the last of whom, the fiery heat-god Kagu-Tsuchi, at his birth fatally burned his mother. So enraged was Izanagi at Kagu-Tsuchi for causing Izanami's death, that he hacked him up with rapid strokes of his sword, only to produce other deities out of the flying fragments.

The historically important part of this story is its sequel. When Izanami died and went to the underworld (the Land of Yomi), in due time the inconsolable Izanagi followed after her, hoping to get her to return to the upper world with him. But he had not come in time. She had begun to decompose, and was unsightly. When he neared her in the darkness, she asked him not to look at her. But he lit the end tooth of the comb by which he kept his hair in place, and saw her lying before him horribly swarming with maggots. "Thou hast put me to shame," she screamed; and, as he fled back, sent the Ugly Females of Yomi to pursue him. When by various stratagems he delayed this pursuit, she sent after him eight Thunder deities, generated in the decay of her own body, and fifteen hundred warriors of Yomi. When he fought these off, she herself took up the chase. As he fled into the upper world he picked up a rock which it would have taken a thousand men to lift, and blocked up the pass of the underworld with it. The two erstwhile loving deities, standing on opposite sides of the rock, exchanged angry farewells. Finally, Izanagi, who was now covered with pollution, went down to the ocean to bathe his august person. As he threw away his staff, his girdle, and the rest of his apparel, each item turned into a deity. But the major event was still to come. According to the Kojiki, when he stepped into the water and, in a typically Japanese act of purification, washed away the filth out of his left eye, he produced the most highly revered of the Japanese deities, Amaterasu, the goddess of the sun. This was an important creation. After that, he produced the moon-god, Tsuki-yomi, from the washing of his right eye, and the storm-god, Susa-no-wo, from his nostrils.

Years later we find the sun-goddess Amaterasu looking down from her seat in heaven and becoming concerned about the disorder in the islands below. The storm-god's son was ruling there, but she was not satisfied. She finally commissioned her grandson Ni-ni-gi to descend to the islands and rule them for her. Her charge to him was in words which many a child in Japan once knew by heart: "This Luxuriant-Reed-Plain-Land-of-Fresh-Rice-Ears is the land which thou shalt rule." Ni-ni-gi obeyed. He first ruled from the island of Kyushu. In a later time, his great-grandson Jimmu Tenno, the first human emperor, embarked from Kyushu on a conquest of the province of Yamato, on the central Japanese island, Hondo, and set up his capital there, in the year set by tradition at 660 B.C.

Meanwhile the leading families of Japan and the whole Japanese people descended from the minor deities, or lesser *kami,* residing on the islands.

Thus we are to understand that the Emperor of Japan is a descendant in unbroken line from the sun-goddess Amaterasu, and that the islands of Japan have a divine origin, and so also the Japanese people.

It will be observed that this Old Shinto account of things is concerned with Japan alone; no other countries are considered. Moreover, Japan is regarded as full of gods and goddesses. The polytheism is almost unlimited. It was characteristic of the earlier Japanese to deify everywhere, to see a god or godling in every kind of force or natural object. They called their country "the Land of the Gods," and in later times estimated that their deities must number some "eighty myriads" or even some "eight hundred myriads." We may observe further that the chief place in the pantheon was given to the sun-goddess Amaterasu, whose temple at Isé is the holiest shrine in Japan; but she has never been regarded as more than the first among her peers. Associated with her were not only those born with her—Tsuki-yomi, the moon-god, and Susa-no-wo, the unmoral and capricious storm-god—but also a vast company of deities, such as the wind deities, "Prince of the Long Wind" and "Lady of the Long Wind"; the god of lightning, "Terrible Swift Fire Deity"; the thunder-god, "Fierce Thunder Male Deity"; the rain-god, "Fierce Rain Chief"; the general mountain god, "Dark-Mountain Possessing Deity," under whose aegis many local mountain deities, like the goddess of Mount Fuji, performed their functions; the fertility deities, such as "High August Producing God" and "Divine Producing Goddess"; the food deities—Inari, who is the grain-goddess, and the still very popular Toyo-Uke-Hime, the food-goddess, today widely worshiped by peasants and especially honored at the outer shrine of Isé; phallic deities; the gods of healing and purification; star-gods and goddesses; the deities of the sea (of whom there are those of the middle, the bottom, and the surface of the sea); not to mention river-gods, harbor-gods, mist-gods and deities of trees, leaves, rocks, earthquakes, volcanoes, and so on.

We need draw out the list no further. It is obvious that the Shinto myth pictured a pristine Japan thronging with deities.

II THE SHINTO MYTH IN JAPANESE HISTORY

But the myth of Shinto is itself a composite affair, and the understanding of its true significance requires a study of the circumstances surrounding its origin, for only thus may we account for the function which the myth has served.

The Composite Nature of the Myth

That the myth reflects a primitive response to Nature, not far advanced above animism, is clear. It is the opinion of D. C. Holtom, a leading authority, that Izanagi and Izanami are Japanese forms of those familiar figures in the world's cosmogonic myths, "the Sky-Father and the

Earth-Mother"; and that the details of the myth fit into the general pattern of world-wide descriptions of seasonal change in vegetation, typified by the Cybele-Attis myth of the Western world. He urges that the death of Izanami is caused by the earth-burning god of summer heat (which is his interpretation of the meaning of Kagu-Tsuchi); so that when Izanagi hews up the fiery god with his sword, thus producing lightning, thunder, and rain deities, what is signified is the vengeful onslaught of the quenching rain-storm upon the drought-child that has burned its earth-mother. The search of Izanagi for Izanami in the under-world is, Dr. Holtom says further, clearly in line with the chthonian myths of the West: the disappearance of the earth-mother has brought about the death of vegetation, and the sky-father endeavors to find her and return her to the world. His is a seeking which "re-echoes the search of the Egyptian Isis for the body of Osiris." [2]

Much may be said for this interpretation of the Japanese myth, but it explains the myth only in part; for interwoven with this portion of the story, and cutting it short, are other parts dealing with the sun-goddess and her struggles with her unruly brother, the storm-god. The story of these quarrels is susceptible of two different interpretations. The first interpretation sees in them a mythological treatment of the unending contest between sun and storm-cloud; the other reading finds in their geographical references an indication that Amaterasu represents the people of the southern island of Kyushu, and Susa-no-wo the settlers in Izumo, two groups which in the early years of immigration from the continent of Asia struggled with each other for ascendancy. The total myth represents therefore the combination of several strands of tradition, originating from different clans among the ancient population of Japan.

The Social Background of Old Shinto

The Japanese are a mixed people, parthly Korean, partly Mongolian, and partly Malayan; their ancestors came at different times from the Asiatic mainland and South Pacific islands, and succeeded in displacing and driving northward the aboriginal Ainu. Apparently the civil condition of ancient Japan was that of a loose conjunction of tribes and clans, each more or less independent and with its own traditions of nature and chieftain-worship. Magic, taboo, and religion were commingled in the fashion that is characteristic of a primitive society. The fox was worshipped as a messenger of the gods. Bows and arrows were fetishes of so high an order that they were offered the reverence accorded to the gods. The constant warfare with the slowly yielding but still fierce Ainu gave a military color to the whole of life. Great warriors were treated with exaggerated respect, whether living or dead. The people recognized and reverenced innumerable *kami,* their name for any being endowed with more than usual power or force—gods, men, or animals.

Clothed though they were in rough garments, and primitively housed, the Japanese already showed the passion for personal cleanliness which is so characteristic of them today. Their attitude toward the dead was marked by a dread of pollution; so that when a death occurred, the funeral was immediately held, and after the ten-day mourning period was at an end, the whole family went into the water to wash. In many cases the survivors abandoned the primitive structure that had been the home of the dead person, and built a new one. This practice imposed a peculiar difficulty upon the early emperors; each new emperor perforce abandoned the old capital and built a new palace in another part of the country; and this meant that with each accession to the throne the government was temporarily disorganized, and the people were obliged to orientate themselves afresh to yet another capital.

There were, it seems likely, three main centers of culture about the time of the 1st century B.C., one in the southwest on the island of Kyushu, another at Izumo, on the western verge of the main island, and a third at Yamato, at the northern end of the Inland Sea. Later times have undoubtedly oversimplified the factors present in the situation, but there are indications that on the island of Kyushu the tribal cults were mainly concerned with gods of the sea; and upon the central island, the Izumo clans worshipped the storm-god Susa-no-wo, while the Yamato clans adored the sun-goddess, regarded as the ruler of the heavens and as the ancestress of their chieftains. The Yamato clans, probably in the 1st century A.D., sealed their ascendancy over the other groups in two ways: by placing their chieftain on the somewhat shaky imperial throne as a descendant of the sun, and by combining the myths of the various tribal cults under one comprehensive "Way of the Gods."

The Effect of Chinese Religion and Culture on Old Shinto

But, however arrived at, this Old Shinto was formless and without any particular sense of direction; it became a clearly worked out pattern of national culture only when Chinese civilizing influences began to operate in Japan in the 5th century A.D. The transformation effected then in the national life and outlook * is one of the most remarkable instances of its kind in history. The Japanese eagerly made their lives over by adapting Chinese ideas and procedures to their needs. They went about it very thoroughly.

Always adept in improving their methods and skills in the practical arts, once the way is shown, they quickly learned all that the Chinese could teach them about pottery-making, metal working, wood carving, farming, horticulture, gardening, silkworm culture, road and bridge building, and canal dredging. Almost at a bound the people passed from a primitive to a relatively advanced type of material culture. In the realm of social relations, Confucian ideas brought about permanent changes of emphasis in morals. There followed in particular a powerful re-enforcement of the ideal of filial piety. Old Shinto had been mainly a haphazard cult of nature-worship, loosely tied in with ancestor-worship; it now took on the aspect of history's most comprehensive ancestor-cult. Not only did the emperor's descent from the sun-goddess receive stress, but the higher officials began to trace their own descent from the deities most closely related to the sun-goddess, while the common people were supposed to be descendants of the more distantly related deities; so that the mythological basis was laid for the claim (so greatly emphasized during the last decades of the 19th century and the beginning of this) that the whole people were organically related to the emperor by a divine family relationship.

But an even greater impact was made upon the Japanese by Buddhism, coming by way of China largely. When this religion came to Japan in the 6th century, it brought with it an exciting literature, a new, rich art, and fresh insights in every field of human thought and action, especially in logic, medicine, and social service. Buddhism broke down Japanese provincialism by bringing the overseas world into the religious picture; for in the eyes of the Buddhist priests, the seats of religious reality and authority lay, not in Japan, but in India and China. The conservative, provincial-minded clan leaders were affronted by this, but Buddhism had so much to contribute to Japan that its best, most progressive minds were irresistibly attracted to it. From the first it made its conquests in the highest quarters. After a short period of resistance, the members of the imperial family adopted Buddhism wholeheartedly. The aristocracy of the court followed suit. As temples multiplied, the common people were gradually won over.

One important result of the new ferment of ideas was the attempt,

* Sometimes called "the first great transformation of Japan," to distinguish it from "the second great transformation" in the 19th century.

under imperial sanction, to put into writing the native myths and traditions still current among the local clans. In 620 A.D. appeared the *Kujiki*, or Chronicle of Old Events, which gave the history of the emperors from Jimmu Tenno onward; in 712 A.D. the more comprehensive *Kojiki*, or Chronicle of Ancient Events, with which we have already become acquainted, was completed, it being intended as a history of Japan from the creation of the world to the middle of the 7th century A.D. Paralleling it, with variations and additions* that give it greater historical accuracy, was the *Nihongi*, or Chronicles of Japan, issued in 720 A.D. Almost a century later, about 806 A.D., appeared the *Kogoshui* or Gleanings from Ancient Stories, a defence of the practices of one of the ancient priestly guilds connected with Shinto. Still later, in the first quarter of the 10th century, came the *Engi-shiki*, an important compendium of Shinto rites and ceremonies, especially those relative to the imperial cult. All these treatises showed the influence of Chinese and Buddhist ideas. Foreign modes of thought were evident, for example, in the opening paragraphs of the Kojiki and Nihongi, much as the influence of Greek philosophy shows in the first chapter of the Fourth Gospel. The Kojiki and Nihongi were deeply indebted to overseas thought for their political orientation, which led them to endow the imperial line with a sovereignty reaching back to remote time and grounded in a divine order of things.

Ryobu or Mixed Shinto

By the 8th century, when Buddhism had obtained a prevailing influence over the governing classes, a closer integration of Shinto and Buddhism seemed desirable. Opportunely, certain Buddhist priests of the Hosso and Shingon sects made the discovery, through a series of religious visions, that the native gods of Japan were in reality Buddhas and Bodhisattvas who had "reappeared" on the Japanese islands. Amaterasu, the sun-goddess, was identified as a manifestation of the Buddha Vairocana; Hachiman, the war-god, was found to be the guise assumed on Japanese soil by the Bodhisattva Kshitigarbha, and so on. The result of accepting these identifications was the so-called *Ryobu* or Mixed Shinto (literally, "the Two-fold Way of the Gods" †). In this syncretism, the deities of the Buddhist pantheon were given the honored position

---

* One interesting feature was the addition of a social register of aristocratic families!

† Another translation is "two-seated," i.e. seated abroad and in Japan at the same time.

of "the Originals," while the deities of the Shinto pantheon were thought
to be their Japanese appearances or manifestations.

It is not surprising that Shinto almost succumbed in this crisis. (In
India Hinduism reabsorbed Buddhism by a similar rapprochement, and
at this same period of time.) Certainly, Ryobu or Two-sided Shinto had
immense influence on the thought of Japan. It won the intellectuals. In
ensuing years most of the Shinto shrines made room for Buddhist worship in the "Inner Sanctuary," and were quite generally served by Buddhist priests. The latter introduced into the old Shinto rites images,
incense, sermons, and elaborate ceremonies. The simple primitive appearance of the Shinto shrines was greatly altered by the exterior
application of the intricate ornament of Buddhist temples, and by the
addition to the shrine property of pagodas, drum-towers, large bells,
assembly halls for preaching services, and the like; even the unadorned
Shinto gateway, or *torii*, was supplied with curves and ornate decoration. So pervasive did the Buddhist influence become, that it is quite
true to say with W. M. Horton, that "down to the Meiji era, Japan might
fairly be described as a Buddhist nation," though one adds, as Dr.
Horton aptly does, the qualification that this only holds good "in the
same sense in which certain western nations have been described as
'Christian.'" [3] A deadly parallel!

Japanese appropriation and adaptation of Buddhism (especially in
its Pure Land form) continued to the beginning of the 13th century,
when public order dissolved in four hundred years of feudal strife, during which the emperor, his religious headship of the nation thoroughly
obscured by Buddhism, vainly strove to control the powerful nobles and
the *samurai* or military class. At the end of the 16th century a *shogun*
or dictator arose from the Tokugawa family, who unified the political
order and brought an end to the centuries of feudal warfare. This
marked the beginning of the period of the Tokugawa Regime (1600 to
1867 A.D.). It was a period of some importance to Shinto, for during it
occurred its own revival or renaissance.

The Revival of Shinto in the 17th Century

The revival of Shinto was not unprepared for. During most of the
period of its near-absorption into Buddhism, it found exponents, such as
the Urabe priesthood at the Kasuga shrine at Nara, and the Watarai
priesthood associated with the Outer Shrine at Isé, who sought to restore it to primacy. (A typical argument reversed the thesis of Ryobu
Shinto, and made the Japanese kami the "originals" and the Buddhist

deities their "appearances.") They strove to return to the emperor the authority of a god in human form; so they laid primary stress on the doctrine that he was directly descended from the greatest divine "original," the sun-goddess Amaterasu. By the 17th century notable developments in the renaissance of Shinto occurred. Political events, such as the Tokugawa shoguns' bloody supression of Christianity,* and the subsequent closing of the ports of Japan to foreigners for two centuries, undoubtedly encouraged Shinto scholars in their nationalistic return to the native "ancient learning." Be that as it may, during the 17th and 18th centuries three great scholars, Mabuchi, Motoōri, and Hirata, took advantage of the anti-foreign feeling of the time to revive what they called "Pure Shinto," or the "True Ancient Way." The second of this group was perhaps the greatest scholar in Japanese history. His commentary on the *Kojiki* is still authoritative. But his conclusions were as subjective as his scholarship in other respects was factual. Scorning to take the position of his contemporaries, who saw and unhesitatingly acknowledged, the dependence of Japanese learning on Chinese sources, he firmly upheld the superiority of the Ancient Way of Japan, declaring:

"From the central truth that the Mikado is the direct descendant of the gods, the tenet that Japan ranks far above all other countries is a natural consequence. No other nation is entitled to equality with her, and all are bound to do homage to the Japanese sovereign and pay tribute to him." [4]

He repudiated the suggestion that, since the Japanese had no native system of ethics, they must borrow one from Confucianism. Only a depraved people need an ethics, he said; the Japanese, by reason of their divine motivation, were so naturally upright in their lives that they were in no need of a moral code, and consequently had never had one. They should therefore give up forever all foreign modes of thought and action, and walk in simplicity the ancient Way of Shinto.

The Restoration of 1868

The effort made in the 17th century revival to disentangle Shinto from its Confucian and Buddhist infusions did not change the habits of the people; it aroused discussion and little more; nevertheless, the fruitage of the movement, and the vindication of the Shinto myth, came in the 19th century, when the "second great transformation of Japan" took place.

* Which had entered Japan with Francis Xavier in 1549 and a generation later numbered 300,000 converts.

The necessity for this transformation was borne in upon the Japanese rather suddenly. Though they strove to remain a "hermit nation," they could not prevent American whaling ships from appearing off their coasts and from time to time suffering shipwreck. The sailors who reached shore were sometimes killed as "foreign devils," and it took many months for those who did not meet this fate to be repatriated through the Dutch traders who were the only foreigners allowed in Japanese waters. But this was not the sole problem of the whalers. Their vessels often ran out of water and provisions by the time they reached Japan, and they naturally desired to be able to put into port to stock up. President Fillmore, aware of this need and also anxious to open Japan to foreign trade, appealed by letter to the ruler of Japan to open up a few ports to American ships. Carrying this letter, Admiral Perry entered Tokyo Bay in 1853, with four gunboats, and managed to deliver the President's message to the shogun. He sailed away to China, promising to return in the spring for an answer. The shogun circulated the President's letter among the Japanese feudal lords, who thereupon formed into three parties: the liberals, the compromisers, and the anti-foreign party, the last being much the largest and rejoicing in the adherence of the anti-foreign emperor, Komei. Admiral Perry returned in 1854 with ten ships and a force of 2,000 men. The shogun yielded to this persuasion, and concluded a treaty providing for kind treatment of shipwrecked sailors, permission for foreign vessels to obtain stores and water ashore, and the opening to trade of three unimportant ports. In concluding this treaty, the shogun did not obtain the sanction of the throne—an old habit of the shoguns. But for once the emperor entered into a determined struggle with him; in the course of which the shogun was at last led to abolish his own office, retire to the background, and leave the way open for restoration of the emperor to sovereignty over the nation, an event which occurred in 1868.

But the shogun had allowed a process of westernization to begin which could not be stopped. The reactionary clan leaders tried to stop it; but after the startling experience of having some of their coastal defences shattered by the guns of American, British, French, and Dutch ships, the anti-foreign leaders began to realize the military impotence of Japan, and abruptly about-faced. They decided then and there to bring the military might of Japan up to a par with that of the Western powers, and therefore entered, along with the liberals, upon the process of modernizing and industrializing Japan. It was a mighty task of transformation, and it was accomplished with amazing speed and thoroughness.

The conservatives soon found that the adoption of Western

economic and industrial methods, even when these were adapted to
Japanese requirements, involved momentous changes in culture and outlook. But this made them all the more resolved to preserve somehow
the ancient military ideals and values in the modern setting. They saw to
it that in the Constitution of 1889—an important step in the national
reorganization—the army and navy were not placed under civilian control
but were made responsible to the emperor alone. And, what is of chief
interest to us here, they raised the old Shinto myth of the emperor's
descent from the sun-goddess to high place in the national life by in-
corporating it, by indirection, in the Constitution itself,* and then went
about developing a state cult which could be expected to give it a continuing force in the nation's life. To this end they felt that the myth
should be isolated from its Buddhist involvements and made to stand
clear.

Accordingly, one of the first acts of the Emperor Meiji, after the
Restoration, was to disestablish Buddhism, make Shinto the state religion, and order the elimination of all Buddhist elements, including
priests, from the Shinto shrines. A good deal of purging was done, some
of it violent; even Buddhism as such was brought under attack; but so
closely were Shinto and Buddhism intermingled, that the national return
to a "pure" Shinto proved impracticable. The common people continued
to favor both religions. In 1877 Buddhism was given leave to exist by
being granted autonomy. In the Constitution of 1889 the complete religious liberty of all citizens was guaranteed, though the government
showed where its official heart lay by setting up a department, called
the Department of Shrines, to express its attitude of special regard and
care for the refurbished and re-defined national faith. This department
was subsequently divided into a Bureau of Shinto Shrines, under the
Department of Home Affairs, and a Bureau of Religions, under the
Department of Education. The division was made advisable by the
official distinction drawn by the government between "State" Shinto and
"Sectarian" Shinto, a matter which requires our further attention.

III STATE SHINTO TO 1945

State Shinto may be defined as the government fostered program of

---

* "Article I: The Empire of Japan shall be reigned over and governed by a line
of Emperors unbroken for ages eternal.
"Article III: The Emperor is sacred and inviolable."

patriotic rites which was conducted until 1945 * in shrines removed from sectarian control and made national property. Its purpose was the systematic cultivation of patriotic feeling within the nation. Age-old traditions were stressed by it, because it rose initially out of the need of keeping the Japanese people true to "the spirit of ancient Japan" through all the revolutionary changes wrought in the economic, educational, and political life of the nation by the adoption of the civilization of the West.

Western Ideas and Agnosticism in Japan

The upheaval of Japanese life and culture which accompanied the wholesale importation of Western ideas in the post-Restoration era at first adversely affected the fortunes of Shinto. The people in their bewilderment turned away for a time from the officially sanctioned state shrines. The simultaneous resurgence of Buddhism, fighting for its life, and the re-entrance of Christianity, raised as it were from the dead, helped to produce a religious attitude among the people which portended the end of the old native faith. But all religions suffered. Disbelife and agnosticism became widespread. The impact of Western science upon the students in the newly-founded universities hastened this tendency. Students began to laugh all religions out of court; and so far did this scepticism ultimately extend, that a census of student opinion in the University of Tokyo two decades after the opening of the present century showed that "out of a total of 4,608, 2,989 listed themselves as agnostic, 1,511 as atheists, and only 118 as adhering to Christianity, Buddhism or Shinto"[5]—a truly extraordinary expression of religious disbelief and indifference.

The Government Attitude before 1945

The Japanese government from the first took measures to save Shinto from extinction. Its strategy was both defensive and offensive. On the side of defence, it encouraged a reinterpretation of the Shinto myth that would make it acceptable to the critical intelligence of the nation. The view which received semi-official sanction was to the effect that the deities of the national myth were originally human beings with superior

---

* The American occupation authority caused its compulsory features to be abolished in that year. Worship at the former state shrines is now on a purely voluntary basis. See further infra.

gifts. The Sun-goddess was a noble woman ruler of a clan that had flourished in the dawn-age of Japanese history, and she laid the foundations of Japanese culture and national organization. This view took advantage of a curious ambiguity in the Japanese term for deity (*kami*). *Kami* means any being that has unusual power or is exceedingly awe-inspiring or superior in potency.* In the words of the famous scholar Motoōri, uttered over two hundred years ago:

"Speaking in general, it may be said that *kami* signifies in the first place, the deities of heaven and earth that appear in the ancient records and also the spirits of the shrines where they are worshipped. It is hardly necessary to say that it includes human beings; also such objects as birds, beasts, trees, plants, seas, mountains, and so forth. In ancient usage, anything whatsoever which was outside of the ordinary, which possessed superior virtues, or which was awe-inspiring was called *kami*."

Motoōri added:

"The *kami* of the Divine Age were for the most part human beings of that time, and because the people of that age were all *kami*, it is called 'the Age of the Gods.' " [6]

Availing themselves of this interpretation of the meaning of the word for deity, Japanese scholars humanized and rationalized the whole of Japanese mythology, and thus tried to make their peace with historical science as that is understood in the Western World. To cite a typical instance, a Japanese professor declared:

"Shinto, as the Chinese characters read, is the way of the Gods. What are gods? There are many things which go by the name 'gods.' In Greece, there is a god of stars; in India, Buddha is a god; in Occidental countries, they have one god, the ruler of Heaven. Thus, we find there are various gods in the world. Gods, in our country, are our forefathers. It is hardly necessary to mention that the Goddess Amaterasu is enshrined in Isé shrine; so are the Emperor Jimmu in Kashiwabara shrine, Emperor Ojin in Hachiman shrine, Emperor Kammu in Heian shrine and Emperor Godaigo in Yoshino shrine. To enshrine forefathers as gods is peculiar to our people. It is not seen in any other civilized countries of the world. It is true that in our country there also existed and exists even now to a certain extent the worship of animals, rocks, trees and mountains, but gods as taught by Shinto are our ancestors worshipped as gods . . . In mystical groves, with sacred torii, the spirits of our forefathers are enshrined." [7]

Although this argument has no sound historical basis so far as the

* A close analogy exists between this potency and the South Sea conception of *mana*.

major gods are concerned, because it flies in the face of the fact that in the Shinto myth Amaterasu, Susa-no-wo, Izanagi, and Izanami stand for aspects of Nature—the radiant sun, the storm, ancient father-sky, teeming mother-earth—and by no means for apotheosized human beings of the past, the argument nevertheless has had an attraction for intelligent Japanese, anxious to be in harmony both with science and the national tradition.

In another direction, the Japanese government endeavored to save Shinto by making it over into a positive force, a national institution of an ethical and historical character. The official government view was that Shinto was not a religion, properly speaking, but a formulation of national ethics and a cult of loyalty to national institutions. In order to make this clear, the Restoration (or Meiji) government in 1882 officially separated what is known as *Jinja-Shinto* or State Shinto, from *Kyoha-Shinto* or Sectarian Shinto; and the latter was disestablished (i.e. deprived of government financial support) and given the status of an independent religion on the same footing with Buddhism and Christianity. State Shinto was declared to be no more than a system of state ceremonials whose patriotic object it was to unify the popular mind in accordance with "the national morality." The official position based itself on declarations made by the Emperor Meiji from 1870 to 1890, when Japan was being reorganized to take its place in the modern world. Especial stress was laid on the famous Imperial Rescript on Education, issued in 1890, and regarded as the basis of the school system of Japan. The rescript reads:

Know Ye, Our Subjects:

Our Imperial Ancestors have founded our Empire on a basis broad and everlasting, and have deeply and firmly implanted virtue; Our subjects ever united in loyalty and filial piety have from generation to generation illustrated the beauty thereof. This is the glory of the fundamental character of Our Empire, and herein lies the source of Our education. Ye, Our subjects, be filial to your parents, affectionate to your brothers and sisters; as husbands and wives be harmonious, as friends true; bear yourselves in modesty and moderation; extend your benevolence to all; pursue learning and cultivate arts and thereby develop intellectual faculties and perfect moral powers; furthermore, advance public good and promote common interests; always respect the Constitution and obey the laws; should emergency arise, offer yourselves courageously to the State; and thus guard and maintain the prosperity of Our Imperial Throne coeval with heaven and earth. So shall ye be not only Our good and faithful subjects but render illustrious the best traditions of your forefathers.

The Way here set forth is indeed the teaching bequeathed by Our Imperial Ancestors, to be observed alike by their descendants and the subjects, infallible for all ages and true for all places. It is Our wish to lay it to heart in all reverence, in common with you, Our subjects, that we may all attain the same virtue.[8]

It was generally accepted in Japan that this declaration outlined the essential elements of State Shinto and expressed the true spirit of the Japanese people. For this reason successive Ministers of Education issued orders to school officials like the following:

> Especially on the days of school ceremonies or on some date determined according to convenience, the pupils must be assembled and the Imperial Rescript on Education must be read before them. Furthermore, the meaning must be carefully explained to the pupils and they must be instructed to obey it at all times.[9]

Another order, dated 1911, goes further:

> The sentiment of reverence is correlative with the feeling of respect for ancestors and is most important in establishing the foundations of national morality. Accordingly, on the occasion of the festivals of the local shrines of the districts where the schools are located, the teachers must conduct the children to the shrines and give expression to the true spirit of reverence.[10]

These and subsequent orders, involving a daily bowing in school assemblies before the picture of the emperor, gave no end of trouble to Christian groups. But leading Japanese nationalists, refusing to see the ambiguity in the government's position, contended that Shinto shrines had no more than the significance of the memorial statues to be seen in London, Paris, or Berlin. "Foreigners," one spokesman said, "erect statues, we celebrate at shrines." [11] So they saw no reason why all citizens might not, without inconsistency, present themselves on patriotic occasions at the shrines, and participate in the ceremonies conducted there.

State Shrines before 1945

The shrines which the government set apart and nationalized numbered about 110,000. Not included were the countless, unlisted wayside shrines, too small to mention in the records of the Department of Home Affairs or too remote to be readily accessible. Many of these were memorial in character, being dedicated to legendary heroes or ancient clan figures; others were small temples erected in honor of the fox, the messenger and symbol of the grain-goddess Inari; and still others were placed in factory compounds, on the roofs of department stores, or in the small space between stores in a business district. The recognized shrines were served by some 16,000 priests, who were appointed by the government, and were officially instructed not to conduct religious ceremonies. (They were not allowed, for instance, to conduct funerals.) In the rural districts one priest often served a large number of scattered shrines, while at the great shrines a staff of ten or more were in attendance.

The state shrines were, as tradition demanded, in appearance just what their name, *jinja*, implies—"god-houses." In most cases they were unpainted Japanese houses of an ancient design; and since the exposed wood surfaces showed the effects of weathering in course of time, it was common to follow the example set at the Grand Imperial Shrine at Isé, and to tear down the shrine every twenty years and rebuild it.

The Grand Imperial Shrine at Isé

The most honored of all State shrines was the Grand Imperial Shrine at Isé, sacred to the sun-goddess Amaterasu. This shrine was of such importance to the government's nationalistic aims that citizens were for years bred up in the notion that from ancient times the people of Japan made pilgrimages to this shrine once in a lifetime "without fail." Isé is situated some two hundred miles southwest of Tokyo near the mouth of the beautiful bay which bears its name. There the shrine of the Sun-goddess still stands, linked with that of the Food-goddess, Toyo-Uke-Hime; and between is a shrine-lined avenue four miles long, running through a forest of magnificent cryptomeria trees. Both shrines, unless they are no longer maintained with the old care, are made of unpainted cedar wood and are in the style of Old Shinto. In each case the super-structure rests on piles driven into the ground. The roofs are thatched, and are secured at the top by three long planks, two fitted so as to form a ridge, and the third laid flat along the ridge to keep the rain from entering there. This third plank is weighted down by the very ancient device of laying short sections of round logs at right angles to it along the whole interval between the end-rafters. A narrow, railed veranda, also on piles, runs around the building. (See cut on next page.)

From time immemorial Amaterasu has had "The Inner Shrine." [*] The shrine itself stands within two sacred fences, through which only authorized priests and officials of the government were in times past allowed to enter. The most treasured possessions of the shrine have been the "divine Imperial regalia," the three precious symbols of the Sun-goddess —a mirror, a sword, and a string of ancient stone jewels. The most highly

[*] As being less holy, the shrine of the Food-goddess stands in a smaller area than that of the Sun-goddess and is called "The Outer Shrine of Isé."

valued of these, both in itself and for its symbolic meaning, has been the mirror, long declared to be the one with which the Sun-goddess was lured from the cave to which she once retreated in high dudgeon at the misdeeds of her brother, Susa-no-wo.* How the "divine Imperial re-

* The old story is that the Sun-goddess locked herself in the Rock-cave of Heaven and left the world in darkness, save for the light of the moon and the stars. So the deities of the world (eighty myriads of them!) gathered outside the rock door and put on a serio-comic show to draw the offended deity out again into the open. They placed in front of the door a freshly dug up *sakaki* tree, the most sacred of all trees, and hung on its branches a newly-forged and very brightly polished metal mirror, a string of "carved" stone jewels, and blue and white offerings of cloth made from the inner bark of the sacred tree. Then Ame-no-uzume, the phallic goddess, danced so outrageously, to the rhythmic chanting of the other deities, that the sound of the laughter shook heaven and earth. Overcome with curiosity, the Sun-goddess peeked out, saw her own face reflected in the mirror hanging from the branches of the sakaki tree, and took a half-step to meet the beautiful rival she thus beheld. Immediately, Te-chikara-wo (Strength-of-hand Deity) took her by the arm and drew her forth, while all the other deities shouted for joy. From this ancient myth of the reappearing of light in the world (after an eclipse?) Shintoists have derived the symbols of the mirror and the string of jewels and also their practice of using in their ceremonies and on altar-tables purification wands, called *nusa* and *gohei,* made to simulate branches of the sacred sakaki tree. The myth also provides the rationale for the two tall poles set up for formal ceremonies in front of the "worship sanctuary," on either side of the approach from the *torii,* the pole on the right bearing suspended, amid a flutter of silk streamers in five colors, a metal mirror and a string of stone jewels, and the pole on the left a small sword. In this latter case, the sword-symbol refers back to the exploit of the storm-god, Susa-no-wo, in slaying a dragon, whose tail terminated in an imbedded sword-blade, of a miraculous potency, which the storm-god extracted and presented to the Sun-goddess.

Inner shrine at Isé. (From contemporary photograph)

galia" reached earth is explained by the story that the Sun-goddess gave them to Ni-ni-gi, her grandson, when she sent him down from Heaven to rule the Japanese empire.* The school books of Japan used to teach that from that time on the successive emperors, in a single dynasty unbroken through the ages, handed on the three sacred treasures as "symbols of the Imperial Throne." [12]

Such was the sacredness of these treasures, that so great a person as the emperor directly concerned himself with the conduct of the state ceremonies of the Grand Imperial Shrine of Isé, though he was seldom present in person. An old school-text explains the matter thus:

> The reverence accorded the Grand Imperial Shrine by the Imperial Family is of an extraordinary nature . . . At the time of the Festival of Prayer for the Year's Crops (Kinen Sai), at the Festival of Presentation of First Fruits (Niiname Sai), he dispatches messengers and presents offerings. At the time of dispatching the Imperial messenger the Emperor personally views the offerings and delivers a ritualistic report to the messenger. Also, the Emperor does not withdraw prior to the departure of the Imperial messenger. Again, on the day of the Festival of the Presentation of First Fruits a solemn ceremony of distant worship (toward the Grand Imperial Shrine) is carried out. Each year at the Ceremony of Beginning State Affairs the first thing done is to receive a report relating to the Grand Imperial Shrine, and whenever there is an affair of great importance either to the Imperial Family or to the nation it is reported to the Grand Imperial Shrine. Furthermore, at the time when the Emperor carries out the Ceremony of Accession to the Throne, he worships in person at the Grand Imperial Shrine.[13]

On at least one other occasion of national importance the emperor customarily went to the Grand Imperial Shrine at Isé. It was when war was declared upon some foreign power. He reported this solemn fact in person, as a matter of life and death import for the nation.

State Ceremonies of the Past

In the past the emperor also played a part in the greatest of all state ceremonies—the *O-Harai* or Great Purification. This was performed not only at Isé but at a number of other shrines, twice each year, in June and December. It was in essence a national purgation by a purification ritual. Before the performance of this ceremony the priests sought to attain inward as well as outward cleanliness by abstaining from all food. During the ceremony itself they waved slowly above the people the *nusa* or purification wand, read the ritual, and accepted penalty-

---

* There are good grounds for believing, however, that they are really ancient gifts from the Chinese court.

offerings. Meanwhile the people rubbed against their persons small straw or paper effigies representing themselves, thus transferring their guilt to their person-substitutes. The priests collected and threw the effigies into some body of water—lake, river, or ocean as the case might be; and the guilt of the people was thus borne away. At the proper moment during the festival, the emperor, as a descendant of the forgiving Sun-goddess, pronounced from the imperial capital the absolution of the sins and impurities of the nation.

The waving of the purification wand during this and other ceremonies has been an important feature of Shinto ceremonies. The origin of the wand itself, though traced back to the ritual use of the branches of the sacred *sakaki* tree by the deities of Heaven, is clearly magical: its many analogues in the aversive magic of primitives throughout the world would make a long list. Other practices before and during Shinto ceremonies have a similar magical derivation. Instances are: the hanging of a taboo rope between the uprights of the *torii* and beneath the eaves of shrine buildings; the flying of streamers, banners, and flags from poles; the use of straw and paper objects twisted into zigzag shapes and placed about the interior of the shrines; and the wearing of grotesque masks by performers in festival processions.

While in the past the emperor customarily took part in the great ceremonies of the year, the priests at Isé and elsewhere conducted by themselves the day-to-day ritual of the state shrines. The services were of the utmost simplicity, consisting merely of a ceremonial approach to the inner shrine with offerings, the ritualistic presentation of the offerings, the reading of ritualistic prayers (called *norito*), the removal of the offerings, and finally the quiet withdrawal of the worshipers and priests. The offerings have usually been of two kinds: food-offerings and cloth-offerings. The former have consisted typically of raw or cooked rice, rice-brandy (*sake*), fish, fruit, vegetables, cakes, salt, and similar food-stuffs. The cloth-offerings have sometimes included money, paper, jewels, or art-objects, but normally consist of lengths of silk, cotton, and linen. These offerings are not only made to the gods but are also often proferred in the spirit of thanksgiving to the ever-glorious ancestress of the imperial family and the local clan leaders and heroes, whose spirits from remote time have guided the nation.

IV SHINTO AND THE WARRIOR

The Way of the Gods has from the beginning been easily reconcilable with the Way of the Warrior. In fact, the affinity of Shinto with the Warrior's Way was long ago made clear in the code practiced by the *samurai*, the military class of the feudal period of Japan. This code was called *Bushido*, literally "the warrior-knight-way." It was the Japanese equivalent of the code of chivalry of medieval Europe, and had a comparable influence. Indeed, when its general provisions became known, the entire nation came under its spell, and has more or less remained so.

The Bushido Code

Bushido did not consist of finally fixed rules. It was a convention; more accurately, it was a system of propriety, preserved in unwritten law and expressing a spirit, an ideal of behavior. As such, it owed something to all the cultural and spiritual forces of the feudal era. Shinto supplied it the spirit of devotion to country and overlord; Confucianism provided its ethical substance, Zen Buddhism its method of private self-discipline; and the feudal habit of life contributed to it the spirit of unquestioning obedience to superiors and a sense of honor that was never to be compromised.

A missionary who knew the Japanese well has set forth the Bushido ethical code in the following eight attitudes:

1. Loyalty.
This was due first of all to the Emperor and under him to the lord whom one more immediately serves. One of the most familiar proverbs says, "A loyal retainer does not serve two lords."
2. Gratitude.
It may surprise some to hear that this is a Japanese characteristic, but the Christian doctrine that the spring of a right life is not duty, but gratitude, is one that is readily appreciated by the Japanese.
3. Courage.
Life itself is to be surrendered gladly in the service of the lord. An American cannot fail to be touched by the noble words of a young warrior of ancient times to the effect that he wanted to die in battle for his lord and feared nothing so much as dying in bed before he had a chance to sacrifice his life for the object of his devotion.
4. Justice.
This means not allowing any selfishness to stand in the way of one's duty.
5. Truthfulness.
A knight scorns to tell a lie in order to avoid harm or hurt to himself.

6. Politeness.

It is the mark of a strong man to be polite in all circumstances, even to an enemy.

7. Reserve.

No matter how deeply one is moved, feeling should not be shown.

8. Honor.

Death is preferable to disgrace. The knight always carried two swords, a long one to fight his foes, a short one to turn upon his own body in the case of blunder or defeat.[14]

The readiness to commit suicide last mentioned is perhaps the most startling feature of the Bushido code. Yet suicide was the accepted form of atonement for failure or misjudgment. The warrior-knight was always preparing himself in thought and in mood for it. The kind of suicide he mentally rehearsed was *harakiri*,* a ceremonial method of disembowelment, carried out coolly and deliberately according to rule, without any expression of emotion. (Women in a similar action cut their jugular veins by a method called *jigai*.)

No story better illustrates the Bushido spirit than the famous tale of old Japan, known as "The Forty-Seven Ronins." A certain lord, we read, was repeatedly insulted by a superior, till, goaded beyond endurance, he aimed a dagger at his tormentor, and missed. A hastily summoned council of court officials condemned him to commit harakiri, and ordered his castle and all his goods to be confiscated to the state. After the noble lord had ceremonially killed himself, his samurai-retainers became *ronins*; that is, men cast adrift by the death of their lord but in duty bound to avenge him. The court official who had brought on the tragedy, and was the object of their vengeance, thereafter kept to his castle, surrounded by a heavy guard. His spies reported that the leader of the ronins had embarked on a career of drunkenness and debauchery, evidently too craven to do his duty by his dead lord. They did not suspect that this was a ruse adopted by the ronin leader to throw the enemy off guard. The ruse succeeded. A less strict watch began to be kept in the enemy castle, and finally half of the guard was sent away. Then the forty-seven ronins secretly came together, and on a snowy night stormed the castle and captured the enemy of their dead lord. The leader of the ronins respectfully addressed the captive noble, saying: "My lord, we are the retainers of Asano Takumi no Kami. Last year your lordship and our master quarreled in the palace, and our master was sentenced to harakiri, and his family was ruined. We have come

---

* Or *seppuku*, the more classical term.

tonight to avenge him, as is the duty of faithful and loyal men. I pray your lordship to acknowledge the justice of our purpose. And now, my lord, we beseech you to perform harakiri. I myself shall have the honor to act as your second, and when, with all humility, I shall have received your lordship's head, it is my intention to lay it as an offering upon the grave of Asano Takumi no Kami." [15] But the enemy lord sat speechless and trembling, unable to perform the act required of him; so the leader of the ronins leaped upon him and cut off his head, with the same dagger with which his own lord had killed himself. All the ronins then went in a body to the grave of their dead lord and offered to his spirit the washed head of his enemy. After that they waited quietly until the government sent word that they should atone for their crime by committing harakiri themselves; and this they all did, without exception. The whole of Japan rang with their praises; and ever since they have lived in Japanese imagination as peerless exemplars of the Bushido spirit.

Bushido and the Modern Warrior

That Bushido has greatly influenced the ideals cherished by modern Japanese is beyond doubt. When General Nogi, who became the military hero of the Russo-Japanese War, heard in 1894 that war with China had been declared, he left home for the front instantly, without stopping to say goodby to his wife; and when the Emperor Meiji died in 1912, the old general and his wife committed suicide (harakiri and jigai respectively), believing that by this devoted act they had made possible their personal attendance on their sovereign in the next world. Many other instances of the Bushido or samurai spirit could be cited. One such instance has been supplied by a certain Lieutenant Sakurai, who was crippled in the siege of Port Arthur during the Russo-Japanese War, and afterwards wrote a religio-military book, entitled *Human Bullets*, which was for many months a best-seller throughout Japan. The title of this book is an apt description of the soldiers who flung themselves at Port Arthur with an unparalleled disregard of self-preservation, a swarm of men whom the machine guns of the Russians, which poured death into them at point-blank range, could not stop. Many of them exhibited an incredibly eager desire to make the supreme sacrifice in battle, since such a death is always thought of as patriotism's perfect gift. Lieutenant Sakurai himself, burning with devotion to emperor and country, gathered his men around him before one assault and passed among them a cup of water, saying: "This water you drink, please drink as if at your death-moment." * ¹⁶ They resolved to be a "sure-death" band, and went into battle with a firm determination to give their lives in the attack, or at any rate to fight with complete disregard of personal safety, until they should either conquer or die.

Experts on the subject of Bushido would probably say that the suicide-complex is a distortion of the original spirit of the warrior-way. Warriors were to be loyal to lord and country, and filial to parents; they were to be brave and fearless in battle, incapable of flinching from danger or death, but they were not to throw their lives away in unthinking bravado; on the contrary, they were to make them count to the utmost in preserving the security of home and country; that is, they were to make their lives last as long as possible. However, this rule was subject to one exception: unbearable humiliation or disgrace justified honorable men in committing harakiri. Thus a warrior, especially one charged with responsibility, was expected to commit harakiri when captured in battle or unsuccessful in carrying out an important mission.

Shinto and Official Militarism

The high regard in which warriors have been held in Japan led, be-

* His intense patriotism always had this touch of formality in it. Thus, when at three o'clock in the morning the cannon which roared from the hill-top of the old castle in his home-town told him he was to depart for the front, he jumped out of bed, cleansed his body with pure water, donned his best uniform, bowed to the east where the emperor resided, solemnly read over his Majesty's declaration of war, and told his Majesty that his humble subject was just starting for the front. While he offered what he thought were his last prayers before the god-shelf, he felt a thrill going through him, as if his ancestors were solemnly saying: "Thou art not thine own. For His Majesty's sake, thou shalt go . . . to bear the crushing of thy bones and the tearing of thy flesh. Disgrace not thine ancestors by any act of cowardice." ¹⁷

About the same time, an acquaintance of his, who "had promised his parents, brothers and friends that he would be among the first to help win battles," was lodged in a Buddhist temple to wait for a later summons. "This was too great a humiliation for him to bear," says our lieutenant. "He thought it better to kill himself so that his spirit, freed from the shackles of the body, might be at the front to work with his living comrades. . . . Late one night when his friends were fast asleep, he scribbled a line of farewell to this effect: 'I am more sorry than I can possibly bear not to be at the front with the others. No one would take me in spite of my entreaties; I will prove my loyalty with death.' Thus prepared, he drew a dagger from a white-wood sheath and cut across the abdomen. . . . But good Heaven seemed to take compassion on such a faithful soldier. His friends awoke and came to the rescue. He was sent to the hospital." "Cold reason may call this man a fool, or a fanatic, but his heart was pure and true," adds our lieutenant.¹⁸

fore and during World War II, to special commemorative services dedicated to the soldiers who had laid down their lives for their country. Throughout Japan, on the designated memorial day, Shinto priests said liturgies before special shrines called "soul-inviting-altars," in which the spirits of the heroic dead were invited to reside during the ceremony to receive homage. The Japanese government maintained in Tokyo a Shinto shrine where an annual ritual of national importance was performed in honor of the army and navy dead. This shrine—the Yasukuni-jinja—was regularly used by military and naval leaders for ceremonies designed to instill in the armed forces the highest patriotism. The names of all the war dead were preserved in it—and still are.

In those years the military ardor of the warrior was fed from yet another source, the publications of professors in the Shinto departments of the imperial universities. The extremes to which a religious nationalism sometimes goes is well illustrated in the following interesting argument by a well-known professor. He declared that Shinto is the faith at the basis of all religion; it is the religion of religions. The proof he offered for this broad assertion was, that in the opening sentences of the Kojiki the first deity mentioned, namely Ame-no-mi-naka-nushi-no-kami ("The Deity Who Is the August Lord of the Center of Heaven"), is none other than the God who has been recognized in all other religions and philosophies as the unchanging foundation of all things, "the great Life of the Universe." Shinto thus has had from the beginning, he declared, a conception of a great all-inclusive Spirit, manifested in the life of each individual human being; and this makes it so comprehensive a faith that it may be regarded as including all other religions! Buddha, Confucius, Lao-tzu, and Jesus Christ were all missionaries of Shinto, unconscious of it though they may have been.* But Shinto has been unique in one respect, and in this fact has demonstrated its superiority. The uniqueness consists in this: politics and religion have not been divorced by it; the Japanese emperor, supreme politically, has also been supreme religiously, since his line goes back unbroken to the Sun-goddess Amaterasu, and behind her to the all-inclusive spirit that is "the great Life of the Universe." The emperor therefore has represented in living person the will of the great Spirit-behind-the-Universe, who is being worshipped under many names in other lands, but who has expressed his original intent best through the Emperor of Japan. The professor whom we are here following therefore declared: "The Emperor is god revealed in men. He

* Several Shinto books have in fact attempted to give plausibility to a story that Jesus did not die on the cross; a younger brother was crucified in his stead; and Jesus then traversed Asia and died in northern Japan, his spiritual home-land!

is manifest Deity." "The Emperors of our country are persons equipped with qualities without parallel in the world; they are both the centers of (religious) faith and of temporal power." Hence:

The center of this phenomenal world is the Mikado's land. From this center we must expand this Great Spirit throughout the world . . . The expansion of Great Japan throughout the world and the elevation of the entire world into the Land of the Gods is the urgent business of the present and, again, it is our eternal and unchanging object.[19]

The Japanese military were not slow in availing themselves of this point of view. They made it part of their war-talk that conquest was the holy mission of Japan. Certainly in such words we may see the logical outcome of a nationalism infused with all the values of religion. From the military point of view, it seemed a useful faith: inspired by its hopes, the Japanese people were empowered to fight for what seemed to them their manifest destiny in Asia, and ultimately in the entire world.

But the military point of view brought disaster. Perhaps that disaster may yet be retrieved, if the Shinto myth is relegated to its true place in poetry and folklore, and the Japanese people move on to a synthesis of the best of their cultural and aesthetic values with the science, religion, and philosophy of the West—a synthesis wrought out of living under a new democratic order of life.

V   SHRINE SHINTO TODAY

When in 1945 the 110,000 shrines formerly under the control of the Home Ministry were cut off from state supervision and subsidies, the first effect of this disestablishment and of the return of the shrines to local control was a measure of confusion and paralysis. Attendance at the shrines fell off sharply; and the priests, accustomed to the now obsolete rituals and prayers that had been supplied to them by the Home Ministry, were thrown on their own resources, although they were sometimes untrained and unprepared. But after a period of readjustment, a more genuine religious situation than before was established and the shrines began to regain their popularity. While a number of shrines have fallen into disuse, others are kept in repair by local shrine associations, and some 86,000 are maintained by a nation-wide Shrine Association supported by private funds and voluntary gifts. Most of the shrines are therefore back in business and enjoy genuine popular support.

Famous torii of the Itsukushima shrine on an island of the Inland Sea near Hiroshima; stands in water at high tide and therefore must have cross-braces that complicate its structure.

The typical village shrine occupies a low knoll, where it reposes among cryptomerias and pines that give it a delightful woodland setting. Its rectangular space is hedged about by a sacred fence, pierced on one side by an exactly centered opening. Here stands the *torii,* the world-famous Shinto gateway, which has been to its shrine what a pagoda is to the Chinese temple or a minaret to a Moslem mosque.* Behind the torii a shaded path leads through other torii to the outer-shrine or *haiden,* which is the sanctuary for worship. This is a small building with a bell hung under its eaves.

As the worshiper draws near the *haiden,* he steps aside to wash his hands and cleanse out his mouth at the "water-purification place." He removes his hat, coat, and scarf. Then he approaches the outer-shrine; bows before it; claps his hands decorously (the distinctive Japanese way of obtaining the gods' attention); bows; rings the bell; bows again, or, if he has ascended the steps of the outer-shrine, kneels on the top step

* In its simplest and oldest form a *torii* is constructed of three smooth tree-trunks, two forming the uprights and one lying horizontally across their tops so as to project on either side, a cross-brace two or three feet from the top holding all in place.

and bows, head low to the floor; leaves an offering on a cloth or drops it in the treasury-box provided for the purpose; prays; bows again in meditation and reverence; and then retires quietly, pausing to turn round and bow low as he goes.

A little beyond the outer-shrine, and often connected with it by a covered passageway, stands the inner sanctuary or *hondon*. This the worshiper does not enter; but he knows that the chief treasure of the shrine is housed within it, an object called the *shintai* or "god-body"— a precious object which is never allowed to be seen, except in those rare instances where it is a large rock, a hill, or a tree. Usually it is small enough to go into a treasure chest. It is often an object of little value in itself, perhaps an old sword, a mirror, a crystal ball, or a bit of ancient parchment with writing on it. In all likelihood it is an object which the ruling local clan in olden times prized as an intimate possession, or manufacture, of the powerful clan ancestors. In any case, it has become symbolic of the superhuman, and is therefore often called the "spirit-substitute," that is, the outward representation of an invisible spiritual presence. Being precious, it is usually wrapped in finely woven cloths and enclosed in several sacred caskets, one inside the other, the whole covered over with another fine cloth. Seldom moved, it is carried once a year during the annual village festival in a shrine-on-wheels, or in a palanquin, through the streets; while before and behind it, amidst banners and streamers, musicians in hideous masks make weird music, actors on floats portray historical scenes drawn from local story, and singing girls posture to the sounds of drum and flute.

The meaning of the *shintai* has varied, of course, with the faith and education of the worshiper. The more devout among the common people have clearly associated the sacred object with one of the old gods of the land or with a deified ancestor, and have even offered prayers to it as though it had ears to hear. Perhaps, however, the majority no longer find in it a distinctly religious value; it signifies instead the locus of a magical power of some sort or the seat of a good luck agency to be coaxed into friendliness. The educated person is more discriminating and comes to regard it as an object symbolic solely of the ongoing virtue and spirit of deified ancestors and great men of the past.

IV   DOMESTIC AND SECTARIAN SHINTO

The ambiguity which once enshrouded the government position has been absent in domestic and sectarian Shinto. Although among the sects there have been ethical culture groups committed to a disavowal of religious interests, the motives of the majority of those supporting the sects have been frankly and unreservedly religious.

Shinto in the Home

The heart and center of domestic Shinto (the Shinto of the home) has been the *kami-dana* or god-shelf. Most private homes possess one. On it are placed memorial tablets made of wood or paper, each inscribed with the name of an ancestor or of a patron deity of the household or locality. Sometimes Amaterasu, sometimes Inari, the goddess of rice, or both, are honored by the presence of their symbols. In most cases a shrine, or *miya*, containing a sacred mirror, or strips of paper with sacred texts written on them, or talismans obtained at Isé or elsewhere, occupies the center of the god-shelf. The god-shelf itself in this case becomes a temple area in miniature. It may be the repository of any object surcharged with family history and significance. (The writer knows of a Japanese farmer, so grateful for kindness rendered during illness in his family by a Christian missionary, that he rescued a pair of the latter's cast-off shoes from an ash-pile and put them on his god-shelf. One can scarcely conceive of a higher compliment.)

Unless in abeyance through neglect or discontinuance, the domestic rites are still performed daily. They may involve no more than the bringing of a small offering of food and the murmuring of a prayer. However, special occasions, or crises in the family life, call forth more elaborate rites, such as the lighting of tapers, and the offering of rice-brandy, sprigs of the *sakaki* tree, and cloth, as supplements to the usual food-offerings, while the whole family sits on the floor before the god-shelf, with bowed heads, in heedful silence.

Usually domestic religious life is not exclusively Shinto in character. Buddhist priests are often called in to perform rites connected with important aspects of family life. This is especially true after a death, the Buddhist priest being a "funeral specialist" whose services are as indispensable in Japanese society as those of a funeral director in our own. The family may also maintain in addition to the *kami-dana,* but usually in another room, a Buddhist altar (or *butsu-dana,* the Buddha-shelf), on which are placed wooden tablets bearing the "heavenly names" of the departed, which the Buddhist priest makes known. The priest may say masses here at stated intervals—another instance of how Buddhism vies with the native religion for the adherence of the family.

The Shinto Sects

During the years that the government sponsored the supposedly non-religious ceremonies of State Shinto, a sphere for Sectarian, that is to say, religious Shinto was allowed. Under the provisions of the Constitution of 1889, which granted religious liberty to all citizens, Shinto sects were free to formulate their own beliefs and ceremonies, but obliged also to find their own means of support, just as were the various branches of Buddhism and Christianity. Of the thirteen sects recognized by the Bureau of Religions before the Second World War, about one half came into existence after the Restoration of 1868. Any attempt to classify these self-propagating religious orders reveals their generally eclectic character. In D. C. Holtom's classification, only three of them can be called Pure Shinto sects. Of the others, two sought amalgamation with Confucianism. Three were called Mountain Sects, because they specialized in the ascent of steep mountain slopes, the object being to experience on the summits ecstatic communion with the great spirits of Japan. Of these last-named sects two centered their faith upon Mount Fuji as the best symbol of the national life and the most sacred object in all the world. The Purification Sects, so-called, of which there were two, emphasized the regard for ceremonial purity which ran through Old Shinto, but they also adopted Hindu methods of cleansing the soul and mind, especially deep breathing and fire-walking. The most interesting, and the most influential, of the sectarian orders were the faith-healing sects, three in number. One of them, the Tenri Kyo, has been aptly called the Christian Science of Japan. It was founded by a woman, and had the strongest popular appeal of any of the sects.

Since World War II, with the withdrawal of the government from the sphere of religion, the sects have very greatly multiplied. Some 800 are now registered with the government, and these include sects with every variety of religious belief, many of them no longer recognizably Shinto in character. The more syncretistic sects adapt to their needs not only the doctrines of many foreign religions but also certain theories drawn from psychology and other sciences, in the hope of attaining ultimate truth and personal spiritual security.

SUGGESTIONS FOR FURTHER READING

Anesaki, M. *The History of Japanese Religion.* K. Paul, Trench, Trubner, 1931
Aston, W. G. *Shinto, the Way of the Gods.* Longmans, 1905

Bunce, W. K. *Religions in Japan.* Tuttle (Vermont) pb, 1955

Chamberlain, Basil H., trans. *The Kojiki.* 2nd ed. J. L. Thompson and Co., Kobe, 1932

Hibino, Yi. *Nippon Shindo Ron, or the National Ideals of the Japanese People.* Cambridge, 1928

Holtom, D. C. *Modern Japan and Shinto Nationalism.* University of Chicago Press, 1943

————. *The National Faith of Japan.* E. P. Dutton, 1938

Sakamaki, Shujo. "Shinto: Japanese Ethnocentrism" in *Philosophy—East and West*, ed. Charles A. Moore. Princeton University Press, 1944

Sansom, G. B. *Japan: A Short Cultural History.* Century, 1931

Wheeler, P., ed. and trans. *Sacred Scriptures of the Japanese.* Schuman, 1952

PART FOUR

The Religions of the Near East

Foreword to
PART FOUR

THE AVERAGE WESTERN READER WILL FIND HIMSELF IN A MORE FAMILIAR atmosphere when he turns from the religions of the Orient to those of the Near East. The prevailing ideas are more easily comprehended. It is not that the religions of India and the Far East are so difficult, as that they have created in him a sense of strangeness. He is not fully at home with the pantheists, for example, or with the believers in re-incarnation; he has not experienced enough aesthetic self-identification with Nature and its underlying structural forces to share in full the Orient's distinctive mysticism. Nor does he readily impersonalize God, as Heaven, the Tao, Brahman-Atman, or the Adi-Buddha are imperson-alized in the East. Accustomed as he is to having religion lay down a moral code for daily observance, he misses in the Oriental religions the preoccupation with ethics which he expects to find in them.

In the religions of the Near East he finds a more familiar per-spective. God is a person, more or less anthropomorphically conceived, with a very pronounced interest in good moral behavior. Pantheism gives place to a spiritual pluralism, in which God, the Creator and Sustainer of the universe, joins with the spiritual host of good men and angels in forming a community of beings devoted through good and evil to the realization of the Good. Religion is a way of mastering life and the world, not of negating, nor of identifying oneself with, them. Asceticism is a minor and not quite natural kind of behavior. Nature is a subordinate reality, a created thing, merely the stage on which the drama of divine-human relationship is enacted. When its usefulness is at an end, it will be destroyed.

Let us say, then, that in their most representative forms the Near East religions, with some minor exceptions here and there, give a high value to human individuality, and conceive of the relationship between God and man as a person-to-person encounter, in which the moral element is prominent.

Above all, man stands apart from Nature in a spiritual relationship with God, and is not caught up along with Nature, as the Orient tends to believe, in the multiple self-manifestation of a reality more ultimate than all gods, men, and other natural forms and forces taken together. The divine, the human, and the natural are not merged together into the ineffable One, but stand out distinctly in a situation that is fundamentally moral.

A consequence of this is that in the Near East religions the characteristic question of the religious man is, What does God want me to do? What is His will? And a further development naturally follows: God is seen to have revealed himself and His will in history. Two marked characteristics of the Near East religions are therefore great interest in the historical religious fact and intense moral activity as the issue of personal encounter with the one God.

12 Zoroastrianism: The Religion of Ethical Dualism

IN OUR STUDY OF THE STRUCTURE OF RELIGIOUS EXPERIENCE AROUND THE world we have come to an interesting point. More clearly than is usual in the history of human thought, we see in the evolution of Zoroastrianism and its neighboring faith, Hinduism, the effect of environment on the beliefs and attitudes of kindred peoples. The religion of Zoroaster had the same source as the religion of the Vedic Aryans. When the Indo-European wanderers who sometime at the beginning of the second millennium before Christ, or earlier, came to a parting of the ways somewhere near the Caspian Sea, one portion, perhaps the larger, went on to India, the other penetrated into present-day Armenia, Azarbaijan, and the mountain valleys forming the northwest fringes of the Iranian plateau. This physical separation was destined to be paralleled by a cultural one.

In the land of Iran, as the historians prefer to call ancient Persia, the soil was hard and arid, the climate dry and rather bracing. The inhabitants therefore tended to be aggressive and realistic, because it was necessary for them to be attentive farmers and herdsmen. In the somewhat enervating climate of India, on the other hand, human life tended to become recessive physically, yet rich in romantic and philosophical interests. There is more time for thought in India, perhaps because more time is taken for it. On the Iranian plateau the situation was quite otherwise. Thought and life were concerned largely with this world, and the exciting, if difficult, struggle for existence. Morality while pursuing the business of life became one of the chief concerns of re-

464

ligion, and the mood of asceticism was far removed from most men's minds.

Suppose that the Aryans of India and the Aryans of Iran had remained together, living side by side on the plains somewhere in southeastern Europe, as they once did; would they have developed so great a difference as that between Zoroastrianism and Hinduism? It is fruitless to ask. They separated, and time and circumstance swung them poles apart.*

The story of Zoroastrianism is not easy to tell. Our sources are not clear and authentic, as they were in our study of the religion of the Vedas. The sacred book of the Zoroastrian faith, the *Avesta,* is more or less a miscellany, without cohesion; indeed, it is but the remnant of a far larger body of literature, a great part of which has perished. The portion of the Avesta most important for us is the *Yasna,* because it contains the *Gathas* or Hymns of Zoroaster, written in an ancient dialect (Gathic, a language closely related to the Vedic) and containing our only really trustworthy information on his life and thought. The other portions of the Avesta—the *Vispered,* the *Vendidad,* the *Yashts* or "songs of praise," and the *Kordah Avesta* or "little Avesta"—are less reliable because of their later date and change in emphasis and world-view.

Our best course, in view of the difficulties, is to begin with Iranian religion before Zoroaster, then to take up the life and teaching of Zoroaster himself, and finally mark the changes which were introduced into his religious system in later times.

I IRANIAN RELIGION BEFORE ZOROASTER

There is difficulty in determining the facts here because virtually all we know of the popular religion of Zoroaster's day is derived from the hostile references to it in the Avesta. Some further light is obtained from recently discovered inscriptions which confirm and supplement what we gather from the Avesta; but that is all.

We know, however, that the popular religion of the Iranians was practically the same as that reflected in the Vedas.

The common people worshipped powers known as *daevas,* a name identical with the *devas* or "shining ones" of the Rig-Veda. They were

* It should be added that a thousand years later a much larger group of Indo-Europeans, well provided with horses, came south to join the Aryans in Iran and to push beyond them toward the Persian Gulf.

personifications of the powers of nature—sun, moon, stars, earth, fire, water, and winds.

Prominent among them was Intar or Indara (the Vedic Indra), the dragon-slayer and rain god, but he was not of as paramount importance as he was among the Aryans of India; he was overshadowed by Mithra (Vedic Mitra), a very popular god, who seems to have been widely known among Aryan folk everywhere. In the Hittite inscription of 1400–1300 B.C., found in Asia Minor, he is mentioned under the name of Miidraashshiill, and he was, it appears, the chief god of the Mitanni, an Aryan group then controlling the mountain areas fringing the Mesopotamian plain on the north. The Iranians on their part gave him highest honors. He was to them the god of war and the god of light (whence the Greeks and Romans drew the inference that he was a sun-god; and this may have been true); particularly, he stood for the quality of loyalty and faith-keeping. In a later *yasht* (song) of the Kordah Avesta he is portrayed as the god "to whom the princes pray when they go forth to battle"; and in his function of supporter of the sanctity of treaties (Mithra seems to mean "treaty" or "pact") he sees to it that, wherever bad faith exists,—

The steeds of the deceivers refuse to bear their riders; though they run they do not advance, though they ride they make no progress, though they ride in their chariots they gain no advantage; backwards flies the lance hurled by the enemy of Mithra. Even if the enemy throw skillfully, even if his lance reach his enemy's body, the stroke does not hurt. The lance from the hand of Mithra's enemy is borne away by the wind.[1]

Along with Mithra there appears a god called in the Hittite inscription Uruwanaashshiil, who was known to the Greeks as Ouranos and is to be identified with the Vedic Varuna, the god of the domed sky and lord of the moral order. He had a high ethical character. We shall have need to mention him again.

We learn also of a conception of an underlying order of the world, whether natural or moral, called Asha or Arta, whose attributes are Right, Justice, and Divine Order (this is certainly the Vedic Rita); of the heavenly twins, the Nasatya or Asvins (in the Hittite inscription called the Nashaadtianna), who were reduced by the later Persians to one being; of Vayu, the Wind, under the double aspect of good and bad winds, blowing from the beginning of time; of the ruler of the dead, the first man to die, Yima (the Vedic Yama); and of the Fravashi or Fathers, the beloved and protective ancestral spirits (the Vedic Pitaras).

These divine powers (and others whose names are lost to us, but were in every case probably akin to the names of gods in the Rig-Veda) were worshipped and sacrificed to under the open sky, beside altars, with the aid of priests, fire-worship, and the sacramental use of the intoxicating beverage prepared from the sacred *haoma* plant (the Vedic *soma*).

The fire worship of the ancient Iranians is of particular interest, not only because of its likeness to the fire ceremonies of ancient India, but also because of its historical importance in Zoroastrianism down to the present day. The Vedic name Agni is not mentioned in the literature; but undoubtedly it was he who was invoked and worshipped. Along with the ceremony by which the sacrificial fire was lit and reverenced, the grass around the altar was consecrated, sprinkled with haoma juice, and made the table upon which were laid portions of the sacrifice for the invisible divine guests, the gods. The sacrifice might be a cereal one, but was usually that of an animal of some kind. In the latter case the victim about to be sacrificed was touched with the *barsom*, a bundle of boughs which was worshipped as supernatural, and held before the face during the adoration of the sacred fire. The ceremony of the pressing of the haoma juice and the sacramental use of the sacred liquid were, one is led to conclude, so similar to the ceremonies of the kind in Vedic India that the reader is referred to the chapter on Hinduism for details.

In general, the ancient Iranians, for the most part settlers who put their livestock out to graze and cultivated gardens, followed a religion ill suited to their mode of life and developing economy. Its animal sacrifices were becoming increasingly burdensome. What to nomads seemed natural and reasonable enough and involved no great economic sacrifice, to settlers was far too costly. Change at last became overdue. So doubtless it seemed to many a good husbandman, whose inarticulate religious experience ran counter to much of the teaching of the priests. The priests were complacent with the traditional state of affairs, and desired no reform; but the need they ignored they ignored at their peril, for Zoroaster was not an easy-going person.

II THE LIFE AND TEACHINGS OF ZOROASTER

Life

Zoroaster was the son of a landed proprietor, probably of Aryan stock. This seems to be the inference from his teachings and career best supported by the facts. His name itself suggests a rural setting. Zoroaster, the designation by which he is known in Europe, is taken from the

Greek corruption of the old Iranian word Zarathustra, and the last part of the old name, *ustra,* means "camel." *

The date of Zoroaster's birth is very uncertain. Persian tradition places the time at 660 B.C. This date, with misgivings, is accepted by most modern scholars; but others, with some plausibility, contend that Zoroaster must have lived at an earlier period, perhaps as early as 1000 B.C.

Another elusive matter is the determination of his birthplace. Was he born in Media or in Bactria? It seems likely he was born in the former province † and did his work in the latter.

According to tradition, he received instruction in youth from a tutor; assumed the *kusti* or sacred thread (note once more the parallelism with Indian custom) at the age of fifteen; was known for his compassionate nature, expressed especially in solicitude toward the aged and toward cattle in time of famine; and at twenty left his father and mother and the wife they chose for him, to wander forth, seeking an answer to his deepest religious questionings. He sought enlightenment from all he met who would submit to inquiry.

> On one occasion, upon inquiring in open assembly, what may be accounted as the most favorable for the soul, he is told, "to nourish the poor, to give fodder to cattle, to bring firewood to the fire, to pour Hom-juice into water, and to worship many demons." Zoroaster gives proof of his eclectic tendency by performing the first four of these injunctions as worthy of a righteous man to do; but demon-worship he absolutely denounces.[2]

According to Greek sources, he kept silent for seven years and lived in a mountain cave; and this tradition reached Rome in the form of the wonder-rousing story that he lived for twenty years in desert places subsisting on cheese!

At the critical age of thirty (so often a time of crisis in the lives of religious geniuses) he received a revelation. Legend magnifies the original event into a series of miraculous visions. The traditional scene of the first and most startling vision is laid on the banks of the Daitya River near his home. A figure "nine times as large as a man" appeared before Zoroaster. It was the archangel Vohu Manah (Good Thought). Vohu Manah questioned Zoroaster and then bade him lay aside the "vesture" of his material body, and, as a disembodied soul, mount to the presence of Ahura Mazda, "the Wise Lord" and Supreme Being, holding court among his attendant angels.[3] A curiously vivid detail of the account

---

* Suggestive proposals for the translation of all of Zoroaster's name are: "One who plows with camels" and "One whose camels are old."

† In Azarbaijan probably.

records the fact that, as soon as Zoroaster appeared in the celestial assembly, he no longer beheld his own shadow upon the floor, "on account of the great brilliance of the archangels," who encircled him.[4] Ahura Mazda then instructed Zoroaster, called now to be a prophet, in the doctrines and duties of the true religion.

During the next eight years Zoroaster is said to have met in vision each of the six principal archangels, and each conference made more complete the original revelation. So runs the tradition.

But in the Gathas, where we have presumably Zoroaster's own words, the references to these revelations furnish us with more authentic, if fragmentary, details. Thus:

"As the holy one I recognized thee, Mazda Ahura, when Good Thought (Vohu Manah) came to me and asked me, 'Who art thou? to whom dost thou belong? By what sign wilt thou appoint the days for questioning about thy possessions and thyself?'

"Then said I to him: 'To the first (question), Zarathustra am I, a true foe to the Liar, to the utmost of my power, but a powerful support would I be to the Righteous, that I may attain the future things of the infinite Dominion, according as I praise and sing thee, Mazda.'

"As the holy one I recognized thee, Mazda Ahura, when Good Thought came to me. To his question, 'For which wilt thou decide?' (I made reply), 'At every offering of reverence to thy Fire, I will bethink me of Right so long as I have power. Then show me Right, upon whom I call.' . . .

"And when thou saidst to me, 'To Right shalt thou go for teaching,' then thou didst not command what I did not obey: 'Speed thee, ere my Obedience * come, followed by treasure-laden Destiny, who shall render to men severally the destinies of the two-fold award.' " [5]

The ten years which followed his divine call were to Zoroaster years of private exaltation but of public discouragement. He began immediately to preach, but was without success. Discouraged, he was visited by severe temptation, in which the Evil Spirit, Angra Mainyu, bade him renounce the religion of the worshiper of Mazda. "But Zarathustra answered him: 'No! I shall not renounce the good Religion of the worshipers of Mazda, not though life, limb, and soul should part asunder.' " [6]

At last he was rewarded. After ten years he won his first convert —his own cousin Maidhynimaonha.

Then somewhere in eastern Iran, he found himself, it is said, in the court of an Aryan prince by the name of Vishtaspa.† With renewed

---

* Sraosha, Obedience, the angel of Judgment, under whose care the dead are.

† Or Hystaspes. Some authorities think he may have been the father of Darius, for the latter bore this name and was satrap of Parthia. But this supposition seems in conflict with the linguistic age of the Gathas.

hope, he began a two years' effort to win this ruler to his faith. Vishtaspa, all but hidden from view in the mass of laudatory tradition gathered round him, gives the impression of being an honest-hearted man, simple and sincere in his habit of life. But he was dominated by the Karpans so detested in the Avesta, a greedy throng of priests. With their numerous animal sacrifices, and their magical procedures designed to make the crops grow, protect the cattle, keep the marauding nomads of the north (the Turanians) at a distance, and frustrate demonic influences of all sorts, they roused Zoroaster's intensest opposition. During the struggle with him they managed to have him cast into prison; but in the end, after two hard years, aided, tradition tells, by his wondrous cure of Vishtaspa's favorite black horse, and helped by the sympathetic support of Vishtaspa's consort, Hutaosa, he won the monarch over to his faith.

The conversion was complete and unreserved. Vishtaspa put all his power behind the propagation of the faith. The whole court followed the monarch into the new religion. The king's brother, Zain, and his gallant son, Isfendir, were of special importance as converts. Two brothers, both nobles who stood high in the councils of Vishtaspa, Frashaoshtra and Jamnaspa by name, became Zoroaster's kin by marriage; the former gave Zoroaster his daughter, Huovi, to wife; and the latter married Pourucista, Zoroaster's daughter by his first wife.

The next twenty years, as the late and not too trustworthy tradition records, were spent in vigorously promulgating the faith among the Iranians and in fighting two holy wars in its defence. The first of these saw the rise of Isfendir to great heights of heroism in routing the invading Turanians. But, if tradition can be credited, the second invasion of the Turanians, which took place when Zoroaster was seventy-seven years of age, was at first successful, and led to Zoroaster's death; the later writers of the Avesta state, over a thousand years after the event, that when the Turanians stormed Balkh, one of their number surprised and slew him before the fire-altar at which he was officiating.

Whether or not this was the manner of it, Zoroaster's death did not mean the extinction of the faith. He had planted the roots of his new faith deeply in the rich soil of Iranian folk-consciousness, where it was destined to flourish.

Teachings

The religion which Zoroaster taught was a unique ethical monotheism. Like the Hebrew monotheist, Moses, he was a great original, even though he based himself solidly on inherited beliefs.

In calling the supreme god of his unquestioning faith Ahura Mazda ("Wise Lord"), he did not resort to invention. The name was already current. Nor was the god denoted by it hitherto unknown. Ahura Mazda was, there is little doubt, no other than the god of the moral and natural order whom the Aryans of India worshipped under the name of Varuna. It seems that Zoroaster's clan had long given their special allegiance to this highly ethical deity. Though the god was no longer called Varuna, many scholars, seeing in what aspects he was viewed (he is described in the Gathas as "clad with the massy heavens as with a garment" [7]), have concluded that the honorific title had come to take the place of his ancient name, just as in India the title "Auspicious" (Shiva) dispossessed the ancient name Rudra. That Ahura Mazda was an honorific designation is quite apparent. Mazda means "the wise" or "the full of light." Ahura is the same word as the Vedic Asura, meaning "lord," and was an Indo-European name for outstanding figures among the devas or gods.

Incidentally, it is interesting to follow out the curious twist given by Zoroaster on the one hand and the Vedic Aryans on the other to the words for lord and god. The Indo-Aryans, like the Romans and Celts on the other side of the world, called their *good* spirits *devas* (Roman *deus*, Celtic *divin*, and English *deity* or *divinity*); but their experience of the capricious natural forces of India somehow caused the name *asura* (lord) to be applied exclusively to *evil* spirits, the sublime and awful lords of mischief. (This shift in meaning may be seen taking place between the earlier and later hymns of the Rig-Veda.) In Iran, on the other hand, Zoroaster attached to these words quite the opposite meanings. In Mazda he saw the one true Ahura to whom his entire devotion should be paid, the sublime and awful "Lord" who was perfect wisdom and goodness. But he feared that Mazda would not be recognized in the same way by the masses of his people. Under the leadership of the priests of the old religion, they worshipped a host of *daevas*—gods called by many ancient Aryan names; they even ignorantly adored as daevas the fire on the altar and the intoxicating juice of the haoma plant. The corrupt priests made magic with the aid of these deities. The wild nomads of Turan, who were the scourge of all good settlers, sacrificed to these deities before they made their raids on Iran, to carry off the grain and cattle and gut the barns and homes with fire. There could be only one conclusion for Zoroaster. One and all, he declared roundly, these daevas were malicious devils masquerading as good spirits, fathers of lies deceiving the very elect. They wrought evil and turned men from following Ahura Mazda. Their worship must be stamped out!

Opposing himself squarely and uncompromisingly, therefore, to the popular religion, Zoroaster set forth his religious system in a few clear-cut conceptions.

1. He took a firm stand, to begin with, on the revelation he had received. The Gathas again and again set forth his claim that he had been called to his prophetic mission by Ahura Mazda himself, and that the religion he taught was the final and perfect religion.

2. He gave all his devotion to one god. Ahura Mazda was, to him, the supreme deity—that is to say, supreme in creation, supreme in value, and supreme by anticipation of the final apocalyptic event by which he would forever crush all evil and establish right and truth. In contra-distinction to some of his later followers, Zoroaster believed that by the will of the one supreme Lord Mazda all things had come into being. As the following sentences from the Gathas declare, Mazda caused dark-ness as well as light.

> Who is by generation the Father of Right (Asha) at the first? Who de-termined the path of sun and stars? Who is it by whom the moon waxes and wanes again? . . . Who upheld the earth beneath and the firmament from falling? Who made the water and the plants? Who yoked swiftness to winds and clouds? . . . What artist made light and darkness, sleep and waking? Who made morning, noon, and night, that call the understanding man to his duty? . . . I strive to recognize by these things thee, O Mazda, creator of all things through the holy spirit.[8]

3. He had a rich conception of Ahura Mazda's way of accomplish-ing results. Mazda expresses his will through a Holy Spirit (Spenta Mainyu) and various modes of divine action, called the "Immortal Holy Ones" or Amesha Spentas (the Ameshaspands of later Persia). These modes of ethical activity bear such names as Vohu Manah (Good Thought or Sense), Asha (Right), Kshathra (Power or Dominion), Haurvatat (Prosperity), Armaiti (Piety), and Ameretat (Immortality). Asha (or Arta) is the Vedic Rita; Vohu Manah is the divine mode which conducted Zoroaster to Ahura Mazda for his first revelation (here the allegorical meaning that Zoroaster was led by inspiration to the true God seems to suggest itself); Armaiti, Kshathra, Haurvatat, and Amere-tat are gifts of Ahura Mazda to man and also forces and facts in their own right. All of them are abstract qualities or states, and it is a little perplexing to know just what Zoroaster's conception of them was, whether he felt that they were good genii of Ahura Mazda, with their own being and individuality, or whether he meant to give them no more

than the force of conveniently personalized abstractions.* Other modes of divine expression are named besides the Amesha Spentas—for example, Obedience (Sraosha), the Ox-Creator or spirit that protects cows (Geus Urva), and still others. But none of these are very clearly visualized as divine beings with independent personalities; at all events they are kept subordinate to Ahura Mazda as agents of his divine self-expression. In short, Zoroaster gives us a rich conception of deity without abandoning monotheism.

4. But, though Ahura Mazda is supreme, he is not unopposed. This is an important belief of Zoroaster. Over against Asha (Right or Truth) is Druj (the Lie). Truth is confronted with Falsehood, Life with Death. The Good Spirit (Spenta Mainyu) is opposed by Angra Mainyu, literally, "the Bad Spirit." It is characteristic of the Gathas to lay continual

---

* If the latter was his meaning, he was using language in much the same way as poets do, as in the lines of W. W. Story:

> "Brothers, unite—rouse in your might,
> For Justice and Freedom, for God and the Right!"

James Hope Moulton was one leading authority who inclined toward this interpretation of Zoroaster's use of his abstractions. He wrote: "The inference seems inevitable that Asha and Vohu Manah are not archangels at all, but divine attributes within the hypostasis of Deity. Piety (Armaiti) and the Ox-Creator would seem to be likewise definable. And if so, there is no reason why we should not include Dominion (Kshathra), Welfare or Salvation (Haurvatat), and Immortality (Ameretat), which are clearly concepts of the same order, although we cannot make a dogmatic statement. In any case we see that this profound thinker's instinct not only grasped the supreme truth of the Oneness of God, but realized the vital corollary that there must be diversity within the Godhead if the unity is to be a fruitful doctrine." [9] But that this high abstractness was modified by Zoroaster himself was admitted by Moulton in an earlier book, in noting the fact "that Armaiti is clearly the genius of the Earth in the Gathas," that there is a connection between Kshathra and metals, and "that Haurvatat and Ameretat are Water and Plants." One might almost suggest, he added, that Zarathushtra "drew from the popular religion what suited him." [10] The German scholar B. Geiger and the American authority A. V. W. Jackson are more inclined to think the Amesha Spenta were real archangels who were endowed with abstract names to accent the changed character they now displayed in Zoroaster's purified faith. More recently, Jacques Duchesne-Guillemin in *Zoroastre* (Paris, 1948) draws the following parallels: the two Vayus with the two Mainyus, Varuna with Rita or Arta, Mitra with Manah (Thought), the two Nasatya with Haurvatat and Ameretat, and the river or water goddess with Armaiti. In the overall Zoroastrian scheme, "at the height of the hierarchy" Ahura Mazda is *"the father"* of Spenta Mainyu (Yasna 47.3), Arta or Asha, and Vohu Manah, the first of these three being especially close, almost to the point of complete identity. At any rate, the Holy Spirit proceeds from the father as a son. If the father and this son are regarded as one, then a trinity emerges, composed of the Wise Lord, Justice (or Right), and Good Thought.

emphasis on the fundamental cleavage in the world of nature and in the life of man between right and wrong, the true religion and the false. This cleavage began with Creation.

Now the two primal Spirits, who revealed themselves in vision as Twins, are the Better and the Bad in thought and word and action. And between these two the wise once choose aright, the foolish not so. And when these twain Spirits came together in the beginning, they established Life and Not-Life, and that at the last the Worst Existence (Hell) shall be to the followers of the Lie, but the Best Thought (Paradise) to him that follows Right. Of these twain Spirits he that followed the Lie chose doing the worst things; the holiest Spirit chose Right.[11]

Again:

I will speak of the Spirits twain at the first beginning of the world, of whom the holier thus spake to the enemy: "Neither thought nor teachings nor wills nor beliefs nor words nor deeds nor selves nor souls of us twain agree." [12]

Thus, at the beginning of the world, the good spirit going forth from Ahura Mazda was met and opposed by an evil spirit—the spirit called in later times Shaitin or Satan.

The language is vague and inconclusive on the point of Ahura Mazda's responsibility for the existence of the evil spirit, Angra Mainyu. Did Angra Mainyu exist with Ahura Mazda from the beginning, or did Ahura Mazda create the Evil One? Or was the fact simply this: that Ahura Mazda did not create the Evil One, but discovered it was just the natural thing to find evil where there is good, and darkness beside light? The last view, on the whole, seems to prevail throughout the Gathas; but it is not difficult to see how the belief expressed in the later Avesta, that the spirit of evil is an arch-fiend who has been always opposed to Ahura Mazda, could grow out of it.

5. Although only a few words are needed to state it, it was perhaps Zoroaster's cardinal moral principle, that each man's soul is the seat of a war between good and evil. This war in the breast is of critical importance. In creating man Ahura Mazda gave him freedom to determine his own actions and hence the power to choose between right and wrong. Though Ahura Mazda seeks always by the power of his good spirit (Spenta Mainyu) and through Vohu Manah to commend the Right, he has not made man inaccessible to Angra Mainyu's evil suggestions. So it is required of each man to decide the issue of the war in his own bosom, and to choose either the Good or the Evil. The good man chooses aright.

6. Good and evil are not clearly defined; but we cannot rightly expect the Gathas, which are devotional hymns and not theological treatises, to be precise. The Gathas, however, give us an indication of the *practical difference* between right and wrong. The good people for example, were to Zoroaster those who accepted the true religion, and the evil were those who rejected it, especially those who continued to practice the old popular religion with its worship of the daevas. The daevas, it seemed clear, had allied themselves with Angra Mainyu, the evil spirit; and so those who followed them were living in a condition fraught with evil. Such people were not merely to be shunned: "Resist them with the weapon!" [13] If it is good always to speak the truth and to aid all those who follow Asha and Vohu Manah, it is evil to help the bad, to do them favors, or give them gifts. The good—and here is an insight into Zoroaster's practical common sense—till the soil, raise grain, grow fruits, root out weeds, reclaim waste land, irrigate the barren ground, and treat kindly the animals, especially the cow, that are of service to the farmers. In their personal relations they are truth-speakers; they never lie. The evil have no such interests; they do not concern themselves about agriculture. That is their condemnation.

He that is no husbandman, O Mazda, however eager he be, has no part in the good message.[14]

Angra Mainyu is always busy against husbandry:

The Liar stays the supporters of Right from prospering the cattle in district and province, infamous that he is.[15]

The Turanian nomads represented evil at its worst. They prepared for their raids by worshipping the daevas, after wickedly slaying cattle as sacrifices for the altar. Then they fell upon the fields and destroyed their produce. Such is the evil one may expect from daeva-worshipers! The good man would say, in the words of an old Zoroastrian pledge:

"I repudiate the Daevas. I confess myself a worshipper of Mazda, a Zarathustrian, as an enemy of the Daevas, a prophet of the Lord, praising and worshipping the Immortal Holy Ones (the Amesha Spentas). To the Wise Lord I promise all good; to him, the good, beneficent, righteous, glorious, venerable, I vow all the best; to him from whom is the cow, the law, the (celestial) luminaries, with whose luminaries (heavenly) blessedness is conjoined. I choose the holy, good Armaiti, she shall be mine. I abjure theft and cattle-stealing, plundering and devastating the villages of Mazda-worshippers." [16]

7. Of religious ceremonial little is left. The old Aryan ritual is purged (almost to the vanishing point) of magic and idolatry.

But there was one feature of the old ritual which Zoroaster retained. According to tradition, as we have seen, he was done to death while serving before the Sacred Fire. In a previous quotation from the Gathas we have heard him say, "At every offering to thy Fire, I will bethink me of Right so long as I have power." Elsewhere he declares the sacred fire to be a gift of Ahura Mazda to mankind. But Zoroaster did not worship *the fire,* as his ancestors had done, or as some of his followers later did; it was to him a precious symbol of Ahura Mazda, and no more, through which he could realize the nature and essence of the Wise Lord. So, at least, his language, and the logic of his whole position, presuppose.

8. What, finally, is to be the issue of the long struggle between Good and Evil? Will Ahura Mazda forever be opposed? Will Angra Mainyu, the Liar, always afflict man and lead him astray?

Whatever misgivings his later followers may have had on the subject, Zoroaster had no doubt that Ahura Mazda would, in the fulness of time, triumphantly overthrow all evil. He did not believe that the influence of Evil is as eternal as Good. He was thoroughly optimistic. Good would yet outlast and outwit Evil.

How?

For the first time in a world religion, eschatology, the conception of "last things" or the end of the world, comes into prominence. According to Zoroaster's teachings, a *general resurrection* will take place at the end of the present world order. The good and evil will then be subjected to an Ordeal of Fire and Molten Metal. By this fiery test, as a later amplification of the original teaching declares, the evil will be made known by their terrible burning, but the righteous will find the Fire kindly and the Molten Metal harmless, as soft and healing as milk. In the Gathas, the picture is so much less clearly defined, that it remains in doubt whether the forces of evil, including Angra Mainyu, will be entirely consumed by the fiery Ordeal, or will survive to be hurled into the abyss of the "Abode of Lies" (Hell).

If the latter conception is the correct one, some consistency can be read into the rather confused imagery of *individual judgment.* Individual judgment follows shortly after death, and the state of the soul remains fixed thereafter until the general resurrection at the end of the world. The references to it—marked by excessive brevity—may, with a little forced interpretation, be made to yield a picture replete with picturesque detail. Each soul, good, or bad, must face judgment at the

Bridge of the Separator (the Chinvat Bridge), which spans the abyss of Hell, and at its farther end opens on Paradise. At this bridge the record of the soul is read. The balance of merits and demerits is cast. If good deeds predominate over evil, the "pointing of the hand" (of Ahura Mazda?) will be toward Paradise; but if evil overbalances good, the hand will point to the abyss below the bridge. The crossing of the bridge is most dramatically conceived. The righteous, guided by Zoroaster, will have no difficulty; but the evil, already condemned by the judges, will find themselves in no case able to go beyond its center. Why? Zoroaster held the profound doctrine that a man's Self fixes his destiny. He said of the evil:

"Their own Soul and their own Self * shall torment them when they come to the Bridge of the Separator. To all time will they be guests for the House of the Lie." [17]

Staggered by their own guilty consciences, they will of themselves fall to their doom.

They will dwell in "The House of the Lie," the Gathas' hell, a place called "the worst existence," the abode of "the worst thought," an ill-smelling region, most dreadful to the Iranian imagination because it is so foul. In its lightless depths sad voices cry out, but each sufferer is forever "alone." On the other hand, the righteous will dwell beyond the great Bridge in "The House of Song," the Gathas' Paradise, described as "the best existence," the abode of "the best thought," where the sun shines forever, and the righteous enjoy spiritual bliss, happy in their ever-joyous companionship.

Zoroaster believed so earnestly that the Good Religion of Ahura Mazda would win enough adherents to bring about the eventual defeat of evil, that he had the stout hope that some of these adherents would be, like him, "Deliverers." † He therefore had no doubt of Ahura Mazda's ultimate triumph—but he also felt strongly, let no man who sees the nature of the struggle between Truth and Falsehood fail meanwhile to ally himself with Truth!

Such was the militant note with which Zoroaster brought his moral challenge to the folk of his time. How far he was in advance of his age, let those who read further judge.

---

* Or "their own *daena*." *Daena* is variously translated. It stands for the moral center of the personality, the higher nature; specifically, the conscience.

† The word here used is *saoshyant,* and after Zoroaster's day it was destined to have a significant history, as we shall see.

III THE RELIGION OF THE LATER AVESTA

It is typical of the fragmentary records of early Zoroastrianism that we cannot trace in them the growth and spread of that faith through the plateau of Iran and in the Zagreus Mountains. When again Zoroastrianism emerges clearly into the light of history it is the religion of the kings of the Achaemenian dynasty, the rulers of the Persian Empire founded by Cyrus the Great, who in 538 B.C. overthrew Babylon and put an end to the Chaldaean Empire. What had happened meanwhile is largely a matter of conjecture. There was probably a rapid spread of Zoroastrianism among the Aryan princes; wars in its behalf were doubtless freely and fiercely fought; and at least in Media Zoroastrianism rose to ascendancy and won the influential support of a Median group known as the Magi.

It is somewhat of a mystery who the Magi were. They probably were not of Aryan stock. But they were known as far west as Jerusalem for their skill in the practice of magical arts. (The word *magic* is of course derived from them.) Babylon knew of them, even before that great city fell under the successful onslaught of Cyrus. It appears that when Zoroastrianism first came on the scene they opposed it, but becoming convinced that their special talents as priests could be used in its propagation, they adopted it, and became its leading exponents in the Mesopotamian world.

Cyrus the Great was a Zoroastrian, but not a very strict one, since for political reasons, when he first extended his sway over the Chaldaeans, he sought their support by appearing to be a worshiper of the Babylonian god Marduk. But Darius I and Xerxes after him did no such compromising; they uniformly honored Ahura Mazda, in their many inscriptions, as supreme Lord of Heaven and Earth. Their religion was not any longer precisely that of Zoroaster, as presented in the Gathas; but they believed firmly that Ahura Mazda and the agencies of his divine working and favor were with them.

It was in these days that world-history hung in the balance. Darius first, and Xerxes later, turned their hopes to world-conquest. Summoning the resources of the great Persian Empire to their aid, they marched toward Europe. Xerxes invaded Greece, and perhaps only the disaster of Salamis prevented Zoroaster's faith from becoming a major religion of the Western World.

In so brief a time Zoroastrianism rose to the apex of its claims to world-wide validity.

However, it made its way to this height of influence at a cost—the ᴄost of modification of the ideas of the founder, the sacrifice of the integrity of his philosophy of life to the brightening of its color and popular appeal.

The account of these developments, which follows, strives to present within the briefest compass consistent with truth a picture of the changes which entered Zoroastrianism—changes which must be called typical of any religion founded by a prophetic personality but propagated by priests and kings.

1. A highly worshipful attitude came to be taken toward Zoroaster himself. To the adoring eyes of his later followers, that very human man, "the shepherd of the poor" who appears in the Gathas, became a godlike personage whose whole existence was attended by supernatural manifestations. Heaven and hell were thrown into commotion by him. His coming was known and foretold three thousand years before by the mythical primeval bull; and King Yima, in the golden age, gave the demons warning that their defeat was impending. The demons, thus forewarned, strove to prevent the occurrence of what they so much feared. They noted with consternation the manner of Zoroaster's conception. The Glory of Ahura Mazda united itself with Zoroaster's future mother at her birth and rendered her fit thereby to bear the prophet. At the same time a divinely protected stem of a *haoma* plant was infused with the *fravashi* * of the coming prophet; and at the proper time the parents of Zoroaster drank its juices mixed with a potent milk, which the demons vainly sought to destroy and which contained the material essence (body protoplasm) of the child about to be conceived. After his birth, at which all nature rejoiced, and at the moment of which he himself laughed aloud, demons and hostile wizards surrounded him with every sort of hazard. His own father was rendered by magic arts indifferent to his fate. The baby was almost killed in his cradle, burnt in a huge fire, and trampled to death by a herd of cattle (whose leading ox, however, stood above him and saved him, exactly as did a leading horse, in a similar event where demons stampeded a herd of horses); he was placed in a cave with wolves whose young had been killed, and sad would have been his plight if these savage creatures had not allowed a ewe to enter and suckle him!

According to the highly elaborated tradition, the same sort of miracle attended his adult life. The *Zartusht Namah* (composed about 1200 A.D. from earlier material) thus tells the famous story of the healing of Vishtaspa's horse:—Zoroaster had been imprisoned as the result of a

* See section 2 below, p. 481 ff.

plot of the hostile nobles (Kavis) and priests of the daevas (Karpans). Thereupon King Vishtaspa's horse fell to the ground, unable to move, its four legs drawn up toward its belly. Zoroaster sent word from his cell that he could cure the animal. But he promised to act only on one condition—that the King would grant a boon for each leg he restored. Zoroaster was summoned to the King's presence. The first boon asked was that Vishtaspa accept the Faith. When the King agreed, the right leg was straightened. As readily the King granted the other three boons —that the King's son Isfendir should fight for the Faith, that the Queen should also become a convert, and that the names of those in the plot against Zoroaster should be revealed and the plotters punished—in consideration of which, one by one the quivering charger's legs were restored to use and it leapt to its feet, full of strength and fire. At one stroke Zoroaster had routed his enemies and multiplied his converts.

His miraculous powers should have afforded no one surprise, one observes, if his first appearance at Vishtaspa's court was, as some writers record, an entrance through the palace roof, which opened of itself to admit the prophet, holding in his hand "a cube of fire with which he played without its hurting him." [18]

Zoroaster was highly venerated in antiquity. The Greeks and Romans were much impressed by what they heard of him and his religion. How greatly they were impressed is evidenced by the astonishingly numerous references to him in the extant literature and by the fact that Plato was reportedly prevented, shortly after the death of Socrates, from going to Persia to study Zoroastrianism at first hand only by the outbreak of the War of Sparta with Persia in 396 B.C.

2. A change came over the monotheism of Zoroaster. In theory— that is to say, according to the official creed of the later Avesta—Ahura Mazda (or Ormazd as he came to be called) was always adored as a supreme deity, transcendent and without equal. He was held to be too great and spiritual to have images made of him, as though he could be contained in wood or stone. But he was no longer godhead undivided. The old Aryan nature worship, which Zoroaster condemned and fought, crept back into the faith, and placed powerful figures around him to share his powers. Thus Vohu Manah (Good Thought), upon hearing in the lowing of the cattle a prayer to him to plead their cause, assumed certain agricultural functions and became the guardian divinity of the cattle. Asha (Right) became the guardian divinity of fire, and Kshathra (Dominion) the lord of metals. Since the other Amesha Spentas had feminine names they became female archangels. Armaiti (Piety) became the goddess of the soil, Haurvatat (Prosperity) the goddess of waters, and Ameretat (Immortality) the goddess of vegetation.

But these Holy Immortal Ones, perhaps because of a certain artificial quality about them (they were at least not suited to popular mythology), seemed much less important than the *Yazatas* or angels, of whom about forty are named. That they came back into Zoroastrianism trailing clouds of glory from a far past is evident in the Yasht which speaks of the Yazatas as rising by "hundreds and thousands." They bore a distinct Aryan character, with many reminders of the Rig-Veda; for included among them were Ushas, the dawn goddess, and Vayu, god of the wind. But greatest of them all was *Mithra*. Though Zoroaster apparently would have nothing to do with this radiant divinity, the people clung to him. In the later Avesta he returns to his earlier prominence. His name is regularly mentioned along with Ahura Mazda's in the inscriptions of the later Achaemenian kings, those of Artaxerxes, for instance. Theologically, he was of course subordinate to Ahura Mazda, but in the religion of the masses he attained a supreme stature as the god of light, the rewarder of those who spoke truth and kept faith, and the chief support of those who relied on him to aid them in the struggle with the powers of darkness in this life and the next. One of the unique features of this later Zoroastrianism is the extraordinary claim that Ahura Mazda himself offers sacrifices to Mithra! ° No wonder that one leading scholar says: "It must be allowed that monotheism is submitted to a severe strain when Ahura Mazda himself offers worship to angels like these." [19]

Also brought back (albeit refined of the character of excess) was *Haoma*, the sacred intoxicant, "the enlivening, the healing, the beautiful, the lordly, with golden eyes." Animal sacrifices—this would have horrified Zoroaster—were made to him. He became again "the averter of Death," associated, as in the Rig-Veda, with long life and the immortality of the soul.

There were also the *Fravashis*. These beings are hard to describe because of their rather mixed character. Originally, they seem to have been the ancestral spirits, guarding, and expecting worship in return from, the living; but later their significance broadened, until they stood for ideal selves, who were also guardian genii, both of men and gods. Each living man was finally thought to have a *fravashi*, or eternal element, and so also certain beings not yet born, namely, "the Saoshyants who are to restore the world." Much more, the Amesha Spentas, the Yazatas, and Ahura Mazda himself were assumed each to have a *fravashi*! Carefully narrowing down this meaning, we arrive at the conclusion that such *fravashis* are the spiritual or immortal parts of living personalities, which, like the human souls in Plato's philosophy, exist

° And both Ahura Mazda and Mithra worship Vayu, the Wind! (Yasht 10:123, 15:2-4).

before birth and survive after death; here they have the added function of subsisting as ideal or better selves separately from men and pulling them heavenward and away from danger. Prayer and sacrifices were owing to ancestral *fravashis* in return for their indispensable service in the work of salvation.

So far did the process of fitting out Ahura Mazda's realm with assistant deities go that the Persians availed themselves of opportunities provided outside the Aryan scheme of things. In one of his inscriptions, Artaxerxes II (404–358 B.C.) for the first time mentions a female deity named *Anahita*, "the Spotless One." His high regard for her is evidenced by the fact that he erected images to her in Babylon, Susa, Ecbatana, Damascus, and Sardis. Her origin was not of the best. She was, it appears, one of the many forms taken by the Babylonian goddess, Ishtar, whom we have met in another connection. In the Yasht in which Anahita's praises are sung, she is called the goddess of the waters let down from heaven to fructify the earth in all its seven regions; she brings increase to vegetation and to flocks and herds; and she awakens in human beings, Ishtar-like, the powers of reproduction, her blessing resting especially on women, that they may have easy births and abundant milk.

In all this we see monotheism relapsing into polytheism, a not uncommon fact in the history of religions. In all faiths there is a joyful acceptance of prophetic utterances and ideals in difficult and degenerate days; but reform is generally succeeded by relapse, a falling away from "thoughts that are high and deeds that are noble" to a more comfortable accommodation of doctrine and practice to the easy-going ways of the masses of men "who like not thinking better than to follow habit."

3. The doctrine of evil was developed further and approached an almost complete ethical dualism. Like the good angels, the spirits of evil were more sharply individualized than they were by Zoroaster. Angra Mainyu, of whom Zoroaster had spoken bitterly, although not in very concrete terms, as being from the beginning of creation in opposition to Ahura Mazda's Spirit of Good, now became the arch-fiend, and was set over against Ahura Mazda in dualistic fashion. Portions of the later Avesta almost made Angra Mainyu co-equal with as well as the contradiction of Ahura Mazda. For example, the world was regarded as their joint creation. In the first chapter of the Vendidad, Ahura Mazda is portrayed as telling Zoroaster the story of his struggle with Angra Mainyu at the creation of the world. He pictures himself creating the various Iranian districts and endowing them with every excellence; unfortunately, as he admits, Angra Mainyu was on hand, too, busily cre-

ating an evil for every good—killing frost of winter, excessive heat of summer; snakes, locusts, ants; the wicked rich, evil sorcerers, non-Aryan lords of the land; human vices, lust, witchcraft, doubt, disbelief, and so on; not to speak of such unpardonable offences as burying of the dead or cooking of carrion, practices peculiarly abhorrent to the orthodox Zoroastrians of later days. Angra Mainyu's capacity for mischief was in fact boundless. The twenty-second chapter places the number of diseases created by him at 99,999, a stupendous number to the people of that time. But there was a final touch. He was the author of Death.

The evil power that Angra Mainyu possessed was many times multiplied by the demons he created to assist him, such as Aka Manah (Bad Thought), Andar (the Vedic Indra), Naonhaithya (the Vedic Nasatya, "the heavenly twins," here reduced to one being), Sauru, Fauru, Zairi, and others. Besides these there were also "numberless myriads" of evil spirits, daevas (devils) all of them. In this connection we must not overlook *Druj* (the Lie), now appearing in the likeness of a female demon so destructive of righteousness among men that even Ahura Mazda, in one Yasht, exclaims: "Had not the awful Fravashis of the faithful given help unto me . . . dominion would belong to the Druj, the material world would belong to the Druj!" [20]

This is one way to solve the problem of evil, to say that all good comes from God, all evil from the Devil. But consistency demands that the Devil, if he is the true author of evil, be co-eternal with God from the beginning of time; otherwise, God created evil in the beginning. Only a few Zoroastrians embraced this logical corollary of their position. A powerful group among the Magi, attempting to avoid so unsatisfactory a conclusion, proposed as early as the 4th century B.C. a doctrine which was rejected by the main body of Zoroastrians but which seems a strange fore-shadowing of modern physical theory. They suggested that both Ahura Mazda and Angra Mainyu sprang from a unitary world-principle called Zervan (Time or Space; or was it Space-Time?); and God and Devil were thus made co-equal in length of years. But even in the working out of this doctrine the ultimate victory of Ahura Mazda was declared to be certain, and opposition to evil was still made the first duty of every right-thinking man.

4. Though man's conflict with the demons on the great battlefield of life is described as fundamentally moral, in the later Avesta, especially in the Vendidad, it becomes more and more a struggle against the demonic attempt to fasten ceremonial impurity on man. In consequence of this shift of interest, ancient procedures designed to preserve life by aversive magic made their way back into the religion of Zoro-

aster. To counteract the power of demons over a man involved in ceremonial impurity the Vendidad provided, not ethical and moral instruction, but directions for the use of powerful *manthras* (cf. the Vedic and Hindu *mantras*), passages taken from the Gathas of Zoroaster for use as spells and incantations. In fact all the Gathas become useful primarily as "spells of ineffable power, to be repeated without flaw, by men who may or may not understand them." [21]

Besides the manthras, an effective means of daunting evil and avoiding its touch, defiling as pitch, was the offering of libations of *haoma*-juice. To this day the Parsis of India take the twigs of a sacred plant, pound them in a mortar, and mix the juice pressed from them with milk and holy water, the resulting fluid being in part offered as a libation, and in part drunk by the officiating priests. This procedure is almost identical with that performed thousands of years ago by the Indo-Aryans on the banks of the Indus River.

But more directly effective were the methods of cleansing one's person of defilement and thus getting rid of contaminating influence. According to the Vendidad, contact with the human dead is the source of greatest defilement. Anyone touching a corpse must immediately be purified by ablutions with water, or, in certain contingencies, with the urine of cattle. To modern as to ancient Parsis, corpses have always been so defiling that they are not allowed to enter the earth, lest they

Zoroastrian Tower of Silence. (Drawing based on photographs)

corrupt the ground; nor fall into the water, lest they render it unfit for any use; nor be burned on a funeral pyre, lest they defile the flame. In the early days of Zoroastrianism the dead were laid on a bed of stones or a layer of lime, or encased in stone, to keep them isolated from earth and water; today they are placed in stone "Towers of Silence," open to the sky, so that birds of prey may feast on them. Any portion of a dead body, or, for that matter, any part severed from a living body, as for example nail-parings or hair cut from the head or beard, is unclean. Spitting, especially in the presence of another person, is forbidden. Even the exhaled breath is defiling; so that, down to the present day, priests wear cloths over their mouths while tending the sacred fire. Creatures that are known to feed on dead flesh—maggots, flies and ants— are loathed. They are creations of Angra Mainyu, as are also snakes and frogs. In times past the Magi have killed hundreds of thousands of them as an act of piety. Direct contact with any of them requires that the person involved must be cleansed and purified without delay.

This shift from moral regeneration to considerations of ceremonial purity marks much of the history of Zoroastrianism.

5. In one more direction the religion of Zoroaster grew ever more elaborate: the doctrine of the future life was worked out in graphic detail, highly stimulating to the imagination.

Much attention was paid to the drama of individual judgment. This was not supposed to take place until the fourth day after death. For three nights, it was thought, the soul of the dead man sits at the head of its former body, and meditates on its past good or evil thoughts, words, and deeds; during this time it is comforted, if it has been a righteous soul, by good angels, and tormented, if it has been wicked, by demons hovering about ready to drag it off to punishment. On the fourth day the soul makes its way to the Chinvat Bridge, to stand before its judges, Mithra and his associates Sraosha and Rashnu, the last of whom holds the dread scales for the final weighing of merits and demerits. Judgment rendered and sentence passed, the soul then walks onto the Chinvat Bridge. Here, according to the Pahlavi text called the *Bundahishn,** in the middle part of the Bridge,—

there is a sharp edge which stands like a sword; . . . and Hell is below the Bridge. Then the soul is carried to where stands the sharp edge. Then, if it be righteous, the sharp edge presents its broad side . . . If the soul be

* This is one of the theological works written at a late date (probably after the Moslem conquest) in Pahlavi, then the language of southwestern Iran. The two most important works in this literature are the book here cited and the *Denkart,* a collection of religious lore.

wicked, that sharp edge continues to stand edgewise, and does not give a passage . . . With three steps which it (the soul) takes forward—which are the evil thoughts, evil words, and evil deeds that it has performed—it is cut down from the head of the Bridge, and falls headlong to Hell.[22]

In a further account of the crossing, this text adds an attractive picture of how the righteous soul is guided over the Bridge by its own *daena,* or conscience, in the form of a beautiful maiden, and how the wicked man is confronted by an ugly hag (the personification of his own bad conscience). A late text gives us this amplified description:

> When (the righteous soul) takes a step over the Chinvat Bridge, there comes to it a fragrant wind from Paradise, which smells of musk and amber-gris, and that fragrance is more pleasant to it than any other pleasure.
>
> When it reaches the middle of the Bridge, it beholds an apparition of such beauty that it hath never seen a figure of greater beauty . . . And when the apparition appears to the soul, (the soul) speaks thus: "Who art thou with such beauty that a figure of greater beauty I have never seen?"
>
> The apparition speaks (thus): "I am thine own good actions. I myself was good, but thine actions have made me better."
>
> And she embraces him, and they both depart with complete joy and ease to Paradise.

But if the soul be that of a wicked man,

> when it takes a step over the Chinvat Bridge, there blows to him an exceedingly foul wind from Hell, so foul as is unheard of among all the stench in the world. There is no stench fouler than that; and that stench is the worst of all the punishments that are visited upon it.
>
> When it reaches the middle of the Chinvat Bridge, it sees an apparition of such extreme ugliness and frightfulness that it hath never seen one uglier and more unseemly . . . And it is as much terrified on account of her as a sheep is of a wolf, and wants to flee away from her.
>
> And that apparition speaks thus: "Whither dost thou want to flee?"
>
> It (the soul) speaks thus: "Who art thou with such ugliness and terror that a figure worse than thou art, uglier and more frightful, I have never seen in the world?"
>
> She speaks (thus): "I am thine own bad actions. I myself was ugly, and thou madest me worse day after day, and now thou hast thrown me and thine own self into misery and damnation, and we shall suffer punishment till the day of the Resurrection."
>
> And she embraces it, and both fall headlong from the middle of the Chinvat Bridge and descend to Hell.[23]

Thus did the later Zoroastrians elaborate the doctrine of their founder that a man's own self—his own moral consciousness—determines his future destiny.

In these later accounts it was held that those whose merits and demerits exactly balanced were sent to Hamestakan, a sort of limbo, located between earth and the stars. Hell, they believed, had several levels, the lowest deep down in the bowels of the earth, where the darkness could be grasped by the hand and where the stench was unbearable. Heaven, on the other hand, presented ascending levels, corresponding to good thoughts, good words, and good deeds, and located respectively in the regions of the stars, the moon, and the sun. Through these ascending stations the good soul passed, until it reached highest heaven, Garotman or Garo-demana, "The House of Song," the realm where the Best Thought dwells, and where it would enjoy felicity beyond earth's highest joy until the day of Resurrection and the Final Judgment of all souls.

In estimating when the Final Judgment would come, the later Zoroastrians developed a theory of world-ages, each lasting three thousand years. They said Zoroaster had appeared at the beginning of the last of these aeons. He would be succeeded by three savior-beings, each appearing at intervals of a thousand years: one, Aushetar, born a thousand years after his time; the second, Aushetarmah, two thousand years later; and the last, Soshyans (Saoshyant) at the end of the world; and Zoroaster would be their father! For it was said that Zoroaster's seed was being miraculously preserved in a lake in Persia, and at intervals of a thousand years three pure virgins would bathe there and conceive the great deliverers.

With the appearance of Soshyans, the last Messiah, the "final days" would begin. All the dead would be raised; Heaven and Hell would be emptied of their residents, in order to make up the great assembly where the final Judgment would be passed upon all souls. The righteous and the wicked would be separated; and a flood of molten metal would pour out upon the earth and roar through Hell, purifying all regions with its scorching fires. Every living soul would have to walk through the flaming river; but to the righteous it would seem like warm milk, since there would be no evil in them to be burned away; while to the wicked it would bring terrible agony, a purifying burning proportioned to their wickedness, which would sear all the evil out of them and allow the survival only of their goodness. In a final conflict, Ahura Mazda and his angels would hurl Ahriman and his devils into the flames, and they would be utterly consumed.* Then all the survivors of the fiery trial

---

* This conception of Ahriman's end is not universal. Some of the later conceptions assert that at the Resurrection men will drive him into outer darkness, there to hide himself, or, as others say, to be destroyed at last.

would live together in the new heavens and the new earth, in utmost joy and felicity. Adults would remain forever at forty years of age and children at fifteen; friends and relatives would be reunited forever. Even Hell, at last made pure, would be brought back "for the enlargement of the world"; and the world in its totality would then be "immortal for ever and everlasting." [24]

IV THE ZOROASTRIANS OF THE PRESENT DAY

The changes in Zoroastrian doctrine which we have just reviewed began during the reigns of the Achaemenian kings and were resumed, after a prolonged period of disturbance occasioned by the invasion of Alexander the Great, during the time of the Sassanian dynasty (226–651 A.D.). The influence which Zoroastrianism during this time wielded on orthodox Judaism and the pre-Islamic Arabs, among them a young camel-driver from Mecca, was very considerable, so far as ideas were concerned. Indeed, the young camel-driver was so obsessed by visions of the approaching Last Judgment foretold alike by Zoroastrians, Jews, and Christians, that he became a shouting prophet among his own amused and scornful townsmen, and then, in flight from his native place, began a career as soldier-prophet which in its effects not only transformed Arabia but shook the Jewish and Christian worlds to their foundations and almost extinguished Zoroastrianism.

The Effects of the Moslem Conquest

The successors of Muhammad conducted their conquests with almost incredible swiftness and thoroughness. In 636 they took Syria from the Christians and in 639 Egypt. During the decade following 637 the empire of the Sassanids was overrun, and in 651 (or 652) the last of the Sassanid rulers was surprised and slain, and Zoroastrianism suffered a severe blow. But for a century or more, the Arab conquerors attempted no wholesale methods of force in bringing about conversion, because the Qur'an provided that peoples "to whom a Book (i.e. a scripture) has been given" were to be treated generously, and the Zoroastrians, like the Jews and Christians, had "a Book," in fact a whole library of sacred texts. It was some time after the Moslem conquest that pressure was exerted; and then the Arabs were not directly responsible. Nevertheless, within a hundred years of the Arab conquest, a great number of Zoroastrians determined to leave Persia. They first moved to a city far down the coast, near the mouth of the Persian Gulf; then removed to an island off the coast of India, and finally to India itself. Other emigrant bands of Zoroastrians joined them; and among the tolerant Hindus, by whom they were called Parsis (i.e. Persians), all were allowed to pursue their religious rites and duties in freedom. We shall see shortly how well they fared.

Their co-religionists who remained behind in Persia were not so fortunate.

The Gabars

The Zoroastrians of Persia did not give themselves this name (a name which was fastened upon them by the Moslems and means, loosely, "infidels"); they called themselves Zardushtians ("Zoroastrians") or Bah-dinan ("those of the Good Religion"); but long persecution made them keep this name to themselves and hide away their light. To this day their clothes are rough and of a dull yellow, and their manners are subdued. But they have clung tenaciously to their faith. The priests are initiated according to the ancient rituals, keep the sacred fires fed in their unpretentious fire-temples, and follow strict rules in performing all their offices. The layfolk are faithful to the old rites; they want no abbreviations of ceremony at the investiture of their boys with the sacred shirt (the *sudra*) and the sacred thread (the *kusti*: a three-ply cord, symbolizing good thought, good words, and good deeds, and worn as a girdle); and they want the full rites at marriages and at funerals, which end with placing the corpse for the vultures to eat in "towers of silence" (*dakhmas*: for further description of which see below). They are careful, too, to observe the ancient purification rites, on the many occasions when they are polluted by contact with unclean things and persons. Like the Jews, they suffered for centuries from the old vicious circle into which religious persecution drew them: their sufferings made them secretive, and their secretiveness made them suspect. But recently, the more tolerant government of modern Iran has removed their civil disabilities, and their lot has greatly eased. They number about eleven thousand now.

The Parsis in India

More fortunate, the Parsis of India have increased to over one hundred thousand souls, most of them still in Gujarat, the province in the Bombay Presidency to which they first came. An outsider in Bombay soon recognizes them, not only by their relatively light complexion and Aryan features, but by their dignified mixture of ancient and modern dress. The men commonly wear European clothes, except for the snugly fitting white trousers which give their legs a spidery appearance; and they never appear with uncovered heads in or out of doors, the common head-gear being a shiny hat of stiffened cloth, darkly colored, rimless, and sloping back from the forehead. The women drape their brightly colored Indian saris over dresses of European style, and go about freely with unveiled faces. The priests with their white turbans, full beards, and immaculate white garments appear in purely ancient garb.

The Bombay Parsis are often seen by travelers gathering at evening on the sands of the city's Back Bay, in order to face the setting sun and "adore" for a few moments, according to ancient custom, the shining waters rolling in from the West.

As a class the Parsis are wealthy, and may deserve their reputation of being the most progressive community in India. They are frequently described as India's best business men and most competent industrialists; they are said to control the best hotels, the biggest stores, and the new Indian air service. Not only can they make money, but they are famous for their many and large benefactions. Yet in their dealings with non-Zoroastrians they still preserve a certain self-protective dignity, a kind of ceremonial coldness; and, like the Gabars of Iran, they let no outsiders, however trusted, share their more sacred rites or look upon the holy fires burning in their fire-temples.

The ceremonial life of the Parsis is regulated by the priesthood, which is hereditary and traces its descent to the ancient tribe of Magi. Their high priests are called *dasturs*, and many of them are highly educated; yet the ceremonies in the fire-temples are not performed by them, but by a specially trained class of priests called *mobeds,* whose ritual of initiation is very exacting and who keep themselves constantly purified by cleansing rites. These priests memorize fully half of the Avesta, without as a rule understanding a word of it, since it is composed in what is now a dead language. In this they do not greatly differ from the ordinary worshipers, who also memorize the more sacred passages of the Avesta and repeat them during ceremonial procedures.

The Fire-Temples and Their Worship

In both Iran and India the fire-temple is not distinguishable from other buildings when viewed from the street. But the worshipers know the fire is kept there, and that it is better if the outsider is not made too curious by a distinctive exterior. In Iran the fire-temple may be merely a room in a quiet part of a dwelling; in India the whole building usually is devoted to the fire-keeping and the ceremonies. The Indian temples are not equally holy, however. Some, where the fire is more ancient or is purified to a greater degree, are holier. This matter of purifying the fire is distinctive of Zoroastrians and is of more than ordinary interest. The more holy fire has to be compounded of sixteen different fires, all purified after a long and complicated ritual. One such fire is obtained from the cremation of a corpse.

A number of sandalwood logs are kindled from the cremation. Then above the flame, a little too high to touch it, a metal spoon is held, with small holes in it, containing chips of sandalwood. When these ignite, the flame is made to kindle a fresh fire. This process is repeated ninety-one times, to the accompaniment of recited prayers.[25]

Other fires, purified to a greater or less degree by a similar use of spoons, are obtained from flames kindled by a bolt of lightning, from fire produced by flints, and from fires in idol-temples, distilleries, and homes. Finally the sixteen purified fires are brought together by priests (who hardly dare to breathe through the covering over their mouths) into one urn, and placed in the fire-chamber of the temple.

The fire occupies the center of an inner room, resting in its ash-filled urn on a four-legged stone pedestal. It is fed day in and day out by the attendant priests with pieces of sandalwood. During the performance of their offices in the fire-chamber the priests always wear a cloth over their mouths, so as to prevent a single breath from coming directly upon and contaminating the pure flame; and they may not cough or sneeze, at any rate not near the fire.

The worshipers come individually, at any time they wish to. Inside the entrance each washes the uncovered parts of his body, recites the Kusti prayer in Avestan, and then, putting off his shoes, proceeds barefooted through the inner hall to the threshold—no further—of the fire-chamber, where he gives the priest his offering of sandalwood and money, and receives in return a ladle-ful of ashes from the sacred urn, which he rubs on his forehead and eyelids. Bowing toward the fire, he offers prayers (but not *to* the fire, for it is only a symbol); and then he retreats slowly backward to his shoes, and goes home.

Perhaps the most important visit to the fire-temple is on the Parsi New Year's Day. On that day the worshipers rise early, bathe, put on new clothes, go to the fire-temple, worship, and, after giving alms to the poor, spend the rest of the day in exchanging greetings and in feasting.

That Parsi practices in general are based on the religion of the later Avesta, and not simply on the religion of Zoroaster himself, is evident from the briefest study of the annual ceremonies. One festival honors Mithra, whose seat is the sun, and who enjoins upon his devotees truth and friendship—faith-keeping. A very solemn festival is that in honor of Farvardin, the deity who presides over the Fravashis or the spirits of the departed ancestors. During this festival, which lasts for ten days, the Fravashis revisit the homes of their descendants. To give them welcome the worshipers attend special ceremonies for the dead on the hills before the Towers of Silence. Still another festival honors Vohu Manah, regarded as the guardian of cattle; during this period the Parsis practice special kindness to animals. Other feasts commemorate the six phases of creation—heaven, water, earth, trees, animals and man.

The Towers of Silence

The *dakhmas,* or Towers of Silence, provide the Parsis with an approved way of disposing of their dead without contaminating soil and water with spoiling flesh. A dakhma is in essence a stone floor with a circular brick or stone wall around it. The floor is built with a pit in the center, and is in three sections—the highest section for men, the next for women, and the lowest for children. The corpse is brought to the dakhma by six bearers, followed by the mourners, all in white. After a final viewing of the remains by the funeral procession, the body is taken inside the Tower, laid in a shallow pit on its proper level, and partially uncovered by a thorough slitting of its clothes with scissors. As to what follows:

As soon as the corpse-bearers have left the Tower, the vultures swoop down from their post of observation round the wall, and in half an hour there is nothing left but the skeleton. Quickly the bones dry, and the corpse-bearers enter again after some days, and cast the bones into the central well, where they crumble away.[26]

For obvious reasons, the Towers of Silence are situated on hill-tops in vacant land. There are seven in the vicinity of Bombay, where deaths occur frequently enough to attract a constant attendance of vultures. In other parts of India where the Parsis are not numerous, as in Calcutta, there is occasional difficulty in attracting vultures at the right time. In communities too small to have a dakhma, interment in lead coffins or in underground stone chambers is common.

At this point we conclude our study of the Zoroastrian faith. A great deal more might have been discussed—for example, the fact that the Parsis are divided into two sects over the question of the yearly calendar, and much else. But enough has been told to give a clear picture, it is hoped, of the course any religion may run, which has had only one great prophet in its whole history.

SUGGESTIONS FOR FURTHER READING

Dhalla, M. N. *History of Zoroastrianism.* Oxford, 1938

———. *Zoroastrian Civilization.* Oxford, 1922

Darmesteter, J., trans. *The Zend Avesta.* In the Sacred Books of the East series. Oxford, 1883

Duchesne-Guillemin, Jacques. *Zoroastre,* Paris, 1948

Ghirshman, R. *Iran from the Earliest Times to the Islamic Conquest.* Penquin Books pb, 1954

Henning, W. B. *Zoroaster, Politician or Witch Doctor?* Oxford, 1950

Herzfeld, Ernest. *Zoroaster and His World.* 2 vols. Princeton University Press, 1947

Jackson, A. V. W. *Zoroaster, the Prophet of Ancient Iran.* Columbia University Press, 1898

———. *Zoroastrian Studies.* Columbia University Press, 1928

Modi, J. J. *Religious Ceremonies and Customs of the Parsis.* 2nd ed. Luzac, 1954

Moulton, James Hope. *Early Zoroastrianism.* Constable, 1913

———. *The Treasure of the Magi.* Oxford, 1917

Pavry, Jal Dastur Cursetji. *The Zoroastrian Doctrine of the Future Life.* Columbia University Press, 1926

13 Judaism: The Discovery
of One God in Nature
and the Social Process

IT MAY BE SAID THAT ONE GREAT THEME DOMINATES THE COURSE OF JEWISH religion; this is the theme that a single righteous God is at work in the social and natural order. This theme was not immediately arrived at; but somehow it seems implicit from the beginning. Only morally and socially sensitive minds could conceive of history in such terms or develop a group consciousness of such a god.

Being socially sensitive, the Hebrews were historical-minded, and not in any casual or intermittent way, but steadily. This fact needs a little stressing. The Old Testament is as complete a record of the nation's history as the Hebrew historians could make it. That their work, from the 8th century B.C. onward, was fundamentally sound, is more and more evident as modern archaeological research proceeds with the task of unearthing the vestiges of the early Palestinian cultures. At the same time it should not be overlooked that the Hebrews wrote religious, not secular, history, and the facts they cited and the traditions they used no longer have quite the values for us that they had for them. In fact, their narratives contain meanings and significances hidden away in them to which they paid no heed because they took them for granted. But we must bring these matters out into the light. It is highly rewarding to do so. When the necessary interpretations and reconstructions have been made, the Old Testament record gains in meaning.

I THE RELIGION OF THE PRE-MOSAIC
HEBREWS

The Hebrews were Semites, originally bred in the Arabian Desert near its northern borders, where they wandered for centuries. As have other Semitic groups before and since, they camped on Arabia's northern steppes, beside oases or in areas of sparse vegetation, crossing and recrossing the desert's undulating wastes of flat stone, thinly covered with pebbles or shifting sand. At each encampment they erected straggling camel- or goat-skin tents, pitched close to the ground. Under such shelter their communal life ran its self-contained course. Each tribe lived to itself, and the day's routine was ordered by a single authoritative voice, that of the ruling elder or patriarch, to whom the word sheikh is now applied. In those far-off times the implements and weapons they possessed were of stone, and their beliefs were in their early formative stages. Suspicious of all strangers, and yet open-handed to a fault to any they received into their tents, they huddled together in the vast expanse of the desert, as if back to back against a hard and grudging world.

That their lives had the character of comradely cohesion at home but fear and caution as they faced outward toward the world is attested by their religious beliefs and practices.

Animism and Tribal Gods

The desert heritage with which the Hebrews began suggests a transition from dynamism and animism to polytheism and monotheism. The earlier types of belief persisted alongside of, or as vestiges contained within, the later.

The veneration of stones and pillars was universal. Certain heaps of stones were particularly viewed with respect. A desert people will honor its landmarks. The Semitic name for a pillar-like rock that was sacred (*mazzebah*) was often on the lips of the earliest Hebrews; and the word *gilgal*, used later by the Hebrews as the name of a town in Palestine, meant a circular series of pillars. Stones and pillars provided convenient objects around which religious ceremonies and sacrifices might be conducted; but originally they had their own awesome significance, perhaps because of their odd shape, or suggestively human appearance, or striking position on a mountain top or athwart a much traveled way. At first the stones were themselves felt to be alive (dynamism or animatism); then they were regarded as the abiding-places of indwelling-spirits (animism); finally demons, or godlings and goddesses, were thought to make their local habitation there (poly-demonism or polytheism).

It was natural among a desert people, unused to seeing enough of them, that wells, springs, and streams had a specially sacred character and usually were credited to the creative power of spirits or gods which had brought them into being and could readily, if angered, dry them up again.

Trees in general, but evergreen trees in particular, were, it was felt, full of spirit-energy. Groves became holy places. But trees were some-times as much dreaded as beheld with rejoicing, for a desert people must fear being entangled in a thicket—the lair of wild beasts and the ambush of demons—and, moreover, trees may draw down the lightning or even be animated demonic beings themselves. On the other hand, some trees whispered wisdom in the rustling of their leaves; they were protective spirits, giving relief and shelter; and under certain conditions they were capable of delivering oracles, should the rare individual who could understand their language be there to hear.

Of the "beasts of the field," serpents were universally feared (and as universally revered) for being demoniacally sly and cunning, if not indeed possessed by fiery spirits (known to the later Hebrews as *sera-phim*, "burning ones"). Goats were regarded as incarnations of "hairy ones" (Hebrew *se'irim*). As for the untameable wild things of the desert—the panthers, leopards, hyenas, wolves, and foxes—they were the savage flock of demon gods of the wasteland. The untameable swift-footed ostrich and the birds of prey were demonic, too.

But the first Hebrews believed in many more spirits besides these. They believed in spirits having a human shape, though possessed of an inhuman character, like the *jinn* of later Arabia; and they let their imaginations play with the thought of seductive female night-demons (like glamorous Lilith in the Hebrew tradition, who led Adam astray). The raging desert wind that brought the sand-storm was a malevolent demon; he was connected with pestilence and ruin. There were many others of a like evil disposition; but of course there were as well multi-tudes of beneficent spirits.

And here we come upon a fact of some importance in the present study. All the spirits that possessed any degree of power or dynamism were given a name universally current among Semitic peoples—it was *el* (sing.) or *elim* or *elohim* (pl.), a word with the general meaning of "superhuman being" or "divinity." This term was broad and inclusive; it was applicable to major and minor divinities alike; and although it usually designated the more beneficent powers, it was also applied to demons. As a rule it referred to no specific supernatural individual, unless hyphenated with a descriptive adjective or with the name of a locality. This held good until among the Aramaeans and the Hebrews it came to mean, whether in its singular or plural form, but one God. (Just so in Europe god became God.) °

Other words used as appellations of the gods in the Semitic world were Adonis or Adoni (Hebrew Adonai) meaning "Lord"; Malak or Moloch (Hebrew Melech) meaning "King"; Bel or Baal meaning "Land-Lord" or "Possessor of the Land"; and Rabb (Hebrew Rabbi) meaning "Master."

An examination of these names for the gods reveals a significant fact. The Semites thought of their relationship to their high-gods as being direct and personal. Perhaps the desert simplified the relationship of god and man by reducing nature to an empty waste. At any rate the Semites adopted toward their gods an attitude which was not like that of frightened or wondering humans approaching the more or less impersonal and mysterious powers of nature, but rather like that of subjects in the presence of a king or, more intimately, like that of sons before a father.

By the time this point was reached, we note further, a distinctive *choice* had been made, either by the gods or by men. Not all the gods could be "father" or "personal lord" to the same men; intimacy cannot be general. What happened was this: one, or at most several, gods chose, or were chosen by, a larger or smaller group of men (a clan) for closer, more intimate connection than that of all the gods to all men. The bond was "peculiar" and familiar, and tended to be binding on both sides.

From the beginning the Hebrews seem to have had this sense of being "chosen" and of making a choice. The case of Abraham is instructive.

Abraham and the Migration to Palestine

Abraham stands in a somewhat new light today. Recent discoveries of long-buried documentary material in Iraq, Syria, and Palestine have placed him in a rather exciting setting, highly fluid and shifting. As the

---

° How the plural of *el* (*elohim*) could stand for one being may perhaps be explained thus: the many gods were eventually considered to be names of but one true God (as we have already seen happen elsewhere in the world); and then the plural term signified "The One who is All," or "the All-god."

Biblical tradition tells us, his forefathers pressed out of the desert in the same way that other Semitic groups had done—the groups which earlier became Babylonians, Aramaeans, Phoenicians, Amorites, and Canaanites. His tribe dwelt for a time in Babylonia, near a place called Ur of the Chaldees; and there Abraham is said to have been born. Under the leadership of their sheikhs his people then migrated along the border of the Mesopotamian plain westward to Harran, a semi-barren place on the extreme northern verge of the Arabian Desert. This migration was made possible for them because the social situation there had for some time been so disturbed that population shifts were constantly taking place; at any rate, newcomers were not immediately driven away. But the tribe of Abraham did not stay long. It had reasons to move again.

Briefly, in the 19th century B.C., after the death of its great Amorite king, the law-giver Hammurabi, the Sumero-Akkadian Empire in the Mesopotamian valley suddenly crumbled under the onslaughts of barbarians from the northwest and northeast. These barbaric invaders were themselves pushed into action. Behind them was the enormous pressure of the Indo-Iranian (Aryan) irruption into the south-lands. (Once more we are confronted by these extraordinary people, whom we have already followed into India and Iran, and whose fellow Indo-Europeans we found in Greece, Italy and Northern Europe.) Syria and Palestine were equally, if not more, disturbed. The Hittites and Hurrians of Asia Minor were driven, some westward, some southward. The population of Palestine was swollen with refugees of many kinds, Hurrians (the Biblical Horites), Amorites, Aramaeans, and non-Semitic peoples from further north. And, apparently, the early nomadic tribe with which tradition has associated Abraham followed or was swept along in the general movement southward. A moving group of associated peoples, most of them Semitic, whom the Egyptians were to call the Hyksos, were gathering and surging toward the Nile.

The story of Abraham as told in Genesis is the interweaving of several strands of tradition of varying age. This has led some historians to doubt all that is told about him. But so great a degree of scepticism seems, on present evidence, unwarranted. It is fairly certain that he was not the only tribal leader of the Hebrew (Habiru?) * migration; but he may have been so typical of his group that legend later centered on him. The gist of the story is this: Abraham's personal religious experience led him to place all his faith in a single protective deity, whom he chose, or who chose him, an *El* whom he called El-Shaddai ("the El of the Mountains"), a god who was probably from the vicinity of Harran. For him, this being far overshadowed the ancestral spirits or household gods represented by the *teraphim*—the wooden or stone images kept by his family for use in domestic magic and worship. When he longed to migrate with the group of which he was the leader to the safer and more favored grazing lands in the southwest, El-Shaddai encouraged him to go there. So Abraham took the long journey, in full faith in the promises of his divine patron (whose favor he enjoyed to such a degree he is called in the old tradition "the friend of God"), and with his flocks and herds and the members of his small tribe came to the land where the Canaanites dwelt. Once safely there, he made his home on the limestone ridge which forms the main contour of the land, and after his death his place was taken successively by his son Isaac and his grandson Jacob.

Then, according to the tradition, a terrible famine smote the land. Unable to eke out an existence any longer, the descendants of Abraham migrated once more, this time to the borders of Egypt—here the story of Joseph explains the sequence of events—where lay the fertile Land of Goshen.

* See infra p. 509 ff. for discussion of this suggested identification. Abraham is the first Old Testament figure to be called a Hebrew. His descendants were commonly called after his grandson Jacob or Israel and thus bore the name of "the children of Israel" or "Israelites." This last name is preferred by many recent scholars to "Hebrews."

Historians are now inclined to supplement this account considerably. They suppose Abraham to have migrated from Harran at the
time when an Indo-Iranian invasion seemed near (about 1800 B.C.). He
may have been in the forefront of the push of displaced peoples
toward the south. Scattered groups of these peoples, coalescing into
the invaders called the Hyksos ("Foreign Rulers"?), pushed past his
descendants, who were still on the hills, down along the sea to Egypt,
which they mastered and continued to dominate from about 1750 to
about 1580. The tribe of Abraham, and no doubt others, were drawn
along, or simply followed behind, to the more fertile lands of the Nile
delta, where the Hyksos treated them as allies. At any rate the Hyksos
used Semitic terms for the names of towns and appointed Semites as
officials under them (as in the famous case of Joseph).

For generations all went well. The Israelites in particular prospered
and multiplied. Then the Egyptians arose and expelled the Hyksos
(1580–1560 B.C.), and recovered control of the whole Eastern Mediterranean coast. The Israelites were not included in this expulsion of the
hated ruling caste. For a century and a half no attempt was made to
reduce them to a lowlier status than that of their Egyptian neighbors.
But there came to the throne of Egypt a mad pharaoh (Ramses II?)
whose passion was the building of great public works, including whole
cities and monumental temples. Needing large forces of free labor, he
turned his eyes toward his northeastern border upon the Israelites,
pounced on and made slaves of them. They were compelled, under the
lash, to give their forced labor to the pharaoh's public works. Nothing
appeared able to save them except either a catastrophe overwhelming
Egypt or a leader arising in their own midst to rescue them from their
plight. One at least, if not both, of these conditions for their escape
was met.

II   MOSES AND THE COVENANT WITH
YAHWEH

The high place which Moses has held in Hebrew-Jewish devotion is
richly deserved. Recent scholarship, while denying to him the authorship of the Pentateuch and the extremely complicated legal provisions
of the Law (the Torah), has vindicated his place of highest honor in
the early history of Israel. He was a creative personality of the first
order. Unfortunately the exact details of his work are shrouded from us
in tradition.

The story of Moses has come down to us in the narratives (known to scholars as J and E) intertwined in Exodus and Numbers. The written form of these traditions dates from three or four hundred years after his time. They have preserved for us the famous tale of Moses' infancy.

Then a new king arose over Egypt, who . . . said to his people, "See, the Israelite people have become too numerous and too strong for us; come, let us take precautions against them lest they become so numerous that in the case of a war they should join forces with our enemies and fight against us." . . .

So Pharaoh commanded all his people, "Every boy that is born to the Hebrews, you must throw into the Nile, but you are to let all the girls live." Now a man belonging to the House of Levi went and married a daughter of Levi. The woman conceived and bore a son, and seeing he was robust, she hid him for three months. When she could no longer hide him, she procured an ark of papyrus reeds for him, and daubing it with bitumen and pitch, she put the child in it, and placed it among the reeds beside the bank of the Nile. His sister posted herself some distance away to see what would happen to him. Presently Pharaoh's daughter came down to bathe at the Nile, while her maids walked on the bank of the Nile. Then she saw the ark among the reeds and sent her maid to get it. On opening it, she saw the child, and it was a boy crying! She took pity on him, and said, "This is one of the Hebrews' children." Thereupon his sister said to Pharaoh's daughter, "Shall I go and summon a nurse for you from the Hebrew women, to nurse the child for you?" "Go," said Pharaoh's daughter to her. So the girl went and called the child's mother, to whom Pharaoh's daughter said, "Take this child away and nurse it for me, and I will pay the wages due you." So the woman took the child and nursed him; and when the child grew up, she brought him to Pharaoh's daughter, and he became her son. She called his name Moses (drawn out); "For," said she, "I drew him out of the water."[1]

The tradition continues that Moses, when grown to manhood, saw one day an Egyptian beating an Israelite, "one of his people"; moved by ungovernable rage, to which he allowed full scope because they were in a lonely place, he smote the Egyptian and killed him. The next day, finding that the deed was becoming known, he fled eastward beyond the Red Sea to the land of Midian, where, while in hiding, he joined the household of a Midianite priest by the name of Jethro (or Reuel). He married Jethro's daughter Zipporah, and had two sons by her.

"In the course of this long time," continues the story, "the king of Egypt died"; and far away in Midian the greatest single event in Hebrew history took place.

While Moses was tending the flock of his father-in-law, Jethro, the priest of Midian, he led the flock to the western side of the desert, and came to the mountain of God, Horeb. Then the angel of the Lord appeared to him in a flame of fire, rising out of a bush. He looked, and there was the bush burning with fire without being consumed! . . . When the Lord saw that he turned aside to look at it, God called to him out of the bush "Moses, Moses!" he said. "Here I am!" said he, "Do not come near here," he said; "take your sandals off your feet; for the place on which you are standing is holy ground." . . . Then Moses hid his face; for he was afraid to look at God. "I have indeed seen the plight of my people who are in Egypt," the Lord said, "and I have heard their cry under their oppressors; for I know their sorrows, and I have come down to rescue them from the Egyptians and bring them up out of that land to a land, fine and large, to a land abounding in milk and honey, to the country of the Canaanites, Hittites, Amorites, Perizzites, Hivvites, and Jebusites . . . So come now, let me send you to Pharaoh, that you may bring my people, the Israelites, out of Egypt." . . . "But," said Moses to God, "in case I go to the Israelites and say to them, 'The God of your fathers has sent me to you,' and they say to me, 'What is his name?' what am I to say to them?"

The reply of God to Moses' question is a very important one, no less to the modern historian than to the Moses of this tradition, who did not know the answer.

"I am who I am," God said to Moses. . . . God said further to Moses, "Thus you shall say to the Israelites: 'Yahweh ° . . . has sent me to you.'" [2]

Behind the elaborations of later tradition embroidering the original historical incident, we may perceive the element of fact. Moses had had a direct, personal experience with a god of strong and determined character. It became evident that this vital being, Yahweh, was not just a nature god, although he dwelt on the wild slopes of a wilderness mountain, and descended upon it in fire and smoke.† These elements

---

° That this was a new name for the Israelites to give to the God of Abraham, Isaac, and Jacob seems evident. Little doubt now exists that Moses introduced them for the first time to the worship of Yahweh (or Jehovah, as another vowel pointing reads). It is significant that in Exodus 6:3 Yahweh is seen admitting that, though he appeared to Abraham, Isaac, and Jacob as El-Shaddai, he was not known to them as Yahweh.

† The ascriptions of nature-power are vivid enough. According to Exodus 19:18, "Mount Sinai was completely enveloped in smoke, because the Lord had descended upon it in fire." In Deut. 4:9–12, passim, we read: "Take care . . . that you do not forget the things that you saw with your own eyes . . . ; but that you impart them to your children and your children's children—the day that you stood before the Lord your God at Horeb . . . at the foot of the mountain, while the mountain flamed with fire up to the very heart of the heavens, shrouded in darkness, cloud, and gloom." Similarly, we read in Exodus 24:17: "The glory of the Lord looked to the Israelites like a consuming fire on the top of the mountain."—Translations from *The Bible: An American Translation* (University of Chicago Press, 1935). Quoted by permission of the publishers.

of Nature were his instrumentalities; he himself was distinct from them, a god behind the scenes, who could take into his keeping the destinies of a whole nation, and swear a solemn compact with them, promising to give them in return for their loyalty and obedience, peace, prosperity and plenty, rain and sun in their season, cattle on a thousand hills, victory in war, children and long life. He was a just god, but a god of strong feelings, happy in the loyalty of those who obeyed him, but jealous if they were unfaithful.

The full character of Yahweh was, of course, not known to Moses at once; Moses' experience simply made him aware of a task, this task being the leading of the Israelites out of Egypt to Sinai, where the god who wanted a people could make a covenant with the people who needed a God.

It is not necessary here to go into the well-known story of how Moses hurried to Egypt, to win the Israelites over to his plan, how during their farewell Passover Yahweh, according to Exodus 12, "passed over" them but slew Egypt's firstborn, and how Moses finally led the Exodus by crossing the Red (or Reed) Sea with all his people, just before the pursuing Egyptians drove up in their chariots in the attempt to turn them back. Apparently the Egyptians could not spare enough fighting men to prevent the Israelites' escape. There seems to be some historical warrant for saying that the Exodus came at a time when catastrophe threatened Egypt from the north and west, as a result of invasions of barbaric enemies from Libya and of pirates sailing up the mouths of the Nile to lay waste the wealthy cities along its banks. The distraction of Egypt by these dangers could have, and perhaps actually, furnished the Israelites with their opportunity.

However, the leadership of Moses made its greatest contribution, not in Egypt, but at the foot of the sacred mountain, called in one strand of tradition Sinai and in another Horeb. The exact location of this mountain is still debatable. It has traditionally been located on what is known as the Sinaitic Peninsula; but many recent scholars place it nearer the head of the Gulf of Aqaba or in the region of Kadesh-Barnea, a little to the southwest of the Dead Sea. The location matters little. What took place, in any event, is that Moses served as the intermediary between his followers and Yahweh, the god who had sent Moses to deliver them out of Egypt, had thus far saved them from all their perils, and who now desired to make a covenant relationship with them. According to the tradition, the terms of the Covenant were made known in the following manner. Leaving the people at the foot of the mountain, Moses went up the slope to commune with Yahweh; and after some days he returned with the knowledge of Yahweh's will for the people. This will, summarized in "commandments," inscribed on two tablets of stone, was subsequently amplified into the many provisions of the Torah or Law.

Two lists of commandments are given in the records. One—the formulation of a high ethical code—is familiar to us as the Ten Commandments. It is doubtful, however, that we have it in its original form. Evidently what we have is the full and elaborated form of later days. For one thing, it was not until much later than the time of Moses that Yahweh was identified as the maker of sky and earth and sea and all that they contain.

The other list of Commandments is not nearly as fine nor as influential as the first; it is indeed largely ritualistic in character. Some scholars, seeing in this fact evidence of priority in time, prefer it as the earlier list. It is very interestingly introduced into the records thus:

The Lord said to Moses,
"Cut two stone tablets ° . . . and in the morning ascend Mount Sinai, and present yourself there to me on the top of the mountain. No one is to ascend with you, nor is anyone to be seen anywhere on the mountain, nor must the flocks and herds graze in front of that mountain."
So Moses cut two stone tablets . . . and rising early next morning, he ascended Mount Sinai, as the Lord had commanded him, taking the two stone tablets in his hand. Then the Lord descended in a cloud, and took up a position with him there, while he called upon the name of the Lord. The Lord passed in front of him, proclaiming,
"The Lord, the Lord, a God compassionate and gracious, slow to anger, abounding in kindness and fidelity, showing kindness to the thousandth generation, forgiving iniquity, transgression, and sin, without leaving it unpunished however, but avenging the iniquity of fathers upon their children and grandchildren down to the third or even the fourth generation."
Then Moses quickly bowed his head to the ground, and made obeisance.[3]

This passage is followed by Yahweh's announcement that he wishes to make a compact or covenant with the Israelites in the following specific terms:

You must not make any molten gods for yourselves.
You must keep the festival of unleavened cakes, eating unleavened cakes for seven days, as I commanded you . . .

° The account adds, "like the former ones." This is considered by scholars an editor's addition necessitated by the earlier use of the story (from the E narrative) telling of the inscribing (by Yahweh's finger) of the Ten Commandments on two tablets of stone, tablets which Moses later broke (see infra). The account here quoted is from the J narrative, the older of the two traditions.

Whatever first opens the womb belongs to me, in the case of all your livestock that are male, the firstlings of oxen and sheep; a firstling ass, however, you may redeem with a sheep, but if you do not redeem it, you must break its neck; any first-born son of yours you may redeem.

None may visit me empty-handed.

Six days you are to labor, but on the seventh day you must rest, resting at ploughing-time and at harvest.

You must observe the festival of weeks, that of the first-fruits of the wheat harvest, and also the festival of ingathering at the turn of the year; three times a year must all your males come to see the Lord God, the God of Israel . . .

You must not offer the blood of a sacrifice to me with leavened bread.

The sacrifice of the passover feast must not be left over night until morning.

The very first of the first-fruits of your land you must bring to the house of the Lord your God.

You must not boil a kid in its mother's milk.[4]

Very clearly, however, this could not have been the original compact with Yahweh, since it presupposes an agricultural, not a nomadic, community, and one, moreover, long established in its own land.

The *precise* terms of the covenant are therefore irrecoverable. Later tradition has too thoroughly obscured the original situation. Nevertheless, the nature of the ceremony by which the pact was sealed between Yahweh and those who were thenceforth to be his people may be preserved in this important passage:

Then Moses . . . recounted to the people all the regulations of the Lord and all the ordinances; and the people all answered with one voice,

"All the regulations that the Lord has given we will observe."

So Moses . . . built an altar at the foot of the mountain, along with twelve sacred pillars, one for each of the twelve tribes of Israel. Then he sent the young men of the Israelites to offer burnt-offerings and to sacrifice oxen as thank-offerings to the Lord, while Moses himself took half of the blood, and put it in basins, dashing the other half on the altar. He then took the book of the covenant, and read it in the hearing of the people, who said,

"All that the Lord has directed we will obediently do."

Then Moses took the blood and dashed it on the people, saying,

"Behold the blood of the covenant which the Lord has made with you on the basis of all these regulations." [5]

Later times were well aware of the significance of such a ritual. One and the same blood was splashed on Yahweh's altar and on the people, and this made them "of one blood," that is, indissolubly joined in a single whole, and made one body. It was a very solemn act of union and community. Other Semitic groups sometimes practiced rituals similar to it. This covenant had a markedly legal and *contractual* character. The people bound themselves to Yahweh by a solemn legal agreement, such as men might contract with each other and ratify in blood.

When the Israelites prepared to journey on they had the problem, not so much of leaving Yahweh behind on his mountain (for they believed he could go with them in spirit and power), but the problem of providing a medium of communication with him. At Sinai Moses went up the mountain, and God talked to him. If they left the mountain behind, what then? The solution of the problem was the ancient one of providing a meeting-place for God and his people, that is, a shrine or sanctuary. So they devised a portable "tent of meeting" (the "Tabernacle of the Lord"), and reserved it for purely sacred use. At each encampment it was set up by ritualistically proper persons (tradition says these were members of the tribe of Levi, from whom sprang the priests of later days), and in the silence of its interior Moses was able to listen as Yahweh spoke to him.

It is quite unlikely that the Tabernacle had an unfurnished interior. The persistent and early tradition may be credited that within it stood a box or chest, in which were contained two stone tablets, marked with the terms of the covenant. This was the famous Ark of the Covenant, which played such a vital part in later Hebrew history. In Moses' day, tradition insists, whenever the Israelites were on the march, they reverently bore the Ark in the van. Carried into battle, it gave strength to the warriors' arms. So holy a thing did it become that none but priests dared to touch it, for fear of being felled by the power it possessed.

Tabernacle of Moses with Sinai in the distance. (After drawing in G. E. Wright, *Biblical Archaeology*)

In a very natural way a ritual of worship was developed which became more and more elaborate with the passing of years. The oldest elements of this ritual were the annual celebration of the Passover and the weekly observance of the Sabbath. The Passover was an ancient Semitic festival appropriated to Israelite uses. Through it they celebrated the memory of their escape from Egyptian bondage. It was a spring festival, taking place during the night of the full moon nearest the spring equinox, and centering in each family's hurried eating between twilight and dawn of a sacrificial sheep (or goat) taken from the flock, after its blood has been smeared on the doorposts of the tent or on the lintel and doorposts at the entrance to a dwelling; the whole sheep was to be consumed, either by the eaters or in the fire, nothing was to be left over. The Sabbath Day also appears to have an ancient date, originating long before the time of the Exodus. It set aside the seventh day of the week as a pious period of rest, sacred to the Lord.

Of an early origin also were the new-moon festivals (more or less frowned upon and modified by the strict of later days), the feast of sheep-shearing, circumcision (common to most Semites and to adjacent peoples), the taboo upon food before battle, and blood revenge.

Mosaic religion may thus be seen to be in transition from the primitive to the more developed ethical type of religion. That the people were not quite prepared for the practice of Yahwism in its purity is implied by the story of the apostasy of Aaron at the foot of Mt. Sinai. The story * runs that when Moses went up the mountain for forty days and forty nights, the people became restive.

When the people saw that Moses was long in coming down from the mountain, the people gathered about Aaron, and said to him,

"Come, make us a god to go ahead of us; for this is the way it is with Moses, the man who brought us up out of the land of Egypt,—we do not know what has become of him."

So Aaron said to them, "Tear off the gold rings which are in the ears of your wives, your sons, and your daughters, and bring them to me."

So all the people tore off the gold rings which were in their ears, and brought them to Aaron, who took the material from them, and pouring it into a mold, made it into a molten bull, whereupon they said,

"Here is your god, O Israel, who brought you up out of the land of Egypt!"

On seeing this, Aaron built an altar in front of it, and Aaron made proclamation, "Tomorrow a feast shall be held to the Lord."

So next day the people rose early, and offered burnt-offerings, and

* So much edited by later hands as to contain obviously self-contradictory elements.

presented thank-offerings; the people sat down to eat and drink, after which they rose to make merry.

Then the Lord said to Moses, "Go down at once; for your people whom you brought up out of the land of Egypt have acted perniciously . . ."

Moses then turned and descended from the mountain . . .

As soon as he came near the camp, he saw the bull and the dancing, whereupon Moses' anger blazed, and he flung the tablets [of the Commandments which he was carrying] from his hands, and broke them at the foot of the mountain; then he took the bull which they had made, and burned it up, and grinding it to powder, he scattered it on the surface of the water, and made the Israelites drink it. Then Moses said to Aaron,

"What did this people do to you, that you have let them incur such great guilt?"

Aaron said, "Let not my Lord's anger blaze; you know yourself how bad the people are. They said to me, 'Make us a god to go ahead of us!' . . . So I said to them, 'Whoever has any gold, let them tear it off'; and when they gave it to me, I threw it into the fire, and out came this bull!" [6]

This sort of apostosy was to be not infrequent in the years to come.

III YAHWEH AND THE BAALS

After wandering in the wilderness for a number of years (forty, according to tradition), the Exodus-Hebrews or Israelites felt themselves strong enough to invade Canaan.

It is not easy to reconstruct the story of the "conquest" from the accounts of Joshua and the Book of Judges. According to them, the main assault of the invaders was led by the "Joseph tribes," Ephraim and Manasseh, which fought their way across the Jordan under the generalship of Joshua,* took Jericho, and from this base spread their bloody conquest through central Palestine, in time capturing Shechem, Shiloh, and Samaria, to make good their control of the central territory. Judah and Simeon, invading from the south, possessed themselves of the highlands in the vicinity of the walled city of the Jebusites. In this they were assisted by the non-Hebraic Kenites on the south. Two tribes, Reuben and Gad, remained behind east of the Jordan. Others made their way among the northern Canaanites (with less of fighting than immigrating), slowly penetrating and permeating the valley of Esdraelon and the north country. Dan, after an abortive settlement in the south, eventually occupied the extreme north, and Zebulun went northwestward toward the Phoenician coast and came to amicable terms with the Hittites; while still other tribes, like Issachar, Asher, and

---

* Moses' successor. Moses died just before these events.

Naphtali, were content with agricultural serfdom to Canaanite overlords who lived in the walled towns near the Lake of Galilee. In the process of occupying the land some of the tribes were either dissipated or absorbed, like Simeon and Benjamin.

The tradition does not hide the fact that this was a long process. The Canaanites had strong walls around their principal cities and villages, and possessed chariots and arms far superior to the crude weapons of the Israelite fighting men. On the heights where Jerusalem stood, a powerful tribe of Jebusites lived secure within the city's thick stone walls, and were destined to repel every attack made on them for two hundred years. Elsewhere as well, the Israelites had to content themselves with possession of the open country, because the Canaanites beat off their attacks on the towns from the top of their battlements. But the invaders in the end, by whatever means, made the land theirs.

Their dominance of the land was not secure, however, until their external enemies were beaten off. This was a long drawn out struggle. Their Semitic enemies from the east, the Edomites, Moabites, and Ammonites, constantly harassed them by seeking to enter the land. But the most formidable enemies were the Philistines, a non-Semitic people who had descended upon the southwestern coastal plain from the islands of the Mediterranean. Their original home, we learn from other sources, was Crete; and when driven out of it, they turned pirates. They may actually have assisted the Israelites in their escape from Egypt by harrying the cities of the lower Nile. Unable to make a landing in Egypt, they sought a territory to colonize further north and found it on the south Palestinian shore. Gradually they spread inland, and, with five fortified towns at their back, began to ascend the hills. The Israelites fought with them for generations, and barely held them off.

This story is now being amended and supplemented by historians, who do not question its substance so much as its narrowing of attention too exclusively to but one group,—the Israelites or Exodus-Hebrews. New evidence has come to light of turmoil within Canaan caused by "outsiders" or "wanderers" known as *Habiru*, some of whom may be unhesitatingly identified as non-Exodus Hebrews, who had not gone down to Egypt but who joined forces with the Exodus-Hebrews (the Israelites) when they entered Canaan. Others of the same or similar grouping had for years been appearing in Mesopotamia, Syria and northern Egypt. They were probably Semites from the desert and had no fixed location nor occupation, for they wandered about sometimes as shepherds, sometimes as musicians, smiths and craftsmen, and sometimes as mercenaries for hire or free-roving guerrillas. (The Akkadians called them Khapiru and the Egyptians Apiru.) They were often very troublesome to local authorities and needed only organization into a group with common beliefs and purposes to be a menace. The famous Tell-el-Amarna Letters, found in Egypt by a peasant woman in 1887, and identified as dispatches sent by the Egyptian governors and minor officials in Canaan to the pharaohs from about 1400 to 1350 B.C., contain frantic appeals for help against groups of Habiru who were coming from the east and northeast and threatening to overrun the country.

"There are no lands left to the king, my lord. The Habiru plunder all the countries of the king!"

"The country of the king is fallen away to the Habiru. And now also a city of the country of Jerusalem (its name is Beth-Shemesh), a city of the king, has gone over to the men of Keilah. May the king send mercenaries that the land may remain unto the king. If there are no mercenaries, lost is the land of the king to the Habiru!" [7]

The alarm of the officials gradually subsided. The Habiru did not make a conquest. Their inrush was an infiltration process in the main, for the Canaanites were able to retain a string of fortresses and walled towns across the land, while the semi-nomadic "outsiders" settled in the unoccupied hill country and made themselves at home.

Some time later, if our reconstruction—a precarious matter at best —is correct, the Exodus-Hebrews, inspired by the Mosaic faith in Yahweh, entered the land, made common cause with the Habiru (whence their own later name of Hebrews?), and by vigorous assaults on important Canaanite towns put themselves in the position to become masters of the whole land eventually, and what is equally important for our story, so impressed their Habiru allies with their superior *élan* that Yahweh was adopted by the latter as their own Lord of Hosts.*

* All this must be regarded as conjectural. There are other interpretations of the historical evidence. Some authorities would make the Exodus-Hebrews enter the south a century or so *after* the Habiru, led by Joshua, invaded the central areas of Canaan. More recent views support the order of events suggested in the text above. See W. F. Albright, *The Archaeology of Palestine* (fully revised, Pelican Books, 1960); Kathleen Kenyon, *Archaeology in the Holy Land* (1960); G. Ernest Wright, *Biblical Archaeology* (1957); and *Adam to Daniel*, an illustrated guide to the Old Testament and its background, printed in Israel (published by The Macmillan Co., N. Y.), the editor being Gaalyahu Cornfield, assisted by Bible scholars, historians and archaeologists in Israel. These books achieve a noteworthy reconciliation of the biblical narratives with the latest archaeological findings.

It may be added that W. F. Albright and the Israeli scholars, B. Mazar and S. Yeivin, consider that the conquest of Canaan occurred in two or more waves and was carried out by different groups of tribes over several generations, first by the Joseph (or Rachel) tribes, then by the Leah tribes.

But this, assuming it occurred, was not the only triumph of the Exodus-Hebrews. As the years passed, they succeeded in imbuing their Canaanite neighbors as well as themselves and their allies with a sense of nationhood. The increasing menace of the Philistines caused the feeling of difference to be forgotten, especially when, under the seer Samuel, and the first king, Saul, strong efforts were made to throw the Philistines back upon their coastal plain. These efforts began to bear fruit at last, for though in the generation before Saul the Philistines had captured the Ark of the Covenant in battle (and then, in fear induced by bad luck, had returned it in a cart drawn by cows turned loose across the frontier), they now began to taste repeated defeat. Saul took his own life when defeated at Mt. Gilboa, but his successor, David, finally routed the Philistines and broke their fighting spirit.

David also captured at long last the city of the Jebusites (Jerusalem), made it his capital, and planned a Temple in it to house the Ark of the Covenant properly, a project which was left for his son Solomon to carry out, as indeed he did.

All this while, the religion of Yahweh had undergone many changes, resisted many more, and risen to new heights of insight.

Great changes were necessarily involved in the passage from nomadic to agricultural and urban life. When the Hebrews came in from the desert, they moved among a people with a well-developed culture and religion. They had much to learn from their new neighbors.

The Canaanites had developed a thorough-going nature-worship, growing out of their agricultural life. Their gods were, in general character, farm-gods. The class name by which they were known was *baal,*

Solomon's Temple with folding doors and two upright columns before it called Jachin and Boaz. (After drawing in G. E. Wright, *Biblical Archaeology*)

which, as we have seen, means "owner" or "possessor" (of the soil). Every stretch of fertile ground owed its fertility to the presence of some baal, who held sway, like a feudal lord, within his own boundaries; though, like a feudal lord, he himself was in turn subject to the two supreme lords of all lesser baals, the elevated but inactive god El, who, if we can judge from recently recovered documents, resided in the "Source of the Two Deeps" in highest heaven, and the subordinate but active storm god and chief of the lower gods, the great Baal of Heaven. El's consort was Ashirat, known to the Hebrews as Asherah, and the great Baal was associated with his sister Anath and the equally virgin but fertility-giving and fruitful Astarte. One may conclude that these heavenly powers were represented on earth by baals acting in the soil, and that each earthly baal in his sphere of operation at will imparted or withheld fertility power in the soil. The plant-cycle was so closely associated with him that its various stages were considered his birth, life, and death, and were ritually celebrated. At his death (the decay of vegetation °) those who owed most to him ceremonially wept at the remembrance of his past goodness; while in a number of districts it was even the custom to tear the hair in grief at his passing. At his birth (revival), it was common to hold festivals of rejoicing during which, in their gayest attire, the celebrants streamed together to the nearest shrine, to dance and sing and give themselves up to orgiastic ceremonies, designed in part to assist him and in part to make recognition of his fertility power renewed in them.

The numerous baals whose presence was recognized on the hill-tops, in the valleys, and at springs and wells all over the land, had each their places of worship; and on elevated ground, either within the walls or upon a nearby dominating height, each city built a sanctuary in honor of its patron baal, whose name was hyphenated with that of the city. The priests in charge of these "bamoth" or "high-places" conducted the worship in an open-air court facing the shrine of the god. An image of the god might occupy the shrine and be dimly seen by the worshipers, and near the altar outside stood a stone pillar, the mazzebah, a phallic symbol of the god. Perhaps also there would be a wooden column or pole, called the asherah, representing the goddess who was the god's consort (the baalah). Many sanctuaries boasted also bull-images and bronze snakes, these being very popular representations of the fertility power of the god.

Sacrifices were of two kinds: (1) gift sacrifices, either of the first-fruits of field or tree (a debt necessarily owing) or of animal flesh

---

° In Palestine vegetation dried up at the beginning of summer and revived with the autumn rains.

burnt upon the altar, and (2) communion sacrifices, through which the god and his people partook together of the sacrifice and thus strengthened the bond between them.

There were three main festivals, in spring, early summer, and fall; and during them the role played by the fertility goddesses was given prominence. By far the most important was Astarte (Hebrew Ashtoreth and Babylonian Ishtar). She embodied all the qualities of the Egyptian Isis, the Grecian Demeter, and the Roman Venus. The cypress, the myrtle, and the palm were sacred to her, as being ever-green; and her special symbol was a two-horned cow. In her own person, she was usually represented as naked, like Anath and other baalahs, who played similar roles. Nor was she always thought of as gentle and kindly. There was something of the uncontrollable about her; she was, when roused, a very primitive force; and, like Kali in India, had a black or terrible side: she sometimes took sword in hand, sprang naked upon a horse, and rode forth to bloody slaughter—perhaps because sex has its deadly as well as life-giving side. It was in connection chiefly with her worship that the Canaanites practiced temple-prostitution. The men and women attendants who ministered in her sanctuaries for this purpose were called Kedeshoth, meaning "consecrated persons," a euphemistic term of respect. In the divine marriage between Astarte and Baal, which the Canaanites celebrated in the autumn, she was literally the soil become a wife, and he was the husband of the land who fertilized her.

The Hebrews found it natural to adopt the greater part of these concepts. Those among them who continued to be herdsmen, or who still lived in a semi-nomadic condition, felt no need of other help than that given by Yahweh, the god of mountain and storm, who had been their guide in the wilderness, and was mighty still in war and in peace. But those who took up agriculture found themselves in a different case. They had practically everything to learn; the art of husbandry had to be acquired by them almost in its entirety. The educational feat here required was as great as that which would confront an Eskimo taking up farming in Connecticut. The analogy is far from perfect, however, because, though the modern farmer must know his tools and seeds and have at least a rudimentary knowledge of the chemistry of the soil, the ancient farmer had to have in addition to an understanding of his materials a thorough grasp of the spirit-lore of his locality, and this involved so much of magic and religion as to make it difficult for him to resist taking over the whole of the local religion. This is why, in the more fertile north, Israel * was less true to the religion of Yahweh than were the people of rock-bound Judah, with its large class of shepherds,

* The ten northern tribes.

not dominated by Canaanite influences. Without resigning their faith in Yahweh as the god who presided over the destiny of the whole people, and guided them in war, the Hebrew farmers went with the Canaanites to the village high-places, gave of their first-fruits to the local baals and ashtoreths, brought gift-offerings and peace-offerings, and learned how to make whole-burnt offerings. They also observed the festivals of their Canaanite neighbors at the beginning and end of the wheat harvest and in the autumn.

Only gradually did the conviction arise that Yahweh controlled the processes of agriculture too. This insight may have come first to those who on the highlands and in the border regions remained true through thick and thin to the Mosaic tradition; but it probably also dawned as well on others who participated freely in baal-worship, but who saw for themselves: "Under these forms of baal-worship we worship Yahweh, for he is the Baal of Heaven and all the power behind the ashtoreths." Though in the period of the Judges the Yahweh shrine at Shiloh held only the Ark of the Covenant, in later times the sanctuaries at Bethel and at Dan contained bull-images (golden calves) *which were regarded as symbols of Yahweh*; and this could have only one meaning, namely, that Yahweh had taken over in addition to his older functions those which the bull represented: the god who had led the Israelites through the desert was now proving his capacity to bring fertility to field and flock.

The sense that Yahweh was over all and in all was thus being engendered. And yet the transition to this insight was precariously made. It looked for a time as if Yahweh was not assimilating Baalism to himself but was instead being absorbed by it, even submerged beneath it. Hence Hosea was moved vehemently to exclaim:

> "My people ask a piece of wood to guide them,
> a pole gives them their oracles!
> For a harlot-spirit has led them astray,
> they have left their God for a faithless way;
> they sacrifice on mountain heights,
> and offer incense on the hills,
> below the oak, the terebinth, the poplar—
> so pleasant is their shade.
> So your daughters play the harlot,
> matrons commit adultery.
> But I will not punish your daughters for harlotry,
> nor your matrons for adultery,
> when the men themselves go off with harlots,
> and sacrifice with temple-prostitutes.

This brings a senseless people to their ruin—
liquor and lust deprive them of their wits." [8]

At long last, inspired by a conception of Yahweh that made him greater than he ever was before, the prophets had risen to protest.

IV PROPHETIC PROTEST AND REFORM

The danger that lay in the *baalization* of Yahweh has been well expressed by several modern scholars. It might be called the danger of *naturization*—that is, of absorption into the agricultural milieu. As Max Loehr puts it: "Baalism saw the activity of the god in natural phenomena. In the annual cycle of the sprouting and decay of vegetation, in the fertilizing rain and the destructive heat of the sun, in the swelling and ripening of the fruits of garden and field, or in their destruction by the forces of nature, the benignant or wrathful god made himself known, the god whom the Old Testament usually names Baal. It was a nature religion whose worship issued in the materializing of the godhead. Genuine Yahwehism, on the other hand, regarded history as the sphere of divine action. It separated nature and God." [9] Rudolph Kittel says even more emphatically: "Those who take a short-sighted view of the period succeeding the death of Moses always take it amiss when it is described as a retrograde period. This was the fact. . . . The nature-elements in Yahweh, instead of being overcome by the higher aspect of his being, were associated in Canaan with the nature-elements in Baal and threatened to submerge the moral and spiritual elements . . . This was the situation in Israel against which the later prophets waged so fierce a war; for they saw that the exalted God of Moses was in danger of being degraded into a mere local nature-power. This then was the root cause of the appearance of the great prophets and of their frequent opposition to their nation." [10]

The Origin of Hebrew Prophecy

The great prophets did not appear suddenly, without a background of preparation. Predecessors "made straight the way" for them. These early "prophets" came during the time of the Judges, before 1000 B.C., and were known as *nebiim*. Like the dancing dervishes of the Orient today, they were ecstatics, who felt that when they were excited with religious frenzy they were full of the spirit of Yahweh and had access to his truth. In I Samuel 10:5 f., Saul, who had just been anointed as the future king, is sent off by the aging Samuel with this prediction: "As you approach the town [of Gibeah], you will meet a band of dervishes [nebiim] coming down from the height with lutes, drums, flutes, and lyres playing in front of them, while they prophesy; the spirit of the Eternal [Yahweh] will then inspire you till you prophesy along with them and become a different man." But when this befalls Saul, he learns that he has not won favor with the people. They say scornfully, "Is Saul now numbered among the prophets?"

The first nebiim, leaping in convulsive frenzy, were prone to irrational utterance, unintelligible even to themselves; but alongside of, and perhaps associated with them, arose men of a cooler spirit, who were the real predecessors of the later prophets: such were Nathan in the time of David, and Ahijah in the time of Solomon, prophets who appeared before kings and people to speak the unvarnished, sensible truth from Yahweh. Their intelligent and inspired behavior may be explained as due perhaps to a new kind of training for prophecy instituted about that time. Some of the nebiim were being gathered into organized schools or guilds and trained to serve their function with greater intelligibility. This certainly was done in Elijah's time, for he belonged to such a group.

Elijah and Elisha

With Elijah, the prophetic protest against degrading the ethical religion of Yahweh to mere nature-worship was begun in earnest. Appearing in the northern kingdom in the time of King Ahab, when that monarch was yielding to the strong pressure of his "wicked" wife, Jezebel, to make the Tyrian variety of Baalism dominant in Israel,* Elijah made a truly noteworthy stand in behalf of Yahwism. The Hebrew historians say that when he began his reforming work there were only seven thousand men in Israel who had not bowed the knee to the Tyrian Baal, nor kissed him, but that before he was done he had reduced the worshipers of this Baal to so much less than that number that they could be crowded into one building. He was not a merciful man. Yahweh was to him a god of stern, unyielding righteousness and justice. When Jezebel contrived to have Naboth stoned, so that Ahab could take his vineyard, Elijah stormed into the presence of the king standing in the vineyard and uttered such terrible imprecations in the name of Yahweh, that the king rent his garments, hastened away to

* Baal-Melkart, god of Tyre, was the deity put forward.

put on sackcloth, and fasted in terror. In the story of the trial of the respective powers of Yahweh and the Tyrian Baal on Mt. Carmel, which, as it stands, is one of the most dramatic in religious literature, Elijah keeps to the stark issue, who is real, Yahweh or Baal-Melkart, and makes good his claim that Yahweh is real, and Baal-Melkart is not.

But during Elijah's lifetime no substantial progress could be effected in permanently discrediting Baalism. The opposition of the royal house was too strong, and the people as a whole were hard to change. When Elijah suddenly and, it was felt, supernaturally disappeared, his reforming work was continued by his disciple Elisha, who encouraged a certain Jehu to carry out a sweeping political and religious revolution. This was one of the most bloody in Hebrew history. Jehu, a violent man, whose headlong charioteering gave rise to the saying, "He drives like Jehu," annihilated the royal house, and then destroyed every vestige of the cult of the Tyrian Baal. So great was the slaughter, that a century later Hosea denounced it.

The sum of the matter is this: that Baalism in general received a telling blow from the activities of Elijah and Elisha, yet not a death blow; it recovered. One permanent and important result, however, was accomplished; the right of Yahweh to supremacy in Palestine was never afterward denied or even doubted. Baalism could be practiced only as a local cult, either because Yahweh's function was not conceived to be locally agricultural, or because Yahweh was held to have made over the local baals into his ministrants. This was a great gain for the stricter followers of Yahweh, for it put them in a tactically good position. On the other hand, it was a gain that was not immediately apparent; too large a loophole had been left for the continued practice of Canaanitish rites, and during the next century the common people, reluctant to part with the baals, availed themselves to the limit of their opportunity in this direction.

Or so Amos and his successors charged.

Amos

Amos, the first and perhaps greatest of the 8th century prophets, came from the border-land of the south, where the debasement of Yahwism to the level of a nature-cult had not progressed as far as elsewhere. He thus resembled in place of origin his great predecessor Elijah, who also sprang from the borders of Canaan, from the town of Tishbe, beyond Jordan. This fact has significance, since it suggests that prophetic reform was motivated by the more spiritual insights of the outlying districts which had remained true to the Mosaic tradition. Amos came from Tekoa, a small town about twelve miles south of Jerusalem, and was by occupation a herdsman and pruner of sycamore trees. In marketing sheep he drove them to the populous commercial centers of the North * and thus became acquainted with social and religious conditions there. This was about the year 760 B.C., during the reign of Uzziah in Judah and Jereboam II in Israel. What he saw set him to brooding. As a herdsman who enjoyed social equality among his fellows in Tekoa, he could not fail to note that under the more complex economic conditions of the North the independence of the farmers had been destroyed in the rise of great landlords, who had bought up farm after farm and who manipulated the grain markets to their own enrichment. The whole social structure had become abnormal. The wars of the past had nearly wiped out the middle class. Rich and poor alike were morally adrift. There was increasing laxity in religion and morals everywhere. Integrity was gone, and justice, mercy, and spiritual religion with it. While he reflected upon all this, suddenly he had visions foretelling the doom imminent over the North. Though he came from Judah, he did not hesitate. He hastened into the northern kingdom. Yahweh had called him to prophesy.

What he said in Bethel and elsewhere he (or some associate) set down in writing, casting his messages into poetic diction and rhythm, so as to give them a high literary quality and a measure of permanency. His thundering words were a prophecy of doom grounded in deeply significant convictions.

That he was appalled at the social injustice and moral laxity on every hand is evident from the strength of his condemnation:

> The Eternal † declares:
> "After crime upon crime of Israel
> I will not relent,
> for they sell honest folk for money,
> the needy for a pair of shoes,
> they trample down the poor like dust,
> and humble souls they harry;
> father and son go in to the same girl
> (a profanation of my sacred shrine!),

* The Northern Kingdom (Israel), formed by the rebellion of the ten northern tribes against Rehoboam, the son of Solomon.

† This is one possible translation of "Yahweh" and is so used here and infra. Other possible translations are "I am that (or Who) I am" or "He that causes to be," i.e. the Creator.

they loll on garments seized in pledge,
by every altar,
they drink the money taken in fines
in the temple of their God. . . .

"Woe to the careless citizens,
so confident in high Samaria,
leaders of this most ancient race,
who are like gods in Israel!—
lolling on their ivory diwans,
sprawling on their couches,
dining off fresh lamb and fatted veal,
crooning to the music of the lute,
composing airs like David himself,
lapping wine by the bowlful,
and using for ointment the best of the oil—
with never a single thought
for the bleeding wounds of the nation!" [11]

To punish these social sins and injustices, Amos predicted, the dreaded Foe from the North would overrun the land, laying its forts level, plundering the palaces, and carrying the citizens away into exile.

But his indictment did not rest on charges of social iniquity alone. Amos declared that Yahweh was sick of the national apostasy in religion, and despised the heathenish temple rites, even though they might be offered in his name.

Your sacred festivals? I hate them, scorn them;
your sacrifices? I will not smell their smoke;
you offer me your gifts? I will not take them;
you offer fatted cattle? I will not look at them.
No more of your hymns for me!
I will not listen to your lutes.
No. Let justice well up like fresh water,
let honesty roll in full tide." [12]

No wonder that Amaziah, the high-priest at Bethel, feared the fiery prophet from Judah, and charged him in the king's name: "Be off to Judah and earn your living there; play the prophet there, but never again at Bethel, for it is the royal shrine, the national temple." But Amos answered: "I am no prophet, no member of any prophets' guild; I am only a shepherd, and I tend sycamores. But the Eternal took me from the flock; the Eternal said to me, 'Go and prophesy to my people Israel.' Now then, listen to what the Eternal says. . . ." [13] He had his say. He would not rest with less.

Amos opens a new epoch in creative religion. In the course of uttering his fearsome indictment, he revealed a conception of the nature and jurisdiction of Yahweh far in advance of the people of his time. Yahweh was going to *send* the Foe from the North; and was about to punish, along with Israel, the Philistines, the Ammonites, the Moabites, and the people of Damascus. Phoenicia and Edom were not beyond his chastisement. Unlimited power over the forces of Nature was his; he had brought on a drought three months before the harvest, smitten the fields with blight and mildew, settled a cloud of locusts on the land, slain the soldiers of the army of Israel with an Egyptian plague, and sent a shattering earthquake, resembling the shaking of Sodom and Gomorrah. His might had been exhibited on a *world-wide* arena.

Hosea

If Amos was the prophet of the righteousness of God, then a younger contemporary of his, Hosea, must be called the prophet of God's love. Unlike Amos, Hosea was a native of the North and enough accustomed to the social conditions there to be less appalled by them; his deepest concern was therefore not moral but religious. The state of the text of his prophecies leaves us in some doubt as to the exact circumstances of his personal life. It seems probable, however, that he married a woman who was unfaithful to him and left him; he could not acknowledge her children as his own; yet, after years of infidelity on her part, he was able to take her back into his home, reclaimed and regenerated. As Hosea contemplated his domestic trials, he began to see a similarity between his inner history and the experience of Yahweh with Israel. Yahweh, too, suffered on account of the unfaithfulness of his people. Unfaithful they were in more than one way. Too blind to see that the political and social doom overhanging them was the inevitable result of abandoning the true God, they were seeking to forestall disaster by the political device of running after "foreign lovers," one party courting Damascus, another Egypt, a third climbing to the throne through alliance with Assyria. Religiously, they were wooing alien gods and futile native baals, their unholy religious paramours. Hosea put into Yahweh's mouth these woeful words, ending on the note of inalienable love, anxious still to forgive:

> "Bid her ° clear her face of harlotry,
> and her breasts of adulterous charms;
> or I will strip her naked,

° I.e. Israel.

bare as the day she was born;
I will make her like a land forlorn. . . .
On her children I will have no mercy,
for they are born out of wedlock;
their mother has played the harlot,
she who conceived them has been shameless;
she said, 'I will follow my lovers,°
who give me my bread and water,
my wool, flax, oil, and wine.' . . .
Little she knew it was I who had given her
the grain and oil and wine. . . .

"I will bring all her gaiety to an end,
her festivals, new-moons, and sabbaths,
to punish her for all the days
when to the Baals she offered incense,
decking herself with rings and jewels,
running after her lovers,
and forgetting me," says the Eternal.

"Now then I will block up her path
with a thorn-hedge,
and bar the road against her,
till she cannot find her way;
she will pursue her lovers and miss them,
seek them and never find them.
Then at last she will say,
'Let me go back to my first husband,
I fared better with him than today.'

"So I will allure her, . . .
and speak to her heart; . . .
then shall she answer me
as in her youthful days,
when she came up from Egypt's land. . . .

"On that day, the Eternal declares, she shall call me,
        'My husband,' no more 'My Baal';
I will betroth her to me for ever,
betroth her in a bond
of goodness and of justice,
in kindness and in love." [14]

It is doubtful whether Hosea received in his time the hearing that
Amos did. He quotes his contemporaries as shouting angrily: "A prophet

° I.e. the Baals.

is a crazy fool, a man inspired is a man insane!" [15] He discovered that within the very temple of God men are hostile to the prophet, God's watchman. Surely, if he lived to see the holocaust of the Assyrian conquest of the Northern Kingdom, he must have felt that the God of love had wooed Israel in vain, and that all he had predicted in that event had been fulfilled.

Isaiah

The Southern Kingdom, meanwhile, came in for its share of prophetic admonition. About 740 B.C., at the close of the reign of King Uzziah, a young man of good family appeared on the streets of Jerusalem in a prophetic role. His name was Isaiah. He had just had an experience of the reality of Yahweh that had moved him deeply. He told of it in these words:

"In the year that king Uzziah died, I saw the Lord seated on a high and lofty throne; his trailing robes spread over the temple-floor, and seraphs hovered round him, each with six wings—two covering the face, two covering the body, and two to fly with. They kept calling to one another,
  'Holy, holy, holy, is the Lord of hosts,
  his majestic splendour fills the whole earth!'
At the sound of the chant, the foundations of the threshold shook, and the temple began to fill with smoke. Then I said, 'Alas! I am undone! man of unclean lips that I am, living among a people of unclean lips! I am undone, for mine eyes have seen the King, the Lord of hosts!' But one of the seraphs flew towards me with a live coal in his hand, which he had lifted with tongs from the altar; he touched my mouth with it, saying,
        'Now that this has touched your lips,
        your guilt is gone, your sin forgiven.'
      Then I heard the voice of the Lord saying,
        'Whom shall I send?
        Who will go for us?'
      I answered, 'Here am I; send me.' " [16]

Conscious of his divine commission, Isaiah remained active for nearly forty years as prophet to the people at large and special adviser to the Judean kings. In a time of uncertainty he stood unswervingly for trusting in the providence of God. He was the prophet of Faith, of confidence in Yahweh beyond doubt or shaking; and he was forever warning the rulers of Jerusalem that the city's safety lay in ceasing to make leagues with the nations round about, and relying upon the only trustworthy ally, Yahweh. "Your strength," he warned, "is quiet faith." [17]

In giving advice to Judah's kings this was his constant declaration. Thus, when the Northern Kingdom had been destroyed by the Assyrians (722 B.C.), and the Assyrians were camped before Jerusalem under the mighty general, Sennacherib, he sent panic-stricken King Hezekiah, who besought him to call upon Yahweh, assurances that the city would not be taken.[18] His prophecy was wondrously fulfilled. The Assyrians suddenly raised the siege.*

But Isaiah was certain that the faithless and wicked would not survive to enjoy future security. They would perish by the sword or languish in miserable exile, far from the comfortable hills of home. As he looked about him, he saw many who were doomed to death or exile. In the manner of Amos, he saw nothing but woe in store for the socially-sinning "soldier and warrior, governor and prophet, seer, sheikh, and official," for "the men who add house to house, who join one field to another, till there is room for none but them," for "those who get up early for a drinking bout, who sit far into the night, heated by their wine," or for "those who think themselves so wise, . . . who let off guilty men for a bribe, and deprive the innocent of his rights," "the unruly men," the rulers of the city, "hand in hand with thieves, every one fond of his bribe, keen upon fees, but careless of the orphan's rights, and of the widow's cause." [19]

Like Amos too, he records Yahweh's impatience with the elaborate ritual of the Temple. Slaughtered rams, the fat from fatted beasts, the blood of bullocks and goats, offerings, the smoke of sacrifice, gatherings at the new moon and on the Sabbath, fasts and festivals, are "a weariness" to Yahweh; though the worshipers stretch out their hands, he will never look at them, and though they offer many a prayer, he will not listen. Their hands are stained with blood! They are not really true to Yahweh!

It is not just blind fate that determines events. Yahweh is the moving force and contriver behind human history. He will punish and destroy the wicked everywhere, in Moab, in Edom, in Damascus, in Egypt, but no less in Judah. The wicked will destroy each other by Yahweh's contrivance. Assyria is doomed like all the rest, but meanwhile Yahweh has use for this exterminator of the nations, a use like that of a club swung in anger or a rod wielded in wrath. It will do its work well. Justice will be done even in the plundering and spoiling of the nations.

If Isaiah was as inflexible as Amos in the pronouncement of doom,

---

* According to tradition, a plague struck them. But there is evidence that Sennacherib accepted a heavy ransom to withdraw his forces.

he saw, however, like Hosea, that pity and love are at the heart of Yahweh's divine plan. The purging of the nations is in the interest of spiritual betterment, a kindlier world.

> "Come, let me put it thus,"
>   the Eternal argues:
> "Scarlet your sins may be,
>   but they can become white as snow,
> they may be red as crimson,
>   and yet turn white as wool.
> If only you are willing to obey . . ." [20]

After the Day of Doom, there will be a return of blessedness to the "remnant" who have lived through all the trouble and relied upon Yahweh for all good. Peace, prosperity, and health will be theirs. Upon them Yahweh will have mercy; them he will abundantly pardon.

And here we come to the passages in Isaiah which have had great historic importance—the golden dreams of the New Age that shall dawn after the terrible day of Wrath and Doom is past. After-generations lingered over them, and relied upon Isaiah's authority in indulging the eager hope of their fulfilment. Some scholars, it is true, and with good warrant, dispute the authenticity of these passages; in them Isaiah is seen, perhaps before the time was ripe for such pre-vision, painting a rosy picture of a warless world and of the benign rule of a great Prince of Peace, the Messiah, who should spring from the seed and lineage of David and bring in the New Day; but these poems of hope and vision came out of the afflictions of his period in history, and so, for our interests in this study, it matters little whether they are from Isaiah's own hand or not. Isaiah was a grieving witness of the spoliation and dismemberment of the Northern Kingdom, and he would quite naturally have dreamed these dreams and seen these visions, which forecast the gathering together from the four corners of the earth and repatriation not only of the scattered of Judah, but of Israel too.

Of the prophecies attributed to Isaiah, consider the two notable passages which follow, both probably reworked or even written by later hands, the first dealing with the New Jerusalem, the second with the peaceful prince who is to sit on David's throne in the New Age.

> In after days it shall be
> that the Eternal's hill shall rise,
> towering over every hill,
> and higher than the heights.
> To it shall all the nations stream,
> and many a folk exclaim,

"Come, let us go to the Eternal's hill,
to the house of Jacob's God,
that he may instruct us in his ways,
to walk upon his paths."
For instruction comes from Sion,
and from Jerusalem the Eternal's word.
He will decide the disputes of the nations,
and settle many a people's case,
till swords are beaten into ploughshares,
spears into pruning hooks;
no nation draws the sword against another,
no longer shall men learn to fight.
O household of Jacob, come,
let us live by the light of the Eternal! [21]

From the stump of Jesse a shoot shall rise,
   and a scion from his roots shall flourish;
on him shall rest the spirit of the Eternal,
   and the spirit of wisdom and insight,
the spirit of counsel and strength,
   the spirit that knows and reverences the Eternal. . . .
Justice shall gird him up for action,
   he shall be belted with trustworthiness.
The wolf shall couch then with the lamb,
   the leopard's lair shall be the kid's;
the lion shall eat straw like any ox,
   wolf and lion shall graze side by side,
   herded by a little child;
the cow and the bear shall be friends,
   and their young lie down together;
the infant shall play at the hole of an asp,
   and the baby's feet at the nest of a viper.
None shall injure, none shall kill,
   anywhere on my sacred hill;
for the land shall be as full of the knowledge of the
Eternal as the ocean-bed is full of water.
And the scion of Jesse who is to rally the peoples,
him shall the nations then consult,
   and his seat shall be famous.[22]

Micah

Inspired by Isaiah, a young man who came up from the country to
Jerusalem, Micah by name, began to prophesy on the eve of the fall

of the Northern Kingdom in 722 B.C. The prophecies attributed to him are remarkable for two utterances, here quoted, one against the prophets who truckled to popular self-complacence about the supposed inviolability of Jerusalem, the other a notable definition of the essence of spiritual religion.

> "And as for the prophets," the Eternal says,
> "who lead my folk astray,
> who cry 'All's well!' if they get food to eat,
> and open war on any who refuse them,
> it shall be night for you, devoid of vision,
> so dark you cannot divine;
> the sun shall set upon the prophets,
> daylight shall darken over them,
> till seers are shamed,
> and the diviners blush,
> in mourning, all of them,
> because no answer comes from God."
> . . . . Listen to this, you. . . .
> priests pattering oracles for pay,
> prophets divining for money,
> . . . saying, "Surely the Eternal is among us;
> no evil can befall us!"
> Therefore on your account
> shall Sion be ploughed up like a field,
> Jerusalem shall become a heap of ruins,
> the temple-hill a mere wooded height.[23]

> How shall I enter the Eternal's presence,
> and bow before the God of Heaven?
> Shall I come to him with sacrifices,
> with yearling calves to offer?
> Would the Eternal care for rams in thousands,
> or for oil flowing in myriad streams?
> Shall I offer my first-born son for my sin,
> fruit of my body for guilt of my soul?
> O man, he has told you what is good;
> what does the Eternal ask from you
> but to be just and kind
> and live in quiet fellowship with your God? [24]

The Deuteronomic Reform

After Micah, the prophets were silent for seventy years. Were they suppressed? That seems likely. For, when the danger of an Assyrian siege of Jerusalem had passed, and King Manasseh sat upon the throne, a serious relapse from ethical Yahwism again set in. Two factors seem to have been in operation. One was a popular ebb-movement back to the Canaanitish form of Yahweh worship. The people were loath to give up the festive gaiety of the high places and altars; they feared the possible ill effects of relinquishing the magic arts, amulets, household spirits, and images, on which they had depended for so long. Besides, the sternly ethical religion of the prophets appeared to them bare and cold compared with the half-heathenish syncretistic religion which so pleased their senses and their imagination. Apostasy became well-nigh universal.

The other factor in the relapse was an official sponsoring of Assyrian cults for reasons of state. Judah was, it must be remembered, a tribute-paying vassal of Assyria. In the very Temple itself, therefore, shrines were erected and offerings made to the gods and goddesses of Assyria. Something like this had happened before, but not to the same extent. In an earlier time Solomon had sought to please his many wives by filling Jerusalem with shrines to foreign deities, but he had not erected them in the Temple area, and at best they had only a sub-rosa status. When King Ahaz, in Isaiah's day and against the protests of that prophet, tried to save Judah by accepting vassalage to Assyria and paying tribute for the "protection" of the Great King, the obsequious monarch set up an altar before the Temple which was a faithful copy of those used in the imperial Assyrian worship; the old Yahweh altar was put to one side; images of Assyrian sun-steeds were given a place in the Temple area, and an arbor for the worship of Tammuz (Adonis) was erected on the roof of a Temple building. These profanations of Yahweh's holy shrine were suppressed in the puritanical reforms instituted under Isaiah's guidance by the next monarch, Hezekiah; but Assyrian pressure and popular religious laxity sufficed to restore them in the reign of King Manasseh, which followed. But Manasseh went far beyond the point reached by his grandfather, Ahaz. He built altars for the sun and star gods of Babylon and Nineveh in both the inner and the outer courts of the Temple. He set up an asherah within the temple area in honor of Ishtar, Queen of Heaven, to whom the people flocking there burnt incense, poured out libations, and offered cakes baked with her image on them. Not neglecting the nearer Semitic deities, Manasseh erected altars to various Baals and sacrificed a son by giving him to the fires of the child-devouring Molech.

Between the state policy of fostering Assyrian forms of worship and the popular drift away from strict ethical conduct, the religion of Yahweh seemed about to suffer entire eclipse.

But not so. Two things happened. Suddenly the prophets began to find again their voices—Zephaniah, Habakkuk, Nahum, and the greatest of all, Jeremiah. And as the Assyrian world-empire began crumbling and falling, the grandson of Manasseh, the good king Josiah, directed a great religious reform.

King Josiah's reform came in this way. In 621 B.C. the king authorized the high priest to make a number of overdue repairs on the Temple, and the high priest subsequently reported a momentous "find." A previously unknown "book of the Law" had, he said, been discovered, laid away in a hiding place. This book, he declared, dated from the Mosaic era.* When the king saw it and heard its provisions, he rent his garments and charged his councilors to find out from Yahweh if it was genuine, a true statement of divine law. The councilors consulted a prophetess called Huldah, who vouched for its authenticity. The king then summoned the people to a great assembly and led them in swearing a solemn convenant to keep with all earnestness and zeal the statutes written in the newly discovered code.

The reform thus determined upon began with a clean sweep of all the religious practices condemned by the code. The Second Book of Kings gives a vivid account of this phase of the reform:

> Then the king commanded Hilkiah, the high priest, and the second priest and the keepers of the threshold to bring out of the temple of the Lord all the vessels that were made for the Baal and the Asherah and for all the host of the heavens; and he burned them outside Jerusalem in the limekilns by the Kidron, and carried their ashes to Bethel. He also removed the idolatrous priests . . . and those who offered sacrifices to the Baal, to the sun, the moon, and the constellations, and all the host of the heavens. . . . He tore down the houses of the devotees of the fertility cult which were in the house of the Lord, where the women wove tunics for the Asherah . . . He tore down the high places of the Satyrs, which stood at the entrance of the gate of Joshua . . . He also defiled Topheth, which is in the valley of the son of Hinnom, that no man might make his son or his daughter pass through the fire to Molech. He took away the horses which the kings of Judah had given to the sun, . . . and he burned the chariots of the sun with fire. Also the altars which were on the roof, and the altars which Manasseh had made in the two courts of the house of the Lord the king demolished and beat them down there, and cast the dust into the Brook Kidron. Moreover the high places that were east of Jerusalem, which Solo-

---

* Now embodied in the Book of Deuteronomy, this document is known to scholars as "D" or the Deuteronomic code. It was undoubtedly a contemporary attempt to codify Hebrew ethical law; its "finding" was *possibly* a pious fraud, honestly intended to promote the public good.

mon had built for Ashtart, the abomination of the Sidonians, and for Chemosh, the abomination of Moab, and for Milcom, the abomination of the Ammonites, the king defiled. He shattered the sacred pillars, and cut down the sacred poles, and filled their places with the bones of men.[25]

The king did not stop with Jerusalem and its immediate environs. He ranged through the whole of Judah and as far as Bethel, demolishing and beating to dust the altars, pillars, and asherahs of the high places and sanctuaries.

One very important feature of the reform followed upon this. The king fetched away all the priests from the sanctuaries of Yahweh outside of Jerusalem, and centralized Yahweh worship at Jerusalem; it was held that proper sacrifices could be offered only there.

Further phases of the reform were concerned with the ethical injunctions of the Deuteronomic code. A new social idealism spread through the land. The code called for greater humanitarianism toward slaves, more consideration for the needs of the poor. The old law of blood vengeance stood condemned in the light of the new law running: "Everyone is to be put to death for his own sin." [26] Though savage and cruel elements still remained to mark the new code with reflections of a more primitive era, there was genuine ethical advance toward justice and righteousness.

But the reform begun with such thoroughness failed of complete success. This was in large part due to its too great severity in one respect—the centralizing of religion in Jerusalem; for this had the effect of subtraction from the local community for the sake of addition to Jerusalem. The Jerusalem priesthood now had an absolute control over Yahwism and, moreover, a vested interest in it. The rural and village priesthoods were abolished, and the rural common people, expected now to go to Jerusalem "to find their chief joy," suffered a greatly diminished sense of the immediacy of the Divine presence in their localities. Yahweh, truly enough, had become ineffably holy and transcendent, and his stern will was clearly known from the pages of a sacred book; but he was a less intimate presence, not so near as before. The common people, finding it hard to attain to so high and intellectual a faith, relapsed disastrously into the emotionally more satisfying rites outlawed now by the Law as well as by the prophets.

Jeremiah

This great prophet, a man of intensely human quality, but condemned by circumstances to the distasteful public role of a Cassandra, began to prophesy when in his early twenties. He came of a priestly family, which before the Josianic reforms ministered in the sanctuary at Anatoth, a small town four miles northeast of Jerusalem. Stirred by the disaster threatening his wayward nation, he felt called by Yahweh to prophecy.

> The word of the Lord came to me, saying,
> "Before I formed you in the womb I knew you,
> And before you were born I set you apart,
> I appointed you a prophet to the nations."
>   Then said I,
> "Ah, Lord God! I cannot speak;
> For I am only a youth."
>   But the Lord said to me,
> "Do not say, 'I am only a youth';
> For to all to whom I send you shall you go,
> And all that I command you shall you speak . . ."
>   Then the Lord stretched forth his hand, and touched
> my mouth. And the Lord said to me,
>   "See! I put my words in your mouth." [27]

The prophetic ministry which Jeremiah performed was mostly that of warning the nation—always in vain—of disasters which might be forestalled or averted with Yahweh's help. So difficult was his task that at times, in later days, his heart failed him, and he gave vent to very human outbursts at the thanklessness of it all.

> I have become a laughing-stock all day long,
> Everyone mocks me.
> As often as I speak, I must cry out,
> I must call, "Violence and spoil!"
> . . . . If I say, "I will not think of it,
> Nor speak any more in his name,"
> It is in my heart like a burning fire,
>   Shut up in my bones;
> I am worn out with holding it in . . .
> Cursed be the day on which I was born,
> The day on which my mother bore me—
>   Let it not be blessed!
> Cursed be the man who brought the good news to my father,
> "A son is born to you"—
>   Wishing him much joy!
> . . . Why came I out of the womb,
> To see trouble and sorrow,
> That my days might be spent in shame? [28]

But although he became highly unpopular, Jeremiah never shrank from saying exactly what he felt the Lord meant him to say. When kings consulted him, he never broke the bad news gently. No threatening mob could make him speak softly. He was not an ingratiating person. Only one loyal friend stood by him through all the bitter days when he was reviled by kings, princes, common people, and fellow prophets. This was Baruch, his private secretary, the man who wrote down Jeremiah's prophecies at the prophet's dictation and afterward added valuable biographical notes to explain how the prophecies came to be uttered and what consequences ensued.

Jeremiah came at one of the most difficult and perplexing periods in Judah's entire history. He began his career when the Assyrian empire was in decline, and a terrifying invasion of Scythian plunderers swept down through Syria and along the Palestinian coast toward Egypt. Judah was in a panic of fear. Not long after the Scythian hordes withdrew into the north, a momentous change occurred in the East: Nineveh fell, and the Assyrian empire gave place to the Babylonian. Immediately there began a titanic contest between Egypt and Babylon for supremacy in the East. Judah became the seat of international intrigue, Egypt hoping to win to its side the little hill country, with its almost impregnable fortress-capital, and in good part succeeding. Yet during the tortuous contest the good king Josiah fell in battle opposing the very Egyptians who proposed to be his allies. Shortly afterward Egypt met with a stunning defeat at the hands of the Babylonians at Carchemish. Judah, now bereft of its good king and of its boastful ally from the Nile, came again under the control of an Oriental power; heavy annual tribute was exacted of her by the Babylonians. Then Egypt resumed her intrigues, making fresh promises. In Jerusalem king and people lent a ready ear.

But Jeremiah had the clear eye and good sense to see the folly of rebelling against the mighty Chaldaean power. He aroused the fierce displeasure of his compatriots by denying that Yahweh would keep the city inviolable, should Judah rebel and the Babylonians attack. Rather the contrary, he declared. He appeared one day in the Temple to deliver a scathing arraignment of the apostate people, and shouted: "Thus says the Lord: 'I will make this house like [ruined] Shiloh, and will make this city a curse to all the nations of the earth.' " His life was immediately in danger; for we read:

When Jeremiah had finished speaking all that the Lord had commanded him to speak to all the people, the priests and the prophets laid hold on him, saying,

"You shall die! How dare you prophesy in the name of the Lord, saying, 'This house shall become like Shiloh, and this city shall become an uninhabited waste'?"

Thereupon all the people crowded around Jeremiah in the house of the Lord.

When the princes of Judah heard the news, they came up from the palace and took their seats at the entrance to the new gate of the house of the Lord. Then the priests and the prophets addressed the princes and all the people saying,

"This man deserves to die; for he has prophesied against this city in the terms which you have heard."

Then Jeremiah addressed the princes and all the people, saying,

"The Lord sent me to prophesy against this house and this city all the words which you have heard. But now, if you amend your ways and your doings, and listen to the voice of the Lord your God, the Lord will repent of the evil which he has pronounced against you. As for myself, see! I am in your hands. Do to me as you think right and proper. Only be well assured of this, that, if you put me to death, you will be bringing innocent blood upon yourselves, upon this city, and upon its people; for the Lord has truly sent me to you, to speak these words in your hearing."

This firm speech completely changed the situation. Jeremiah was saved.

Then the princes and all the people said to the priests and the prophets,

"This man does not deserve to die; for he has spoken to us in the name of the Lord our God." [29]

It required only that the elders of the land should remind the assembly how Micah had prophesied in an earlier day that Jerusalem should become a ruin; * and Jeremiah was released.

It will be noted that Jeremiah's fellow-prophets united with the priests against him. Their constant opposition was a sore point. On one occasion he appeared in the streets with a wooden yoke upon his neck. This he said symbolized the yoke of the king of Babylon which would be laid upon the necks of the people. While he was walking through the Temple, a rival prophet named Hananiah stepped forward, bringing an opposite word from the Lord; he took the yoke from Jeremiah's neck and broke it, saying: "Thus says the Lord: 'So will I break the yoke of Nebuchadnezzar, king of Babylon, from the neck of all the nations within two years.'" Jeremiah retired to ponder this, and then came back to cry out that Hananiah, the false prophet, had made the people trust in a lie, and that the Lord would bind them with iron: he would put an unbreakable "yoke of iron on the neck of all the nations," that they might "serve Nebuchadnezzar, the king of Babylon." [30]

* Micah 3:9-12. See p. 526, supra.

The other prophets in Jerusalem seemed to Jeremiah no better than Hananiah. He pronounced severe judgment on them:

> Thus says the Lord of hosts:
> "Listen not to the words of the prophets
>   who prophesy to you!
> They fill you with vain hopes;
> They speak a vision from their own minds,
>   Not from the mouth of the Lord. . . .

"Behold, I am against the prophets who deal in lying dreams," is the oracle of the Lord, "and tell them, and mislead my people by their lies and their bombast—when I neither sent them nor commissioned them." [31]

When Judah recklessly revolted against Babylon, and the city was invested by the army of Nebuchadnezzar, Jeremiah exhausted the patience of the princes by openly telling the people that the city was doomed, and that those who stayed in it would die by the sword, famine, and pestilence, but those who would go and surrender to the Chaldeans would escape and have their lives given them as a prize of war. The rulers of Jerusalem naturally complained to the king that Jeremiah was disheartening the soldiers defending the city, and they urged that he be put out of the way. So Jeremiah was thrown into a dry cistern in the court of the royal guard, where he sank in the mud and was left to die. Had not an Ethiopian guard pricked the king's conscience with a description of Jeremiah's plight, he would surely have perished; as it happened, the king had the prophet secretly drawn up to terra firma. He was not set at liberty again until the city fell to the Babylonians.

This was not the first nor the last time Jeremiah was in danger. Once he had been arrested and put in the stocks for twenty-four hours; at one time his fellow-townsmen at Anatoth had plotted to put him to death; he and Baruch had had to go into hiding during the reign of King Jehoiakim, after that monarch became coldly enraged during a private palace-reading of a scroll of Jeremiah's sermons; the king cut up the scroll with his penknife piece by piece as it was being read to him and flung the pieces into the fire in the brazier before him, and then ordered Jeremiah's arrest. The danger passed, but the prophet was never to know peace thereafter. When Jerusalem was destroyed in 586 B.C., Nebuchadnezzar freed him as a friend and allowed him to remain in Judah along with the handful of citizens—the rabble really—who were not taken into exile. Jeremiah tried to reconcile those left behind with him to their lot, but Gedaliah, the able governor appointed by Nebuchadnezzar, was assassinated, and the conspirators kidnapped Jeremiah and carried him to Egypt, where he prophesied briefly before he came to his unknown, perhaps violent, end.

A reading of Jeremiah's sermons brings clearly before us his forthright, gloomy, suffering personality. The passages in which he predicts dire doom are still harrowing to read and must have been almost unendurable to hear; certainly they burn with the prophet's own anguish. Yet Jeremiah was not an ultimate pessimist; he had grounds for hope. He predicted that, after Yahweh had finished using Babylon as the means of accomplishing his just punishment of the nations, Babylon itself would be punished. Then the people of Judah, and those also of Israel, would "serve aliens no more" but would return to Judah to "serve the Lord their God, and David their king," whom Yahweh would raise up for them.

> "For I am with you to save you,"
> is the oracle of the Lord;
> "And I will make a full end of all the nations
> among whom I scattered you;
> But of you will I not make a full end." [32]

Having corrected them "in just measure," Yahweh would make a "new covenant" with his people, Jeremiah said.

At this point Jeremiah made an original and distinctive contribution to the prophetic tradition. The new covenant that was to be made was to be between Yahweh and redeemed *individuals*. Former prophets had concentrated on the public, socially experienced relationship between Yahweh and the Hebrews—the basis of the old covenant; Jeremiah advanced the idea of a valid, subjective experience of relationship between Yahweh and the individual.

> "Behold, days are coming," is the oracle of the Lord, "when I will make a new covenant with the household of Israel and with the household of Judah, not like the covenant which I made with their fathers on the day that I took them by the hand to lead them out of the land of Egypt—that covenant of mine which they broke, so that I had to reject them—but this is the covenant which I will make with the household of Israel. . . . I will put my law within them, and will write it on their hearts . . . And they shall teach no more every one his neighbor, and every one his brother, saying, 'Know the Lord'; for all of them shall know me, from the least of them to the greatest of them."

Jeremiah accompanied this prediction with a succinct statement of individual responsibility:

"In those days shall they say no more,
  'The fathers have eaten sour grapes,
  And the children's teeth are set on edge';
but everyone shall die for his own guilt—everyone who eats
the sour grapes shall have his own teeth set on edge." [33]

In other words, Jeremiah brought men face to face with God as individuals who were responsible directly to Him for their conduct; they could no longer say that He dealt with men only through their group relationships.

This was a proposition of great importance; for its logical corollary was: if the human relationship to God is a direct and personal relationship, then the approach to God through Temple sacrifice may not be all-important, may even be no longer requisite to the highest spiritual living of the individual.

V THE BABYLONIAN EXILE

As so often happens with fanatical nationalist groups, the pro-Egyptian party in Jerusalem brought about the very disaster they most hoped to avert—the collapse of Hebrew national sovereignty. They persuaded the aging King Jehoiakim to withhold tribute from Nebuchadnezzar, king of Babylon, and to make a stand for national independence, relying upon Egypt's military backing. When Nebuchadnezzar learned of this, he moved quickly, displaying in every decision an unyielding determination to crush Judean rebelliousness for good and all. In 597 B.C. he invested Jerusalem with his full forces. After a three months' siege the new king, Jehoiakin, who had just succeeded to the throne,* surrendered the city in order to avoid its total destruction. Nebuchadnezzar looted the Temple and carried away captive to Babylon the king and ten thousand of the citizens, or, as II Kings describes them, "all the nobles, and all the renowned warriors, and all the craftsmen, and all the smiths," as well as "all the strong men fit for war." [34] At Babylon the king was thrown into prison and the people were settled as colonists on the River Chebar, a large canal running to the southeast out of Babylon. Those who were left behind in Judah were placed under the rule of the deported king's uncle, Zedekiah, the third son of Josiah. In 588, after nine years of wavering loyalty to Nebuchadnezzar, Zedekiah too rebelled.

This time Jerusalem was not spared. In 586 B.C. after a siege lasting

---

* Jehoiakim died during the siege.

a year and a half, during which the Egyptians coming up to relieve the beleaguered city were decisively driven back by the besiegers, Jerusalem was taken. The Babylonians and their allies * systematically looted, burned, and destroyed all the buildings in the city, including the Temple, whose holy Ark was never again heard of; and they laboriously tore down the city walls. The city was so thoroughly laid in ruins that it was not completely rebuilt for over a century and a half. Before being carried away in chains to Babylon, King Zedekiah was forced to witness the execution of his sons and then had his own eyes put out. All of the inhabitants of Jerusalem, except Jeremiah and a handful of the poorest and lowliest citizens, were taken away. The towns around Jerusalem were drained of their upper classes. Meanwhile, many of those who could do so fled southward toward Egypt. The nation was disrupted. One part was in Babylonia. Another portion reached Egypt and settled in scattered communities along the Nile and its delta. A third portion stayed on in the ruined homeland. So profound was the change in national status that historians referring to the people who survived the fall of Jerusalem in 586 drop the name Hebrew and speak of them henceforward as Jews.

Yet the Babylonian Exile was not as disastrous to the Judean captives as the Assyrian deportation had been to the lost Ten Tribes. Nebuchadnezzar's hostility was of a political kind; it had only been directed against the continuance of Hebrew national sovereignty and not against the people as individuals. Once the Jews had been transported to the environs of Babylon, he allowed them comparative freedom. They could live together and follow their old ways of life and culture without disturbance. The region in which they were settled was part of a rich alluvial plain, intersected by irrigating canals, and therefore from an agricultural standpoint far superior to Palestine. Moreover it lay between two of the greatest cities of the world—Babylon and Nippur—and hence provided economic advantages of an unusual kind. So that those who made themselves at home and developed their opportunities throve wonderfully.

At first, of course, it was hard to feel at home. Of this we have the clearest sort of evidence. The Old Testament contains no passage so full of mingled pathos and unhappy rage as the Psalm which runs:

> By the rivers of Babylon,
> There we sat down, and wept,
> When we remembered Zion.
> Upon the poplars, in the midst of her,

---

* The Edomites, Samaritans, Ammonites, and others, who came in for the kill.

We hung up our harps.
For there our captors
Demanded of us songs,
And our tormentors, mirth:
"Sing us some of the songs of Zion."

How could we sing the songs of the Lord
In a foreign land?
If I forget you, O Jerusalem,
May my right hand fail me!
May my tongue cleave to my palate,
If I do not remember you;
If I set not Jerusalem
Above my highest joy!

Remember, O Lord, against the Edomites,
The day of Jerusalem!
They who said, "Raze it, raze it,
To its very foundations!"
O daughter of Babylon, destructive one,
Blessed be he who requites to you
The treatment that you dealt out to us!
Blessed be he who seizes your little ones,
And dashes them to pieces upon a rock! [35]

But the mood of irreconcilability with their lot passed. Economically the situation became better than tolerable. Those who farmed the rich soil found themselves harvesting big crops. Stony Judah had never yielded such. Many Jews, freed from farming, entered government service, as soldiers and officials. Others, turning their economic opportunities to advantage, became merchants and traders, following a direction which many of their ethnic brethren were even now pursuing in Egypt and Syria, and were to pursue increasingly down the centuries. It would not be long now before their great success would lead a Jewish writer (the author of Esther) to recognize the existence of anti-Semitism in Babylonia; he would make Haman say to King Xerxes in Susa: "There is a certain people scattered abroad and dispersed among the peoples throughout all the provinces of your kingdom, and their laws are different from every other people. . . . If it please the king, let it be prescribed that they be destroyed." [36] The Jews had entered upon the long and troublous course of anti-Semitic persecution across the face of the earth.

The Origin of the Synagogue

Yahwism had now to pass a crucial test. Would the exiled people consider that their Palestinian god had failed them and that the deities of foreign peoples were greater? Or would the viewpoint of the major prophets, that Yahweh was with his people everywhere and directed the destinies of other peoples besides the chosen race, prevail? Apparently some gave up Yahweh to follow the gods that had prospered Babylon. An older apostasy recurred in Egypt. Among the refugees who kidnapped Jeremiah and dragged him off to Egypt were men and women who thus defied the old prophet: "We will not listen to you, but will assuredly . . . [offer] sacrifices to the queen of the heavens,* and . . . [pour] libations to her, as we did, both we and our fathers, our kings and our princes, in the cities of Judah and in the streets of Jerusalem. For then we had plenty to eat, and were well, and met with no trouble; but since we gave up offering sacrifices to the queen of the heavens . . . we have been destitute of all things, and have been consumed by sword and famine."[37] These folk were lost to Yahwism. But those with whom the future of Judaism lay were not shaken in their faith: it widened and deepened. Yahweh was in Egypt, and in Babylonia, with them; of this they were assured.

To the faithful in Babylonia there was only one place in the world where sacrifices could be offered to Yahweh, and that was on the altar in the Temple at Jerusalem. This means of approach to the High God was now denied to them. But they could draw near to him in other ways. They could, for example, gather together on the Sabbath day in their homes, read to each other the scrolls of the Law and the writings of the Prophets. Besides these they could read aloud the early histories of their people, in various recensions, not yet finally combined into a canonical text. After reading from these texts, someone might lead in prayer. It became a practice to hold such gatherings every Sabbath day.† Out of them came the synagogue of later days. The sermon so familiar to Christian church-goers originated here too, for one of the chief features of the Sabbath meetings of the Jews in Babylon came to be an exposition and interpretation of some portion of the sacred texts directed to the correction or comfort of the hearers.

Along with the establishment of this form of worship there came a marked increase in literary activity. Copies of the older writings were prepared for use on the Sabbath day and during the festivals of the Jewish year; and those who feared that the new generation growing up

---

* Ashtart (=Ishtar).

† Some authorities think this custom had already been begun in the villages of Judah after the Deuteronomic Reform, as an attempt to worship God without animal sacrifice.

in Babylon might forget the traditions which were still unrecorded made haste to write these traditions down and to revise and enlarge the older histories and codes by addition and expansion. Writings also appeared reflecting contemporary religious insights. Many psalms, such as the one quoted on a previous page, were composed. And two great prophets appeared to pour out their inspired .thoughts in speech and writing.

Ezekiel

Very little is known about the life of Ezekiel. It is possible that much of the book credited to him was written in his name at a later time. He was apparently a leader of what has been called the Deuteronomic circle among the exiles—those who leaned heavily upon the Deuteronomic code and interpreted the whole of Hebrew history in its light, going so far as to rewrite much of Judges, and the books of Samuel and Kings in accordance with Deuteronomic value-judgments. Ezekiel came of a priestly family of Jerusalem, was carried captive to Babylonia in 597 B.C., and lived in a Jewish community by the River Chebar. For twenty-two years or more he was active as prophet and self-styled "watchman to the household of Israel," [38] exercising pastoral oversight and care over his fellow-exiles and dreaming always of the restoration and regeneration of his people.

In his visions and allegories, written down in fervid and florid phrase, a major concern emerged: when the exile should end, as it soon would, and the people returned to the homeland, what was to be the constitution under which they were to live, and, especially, how were the services in the restored Temple to be conducted? Here Ezekiel showed himself to be what he has been called, "a priest in the prophet's mantle." [39] Whereas Jeremiah realized in his day that the Temple and its divine services would soon come to an end, but that he could do without them, Ezekiel knew that "it was only a question of time before the Temple and its divine services would be restored, and he could not do without them." [40] So he concentrated on envisioning their restoration and did it in detail and with great enthusiasm. His minute descriptions of the Temple to be and its ceremonies, and his statement of the philosophy of worship which inspired him, had a very great influence on later Judaism.

Ezekiel's philosophy of worship combined the new emphasis on individual responsibility—new since Jeremiah and the issuance of the Deuteronomic code—with an exalted conception of Yahweh as a being sublimely transcendant and holy. The sinner needing pardon would not find Yahweh melting with love and forgiveness at the first sign of remorse. The holiness of Yahweh required the sacrificial approach of chastened individuals gathering in the Temple in a state of physical and ritual purity, under the guidance of expert priests. In his infinite sanctity, Yahweh had now withdrawn so far from the world of men that it was only through intermediaries, human and divine,* that he could be reached.

Perhaps this emphasis on the remoteness and absoluteness of the Lord God was an effect of the expanding view of his movements in history which the exiles had. Did not the Lord God rule the nations with a rod of iron? Was he not using individual men and single nations as means to inscrutable but holy and righteous ends? Was he not bent upon making his name known to all mankind? Questions such as these oppressed the minds of Ezekiel and his contemporaries and made them aware that God had other objects in view than just the showing of loving kindness and tender mercy to a chosen few. Ezekiel expressed their awareness in one saying of his:

"Thus says the Lord God: It is not for your sake that I am about to act, O household of Israel, but for my holy name which you have caused to be profaned among the nations to which you came. . . . and when I restore my holiness in their sight, through my dealings with you, the nations shall know that I am the Lord." [41]

Nevertheless, the Temple alone could offer the conditions of a proper approach to such a God—an approach of purified persons, in the beauty of holiness, seeking to add to the glory of God by fulfilling his Law.

Deutero-Isaiah

To this, the Great Unknown Prophet of the Exile, scholars have given a cumbrous name meaning Second Isaiah. His prophecies are preserved in the latter part of the book of Isaiah, approximately from the fortieth chapter on. Nothing about his life or identity is known; but fortunately his mind and spirit do not thus elude us. In ethical and religious insight his prophecies bring us to the culminating point of the Old Testament.

The central problem with which Deutero-Isaiah was concerned loomed large in the minds of the exiled Jews. It was the problem of

* Priests and angels.

the evil that had befallen them. Why had Yahweh brought so much suffering upon them? The old answer that it was because of their sins —while acknowledged to explain much—was not wholly satisfactory; for it was evident that the people of Babylonia, who now prospered, were as bad as, even worse than, the Jews had ever been. Deutero-Isaiah did not reject the conventional explanation; he saw truth in it. But he did not think the sufferings of the Jews could be entirely explained on that basis. He set his people's trials against a world background; they were, he declared, a part of Yahweh's plan of world redemption.

The conception here is magnificent in scope. Yahweh becomes without any qualification the only God: "there is no other." His sphere of action is the whole world. Whatever he does must be seen against a cosmic background.

> Have you not known? have you not heard?
> The Lord is a God everlasting,
> The Creator of the ends of the earth.[42]

He is the first, and the last: "before me was no God formed, and after me there shall be none." [43] He alone created the heavens and the earth, and he gives breath to the peoples. He controls all history; forms the light, and creates darkness; makes peace, and creates evil. This holy Lord of Hosts, who says from his seat of world power, "As the heavens are higher than the earth, so are my ways higher than your ways, and my thoughts than your thoughts," [44] nevertheless dwells as an immanent Savior and Redeemer in the hearts of the contrite and humble in spirit.

> For thus says the high and exalted One,
> Who dwells enthroned for ever, and whose name is Holy:
> "I dwell enthroned on high, as the Holy One,
> But with him also that is contrite and humble in spirit." [45]

Furthermore, God's redemptive purpose is not limited to one area or one people; it is universal; he means to save all mankind, Gentiles as well as Jews.

At this point Deutero-Isaiah brought forward his most original conception, the finest fruit of his experience of living among the Gentiles. To bring the saving knowledge of himself and his holy will to all mankind God needs a messenger, a Servant. Israel is that servant, and may say:

> Listen, you coast lands, to me;
> Hearken, you peoples afar!
> The Lord called me from birth,
> From my mother's womb he gave me my name. . . .
> He said to me, "You are my servant,

Israel, through whom I will show forth my glory." [46]
"I the Eternal have called you of set purpose,
And have taken you by the hand;
I have formed you for the rescuing of my people,
    For a light to the nations." [47]

The Jews were thus a chosen people, chosen not to be the recipients of
unearned favors, but to serve as bearers of light. It was not that they
were to be active missionaries, it would seem, but that in their characters and lives the nations would see the presence of the Lord.

But, alas, they had been blind and deaf to their world mission, and
had had to be refined and purified "in the furnace of suffering." The
Lord had to give up the chosen people to spoilers and plunderers, because they had sinned, and would not walk in his ways, nor listen to
his instructions. "So he poured upon them the heat of his anger, and
the fierceness of war." [48] This punishment had to be. It was forced upon
God by the chosen people's sins. But the prophet brought comforting
word that the Lord God now declared that Jerusalem's guilt was paid
in full, and her people would therefore not have to suffer any more
afflictions.

The suffering had not been in vain. Not only had it purified the
nation, but it had gone straight to the hearts of onlooking Gentiles and
vicariously redeemed them. This conception is wrought out in one of
the greatest religious odes ever written. The nations of the earth are
heard saying of the Suffering Servant:

He was despised, and rejected of men;
A man of sorrows, and acquainted with grief:
    And as one from whom men hide their face he was despised,
    And we esteemed him not.

Surely he hath borne our griefs,
And carried our sorrows:
    Yet we did esteem him stricken,
    Smitten of God, and afflicted.

But he was wounded for our transgressions,
He was bruised for our iniquities:
    The chastisement of our peace was upon him;
    And with his stripes we are healed.

All we like sheep have gone astray;
We have turned every one to his own way:
    And the Lord hath laid on him
    The iniquity of us all.[49]

Deeply moved, the Gentile kings and their people understand at last that through the sufferings of God's servant, Israel, righteousness is recommended to them and they are led to practice it; the ethical character of the true God has been revealed to them in the moral nature of his stricken servant.

Thus Deutero-Isaiah justified the ways of God to the Jews. But he not only looked into the past, he saw into the future. The next phase of God's redemptive plan, he declared, was a glorious restoration of the Jews to Jerusalem, where the work of redemption could proceed into all the world as from a center, amid the joy of all believers. This was to be effected through Cyrus, the Persian war-lord, who by God's direction would tread down rulers as a potter tramples clay, overthrow Babylon, and release the Jews. (We shall see that Cyrus fulfilled these expectations.) Then after their return to the homeland, the Jews would minister to the nations in the Lord's name. All the world would flock to Jerusalem to worship God, saying,

> "With you alone is God, and there is no other,
> no God besides;
> Truly with you God hides himself,
> the God of Israel is a savior." [50]

But not only would the world come to Jerusalem; Israel would go out into the world.

> Thus says the Lord God:
> "Behold! I will lift up my hands to the nations, . . .
> And they shall bring your sons in their bosom,
> And your daughters shall be carried on their shoulders.
> And kings shall be your foster fathers,
> And their queens your nursing-mothers." [51]

Salvation would reach to the ends of the earth. Evil would be destroyed. Eternal light would arise.

Through the appeal of his high moral idealism, Deutero-Isaiah was to have a great influence on the best minds of later Judaism; and even more was he to influence early Christianity. Some understood him; others did not. His prophecies were searched again and again by those who waited expectantly for the coming of a Messiah. His descriptions of the Suffering Servant were so concrete and individualized that later generations readily concluded that he was speaking in them, not of a nation, but of a Messiah; and so they looked for a person who should some day redeem the world through his suffering. The early Christians found in Jesus of Nazareth one who fitted these descriptions perfectly.

VI THE RISE OF JUDAISM IN THE
RESTORATION PERIOD

In 538 B.C. Cyrus the Great took Babylon, and made it the capital of a new empire, which was ultimately to stretch from the Persian Gulf to the Black Sea and from the Indus River to the Greek cities on the Ionian Coast. When he looked about him, he found grouped together in the heart of Babylonia an unassimilated captive people, with ways different from the ways of other peoples; and on inquiring about them, he heard their plaints. In order to win their friendship and at the same time to have them go off to the border near Egypt and set up a buffer state, he gave them permission to return to Jerusalem. The "Return" so longed for by the first generation of exiles was now possible.

The Return to Judah and Jerusalem

An expedition of returning Jews was organized at once. According to later Jewish historians, Cyrus issued a decree giving them a privileged status; he not only restored to them the Temple vessels carried away by Nebuchadnezzar in 586 B.C., but even made funds available for the expedition! Apparently, the leaders of the return were two: Zerubbabel, a grandson of King Jehoiakin and hence as a lineal descendant of King David a person with Messianic possibilities, and Joshua, a priest of the highly revered Zadokite branch of the Levite tribe. Though it was evident from the first that many Jews were not going to return, since Babylonia was their home now, thousands did. The latter were idealistically described by Ezra a century later as those "whose spirit God had aroused to go up to build the house of the Lord which is in Jerusalem." [52]

Upon arrival at Jerusalem, the first act of the returning exiles was to erect an altar on the site of the ruined Temple and begin regular morning and evening sacrifices. The rebuilt altar was made the center of a communal life organized on lines like those suggested by the prophet Ezekiel. The Temple area was gradually cleared of debris, and amid shouts of joy and the weeping of the older folks, the foundation stone was laid for the reconstruction of the Temple.

But the community soon proved unable to proceed with the task. Most of the people chose to live in the surrounding fields and villages, not in Jerusalem itself, where the heaps of burnt-over ruins discouraged home-making. But conditions outside of Jerusalem were scarcely better. Virtually no economic opportunities awaited the newcomers. Moreover, the "peoples of the land," that is, the non-exiles, had taken possession of the properties of the exiled upper classes and were undoubtedly annoyed to see so many returning claimants to old homesteads; for they could themselves claim sixty or seventy years of squatter's rights. But there were further factors of contention. The returning exiles had for seventy years idealized Jerusalem and the Law, and they looked with disdain upon the non-exiles, because they had lapsed from the Deuteronomic standard, and had, moreover, intermarried with Edomites, Ammonites, and Samaritans. So on their part, the non-exiles, disgruntled at being treated as religious and social inferiors, withheld cooperation from the rebuilding of the Temple and other reconstruction projects. No wonder, then, that a stubborn depression, both spiritual and economic, overwhelmed the community, and for fifteen years the Temple lay untouched.

Then at the urging of the prophets Haggai and Zechariah the rebuilding was resumed. Haggai had indignantly scolded: how could the people expect prosperity as long as they left the Lord's house in ruins? Both prophets encouraged the community to resume the work quickly because of the great hope which they held out: there would be a shaking up of the world powers and Judah would again become an independent kingdom, with Zerubbabel, the descendant of David, becoming their crowned head, as Yahweh's Messianic "Chosen one." This hope animating them, the Jews made haste to complete the Temple. It was not like Solomon's, but it was strongly built and in the correct dimensions. Then they settled back to wait for signs of the Lord's favor. And no change in the situation came.

A century passed. The prophetic hopes concerning the restoration were plainly unrealized. Were they unrealizable? Some apparently thought so, for on every hand there were multiplying signs of ebbing faith. The writer of the book of Malachi, who prophesied at this time, accused the people of slackening zeal, of cynicism, of lack of respect for Yahweh; he said they did not pay their tithes properly, brought defective animals to the sacrifices, were not reverent during the Temple ceremonies. How could they hope for the Lord's blessing?

When knowledge of this state of affairs reached Babylonia, the faithful Jews there were disturbed. One of their number, a young man who was a favorite cup-bearer to King Artaxerxes (I or II?), on receiving fresh reports of the woeful condition of Jerusalem and its inhabitants, came before the king at Susa with a sad countenance. The king inquired the reason for his melancholy, and, learning the cause, generously sent the young man, whose name was Nehemiah, upon a special mission, with the powers of a governor, to Jerusalem, to oversee the rebuilding of the city's walls and to reorganize the community. Nehemiah set out for Jerusalem, accompanied by army officers and horsemen, and provided with enabling letters to the authorities. Before or about the same time Ezra the Scribe and some seventeen hundred Babylonian Jews, many of them handpicked for the work of reform, left for Jerusalem to push the spiritual renewal which was to parallel Nehemiah's rebuilding of the walls.* The story of Nehemiah's successful leadership is dramatically told in the autobiography bearing his name. It was due entirely to his executive genius and energy that the breaches in the walls and the burnt gates of the city were repaired at last, after over one hundred and fifty years of lying in ruin.

The Establishment of a Priestly State

Seeking the spiritual renewal of the community, Ezra the Scribe summoned the Jews before the Water Gate. Here the assembly heard read to them a book of the Law (presumably the Holiness code from Leviticus †), and bound themselves by a solemn covenant and oath to observe its provisions. A new theocratic state was inaugurated, with power vested in the priests. It reestablished the Mosaic covenant but might be called a new one at the same time. What occupied the center of attention—then and for the next four hundred years—becomes clear in the following quotation from the pledge the assembly adopted under oath:

"We make and sign a binding covenant . . . and take oath, under penalty of a curse, to walk in the law of God which was given by Moses the servant of God, and to be careful to observe all the commands of the LORD our Lord, and his ordinances and his statutes; and that we will not give our daughters to the peoples of the land or take their daughters as wives for our sons; and that, if the peoples of the land bring wares or any grain on the Sabbath day to sell, we will not buy from them on the Sabbath or on a holy day; and that in the seventh year we will leave the land fallow and refrain from the exaction of any debt.

"We also lay upon ourselves the charge to give the third part of a shekel yearly for the service of the house of our God, for the bread that is arranged in layers, and for the regular burnt-offering, for the sabbaths, the

---

* It is here assumed that Ezra and Nehemiah were in Jerusalem about the same time. The facts are susceptible of another interpretation. It is possible that Ezra arrived first and that Nehemiah came later and completed the work which Ezra had begun. Scholars are divided on the sequence of events.

† Leviticus xvii–xxvi.

new moons, the fixed festivals, and the holy things, and for the sin-offerings to make atonement for Israel, and for all the work of the house of our God. Moreover, we will cast lots, the priests, the Levites, and the people, concerning the wood-offering, to bring it into the house of our God, . . . to burn upon the altar of the LORD our God . . . ; and to bring the first produce of our ground and the first of all fruit of every kind of tree year by year to the house of the LORD; also the first-born of our sons and of our cattle, as it is written in the law, and the firstlings of our herds and our flocks, . . . and our first batch of baking, our contributions, the fruit of every kind of tree, the wine, and the oil, to the priests in the chambers of the house of our God; and the tithes of our ground to the Levites, since they, the Levites, take the tithes in all the cities dependent on our agriculture. Now the priest, the son of Aaron, shall be with the Levites, when the Levites tithe, and the Levites shall bring up the tithe of the tithes to the house of our God, to the chambers into the treasure house." [53]

In thus laying primary stress on first-fruits, and tithing, and sacrifices, and fixed festivals, the Jews of Ezra's time established upon the foundation of the old pre-exilic faith—called conveniently the Religion of Israel—the clear-cut, legalistic religion named Judaism. The chief figures of the reorganized faith were priests; its infallible guide was a book of the Law (the Torah); its concern was directed toward matters of ritual: what was clean and unclean, purifications and expiations, permissions and prohibitions, and general obedience to the scriptural law. And when after a struggle, in which Ezra and Nehemiah had to exert all their authority, foreign wives were put away, together with their children, and intermarriage with non-Jews prohibited on pain of ostracism, the Jews entered upon the process of becoming a racially as well as religiously exclusive group.

Much future history, however, is anticipated in a revealing passage from Nehemiah, written of his second governorship, when presumably Ezra was dead and he himself had been away in Susa:

In these days I saw in Judah men treading wine presses on the Sabbath and bringing heaps of grain loaded on asses, also wine, grapes, figs, and all kinds of burdens which they brought into Jerusalem on the Sabbath day; and I protested on the day when they sold provisions. Tyrians also dwelt therein, who brought in fish and all kinds of wares, and sold them on the Sabbath to the Judeans and in Jerusalem. Then I contended with the nobles of Judah and said to them,

"What evil thing is this that you are doing, and thereby profaning the Sabbath day? Did not your fathers do this and did not our God bring all this misfortune upon us and upon this city? Yet you are bringing more wrath upon Israel by profaning the Sabbath."

Accordingly when the gates of Jerusalem began to be in darkness, before the Sabbath, I commanded that the gates be shut; and I gave orders that they should not be opened until after the Sabbath. Also I put some of my servants in charge of the gates, that none should bring in a burden on the Sabbath day. Then the traders and sellers of all kinds of wares lodged outside Jerusalem once or twice. So I warned them and said to them,

"Why do you lodge in front of the wall? If you repeat it, I shall arrest you."

From that time on they came no more on the Sabbath. ° [54]

These details have been given to show the situation: the common people continued to err, and yet the way of life established for them in law and in authority—a theocratic, ceremonial legalism—was laid inescapably upon their consciences and dominated all thought. As time went on it would claim them more and more. In considering the post-exilic period down to the end of the 4th century B.C., we cannot fail to see that, however great their laxity at times, the people gave their increasing loyalty to the regular round of religious duties prescribed for them. The weekly Sabbath day observances drew them to the Temple at Jerusalem or to the gathering-places in the outlying towns and villages which later acquired the Greek name for such places, synagogues. The annual festivals and fasts became a matter of ingrained custom. These were the *Passover* and the week-long *Feast of Unleavened Bread* which accompanied it in the first month of the year (March or April); the *Feast of Weeks* (or First Ripe Fruits) ending in *Pentecost* in the spring; and the *Feast of Trumpets* (later called "Rosh Hashanah" or New Year), followed ten days later by the fast of the *Day of Atonement* or *Yom Kippur,* and in fifteen days by the *Feast of Booths* or *Tabernacles,* all in the seventh month (September or October). The purely ethical religion of the prophets could not by itself firmly hold the common people, but these observances did.† Later Judaism had been born.‡

° Nehemiah found to his horror that the portion of the Levites had not been given them, so that the Levites and the singers at the services in the Temple were obliged to cultivate their own fields for a living. So he had to bring pressure upon the Judeans to pay their tithes. Also he found that some Jews had married foreign women, and that their children spoke foreign languages and "none of them could speak in the Jews' language." Here he felt he had to take direct action, reporting: "I contended with them and cursed them and beat some of them and pulled out their hair and made them swear by God"; [55] after which they sent their foreign wives off. He even found a prominent priest married to a foreign woman, and exiled him.

† For a fuller description of these observances as practiced at a later time, see the last topic in Section XI of this chapter, beginning on page 576.

‡ Many scholars prefer to call the pre-exilic Hebrew faith "the Religion of Israel," and reserve the name "Judaism" for the religion of the postexilic Jews whom we are here studying.

Further, the racial exclusiveness of the Jews threw them more and more as the years passed upon their own religious authorities, both human and literary. Their supreme ecclesiastical personage was the high priest, who lived in the Temple at Jerusalem; he was a descendant of Zadok, a royally appointed priest of King David's time, said to be descended from Aaron, the brother of Moses. He was both the religious and the civic ruler of Jerusalem. Under him were the ordained priests, who ministered in the Temple during religious ceremonies, and the Levites, who had the status of Temple servitors and were in charge of the musical services and the temple property. Authority was also vested in the learned profession of scribes, from which the rabbis sprang. The scribes had once been a more or less secular order, but they were now a religious class devoted to copying and interpreting the Torah and other sacred writings. Those of their number who developed a special talent for preaching in the synagogues came to be known as rabbis or "teachers." The rabbis performed a double service for the common people, which gave them increasing importance as time went on. In the first place, they met the growing need for a professional exposition of the sacred books, all the more necessary because Hebrew was being superseded as a spoken language by Aramaic, the mixed language that prevailed throughout Syria and Palestine, so that the common people could no longer understand their own Hebrew writings without the aid of an interpreter.* In the second place, the rabbis helped to decentralize religious worship and make genuine group religious experience possible again in the villages—something that King Josiah's reformation in 621 B.C. had made difficult.

The priests and the scribes were not idle in providing authoritative religious literature for the people. Though the days of oral prophecy had virtually ended, testifying through the written word to the power of the holy and transcendent God of Israel in nature and history had become more and more common. In Babylonia and in Jerusalem the priests and scribes were diligently engaged in literary labors. They circulated copies of the writings of the more recent prophets, Malachi Obadiah, Ezekiel, Haggai, Zechariah, and Second Isaiah; and they reedited the writings of the older prophets. The five books of the Torah were being finally completed: "J," "E," and "D" were dovetailed into one complete work, then recombined with "P" or the Priestly Code. This last document, newly written, furnished the strictly monotheistic first chapter of Genesis and many legal provisions interspersed through the

---

* A translation of important texts into Aramaic was finally made and called the *Targum*. An earlier translation into Greek, begun in the 3rd century B.C. in Alexandria, is known as the *Septuagint*. See p. 556 for further details.

five books, including "H," the Holiness code used by Ezra and Nehemiah in their reforms. Joshua, Judges, Samuel, and Kings were further revised, and expanded by the addition of new material. A group of priests, with a Deuteronomic slant, worked on Chronicles, Ezra, and Nehemiah. The singers in the Temple were using and composing the chants which were later to furnish much of the Book of Psalms. Quite another type of poetry, the erotic, had already found embodiment in the Song of Songs. Fully two-thirds of the Old Testament as we know it today was in existence.

The significance of the new shift in interest has been well stated by a Jewish historian, thus:

> All through the 5th century there was a steady reaction against religious laxness, a reaction sponsored by the scribes, who were becoming ever more influential. The scribes, forerunners of the Pharisees, were the interpreters of the law, the leaders in the synagogues. . . . "Turn it and turn it again," the scribes admonished their people, "for everything is in it." And the Jews responded with unparalleled devotion. All existence was centered in the law. The Jews became a people of the book. The early Hebrews had created the Bible out of their lives; their descendants created their lives out of the Bible.[56]

Or as a group of Jewish scholars has pointed out, in commenting on the effects of Ezra's reform:

> Henceforth, the distinguishing mark of a Jew would not be political identity but adherence to the Torah, even if he lived outside Palestine and did not participate in the Temple cult. After the Exile, Jewish nationality became identified with ethnic solidarity—common descent, destiny, religion, and culture—rather than territorial status.[57]

"Schools of expounders" arose to deduce new laws from the old, in order that the ancient Torah might be made applicable to and practical in the life of later generations. These schools of the scribes were ultimately to become the solidly learned Pharisaic schools of the 2nd and 1st centuries B.C. From the first they provided valuable insight on the problem of divising workable laws or conditions not dreamt of in the day of Moses. Improvements were made in civil law and Sabbath practices. But that there were drawbacks is also indicated by the historian we have just quoted:

> It was inevitable that the endless spinning of meanings from the old texts should go to extremes and become burdensome. The Biblical law which prohibited the eating of meat torn in the field was based upon the sensible hygienic principle that carrion was dangerous as food. In the hands of the

dialecticians the law was elaborated into a complex dietary machinery. If meat torn in the field was prohibited, why not also meat torn in the city? But what was torn meat? If it were not properly slaughtered, it was surely torn. What was proper slaughter? A whole code, the basis for the practice of *Shehita* (ritual slaughter), grew up to meet these problems—rules governing the knife to be used and the manner of using it, rules governing the competency of the ritual slaughterer and his training, the prayers to be recited when the throat was cut and when the blood was covered with ashes.° A simple Biblical precept grew into a labyrinth of observances.[58]

VII NEW TRENDS OF THOUGHT IN THE GREEK AND MACCABEAN PERIODS

In 332 B.C. the Palestinian theocracy came under a new control— that of far-away Greece. Alexander the Great drove the Persian armies out of Asia Minor and Syria, and then seized Palestine on his way to the conquest of Egypt. After founding on the Egyptian coast, and naming after himself, the new city of Alexandria, which he hoped would become a culture center that would revolutionize the civilization of the regions bordering on the southeastern Mediterranean, he turned his attention to what was left of the Persian Empire and brought it tumbling down at his feet.

General Characteristics of the Hellenistic Influence

In Alexander's motivation his personal ambition without a doubt played the more considerable part; but he also started out with a naive and altruistic passion for the spread of Greek civilization through the East. Yet he had no notion of imparting Greek civilization by force. He believed in the self-evidencing power of truth, and planned to convert the world to the Greek view of life by education and example. So in Alexandria and at other strategic points he ordered the establishment of new cities, which were to be laid out by Greek architects and provided with colonnaded municipal buildings, gymnasiums, open air theaters, and libraries like those at Athens. He encouraged Greek, Egyptian, Persian, and Jewish colonists to live in these model cities, under municipal governments that allowed each national group to live in its own

---

° Without such slaughter the flesh would not be *kosher* or "fit."

quarter of the city and yet have a democratic share in certain processes of city government.° Of course, no little pressure was brought to bear on each citizen to induce him—entirely of his own free will!—to put on Greek dress, speak in Greek, build and furnish his home in the Hellenistic modes, and read and discuss Greek philosophical and political works, so far as his education allowed.

Alexander seemed to respect and favor the Jews. He wanted them in Alexandria, and in later days they filled two of the city's five sections. (They may have numbered 1,000,000 souls there!) He hoped to make places for them elsewhere. The Jews, for their part, were more influenced by his cultural proposals than by those of any foreigner in their whole history. For one thing, the Hellenism for which he stood combined a new breadth of culture with unprecedented religious and racial tolerance. For another, it seemed to hold a great promise of vital world relationships overflowing into the economic and political back-eddy that was Judah. The Jews wanted to be on good terms with the rest of the world. They may have been suspicious at first of the Hellenic colonists set up in model communities throughout Palestine; but these colonists proved after all to be persuasive exponents of Hellenism, because they were amusing, fraternal and peaceful. In three generations, the higher class Jews were freely admitting Greek words into their everyday speech and calling their children by Greek names. The cultured classes, and especially the Jerusalem priests, were, as might be expected, more profoundly influenced than the common people. Without giving up their religion, they welcomed the external features of Hellenistic civilization; so much so that, in the heyday of the Greek influence, the sacrifices were sometimes left half burnt on the altar at Jerusalem while the priests rushed off to some stadium to see the Greek athletes performing in the games! Yet there was a strong counter-current. The plain people were slow as always to adopt foreign ways. And the scribes and rabbis held back; with a stubborn loyalty to the Torah and the Jewish way of life, they kept resistance to Hellenism and all its ways and works alive among the "quiet in the land," the conservatively Jewish "pious ones" or *hasidim*, as they were called.

The process of Hellenization was retarded but not interrupted by the contention for the possession of Palestine which followed Alexander's early death in Babylon. During a hundred years, unhappy Palestine was overrun again and again by the armies of the Seleucids (of Syria) and the Ptolemies (of Egypt). Though the latter, the kindlier and

---

° For example, each city was to be ruled by a council annually elected by the people.

therefore the preferred overlords of the Jews, were in the ascendancy most of the time, at the beginning of the 2nd century B.C. the Seleucids finally triumphed. There was peace after that for a while, and Palestinian Judaism might have gone over even more completely to Hellenism than had yet been the case had not a headstrong Seleucid king caused his Jewish subjects to revolt against him and return to the ways of their fathers.

The Period of Independence under the Maccabees

It had now become a fact that, as long as their religious life was not interfered with, the orthodox Jews endured a good deal of oppression, but when their religion was endangered they incontinently rebelled. This was something that Antiochus Epiphanes, king of Syria, did not understand. Anxious to hasten the lagging process of welding all the peoples of his kingdom into a Hellenistically-minded whole, he determined to use force to make the Jews worship Zeus and Dionysus. He therefore forbade the Jews, on pain of death, to keep the Sabbath, own any copies of their sacred writings, or practice circumcision. He erected on the altar of burnt offering in the Temple at Jerusalem an altar to Zeus of Olympus, and here sacrificed pigs (always an abomination to the Jews). Further he commanded all Jews to join in similar sacrifices, not only at Jerusalem but in the villages. The horror and indignation of the faithful passed all bounds. When, then, an aged priest called Mattathias was ordered by a Syrian commissioner to participate in a sacrifice to Zeus at the village of Modin, he murdered the commissioner, and raised the standard of revolt. With his five sons at his side, and backed by many followers from among the orthodox Jews who rushed to him from every quarter, he took his stand in the wilderness; his able son Judas Maccabeus astounded the Syrian commanders by defeating four of their armies and forcing a fifth to retreat. In 165 B.C. Judas accomplished the surprising feat of recapturing all of Jerusalem except its garrisoned castle. The Temple was then purged of its "abominations," and the Jewish worship restored. Palestinian Judaism had been saved. In the subsequent phases of the campaign, the Syrians were obliged to quit Judea. Judas was killed in 161 B.C. and the leadership passed to his brother Jonathan, and after him to the last of the brothers, Simon, who was made high priest. Simon's son, John Hyrcanus, jeopardized the future by imperialistically adding Idumea (Edom), Samaria, and Perea (the region beyond Jordan) to Judea, so that his kingdom approached King David's in size. He forced the Idumeans to accept Judaism at the point of the sword—a bad precedent. Though the Jews seemed here to be overreaching themselves, the period of Jewish independence lasted to 63 B.C., and might have lasted longer had it not been for the strife which broke out between divergent parties among the Jews themselves.

Before we tell that story and add the tragic aftermath, we need to examine the foreign ideas and modes of thought that now made an influx into Judaism and laid the basis for the rise of the postexilic Jewish parties.

Gentile Influences on Thought during the Greek and Maccabean Periods

In the theology and literature of these periods may be seen the influence of Greek and Persian ideas about nature and history. Written or being written were the books of Proverbs, Job, and Ecclesiastes, now in the Bible, and Ecclesiasticus and the Wisdom of Solomon, contained in the Apocrypha. Considered together, they are usually referred to as the *Wisdom Books*. Ruth, Esther, Jonah, and the Book of Psalms made their appearance at this time, too. Finally, the last of the Old Testament books to be completed was Daniel, and along with it a host of extracanonical books in like vein, giving expression to fervid Messianic hopes.

The Wisdom literature shows the influence of Greek ideas, although one cannot say that these ideas were either dominant or the basic motivating factors. One may only say that Hellenism confirmed many thoughtful Jews, discouraged by the trend of their history, in their disillusionment and quiet scepticism; and that, beyond this, it developed in them the rationalistic attitude of submitting every belief to the test of reason, and thus cultivated a taste for the more intellectual types of speculation. To take an example, the latest portions of Proverbs assimilate certain speculative concepts of Greek philosophy. Most of Proverbs is very old. It was begun in the days before Solomon as a translation and paraphrase of Egyptian collections of wise sayings about the nature and conduct of life. Solomon is said to have been attracted to these sayings and to have added some generalizations of his own.

The collection grew slowly with the years by the accession to it of other independent collections, until by about 250 B.C. it assumed its present form. On the whole, it is pitched in a key of quite unecclesiastical lay-wisdom, in the spirit of *Poor Richard's Almanac*, Benjamin Franklin's contribution to the practical wisdom of early America. Morality is for the most part regarded not so much as the law of God (though that is not denied, certainly) but as the demand of reason and common sense. In its latest sections, however, Wisdom is personified as God's consultant at creation—a Greek notion, the' word for Wisdom being "Sophia" or "Logos," and signifying in either case a combination of reason and sound judgment.

Another book that requires for its explanation the presence of Hellenism is Ecclesiastes. The writer seems to have had a knowledge of both Judaism and Hellenism, but to have been thrown into such mental confusion by the attempt to reconcile them that he could see no worth in human thought or effort. All that seemed to him good he summed up in such words as these: "I know there is nothing good for man but to be glad and enjoy himself while he lives." Everything else involved futility, a vain striving to hold the wind. Perhaps the writer had read the older book, Job, and had been unable to solve its fundamental problem, Why does not God make it the rule that the righteous prosper and the wicked suffer? But no, the righteous suffer and the wicked prosper. Ecclesiastes only vaguely catches Job's suggestion that the wise and pure in heart may transcend their suffering by rejoicing in the wisdom and majesty of God revealed in the awesome design of the world.

The Hellenistic influence on Judaism reached its height at Alexandria in Egypt rather than in Palestine. There near the time of Christ it made itself felt in the book called the Wisdom of Solomon and in the writings of the Jewish philosopher *Philo*, who consciously tried to synthesize Greek and Jewish thought by identifying the Wisdom of Jewish theology with the Logos of Greek philosophy. His teaching that contact with the Supreme Being, in the fullest spiritual sense, was the work of the divine Logos as the mediator of the power or activity of God was to have great influence on the thought-forms to be found in the prologue of the Fourth Gospel and in the writings of the early Christian Fathers.

Another effect of the pervasive Greek influence was the translation of the books of the Old Testament into Greek by a group of scholarly translators, traditionally said to have numbered seventy (whence the name of the translation, the *Septuagint*). This translation was begun in the 3rd century B.C., but was not completed until near the time of Christ.°

But the influence of Hellenism on the religious conceptions of the main body of Jews was less enduring than that of Zoroastrianism, chiefly because the former was philosophical and secular in spirit, while the latter was religious and could offer supplementation to already existing beliefs.

It is easy but hazardous to seek exact conclusions concerning so elusive a thing as "influence"; but the Jews came to know Zoroastrianism from observations near at hand in Babylonia, and certain Persian beliefs about Satan, the angels, the after-life and the Messianic Deliverer supplied what must have seemed missing elements in the old Jewish beliefs. Before they met the Satan of the Zoroastrians, the Jews had pondered the old stories about the serpent in the Garden of Eden and the fallen angels who had taken wives from among the daughters of men before the days of Noah. Then, too, there was the Adversary among the heavenly beings surrounding Yahweh who obtained permission to afflict Job and make him curse God. These stories antedated the Exile, and in none of them is there the suggestion that the Spirit of Evil is a cosmic being, manifested from the beginning of time, and of a strength and creative power almost equal to that of the Spirit of Good. But after the Exile the Adversary among the heavenly beings became, for at least some of the Jews, an evil and infinitely malicious power, wholly in opposition to God—in fact almost a rival sovereign, with attendant devils to match the angels who stood before God. In another direction, She'ol, the shadowy land of the dead, was replaced by a heaven and a hell; and some Jews began also to speak of a resurrection from the dead at the last day and of a last judgment, a final reward of the good and condemnation of the evil. Long before the Exile the prophets foretold, of course, a Day of Doom and a purging of the nations; but now many Jews believed this with Persian alterations. Let us see what some of these changes specifically were.

° A word should be said about the importance of this translation. It is now apparent that the translators used only the most authentic manuscripts. Scholars have long believed this to be the case. The Septuagint proved to be the most reliable check they had upon the accuracy of the Hebrew manuscripts that had survived before 1947, none of which could be dated before the 10th century A.D. The discovery from 1947 on of the *Dead Sea Scrolls* has confirmed this earlier belief, for these oldest of Hebrew manuscripts (dated from the two centuries before Christ) are in accord at nearly every point with the Septuagint.

It may be added that the Dead Sea Scrolls have also confirmed the belief that the Latin translation (the Vulgate) made by St. Jerome in the 4th century A.D. was the result of his careful choices among variant readings in the Hebrew manuscripts he was able to gather.

1. The ancient Hebrew belief in demons, which scarcely rose above the animistic level and never implied strong resistance to Yahweh, much less a systematic or sustained opposition, now became the belief that the demons were *organized*; they had a leader, a head. This head was variously named, but the most common name for him was Satan (Shaitin). One of his first appearances under this name is in a passage in the prophecies of Zechariah, where he is described as contending with an angel-messenger of the Lord. As the Tempter, he was also read back by editors and revisers into the historical books; and the writers of "P" put him into the Garden of Eden.

2. The angels who, according to old belief, were Yahweh's divine messengers now were thought of as arranged in a hierarchy. In the Hellenistic and Maccabean periods this hierarchy consisted of seven archangels: Raphael, Uriel, Michael, Raguel, Saraqiel, Gabriel, and Jeremiel. The most prominent of these was Michael, with Gabriel coming next in importance.

3. The older Jewish belief that the dead descend to a colorless existence in the pit of She'ol, a land of forgetfulness not unlike the Greek Hades and the Babylonian Aralu, was in large part superseded by a belief in the resurrection of the body to an after-life of full mental vigor and awareness.

4. The prediction of the older prophets that there would be a Day of Yahweh in which the enemies of Israel would be carried down to doom, after which a new kingdom would be set up, with a Messianic king of Davidic lineage on the throne, underwent a radical change. This may have been a natural development and not a Zoroastrian suggestion; probably it was both; but at any rate, the older hopes being unfulfilled and seemingly unfulfillable, the expectation now was that the coming of God's agent of deliverance would be from the clouds of heaven at the end of the world.

5. It looks as if the idea of a last judgment, a comparatively new concept, was taken over into Jewish apocalypticism with little basic change from Persian sources, although the locale was shifted.

This must suffice as a brief and somewhat speculative account of the influx of alien thought into Judaism. It raises a question for us. Was there, then, little opposition among the Jews to Gentile thought-pressures? Not so, at all. Considerable opposition did arise, as we shall see in the next section. Yet, as one might suspect, attitudes were sharply divided. Some did not accept anything alien; some did. The books of Esther, Ruth, and Jonah reflect these differences. Esther was written by a Jewish nationalist, fired by a fierce hatred of the peoples who had anti-Semites among them. But the more tolerant and forgiving view toward aliens was given immortal expression in two stories, one concerning Ruth, the beautiful Moabitess, who found acceptance among Jews, married one of them, and became an ancestress of King David, and the other concerning Jonah, the rebellious and anti-Gentile prophet, whom the Lord firmly bent to his more inclusive purposes.

The Rise of the Postexilic Jewish Parties

Had Judea remained isolated from the rest of the world, there might perhaps have been among its people no divisions into parties; there might have been only the old clash between the popular majority and prophetic minority, which characterized the pre-exilic era.

Choices between cultures are seldom clear and simple; in any one instance of choice it is not often possible to leave out the bearing of what is desired by parties in power and what coincides best with local opinion, personal popularity, and means of livelihood. In Judea it was the priests, or at least the higher orders of the priesthood, who were the internationalists. This certainly seems a paradox; for priests are notoriously conservative and careful in their tolerances. But in this case the priests were the party in power; the high priest had become the civic as well as religious head of the country, and raised taxes, collected tribute money, and grew wealthy along with the other members of the high priestly families. His actions were subject to some slight check by the Gerousia, the council of Jewish elders later known as the Sanhedrin; but in most respects he was archbishop, prime minister, and foreign secretary all in one. This meant that the higher orders of priests were constantly engaged in regulating the international relations of Judea. The psychological effect of this was to make them discriminate for purposes of official policy between the essential or unchangeable in Judaism, as they saw it, and the matters that seemed open to change and compromise. The rule which they evolved, without much thought, was this: new and foreign ideas in *religion*, that is, ideas not found in the Torah, were to be frowned upon, but *cultural innovations* tending to improve foreign relations abroad and living conditions and standards at home were to be welcomed.

Out of this rose the important party of the *Sadducees* (a name very likely derived from "Zadokites," a word for the group of great families which formed the ruling clan of priests). The members of this wealthy, aristocratic, and worldly group dissociated themselves from the emotional ardors of the masses, believed in the "reasonable" views of the ancient fathers, as embodied in the written law, and thought well of the teachings of the Greek intelligentsia. In the realm of religion they rejected the spreading popular belief in angels, the new apocalyptic ideas, and particularly the conceptions of the resurrection of the body to full consciousness in after-life. In matters of culture they were so liberal to foreign points of view that they were called "Hellenizers," the implication being that they were active propagandists for the Greek view of life.

This kind of thing was held quite unacceptable by the Hasidim, the "pious ones" or "puritans," already mentioned, who were described as "the quiet in the land." These were the ones who rallied so quickly to fight beside Judas Maccabeus in the war for independence. They had no interest in politics as such, much less in internationalism, or Greek culture. Their one major intellectual passion was the Jewish religion. From their ranks sprang the powerful party of the *Pharisees*, to which most of the scribes and rabbis and many of the lower orders of the priesthood belonged. The Pharisees believed that the Sadducees were lost souls. The world with which the Sadducees compromised was under a sentence of doom; God meant to destroy it, and bring in a New Age. The Pharisees eagerly embraced the new Messianic concepts involving the resurrection of the dead and the last judgment. Yet their dreams were harnessed to some very practical considerations. In the interim before the end of the world, which would come only when God judged the time was ripe, they believed their prime duty was to be loyal to the Law "written" and "unwritten," not only in letter, but even more in spirit. That meant careful study of the scriptures and "traditions," together with moral obedience, ceremonial purity (they had to keep themselves unspotted from unclean persons and things), and, above all, spiritual growth and development, the result of "living unto the Lord."

When John Hyrcanus and his Maccabean successors became too enamored of their despotic power, and over-sympathetic with Sadducean ideas, the Pharisees swung from support of the ruling family to fierce opposition. Sporadic open revolt was met with violent suppression and bloody massacre. When, in their turn, the Pharisees won an advantage, they took revenge in retaliatory bloodshed. The final result was civil war. But a stalemate resulted, and the Roman general Pompey, then resident in Syria, was called upon to arbitrate the issue. In 63 B.C., Pompey came down from Syria, and promptly took the country over. It became a Roman province.

VIII   THE ROMAN PERIOD TO 70 A.D.

The Romans had been called in to umpire a dispute. That they seized the opportunity to make themselves masters of Palestine hardly pleased the Jews. The swift and bewildering succession of political changes, which followed, increased the sense of frustration and outrage. One source of deep resentment was the fact that a certain Antipater, an Idumean, and therefore, even though he professed Judaism, racially unacceptable to the Jews, had been active behind the scenes in winning Roman favor and gaining personal power. The grudging approval he won from the Jews, when he got the Romans to make Hyrcanus II, of the Maccabean family, the high priest, was withdrawn after the overthrow of Pompey, when Julius Caesar rewarded him for his services by making him a Roman citizen and the procurator of Judea; for thus an Idumean became the civil ruler of Judea and the political superior of the high priest. In 40 B.C. Antipater's son Herod, whose favorite wife was a Maccabean princess, was chosen by Augustus Caesar to be King of Judea. It took three years of fighting, but Herod established himself as the absolute ruler of Palestine. In spite of the peace and prosperity which he brought, and his remodeling of the Temple into a thing of marble beauty, the Jews hated him. When he died horribly of a cancer in 4 B.C., they rejoiced loudly.

Meanwhile, significant factors in the religious situation were operating.

The Messianic Expectation at Its Height

From the coming of the Romans to the time of the destruction of Jerusalem in 70 A.D., the Messianic expectation increased its hold on thousands of suffering Jews. Deep in their hearts was the feeling that, if God cared at all for his chosen people, he would act soon. The ardent hope of a supernatural deliverance from their unmerited suffering grew by what it fed on—an increasing flood of apocalyptic literature. Most of it followed the pattern of Daniel,* which had set the fashion of rehearsing the history of the Jews, from the Exile to the time of writing, in the cryptic terms of beasts with wings and images breaking under blows, to signify in symbols the end of the wicked world-order and the resurrection of the righteous dead to join the righteous living in the enjoyment of a better world. There is not space here, nor necessity, to mention by name and assign to their decades the books which followed

* Written during the early years of the Maccabean revolt.

Daniel's pattern.* It will be enough to give a general picture of the Messianic expectation when it reached its height.

The central belief was that divine intervention would bring about a radical change in the world-order. Through his Messiah, God was going to gather together "his own," both living and dead, and live with them in blessedness forever. That necessitated first the "end of the age," as some held, or the end of the world, as others believed. The "end" would be foretokened by certain last evils—wars and rumors of wars, distress, fear, famine, plagues, the rise to power of even more wicked rulers on the earth, and the like. The discerning would recognize in them the "signs of the end." At the last moment, with the sounding of "the last trump," the Messiah would appear in the clouds, with all the heavenly angels round him; he would be a supernatural personage, someone "like a man," and to be called the Son of Man, but bearing as well other titles, such as the Christ, the Elect One, the Son of David, the Lord's Anointed, the Righteous Judge, the Prince of Peace, and the like. At his appearing the righteous on earth would be caught up to him in the air (many said), and the dead would rise from their graves. The older views held that only the justified Jews would join the Messiah, but later expectations offered hope to the righteous Gentiles that they also would be among the redeemed; finally, the Zoroastrian view was accepted that all human souls, good and bad, would be summoned to a Last Judgment. Before the Messiah's seat they would be separated into the redeemed and the lost. The bad would be sent away into everlasting hellfire, and the good would enter a state of blessedness with their Lord and King. This state of blessedness was variously conceived. Some writers thought it would be enjoyed on earth in a restored Garden of Eden, an earthly paradise; others placed it in one of the lower heavens. (There were thought to be seven heavens in all, God occupying the highest level, along with his attendant angels.) Some combined the divergent conceptions, picturing an earthly paradise centered in a New Jerusalem to be inhabited by the Messiah and his chosen ones for a millennial period before the Last Judgment, and a heavenly paradise to be occupied by the redeemed after judgment was given. The heavenly paradise was most enthusiastically described as a place of green meadows, flowing streams, and fruit trees, where the righteous would banquet together with great joy and sing to the glory of God forever.

So great was the distress of devout Jews in the period we are describing, and yet so high their faith, that the near fulfilment of these

* Many of the books were lost and the dates of those existing are hard to determine in any case.

dreams seemed completely reasonable; in fact, the world would not have seemed rational otherwise.

But not all the Jews believed alike about these matters.

New Jewish Parties in the Roman Period

Throughout this period the old parties continued to function; the Sadducees were more concerned than ever in politics, and the Pharisees, with a majority representation in the Sanhedrin, the deliberative body of organized Judean Judaism, regarded themselves as the true carriers of the Jewish religion. The schools which the latter maintained were the best in Jewry and boasted such great teachers as Shammai and Hillel.

But two new parties, with a distinct political orientation, now sprang up. One got the name of the *Herodians,* because they supported the house of Herod. They came into existence as a party in 6 A.D. when Augustus Caesar, at the request of a Jewish deputation, deposed Herod's son Archelaus as ethnarch of Judea and appointed a Roman procurator in his stead. The Herodians were not inhospitable to Greco-Roman culture, but they wanted home rule, at all costs.

A far different group were the *Zealots.* They were passionate upholders of a policy of rebellion against Rome. The northern district of Galilee was their home base and stronghold. As an organized group they made their first appearance in 6 A.D. under the leadership of a certain Judas the Gaulonite or Galilean, who led a revolt against the taking of a census by the Romans. The revolt was bloodily suppressed by the Roman general Varus; but this did not bring to an end the Zealot agitation. The Zealots all believed that meek submission to "Roman slavery" meant forsaking God, their only Lord and Master; and they were convinced that by taking the sword they could hasten the Messiah's coming or even be rewarded by finding the Messiah in their midst. (On occasion they thought one of their own number was the Messiah.) The Romans called these super-patriots, who hid out in the hills and fought in guerrilla fashion, "bandits" and "robbers"—a not unfamiliar proceeding among conquerors.

A third new group, which entirely dissociated itself from politics, bore the name of *Essenes.* They lived in various places throughout Palestine, some in the villages, others in the open country. In preparation for the Messiah's coming they withdrew from the "corruption" of civilized society into monastic seclusion, where they fasted and prayed, ate together, washed themselves frequently in prescribed ceremonial ablutions, observed the Sabbath strictly, and engaged in daily chores

of farming and handicraft. They practiced non-violence, meekly awaiting the world's end. As we learn from the famous *Dead Sea Scrolls,*
the main group withdrew to a level hilltop south of Jericho under the
cliffs rimming the western shore of the Dead Sea. As early as in the
2nd century B.C., they sought this especially barren and isolated site
in order to remain unmolested in their utter absorption in religious
study and devotion. The founder of the community, as an expounder
of the Law or Torah, bore the name "The Teacher of Righteousness."
From his time on, they held property in common, ate common meals,
and worshipped and studied together, devoting themselves especially to
copying scrolls for their library on a long table of solid plaster. Under
the regimen described in the scroll known as the *Manual of Discipline,*
they formed a decidedly other-worldly covenant community. They practiced baptism as a rite of cleansing following on confession and repentance of sins, and it was repeated in individual cases whenever this
seemed spiritually necessary. They called themselves, in a manner suggestive of the early Christians, followers of "the Way," and "sons of
light," for they conceived themselves to be under the rule of "the Prince
of Lights," and opposed themselves therefore to the "sons of darkness"
under the "Angel of Darkness"—a set of concepts with a Zoroastrian
rather than Hebrew coloring. Leadership of the community, until its
complete destruction in 68 A.D., during the Jewish War, by a Roman
legion, was exercised by a group of chosen priests and laymen, perhaps
twelve in number.*

And then, as always, there were the unorganized common people,
many of them indifferent to religion, though keeping up some of its
forms, like circumcision and hanging up the mezuzah on the doorpost,
and others very pious in a quiet kind of way. These, when confronted
by the challenging point of view of a young carpenter from Nazareth,
listened to him gladly, just as with some astonishment they had earlier
given ear to the prophetic personality, John the Baptist, who counseled
repentance, because, he insisted, the end was near. Both won large
followings; but Herod Antipas beheaded the one, and the other was
crucified. The main stream of Judaism was tending elsewhere, irresistibly, toward tragedy.

IX THE GREAT DISPERSION

The discontent of the Jews had been leading steadily to a gruesome

---

* If we are to go by a rather obscure reference in the *Manual of Discipline,*
twelve may have been the number, but this is conjectural.

climax. Bloodshed and turmoil, with only brief intervals of quiet, kept all Palestine seething for sixty years after the desperate revolt of Judas the Galilean in 6 A.D. The Romans were aware that the one indispensable condition of keeping the peace was to let the Jewish religion alone, and they made it their policy to do so. In other directions they used a grim force. At the beginning of the 1st century Palestine was divided into four districts—three ruled by sons of Herod, the fourth (Judea, Idumea, and Samaria) governed by a Roman procurator residing at Caesarea on the coast below Jerusalem. In deference to Jewish feeling the procurators never brought the Roman imperial standards with their image of Caesar into Jerusalem, nor required that the statue of the emperor be erected in the Temple and made the object of worship; they were satisfied officially with the Jewish agreement to offer a daily sacrifice *for* the emperor on the Temple altar. But the Jews were touchy; or, from another point of view, forever on their guard. When Pilate thought that he might meet with no objection if he brought the imperial standards into Jerusalem in the darkness of the night, he found he had failed to reckon with Jewish alertness; when, again, he assumed that the Jews would take no offense at his seizing and applying Temple funds to the extension of an aqueduct into Jerusalem, he discovered they were offended to the point of revolt. A slight improvement of the condition of ill-will came during the reigns of Caligula and Claudius when Herod Agrippa I, a grandson of Herod the Great, ruled the whole of Palestine, and the procurators were recalled. But when the well-liked Herod Agrippa died, the sending of procurators was resumed. As one succeeded another, disorder mounted; there were "bandits" everywhere, and rioting broke out in Jerusalem; a lax high priest was assassinated; there was conflict between Jew and Gentile, Jew and Samaritan, Jew and Roman. A frightened people was struggling desperately for self-determination.

The stage was now set for open rebellion. It came in 66 A.D., toward the close of Nero's reign. The war was begun with terrible determination on both sides. The Jews had been divided among themselves about having a war at all, but once the issue was joined, they entered the struggle together, still quarreling. The Romans on their part had lost all patience and would stand for no more "folly." Their forces were led by Vespasian, until Nero's death took him to Rome to be crowned emperor; he then appointed his son Titus to subdue the Jews. Titus did so. The struggle was unbelievably savage and bitter. After Titus finally invested Jerusalem, he more than once pled with the Jews to surrender, but they would not. The superhuman resistance of the city's

defenders nearly baffled their besiegers, even though the Roman cata-
pults threw huge stones a quarter of a mile into the defences, and the
battering rams, devastating in their weight and force, broke down wall
after wall. Yet as soon as one wall was breached, another was found
behind it. The defenders, starving and half maddened with horror, were
driven back until they were at bay within the Temple area. The heroic
resistance continued even after a brand hurled through the air set the
Temple on fire, and the assaulting forces broke into the enclosure. Then
the defenders retired to make a last stand in the upper city. At the
end of another month they could resist no more. Amid indescribable
slaughter, the city was razed, and Titus went away to Rome, laden
with plunder, to be borne in triumph under the beautiful arch which
bears his name, and stands proudly still in the ruins of the Roman
Forum, a mute testimony to Jewish valor.

More than the city was destroyed: the priests and their sacrifices,
and with them the Sadducean party, passed from the scene of history,
never to have importance, or even reality, again. The Zealots, Essenes,
and Herodians were the next to follow them off the stage. Only the
party of the rabbis—that is, the Pharisees—and a rising heretic sect
called the Christians, were destined to wield influence through the coming years. The Romans had succeeded, for the moment, in decentralizing
the Jewish religion. The bonds joining each outlying synagogue with
the Temple were sundered. Set adrift, the Jews had no reason to turn
their faces in worship to Jerusalem, except in sorrow and mourning.

After 70 A.D. the Jewish dispersion reached the proportions of a national migration. Some of the inhabitants of Jerusalem fled east to
Babylonia and southeast into the Arabian Desert, where they were beyond the power of Rome. Others went to join friends and relatives all
over the Mediterranean world. Many who had no such ties emigrated
to Jewish communities in Syria, Asia Minor, Rome, Egypt, North Africa,
and far-off Spain.

But not all went away. Some retired to the rural parts of Palestine,
hoping to be able to go back to Jerusalem some day and restore it.
The Zealots, unwilling to believe their cause hopeless, continued active
in the hills, eluding the Romans who lay in wait for them.

Then sixty years after the fall of Jerusalem a last, bloody revolt
broke out in Palestine. On a visit to Judea the emperor Hadrian had
seen for himself that Jerusalem still lay in ruins after over half a century, and had reissued his previous order drawn up in Rome, that the
city be rebuilt and that a temple to Jupiter Capitolinus be erected on
the site of the razed Jewish sanctuary. As soon as Hadrian left Syria,

Judea rose to arms. The most learned Jew of the day, Rabbi Akiba, had urged a Messianic aspirant, called Bar Kokba, to be the military leader of a new war for liberation. In high anger Hadrian ordered the Jews to be butchered into submission, at the same time intensifying their opposition by forbidding the observance of the Sabbath, the practice of circumcision, and the study of the Torah. The struggle lasted three and a half years. Judea was virtually depopulated. The Romans then proceeded to the rebuilding of Jerusalem as planned; but it was constituted a Roman colony in which only non-Jews were allowed to live, and its name was changed to Aelia Capitolina. With despairing eyes the patriots who drew near the city beheld the new temple to Jupiter standing where the old sanctuary had been; but they were forbidden by imperial edict to set foot in the city or linger near it, on pain of death. Only on the anniversary of the destruction of the Temple—the ninth day of the month Ab—were they permitted to pay the sentries for the forlorn privilege of leaning against a remnant of the foundation wall of the old Temple and bewail the loss of their national home and the complete dispersion of their nation. That "Wailing at the Wall," begun then, has continued, in spite of interruptions, to the present day, when it is once more halted.

X   THE MAKING OF THE TALMUD

But the Jews would not give up. Though cured apparently—then —of the Zealot delusion, and persuaded also of the truth in the saying of the rejected Jesus: "Those that take the sword shall perish by the sword," they defended themselves from this time forward by religious and cultural cohesion,—a form of nonviolent resistance, under the direction of their intellectual and moral leaders, the rabbis, which was destined to survive every persecution of the future.

In the year 69 A.D., while Titus was before Jerusalem, a leading rabbi, with the name of Johanan ben Zakkai, escaped through the Roman army to the seaside town of Jabneh (Jamnia), where he began teaching in a "house of learning," * in a far-sighted endeavor to save Judaism from extinction by systematizing its laws and doctrines and adapting it to the changes now upon it. He was a follower of the great rabbi Hillel of the previous century, and he took his task seriously. Not

---

* Or "school" such as existed in connection with most synagogues throughout the Jewish world.

only did he gather about him students and scholars who were to devote themselves earnestly to study and interpretation of the Scriptures and the Traditions, but now that the Sanhedrin was defunct, he organized the leaders among them into a new council to fix the dates of the Jewish calendar—a task which had to be done each year—and to make such necessary regulations for Judaism as a whole as needed to be made. Gradually this body became the one recognized authority throughout the Jewish world that could pronounce on the true meaning and right practice of Judaism. Its president, with the title of Patriarch, was officially recognized by the Romans (until 425 A.D.) as the supreme head of all the Jews in the Roman Empire.

During the sixty years of the school's existence at Jabneh much work was accomplished. In addition to making a detailed study of the written law (the Torah), the school exactly recorded and defined the unwritten law (the Halakah), conveyed through the traditions of the past and in the interpretations and opinions (the Midrash) of learned rabbis. This produced a vast accumulation of rules and judgments, which had at last to be sorted out. It was Rabbi Akiba (the same who backed up Bar Kokba in the disastrous rebellion during the reign of Hadrian) who discovered how to group the material of the unwritten law under six major heads, and thus simplified the task of classifying and codifying the whole body of tradition.

The repressive measures following in the train of the war under Hadrian brought a sudden end to the school at Jabneh. Akiba perished during the conflict, and other rabbis and scholars lost their lives. But those who survived smuggled the scrolls of Jabneh into Galilee, where work on them was presently resumed at Usha, near the seaport of Haifa, and then at various other places, such as Sepphoris and Tiberias, further inland. Such repeated removals only increased the rabbis' sense of urgency.

The Mishnah

The schools in Galilee developed outstanding "masters," chief among them being Rabbi Meir and Rabbi Judah.* Their names are associated with the compilation of the great *Mishnah* (Repetition), a voluminous collection, under Akiba's six headings, of some four thousand precepts of rabbinic law, intended to "interpret" and adapt the original Torah to the conditions of the 2nd century. The Mishnah was

---

* Who was also Patriarch.

a large and rambling work which quoted the legal decisions of the outstanding rabbis of past generations, pausing sometimes to give the varying points of view of noted rabbis on disputed points. After it left
Rabbi Judah's hands, it acquired an authority almost as great as that
of the Torah itself. Certainly it met a real need. The "Law of Moses"
was all but inapplicable in the 2nd century, and the Mishnah provided
detailed guidance for the Jews who needed new ways to hold fast to
their ancient faith. Completed by about 220 A.D., the Mishnah contained
the decisions and judgments of almost one hundred and fifty of the
sainted teachers (*Tannaim*) of Israel, and gathered its material from a
period of six centuries. The range of its subjects was great, as may be
seen by a glance at its contents. One section was concerned with the
seasonal festivals and fasts; another with prayers, agricultural laws, and
the rights of the poor; a third with "women," that is, the laws relating
to marriage and divorce; a fourth with civil and criminal law; a fifth
with "consecrated things," particularly the ritual of offerings and sacrifices; a sixth with laws respecting what was clean and unclean in
persons and things, and prescriptions as to how a Jew was to purify
himself when polluted.

One reads the Mishnah's pages with a sense of wonderment at its
microscopic examination of every phase of Jewish life, and cannot withhold his sympathy, in spite of the overstrained interpretations and tortuous reasonings. It may seem hard to believe, as Lewis Browne suggests, that the rabbis who compiled the laws in the Mishnah were sane.
"But they were very sane, those rabbis. They saw how near their people
were to death. Panic-stricken they clutched at every imaginable regulation that might keep Israel alive." [59]

The schools in Galilee flourished for a century, and then declined
in importance. The Mishnah proved to be their one *magnum opus*. The
economic and spiritual inanition of the Palestinian area somehow operated to rob them of their creative power. Their schools continued to
exist for two centuries more, and made a contribution to Jewish learning
through the Palestinian Talmud, but this was an incomplete and inferior
work. Intellectual leadership had long since passed to the scholars of
Babylonia.

The schools in Babylonia were of long standing. They were the
expression, in fact, of an uninterrupted community life going back as
far as 586 B.C., when Nebuchadnezzar carried away into exile the greater
part of the people of Jerusalem. It is estimated that after the destruction of Jerusalem in 70 A.D. the refugees who fled to Babylonia swelled
its Jewish population to nearly a million persons. The importance of

this group was increased during the Parthian dominance of Babylonia by the fact that the government recognized a Jew of reputedly Davidic lineage, called the Resh Galuta or Chief of the Exile, as their civil head. But far greater importance for Judaism at large can be claimed for the deep learning and great ability of the rabbis in the Babylonian schools. Out of their labors came the ponderous work known as the *Gemara* (or Supplementary Learning).

The Gemara and the Talmud

The completion of the Mishnah did not bring an end to the process of exploring and defining the details of orthodox Jewish religion and life. Indeed the Mishnah itself became the basis of further commentary, since in many parts it was so concise as to be very nearly cryptic and therefore itself in need of elucidation; moreover, it was devoted chiefly to the study of the unwritten Law (the Halakah), and contained a relatively small portion of the oral traditions which the Jews called the Haggadah, a name by which they meant the nonjuristic traditions—the historical, moral, and religious instruction included in rabbinic lore. The Haggadah was the remembered substance of countless school and synagogue homilies. In itself it was more interesting by far than the Halakah or legal traditions; for its purpose was the instruction and edification, if not entertainment, of the layman, through graphic discourse illustrating the meaning of moral and religious truths. It abounded in stories from Jewish history, anecdotes of great and wise men, vivid anticipations of reward and punishment here and hereafter, and pithy comments on Bible truths by the great rabbis and teachers of Israel. Therefore, when the basic and indispensable Mishnah was completed, the Palestinian and Babylonian scholars busied themselves with recording and coming to agreement on the unrecorded portions of the Haggadah and indeed of every scrap of Jewish learning which was not in the Mishnah, so that nothing might be lost.

Then in the second quarter of the 3rd century, just after Jewish intellectual leadership had passed to the scholars of Babylonia, the tolerant Parthian rule was replaced by the severe reign of the Sassanian dynasty, dominated by the Magi—that is, the Zoroastrian priesthood. After centuries of security and prosperity the Babylonian Jews began to experience persecution. They were forbidden to bury their dead in the ground, because in the Zoroastrian view that would pollute the soil, and were ordered to send in a portion of all their table meat to be sacrificed on the Zoroastrian altars. Because the Magi of that period had a fanatically high regard for fire as a symbol of deity, they prohibited its religious use by all non-Zoroastrians. Immediate difficulties with the Jews arose as a result, for the Mishnah instructed them to light a Sabbath lamp before dark on Friday and keep it burning until the holy day ended—an observance which is orthodox practice to this day. Attempts to enforce the prohibition led to rioting and massacre. In the ensuing troubles some of the schools and academies were raided and closed.

The upshot of the new difficulties—which, however, never reached the proportions of an annihilating persecution—was a still greater zeal to preserve Jewish learning. The vast accumulations of rabbinic commentary were at last put in order. All unrecorded Halakah and Haggada were brought together in the Gemara, the *magnum opus* of the Babylonian schools. When this was combined with the Mishnah, the *Talmud* was the result.

The Talmud was completed by the end of the 5th century. It marked an epoch in Jewish history. In all the years since its completion it has never been superseded as an authoritative compendium or even encyclopedia of descriptions and definitions in detail of every aspect of orthodox Jewish belief and practice. Its six major parts and sixty-three volumes have been as meat and drink to the tragic Jews who fled from east to west and back again during the long ordeal of the Middle Ages. Its physical bulk has had—and this constitutes a rather exceptional circumstance—no little relation to its spiritual inexhaustibility. It has served as a rampart of moral resistance that rose higher and stood firmer than the brick and stone of the ghetto walls that Europe raised to hem the Jew in. Though condemned as magic and as devil's lore, burned in the market-places by angry civil authorities, or torn apart page by page and thrown on the waters, the Talmud always survived to feed the souls of a persecuted people determined to live by its regulations or have no further part in life. Others might laugh at what was contained in it, but to the Jew it was the wisdom which is of God.

XI THE JEW IN THE MIDDLE AGES

At the beginning of the Middle Ages the situation of the Jewish people was profoundly affected by the impact upon them of two religions: Christianity and Islam. The first was inclined to be hostile; the second tolerant, if not friendly.

The relationship between the Jews and the Christians had never been good, even from the beginning. Because, from the 1st century on, the official attitude of Judaism was always defined by the rabbis, the Christian claim that Jesus was the Christ (that is, the Messiah) was flatly denied by the Jews from the moment it was made. The Christians, however, never quite gave up hope that the Jews might be persuaded to accept Jesus as the Christ. For two centuries and more, their missionaries and apologists tried with earnest persistence to win the Jews over to their faith; but their success was small in proportion to the efforts they expended. The Jews were for the most part adamant against the Christian teaching, especially after St. Paul carried the Christian gospel into Europe, and the Greeks who entered the Church, in giving expression to their fine flair for philosophical interpretation, placed the life of Jesus in the cosmological setting of Greek philosophy, and developed a theology around the figure of Jesus that was breathtaking in its speculative sweep and daring. It should be remembered that the rabbis, primarily concerned as they were with saving Judaism from dissolution, seldom strayed from the study of conduct of life; meticulous in details, they kept their eyes on what was written in the Law, not disdaining to be common-place and even humdrum in their interpretations; above all, they took off on no high flights of philosophizing: the Talmud is proof of that. Consequently they viewed "the Hellenizing of the Christian religion" with scorn, refusing to see any virtue in it. Why should they accept the vague and cloudy propositions of theological speculation in exchange for the concrete ethical realities of a holy way of life sanctioned by long tradition and deriving from God? The antagonisms implicit in this situation became a political actuality after the conversion of the emperor Constantine in 312 A.D. and the subsequent elevation of Christianity to the status of the state religion. The Christian bishops, who now became great powers in the world, were in no amiable mood when they found that the Jews only stiffened their resistance to Christian pressure, with the state behind it. As the Middle Ages advanced, hostility between Christians and Jews intensified, and occasionally broke out into violence.

The Moslems at first treated the Jews better. In Palestine, Syria, and Babylonia, they displayed toward the Jews not only tolerance but kindness, partly because the Jews looked upon them as deliverers from the Christians and Zoroastrians, and therefore lent them their service as spies and scouts, and partly for the reason that culturally, racially, and religiously there was a marked resemblance between them. The rabbinical schools in Babylonia therefore throve once more; the "Prince of the Exile" (the Exilarch) became a powerful figure in the Moslem court at Baghdad; and the Jewish traders, following in the wake of Moslem conquerors, turned almost overnight into wealthy merchants who trafficked from one end of the Mediterranean world to the other. But it was too good to last. Economic conditions took a turn for the worse. The Turks came; the Jews again began to be oppressed. So in the 10th and 11th centuries many Babylonian scholars took their precious scrolls and set forth with their folk for Spain, at the other end of the world, where, since the 8th century, Jewish learning had been enjoying a heyday under the tolerant rule of the Moors. Here they joined forces with their Spanish brethren in creating the "golden age" of Jewish philosophy and science in the West.

New Thought in Babylonia and Spain

It took the combined resources of eastern and western Judaism to produce this notable Spanish interlude. Jewish scholarship in the West had at least these advantages: it was the beneficiary, first of Arabic science, which excelled in mathematics and astronomy and had rediscovered Aristotle, and next of a renaissance of Jewish poetry and belles lettres, then in progress (11th century). But the scholars from Babylonia were also ripe for creative advance. They were not narrow Talmudists; something had happened to them before they left Babylonia that freed them from too confined an adherence to the Talmud's text. This was the Karaite heresy and the corrective reaction, led by the great scholar Saadiah, which followed in its wake.

Acceptance of the Talmud as an infallible guide of life never was universal throughout the Jewish world. Occasionally Messianic aspirants would release their followers from obedience to its regulations and lead them "back to the Torah." But this was perhaps the least important reaction against the Talmud. There was greater disturbance when it was argued that the Talmud was a departure from the truths divinely revealed to ancient Israel. A significant protest of this kind was led by the scholar Anan ben David of Baghdad, a candidate for the title of Exilarch, rejected (767 A.D.) for his heretical views, who declared that the supreme authority in Jewish life was what we call today the Old Testament, and not the Talmud. The new sect he founded was nicknamed "The Children of the Text" and more commonly bore the name of Karaites (Readers). As a movement, it resembled in some respects the Protestant Anabaptist reaction against Catholic scholasticism and ritual, though it was even more extremely literalistic. Generally among the Karaites the eating of almost any meat was forbidden; the Sabbath lights enjoined by the Mishnah were not kindled; recourse to physicians was regarded as lack of faith in the scriptural promise: "I am the Lord that healeth thee"; and many ancient practices that had fallen into disuse were revived, in spite of the anachronisms involved. Although, because it stressed the full validity of individual interpretations of the ancient scriptures, it broke up into many divergent sects (like Protestantism again) and subsequently declined, the Karaite sect spread thinly through the Jewish world and up into Russia, where a remnant of the sect still survives. Its chief historical importance lies in the fact that it awoke orthodox Jews from their complacency with strictly logical juristic deductions from divine Law, and stimulated a re-examination retrospectively of the Talmud's indebtedness to the Old Testament and, in terms of contemporary interests, of its general suitability to the times. Just this was attempted by Saadiah ben Joseph (882–942 A.D.), head of the Sura Academy in Babylonia.

Saadiah, realizing that the Karaites were obeying a sound impulse in returning to the original Hebrew scriptures (now no longer read by the rabbis themselves, because Hebrew was by this time a dead language), began the translation of the Old Testament into Arabic, in order that his fellow-Talmudists might see how their position was based in scripture. Beyond this, he also tried to demonstrate the reasonableness of that position by reference to the Arabic translations of Greek philosophical and scientific works. Revelation and reason (scripture and philosophy) were, he said, complementary; both were needed. So he attempted a new systematization of Jewish thought, harmonizing it with the best in world-thought, and thus became the father of medieval Jewish philosophy.

When the Babylonian scholars migrated to Spain, they took Saadiah's liberal conceptions with them, and these ideas of his helped to shape the course taken by enlightened Jewish opinion there.

In Spain, the fruitful meeting of eastern and western influences produced a mental quickening so marked, that Spain quickly became the chief center of Jewish learning and culture. In the Jewish Academy of Cordova, founded in the 10th century, a succession of distinguished scholars encouraged the fresh expression of Jewish learning and insight in literature. In the 11th and 12th centuries, Ibn Gabirol, Judah Halevi, and Ibn Ezra wrote books of verse and learned treatises with great clarity and power. So deeply devotional were many of their hymns and religious essays that portions of them have since found their way into the liturgy of the synagogues.

Moses Maimonides

Even more famous was the great 12th century scholar Moses ben Maimon (1135–1204), who is usually called Moses Maimonides. Born in Cordova, he and his family fled during his youth from persecution (this time Moslem), which drove them through Spain and across the world to Cairo, where he wrote two great commentaries—the one systematizing the Mishnah and reducing it to thirteen cardinal principles,* the other simplifying and condensing the whole of rabbinical law by what amounted to a rewriting of the Talmud. His greatest work was his *Guide to the Perplexed,* a rational examination of the Jewish faith, conceived in a spirit more than cordial to Aristotle, even while it stood firm on the doctrine of the divine revelation of the Hebrew Law. Reason, he said, could take one far, even though revelation was needed to supplement it. Such revelation, when it came, could not be contrary to reason, but was rational in all its parts. Hence, the miracles are to be explained rationally, and the anthropomorphisms of the scriptures so interpreted that they become mere figures of speech, charged with ethical meanings. The account of creation in Genesis must be interpreted allegorically. By such use of our understanding we get to know the highest truth about God.

But many Jewish scholars were not taken with Maimonides' rationalism; they would have none of him, in spite of the mental stimulus his works provided. Religion, they said, was mystical and dealt with hidden meanings, not accessible to reason, but known only to the truly devout. The most able spokesman for these views was Nahmanides (1195–1270), born in Gerona, Spain, who felt that man cannot compass God's truth with his finite and fallible reason; one must have faith and deep feeling that God is all in all. In similar vein, Hasdai Crescas in the 14th century contended that man can reach God only through love and submission, not through a purely rational search.

The Kabbala

But the conviction that religion has hidden meanings was to receive

* These were in brief: "I believe with perfect faith that God is; that he is one with a unique unity; that he is incorporeal; that he is eternal; that to him alone prayer is to be made; that all the words of the Prophets are true; that Moses is the chief of the Prophets; that the law given to Moses has been transmitted without alteration; that this law will never be changed or superseded; that God knows all the deeds and thoughts of men; that he rewards the obedient and punishes transgressors; that the Messiah will come; that there will be a resurrection of the dead."—See G. F. Moore, *History of Religions,* Vol. II, p. 94 (Scribner's Sons, 1919).

another kind of statement—that of the Kabbala, the books of speculative theology and mystical number symbolism which gave new currency to old accumulations of secret wisdom and esoteric lore, and fascinated their hopeful readers by mysterious arrangements of words and numbers, purporting to reveal the "deeper meaning" in the scriptures. The fact that the ten Hebrew numbers (the *Sephiroth*) are letters of the alphabet had the effect of turning any word or sentence into a number series; and this seemed to the Kabbalists to yield significant results in the case of the various names and attributes of God. Even rabbis and scholars of note gave themselves up to acrostic anagrams and other forms of esoteric word-play.

But the Kabbala also addressed itself to serious metaphysical problems—the problem, for example, of how a perfect God could produce an imperfect or incomplete world; or, to put it in other terms, how the Infinite could bring forth the finite without damaging subtraction from himself. In finding a solution of this problem in the theory of emanations, the Kabbala went back ultimately to such ancient sources as Philo and the Gnostics. A typical line of speculation started with the concept of God as the Boundless (*Ensoph*). From him as light springs from a sun proceeded various emanations, like the Divine Will, which generated Wisdom (male) and Knowledge (female), these in turn generating Grace (male) and Power (female), which latter by their union produced Beauty; from the last three sprang the natural world. Not to carry the matter further, the upshot of these speculations was the conviction that man, who has all these qualities, is the universe in miniature, a microcosm filled with magical cosmic forces, the direction of which can be controlled by efficacious formulas, names, and symbols. The Messiah himself will be identified at his coming by his mysterious name and symbol.

The exciting implications which flowed from these considerations produced in central Europe an abundant crop of false Messiahs who only disappointed the faithful.

The Crusades and the Ghettos

The Jews had by this time long since spread out into France, England, and the Rhineland, where they settled in little clusters, followed similar occupations, and remained true to their faith. Because their religious ceremonies were carried out in virtual seclusion and never came under the direct observation of the general public, they excited curiosity and suspicion. Many on the outside took the attitude that the Jews were a secret order of conspirators against the public welfare.

They were charged with every form of malevolent purpose. The launching of the Crusades, at the end of the 11th century, produced such excitement against "infidels" that an open butchery of the Jews began, starting in Germany, where wholesale massacres took place, and spreading to the rest of Europe. After the butchery ran its course, orders of expulsion followed. In Germany one town after another drove the Jews out completely; they were expelled, at least in law, from England in 1290; and, after two centuries of periodic expulsion and restoration, in 1394 they were denied residence in France. In Spain, persecution of the Jews accompanied the expulsion of the Moors, and in 1492 all unconverted Jews were ordered driven out.

Fleeing in the only direction open to them, eastward, the Jews of Spain and southern European areas found refuge in Turkey and Syria (where they spoke Ladino, Spanish interspersed with Hebrew). The Jews of northern areas went in large numbers to Poland, where they brought the welcome arts of trade and money-lending to that sparsely settled land. But they were not assimilated by the Poles. They spoke a dialect compounded of German and Hebrew, now called Yiddish.

As for those who remained in Italy and the towns of Austria and Germany which had not totally excluded them, they were forced to live in segregated quarters called *ghettos,* usually located in the worst part of town. To add to their distress, in most places where the Catholic Church was supreme there was enforcement of the 13th century law forbidding Jews on pain of death to appear on the streets without the Jew Badge—a colored patch of cloth sewn on to their clothing. This badge became a mark of shame. In most towns, high walls were built around the ghettos, and the Jews were locked in at night; to be seen abroad after dark often meant death, and always a fine.

The Medieval Festivals and Fasts

Meanwhile, the calendar of Jewish festivals and fasts had undergone development and reinterpretation. The ancient Palestinian and Babylonian liturgies, somewhat divergent to begin with, were further, but not radically, modified to meet the particular needs or preferences of the Jews of Spain, Italy, North Africa, Turkey, Persia, and central and western Europe, or to admit Spanish, Kabbalistic and other devotional materials.* Of great importance was the fact that the agricultural inter-

---

* At times, also, for longer or shorter periods, and more or less radically, the ritual was affected by leading Jewish personalities, such as Anan ben David, the Karaite leader; Maimonides; Isaac Lurya; and others. Such rites are today mostly extinct.

ests expressed in the ancient Hebrew rites and ceremonies were no longer in the forefront and therefore the inherited forms had to be charged with historical and ethical meanings that would call out the continued loyalty and devotion of the Jews in every sort of occupation and environment.

The chief festivals and fasts of the year, with considerable local variation, were assigned the procedures, meanings, and dates (determined according to the lunar calendar) which have been standard for orthodox Jews to the present day. They had by now taken approximately the following forms (forms in use today):

In late March or during April, Passover (*Pesakh*), "the anniversary of Israel's natal day," basically a spring festival of thanksgiving for the birth of lambs and the sprouting of grain, was ritually associated with the idea of individual and group liberation and renewal in all times, beginning with the Exodus and continuing through history. As in the ancient period, nothing leavened was eaten for a full week (whence the name "The Feast of Unleavened Bread"). The biblically prescribed eating of the paschal lamb had from the time of the Great Dispersion been gradually set aside, and the chief event of Passover had become the *Seder* Feast, observed on the eve of the first (or else the second) day, by the whole family assembled together, some from a distance, in the home. A ritual called the Haggadah—or Narrative—was read throughout the ceremony. After the Kiddush cup had been passed, the male head of the family washed his hands and assumed the function of the family priest. Parsley dipped in salt water was eaten in remembrance of the trials of captivity. At other intervals further cups of wine, bitter herbs and roots, and unleavened bread were passed. Accompanying each act was the running account of the Haggadah, generally in the form of question and answer, designed to retell the story of the Exodus and explain the purpose of the Passover rite itself—that is, its challenge ever to seek freedom from any bondage. Psalms were sung, and finally the evening meal was served. Afterwards a door was opened, amid a recitation of psalms and lamentations, and Elijah, the hoped-for precursor of the Messiah, was invited to come in and drink of the Elijah Cup, which had stood untouched on the table during the preceding rite. The service ended with a psalm of praise, a prayer, or the recitation of a grace. The solemnity then melted into general rejoicing, in which the children present were encouraged to take a leading part.

For forty-nine days after the Seder Feast, except at the new moon or on the thirty-third day, no joyous occasions, including marriages, were allowed; then on the fiftieth day came *Shebhuoth*—the Feast of Weeks or Pentecost, a day of rejoicing once set aside to commemorate the first fruits of the spring wheat harvest, now modified to include thanksgiving for the giving of the Law at Sinai, which was held to have occurred at the same time of year.

The next great holiday came in September (or early October). It was *Rosh Hashanah,* or New Year's Day. This name took the place of the ancient biblical names, Day of Memorial and Day of Blowing the Alarm (signalized by the sounding of the *shofar* or ram's horn, a custom which is still solemnly observed as a means of summoning the Jew "to ponder over his deeds, remember his Creator, and go back to Him in penitence"). In recognition of the significance of the day, the Talmud called it the Day of Judgment. After it followed the Days of Repentance, and on the tenth day the solemn Day of Atonement (*Yom Kippur*), during which "repentance, prayer, and righteousness" were enjoined upon all the participants in the fast, who, as free agents, were urged to exert their wills to turn from wrong-doing and in true atonement for sin do God's will henceforth.

Five days later came *Succoth,* the eight-day Feast of Booths or Tabernacles, basically a thanksgiving festival devoted to expression of gratitude for the autumnal fruits of vine and tree, and now associated with the thought of God's provident goodness in the days of Israel's wandering in the wilderness and during later times. In addition to the decoration of the synagogue with all sorts of fruits and flowers, a feature of the services was the ritualistic carrying in procession of four products of Palestine tied together—namely, a citron and a palm-branch bound with branches of the myrtle and the willow. Those who could do so erected a booth or tabernacle in or beside their home and ate their meals under it during the period of the festival. (Some even slept there.)

Sounding of the *shofar* in the synagogue. (Modern drawing)

Close on the termination of the festival a special day—*Simkhath Torah*, the Rejoicing over the Law—had as its feature the carrying of the Scrolls from the Ark in procession around the synagogue.

Two festivals not based upon the Mosaic tradition were the *Hannukkah* in December and *Purim* in February or March. The former—the Feast of Lights—was celebrated for eight days, one light being lit in the synagogues and in every home on the first night, two on the second, three on the third, and so on, this being interpreted to commemorate the rededication of the Temple by Judas Maccabeus in 165 B.C.

Purim or the Feast of Lots was associated with the biblical Book of Esther and thus was made to celebrate the deliverance of the Jews from persecution through Esther's patriotic intervention. Gifts were exchanged within the family and sent to friends and to the poor, in the spirit of carnival. There was dancing and singing in the homes.

XII JUDAISM IN THE MODERN WORLD

The Protestant Reformation was the product of many causes; not least among the contributing factors was the return by the Reformers to the study of the Bible in the original Hebrew and Greek. So impressed was Luther in his earlier years by his discovery of the close genetic relation of the Jewish and Christian faiths, that he published in 1523 a pamphlet on "Jesus Was Born a Jew," in which he pleaded: "They (the Jews) are blood-relations of our Lord; and if it were proper to boast of flesh and blood, the Jews belong to Christ more than we. . . . Therefore it is my advice that we treat them kindly. . . . We must exercise not the law of the Pope, but that of Christian love, and show them a friendly spirit. . . ." [60] But Luther retraced in his own life the first three centuries of the Christian era. When he found the Jews solidly resistant to conversion, his anger slowly mounted, until in his later years he began to abuse them savagely. In a pamphlet "Concerning the Jews and Their Lies" (1542), he repeated in a passion of credulous rage all the old rumors concerning the Jews—that they poisoned the wells of the Christians or that they murdered Christian children (presumably, as the current rumor had it, to get blood for the Passover). In his last sermons he hinted that Jewish doctors knew and therefore practiced the art of poisoning their Christian patients. "If the Jews," he growled, "refuse to be converted, we ought not to suffer them or bear with them any longer!" [61]

Luther was, alas, but typical of his age in this. The Reformation brought no permanent improvement in the condition of the Jews of Europe. In fact in the 16th and 17th centuries their fortunes reached a very low point—as low as any in their history: not only did they live in physical ghettos devised by their oppressors, but they themselves retired into mental ghettos of their own creation, which shut the world out,—its science, art, and culture as well as its hostility and evil. Improvement in their lot came, but came slowly.

Eastern Europe

In eastern Europe the Jews were (and have largely remained up to the present time) true to their heritage of ancient patterns of thought and life. In the 17th century a terrible pogrom was wreaked upon them, especially in Poland, by the Cossacks, when these furious Russians rose in rebellion against their feudal lords and went on to slaughter five hundred thousand Jews. This and other pogroms have only confirmed the eastern Jew in his unrelaxing grip upon every article of his inherited faith. But there are characteristic differences in the different areas. In Lithuania and White Russia the emphasis has been on intellectual study of the Talmud and the original Hebrew texts. In these regions the Jews have been consistently anti-mystical; a dry, matter-of-fact scholarship has been rated above emotional fervor. Their characteristic personality was the 18th century scholar, Elijah of Vilna, who became their ruling rabbi; he was an intellectual giant, who was at once Hebrew grammarian, astronomer, author, bitter foe of the mystical Hasidim (about to be described), and founder of a famous academy, to which students came from all over Europe during the 19th century to study the Talmud in the traditional manner of the Babylonian schools of over a thousand years earlier.

South of the Pripet Marshes, in southern Poland and the Ukraine, eastern Talmudism took a warmly emotional and mystical turn, which led finally to the virtual abandonment of the Talmudic point of view and a joyous espousal of the pantheistic vagaries of the Kabbala. Messianism ran riot among them, and more than one unstable soul stirred by their hopefulness ran a career among them as Messiah, only to dash their hopes at last by some false step that brought ruin or disgrace. However, one notable religious personality emerged among them—Israel of Moldavia, affectionately renamed Baal Shem Tob ("The Good Master of God's Name"), a kindly, itinerant faith-healer of the 18th century, who scorned the Talmudists for studying the Law so narrowly that they

had no time to think about God. Thinking about God meant to him
realizing that God is everywhere—in Nature, in human life, and in
every human thought. Religion was feeling God in everything and praying joyously in the wholesome consciousness of God's indwelling. "All
that I have achieved," he used to say, "I have achieved, not through
study, but through prayer." [62] Reviving a name used in postexilic times
two thousand years earlier, he called his followers, who were mostly
common people, Hasidim or "Pious Ones." Hence, the movement initiated by him is called Hasidism.

Central and Western Europe

In central and western Europe, the matter of chief import during
the last two centuries has been the experience of slow, but exhilarating
liberation from civic disabilities, followed by what might be called "a
return to the world." The justice of such a liberation was admitted by
the leaders of the European "Enlightenment" during the 18th century
and was made an actuality by the revolutionary movements in France
and Germany in the 18th and 19th centuries.

The rationalism and scepticism of the 18th century intellectuals in
Europe—which tended to hold all religions up to mockery—led to a
lowering of religious and class barriers in the centers of culture. It
was thus that Moses Mendelssohn, perhaps the greatest modern Jew,
broke through the restrictions barring Jews in Berlin, and reached the
center of its intellectual life. While pursuing his studies there, he became the friend of Lessing, the literary lion of Berlin, and was accorded
the signal honor of having the liberal drama, *Nathan the Wise*, Lessing's
masterpiece, created around his personality. That the great Lessing
should choose a humpbacked Jew as his intimate, and enshrine him in
a serious work of art, was at first astounding, then thought-provoking.
Mendelssohn wrote German, not as the Jews spoke it, but as the Germans themselves desired to write it. A dialogue on immortality, which
he composed on the Platonic model, was read throughout Europe. In
the hope of doing a service to his fellow Jews, he translated the
Pentateuch and other parts of the Old Testament into accomplished
German prose (written out in Hebrew characters), and added a commentary of an advanced liberal character. But the chief work of his life
was his earnest pleading in behalf of his people, that they might be
freed from the ghettos to enter the stream of modern life on a basis
approaching equality with other people. He did not live to see this
happen, but in his own person he showed Europe how worthy the Jews
were to be freed.

Liberalism and Reform

The revolutionary changes wrought by the rise of democracy in America and Europe eventually gave the Jews their full civic freedom. The American Revolution established the political principle that all men are created free and equal. During the French Revolution the Jews of France received the rights of full citizenship. Wherever Napoleon went, he abolished the ghettos and released the Jews into the world at large. After him reaction set in; all through Europe the Jews were faced with the choice: back to the ghetto or become a Christian. Many chose the latter alternative; others submitted to the re-imposition of restrictions, but entered avidly into all underground revolutionary movements looking toward the overthrow of reactionary governments, thereby providing conservatives and future reactionaries with the argument that Jews are by nature subversive. (Those Jews who had never tried to enter European life, but clung to their ancient ways, had of course no part in this.) Finally came the social upheavals of 1848 and after, which had as their consequence, for the Jews of all Europe, the granting of complete equality with other men before the law. The universities opened their doors. From them Jewish doctors, politicians, dramatists, professors, and scientists poured forth into the communal life of Europe. In the vast processes of change accompanying the victory of political democracy, the Jews stood to benefit most.

Not least among the far-reaching consequences of the freeing of the Jews was the effect upon Judaism itself. The Jews found themselves in a world fast throwing aside the vestiges of the past which stood in the path of the liberal movement, and it was natural that they should consider doing the like among themselves. The educated Jew, engaged in the activities of the modern world, began to feel that Judaism should no longer stand aloof behind self-protective barriers but should resume its ancient progressive character. The result of this realization was the movement called Reform Judaism. It made a beginning in such synagogues as the Reform rabbis could control, its usual first innovation being the simplifying and modernizing of the synagogue worship. The Sabbath service was condensed, and most of it was translated into the vernacular. References to the coming of the Messiah, the resurrection of the dead on the last day, or to the re-establishment of Jewish nationality and of the sacrificial rites of ancient Palestine, were stricken out. Organ and choir were installed, and hymns in the vernacular were sung. The fundamental conviction of the movement was stated by Abraham Geiger, its leading exponent, in the words: "Judaism is not a finished tale; there is much in its present form that must be changed or abolished; it can assume a better and higher position in the world only if it will rejuvenate itself." [63] There were both moderates and radicals in the Reform movement. The latter shocked the Jewish world by declaring in 1843 that their principles were: "*First*, We recognize the possibility of unlimited development in the Mosaic religion. *Second*, The collection of controversies, dissertations, and prescriptions commonly designated by the name Talmud possesses for us no authority from either the doctrinal or practical standpoint. *Third*, A Messiah who is to lead back the Israelites to the land of Palestine is neither expected nor desired by us; we know no fatherland but that to which we belong by birth and citizenship." [64] But after 1848 the conservatives fought the Reform movement to a halt, and even drove it into retreat. The movement then transferred itself largely to America, where it is now very powerful.

The Orthodox Jews earnestly fought Reform from its beginning, because it denied the orthodox view that the divine revelation in the Law is final and complete and awaits only its fulfilment. But the proposed changes in belief seemed less dangerous than the threatened changes in way of life. It is perhaps fair to say that the Orthodox Jew of today lays a heavier emphasis on practice than on belief. One need not believe exactly as the rabbis do; but one *must* adhere with absolute fidelity to the practical admonitions of the Law of Moses, as they are interpreted and applied to daily life by the Talmud: the Sabbath lights must be lit and the Sabbath kept as of old; none of the ancient Jewish festivals may be skimped or abbreviated; the dietary laws, with their prohibitions of certain foods and their regulations as to kosher meat, must be observed exactly; and one's life must never be regarded as "holy" or "acceptable to the Lord," unless defilement is avoided precisely as the ancient laws prescribe. So far as conditions permit, the ancient Palestinian mode of life—minus only the daily sacrifices on the altar of the Temple at Jerusalem—must be carefully followed by the Jewish community.

Zionism and the Establishment of a New Nation

Neither Reform nor Orthodox Jews have had plain sailing, however. The astonishing economic and professional successes of the Jews in the second half of the 19th century stirred up a new wave of anti-Semitism in Europe, where pogroms in Russia, vindictive Jew-baiting in Germany, and the famous Dreyfus case in France, convinced many

Jews that their only hope of permanent security lay in the re-establishment of a national home in Palestine. A landmark in the crystallization of this viewpoint was the book by Theodor Herzl on "The Jewish State," issued in 1896. Based on its premises, a Jewish movement rose rapidly to international notice, called Zionism. From the start it gained wide support among Orthodox Jews, and has by now won over many Reform Jews, who at first opposed it as reactionary and impracticable. The Balfour Declaration during the First World War, to the effect that the British Government viewed with favor "the establishment in Palestine of a national home for the Jewish people," and would seek to "facilitate the achievement of this object," changed the political status of the movement overnight. Thousands of Jews went to Palestine during the next two decades; and, under the protection of the British Mandate, laid the foundations of Jewish national life there. The monstrously brutal and murderous persecution of the Jews by the Nazis, and the displacements of the Second World War, accentuated the pressures brought to bear by world Jewry toward the formation of an independent Jewish state. While the world watched, the United Nations Assembly finally, in 1947, voted to partition Palestine and make a Jewish state an actuality. The new state calls itself Israel. It has maintained itself as a nation with vigor and success. Yet the intensity of Arab opposition has not abated and still augurs stormy times ahead for the eastern Mediterranean littoral.

Other Developments

Meanwhile, the need to find a median position between Orthodoxy and Reform resulted in the establishment of neo-Orthodoxy and Conservatism in Europe. These movements were founded in the mid-19th century, and made some headway. In America the Conservative movement experienced a rapid growth. With its own seminary in New York City, and its congregations organized into the United Synagogue of America, it has striven to find common ground between extreme Zionism, on the one hand, and the position taken, say, by the Conference of Reform Jews meeting in Chicago in 1918 some six months after the Balfour Declaration was issued, at which time that body announced:

We hold that Jewish people are and of right ought to be at home in all lands. Israel, like every other religious communion, has the right to live and assert its message in any part of the world. We are opposed to the idea that Palestine should be considered *the home-land* of the Jews. Jews in America are part of the American nation. The ideal of the Jew is not the establishment of a Jewish state—not the reassertion of Jewish nationality which has long been outgrown. We believe that our survival as a people is dependent upon the assertion and the maintenance of our historic religious role and not upon the acceptance of Palestine as a home-land of the Jewish people. The mission of the Jew is to witness to God all over the world.[65] *

The Conservatives see no inherent contradiction in witnessing to God all over the world and having a Jewish state in Palestine as a center from which Jewish culture may be disseminated among the nations. In effect, the Conservatives endorse the *religious* aspects of both right and left. In an essay on "Current Philosophies of Jewish Life," Milton Steinberg says:

Conservative Judaism had its origin simultaneously in America and Western Europe among those Jews who either in theory or practice could no longer be orthodox, and who yet refused to accept what they regarded as the extreme nontraditionalism of Reform. . . . Two motifs dominate conservative Judaism. The first is the assertion of the centrality of religion in Jewish life. . . . The second theme, heavily underscored, is the sense of tradition, of history, of the continuity of Jewish life both through time and in space. It is this feeling of the organic unity of one Jewry with other Jewries which Professor Solomon Schechter, the leading figure in American Conservatism, caught in the phrase "Catholic Israel." This phrase is more than a description. It is intended to serve as a norm for the guidance of behavior. That shall be done by Jews, it implies, which is normal to Catholic Israel: . . . to hold on to the traditional, to sanction modifications slowly, reluctantly, and, if at all possible, within the framework of Jewish law.[66]

Recently a group a little left of center has arisen among the Conservatives calling themselves the Reconstructionists. They advocate wide liberty in doctrine and "creative adjustment" to the conditions of modern life.

The future of Judaism would seem to lie between these divergent groups, each as yet feeling its way more or less anxiously to solid foundations in a tragically unstable modern world. These groups are not sharply divided from each other; for each yearns to have its unity with the others made possible in word, deed, and faith.

SUGGESTIONS FOR FURTHER READING

Albright, W. F. *From the Stone Age to Christianity*. 2nd ed. with new introduction, Johns Hopkins Press, 1957. Also available in Anchor pb

* There still exists an active Jewish minority—The American Council for Judaism, with headquarters in New York—that opposes the idea of a Jewish state.

――――. *The Archaeology of Palestine.* Penguin Books; 3rd ed., fully revised, 1960. A Pelican pb

――――. *Archaeology and the Religion of Israel.* 3rd ed. Johns Hopkins Press, 1953

Anderson, Bernard W. *Understanding the Old Testament,* Prentice-Hall, 1957

Baron, S. W. *A Social and Religious History of the Jews.* 3 vols. Columbia University Press, 1952

Baron, S. W. and Blau, Joseph L., eds. *Judaism. Postbiblical and Talmudic Period.* Liberal Arts Press, 1954. An anthology in pb

Bevan and Singer, eds. *The Legacy of Israel.* Oxford, 1927

Bewer, Julius A. *The Literature of the Old Testament.* Rev. ed. Columbia University Press, 1933

Bright, John. *History of Israel.* Westminster, 1959

Cohen, A. *Everyman's Talmud.* J. M. Dent, 1937

Cornfield, Gaalyahu, ed. *Adam to Daniel: An Illustrated Guide to the Old Testament and Its Background.* Printed in Israel, distributed by Macmillan, New York, 1961

Gordis, Robert. *Judaism for the Modern Age.* Farrar, Strauss and Cudahy, 1955. A Conservative interpretation

James, Fleming. *Personalities of the Old Testament.* Scribner, 1939

Kittel, Rudolph. *The Religion of the People of Israel.* Macmillan, 1925

Kohler, K. *Jewish Theology, Systematically and Historically Considered.* Macmillan, 1918

Lods, Adolphe. *Israel from Its Beginnings to the Middle of the Eighth Century B.C.* Knopf, 1932

――――. *The Prophets and the Rise of Judaism.* Dutton, 1937

Moore, George Foot. *Judaism in the First Centuries of the Christian Era.* 3 vols. Harvard University Press, 1927–1930

Noth, Martin. *The History of Israel.* Harper, 1958

Oesterley and Robinson. *A History of Israel.* 2 vols. Oxford, 1932

――――. *Hebrew Religion, Its Origin and Development.* Macmillan, 1937

Pfeiffer, Robert H. *Introduction to the Old Testament.* Harper, 1941

Pritchard, James B. ed. *The Ancient Near East.* An anthology of texts and pictures compiled from two earlier works: *Ancient Near Eastern Texts* and *The Ancient Near East in Pictures.* Princeton University Press, 1958

Sachar, A. L. *A History of the Jews.* Knopf, 1930

Schauss, Hayyim. *The Jewish Festivals.* Cincinnati: Union of American Hebrew Congregations, 1938

Scholem, G. G. *Major Trends in Jewish Mysticism.* Schocken Books, 1946

Vermes, Geza. *Discovery in the Judean Desert.* Desclee, 1956. Translations and comments on Dead Sea Scrolls

Wright, G. E. *Biblical Archaeology.* Westminster, 1957. With illustrations

14 Christianity in

Its Opening Phase:
The Religion of Jesus

THE STORY OF CHRISTIANITY IS THE STORY OF A RELIGION WHICH HAS sprung from the faith that in its founder God was made manifest in the flesh and dwelt among men. Other religions have developed a conception of incarnation, but none has given it such centrality. In the belief that Jesus is the clearest portrayal of the character of God all the rest of Christian doctrine is implied.

It is not easy to tell the story briefly and clearly. The first Christian century has had more books written about it than any other comparable period of history. The chief sources bearing on its history are the Gospels and Epistles of the New Testament, and these—again we must make a comparative statement—have been more thoroughly searched by inquiring minds than any other books ever written. Historical criticism has been particularly busy with them during the last seventy-five years, and has reached the verdict that in the New Testament the early Christian religion *about* Jesus has overlaid and modified the record of the religion *of* Jesus himself; but there is no unanimity about the degree of modification. It is known that Jesus himself did not write down his teachings, but relied upon his disciples to go about preaching what he taught, from memory. It is generally assumed by historians that after his death some of them did write down his sayings, with occasional notes of the historical setting, before they should be forgotten, and that thus a

587

document, or group of documents, came into being which scholars call Q (from the German word *Quelle* or "source"). It is generally considered that Q was somewhat colored by the prepossessions of the early Christians, and may have had sayings added to it which were mistakenly ascribed to Jesus; but on the whole it was authentic, and quite naturally became primary source material for the compilers of Matthew and Luke. These compilers used a great deal of other material also, both oral and written; for example they drew much of their material from Mark, already existent (65–70 A.D.). The Gospel of John was not written until the end of the century and then largely from private sources which were primarily concerned with the theological implications of Jesus' life and death.

Through all these records runs the often unseen division between what is from Jesus and what is about or concerning Jesus. But when scholars are asked to separate the material that authentically reveals the historical Jesus from the material that reflects the growing Christology of the early Christians, they vary widely in their interpretations. At certain points each student is thrown back, after careful study, upon his own judgment, even his intuitive feeling of what is from the historical Jesus and what is from the early Church. In many cases these decisions on the quality of the evidence are crucial. There is some warrant therefore for saying that every life of Jesus is in some sense a *confessio fidei*. And yet on many other points there has been wide agreement, and the future may see the development of a greater consensus among authorities as to the finally valid interpretation of the life of Jesus. The present chapter contains an essay in that direction.

I THE WORLD INTO WHICH JESUS CAME

That Jesus was born into a part of the world which had only recently been brought under Roman dominion is of some significance, to begin with. One of the last acquisitions of Roman arms was Palestine. The Jews, as we have seen in the chapter dealing with them, had been subjected over and over to a foreign yoke; yet the Roman rule came to seem more intolerable than any. This was due in large part to the fact that the Romans were an aloof, administrative group; they had in particular a purely regulatory feeling concerning local populations; there was no fellow-feeling at all. It had been different with the Greeks, who were an imaginative and responsive people, able to enter into the spirit of a locality and weigh its ideas as though they deserved respect. But the Jews and the Romans were poles apart; there was so little of seeing eye to eye that they were enigmas to each other, and gave up trying to arrive at an understanding.

This hardening of the heart toward each other's natures and cultures precluded any possibility of adjustment, and therefore made it inevitable that their living together in the same land would produce social tumult. This was so much the case throughout Palestine, that in his childhood Jesus must have gained little better than a confusing impression of swift political and social changes taking place all around him. He grew up in an atmosphere of argument, conflict, and bitterness. There was endless talk. Older minds were bewildered by events, and torn by mounting tensions. Even now the historians' picture of the period remains confusing. What then must contemporaries have felt!

The Political Divisions of Palestine in Jesus' Time

About the time of Jesus' birth, Herod the Great died. Three of Herod's sons had escaped the fatal consequences of exciting his suspicion, and so survived. In his will he divided Palestine between them. While that unhappy country trembled on the brink of insurrection, the three sons hurried to Rome to have their bequest confirmed; and Augustus Caesar assigned Judea, Samaria, and Idumea to Archelaus, Galilee

PALESTINE IN THE
TIME OF JESUS

TETRARCHY
OF PHILIP

Tyre

PHOENICIA

GALILEE

Capernaum

Sephoris

Tiberias

Nazareth

SAMARIA

PEREA

MEDITERRANEAN SEA

Jericho

JUDEA

Jerusalem

DEAD SEA

and Perea to Herod Antipas, and the region northeast of the Lake of Galilee to Philip. Archelaus was, however, not given outright control of his district, as the other two sons were. The caution of Augustus proved well founded; for after nine years of incompetence and brutality, Archelaus was accused before the emperor on a number of serious charges and banished to Gaul. His place was taken by a Roman official called a procurator, who was made responsible to the governor of Syria.

Procurator followed procurator, in regular succession. They ruled Judea from Caesarea, on the coast below Jerusalem. Few of them had any sense of the historic forces at work beneath the surface of the Jewish scene. Some of them were rapacious and unscrupulous men, anxious only to make enough money to retire in comfort to Rome. Though they allowed the Jews as much civil and religious liberty as political considerations (that is, Roman imperialism) permitted, they insisted on a kind of remote control over the Jewish religion. For example, they kept the robes of the high priest stored in the Tower of Antonia, and released them only for the ceremonies in which they were worn. This meant that they could control the appointment of the high priest by signifying to whom they would be pleased to release the robes. They also from time to time tried to introduce into Jerusalem battle-standards and shields displaying the image of Caesar as emperor-god; but the Jews angrily protested each time, and the procurators did not insist.

Under these conditions Judea was scarcely happy. Indeed, perplexed almost to despair by the difficulties besetting them, the Jews "strove among themselves"—Pharisees with Sadducees, and Zealots and Herodians with the rest.

The Situation in Galilee

In Galilee, on the other hand, the irritation was less pervasive. There Herod Antipas ruled over a very mixed population. The Jews were barely in the majority. There were many Greek-speaking citizens, as well as Phoenicians from the coast and Syrians from interior regions to the north. In some districts the Jews were outnumbered by these gentiles. Furthermore, across the Jordan, and not under Herod's authority directly, though within the borders of Perea, there were ten self-governing towns,* leagued together on the pattern of Hellenic city-states; these were the Palestinian expression of Alexander the Great's dream of a new international order. Their presence helps to explain why Herod Antipas pursued a policy of internationalism. He hoped

* Hence called, from the Greek, the Decapolis.

that a patient infusion of world-culture into his area would unify his people under his rule. But the Galilean Jews, while predisposed to "suffer fools gladly" so long as their religion was not threatened, were more than a little disturbed when he began to make their key towns over into Greco-Roman cities. One of these cultural ventures was the rebuilding of the largest city in Galilee, Sepphoris, not more than four miles north of Nazareth. This city was, however, outshone in magnificence, if not in size, by the new town of Tiberias, on the western shore of the Lake of Galilee, a city provided with a colonnaded forum, and named by Herod after the reigning Roman emperor. Here the Hellenistic influence reached its apogee in Herod's domain.

Many of the Jews in Galilee might have reconciled themselves to all this, if they had not been obliged to foot the bill. It had formerly seemed onerous enough to have to pay the direct, personal tax for administrative expenses, since only part of it went to Herod Antipas, the rest going to far-away Rome. Now they were obliged to pay additional taxes in the form of burdensome customs duties, not only on goods imported into or exported from the region, but on those shipped from city to city and from farm to market. Tolls were collected, too, at bridges and harbors. And there was a salt tax—always irritating anywhere. The Jews thus found themselves contributing to the expenses of their own subjection. So, when in 6 A.D. Quirinius, the governor of Syria, ordered a census taken of the inhabitants of Palestine, in order that an even more thorough form of tax-assessment might be worked out, there were immediate hostile repercussions among the people. Jesus may have been ten or twelve years old at that time, and must have been keenly aware of the general excitement of the Galilean Jews, which boiled up swiftly into insurrection.

A certain Judas the Galilean, assisted by a Pharisee called Zaddok, organized the *Zealot party* by calling around him the Galilean hotheads, and forming a rebel army which stood ready to fight on the principle: "No God but Yahweh, no tax but to the Temple, no friend but the Zealot." * ¹ Judas and his followers surprised the city of Sepphoris, seized

---

* According to their contemporary, Josephus, "These men agree in all other things with the Pharisaic notions; but they have an inviolable attachment to liberty, and say that *God* is to be their only Lord and Master. They also do not mind dying any death, nor indeed do they heed the deaths of their relations and friends, nor could the fear of death make them call any man their master. And . . . I fear that what I have said does not adequately express the determination that they show when they undergo pain."—Antiquities, XVIII, 1, 6. The fanaticism of the Zealots was due in some measure to the fact that many of them had a family history of death by violence for rebellion. Judas the Galilean's father was killed fifty-two years earlier while engaged in insurrection.

the armory, provided themselves with its store of weapons, and made the city their headquarters. So serious did the revolt become that the Roman general Varus had to bring up two Roman legions to suppress it. He burned and destroyed Sepphoris, and crucified several thousand Zealots in a bloody attempt to stamp the movement out; but its secret spread continued. Jesus was faced with the realities created by it all his life; for one at least, if not two, of the Twelve* had been affiliated with the Zealot party, and he himself was crucified finally, when the crowd in Pilate's courtyard shouted to have Barabbas, known to them as a Zealot, released to them instead of himself.

Not all the Jews of Galilee supported the Zealot cause. The *Essenes* were opposed to violence on principle. They were even opposed to animal sacrifices—a radical departure for that day. Fairly numerous in Galilee, they paid little attention to the strife of the times, but waited patiently for the Lord's Anointed One, the Messiah. Meanwhile they lived by strict rules, in celibate communities, holding their possessions in common, keeping the Sabbath day, laboring in their fields during the other days of the week, and devoting themselves to fasting, prayer, and frequent ceremonial ablutions, much as the Dead Sea community did.

The *Pharisees*, on their part, held themselves from violence largely out of considerations of prudence. They were far the largest party in Galilee and were led by scribes and rabbis whose consciousness of mission was heightened by systematic training. The Jewish parties had all caught the concept of organization from the Greeks and Romans, and knew their hopes of survival depended upon unified leadership. Many attended schools which the Pharisees maintained—academies, we might call them, for in attitude and method they resembled the academies of Greece. The largest of these schools was in Jerusalem and boasted great teachers like Shammai and Hillel. Caught, all of them, in a world of rapid and unpredictable change, the Pharisees made it their principle to live as nearly as conditions permitted according to their traditions. They felt that the only way to hasten the coming of the Messiah, and in the meantime save Judaism in their perverse and wicked generation from extinction, was to be scrupulous in religious practices that linked tradition with every detail of daily living. This meant that they endeavored to keep every one of the Sabbath laws; to fulfil to the letter the regulations for keeping the Jewish festivals; to tithe; to repeat the Shema constantly; to have a mezuzah inside the door and a phylactery on the brow; to be very particular about ceremonial purity, correct treatment of "Holy things," and dietary rules; to have no legal dealings with anyone in the civil courts, because Jews should have recourse only to the

---

* Simon the Zealot and possibly Judas Iscariot.

judicial proceedings set up by their own tribunal, the Sanhedrin; and so on. Though the time was not long distant when they would be obliged to alter many of their old rites and introduce others that would be new, they were at this time critical of all those who did not keep the Law as they interpreted it.

The *Sadducees*, by comparison, were less influential in Galilee, but even more conservative. They were certain that the old cultus and Torah were unalterable; whereas the Pharisees, after much heart-searching, were willing with changed circumstances to alter old customs, if that meant preserving Jewish communities against religious dissolution. But Sadducees and Pharisees alike opposed looseness, opportunism, or radicalism.

Some of the common people, perhaps most of them, were tolerant and easy-going in these things, readily influenced by "the world," and only loosely and vaguely religious. Many, on the other hand, considered themselves strict Jews, attended the services of the synagogues, revered the Law and the Prophets, kept the Jewish festivals and fasts, and went up annually to the Temple in Jerusalem at the Passover. This was not enough, the sterner Pharisees held. If they did not keep themselves free from ceremonial defilement, observe the strict dietary rules, tithe, wash their hands before meals, ceremonially cleanse their persons, their clothes, cups, jugs, basins, and all the food bought in the markets, and do no work on the Sabbath day, they were impure and could not be considered pious. Many of the devout among the common people, however, were sure that one could be deeply devotional, truly religious, without being narrowly legalistic in obeying "the tradition of the elders." It was to this group that the parents of Jesus belonged.

II THE LIFE AND TEACHINGS OF JESUS

Youth

It seems paradoxical to say it, but Jesus was born in 4 B.C. or a year or two earlier. Herod the Great was still alive; and this fact, together with other evidence, such as the testimony of Luke that Jesus was crucified in "the fifteenth year of Tiberius Caesar," compels us to put his birth further back than the year hallowed by long use.* Matthew and

* It was not until the middle of the 6th century A.D. that the Church began to reckon time as before and after the birth of Christ. The monks whose calculations were followed made a mistake in computing the year.

Luke are authorities for the fact that he was born in Bethlehem, south of Jerusalem, while Joseph and Mary were on a visit there. Luke says they were there to register for a census, but he alone suggests such a reason. All the evangelists agree that the home of the family was in Nazareth of Galilee. It was there that Joseph pursued his trade as a carpenter, and up to about his thirtieth year all but a few weeks of Jesus' life were spent there.

Of Jesus' childhood and youth we know little directly. The internal evidence of the Gospels leads us to assume that his parents belonged to the common people, the 'Am ha'aretz, but were deeply religious. Jesus not only went to the synagogue services with them, but came to know by heart long passages from the Law and the Prophets. It may be that he attended the local synagogue school. Somehow he came to know enough of the prophetic tradition to develop a distrust of whatever arid scholarship and legalism the scribes and Pharisees were given to. As to his trade, he was trained to be a carpenter. As a result, his feeling for the common people was strong. We know from the Gospels that he grew up in a large family. There were at least six other children: four boys—James, Joses, Simon, and Jude—and "sisters," how many is not said.* Luke gives us one revealing glimpse into his religious experience as a child. The story of the boy Jesus in the Temple is a witness to many things, but above all to the fact that he was capable of sustained interest in religious matters, an absorption so deep that he did not think of the effect his absence must be having upon his relatives and friends.

The next eighteen years of Jesus' life are often called the silent years, for we have no direct evidence on what took place during them. We may assume, from the fact that Joseph drops out of the story completely, that he died in this interval, and that Jesus, as the oldest son, took over the management of the carpenter business, his brothers helping him. It has been an interesting surmise of recent scholarship that in the early part of this period Jesus worked as a carpenter in Sepphoris, four miles to the north, when that city was rebuilt by Herod Antipas after its burning during the Zealot rebellion of 6 A.D. If that was so, he had first hand experience of working in a city being rebuilt after the Greek manner. But we have greater warrant for assuming that as a carpenter Jesus hewed and installed the woodwork that went into Galilean homes, and constructed ploughshares, yokes, and carts for the farmers near Nazareth.

* Mk. 6:3. Roman Catholics, however, say the other children were not Mary's but children of Joseph by an earlier marriage or of Mary's presumed sister, Mary Cleophas.

Baptism and Temptation

When he was about thirty years old Jesus passed through one of the profoundest experiences of his life. His baptism by John brought to him the same double experience of mystic vision and call that came to Amos, Isaiah, and Jeremiah. It terminated the quiet years at Nazareth, and changed the direction of his life completely.

John the Baptist had appeared suddenly on the banks of the Jordan, with an urgent message, "Repent! for the Kingdom of Heaven is coming!" He had emerged from the desert region beyond the Jordan, where he had been meditating on what appeared to him the crisis of the hour. We are told by the Gospels that he "wore clothing made of hair cloth, and had a leather belt around his waist, and he lived on dried locusts and wild honey," [2]—that is, he had assumed the life of a solitary ascetic. His periods of lonely brooding increased his feeling that the end of the present age was at hand; the Messiah who should judge the world was about to appear and bring in the Day of Wrath which the repentant alone would be able to face. So near did this day seem to him that he is reported to have used the vivid figure, "The axe is already lying at the roots of the trees." Another startling image of his was drawn from the threshing floor; he said the Messiah had already taken up the winnowing fork in his hand, and would "clean up his threshing-floor, and store his wheat in his barn," but would "burn up the chaff with inextinguishable fire." [3] He was not alone in so believing. The Essenes had a similar sense of the imminence of the End; but John did not join them; he had too much of the feeling of social responsibility to retire into mere watchful waiting. He therefore left the desert, and began a career of fiery preaching, in order to warn the unwary. He succeeded in drawing people from all over Palestine to hear him. When these listeners became distressed about their spiritual condition, he took them down into the Jordan and immersed them in the water, to signify their repentance and the washing away of their sins. He became known as *the Baptist*. He was more, however, than a ceremonialist. His instructions to his converts were on an ethical plane of highest urgency. In the interim before the coming of the Messiah, they were to practice the strictest individual and social righteousness. The crowds would ask him, "What ought we to do?" He answered, "The man who has two shirts must share with the man who has none, and the man who has food must do the same." [4] He told tax-collectors not to collect more than they were authorized to, and soldiers not to extort money or make false charges against people, but to be satisfied with their pay. Though he roused the anger of Herod Antipas by condemning his illegal marriage with Herodias, his brother's wife, and was arrested and finally executed while in prison, he had raised up a loyal following which became self-propagating; St. Paul found a circle of his followers in Ephesus thirty years later.

It was natural that Jesus should be attracted. In the first chapter of Mark we have the story given barely and briefly:

> It was in those days that Jesus came from Nazareth in Galilee, and was baptized by John in the Jordan. And just as he was coming up out of the water he saw the heavens torn open and the Spirit coming down like a dove to enter into him, and out of the heavens came a voice:
> "You are my Son, my Beloved! You are my Chosen!" [5]

This experience was profoundly moving and convincing. Ever since his twelfth year Jesus had felt, and been known by his acquaintances to feel, a more than ordinary interest in religious matters. His sensitive intelligence and quick social conscience predisposed him toward a prophetic role in life. Now he was clearly called to assume such a role.

It is significant that he at once retired into the wilderness beyond Jordan to think through the course which he must in future take. In the Christian tradition, this time of meditation and decision is described as a period of forty days during which Satan tried to tempt him. As told by Matthew and Luke, the temptation had three phases. Back of the imagery used we may see the elements of very real issues. Should he continue to work for a livelihood—for bread? Not any longer. Should he use spectacular methods which might attract attention but put him in jeopardy? No, he must not force God's hand, must not put God's choice of him to trial. Should he seek political power as a precondition of redeeming Israel? No, that would be indeed compromising with Satan.

In making his decisions Jesus was guided by what he knew differentiated his position from those taken by the leading Jewish parties. He rejected the methods of the Zealot, because he saw they were futile and self-destructive. Those who take the sword, he later said, will perish by the sword. This conviction others shared with him. Many in Nazareth and Sepphoris knew by bitter experience that the Zealot rebellion of 6 A.D. had brought upon them only death and destruction.* As to the Pharisees, he differed from them chiefly in emphasis. In the diatribe in the 23rd chapter of Matthew he is quoted as saying: "Alas for you, you hypocritical scribes and Pharisees, for you pay tithes on mint, dill, and cummin, and you have let the weightier matters of the law go—justice, mercy, and

---

* The people of Sepphoris and the surrounding towns actually refused in 66 A.D. to support the Zealot-inspired Jewish War which led four years later to the destruction of Jerusalem and the dispersion of the nation.

integrity. But you should have observed these, without overlooking the others." With the Sadducees he had little contact; but he seems to have sided with the Pharisees against them. In another direction, he could not be an Essene. Like John the Baptist, he was too sensitive to his social duty to go into monastic seclusion. Moreover, he was no ascetic. Thoroughly at home with the plain people from among whom he had sprung, he enjoyed wedding feasts and banquets, insomuch that the scandalized Pharisees, afraid of all forms of ceremonial defilement, went about complaining that Jesus ate with tax-collectors and irreligious people, did not observe the dietary rules, and never fasted. They pointed out that even John the Baptist's disciples fasted. But Jesus insisted that fasting should be done in private; not by rule or rote, but in accordance with personal need. And this was not the only respect in which he differed from John the Baptist. He came too freshly from the carpenter's bench and from vital contacts with village folk absorbed in the concrete problems of the everyday world to be carried away by John's fanatic persuasion that the world was about to end suddenly. Moreover, John was too much the preacher: the people had to come to him. Jesus resolved to go to the people, and change them where he found them.

The Beginning of the Galilean Ministry

About the time of John's arrest, Jesus crossed the Jordan and made his way to Galilee, "proclaiming," says Mark, "the good news from God, saying, 'The time has come and the reign of God is near; repent, and believe this good news!'" [6] He produced such conviction of his divine calling that he was immediately followed by four disciples—Simon Peter, and his brother Andrew; James and his brother John, the sons of Zebedee —all fishermen who dropped their nets and followed him. The Lake of Galilee was then surrounded by thriving towns—Tiberias, Taricheae, Capernaum, Chorazin, and Bethsaida. Jesus began his ministry among them, choosing Capernaum as his headquarters because Simon Peter's home was there. At first he spoke in the synagogues, and when the crowds grew too large for that, he preached in the market-places and open fields.

The first chapter of Mark contains a full description of what befell Jesus on the first Sabbath day in Capernaum. It will serve our purpose well to analyze it at some length as a typical day in the early ministry of Jesus. First of all, "he went to the synagogue and taught." Probably there was more than one synagogue in Capernaum, and he went to the one to which he was invited.° The interior of the synagogue was bare and simple. The worshipers faced Jerusalem. Before them was a raised platform, with a reading desk on it; and against the wall or within a recess was a cabinet containing the rolls of scripture. This was the ark. A curtain hung before it, and in front of the curtain stood a lamp, which was always alight. During services the "chief seats" were occupied by the elders and the leading Pharisees, who sat facing the other worshipers. Their voices led in the unison repetition of the Shema—an essential part of every service. At times the worshipers stood, as when the ruler of the synagogue recited prayers and the congregation repeated the appropriate responses. After the Chazzan took from the ark the rolls of the Law and the Prophets, the scripture readings of the day were recited, first in Hebrew, then in Aramaic. After that the ruler himself, or a person chosen by him, addressed the congregation by way of "teaching."

Such was the setting of Jesus' first important utterance in Capernaum. When he began speaking, we are told, his audience was amazed at his teaching, for he spoke "like one who had authority," that is, with great freedom of interpretation and from the fulness of his heart, not drily "like the scribes." Whereupon a startling thing occurred. A man in the audience who believed he had a devil in him which had caused his abnormal physical and mental condition—the universally accepted explanation of certain ailments in that day—suddenly and hopefully interrupted the preacher.

"What do you want of us, Jesus, you Nazarene? Have you come to destroy us? I know who you are, you are God's Holy one!"

Jesus reproved him, and said,

"Silence! Get out of him!"

The foul spirit convulsed the man and gave a loud cry and went out of him.†

° The synagogues were controlled, in matters of doctrine and polity, by the scribes and Pharisees, but the local administration was in the hands of a council of elders, one of whom was elected the "ruler of the synagogue" and had charge of the religious services. He would be in a position to invite Jesus to speak in the synagogue. Another officer, the "chazzan" or attendant, was the synagogue's librarian, having in his care the rolls of the scriptures which were in the "ark"; he was also the caretaker of the building, and if a person with scribal training, the teacher of the synagogue school. Every synagogue had in addition a group of men who collected and disbursed the alms. It was in imitation of them that the Christians appointed deacons.

† This and the next four quotations are from Mark 1:21–45. Translation is from *The Bible: An American Translation*, University of Chicago Press, 1935. Reprinted by permission of the publishers.

Jesus was probably as much surprised as anyone at this evidence of his healing power. (That seems to be indicated in what he did early the next morning.) It should be kept in mind in judging the situation that he had no reason to question the diagnosis of puzzling ailments which was universal in his time, that is, that they were caused by an indwelling demonic power entering the person from elsewhere. His audience certainly had no doubt. We read further:

And they were all so amazed that they discussed it with one another, and said,

"What does this mean? It is a new teaching! He gives orders with authority even to the foul spirits, and they obey him!"

And his fame immediately spread in all directions. . . .

After the synagogue service, the story continues, Jesus went with his disciples to the home of Simon Peter, where Simon's mother-in-law was in bed, sick with a fever. Jesus went up to her, and grasping her hand, made her rise. "And the fever left her, and she waited on them." Then followed one of the crucial episodes of Jesus' early ministry.

In the evening, after sunset, they brought to him all who were sick or possessed by demons, and the whole town was gathered at the door. And he cured many. . . .

The wording here deserves close study. It is interesting to note that the other evangelists in copying from Mark at this point change the word "many" to "all"; but Mark undoubtedly preserves the original tradition. Jesus could not heal people except by their "faith"; and in his perfect honesty he always refused the credit, but said to every healed person such words as: "Go, in peace, and sin no more. Your faith has healed you." *

That Jesus was disturbed by his new-found power and the kind of renown it brought him is implied in the next words:

Early in the morning, long before daylight, he got up and left the house and went off to a lonely spot, and prayed there. And Simon and his companions sought him out and found him, and said to him,

---

* The healing miracles of Jesus, as preserved for us in tradition, present many difficulties; but if we could speak of a *minimum view*, it would be something like this: in a world like that of Jesus' time, where spiritual and nervous tensions were so great, there must have been many instances of functional disorders, greatly aggravated by fears and repressions, and exhibiting many of the symptoms of organic disease, among all classes of the people. The nobility of Jesus' own faith, mediated through a wholesome, sympathetic and challenging personality, remade many lost or sick souls, restored their faith, and caused their alarming symptoms to vanish in an instant. To this minimum view a great deal might be added.

"They are all looking for you!"

He said to them,

"Let us go somewhere else, to the neighboring country towns, so that I may preach in them, too, for that is why I came out here."

But his experience in the other towns was like that in Capernaum. For some days he could no longer go into a town openly, but stayed in unfrequented places, and people came to him from every direction. His popularity was tremendous. People "ran" to him. There seemed to be great promise in him. They were hopeful of great things. When he came again into Capernaum, "such a crowd gathered that there was no room even around the door." On another occasion there were so many people in the house it was impossible to prepare a meal; on still another, so many people gathered along the lake shore that, for fear of being crushed, Jesus had his disciples keep a boat ready to remove him. Subsequently, he found the crowd so great "he got into a boat and sat in it, a little way from the shore, while all the people were on the land close to the water"; [7] and from this vantage point, he taught them.

The Content of Jesus' Teaching

What was it in Jesus' preaching which so attracted the crowds during the early part of his ministry? The answer is, that, for one thing, he spoke in simple and untechnical language about the central issues in religion, always with the use of homely illustrations drawn from Nature and human life. He was a plain man speaking to plain people. Many of his profoundest lessons were given through parables—brief stories which set life in its true perspective. But it would not have been enough if the manner of his teaching had been its only attraction; what he really had achieved was a new synthesis of the religious insights of his people, perfectly exemplified and illustrated in his own personality and experience.

A. RELIGIOUS TEACHING. One thing is obvious in all the teaching which his disciples remembered: the centrality of the religious point of view. From the time of his baptism by John the Baptist, and throughout the rest of his life, the reality of God and of his own intimate relationship with God occupied the central place in Jesus' thinking and determined the consistency of his point of view. He was never moved to set in order his reasons for believing in the reality of God. In that age of universal faith in the Divine existence, no one ever asked him to. What men desired to know then was what kind of a god God was, and what, in view of his character, he might be expected to do. On this point Jesus spoke with profound assurance. God was the sovereign moral personality ruling the universe, the moving spirit behind the course of history, a transcendent being, sternly righteous, who never departed from perfect justice in determining the course of events or the destiny of an individual. But God was also forgiving and merciful, primarily occupied with human redemption, in character and action paternal. Jesus' favorite name for God was Father (or Father in Heaven). It is implied in his teaching that, though God allows men to make their own decisions and, like the Prodigal in the famous parable, take the means at their disposal and waste them in riotous living, he continues to love them throughout the redemptive process of punishment and suffering that inevitably follows, and will forgive them when they return to him. God therefore is utterly good as well as holy. Men should trust him beyond all shadow of doubting, be unanxious, and regularly seek spiritual enlightenment through prayer, especially private prayer in one's chamber or in the solitude of the fields and hill-tops.

Jesus' attitude toward Nature was conditioned by his conception of God. He was truly Jewish in thinking of Nature as the stage-setting of the sublime drama of human redemption. Nature was not the ultimate reality. God worked behind and through Nature. (One might generalize and say, that Jesus was like the Jews in looking through Nature at God, and did not follow the Greek tendency to look through the gods at Nature.) At the same time it is apparent in Jesus' teaching that he looked at Nature directly with delight and trust. The lilies of the field, more beautifully arrayed than Solomon in all his glory, were of God's making, and were, like the birds of the heaven—the ravens and sparrows—fully sustained by God's care. Surely, if men would know how to live with each other in the righteousness of God's kingdom, they too would find in Nature all they needed.*

Jesus' attitude toward his body and the impulses of the natural man within him (to follow the traditional phrasing for a reference to the native impulses of human beings) was similarly confident and trustful, and again typically Jewish. He apparently accepted the body as functionally integrated with the mind and spirit in a working unity. As we have observed earlier, he was no ascetic. He enjoyed wedding feasts and banquets. He never suggested that the body is inherently corrupting

---

* It is a simplification, but the sense of Jesus' teaching at this point is: the trouble lies in the fact that men seek food and clothing *first;* but if they would seek first the Kingdom, food and clothing would come in course; that was God's plan. If we shed the thought-forms of Jesus' time, this is at the heart of his faith.

and defiling, or that the soul is foully imprisoned in the flesh. The body
may indeed become the dangerous instrument of an evil will, or it may
be divided between good and evil, because the will is so divided. In the
latter case, Jesus said, one might use drastic means to regain unity of
the personality: "If your foot makes you fall, cut it off." [8] But on the
positive side, his follower, St. Paul, who had received a Jewish training,
put the whole matter clearly enough in the suggestion that the body may
become the temple of the Holy Spirit.* Jesus, in short, did not distract
his followers from the pursuit of personal and social goodness by suggesting that the body is the chief enemy of good, and ought first to be
subdued.

His attention was directed elsewhere. His primary interest was in
man's doing the will of God. What God most wanted was that men should
become fit for the coming Kingdom of Heaven, by living together as
persons religiously orientated toward him as sons toward a father and
ethically orientated toward each other as brethren. No person was to be
excluded from attempting to reach such fitness. No person was natively
unworthy either of God's grace or man's fellowship. All through Jesus'
teaching appears the concept of the infinite worth of human personality
—the principle which is often called today respect for personality. He invoked this principle particularly in the case of little children, but also in
the case of the disinherited, the sinful, and alien folk, with whom he
was constantly in association. There were to be no exceptions to the law
of love; it was to be inter-racial and inter-national.

These might be called the universal and fundamental elements in
Jesus' religious teaching. They were, of course, clothed in and colored by
the thought-forms of his day. That was inevitable. This places us in some
difficulty, however. While some of the thought-forms he used may properly be called fugitive and now largely unusable, they had great importance at the time, and hence it is necessary to give them serious
consideration. We are here in a hard field of discussion, providing perhaps the thorniest problems of interpretation in the entire field of
historical research; but if the strictest objectivity in seeking to determine the facts be as nearly as possible realized, one may hope to approximate the truth of history, even though *final* proof for any one
interpretation is unobtainable.

It is apparent that Jesus shared with his people the expectation that
the Messianic Kingdom long foretold was about to be ushered in. The

---

* St. Paul, however, was sufficiently influenced by Greek modes of thought to
say elsewhere that the flesh and spirit are "in opposition, so that you cannot do
anything you please." [9]

religious feeling of the Jewish people then centered in this expectation. From his youth up Jesus was under the influence of the hopes raised by it. So that he was responding normally to his environment when he entertained along with his people their general and passionate hope of a new order of things.

Consider the following passages from "Q":

And he said to his disciples,
"The time will come when you will long to see one of the days of the Son of Man. . . . Men will say to you, 'Look! There he is!' or, 'Look! Here he is!' Do not go off in pursuit of him, for just as when lightning flashes, it shines from one end of the sky to the other, that will be the way with the Son of Man. . . . In the time of the Son of Man it will be just as in the time of Noah. People went on eating, drinking, marrying, and being married up to the very day that Noah got into the ark and the flood came and destroyed them all. . . . It will be like that on the day when the Son of Man appears." [10]

In the Gospel of Mark there are passages (modified by the language of the Apostolic Age) which have a similar meaning:

And he said to them, "I tell you, some of you who stand here will certainly live to see the reign of God come in its might." [11]
"I tell you, these things will all happen before the present age passes away. . . . But about that day or hour no one knows, not even the angels in heaven, nor the Son; only the Father. You must look out and be on the alert, for you do not know when it will be time." [12]

If we accept these sayings as going back to Jesus—and they would seem in essence to be his—what is to be said of their meaning? In the first place, the conviction clearly is, that the "end of the age" is imminent, possibly very near. The thrill of expectancy produced by this conviction is hard for us to recreate even in imagination. That it is a strange belief to the 20th century is, of course, no argument at all that only a strange or unhealthy mind could believe it then. The marvel of it is that Jesus did not make more of it. If the critical dissection of the records is on the right track, his disciples made much more of it than he did. For it was almost an obsession among the greater number of unhappy Jews of Palestine, and was a large factor in the lives of the Jews of the diaspora. Not to believe it was unreasonable. In a world where the concept of social evolution and progress did not exist, and where faith in God's direct intervention in human affairs was unquestioned, no pious mind among the Jews doubted that God was soon to work his deliverance, just as he had in the past when his people were suffering beyond endurance.

But in his analysis and weighing of the situation Jesus showed distinct originality.

A careful examination of his use of the more or less fugitive thought-forms of the eschatology of his time conclusively shows that, though Jesus shared the general apocalyptic hope, he transformed it. He took the narrowly conceived, exclusively Jewish messianic kingdom of the less liberal Judaism and made it the universal kingdom of the Father of all men. The "elect" are from the four corners of the earth. A passage from "Q" puts it with the utmost directness:

"You must strain every nerve to get in through the narrow door, for I tell you many will try to get in, and will not succeed, when the master of the house gets up and shuts the door, and you begin to stand outside and to knock on the door, and say, 'Open it for us, sir!' Then he will answer you and say, 'I do not know where you come from . . . Get away from me, all you wrong-doers!' There you will weep and gnash your teeth when you see Abraham and Isaac and Jacob and all the prophets in the Kingdom of God, while you are put outside. People will come from the east and west and the north and south, and take their places in the Kingdom of God. There are those now last who will then be first, and there are those now first who will be last." [13]

Matthew renders part of this passage still more clearly, thus:

"I tell you, many will come from the east and from the west and take their places at the feast with Abraham, Isaac, and Jacob, in the Kingdom of Heaven, while the heirs to the kingdom will be driven into the darkness outside, there to weep and grind their teeth!" [14]

The Kingdom is thus not a collection of righteous Jews only, but a brotherhood including Gentiles. Entrance into the Kingdom is not conditioned by the keeping of the law of Moses, but by broader ethical qualifications. Matthew's paraphrase of the Lukan beatitudes is not false to the fact. It is the pure in heart who shall see God; it is the meek who shall inherit the earth.

Further, it is to be noted that Jesus distinctly lessened the tension of expectation by teaching that the Kingdom is in a real sense already present. It is from "Q" that we derive this teaching: the Kingdom is like a bit of yeast in a large measure of flour; it is like a mustard seed, the smallest of the seeds, but sure in process of time to grow into a tree. Jesus was in no hurry for the consummation of the eschatological hope: we see everywhere that the essential thing to him was *present* unbroken union with God.

And this brings us to the very knotty problem of Jesus' conception of his own relationship with God. Did he consider himself the Son of Man and Son of God in a special sense? Did he think of himself as the Messiah from the time of his baptism, or did he grow gradually into the conviction that he was the Lord's Anointed? Or did his followers endow him with messiahship toward the end of his career and after his death, without any intimation from him that this was due him?

These questions are crucial, and can perhaps never be answered finally. Nevertheless some very definite things can be said about Jesus' sense of unique relationship with God.

God was much more to Jesus than the great august Presence to whom one owes a morning and an evening prayer. The intimacy and rapport of his communion with God in prayer exceeded anything he experienced among men. In teaching his disciples to pray, he communicated something of this experience to them; but there was as well something incommunicable about it, so that they were reduced to wonder. Whatever his use of the terms "Son of Man" and "the Christ" was, it is quite beyond doubt that he knew he was "sent." God had commissioned him to establish his Kingdom. As with Amos, so with Jesus: God "took" him and sent him to men.

Hence he could choose twelve men to follow him. He could preach and teach and heal with authority. He could propound a law superseding that of Moses. He could read to the congregation in Nazareth the great passage from Isaiah:

"The spirit of the Lord is upon me,
For he has consecrated me to preach the good news to the poor,
He has sent me to announce to the prisoners their release and to the
    blind the recovery of their sight,
To set the down trodden at liberty,
To proclaim the year of the Lord's favor!"

and say calmly, "This passage of Scripture has been fulfilled here in your hearing today!" [15]

The sum of the matter is, that Jesus had found a master principle for his life, and that he was completely possessed by it. The central reality in his environment as he saw it, the ultimate fact giving religious value and character to all his world, was God; and in an act of surrender, he gave himself up to the consciousness of the presence and will of God. Thenceforth, completely unified in person and attitude, he went among men, possessed of absolute certitude, never hesitant, never doubting, clothed with power and authority, his whole unified life crying aloud: Nothing is so important to you as that you should hear me, everyone of you: by me God speaks!

B. ETHICAL TEACHING. This religious consciousness of Jesus—analogous to that of the prophets—carried over into his ethical teaching. He spoke with the authority of great moral assurance. And because he could himself move swiftly and easily from one moral decision to another, without prolonged hesitancy, his teaching contains a constant challenge to will whatever may hasten the coming of the Kingdom of God and to be firm in that will.

Taking for granted their knowledge of the scope and requirements of the Kingdom of God, Jesus expected his followers, as truly religious men, to be sincere, immediately and thoroughly sincere, in acting on their insight. According to Luke this seemed so urgent a matter to him that once when he challenged a man to follow him, and the man said, "Let me first go and bury my father," Jesus said to him, "Leave the dead to bury their own dead; you must go and spread the news of the Kingdom of God!" Yet another man said to him, "Master, I am going to follow you, but let me first say goodbye to my people at home"; to which Jesus replied, "No one who puts his hand to the plough, and then looks back, is fitted for the Kingdom of God!" [16]

Besides calling for sincerity and complete self-commitment, Jesus asked his followers to put their moral obligations above all social, legal, or ceremonial demands. It was at this point that he felt most critical of the Pharisees. They * were guilty of certain obvious faults: complacency, self-seeking, the desire for honor and applause, spiritual pride, hypocrisy; but, more profoundly, their gravest shortcoming lay in their neglect of the primary imperatives of the moral law; they had substituted legal and ceremonial practices for a creative and truly regenerating morality. They strained out the gnat, yet swallowed the camel; they cleaned the outside of the cup and the dish, but were themselves full inside of greed and self-indulgence; they were like whitewashed tombs, looking well on the outside, but full inside of the bones of the dead and all that is unclean. Though they paid tithes on mint, dill, and cummin, they let the weightier matters of the Law go—justice, mercy, and integrity. They took the relatively unimportant for the central and significant, and so their religious position had lost all vital significance.

It was indeed characteristic of Jesus, in all his ethical precepts, to transfer attention from the external features of moral behavior to its inward motivation, the spirit or attitude behind it. To concentrate upon outwardly correct behavior according to Jewish law was perversely shortsighted, if not downright immoral! Only if one's heart is right and one is

* One should perhaps note here that Jesus was referring to the Pharisees who had not yielded to the liberals of their own party.

in addition sincere in doing as the heart directs, can one be called a truly moral person. Spirit and motive are all-important. Out of the heart are the issues of life.

Before we look at the application of this principle to morality, we should see clearly that Jesus linked it up with a two-fold concern: concern for one's own inner integrity and concern for the inner health of others. Woe, said Jesus, to anyone who hurts another at the center of his moral being! All three Synoptic Gospels repeat the solemn warning that anyone who causes a humble believer to fall might better have a great millstone hung around his neck and then be thrown into the sea. Harming the moral nature of another is the gravest of crimes.

With the same stress on the inward condition of the personality Jesus reviewed and rephrased the old Hebrew laws. Matthew assembles a series of teachings in which Jesus looks behind a prohibited act to the motive that might cause it. Two examples may be cited. There was the law against murder which had been given to the men of old. "But I tell you that anyone who gets angry with his brother . . . and anyone who speaks contemptuously to his brother . . . and anyone who says to his brother 'You cursed fool!' will have to answer for it." [17] There was the law against adultery. "But I tell you that anyone who looks at a woman with desire has already committed adultery with her in his heart." [18]

But the stress on the spiritual and the inward in morality reached its most significant form in Jesus' teaching about love. This is a teaching that still requires the utmost effort of understanding; for while the command to use the method of love toward friend and foe alike is an absolute principle, its application to the details of conduct is always marked by such relativity that sincere Christians often differ in their judgments as to what that conduct should be.

The absolute principle is contained in the familiar words:

You have heard that [the men of old] were told, "You must love your neighbor and hate your enemy." But I tell you, love your enemies and pray for your persecutors, so that you may show yourselves true sons of your Father in heaven, for he makes his sun rise on bad and good alike, and makes his rain fall on the upright and the wrongdoers. . . . You are to be perfect, as your heavenly Father is.

You must always treat other people as you would like to have them treat you, for this sums up the Law and the Prophets.

"You must love the Lord your God with your whole heart, your whole soul, and your whole mind." That is the great, first command. There is a second like it: "You must love your neighbor as you do yourself." These two commands sum up the whole of the Law and the Prophets.[19]

Recent studies of his disciples' understanding of Jesus' teaching about the love of God and the love of man clearly show that to them God's love for man is so boundless and unlimited that it is poured out on good and bad alike without regard to merit or need and does not diminish when it gets a bad reception; it hates evil, but it loves persons with the same unqualified good will with which a mother loves her child or the father in the parable loved the prodigal son. It was understood that every follower of Christ must love his fellowmen, regardless of merit or desert, in the same unqualified fashion. Evil must be opposed with vigor; but persons must be loved unendingly and with an unlimited capacity to forgive.

The application of this principle to the details of conduct must be left to the judgment of the moment; for the moment often contains unpredictable surprises and one finds himself faced with the quandary, "Which side shall I take in this conflict between groups of my fellowmen? What is evil here and what is good? * And what form of opposition to evil must I adopt which will be consistent with inclusive love for all?" It cannot be said that Jesus' teaching, as it has been preserved, deals specifically with such a dilemma; just the central principle is stated, and the application of it at any juncture is left to the conscience of the individual who espouses it.

In one direction, however, clear guidance is given. The hard rule is laid down that one should not resist with violence evil done to one's own self.

You have heard that [the men of old] were told, "An eye for an eye and a tooth for a tooth." But I tell you not to resist injury, but if anyone strikes you on your right cheek, turn the other to him too; and if anyone wants to sue you for your shirt, let him have your coat too.[20]

The correct interpretation of these words would seem to be, do not engage in embittering and futile personal retaliation; it will only add to the moral confusion if one answers a personal injury with some similar one; rather, then, one should endure a wrong without any display of vengefulness or hatred, and without doing the things that would prolong the bad situation indefinitely, with no improvement. Yet on the other, and more positive, side, the wrong should be endured without moral surrender or compromise. The wrong-doer should be made to understand that his wrong-doing is being resisted, man to man,—yet only with answering goodness, immediately expressed by a gesture—the turning of a cheek, the giving of a coat, the second mile—symbolizing with shat-

* Or, "Which is the lesser evil?"

tering clearness the complete willingness of the wronged individual to live in fellowship with the wrong-doer, should that be made possible.

A complementary teaching warns against rash or ill-considered criticism of another's conduct. For one thing, it is all too often true that the rash critic is himself in need of moral correction; for another, it is always best to be generous and thus call forth love from others.

Pass no more judgments upon other people, so that you may not have judgment passed upon you. . . . Why do you keep looking at the speck in your brother's eye, and pay no attention to the beam that is in your own? How can you say to your brother, "Just let me get that speck out of your eye," when all the time there is a beam in your own? You hypocrite! First get the beam out of your own eye, and then you can see to get the speck out of your brother's eye.[21]

You must be merciful just as your Father is. Do not judge others. . . . Excuse others. . . . Give, and they will give to you; good measure, pressed down, shaken together, and running over, they will pour into your lap. For the measure you use with others they in turn will use with you.[22]

In other words, goodness in any form has an all-conquering power to call forth a response in kind.

The Growth of Opposition and the Retirement to the North

The furore of excitement and interest which attended the journeys of Jesus through the towns and villages of Galilee attracted the attention of the Pharisees and Sadducees in Jerusalem. The former as guardians of the Law and the latter as guardians of the Temple sent investigators to spy on Jesus and render a full report of him. The report when it came in was adverse. Thereupon selected Pharisees and Sadducees were sent to Galilee to heckle and oppose him. Verbal encounters between them and Jesus became frequent, and always threw the radical tendency of Jesus' proposals into sharp focus. A typical encounter occurred when, in passing through the wheat fields on the Sabbath, Jesus' disciples began to pick the heads of the wheat as they made their way through. The Pharisees protested against this as a breaking of the Sabbath law forbidding the gathering of produce from the fields. Jesus retorted: "The Sabbath was made for man, not man for the Sabbath."[23] The Pharisees would not have denied the truth of this assertion, but they disliked its radical tone. They were critical also of other elements in Jesus' teaching. Since physicians were prohibited from working on the Sabbath day, they protested the healings on the Sabbath. On more than one occasion they obliged Jesus to defend himself on this score. They noticed too that some of his disciples ate their food without first giving their hands a ceremonial washing to purify them, and accused Jesus of allowing the laxity. Jesus replied: "Listen to me all of you, and understand this. Nothing that goes into a man from outside can pollute him. It is what comes out of a man that pollutes him." [24] Asked by his disciples to explain, he said: "It is from inside, from men's hearts, that designs of evil come; immorality, stealing, murder, adultery, greed, malice, deceit, indecency, envy, abusiveness, arrogance, folly—all these evils come from inside, and they pollute a man."

What offended the Pharisees most, however, was the freedom with which Jesus interpreted the Law and the Prophets without respecting Tradition. Too often the formula which Matthew uses in recording the Sermon on the Mount appeared in Jesus' discourse: "You have heard that the men of old were told . . . but I tell you. . . ." In short, Jesus had his authority from within. Some Pharisees pitched on this with eagerness. They began to go among the people, zealously spreading the rumor that Jesus' eloquence and ability to draw the people away from the Pharisaic line of reasoning to a broader and (to their mind) dangerously free point of view were proof that he was possessed by an evil spirit which had entered into him; his apparent sincerity was the result of delusion; of a truth he was going against the revelation of God, contradicting Moses, and leading the people astray.

The rumor that Jesus was "possessed" was implanted at Nazareth. When he returned to his home town and taught in the synagogue on the Sabbath day, he wondered at the lack of faith. "A prophet is treated with honor everywhere except in his native place and among his relatives and at his home," he is reported to have said.[25] Mark records, that on an earlier occasion his relatives had come to Capernaum to stop him, because, being not yet won over, they were alarmed at his behavior. The story has a grim note:

His mother and his brothers came. And they stood outside the house and sent word in to him to come outside to them. There was a crowd sitting around him when they told him,

"Your mother and your brothers are outside asking for you."

He answered,

"Who are my mother and my brothers?"

And looking around at the people sitting about him, he said, "Here are my mother and my brothers! Whoever does the will of God is my brother and sister and mother." [26]

The only answer which Jesus could make to the open accusations against him was, "How can Satan drive Satan out? . . . If Satan has rebelled against himself and become disunited, he cannot last." [27] But the Pharisees brushed this aside.

The Zealot group in Galilee meanwhile turned against Jesus because he held the position that those who take the sword will perish by the sword. He could not be the Messiah, with such views, they felt, even though he healed the sick, cast out demons, and drew the multitudes to him with enthralling discourses on matters of religion and morals.

Many of the common people began therefore to fall away from Jesus, in doubt and disappointment. They had been so often deceived and misled; were they being imposed on once more? The enemies of Jesus redoubled their attacks, and threats against his life began to be breathed.

It was under these circumstances that Jesus made his way northwestward into the regions about Tyre and Sidon which were outside of Palestine, and then into southern Syria. This retirement to the north was apparently for the purpose of gaining time to consider further fateful decisions and to prepare his disciples for them. The Twelve were with him when he reached the inland town of Caesarea Philippi.* Here occurred the famous confession of Peter. Jesus said to them, "Who do people say that I am?" They said to him, "John the Baptist; others say Elijah, and others that you are one of the prophets." (It was thus clear that the people had not thought he was the Messiah.) "But," he said, "who do you say I am?" Peter answered: "You are the Christ." † [28] The record says that Jesus warned the Twelve not to say this about him to anyone, and he went on to tell them that he must go to Jerusalem and face suffering and death for the consummation of his mission. The frightened protest of the Twelve, voiced by Peter, met with his stern rebuke. This final step had now become necessary. He began to make his way steadily and quietly toward Jerusalem, timing himself to arrive during the Passover Festival.

Passion Week and Crucifixion

Jews from all over the world had come to Jerusalem to attend the great annual festival of the Passover. The Roman procurator, Pilate, had moved up to the city from the coastal town of Caesarea, to be on hand to see order kept and to quell any attempted uprising. Herod Antipas

---

* The capital of the Tetrarchy of Philip.

† I.e., the Messiah.

had come down from Galilee to enjoy the festivities and to go through
the motions of being a faithful Jew. There was no room in the inns. The
Galileans came prepared to live in tents in the valley between the city
and the Mount of Olives. Many of them knew Jesus, and would welcome him if he put in an appearance. On a borrowed colt, he rode down
the Mount of Olives, accompanied by his disciples, and into the city.
The Galileans greeted him with shouts of joy, and spread palm branches
in the way; but the people of the city said, "Who is this?" and the people
in the procession responded, "This is Jesus, the prophet of Nazareth in
Galilee!"

With his disciples, Jesus did a startling thing; he went to the Temple
and overturned the tables of the money-changers and drove out the
pigeon-dealers and all who were buying or selling things in the precincts
of the Temple. He cried out: "Does not the Scripture say, 'My house shall
be called a house of prayer for all the nations'? But you have made it a
robbers' cave." [29] This act must have had wide popular support, for the
authorities did nothing in direct reprisal.

But the Jewish leaders did not intend to let Jesus go scot free; they
began verbal hostilities, in the hope of discrediting him before the people. For several days, while he taught in the Temple, they attempted to
trap him into some treasonable or blasphemous utterance, but he eluded
them. He urged the plain people to join his movement as the inagura-
tion of the true Kingdom of God, and they listened to him eagerly.

His opponents damaged him in the people's eyes, however, when
he refused to make a declaration against paying the poll-tax to the
Roman emperor. Presented with the dilemma, "Is it right to pay taxes to
Caesar or not?" he made the disappointing reply, "Give Caesar what
belongs to Caesar, give God what belongs to God!" [30] The sheer weight
of the opposition to him must have impressed the people unfavorably;
even the Herodians joined in the opposition. Seeing that this was so,
Jesus began to tell the people, in pungent parables, that though the
Jews had received the first invitation to sit at God's banquet-table, now
because they had refused the invitation, God was going to bring in to
the feast of the Kingdom outcasts and aliens. Matthew represents Jesus
as saying pointedly to the Sadducees and Pharisees, "I tell you, the tax-
collectors and prostitutes are going into the Kingdom of God ahead of
you. . . . The Kingdom of God will be taken away from you, and given to
a people that will produce its proper fruit." [31]

All the evangelists agree that Jesus knew the opposition would con-
trive his death and that he prepared himself for it. In their treatment of
events they clearly reflect the consuming interest of the early Christians

in these final hours and especially in the Last Supper in an upper room in Jerusalem. As the early Christians told and retold the story, Jesus not only foresaw his death but knew who should betray him; and he performed a simple ceremony, during that last meal, to bring home to the Twelve the significance of his death.

> As they were eating, he took a loaf and blessed it, and he broke it in pieces and gave it to them saying,
> "Take this. It is my body."
> And he took the wine cup and gave thanks and gave it to them and they all drank from it. And he said to them,
> "This is my blood." [32]

Later, in the Garden of Gethsemane, he was betrayed by Judas to a crowd of men with swords and clubs, who had been sent out by the high priest. He was haled before the Sanhedrin and condemned to death by Jewish law for blasphemy. Pilate, when asked to carry out the sentence, passed Jesus over to Herod Antipas, as the governor of Galilee; but Herod sent Jesus back to Pilate. The latter endeavored to procure Jesus' release, the early Christians asserted, by offering him to the crowd in his courtyard as the prisoner to be released to them for that year. But the crowd cried for the release of Barabbas, known to Pilate as a robber, but to them as a Zealot insurrectionist. At their demand, Pilate turned Jesus over for crucifixion. At three o'clock in the afternoon, forsaken by all but the women who would not leave him, amidst a howling mob for whom he breathed out the prayer, "Father, forgive them, for they know not what they do," he cried out with a loud voice, "My God, my God, why have you forsaken me?" and, resigning himself into God's care, expired.

No single death in the world's history has so affected the human imagination. To the Christians who have used the cross as a symbol of their faith, it has seemed that in his willingness to suffer death for the redemption of his fellowmen, Jesus has given to them their clearest insight into the quality of the redemptive love of God himself.

To avoid having the body hanging on the cross over the Sabbath day, Joseph of Arimathaea, a member of the Sanhedrin, offered the use of his empty tomb; and the body of Jesus was taken there.

SUGGESTIONS FOR FURTHER READING

Bornkamm, G. *Jesus of Nazareth*. Trans. Irene and Fraser McLuskey with James M. Robinson. Harper, 1960

Branscomb, H. *The Teachings of Jesus.* Abingdon-Cokesbury, 1931. Available as Apex pb

Bultmann, R. *Jesus and the Word.* Trans. L. P. Smith and E. Huntress. Scribner, 1934. Available as Scribner pb

Dibelius, M. *Jesus.* Trans. Hedrick and Grant. Westminster Press, 1949

Goguel, M. *The Life of Jesus.* Trans. Olive Wyon. Macmillan, 1945. Available in 2 vols. as Harper Torchbooks pb

Jeremias, J. *The Parables of Jesus.* Trans. S. H. Hooke. Scribner, 1955

Klausner, Joseph. *Jesus of Nazareth.* Macmillan, 1925. (A Jewish interpretation)

Major, Manson, and Wright. *The Mission and Message of Jesus.* Dutton, 1946. (Especially the section by Manson)

Ricciotti, G. *The Life of Christ.* Trans. A. L. Zizzamia. Bruce, 1945. (A Catholic interpretation)

Scott, E. F. *The Ethical Teaching of Jesus.* Macmillan, 1923

15 The Religious Development of Christianity

To the Christians of the 1st century the events that followed upon the death of Jesus were of greater importance than those that preceded it. It was true for them that the life and teachings of Jesus were of priceless value for their daily life and thought; but yet his resurrection from the dead was of higher value still, for it was their *proof* of his *living* reality as a person, that is, as the undying Lord of Life who was the assurance of their own immortality and the pledge of their unbreakable spiritual oneness with God the Father.

I THE APOSTOLIC AGE

The Resurrection

At the time of Jesus' arrest in the Garden of Gethsemane the disciples scattered and fled. None of them, except John, dared draw near to the place of crucifixion. Peter had hung about while Jesus was being tried, but on being identified by a maid-servant in the courtyard of the high priest as a follower of Jesus, he denied it. Sick with despair and fear, the disciples remained in hiding during the Sabbath day. On the morning of the third day, some of the women, before starting back to Galilee, sought out the tomb to which the body of Jesus had been taken. They found it empty. When they were about to turn away perplexed, they saw, so they later told the at first unbelieving disciples, an angel who convinced them that Jesus had risen from the dead. Then Peter and others experienced seeing Jesus himself. These experiences were repeated in Galilee, when they returned there. By this time despair had given way to an invincible confidence and hope, which was to spread a great new faith throughout the Mediterranean world.

The earliest extant account of the appearances of Jesus after the resurrection is that of St. Paul. About the year 52 A.D. he wrote to the church he had founded in Corinth:

> Now I want to remind you, brothers. . . . [that] I passed on to you, as of first importance, the account I had received, that Christ died for our sins, as the Scriptures foretold, that he was buried, that on the third day he was raised from the dead, as the Scriptures foretold, and that he was seen by Cephas [Peter], and then by the Twelve. After that he was seen by more than five hundred brothers at one time, most of whom are still alive, although some of them have fallen asleep.* Then he was seen by James, then by all the apostles, and finally he was seen by me also, as though I were born at the wrong time.† [1]

Pentecost

The resurrection appearances convinced the disciples that Jesus had been raised from the dead so that he might soon return on the clouds of heaven as the promised Son of Man who should judge the nations at the great assize of the Last Day. His mission on earth, they now believed, had been to prepare the way for his second coming. So all the disciples who could do so—about one hundred and twenty in number—left Galilee and went to live in Jerusalem, where they met in a large upper room for prayer and counsel. The Book of Acts says that among them were Mary, Jesus' mother, and his brothers. The Apostles were the official leaders of the group, but James, Jesus' brother, soon became a prominent figure.

---

* The early Christians spoke of death as a going to sleep until the Judgment Day.

† The interesting thing about what Paul says next is that he goes on the assumption that Jesus rose in a spiritual body, not in a physical one. "It is so with the resurrection of the dead. The body is sown in decay, it is raised free from decay. . . . It is a physical body that is sown, it is a spiritual body that is raised. . . . I can tell you this, brothers: flesh and blood cannot share in the Kingdom of God, and decay will not share in what is imperishable."—This is not what the Church later declared about the resurrection of Jesus, namely, that it was a resurrection of his physical body; nor is it the view of Luke and John; but it is worth noting that one who was converted two years after Jesus' death should hold it.

The next great moment in their common experience is thus recorded:

On the day of the Harvest Festival [the Jewish festival called Pentecost], they were all meeting together, when suddenly there came from the sky a sound like a violent blast of wind, and it filled the whole house where they were sitting. And they saw tongues like flame separating and settling one on the head of each of them, and they were all filled with the holy Spirit and began to say in foreign languages whatever the Spirit prompted them to utter.[2]

To the early Christians the Resurrection was their proof of the truth of the Gospel, and the descent of the Holy Spirit at Pentecost was their guarantee that the power which was in Jesus Christ their Lord was in them too. The Apostles now took courage and began preaching boldly in the streets where but a few weeks before Jesus had encountered an opposition that had ended in his crucifixion.

They met with startling success. Hundreds of converts joined them. The Pharisees and Sadducees in alarm arrested Peter and John, brought them before the Sanhedrin, and ordered them to cease speaking as they did "in the name of Jesus." But on their release they continued their preaching undeterred. Once more they were arrested, with others of their number, and haled before the Sanhedrin. Reminded that they had been ordered to refrain from speaking in the name of Jesus, Peter and the Apostles, we read, answered: "We must obey God rather than men." [3] During the disturbance that followed one of the leading Pharisees checked the rising anger of the other members of the Sanhedrin by suavely suggesting that fanatical messianic movements always destroy themselves in time; one may therefore safely let them alone. This man was Gamaliel, a grandson of Hillel, and like his grandfather one of the great teachers of the rabbinical schools. He proceeded to draw upon history for his argument: "Men of Israel, take care what you propose to do with these men. For some time ago Theudas appeared, claiming to be a person of importance, and a group of men numbering some four hundred joined him. But he was killed and all his followers were dispersed and disappeared. After him, at the time of the census, Judas of Galilee appeared, and raised a great following, but he too perished, and all his followers were scattered. So in the present case, I tell you, keep away from these men and let them alone, for if this idea or movement is of human origin, it will come to naught, but if it is from God, you will not be able to stop it." [4] This counsel prevailed; the authorities contented themselves with flogging the Apostles, in order to disgrace them in the eyes of the people, and let them go.

The Jerusalem Church

Two factors seem to have saved the Jerusalem Church from annihilating persecution: first, the apostles were followers of a dead leader and might be expected to lose their fervor with the passage of time; and second, the apostles obviously kept all the provisions of the Jewish Law. In fact, the Palestinian followers of Jesus went daily to the Temple and honored the Law of Moses as much as any Jew, requiring circumcision of every convert not already circumcised, as if they were just a Jewish sect. But they had made some unorthodox additions to the accepted faith and practice. They believed that Jesus was the Messiah foretold in the Jewish scriptures and that he would shortly reappear on the clouds of heaven as the Son of Man; they met in private homes, such as the home of John Mark's mother in Jerusalem, for group gatherings, which were devoted to "the breaking of bread and prayers"; the believers shared everything they had with one another, sold their property, and belongings, and divided the proceeds according to their special needs; and they all had a vigorous proselyting spirit, and baptized their converts.

But if it appeared true of the Palestinian followers of Jesus, that they acted as if they were just a Jewish sect, this was not true of all the converts. Some began to take the liberties Jesus had taken with the Law of Moses. The situation was this. There were synagogues in Jerusalem for the Jews who had returned from foreign lands and spoke Greek, and these Greek-speaking Jews were notably less impressed by the Temple sacrifices than the Palestinian Jews, and more given than the latter to stressing the passages in the prophetic writings condemning externalism in the practice of the Law. So when any of the Greek-speaking Jews became Christians they eagerly applied the more radical passages from the Prophets to the life and sayings of Jesus and stressed Jesus' criticism of the practices of the Sadducees and Pharisees.

Tension not only appeared between these Christians and the Jewish authorities, but within the Christian group itself. On the one hand, the apostles began to lose touch with the Greek-speaking radicals. On the other hand, the latter made complaints against the Palestinian Christians "that their [i.e., the Greek-speaking] widows were being neglected in the daily distribution of food." [5] To allay this tension, the whole Christian group met, and solved the problem by appointing from their number seven men who were not Apostles to take charge of the distribution of food and the keeping of accounts. One of these seven was a Greek-speaking man by the name of Stephen, who was a leader of the more libertarian wing of the Christian movement. All went well until the Jewish authorities brought him before the Sanhedrin, condemned him, and stoned him to death.

This violent action signalized the outbreak of a great persecution of the church in Jerusalem. The Jewish authorities apparently directed it against those who did not keep the Jewish law; for the Book of Acts says, "They were all scattered over Judea and Samaria, except the apostles." [6]

Thenceforth the Christian movement in Palestine was to have two parties within it, which never lost their sense of being bound together under the name of Christ, but which struggled with each other for the right to be the final interpreters of what Christianity meant. On the one side stood James, the brother of Jesus, now the chief "pillar" of the Jerusalem church, and with him most of the Apostles. They held that Christians must not only follow Christ, but please God by also obeying the Law of Moses. One of the requirements for which they stood was circumcision, and they sent out their emissaries to the out-lying churches to insist on this requirement being met before baptism. It was also considered necessary to observe the distinctions between clean and unclean, and to refuse to sit down to a meal with the uncircumcised. While some of the members of the Jerusalem church showed a willingness to compromise, the extremists carried their insistence to great lengths. They are often called the Judaizers. In time they formed an exclusive group of Jewish Christians called Ebionites or Nazarenes.

Among the Jerusalem Christians who were disposed to make compromises was Peter. He saw that the Holy Spirit had descended freely upon the more liberal Christians. What was more, on visits to the coast towns he found the new faith spreading among uncircumcised foreigners, and the Holy Spirit had come upon them too. He approved of their being baptized, and sat down to eat with them, without being overly careful concerning the Jewish dietary restrictions. But when he was back in Jerusalem he was severely criticized by the Judaizers, and thereafter vacillated before his narrower brethren, without being able to take a bold stand.*

Yet the more liberal elements in the Christian movement were to win the day and remake the heretical Jewish sect into a powerful independent religion which was to spread rapidly through the gentile world. The leader of the liberals was their onetime fiercest persecutor, a man from Tarsus called Saul (or Paul).

---

* Subsequently, he went to Rome, where presumably he was able to follow a freer course.

*Paul and the Spread of Christianity
to Europe*

Paul has been frequently called "the second founder of Christianity." Certain it is that he fought and defeated the Judaizers, who thereafter steadily lost importance in the Christian movement; but, more important, he developed certain basic theological concepts for stating the spiritual effects of Jesus upon the lives of his followers, concepts which enabled Christianity to win the gentile world. To that world, he brought intact the religion *of* Jesus in the vehicle of a religion *about* Jesus.

All this Paul accomplished only after an early career of fierce opposition to Christianity. He was a Jew of the dispersion, born, about the same time as Jesus, in the town of Tarsus, in Cilicia, then an important city, and the seat of a university where the Stoic and Cynic philosophies were taught. Probably Paul here learned something of the Greek mystery-cults and the desire of their adherents to achieve immortality by identification with dying and rising savior-gods. His family was apparently well-off, for his parents had purchased Roman citizenship, and he therefore had the legal status of a free-born Roman. But he reacted adversely to the religious ideas of his Hellenistic environment, and remained a strict Pharisee. Filled with an earnest desire for "the righteousness which is from the Law," he went to Jerusalem and "sat at the feet" of Gamaliel, the leading Pharisaic teacher. Of this period of his life he later wrote: "I surpassed many of my own age among my people in my devotion to Judaism, I was so fanatically devoted to what my forefathers had handed down." [7] He joined furiously in the persecution of the early Church. He was present as an approving spectator at the stoning of Stephen.

When the Christian believers fled northward to Damascus and beyond, he went to the high priest and asked for letters to the synagogues in Damascus, "so that if he found any men or women there who belonged to the Way, he might bring them in chains to Jerusalem." "But," says the Book of Acts, "as he was approaching Damascus, a sudden light flashed around him from heaven, and he fell to the ground. Then he heard a voice saying to him, 'Saul! Saul! Why do you persecute me?'" [8] Blinded by the bright vision, Paul was led by the hand into Damascus, where for three days he could not see, and neither ate nor drank. He believed that the resurrected Jesus, in whom the Christians now centered their faith, had appeared also to him.

So vast a change in Paul's life was now made necessary, that he went off into upper Arabia to think things through. Then he returned to Damascus. He became a Christian leader not only there but also far to the north at Antioch, the third largest city in the Roman Empire, where the new religion was making many converts among the Gentiles. Except for a two week's visit to Jerusalem, after three years, to become personally acquainted with Peter and James, he confined himself to the districts of Syria and Cilicia. Then he set out on his famous missionary journeys, accompanied by men like Barnabas and John Mark. On his first journey he sailed to the island of Cyprus, traveled through it from end to end, embarked for Asia Minor, and established self-propagating Christian groups at Perga, Antioch in Pisidia, Iconium, Lystra, and Derbe. On his second journey he revisited the churches he had already established, and then proceeded to Troas (ancient Troy), whence he sailed to Macedonia on the continent of Europe. After establishing congregations in the principal cities along the coast, he went south to Athens, and then to Corinth, where he founded an important church. On his return he sailed to Ephesus, in Ionia, before going home. His third journey took him around the same circuit.

Although he suffered from some physical malady, which he refers to as "a thorn in the flesh," in these journeys he displayed tremendous energy, zeal, and courage. His strength abounded, he said, because when he felt physically weak, he threw himself upon the strength of Christ, who dwelt within him.

Five times (he wrote) I have been given one less than forty lashes, by the Jews. I have been beaten three times by the Romans, I have been stoned once, I have been ship-wrecked three times, a night and a day I have been adrift at sea; with my frequent journeys, [I have been] in danger from rivers, danger from robbers, danger from my own people, danger from the heathen, danger in the city, danger in the desert, danger at sea, danger from false brothers, through toil and hardship, through many a sleepless night, through hunger and thirst, often without food, and exposed to cold.[9]

Two great spiritual facts animated Paul and gave him his dynamic faith: the "Lordship of Christ Jesus," and "the freedom of the Spirit."

He came to know the freedom of the Spirit during the early days of his conversion. The Christians of Syria and Cilicia were for the most part uncircumcised and without the knowledge of the Jewish Law. In his great hunger to know the secret of true righteousness, Paul had long held the Law (the Torah) to be the one and only condition of a good life enjoying the Lord's favor. But now he was surprised and delighted to discover that those who followed Christ were, quite apart from the Law, more profoundly good than those who obeyed the Law. The righteousness which was in Christ was greater than the righteousness which was from the Law. The reason was, that Christ changed a man's inward disposition and gave him the right relationship to his fellowmen and to God, so that he did what is right from the heart, without having to refer constantly to outward legal requirements. Love was the fulfilment of the Law. Therefore the weary bondage of the Law could be cast aside for the freedom of the Spirit. There was no further need, Paul declared, for circumcision, dietary restrictions, and distinctions between clean and unclean.

It was at this point that the Judaizers came into conflict with Paul. He had it out with Peter, James, and John at Jerusalem, and they gave him their cooperation on the basis that he was to consider himself called to work among the uncircumcised, while they were called to work among the circumcised. At the same time they were not willing to yield all, but insisted on the compromise that the Gentiles need not be circumcised, if they pledged themselves to be chaste, to eat no meat that had been sacrificed to idols, and to refrain from the meat of strangled animals and the tasting of blood. This compromise was a great victory for Paul, for it meant that the Christians would no longer be asked to regard the Jewish Law as in all respects binding.

The Lordship of Christ was another article of faith at the heart of Paul's conviction. To him it meant more even than the messiahship of Jesus. He had joyously accepted Jesus as the messianic savior who had inaugurated the Kingdom of God and would soon return on the clouds of heaven to judge the quick and the dead on the Last Day; but as a missionary to the Gentiles (to whom the messiahship of Jesus, a purely Jewish concept, meant little) he was quick to see and to herald the power of Christ to redeem individuals from sin and death by uniting them to himself by faith. And here Paul made an original contribution to the interpretation of Christ's death and resurrection. Christ, he ardently declared, was a divine being who possessed the nature of God, but who had humbled himself and come down from heaven and assumed human form, and, humbling himself still further, died on the cross, in order that he might rise again, after his victory over death, to the right hand of God as the Lord of life and death. In setting forth this new and glorious mystery, Paul ascribed unqualified divinity to the pre-existent Christ: "He is a likeness of the unseen God, born before any creature, for it was through him that everything was created in heaven and earth, the seen and the unseen, angelic thrones, dominions, principalities, authorities,—all things were created through and for him." [10]

By this great conception—through which Paul expressed his intuition that Jesus was the expression in human history of God's redemptive spirit and love at work since the dawn of creation—Paul quite captivated the Gentiles. They had been brought up under the influence of the Greek mystery religions, which, as we have seen, satisfied the yearning for immortality by providing an experience of union with a resurrected savior-god, thereby deifying and immortalizing the corrupt and perishable self.° But Paul's conception was far more profound and regenerative than any they had known. He not only offered assurance of immortality through union with Christ but provided a means of salvation from guilt and sin in this life; for Christ the deified Lord of life and death had been the blameless Jesus of Nazareth of Galilee, who had proclaimed a high and noble ethics that led to individual and social remaking on the moral plane. Thus mysticism and ethics were in Paul's teaching one and inseparable. To follow Christ meant not only identifying oneself with him through baptism, the Lord's Supper, and the ecstasy of speaking with tongues, but, even more, doing as Jesus did, living as he did.†

This was important in the development of Christianity, for here Paul saved it from an extreme—that of non-ethical mysticism—as dangerous to its balance and truth as the extreme of legalism from which he had earlier rescued it.

The letters which Paul sent to the churches he established furnish abundant proof of the importance he attached to ethics. With eagle eye he watched over his congregations and scolded them like a father for every infraction of the high Christian code of morality. He was far from believing that a capacity for religious ecstasy covers a multitude of sins.

His generosity toward his Christian brethren in Jerusalem brought to a sudden end his missionary career. He had taken upon himself the obligation to raise a collection for the poor in the Jerusalem church, and having done so, carried the funds to Jerusalem himself. Here he ran afoul of the Jews, who mobbed him, and caused his arrest. As a Roman citizen, he appealed to Caesar, anxious as he was at any rate to get to Rome. He

---

° To help them to understand properly the significance of the redemption which Christ wrought in their lives, Paul put it thus: by the mystical experience of baptism, those who believe may identify themselves with Christ in his death and resurrection; for "through baptism we have been buried with him in death, so that just as he was raised from the dead through the Father's glory, we too may live a new life." "You must think of yourselves as dead to sin but alive to God, through union with Christ Jesus" (Romans 6:4, 11).

† "If I can speak the languages of men and even of angels, but have no love, I am only a noisy gong or a clashing cymbal. . . . I want you all to speak ecstatically. . . . But in public worship I would rather say five words with my understanding so as to instruct others also than ten thousand words in an ecstasy" (I Cor. 13:1; 14:5, 19).

was taken, under arrest, to the Imperial City; but if he expected to be
released after his trial, he was disappointed. The authorities continued
to hold him in custody. He had time to write letters to churches and
individuals, but after a period of confinement whose length is not known,
he was executed as a troublesome character, a disturber of the Roman
peace.

But he had by this time fully demonstrated the power of the Christian religion to bring together Jew, Greek, and Roman; mystic, legalist,
and rationalist; all under a common sense of their vital spiritual community in Christ. To such of the culturally divided and spiritually drifting people of the Roman Empire as heard them, words like these from
the powerful letter to the Ephesians—a letter which some scholars now
attribute to a follower of Paul rather than to him, but which in any
case is warmed and vitalized by his spirit—contained "good news":

> You also were dead because of the offenses and sins in the midst of
> which you once lived under the control of the present age of the world. . . .
> We all lived among them once, indulging our physical cravings and obeying
> the impulses of our lower nature and its thoughts, and by nature we were
> doomed to God's wrath like other men. But God is so rich in mercy that
> because of the great love he had for us, he made us, dead as we were
> through our offenses, live again with the Christ. It is by his mercy that you
> have been saved. . . . It is not by your own action, it is the gift of God. It
> has not been earned, so that no one can boast of it. . . .
>
> So remember that you were once physically heathen. . . . At that time
> you had no connection with Christ, you were aliens to the commonwealth
> of Israel . . . ; with no hope and no God in all the world. But now through
> your union with Christ Jesus you who were once far away have through the
> blood of Christ been brought near. For he is our peace. He has united the
> two divisions, and broken down the barrier that kept us apart; . . . for it
> is through him that we both with one Spirit are now able to approach
> the Father. So you are no longer foreigners or strangers, but you are fellow-
> citizens of God's people and members of his family.[11]

II   THE EARLY CHURCH (50–150 A.D.)

The World-Spread of the Early Christian Communities

But in calling Paul "the second founder of Christianity" we should
not exaggerate his immediate influence. Before his time other leaders

than he successfully carried Christianity to Antioch, Alexandria, and Rome. Besides the Apostles we hear of Barnabas, Symeon Niger, Lucius the Cyrenian, Manaen "who had been brought up with Herod the governor," Apollos, and others; all actively engaged in organizing new Christian churches. So rapidly, in fact, were Christian converts springing up along the coasts of the eastern Mediterranean, that it was Paul's ambition to proceed from Rome to Spain, in order to carry Christianity to the farthest bounds of the known world.

The chief successes of early Christianity were in the commercial centers of the Roman Empire, largely because there were synagogues, or at least Jewish quarters, in them, and the Christian message could make its best appeal in places where the Jewish religion was already known. But when the orthodox Jewish communities rejected the new faith, and refused to harbor it, independent Christian communities sprang up among the tradesmen and working people of the great cities and towns, first among the Greek-speaking citizens and then among those who spoke other languages. And not only did the new religion spread westward; it was also carried to the Tigris-Euphrates valley and into Ethiopia.

Opposition and Persecution

By the middle of the 2nd century the Christian religion had become a major problem to the governors of the Roman provinces, especially in Syria and Asia Minor. For one thing the Romans disliked mystery and secrecy. For another the Christians considered themselves *in* the world but not *of* it. Though a few of them here and there joined the armed services of the Roman Empire and took office in the administrative branches of the government, the greater number dissociated themselves from all worldly power. In purely secular matters they were obedient, but on the whole indifferent, to the civil authority. But they absolutely refused to take part in the official patriotic cult which required citizens to take an oath "by the genius" (the divine spirit) of the emperor and to offer incense and wine in honor of the emperor's godhead on the altar before his image. This refusal was a particularly sore point with the Roman administrative officials, less for religious reasons than because it signified disloyalty and rebellion. Moreover, the Christians met secretly, almost always at daybreak or at night, because so many of them were employed during the day. Distorted conceptions of their worship "orgies" were current. The Christians were accused of sexual perversions ("love-feasts") and cannibalism, the eating of human flesh. ("Take, eat; this is my body . . . this is my blood.") In addition, their staying away from theaters, gladiatorial combats, and popular festivals, was interpreted as narrow and intolerant, and aroused rage. "The Christians to the lions!" became a common cry.

A classic expression of official perplexity is contained in the letters of Pliny the Younger, governor of Bithynia (in Asia Minor), to the Roman emperor Trajan. Wrote he:

> It is my custom, my lord, to refer to you all questions about which I have doubts. . . . I have no little uncertainty whether pardon is granted on repentance, or whether when one has been a Christian there is no gain to him in that he has ceased to be such; whether the mere name, without crimes, or crimes connected with the name are punished. . . . Those who were accused before me as Christians . . . asserted that the amount of their fault or error was this: that they had been accustomed to assemble on a fixed day before daylight and sing by turns a hymn to Christ as a god; and that they bound themselves with an oath, not for any crime, but to commit neither theft, nor robbery, nor adultery, not to break their word and not to deny a deposit when demanded; after these things were done, it was their custom to depart and meet together again to take food, but ordinary and harmless food; and they said that even this had ceased after my edict was issued, by which, according to your commands, I had forbidden the existence of clubs. On this account I believed it the more necessary to find out from two maid-servants, who were called deaconesses, and that by torture, what was the truth. I found nothing else than a perverse and excessive superstition. I therefore adjourned the examination and hastened to consult you. The matter seemed to me to be worth deliberation.[12]

Pliny reported, however, that when he found Christians who persisted three times over in saying they were Christians, he ordered them to be executed; "for," said he blandly, "I did not doubt that, whatever it was they admitted, obstinacy and unbending perversity certainly deserve to be punished!"

Christians were publicly done to death in Rome as early as 64 A.D., in the time of Nero. During the century that followed, Roman officials frequently made examples of Christians who refused to worship Caesar's image by throwing them to the lions or burning them at the stake. The number of martyrs was not large, perhaps; but the public commotion was sometimes great, and had far-reaching effects both on the Christians themselves and on the public at large, especially in sharpening the feeling that the Christian religion was to its adherents not only worth living by but dying for as well.

Developments in Worship and Ecclesiastical Organization

Meanwhile the Christian communities were developing into self-contained units with an organized life of their own.

At the time of the Apostle Paul, when the Christians were beginning to look upon themselves as a church called out of the world into a separate fellowship, their services were of two kinds: (1) meetings on the model of synagogue services, open to inquirers as well as believers, and consisting of readings from the Jewish scriptures,* prayer, preaching, and the singing of psalms; and (2) the *agapé* or "love feast," for the believers only, an evening meal in which all present shared, and during which a brief ceremony, recalling the Last Supper, commemorated the sacrifice of Jesus' body and blood. Since this ceremony was couched in terms of thanksgiving, the Greek name for it was *eucharist* ("the giving of thanks").

As the Christian communities grew larger, the common meal was gradually discontinued as impracticable; and the Lord's Supper was observed thereafter at the conclusion of the public portion of the Sunday services, when the unbaptized withdrew in order that the baptized might celebrate together this inner mystery of the Christian faith.

At the same time entrance into the Christian community was formalized into definite steps. Candidates for church membership, of all ages, were first given a systematic course of instruction and testing (catechization), lasting for several months and ending in the rite of baptism, by immersion or sprinkling. (Commonly the catechizing was during Lent and the baptizing at Easter.) The believers appeared in white robes for their baptism; and that rite was followed by confirmation or the laying on of hands, that the Holy Spirit might descend upon each new member. After the laying on of hands came unction (anointing with oil), concluded with making the sign of the cross, while each new member vowed to give up the old gods, and the old morality, and to follow the law of Christ, in perfect assurance of faith.

At first the churches were loosely organized; but by the end of the 1st century the congregations were directed by a board of elders, including one or more superintendents or "bishops." These officers were assisted by deacons. Preaching and instruction were still, however, in the hands of prophets and teachers, who either belonged to the congregation or came from elsewhere, perhaps as traveling evangelists. Out

* Not until the 2nd century were the Jewish scriptures supplemented with readings from the Gospels and Epistles.

of this type of government, there very naturally developed a more rigid and centralized form of organization. By the first quarter of the 2nd century we read of congregations being headed by a single bishop, assisted by elders and deacons; and, when this became general, this permanent head of the congregation included among his functions those of teaching and preaching, with the result that the prophets and traveling evangelists of the early church gradually disappeared from church life.

Doctrinal Developments to the Year 150 A.D.

Growth in doctrine more than matched the growth in institutional forms.

By the year 100 A.D. a Christian literature distinct from that of the Old Testament and in some respects consciously designed to serve as a new scripture (it eventually became the New Testament) had come into being. Its appearance had become necessary with the gradual fading of the first generation's expectation of the imminent return of Jesus on the clouds of heaven—a faith which had once made the writing of a scripture seem superfluous. The eye-witnesses of Jesus' ministry were rapidly dying off by the time fifty years had passed, and the second generation Christians, most of whom now lived far from Jerusalem, demanded a record of the Master's life and teachings. The destruction of Jerusalem in 70 A.D. increased the urgency of this demand.

In the introduction to the previous chapter we reviewed the beginning of this literature. Something further needs to be said here about the nature and content of the completed literature which sprang from these beginnings; for each portion of it is significant of the greater and greater estimates placed upon Jesus' teaching and person as time went on; and all combine to give us a sense of the factors, both Jewish and Greek, which operated in the 1st century of Christian history to make Christianity a great and rich religion.

Of the earliest portions of the New Testament—the epistles of Paul —we need say nothing more, since their doctrinal significance has already been discussed; so it is to the Gospels that we first turn, for each had a distinct Christological purpose in view.

The Gospel of Mark, the earliest and briefest of the gospels, was probably written in Antioch during the years 65–70. According to Papias, a Christian writer of the early 2nd century, it was based upon the recollections of St. Peter as set down by John Mark, who had lived in Jerusalem before he came to Antioch. This gospel shows no interest in

Jesus' birth and youth, but begins with his baptism and gives a vivid account of his ministry, with pointed descriptions of his human feelings. But Jesus is much more than a human being in Mark; he is the Son of God through the experience of divine adoption at his baptism, and the true Messiah, the "Holy One of God." No doctrine of divine incarnation nor any conception of pre-existence such as Paul exhibits are found, however.

Matthew and Luke, going further, provide a basis for the doctrine of the incarnation. Both relate the stories of the Virgin Birth and of supernatural incidents occurring during Jesus' infancy. They concentrate throughout on the divine character of the messiahship of Jesus and the manner in which, as one who came from heaven, he fulfilled Hebrew prophecy of the coming of the Son of Man.

But it is in the Fourth Gospel that we find the divine character of Jesus most clearly presented. The writer sought to write a gospel that would find the living, subjectively experienced Lord of Paul in the historic objectively known Jesus of the Synoptic Gospels. The fundamental thesis of this gospel is, "The Word (the Logos) became flesh and blood and lived for a while among us, . . . and we saw the honor God had given him, such honor as an only son receives from his father." [13] Though we are not allowed to forget the man Jesus who was an objective personage in a world of real persons and things, the divinity of Jesus is the characteristic note of this gospel. Jesus Christ is above all else "the Son of God." He is more than the Son of God in the Hebrew sense of being the Messiah; for, though this simpler messianic significance is implicit, it is merged, even submerged, in the more comprehensive meanings found in the prologue of the gospel. There Christ is represented as the visible bodying forth of the creative impulsion (the Logos) of the unseen and eternal Father and the mode or manifestation in a human person of the love of the Father for men. The Fourth Gospel therefore follows Paul in thinking of Christ as personally come from God, that is, from a state of pre-existence; and connects him not only with the work of redemption on earth but with the creation of the world. In the body of the gospel he is represented as remembering his pre-incarnate life, or at least that he had a pre-incarnate life. This pre-existence, and not his human experience, accounts for his knowledge of God, to whom, therefore, he bears "true" witness; since, having come from heaven, "it is to what he has seen and heard that he gives testimony." What is more, not only are his words "the words of God," but he is himself the Word (the Logos); he is himself that to which he bears witness. To know him is to know the Father.

The Epistle to the Hebrews, written in the decade before the Fourth Gospel, does not use the term Logos (Word), but it is apparent that the writer had something like it in mind. In the first sentence he says that God, who spoke fragmentarily through the Prophets, has now spoken to us fully "in a Son, whom he had destined to possess everything, and through whom he had made the world." The Son while on earth resembled his human brethren in every respect; he shared their flesh and blood, and participated in their nature, even to suffering temptation and agonizing "with tears"; but, because in his essential nature he was divine, his spiritual and psychological endowment was unique. The human Jesus and the divine Father were mutually accessible to each other at all times. In this Jesus differed from his brethren, who can have no such free access to the Father without his mediation as High Priest.

A simpler and less doctrinal conception of the person and work of Christ appeared in the epistles of James and Peter, and in the non-canonical writings of the so-called Apostolic Fathers: Clement of Rome (writing ca. 93–97); Hermas of Rome (ca. 115–140); and the authors of such works as *The Epistle of Barnabas* (ca. 130), *Second Clement* (ca. 160), and *The Teachings of the Twelve Apostles* (ca. 130–160). For the most part, these various writings gave expression to a straightforward adoration of Christ as the heaven-descended revealer of the true nature of God and the giver of a new law of life on the loftiest ethical plane.

Addressed directly not to the religious needs of the growing Christian communities but rather to the world at large were the writings of the Apologists. These were men educated in the best Greek and Roman schools and well versed in ancient philosophy, who sent their defences of Christianity to the Roman emperors or to other non-Christians of high rank and reputation. Among their number were Aristides of Athens; Melito, bishop of Sardis; Minucius Felix, a cultivated gentleman of Rome; and most famous of all, Justin, called the Martyr, because of the nature of his death, who, like his disciple, Tatian, had been successively a Stoic, Aristotelian, Pythagorean, and Platonist. When he turned Christian, he found in his new faith the perfect philosophy. He was far from believing that all other thought-systems were untrue. The divine Logos was at work in the world before the time of Christ, enlightening Socrates and Heraclitus, and imparting truth to such "barbarians" (a truly Greek expression) as the patriarchs of the Old Testament; so that the Greek philosophers and the Hebrew prophets, insofar as the Logos enlightened them, were so far forth Christians before Christ. But Christianity was superior to all other thought-systems, because the Logos not only spoke through Christ; the Logos *was* Christ. Christ perfectly revealed the truth of Divine Reason, and was the peerless Teacher whom all humanity should accept.

The significance of Justin Martyr and his fellow apologists is, that they successfully demonstrated how Christianity, when it chose to appear in Greek dress, could, at whatever sacrifice of its original Hebraic form, not only continue to make a powerful religious appeal, but hold its own with any of the classic philosophies of the ancient world—Platonism and Stoicism especially. It became easier now for Christian writers to invade the field of general philosophy, and to speak of the Christian religion as truly universal in its scope and application—"catholic" was the word they used.

III   THE ANCIENT CATHOLIC CHURCH
   (*150–1054 A.D.*)

The word "catholic" was first applied to the Christian Church in its meaning of "universal." Descriptively, this was an apt designation for a religious faith that now reached into all the provinces of the Empire and into every class of society. But it was too good an adjective to escape a more technical use. It became, in fact, part of the name of *the single* organized institution that expressed the Christian religion after the middle of the 2nd century. With this name, the Catholic Church could stand united in the resolve to maintain itself against its external foes and also to combat heresy and schism within.

In striving to keep both its outer and inner integrity, the ancient Catholic Church developed two things: (1) a system of doctrine, clarified, purged of error, and declared to be orthodox, and (2) an ecclesiastical organization characterized in its own eyes by apostolicity, catholicity, unity, and holiness. We shall now describe the several steps by which these developments were effected.

The Gnostic and Marcionite Heresies

It was Jesus' fortune to appear not only at a time when the Jews were looking for a Messiah, but when the rest of the world was seeking an incarnation of godhead and had, at the same time, evolved the concept of the Logos, without realizing with what richness of meaning it might be endowed were it to be applied to a savior-god appearing in the flesh of a human personality. When Christian thinkers brought the Logos-concept to bear upon Jesus, a whole theology sprang, almost without effort, into being, a theology which combined in the most satisfactory measure both religion and philosophy. Yet there were dangers in the process. A just balance of elements had to be preserved, or the religious value of the new synthesis would be destroyed. It became the task of the Christian bishops and teachers of the 2nd and 3rd centuries to find that balance, and to outlaw all deviations from the orthodox view.

Among the interpretations of the work and person of Christ during the 2nd century that were later declared heretical were the Gnostic and Marcionite doctrines.

The view called Gnosticism (from *gnosis* or saving knowledge) had a marked characteristic running through all its varieties: instead of assimilating philosophy to the Christian religion it adopted the figure of Christ as the final ingredient of a Greco-Oriental syncretism. The Gnostics started with a dualism which radically divided spirit from matter, and regarded the material world as so vile and degrading that God could have had nothing to do with making it. Surrounded by a society of male and female spiritual beings, called *aeons,* the pre-existent Jesus among them, God dwelt far above the evil world. At a lower level lived and labored the creator of the earth, the Jehovah of the Old Testament, a spiritual vulgarian, who produced the evil mass that is the world of matter. The Old Testament and its way of life is hopelessly infected with Jehovah's inferior conception of things. To the Gnostics the serpent in the Garden of Eden, in bringing Adam and Eve to the Tree of Knowledge (that is, of Gnosis!), was a benefactor, not a vile tempter, and did his best to save the parents of the human race from Jehovah's misleading guidance! When Jesus, the compassionate divine aeon, saw how badly things were going on earth, he came down in the masquerade of a body (but his flesh could not have been real, it was appearance merely*), and showed the human souls struggling in their defiling envelopes of flesh how, by an ascetic discipline of the body and the acquisition of saving wisdom for the mind, they could free themselves from their bondage in the material world and gain immortality by an escape from the flesh into pure spirituality of being.

Here were doctrines which the Church as a whole felt indeed it could not countenance without violence to its own historic foundations: that God does not control the entire universe; that the Jehovah of the Old Testament is an inferior being; that the Old Testament must be

---

* This view, called Docetism, was an early heresy, not confined to the Gnostics.

rejected as valueless; that Jesus was not really born and did not truly suffer and die; and that there can be no resurrection of the flesh.

The suggestion that the Old Testament is valueless found, however, a tempestuous advocate in a citizen of Rome, called Marcion. Without joining any of the Gnostic schools (which flourished chiefly in Egypt and Asia Minor), he nevertheless followed their lead in excoriating the God of the Old Testament as a cruelly legalistic and merciless deity, who, though he created the material world, was of an inferior moral quality. The really good God, who created the invisible, spiritual world, was not known to the prophets of the Old Testament; Christ was the first to reveal him. Men are in bondage to the bodies they have received from the God of the Old Testament, but their souls may find redemption through faith in the God of Jesus. Let them then follow Christ and St. Paul in asceticism, celibacy, and scorn of the physical world, and strive to enter the kingdom of the good God, here and hereafter. Marcion increased the alarm his views created by attempting to provide a scripture for his followers; in doing which he edited and brought together the writings of Paul, and the Gospel of Luke, but first expurgated all passages linking Jesus with the God of the Old Testament. Furthermore, he broke away from the church at Rome, and organized a new congregation.

This kind of thing aroused the Christian world to inquire into its basic positions.

The Answer of the Church: The Apostles' Creed and the Canon of the New Testament

The first clear voice within the Church to propose a program for dealing with heretical opinions was Irenaeus, a native of Asia Minor, and the bishop of Lyons (in the province of Gaul). About 185 A.D. he issued a famous book, *Against the Heresies*. It was of determinative importance. In it he argued that the sign of a sound Christian doctrine is its apostolicity. The Apostles had perfect knowledge, and what is not in agreement with their teachings as transmitted in the Gospels and Epistles cannot be accepted. By this touchstone Gnosticism and Marcionism stood condemned. To the retort that Jesus must have imparted a private and esoteric teaching to an elect few—a claim made by the Gnostics—Irenaeus replied that such private wisdom, if it ever existed, would have had to be handed down through the churches founded by apostles; yet, he pointed out, the churches of apostolic foundation had no such traditions. On the whole, then, Irenaeus urged, one must go for sound doctrine to the apostolic writings, the apostolic churches, and their bishops.

This was the answer that appealed to the churches of the West. It was especially pleasing to the church at Rome, where between 150 and 175 A.D. a creed for use at baptism had been framed to oppose the Gnostic and Marcionite doctrines. It came to be called, in accordance with Irenaeus' criterion of orthodoxy, *The Apostles' Creed,* and in its early form it ran (the crucial words being here italicized) as follows:

I believe in God the Father *Almighty* °;

And in Jesus Christ, his *only begotten* Son, our Lord, who was *born* of the Holy Spirit and the Virgin Mary, *crucified* under Pontius Pilate and *buried;* the third day he rose from the dead, ascended into heaven, being seated at the right hand of the Father, whence he shall come to judge the living and the dead;

And in the Holy Spirit, holy Church, forgiveness of sins, and *the resurrection of the flesh.*[14]

The later emendations and refinements of this creed sharpened its significance as a summary of orthodox and apostolic doctrine.

Another result of the Church's attempt to define apostolic tradition was an endeavor to fix a canon of authentic scripture. By the end of the 2nd century the present New Testament canon was virtually agreed upon.† The books now in the New Testament apocrypha were excluded from the canon when a careful weighing of their value had thrown doubt on their apostolicity.

The Church was by these measures placed in a position to preserve itself from dissolution into countless sects, "borne about by every wind of doctrine" and doomed to quick disappearance.

The Triumph of Christianity as the Imperial State Church

Meanwhile the central Roman government remained officially opposed to Christianity. It had come to realize during the 2nd century that the growing Christian Church was the institutional expression of a powerful new religion in the Empire, and that it presented an increasingly

---

° In order to make the point against the Gnostics clear there was added later the phrase: "Maker of heaven and earth."

† This is roughly true, though the canon was not finally fixed until 400 in the West and still later in the East. Several books were removed from the original list, others added.

serious challenge to the old pagan faiths. Since the latter had given to the Roman and Greek civilizations their distinctive moral and spiritual tone, it began to trouble the government, and the schools, that the old religious values were now threatened with total overthrow. Would the Empire survive? The barbarian hordes that were poised along the Danube and the Rhine, ready to come plunging into the Empire whenever the restraints were relaxed, would not be resisted by the pacifist Christians—nor by the Romans themselves, should they be even partially infected by Christian pietism and otherworldliness. Something had to be done. Therefore Marcus Aurelius (161–180 A.D.), himself an admirable person imbued with the highest ideals of Stoicism, initiated during the last years of his reign severe persecutions of Christians in the provinces. Septimus Severus, Caracalla, and Maximimus followed with like attempts to curb the Christian movement.

But not until the middle of the 3rd century did the central government become thoroughly alarmed. The Emperor Decius, returning from the endangered frontier, and sensing in the apathy of the people to their peril weaknesses due to Christianity, issued an order in 250 that every citizen of the Empire must be required to get a certificate from a government official affirming that he had sacrificed to the emperor's image. Failure to possess such a certificate was to be visited with death. In the persecutions that followed there were conspicuous martyrs, the bishops of Rome and Antioch among them. Multitudes were painfully tortured, and yet refused to yield. A great many others surrendered to the government's pressure, whether through fear or weakness, and joined the number of "the lapsed," as the more faithful Christians called them. Still others bribed officials to issue them certificates without their actually having sacrificed in the prescribed manner. In the eyes of the loyal "confessors" they, too, were apostate. The persecution soon ended, and most of the apostates tried to get back into the Church; with the result that some of the stricter Christians created schisms in the churches in protest against the readmission of the returning penitents.* Under the Emperor Valerian the persecutions were fiercely renewed; much church property was confiscated and many among the higher clergy met martyrdom; but when the emperor fell a prisoner to the Persians his orders were rescinded. A final terrible persecution began under Diocletian in 303; successive decrees ordered all churches destroyed, Christian scriptures confiscated, bishops and lesser clergy put to the torture until they

---

* One such schism at Rome was widely discussed. During the persecutions under Diocletian a similar and more widespread schism developed in North Africa and persisted until the Moslem invasion.

sacrificed to Caesar's image, and ordinary Christians forced to sacrifice likewise. But before the persecutions had gone very far Diocletian retired from the burdens of office, and left four coordinate "Caesars" in control. Thereafter the persecutions became more sporadic. Clashes between the caesars soon upset the balance between them, and the son of one of them, a man favorable to Christianity, named Constantine, finally overcame all opposition and became in 323 the sole ruler of the Empire.

Constantine changed the entire situation. Already in 313 he had issued jointly with another contender for power an edict granting freedom of conscience to Christians and equality with other religions to Christianity. Constantine was said to have affirmed meanwhile—whether truthfully or not—that early in his upward struggle he had seen in the heavens the cross of Christ with the inscription "In hoc signo vinces" ("In this sign you shall conquer"); and although he was not baptized, he had vowed to rest his hopes of conquest in the Christian God.* When, therefore, Constantine became undisputed emperor, he set himself to the task of strengthening the Catholic Church. Not only did he restore to the Church its lost properties; he put it in the way of increasing its holdings. He frowned upon heretical sects and sought to heal all schisms; for he wanted unity in the Empire, and hoped to obtain it through a united Christendom. He made the Christian Sunday a legal holiday. He built new churches and ordered others built at pagan expense. Indeed, his interest was almost too great; it amounted to a form of active control. His successors followed in his steps. Christianity was declared in 383 the imperial state religion.

The Arian Controversy and the Nicene Creed

While all these events were in progress, the theological formulation of the Catholic faith had gone steadily forward. Tertullian and Cyprian in North Africa, Clement and Origen in Alexandria, began to clarify and define the still inchoate doctrines concerning the relation of Father, Son and Holy Spirit, and to set forth the claims of the Church to power and authority. But lack of complete agreement among them gave scope to acrimonious disputes.

* This may be a legend with only general truth to sustain it.

Constantine felt that the issues had to be settled by a world council of the churches. The circumstances were these. A learned presbyter of Alexandria, called Arius, differed with his bishop on the question of whether Christ was a finite or an eternal being. Arius held that Christ, even as the Logos, was a created being; he was made like other creatures out of nothing, and so he could not be eternal; neither could he be of the same substance as God. The Son, he argued, had a beginning, while God was without beginning. Arius' bishop took issue with him hotly, asserting that the Son was eternal, uncreated, and of like essence with God. Summoning a synod, the bishop had Arius deposed; but this only caused the controversy to spread all over the East. This was in 321; and Constantine, after failing in conciliatory efforts, called a council of the whole Church to settle the issue once and for all. In the summer of 325 some three hundred delegate bishops, mostly from the East, met at Nicaea, across the Bosphorus from Constantinople, and produced the famous formula of the Creed of Nicaea. With its crucial phrases italicized, its text was:

We believe in one God, Father Almighty, maker of all things, visible and invisible. And in one Lord Jesus Christ, the Son of God, begotten of [literally, "out of"] the Father, as His only Son, that is, from the substance of the Father, God from God, light from light, true God from true God, *begotten, not made, of the same substance* [*homo-ousios*] *with the Father*, through whom all things in heaven and earth were made; who for us men and our salvation came down and was made flesh, became man, suffered, and rose on the third day, ascended to heaven, and is coming to judge the living and the dead. And (we believe) in the Holy Spirit.

Attached to this creed was a rider declaring anathema those who say, "There was a time when he was not" or assert, "The Son of God is of a different subsistence or substance, or is created."

This creed, adopted under pressure from the emperor, who wanted peace, did not immediately solve the doctrinal difficulties or save the peace. The phrases we have italicized were bitterly denounced by many, and were actually revoked by later councils; ° indeed it was perhaps only the ardent, indefatigable, and patient defence of it by Athanasius, bishop of Alexandria, in tract after tract, that finally overbore opposition, and led to its ultimate acceptance. And even then it was several

° One such council substituted for the homo-ousios of the Creed of Nicaea homoiousios, that is, "of *like* substance." "We call the Son *like* the Father, as the holy scriptures call him and teach." [15] But the decision of this council did not stand. The Church later went back to the Nicene formula.

generations before it became sacrosanct and infallible in the eyes of the Church.*

What Athanasius successfully urged upon his at first unbelieving contemporaries in the East was that the issue at stake was no mere verbal matter, no question of words; it was the issue of whether Christ is truly a savior. For the East in general held to the Greek conception of salvation, that it consists in making divine and immortal the sinful mortality of the human being. Athanasius was eventually able to convince the East that only God can bring immortal life down into the realm of mortality; and so Jesus must have been true God, truly so in substance or essence, not just a created being of lower quality, as Arius had urged.

The Christological Controversies and the Creed of Chalcedon

The story of theological difficulties is not ended. Other issues now arose to divide the mind of Christendom. When the Creed of Nicaea laid down the dogma that the Logos or Christ was not of a lower grade of deity but equal in divinity with God the Father, it said nothing about the mode of union of the divine Logos with the human Jesus. So the incarnation itself now became the center of heated theological argument.

Once the distinction was drawn between the divine and the human natures of Christ, it was possible to regard them as being so distinct as to make it difficult to account for Jesus' unified personality; and on the other hand, it was equally easy to see such a dominance of the one nature over the other as to suggest the absorption of the one nature in the other.

The West had no great difficulty here; for among the definitive statements of Tertullian, made over a century earlier, was the generally accepted formula: "We see (in Christ) a twofold state, not confounded but conjoined in one person, Jesus, God and man." [16] The practical-minded West puzzled over the matter no further.

* The familiar *Nicene Creed* which is recited in certain Christian churches today, it should be said, is not the original creed adopted at Nicaea in 325, but an expanded form of it (often called the "Constantinopolitan Creed"), which came into use after the time of the General Council of 381. For completeness, we may add that the later definition says firmly that the Godhead of Father, Son, and Holy Spirit is *one in essence* (or substance), though *in three hypostases* (subsistences or individualized manifestations). When this formulation was translated into Latin, the rather abstract Greek for individualized manifestation became the rater concrete word *persona,* and connotations of distinct and self-contained personality were suggested in a way not intended by the original Greek wording.

Not so the East. It was soon fiercely, and deeply, divided. The great sees of Alexandria and Antioch became especially irreconcilable—until the Moslem conquests hammered them down in common disaster.

The controversy first became heated when Apollinaris, a bishop in Syria, perhaps reacting adversely to the views of his nearest colleagues, asserted that Christ could not have been perfect man united with complete God, for then there would not have been one Son of God, but two sons, one by nature and one by adoption, the first with a divine, the second with a human will. Such a thing seemed inconceivable, religiously abhorrent. Therefore, in Christ a human body with its animating principle ("animal soul" was the actual phrase) was indwelt by the Logos, as the reasoning principle; the union, on the analogy of the unity of a human personality, being so complete that the body of Christ was the body of God, and in crucifying this body the Jews crucified God. Immediately his opponents of the School of Antioch pointed out that under this conception Christ was not truly human, for his manhood was incomplete, without a reasoning intelligence or the power of choice. The Antiochians declared that in Christ a *whole* human being must have been divine; the Jesus of history had a complete human nature, endowed with reason and free will, like all other men, and the Logos dwelt in him as in a temple, in perfect moral unity, such that the Logos and Jesus willed the same things. Nestorius, their chief spokesman, excited riots among the monks of Constantinople, where he became bishop, when he preached a sermon against calling the Virgin Mary "the mother of God," declaring she did not bear a deity, she bore "a man, the organ of deity." [17] Cyril, bishop of Alexandria, now entered the fray on the other side. He admitted that Christ's humanity possessed body, rational soul, and spirit, but it was without personality; the Logos was its personality.

Charges and counter-charges flew thick and fast. A general council was called in 431, and found itself unwholesomely involved in political machinations and imperial pressures. Nestorius was deposed and banished. But the issues remained unsettled. Finally, a general council met in 451 at Chalcedon, in Asia Minor, and formulated a definition of the relation of Christ's natures that became standard Catholic doctrine. It reads:

Following, therefore, the holy Fathers, we confess and all teach with one accord one and the same Son, our Lord Jesus Christ, at once complete in Godhead and complete in manhood, truly God and truly man, and, further, of a rational soul and body; of one essence with the Father as regards his Godhead, and at the same time of one essence with us as regards his manhood, in all respects like us, apart from sin; as regards his Godhead begotten of the Father before the ages, yet as regards his manhood—on account of us and our salvation—begotten in these last days of Mary the Virgin, bearer of God; one and the same Christ, Son, Lord, Only-begotten, proclaimed in two natures, without confusion, without change, without division, without separation; the difference of the natures being in no way destroyed on account of the union, but rather the peculiar property of each nature being preserved and concurring in one person and one hypostasis—not as though parted or divided into two persons, but one and the same son and Only-begotten God the Logos, Lord, Jesus Christ, even as the prophets from of old and the Lord Jesus Christ taught us concerning him, and the Creed of the Fathers has handed down to us.

This creed, like the Nicene, was a triumph for the West, and of course the West accepted it without demur. But the East did not find it so satisfactory. Those who followed the Alexandrian lead dissented as "partisans of the *one* nature" and were called accordingly Monophysites. From them sprang the Coptic Church, of Egypt and Abyssinia, and the "Jacobite" churches of Syria and Armenia, which dissent to this day.

The Nestorians were already declared unsound when the general council convened at Chalcedon. They persisted as a sect in Syria, however; and they found the peoples to the east of them receptive. So they took their doctrines into Persia, and from thence to India and China, which they reached in the 7th century. In Syria Nestorianism survived the Moslem conquest. Nestorian churches also still exist in southern India and northwestern Iran.

The Growth of the Papacy

It was the good fortune of the church of Rome to be on the victorious side in the great doctrinal controversies of the 2nd and 4th centuries. During the Gnostic crisis it was the church of Rome that framed the Apostles' Creed; and it was the same church that led in the formation of the New Testament canon. The superior dignity of the church of Rome was acknowledged by eminent authorites of the West. Irenaeus, from his place in Gaul, urged the western churches to agree with Rome in all matters involving the apostolic tradition. Cyprian, from his place in North Africa, thought of Rome as "the chief church whence priestly unity takes its source." [18]

Aware of all these things, and sure that, if civil authority rested at Constantinople in the person of the emperor, spiritual authority rested at Rome, in his own person, Pope Leo I (440–461) declared that since

St. Peter was the first among the apostles, St. Peter's church should be accorded primacy among the churches. He based his claim on the doctrine that Peter's powers, as defined in Matt. 16:18, 19,* had been passed on to each of his successors. This was a special application, we note, of the doctrine of "apostolic succession," a doctrine which had early been formulated, e.g., by Clement of Rome at the close of the 1st century, and which was generally understood to apply to *all* bishops as the successors, through the laying on of hands at ordination, of *all* the apostles. But Leo held that St. Peter was the first in rank among the apostles, and hence the successors of Peter were the first among bishops.

He and his successors took steps to make good this claim, but their success was in suspense while the Roman Empire fell. Well was it for the pope, indeed, that most of the Empire's invaders—Visigoths, Ostrogoths, Vandals, Burgundians, and Lombards—had already been converted to Christianity by missionaries of the heretical Arian sects.† They were heretics, but they were Christians, so that when Alaric the Visigoth captured Rome, he treated the pope with favor, and spared the churches, while ravin and ruin overwhelmed all else around.

As the inroads of the Barbarians swelled to a disastrous flood-tide, and civilization faltered, the popes drew some consolation from the fact that the Arian invaders were after awhile persuaded to become Catholics.‡

The Rise of Monasticism

Monasticism grew rapidly in the Catholic Church after Christianity was made the imperial state religion. Early tendencies in its direction appeared in the individuals who followed St. Paul's suggestion that men and women believers might well practice sexual abstinence and live as "virgins." But as a movement involving a definite break with society, it did not begin until toward the end of the 3rd century. Its first great representative was St. Anthony of Korma in Egypt. After trying to

* "I tell you, your name is Peter, a rock, and on this rock I will build my church, and the powers of death will not subdue it. I will give you the keys of the Kingdom of Heaven, and whatever you forbid on earth will be held in heaven to be forbidden, and whatever you permit on earth will be held in heaven to be permitted."

† By the great missionary Ulfilas and others.

‡ As a result of the conversion of Clovis, king of the Franks, and the efforts of the British missionary, Boniface.

practice asceticism in his own village, an attempt which failed, he went away into the solitude of the desert. There he was beset by his famous temptations, at peace only when asleep, when awake fasting and praying ceaselessly, but haunted by demons, in male and female form, enticing him to every sin. Egypt was full of lonely exiles and friendless men; its climate was favorable for, and its people respectful toward austerity; the belief was prevalent (in accord with the Gnostic and Alexandrian theologies) that the world and the body were defiling; so Anthony attracted many followers. It was soon apparent, however, that those who strove to live entirely alone often went mad, and just as often failed through lack of guidance; so a communal type of hermit life (cenobitism) was developed by Pachomius, a convert to Coptic Christianity in southern Egypt, who organized monasteries (and one nunnery) under a rule of balanced work and meditation, directed by an abbot.

Both the solitary and communal types of monasticism quickly spread to Syria and Asia Minor. The solitary hermits drew great attention to themselves. Some retired to caves and desert places; some, like Simeon the Stylite, lived on the tops of pillars in ruined cities and had their food lifted up to them on poles; others (the Dendrites) resided in trees; still others, in the same manner as Buddhist monks in China and Tibet, walled themselves up in narrow enclosures and had food tossed in to them or pushed through slits in the wall. But this form of asceticism was never more than the rage of the moment; by far the greater number of hermits gathered together in monasteries (that is, became monks) and maintained themselves by their own husbandry. They early won the favor of Basil, bishop of Caesarea, one of the three great Cappadocians still honored by the Eastern Orthodox churches; and he laid down for them a rule which is universal in the East to this day. By it the monasteries submit themselves to the bishops of their localities, and, in addition to the monastic practices shared with the West, prohibit strong drink and outside or non-canonical reading. Social service among the poor and orphaned is prescribed.

In the West the monastic movement was slow in getting started, but when the Germanic invasions turned society upsidedown, it became popular, and developed many independent orders. For some time each monastery had its own rule, and some were shockingly lax. In the 6th century therefore appeared the Order of St. Benedict, whose founder prescribed for those who joined his order a full life of manual labor in the monastery's fields or shops, serious directed reading, and, above all, worship throughout the day and part of the night. That the Benedictine monasteries, which eventually spread through western Europe, had libraries was in itself a fact of great consequence for the future.

How consistent monasticism was, at least in the case of some individuals, with an active purpose of serving society at large was apparent in the life, first, of St. Jerome, who while in monastic seclusion in Palestine, completed the Vulgate, the translation of the Old and New Testaments into Latin; and in the career also of St. Chrysostom, the "golden-mouthed," who emerged from hermit life to attract great congregations in Antioch by his sermons, and was therefore called to the bishopric of Constantinople (and the jealousies that plunged him into the obscurity of ill-deserved exile).

Another influential representative of the hermit life was Gregory the Great, the first monk to be chosen to the papal office (590–604). An administrator with great personal gifts, he so managed the financial resources of the papacy * that he virtually ruled Italy like a monarch. He laid the foundations of later papal authority in England, in whose conversion to Christianity he took great interest; † and increased his ecclesiastical power in France and Spain. His emphasis on penance and his stress on belief in purgatory brought these aspects of belief and practice for the first time to the forefront in Catholicism; and he anticipated later practice by recommending penitents to seek the aid of the saints. He took it to be a fact that as the apostolic successor to St. Peter, who was "the prince of all the Apostles" to whom "by the Lord's voice the care of the whole church was committed," he should be acknowledged to be the head of the whole church. He thus was the forerunner and model of the powerful medieval popes.

St. Augustine

But the greatest personality of the ancient Catholic Church was Augustine (354–430), bishop of Hippo in North Africa. He was a person in whose temperament almost every human quality was present in great intensity; yet such was the clarity and strength of his mind that he was able to master his unruly passions and harness them to a Christian purpose. Born of a pagan father and Christian mother, he attended the schools of his native North Africa; and at seventeen while pursuing the study of rhetoric, he followed the promptings of his ardently sensuous nature and took a concubine. He rejected the New Testament at first

* The church at Rome now had great land-holdings in Italy.

† England was converted by a kind of Christian pincers movement—from the north by way of Ireland and Scotland, from the south by missionaries sent out from Rome directly. Ireland had been converted earlier by St. Patrick; his converts crossed to Scotland; after they won it, missionaries entered England from Scotland.

as "unworthy to be compared with the dignity of Cicero," [19] whose works he was studying. But Cicero was not enough; so he became an adherent of Manichaeism.* He derived only small comfort from this doctrine, however, for he never became one of the "perfect"; he could only be a "hearer," because he was unable to give up the lusts of the flesh, as Manichaeism demanded. His prayer at that time, he says in his famous *Confessions*, was, "Grant me chastity and continence, but not yet." [20]

At twenty-nine he went to Italy. There, in Milan, he heard the powerful sermons of Ambrose, another of the great personalities of the ancient Catholic Church. His conscience was touched. When his mother, on joining him, urged him to enter upon betrothal to someone of his own class, he sorrowfully sent away his faithful concubine, who had borne him a son, and agreed to do as his mother asked, though on account of the tender years of the girl to whom he contracted himself, he put his marriage off. Then finding himself still a prey to desire, he took another concubine. He almost despaired of himself now; for it seemed indeed true to him, as the Manichaens taught, that the flesh is incurably evil.

Radical changes in his point of view followed from an awakened interest in Neo-Platonism.† He began to consider it true that the temptations of the flesh follow from a falling away from God, rather than from the presence of any positive and inherent element of badness in

---

* This was a philosophical system evolved by a Persian called Mani (215–276). Combined of elements drawn from Zoroastrianism, Buddhism, Judaism, Gnosticism, and Christianity, its characteristic tenet was the dualism of light and darkness, spirit and matter, good and evil. The soul of man is in bondage to vile matter, and must follow the way of asceticism to freedom from the lusts of the flesh. Organized like a religion, it became for a time one of the chief rivals of Christianity; and though its influence waned after Augustine's time, it is interesting that some of the Crusaders returned to western Europe with a revived form of its doctrines and founded the sect of Cathari in southern France.

† An Alexandrian school of philosophy, of which Plotinus (205–270) was the chief representative. All reality consists, according to this school, of a series of emanations, at various removes, issuing from the *One*, the perfect Form, which is the source of all being everywhere. Like water from an overflowing spring, the realities closest to the source of being are the purest and best. Mind or intelligence is the emanation nearest to the One, soul or psyche is further removed, and matter is at the outer edge of being, at such a remove from its source as to suffer from an absence of indwelling divine reason or worth. Man is a union of matter, soul, and mind. His salvation depends on his moving away from immersion in the realm of matter and achieving knowledge of true reality by an intuitive and mystical union with the One. As his soul becomes more intelligent and rational, it becomes more spiritual and divine.

the flesh. In fact, he came to believe that God is the source of all things; and that matter and evil are to be defined in terms of an absence of the creative energy of God, due to spiritual remoteness from the one eternal good Being.

His conversion to Christianity occurred with apparent suddenness. Learning of a Neo-Platonist who had turned Christian, and then of some Egyptian monks who overcame their temptations by simple faithfulness to their monastic discipline, he ran distractedly from his friend Alypius into the farther reaches of a garden, and heard a child's voice from across the wall saying: "Take up and read." Returning to his friend, he seized a copy of the Epistles of the New Testament lying on the bench, and opening it, read: "Not in rioting and drunkenness, not in chambering and wantonness . . . ; but put ye on the Lord Jesus Christ, and make not provision for the flesh to fulfil the lusts thereof." These words brought him to a decision.[21] Thenceforth he lived in strict continence. Baptized by Ambrose, he left for North Africa, resolved to found a monastery; there he became bishop of Hippo, wrote voluminously for the next thirty years, and died while the Vandals were besieging his city.

Augustine was so many-sided that his theology is a synthesis of various trends. One sees in it a Neo-Platonist strain which modifies his basic reliance on Hebraic insights. But he yielded to no one tendency exclusively. So germinal was his thinking, that we should not take leave of him without briefly summarizing his doctrines of God, man, and the Church, and his philosophy of history.

Augustine's mystical personal experience of God kept him from thinking of God as a pure abstraction. God is near and very real, and both in the person of Jesus and through the activity of the Holy Spirit has broken into history and is continuously at work in human hearts. And yet Augustine's conception had a Neo-Platonist tinge. God is the one eternal Being, alone absolutely real and absolutely good. He is the source of all other things, and they depend upon him at every moment for their continued existence. The physical universe especially has only a derived reality, and is scarcely worthy of study in itself.

Augustine adapted this conception of God to his Christian conviction that God is "one in three." In the Trinity he saw no subordination of one member to another, as earlier theologians did. "There is so great an equality in that Trinity," he wrote, "that not only the Father is not greater than the Son, as regards divinity, but neither are the Father and the Son together greater than the Holy Spirit." [22] Going further, he suggested that the Holy Spirit, though equal with the Father and the Son as regards divinity, "proceeds not only from the Father but also from the Son (*filioque*)." [23] Yet again, the Trinity is as united as lover, loved, and love; or as memory, understanding, and will, of which he said: "Since, then, these three, memory, understanding, will, are not three lives, but one life; nor three minds, but one mind; it follows certainly that neither are they three substances, but one substance." [24]

In forming his doctrine of man—which had enormous influence, not only on Catholic theologians, but also on the Protestant Reformers— Augustine drew upon his bitter experiences of his own moral weakness in youth. Man in and of himself is depraved, "the entire mass of (his) nature ruined," [25] "bound by original sin." [26] This is the inheritance we all have from Adam. Adam was created good and with a fine intelligence. But he was endowed with free will; and though he could have chosen not to sin, he, along with Eve, ate of the forbidden fruit, in wilfulness and pride. After that he and all his descendants have been in a state of original sin, from which no one can now escape by his own efforts. It is as though the whole human race were morally diseased.

But God is merciful. Those whom He chooses, He saves by divine grace. Not that they deserve such mercy; it is entirely a free gift. This is the love of God, on which no human claims can be made. And when the divine grace comes, no one can resist it. Uplifted to effort and perseverance—"the perseverance of the saints"[27]—the sinner is changed, justified, sanctified. To others the grace never comes; for they are doomed to damnation.

This hard doctrine involved Augustine in fierce controversy with a British monk called Pelagius, and with others. These men contended that there is no such thing as original sin, all men having an aptitude for goodness. Adam may have left to his descendants a bad example, but no inherited and inescapable moral weakness. Anyone who has faith is justified. But Augustine fought stoutly for his view. He knew from experience how inescapable are pride and lust in a life spent apart from God, and how irresistible is God's sudden grace.

The Church, according to Augustine, is the divinely appointed institution to perform the sacraments which are the means of grace. There is only one Church, and none who are outside of it, whether heathen or heretic, can be saved. In opposition to a purist group in North Africa, called the Donatists, who maintained that the sacraments performed by unworthy priests were ineffectual, Augustine held that the sacraments are instituted of God, not of men, and therefore they communicate grace, regardless of the unworthy character of any man who performs them.

Augustine expressed his philosophy of history in his treatise *The City of God*. When he wrote it, Rome, "the mistress of the world," had been sacked by barbaric conquerors, and the pagan writers of the time were loudly lamenting what they conceived to be the fact, that the city had declined and fallen because the grand old gods that had brought greatness to her had been abandoned for the enfeebling god of the Christians. In defending Christianity against this charge, Augustine boldly contrasted the Earthly City, which in history reached its clearest forms in Babylon and Rome, with the City of God, to which God's elect in every generation have belonged. In his own day, he said, not all those who formed the visible Church were members of the invisible City of God. They, the non-elect, together with all those outside the Church, belonged to the Earthly City, which must decline and pass away. But the City of God will survive even the death of "civilization," and ultimately inherit the earth. So wrote Augustine even while the barbarians hammered at the gates of the cities of his Africa.

It cannot be said that the Roman Catholic Church adopted all of the Augustinian theology; other influences, as we shall see, intervened; but the Protestant Reformation was a return to Augustine just as much as it was a return to Paul and Jesus.

The Division of the Church into East and West

Not only was the Roman Empire brought low by invasions from the north; in the 7th century other invaders appeared in the southeast, and rapidly overran Palestine, Syria, Asia Minor, North Africa, and Spain. The staunch defence of Constantinople checked them for a time in the East; and a Frankish chieftain, by the name of Charles Martel, turned them back in France in 732; otherwise, perhaps, the Moslems would have taken Europe.

The effect of the Moslem conquests on what was left of the Roman Empire was to divide it more seriously than ever. The Emperor Leo III at Constantinople incurred the displeasure of Pope Gregory II by his efforts to obtain reform in the face of the onrushing Moslem peril. Recoiling sharply from the criticisms coming from Arab (and Christian) quarters concerning the "idolatrous" veneration of images and pictures in the Christian churches, the emperor forbade, in 726, their further use —thus fathering the first iconoclastic movement in Christian history. There was immediate remonstrance both in the East and in the West. In the East Leo used his army to enforce his decree. But Rome was far

enough away to make good its disobedience. What was more, the pope
called a Roman synod and obtained an action excommunicating those
who opposed the use of pictures, namely, the emperor and those who
sided with him. The emperor retaliated by removing Sicily and southern
Italy from the pope's spiritual jurisdiction. This left the pope in a precarious situation; for northern Italy was occupied by Lombards, and they
had their hearts set on the conquest of Rome. So the pope called for
help from Charles Martel, whose prowess against the Moslems made his
aid worth seeking. Both Gregory and Charles were to die before that
help was forthcoming; but Charles's son, Pippin the Short, invaded
Italy, brought the Lombard king to terms, and made a present of the
province of Ravenna to the pope. He thus caused the pope to fix the
orientation of the papacy toward the trans-Alpine lands rather than
toward the East, and, without knowing it, laid the foundations of a
huge, unstable, western empire.

The pope gained much; he was now not only the largest landholder
in Italy, with an annual income of over a million dollars, but a temporal
sovereign, the ruler of "the states of the Church," as they came to be
called; and very important these were to him.* Pippin's son, Charlemagne, gained much too. He built up an empire which included almost
all of western Europe—in modern terms, France, northeastern Spain,
Belgium, Holland, most of Germany, Austria, Hungary, and northern

* From 740 to 1870, the popes held firmly to their States of the Church, and
when bereft of them by King Victor Emmanuel, were outraged. In 1929 Mussolini
restored the pope's temporal sovereignty over the Vatican and the grounds immediately around it.

Christian basilica of early design with separate tower. (Ravenna)

Italy. Cordial to the Church, Charlemagne came to Rome and on Christmas Day, 800, was formally crowned Holy Roman Emperor by Leo III. This act signalized the fact that West and East were at the parting of the ways, a fact accepted some years later by Emperor Leo V in Constantinople when he officially recognized the title of Charlemagne, and thus acknowledged that the Empire had fallen in two.

Meanwhile a serious doctrinal split between East and West had been preparing. We have already seen that Augustine thought the Holy Spirit proceeds from the Father *and* the Son. In 589 a Western council, meeting in Spain, added to the Athanasian Creed the word *filioque* ("and from the Son") immediately after the words saying the Holy Spirit proceeds from the Father. The theologians of the East protested the change strongly, believing that to make it meant denying that God is the source of all things. The West held out generally for the "filioque." The rift of opinion hung fire for several centuries. Finally in 876 a synod at Constantinople condemned the pope, both for his political activities and because he did not correct the heresy of the filioque-clause. This action was part of the East's entire rejection of the pope's claim of universal jurisdiction over the Church. The final and complete break came in 1054, when the long-standing schism led the pope to excommunicate the patriarch of Constantinople and the patriarch to hurl back anathemas at the pope. Since then the two branches of the Catholic Church have gone their separate ways.

IV THE EASTERN ORTHODOX CHURCHES

Although until recently the patriarch of Constantinople claimed spiritual supremacy over them, the various bodies of the Eastern Orthodox Church have been virtually independent of each other, divided as they are into units corresponding more or less to the national states in which they have existed. Yet none of them has departed to any great degree from the orthodox tradition accepted in the East. Inasmuch as the ancient sees of Alexandria, Jerusalem, and Antioch early fell into Moslem hands, theological development in those areas virtually ceased after the 8th century. It ceased elsewhere as well. The only real changes have been in liturgy and religious practice. Here leadership was for a long time held by the patriarch of Constantinople, and, when Constantinople fell to the Turks in 1453, it passed to the Slavic Orthodox churches, and particularly to the largest of them all, the Russian Orthodox Church, whose patriarch once said that even as Constantinople had been the second Rome, so Moscow should be the third.

The unity of the Orthodox churches has never been really broken. Although, as a consequence of international changes and conflicts, the various nationalized churches have sometimes had such violent disputes concerning jurisdiction that more than once one branch of the church has excommunicated another, they have all learned to fall back finally on a doctrine of expediency, called "economy," whereby acts of excommunicated church leaders have been first tolerated, and then validated, on the grounds of keeping the churches operating without loss of power and authority.

The General Doctrinal Position

In spite of differences of administration, the various branches of the Eastern Orthodox Church have remained more or less united in matters of doctrine. The ancient creeds are accepted as infallible definitions of orthodox apostolic teaching. There have been local divergencies in faith and practice, but in general the churches have not departed from the doctrinal position reached by the last of their acknowledged Ancient Fathers, John of Damascus, who one century after the Moslems seized Syria made a last effort on the basis of the completed Creeds and the writings of preceding Fathers to systematize the Eastern faith.

The position taken by John of Damascus fairly well characterizes the general attitude of the Orthodox churches—a mystical emphasis on the life-giving incarnation of God in Christ conveyed down to the present time through the seven sacraments and the other rites and devotional practices of the churches. The Western interest in the practical, juridical aspects of the relation between God and man had no great place in the concern of John of Damascus or, for that matter, of the Eastern church before or after him.

There are some interesting aspects in this position. John of Damascus appeared at a time when the Byzantine type of church architecture had been highly developed. The chief external mark of the eastern churches had become a dome resting on a rectangular or octagonal substructure, supported by half-domes and buttresses. In the interior, the nave led to a chancel within which was the altar and to the rear of it a semi-circle of seats for the bishops and presbyters. The pulpit stood outside of the chancel, nearer to the congregation. The floor, walls, ceilings, and screens were richly decorated with pictures and mosaics, representing in the formal manner of symbolical and devotional art the Holy

Trinity, the Virgin Mary, Christ, the Apostles, and many saints and martyrs. Icons, with images shown in low relief against a plaque (such as Christ on the cross and Mary as the Mother of God) were colored in red, gold, and blue; and these, together with multi-colored mosaics of the same subjects, were venerated by the worshipers, prayers being addressed in their direction and even kisses and strokings bestowed on them. In due time some of these images and pictures were credited with miraculous powers and became objects of special pilgrimage. When the Emperor Leo III was moved to order the suppression of such veneration, and there ensued the uproar in the East and West which we have described, John of Damascus came to the defence of images. He declared that the question of icons "is a question for Synods and not for Emperors." He went on to argue that the synods would see in images an incarnation of the Holy Spirit analogous to the incarnation of God in Christ. Again, icons were analogous to the sacraments, in that they conveyed divine grace to the believer. Yet again, they were analogous to books; for "what a book is to the literate, that an image is to the illiterate." Indeed the reverend Father went so far as to put all the rites, creeds, and institutions of the Church in the same position: all alike are chiefly means of conveying divine life and grace to the believer.

It was in accordance with this reasoning that in 787 the Seventh General Council—the last in which the Greek and Roman churches concurred—declared that pictures and images, the cross, and the Gospels "should be given due salutation and honorable reverence (though) not indeed that true worship which pertains to the divine nature. . . . For the honor which is paid to the image passes on to that which the image represents, and he who shows reverence to the image shows reverence to the subject represented in it." [28] (So far the East and West could agree.)

Differences between the Eastern and Roman Churches

But even in the attitude toward images the Eastern and Roman churches have differed. In the East icons are not humanized, and the figures remain symbols, simplified representations of "essential" meanings; as such they are rendered in formalized bas-relief rather than in the round as in the Roman Church. In other words, the East regards icons as signifying divine nature and spirit, whereas the Roman Church on the whole uses images to bring the Virgin and the saints within human range. Hence the attitude to Jesus' mother differs fundamentally in the two churches: the Roman Catholics venerate the Blessed Virgin as one who loves her child and is compassionate and humane to her suppliants; the Eastern churches worship her as the holy Mother of God, the exalted being in whom the human and the divine met in the Incarnation.*

Other points of difference persisting down to the present may be briefly mentioned. The East has a list of sacraments, seven in number, differing from the Roman Catholic: baptism (which is by immersion), chrismation (anointing after baptism with oil consecrated by a bishop), the eucharist, confession, the taking of holy orders, marriage, and extreme unction (which is given not, as in the West, only before death, but in serious illness to encourage recovery). It is held that in the eucharist the bread and wine become the body and blood of Christ, but not as in Roman belief by transubstantiation, rather by a transformation due to the operation of the Holy Spirit. The liturgy of the eucharist has been developed into an elaborate work of devotional art, enriched by antiphonal choral chants, sung in different voices, without instrumental accompaniment, by priests in gorgeous vestments. Long recitatives at a

* A similarly high view is taken of the saints, the Eastern list of whom sounds odd in Roman Catholic ears.

Byzantine icon of the Mother of God, known as Our Lady of the Signs. (15th Century)

high level of devotional poetry and beauty precede and follow the central act of elevating the sanctified bread and wine before the altar. In the eucharist the East uses leavened bread instead of the Roman unleavened wafer, and like the Protestant churches offers the cup as well as the bread to the congregation. (The Roman church "reserves" the wine.) The sign of the cross is made by the priest with candles, of which two in the left hand, with lighted tips meeting, symbolize the union of the divine and human natures in Christ, and three in the right hand, similarly joined, symbolize the Trinity of Father, Son, and Holy Spirit.

The list of differences could be extended. It must suffice to mention but one or two more. Of course the Eastern churches firmly "renounce" as "erroneous" the belief "that a man, to wit, the Bishop of Rome, can be the head of Christ's Body, that is to say, of the whole church." With equal firmness they reject "the erroneous belief that the Holy Apostles did not receive from our Lord equal spiritual power, but that the holy Apostle Peter was their Prince: and that the Bishop of Rome alone is his successor: and that the Bishops of Jerusalem, Alexandria, Antioch, and others are not, equally with the bishops of Rome, successors of the Apostles." [29] They contend that the Pope of Rome cannot be infallible in matters of faith and morals, since several of the popes have been condemned as heretics by the church councils; certainly, they say, the Pope cannot claim to be superior to the church councils.

The Present Situation

The Orthodox churches outside the Iron Curtain have to a large extent recovered from the setbacks received during World War II. Since their admission to the World Council of Churches, they have participated in its activities with considerable evidence of vitality.

As for the Orthodox churches in Russia and the satellite countries, it has been difficult to gauge accurately the developments taking place within them. The old national church of Russia was so clearly identified with the Czarist regime that the 1917 revolution was a major catastrophe to it; but the situation of its disestablished successor, the Orthodox Church of Russia, seems rather to improve with time. Its work in society continues to be restricted, for the Church may engage only in religious activity; it may maintain a certain number of buildings, train and employ priests, and conduct religious services, but formal religious education of the young is prohibited. However, although for some time the Russian government kept the Russian Church from joining the World Council of Churches, it reversed itself in 1961. In November of that year, not only the Russian but also the Bulgarian, Roumanian, and Polish churches sent delegates to the meeting of the World Council at New Delhi, India, and entered its membership. In his letter requesting such membership, the patriarch of Moscow reported that the Russian Church had at that time 30,000 priests, 20,000 parishes, 73 bishoprics, 8 theological schools, and 40 monasteries. Apparently, as long as there was no "subversion" or "counter-revolutionary activity" within the Church, it was allowed to minister religiously to its estimated forty million adherents.

## V	THE ROMAN CATHOLIC CHURCH IN THE MIDDLE AGES

The Great Period of the Papacy

The Roman Catholic Church entered the Middle Ages with a head who was a temporal sovereign quite equal in political and financial position to some of the secular sovereigns of the West. Not only that; the Donations of Constantine, so-called, suggested that he was destined to be the theocratic ruler of the entire West. Whether the popes of the time actually desired such a position or not, there seemed to be no insurmountable obstacle to their attaining it, if they wanted it.

The kings and chieftains of the West, on their part, were willing to concede the spiritual supremacy of the Roman pontiff; but they were equally sure that the Pope ought not to intrude himself into their purely temporal affairs.

Hence arose vexing conflicts between the popes and secular powers. Such churchmen as were elevated to high office at the behest or by the appointment of kings and princes were often easy-going and worldly-minded. Some of them had even bought and paid for their appointment—a practice called *simony*. They were prone to take their churchly honors as a personal prerogative, to do with as they liked; and the farther they were from Rome the more this was the case. In northern areas, especially in Germany, bishops even married and passed their bishoprics on to their sons, in complete disregard of the rule laid down long before by Pope Leo I, that all the clergy, even to the sub-deacons, should be celibate. Again, northern bishops were frequently complaisant toward, and sanctioned, easy divorce among kings and princes, when political marriages proved unsatisfactory. In another direction, conflicts arose between canon law (the law of the church drawn from the decrees of councils, synods, and popes) and the civil law of the various states; and where the state was strong, the canon law was often violated in the administration of parishes and monasteries.

A head-on contest between pope and emperor could not long be avoided. Its outbreak simply awaited the appearance of personalities sufficiently strong to enter upon it. This occurred when Hildebrand became pope in 1073, under the name of Gregory VII. He wasted no time. A new emperor, Henry IV, had ascended the throne in Germany. The pope ordered Henry to conform to the decree that bishops receive their staff of office from the pope and not from the emperor; and he charged the married bishops of Germany to give up their wives. But Henry IV was to prove a formidable opponent. He defiantly appointed a cleric of his own choice to the bishopric of Milan, then under his control. Hildebrand called him to task. Henry held a council with his nobles and bishops and led them in rejecting Hildebrand's authority as pope. Hildebrand replied with a decree falling like a thunderbolt upon Henry, excommunicating him and releasing his subjects in Germany and Italy from their oaths of allegiance to him. Though Henry sent the pope a fierce letter calling him "now no pope, but a false monk," and telling him to "come down, to be damned through all eternity," he was merely blustering. In reality he was hard hit. His nobles told him that, if he were not released from his excommunication within a year and a day, they would depose him.

In great trouble Henry crossed the Alps. It was mid-winter. He followed the pope to a castle at Canossa, and for three days stood in the snow of the courtyard a white-clad, bare-footed penitent, while Gregory considered what to do about him. Finally, the pope, utterly avenged, admitted Henry to an audience, and released him from his excommunication.

The pope's great triumph—one of the most dramatic in history—was short-lived. Three years later he made the mistake of excommunicating Henry again. Henry's answer was a march on Rome which enabled him to drive the pope out of it and set up a rival pontiff. But the contest had reached an inconclusive stage. Soon Gregory and Henry were both dead; and their successors, Henry V and Pope Calixtus II, came to a compromise. Bishops everywhere and in all cases were to be chosen by the church in accordance with canon law, yet before their consecration the German bishops were to appear before the emperor to be invested by the touch of the royal scepter with the temporal possession of their sees. In other words, all new German bishops were to be acceptable to the emperor. Furthermore, it was agreed that bishops should be celibate. Hildebrand's reforms had in great part been achieved.

More powerful even than Hildebrand was Pope Innocent III (1193–1216), a hundred years later. Innocent entered on his office when papal prestige had reached a new height, largely due to his predecessor's effective discipline of Henry II of England.* While Innocent III was conceded, on his accession, to be, without qualification, the spiritual superior of every terrestrial sovereign, he acted on the principle that he was the first among his peers in the temporal sphere also. When Germany was torn between rival claimants to the throne, he crowned one of them, Otto III, Holy Roman Emperor—after wringing large promises from him. When the new emperor forgot his promises, the pope put a rival in the field and with the help of the king of France established him on the imperial throne. He thus proved that he could make and unmake kings. The king of France, too, felt the pope's whip-hand. Resolved to rid himself of his unloved queen, the Swedish princess Ingeborg, the French monarch divorced her. The pope then put all France under an interdict (i.e., religious services were suspended throughout France), and the king, yielding to popular clamor, took back his queen. In Spain the pope first assumed control of Aragon and then granted it back as a fief to its king, Peter. He imposed a similar status upon the rebellious English. Richard the Lion-Hearted's unpopular brother, King John, tried to force his candidate for archbishop on the see of Canterbury, and the pope placed England under an interdict, to last until Stephen Langton, his choice, should be made archbishop. When King John resisted, the pope excommunicated him, declared his throne vacant, and proclaimed a crusade against him. John capitulated, but was not restored to grace until he acknowledged his kingdom to be a fief of the papacy from which a thousand marks were due annually to the pope as a feudal tax!

Within the Church itself, Innocent III became the undisputed head

---

* From the security of his island kingdom Henry II had challenged the Roman pontiff by passing laws limiting the application of canon law in ecclesiastical cases and putting the election of bishops into the hands of the king, to whom these prelates were required to do homage. The archbishop of Canterbury, Thomas à Becket, an old friend of Henry's, had sternly opposed him at this juncture, and Henry's expressions of anger caused four knights to ride to Canterbury and murder the archbishop before the cathedral's very altar. The pope, capitalizing on Becket's popularity, canonized him; streams of pilgrims (precisely like those pictured in *The Canterbury Tales*) poured through the cathedral's doors and wore down the stone floor by kneeling before the new saint's tomb. The king, full of dismay and remorse, withdrew the offending laws, and as a penitent submitted himself to being scourged before Becket's tomb!

of the whole ecclesiastical domain. All disagreements of the higher clergy were ordered to be referred to him, and his decisions were final. He reserved the right to move bishops about among their sees. He forced through the Fourth Lateran Council (in 1215) the acceptance of the dogma of transubstantiation* and the rule that the good standing of a Catholic was conditioned upon periodic confession, absolution, and communion.

The papacy had reached its all-time height of spiritual and earthly power.

Medieval Monasticism

Monastic reform was in the air before the Crusades. (In fact the Crusades were first projected by popes schooled in the reforms initiated by the Cluny Movement of the 10th century.) Significantly, the whole monastic scene in Europe during the Crusades was dominated by the reforming Cistercian Order—French and Benedictine, like the Cluny group—its greatest exponent, as organizer and preacher, being the saintly Bernard of Clairvaux. But the most notable expressions of medieval monastic piety were achieved a little later by the Dominican and Franciscan Orders.

The Dominican Order was in origin a missionary movement, whose first objective was the conversion of the heretical Cathari of southern France; but Dominic (1170–1221), its Spanish founder, had the inspiration to send his "preachers," as imitators of the Apostle Paul, to many other parts of Europe, especially to the university towns, and their success caused his order to grow swiftly. The friars, as his monks were called, were devoted to learning, because they were primarily preachers and teachers sent to the uninstructed and the unconvinced. They dressed plainly in black (whence their name of Black Friars) and were vowed to a mendicant poverty—begging their daily food in the spirit of Matt. 10:7–14. The order was headed by a "master-general" who supervised the work of the "provincial priors" in the Dominican "provinces." At the head of each monastery or nunnery was a "prior" or "prioress," chosen for a term of four years by the monks or nuns themselves, something of a democratic innovation. It was the misfortune of the Dominicans that the popes chose them as Inquisitors; they had no original leaning in that direction. When they followed their own natural path, they had

---

* The doctrine that during the celebration of the Mass the substance of the bread and of the wine is converted into the actual or real body and blood of Christ.

wide success among the higher classes, and produced great writers and teachers, like the theologians Albertus Magnus and Thomas Aquinas; the reformer of Florence, Savonarola; and the mystics, Eckhart and Tauler.

The Franciscans had their great success among the common people. The founder of their order, St. Francis of Assissi (1182–1226), is one of the world's great personalities—as an individual the most winsome of saints, as a world figure Christ in a medieval incarnation. After a gay and frivolous youth, during which his father, a business man, disinherited him for showing no interest in accumulating riches, he underwent after illness a religious experience which led him back to the "rule of Christ" as described in the New Testament. Thereafter he said he was "married to Lady Poverty"; ate the plainest food, wore unadorned, grey garments; possessed no other property than his immediate personal belongings; worked when he could, not for money, which he would not take, but just for the needs of the hour, or begged for his food when work failed; preached to the poor, or, when solitary, to the birds and beasts, in a love of Nature which was a revelation to his hard-headed and practical age; and ministered to the unfortunate, the lepers, the outcast, with a compassion drawn both from his own nature and from his imitation of Christ. His way of life immediately attracted others, and he prescribed for them no more than the New Testament "rule of Christ." When twelve men had joined him, he went with them to Pope Innocent III for recognition of their order, and it was at once granted. Francis attempted no organization beyond sending his grey-clad friars out two by two on preaching missions. Even so, his movement spread like wildfire. It became necessary for others to step in and organize it, putting at its head a "minister-general," who directed the "provincial ministers" of the "provinces," which were composed in turn of local groups under a "custos." A second order, for nuns, was formed under Clara Sciffi of Assissi; and later a third order was created for lay people who wished, while pursuing a livelihood, to fast, pray, and practice benevolence in association with the Order. St. Francis did not oppose the organizers who came to help him, but he regretted the necessity of putting a spiritual movement in leading strings.*

Both the Dominican and Franciscan orders had enormous influence in suggesting that the Christian religion transcends all organization and

---

* Today the Order consists of three branches of varying degrees of strictness: the Friars Minor (dressed in dark brown tunics), the more rigorous Capuchins (grey-clad), and the less rigorous, property-accumulating Conventuals (in black tunics).

reaches into every department of life with an elemental appeal addressed directly to every man's reason and conscience.

Scholasticism

While all this occurred, the schools were busy; for a new world had risen at last out of the ruins of the old, and men now began to study their intellectual heritage.

Since the time of Charlemagne the cathedrals and monasteries had devoted more and more attention to the schools they had founded for boys and young men. Some of the teachers, pursuing truth for its own sake, began to develop an interest in every kind of subject matter. They not only taught what was in the old books—the Vulgate, the Creeds, collections of Canon Law, fragments of Aristotle, Plato, the Stoics, the writings of the Neo-Platonists, the works of St. Augustine, and so on—but they began to compose new treatises, which were circulated among the various monasteries and aroused debate, controversy, and dialectical discussion. As the fame of individual teachers increased, students came from far and near; and the conditions were created for the founding of universities, the first of which were established late in the 12th century. Soon Bologna became famous for canon and civil law, Salerno for medicine, and Paris and Oxford for theology.

Scholasticism was the brain-child of these medieval schools. It quite naturally concerned itself with the *logic* of the Faith. After its first tentative emergence in the time of Charlemagne, it became with time more responsible, philosophically more weighty.* Its dialectical method was applied at last to the really great problem of theology: how to reconcile reason and revelation—a problem which becomes in one direction the problem of the reconciliation of science and religion, and, in another, that of the reconciliation of philosophy and theology.

---

* It is generally agreed that some of the early efforts of scholastic logic were scarcely profound; for, in the words of Guignebert, *Christianity, Past and Present* (Macmillan, 1927), p. 257: "To tell the truth, the dialecticians of the ninth century, and even those of the first half of the tenth, do not always deal in their arguments with really lofty subjects; little by little they perfect their methods through discussions which appear to us extremely puerile. They inquire, for instance, whether God can choose as a Redeemer a woman or a demon or an ass, or even a plant or a stone; they discuss the question whether a prostitute can become a virgin again through Divine grace, or whether a mouse that nibbles a consecrated wafer really eats the Lord's body!" But our possible amusement at this turn of discussion should be tempered with the thought that it was not characteristic of scholasticism generally or of any one place for long.

Augustine had laid one of the bases of Scholasticism by saying, "Faith seeks the support of the intelligence" (*fides quaerit intellectum*); meaning that the intelligence *explores* and *corroborates* or finds *added reasons* for believing in the divinely revealed dogmas of the Church. When Scholasticism was in full swing six hundred years later, this was its position exactly. Its exponents were committed roughly to the following procedure: they took their starting point from the incompletely systematized doctrines set forth in the Scriptures and the Creeds; erected these into a general structure of truth; and then proceeded to fill in this framework with the proper details—that is to say, with the deductions, inferences, and related data necessary to a fully developed systematic theology—all the while using as a test of validity each detail's coherence with the revealed dogma.

The early schoolmen started out with high hopes, drawing heavily upon the opinions of the Church Fathers and the great pagan philosophers. But they soon hit upon serious snags, which no amount of discussion seemed entirely to remove. Among them was the snag provided by the problem of the status to be assigned to unchanging ideas or universals. Were universals real (the position of medieval realism) or names only (the position of nominalism)? * Much depended—much that didn't at once meet the eye—upon the answer. Take the Church, for example. "Church" is a universal. Did the Church exist as an ideal form *prior to* all individual churches, which must then have come into existence to exemplify its nature, or is "Church" a name given to individual institutions with certain marked resemblances and thus bestowed *after* they came into existence? If the answer was in terms of the first alternative, then the Church was indeed a divine institution; if the answer was in terms of the second alternative, then it was a much more human institution than it claimed to be.

The Church was actively behind the realists, yet nominalism had sown such doubts, left such problems, and won so many followers, that the effort of the scholastic theologians to bring philosophy wholly into the service of theology (which they called "the queen of the sciences") proved at last a failure. By the 14th century, Catholic theology had to let philosophy go upon its own way of free intellectual inquiry, untrammeled by tradition and authority.

---

* To put the issue more technically, do universals (class terms), like "man" or "house," exist, as Plato claimed, prior to and as patterns determining the nature of the individual objects bearing their names (realism), or are such universals merely designations for resemblances between objects, and do they have no existence except in thought (nominalism)?

The recovery late in the 12th century of the Aristotelian writings helped to win for philosophy this freedom from theology. Up to the 12th century only fragments of Aristotle's writings had survived the wreck of Roman civilization; but then from Spain there came translations of his works from the Arabic texts studied in the University of Cordova. These translations were later checked against recovered Greek texts. For the first time in seven hundred years the West had before it a systematic treatment of natural science. The final result of its study was a "new theology," ably presented by Thomas Aquinas, the greatest of the scholastics. His synthesis of faith and philosophy, which reconciled without discrediting either, proved to be the most influential scholastic achievement.

Thomas Aquinas

Born in 1227, Thomas Aquinas was a native of Italy, a member of a noble family of part Roman and part German blood. He became a Dominican friar, of such promise, that he was sent to Paris and Cologne to study under Albertus Magnus, another Dominican friar and one of the encyclopedic minds of his time; afterwards he taught, first at Cologne, then at Paris, and finally in Italy, where he wrote his great books—now the standard theological guides of the Roman Catholic Church—the *Summa Contra Gentiles* and the *Summa Theologica*.

In the endeavor to reconcile reason and revelation, philosophy and theology, Aristotle and Christ, he tried to show that natural reason and faith are lower and higher forms of apprehension which are supplementary to each other. By itself human or natural reason, that is, such reason as Aristotle used, can go very far, not only in exploring the natural world, but also in proving the existence of God. It is possible for human reason by its own efforts to establish God's existence, using at least five cogent arguments: an argument from motion to an unmoved mover, an argument based on the necessity of a first efficient cause, an argument from possibility to necessity, an argument accounting for the gradation to be found in things, and a teleological argument drawn from consideration of design in the structure of the world. Nor is this all that reason can do. It can discover without divine help the nature of God; that is, it can by itself establish that God is pure actuality; one and unchanging; perfect, and therefore good; infinite, and therefore possessed of infinite intelligence, knowledge, goodness, freedom, and power. But reason is unable to establish more than general propositions; it cannot know what God hath wrought *historically*, unless it receives divine supplementation of its knowledge; therefore it needs to have added to its conclusions what *revelation* alone can supply, namely, knowledge of the tragic nature of the fall of Adam, by which mankind has been infected with original sin; the facts of the Incarnation and the Atonement; the doctrine of the Trinity; the fact of saving grace through the sacraments; assurance of the resurrection of the body; and knowledge of Hell, Purgatory, and Paradise. Thus a faith based on revelation knows things that are *above* reason, that is, that are beyond reason's unaided power to establish.

Yet faith needs reason none the less. Nothing should be accepted by faith which is *contrary* to reason. There is no risk in this. Candid examination of the Christian revelation shows it to be in no part contrary to reason, but in all parts *according* to reason.

Similar reasoning enabled Thomas Aquinas to reconcile philosophy and theology. Philosophy begins with the world of sense-experience and by the exercise of scientific reflection (reason) ascends to God; theology begins with the revealed truths which are from God and descends to man and the world. Both supplement and need each other.

In his doctrine of man, Aquinas combined Aristotle with the Christian revelation. With Aristotle, he considered that body and soul (matter and form) are functionally necessary to each other. The body without the soul cannot live; and the soul, though immortal, can neither develop nor maintain the characteristics of an individual self without the body. Hence, it is a great comfort to be assured by Christian revelation of the resurrection of the body.

Aquinas clarified the Catholic conception of the sacraments by a similar Aristotelian distinction of lower and higher elements. Every sacrament has two elements in it, a material element (water, bread, wine, oil) and a formal element (the liturgical formulas). Together they make an organic union and supply a means of grace. Present during the performance of each sacrament are the human or affected and the divine or causal elements. When the conditions are duly present, supernatural grace is conveyed through the sacraments to the human recipients as regenerating power. In each case a miracle takes place. Especially is this so in the celebration of the mass. There, at the words of consecration by the priest, the unleavened bread and the wine are transubstantiated, so that without changing in shape or taste, they are the very body and blood of Christ. The miracle of the Incarnation is thus repeated at each celebration of the mass.

Penance, though a sacrament, is not highly sacramental. It is more prolonged and requires greater human participation. It involves contrition, confession (to a priest), satisfaction, and absolution (by a priest). Here, as in all human regeneration, there is a lower and a higher side. In his life on earth the individual finds himself able to attain a certain degree of natural virtue. Without God's aid, he may exemplify wisdom, justice, courage, and temperance. But these will not redeem him; these are but the virtues of the natural man. To attain to eternal life he must attain the theological virtues, which have God for their source and their object, and are nourished by God's grace alone. These virtues, which he cannot achieve by himself, but must have from God, are faith, hope, and love.

To go no further with the summary of Aquinas' synthesis, we may see how orthodox and yet how flexible it is. The whole system is dogmatic from beginning to end, yet science is granted competence in the discovery of truth. Theology is in highest place, but humanism and naturalism are also given roles to play.

Medieval Mysticism

While, under the leadership of men like Thomas Aquinas, the schoolmen were pursuing what the Hindus would call "the way of knowledge," and while, at the same time, the common man was following "the way of works," there were others who cultivated a mystic "way of devotion" that was deeply rooted in the Church's past. Monasticism had always had its mystic aspect; when the monk retired to solitary meditation, he sought to purge himself of evil and lift his soul to ecstatic union with God and the saints. The mystics were those who refused to believe that the direct vision of God himself, or of Christ, or of the saints, had to await the passage from this world to the next; the mystic vision was possible here on earth.

Medieval mysticism had both an individual and a cultic form. In the 12th century the Cistercian leader, Bernard of Clairvaux, tried to bring new vigor into the religious life of his time by preaching and writing of the blessing that came from the mystic's love of the Virgin and of Christ. In his *Homilies on the Song of Songs* he provided later mystics with valuable concepts for the description of their feelings: he saw in Christ the bridegroom of the soul, and so vividly defined this relationship of the Redeemer and his adorers that he made it possible for mystics to interpret their raptures as ideal and heavenly love. It seemed to Bernard that such a relationship would transcend earthly feeling. Love for Jesus can be so warm and personal that the entire being of the enraptured mystic becomes flooded with a sense of tenderness, fervor, and sweetness.*

Hugo St. Victor and Bonaventura in the 12th and 13th centuries carried mysticism into the schools. The Dominican preachers, Meister Eckhart and John Tauler, in the late 13th and early 14th centuries in Germany, succeeded in developing an influential mystic cult in central Europe. Both were impatient of the externalism of the then current Catholicism. To Eckhart even "individuality" was something to be laid aside; it was "nothing." Only the divine spark in the soul is real; it alone matters. Following the same path, the Dominican ascetic, Henry Suso, illustrated in his own life the privations which extremer mystics determinedly underwent. As long as he felt within himself any element of self-love and fleshly desire, he submitted his body to the extremes of self-torture, carrying on his back a heavy cross studded with nails and needles, and sometimes lying down upon it in stern self-chastisement, until at last God did "gladden the heart of the sufferer in return for all his sufferings with inward peace of heart, so that he praised God with all his heart for his past suffering." [30]

Around these German mystics a cult calling itself "The Friends of God" arose and spread through southwestern Germany, Switzerland, and Holland. In Holland the movement led to the founding of a group called the "Brethren of the Common Life," whose members, renouncing sex, lived in separate houses of brethren and sisters, practicing the mystic discipline in semi-monastic seclusion. The finest literary product of this group was a book of simple and earnest piety called the *Imitation of Christ*, by one Thomas à Kempis. No book produced during the Middle Ages has reached so many readers as this, for it commended itself long after as much to Protestants as to Catholics.

In other parts of the Catholic world the disorders of the Church

---

* How profoundly stirring this idea was, may be seen in the hymn which comes down from his day, perhaps from his own hand:

> Jesus, the very thought of thee
>   With sweetness fills the breast;
> But sweeter far thy face to see,
>   And in thy presence rest. . . .
>
> O Hope of every contrite heart,
>   O Joy of all the meek,
> To those who fall, how kind thou art!
>   How good to those who seek!
>
> But what to those who find? Ah, this
>   Nor tongue nor pen can show;
> The love of Jesus, what it is
>   None but his loved ones know.

Christ on the cross. (After crucifix, Swabia, ca. 1200, in Germanic Museum, Nuremberg)

beginning in the 14th century caused many individuals to turn to mysticism for truth and grace. Two great women found in their mystic raptures the power to work for reforms in the church and in the world. Catherine of Siena (1347–1380), energized by a mystic experience of "marriage" with Christ, the heavenly bridegroom, worked among the victims of the Black Plague, and being distressed by the "Babylonish Captivity" of the popes at Avignon, personally persuaded Gregory XI to move the seat of the papacy back to Rome. Almost two centuries later, Teresa of Avila, in Spain (1515–1582) after similar experiences, reformed the Carmelite order. She found guidance and help from a fellow mystic, the ascetic John of the Cross.

It is needless here to extend the list. One and all displayed the irrepressible longing of all high religions to transcend the formal and external limits of human experience and meet God face to face.

The Decline of the Papacy

The papacy was unable to maintain itself on the height of authority and power reached during the 13th century. The factors which led to its decline were many. The unremitting papal pressure at the top only accentuated the divisive effect of a new sense of nationalism rising among the different European peoples from below. France and England, particularly, were able to move toward independence; indeed, the Holy Roman Empire (now "neither holy, nor Roman, nor an empire") broke up into a collection of loosely united petty kingdoms. When this happened, France began to wield a more powerful influence than Italy. There was an immediate clash of interests. The French clergy, forced to take sides, began to distinguish between the spiritual and the temporal authority of the pope; and often sided with the king of France in disputes involving temporal matters. When Pope Boniface VIII (1294–1303) and Philip the Fair fell out, the latter did an epochal thing—a demonstration both of the force of rising nationalism and of the stirring of democracy in western Europe; he called together a parliament such as the English already had; it was the first French States-General, and had representation from clergy, nobility, and commoners. This body gave him full support. The pope thereupon issued the famous bull, *Unam Sanctam,* containing the unqualified words: "We declare, we say, we define and pronounce that to every creature it is absolutely necessary to salvation to be subject to the Roman pontiff." This attempt to bring him to heel only led Philip to call another session of the States-General, during which the pope was defiantly arraigned as a criminal, a heretic, and immoral, and an appeal was issued for a general council of the churches to put the pope on trial. Since neither side would yield, the pope, a spiritual authority without military power, at length suffered the indignity of imprisonment by some of Philip's armed supporters. He was soon released, but the harm was done: in the name of nationalism, rough men had seized the pope's person and put him under duress!

A succession of French popes followed (1305–1377). Fearing violence in Italy, they retired to "Babylonish Captivity" at Avignon, where the power of the king of France over them was so unlimited that rival popes were elsewhere put in the field (1378–1417), thus to the great damage of papal prestige producing what is known as the Great Schism. Thenceforth France and England became increasingly independent. The papal power waned. In the great chorus of liberated voices which was rising, the popes were no longer able to command a hushed silence when they spoke.

The Movement toward Individualism,
Freedom, and Reform

Meanwhile, during the Crusades and especially after the fall of

Constantinople in the 15th century—an event which brought many scholars fleeing to Italy with the literary masterpieces of the ancient Greeks in the original tongue—there began that revival of classical learning known as the Renaissance. Poets and tale tellers like Petrarch and Boccaccio were the literary masters who joined the great Renaissance painters and sculptors in popularizing the "humanist" outlook, with its ever-fresh delight in man and nature. Even the popes became zealous patrons of art and learning, and all but forgot the duties they owed to the Christian world as Holy Fathers.

This was not lost on the common man. With the world rapidly expanding and enlarging on his view, as stories first of the Crusades, then of the discoveries of Marco Polo, of Columbus, and later of Magellan and others were conveyed to him, and with his own life vastly altered by the rise of commercial towns independent of lords and princes, the common man began, in guild-hall and market-place, to question the manners and morals of the clergy, from the pope down, and to criticize the practices of the Church which had recently been established—the sale of indulgences,* obligatory confession, and papal taxation in the form of money fees for baptisms, weddings, funerals, and all appointments to office in the church, and for hundreds of other transactions. Moreover, the common man began to want learning for himself. He knew he could not master the classics of antiquity known to the learned,

---

* It was held that the pope possessed a treasury of the superfluous merits accumulated by the saints and that he had unlimited dispensation of these credits. Indulgences were sold in the form of documents transferring credits to the purchaser's spiritual account.

Scenes from a Medieval mystery play: the presentation of the child Jesus at the Temple; Jesus disputing with the doctors; and Jesus being baptized in the Jordan by John the Baptist.

but he became curious about the Bible. He revelled in the mystery plays that dramatized for him episodes from the Biblical story and moral dilemmas from everyday life. These whetted his appetite for direct acquaintance with the literary sources of these productions.

The common man's criticism of the Church and his hunger for scripture reached more intense forms in northern Europe than elsewhere; and there aroused the English priest, John Wyclif, to condemn papal taxation as greed and the doctrine of transubstantiation as unscriptural, and to send his Lollard priests among the people of England to teach them the leveling doctrines of the Bible directly from translations out of the Vulgate into the English tongue. Wyclif influenced John Huss in Bohemia to lead a popular religious revolt of such proportions that the Council of Constance in 1415 condemned Huss to be burned at the stake. A quite unrelated reform later in the 15th century was led by the Dominican monk Savonarola in the city of Florence; which, after a brief triumph over the lives and spirits of the entire citizenry, procured for Savonarola finally only his own death by hanging.

In vain the Church at large attempted, through the cooperation of bishops, kings, emperors, and by the councils called at Constance and at Basel in the first half of the 15th century, to introduce needed reforms in church life and administration; the only reform they seemed able to effect was the healing of the scandalous papal schism, an accomplishment brought about by forcing the rival popes from office and then restoring a single pontiff to the see of Rome. Otherwise, the situation remained fundamentally unaltered and provocative of greater upheavals to come.

VI THE PROTESTANT REFORMATION

The Protestant Reformation split western Christianity into two irreconcilable groups. It was long in preparation, as any study of medieval thought, even one so brief as ours, shows. It remained only for certain new developments, chief among which was the rise of the middle class to economic and cultural self-sufficiency, to bring it to pass. When the people of Europe gathered into towns along the rivers and coasts, as a consequence of the increase of commerce and trade, wealth was no longer immobilized in land or in produce offered for near-at-hand barter; it became fluid in the form of money; and modern capitalism

was born. Gradually the lords and princes were forced to relax their
hold upon the growing middle class, and thousands of townspeople began to be true individuals. With no immediate overlords save only
burgomaster and town councilors, they gained rapidly in self-confidence
and ability to meet life's problems on their own initiative. Politically,
they began to evolve a point of view which was later to issue in democracy. One John Ball, the so-called "mad priest of Kent," cried out in
England as early as in the 14th century:

> "My good friends, matters cannot go on well in England until all things
> shall be in common; when there shall be neither vassals nor lords; when the
> lords shall be no more masters than ourselves. . . . Are we not all descended
> from the same parents, Adam and Eve? So what reason can they give why
> they should be more masters than ourselves? They are clothed in velvet
> and rich stuffs, ornamented with ermine and other furs, while we are forced
> to wear coarse linen. They have wine, spices, and good bread, while we have
> only rye-bread and the refuse of the straw; and when we drink it must be
> water. They have handsome seats and manors, while we have the trouble and
> the work, and must brave the rain and the wind in the fields. And it is by
> our labor they have wherewith to support their pomp." [31]

In such words lay the seeds of the peasant revolts of the 14th and 15th
centuries in England and central Europe.

It is not surprising that the common man of Europe began to want
his religious competence recognized too—whether in the use of reason
or in the exercise of conscience. Martin Luther very well expressed the
feeling of laymen when he passionately asserted:

> "I say, then, neither pope, nor bishop, nor any man whatever has the
> right of making one syllable binding on a Christian man, unless it be done
> with his own consent. Whatever is done otherwise is done in the spirit of
> tyranny. . . . I cry aloud on behalf of liberty and conscience, and I proclaim
> with confidence that no kind of law can with any justice be imposed on
> Christians, except so far as they themselves will; for we are free from all." [32]

The spiritual fact was, that at the very time when the layman
began to feel his own competence most, the Church seemed to him
most corrupt. The Church had become identified in his mind with a
vast system of financial exactions, rapaciously draining gold from every
corner of Europe to Rome, where luxury, materialism, irreverence, and
even harlotry seemed to reign unchecked among the clergy. Not only
was the Church in his eyes corrupt, it seemed also to be left behind in
the onward sweep of progress. In a changing world, it represented
cramping institutionalism, conservatism, conformity from age to age to

one inflexible law, one worship, one order of life for every individual. Worse still, a yawning gulf had opened between religion and life, and the disparity between the Church and man's need increased more and more, until the pious layman, just a little appalled anyway by the secularizing effects of capitalism and nationalism, began to wish for changes in the Church that would make it serve the needs of men better.

All that was lacking was a leader who should precipitate the needed reforms.

The Lutheran Reformation

In Germany such a man appeared. He was Martin Luther (1483–1546), an honest, impetuous, heavy-set German, who linked conviction immediately and as a matter of course with appropriate action. Born in Saxony, of peasant stock, he absorbed from his environment no particular respect for priests, but a great fear of the wrath of God. His father wanted him to become a lawyer, but midway in his study of the law he responded to his intense religious need and entered a monastery of the Augustinian order, bent on winning God's favor by a pure and arduous conformity to monastic discipline. He punctiliously obeyed all the rules of his order; he swept the floor, fasted, bent over his books, almost froze. But though he wept and prayed and became mere skin and bone, he failed to make God gracious; indeed he was not sure of his salvation. In 1507, he was ordained to the priesthood, and later was appointed a professor in the new university established at Wittenberg by Frederick the Wise, elector of Saxony. There he came to despise Aristotle as an "accursed, proud, knavish heathen" who had led many of the best Christians astray by his emptiness and "false words." [33] The reason for this animus seems to have been the lack in Aristotle of any profound religious conviction. Luther obtained what he most needed directly from the Bible; and on its books, especially the Book of Psalms and the Epistles of Paul, he lectured with growing enthusiasm and comfort to himself.

A journey to Rome in the meantime, even while it deepened his love of the Holy City, confirmed him in the conviction that the papacy had fallen into unworthy hands. He saw in the lives of the priests at Rome, not the poverty and humility of Christ, but pomp, worldliness, and pride. He was later to say:

"It is of a piece with this revolting pride that the Pope is not satisfied with riding on horseback or in a carriage, but though he be hale and strong, is carried by men like an idol in unheard-of pomp. My friend, how does this

Lucifer-like pride agree with the example of Christ, who went on foot, as did also all the Apostles?" [34]

His own inner life was illuminated suddenly by a sentence from St. Paul; its words were determinative in clearing up his own uncertainty: "The just shall live by faith" (Romans 1:17). Faith!—it alone was sufficient! God cannot be *made* gracious by good works; God, like a father, *is* gracious toward His own. All who live in this love and trust know that they are justified by their faith alone, and will gratefully live a life of good works, without any urging, like a child who knows his father loves him. Gratitude, not fear, is the spring of the Christian life.

While Luther was forming these convictions, he was disturbed by the arrival of Tetzel, a papal agent, to sell indulgences in a nearby town. When members of his Wittenberg congregation (he preached in the castle church besides teaching in the university) went to buy these indulgences, he spoke out against their doing so. Urged by friends who felt as he did, on October 31, 1517, he posted on the door of the castle church the famous Ninety-Five Theses, a detailed attack on the selling of indulgences, drawn up in the form of propositions for public discussion. In accordance with the prevailing academic etiquette, he politely invited debate on each point he made; but he hardly anticipated

Luther nailing his theses on church door at Wittenberg.

the effect of his action. So great was the demand both for copies of the Latin original of his Theses and for its German translation, that the university press could not issue copies fast enough to meet the demand from every part of Germany.

The fat was in the fire now. All North Germany began to buzz with talk. There was no thought then on anyone's part of leaving the Church; there was only a demand for reform. Yet there was present a deeper desire—scarcely conscious—for greater freedom from Rome. It was natural that Luther should be immediately attacked by Tetzel and others. His own bishop sent a copy of the Theses to the pope, who promptly ordered Luther to appear at Rome for trial and discipline. The elector of Saxony, who was proud of Luther, intervened, however, and the pope modified his demand to the order that Luther appear before the papal legate at Augsburg, which he did.

All this pressure had the effect, in itself a basic reaction of the entire Reformation, of making Luther search the Scriptures to verify his position and justify his actions. His examination of the Bible convinced him that the Catholic Church had so far departed from its scriptural basis that many of its practices were actually anti-Christian. He was driven to question not only the sale through indulgences of the infinite merits of Christ and the superfluous merits of the saints, but the whole medieval attitude toward penance and good works conceived as transactions made with God for His favor through the necessary mediation of priest, bishop, and pope. True repentance is an inward matter, and puts a man into direct touch with the forgiving Father; therefore, in the words of the 36th Thesis: "Every Christian who feels true compunction has of right plenary remission of pain and guilt, even without letters of pardon." [35] Forgiveness of sins comes through the change wrought in a man's soul by his direct personal relationship with Christ and through Christ with God. Gradually Luther reached the position that the true Church is not any particular ecclesiastical organization but simply the community of the faithful whose head is Christ. The only final religious authority is the Bible made understandable to believers by the Holy Spirit through their faith. So competent is every man of faith, that he is potentially a priest; the church should therefore proclaim "the universal priesthood of all believers." Said he:

> To put the matter plainly, if a little company of pious Christian laymen were taken prisoners and carried away to a desert, and had not among them a priest consecrated by a bishop, and were there to agree to elect one of them, born in wedlock or not, and were to order him to baptise, to celebrate the mass, to absolve, and to preach, this man would as truly be a

priest, as if all the bishops and all the popes had consecrated him. That is why in cases of necessity every man can baptise and absolve, which would not be possible if we were not all priests.[36]

Further, since believers should be enabled to participate in religious exercises to the full, services should be in German, rather than Latin; and they should be simplified and given a clearer intent.

Luther's appearance before the papal legate proved inconclusive. Ordered to recant, he refused, and made good his escape back to Wittenberg. A lull in the papal agitation against him followed, produced by political developments in the Empire; but it ended abruptly when Luther was led into a debate with the Catholic theologian, John of Eck, and forced to admit that he thought the Council of Constance had erred in condemning John Huss. Was Luther now repudiating the authority of the Catholic Church wherever it ran counter to his own judgment of what the Bible meant? It appeared so, and the pope issued a bull of condemnation against him. The Emperor Charles V being called upon to act, Luther was summoned in 1521 to appear before the imperial diet, meeting at Worms. The elector of Saxony consented to this only if Luther were promised safe conduct; which being assured, Luther appeared. He readily acknowledged that the writings issued under his name were his, but would not retract, he said, unless he should be convinced from Scripture that he was in error. While some of his admirers among the German princes looked on, he boldly told the emperor and assembled delegates of the Church: "Unless I am· convinced by the testimony of Scripture or by evident reason—for I confide neither in the Pope nor in a Council alone, since it is certain they have often erred and contradicted themselves—I am held fast by the Scriptures adduced by me, and my conscience is taken captive by God's Word, and I neither can nor will revoke anything, seeing that it is not safe or right to act against conscience. God help me. Amen." [37] Since he was under safe conduct, Luther left Worms unharmed; but it was understood that as soon as he returned home, he could be apprehended for punishment. The diet therefore put him under a ban, ordered him to surrender, and forbade anyone to shelter him or read his books. But Luther could not be found; his prince, the elector Frederick, had had him seized on the way home, and he was hidden away in Wartburg Castle.

Luther used his enforced leisure to good purpose. He set to work on a translation of the New Testament into German. (Some years later, in 1534, he issued a complete translation of the Bible—an epochal achievement in more than one sense; not only did it carry out the

Reformation principle that the Bible must be put into the hands of the common man, but it also gave the Germans for the first time a uniform language, through which they could achieve national cultural unity.)

The Edict of Worms was never enforced. When Luther emerged from hiding, the emperor was busy with wars and quarrels elsewhere, and moreover it was apparent that the German people were largely on Luther's side. Whole provinces became Protestant at one stroke when their princes renounced allegiance to the pope and turned Lutheran. By the time of Luther's death in 1546, his reforms had spread from central Germany into much of southern, all of northern Germany, and beyond into Denmark, Norway, Sweden, and the Baltic states.

Luther did not leave to his followers a fixed system of theology and polity. He himself showed many inconsistencies, due in no small degree to his caution and conservatism. He was in no sense a radical. He had repudiated Thomas Aquinas and Aristotle; yet, as though he were appealing from medieval Catholicism back to the ancient Catholic Church, he found in St. Augustine a man after his own heart; and back of Augustine he rested, of course, on St. Paul. So vehemently did he cling to what he conceived to be Augustine's doctrine of determinism and predestination, that he alienated the humanist Erasmus. Others found him too conservative in matters of worship, inasmuch as he retained the use of candles, the crucifix, the organ, and certain elements of the Roman Mass.* When an attempt was made to bring Luther and the Swiss Reformer Zwingli together, the conference between them broke down because Luther insisted that, while there is no transubstantiation in the Lord's Supper, the body of Christ is spiritually present in, with, and under the elements of bread and wine (consubstantiation). His conservatism appeared, too, in his social and political views. He showed traces of anti-Semitism in later life; and in the peasant revolt of 1524 he disappointed many by siding with the princes. In fact, he laid the basis of German statism by commanding submissive obedience to state authorities on the part of all Lutherans.

Wherever the Lutheran Reformation spread, the Catholic monks and nuns either left the district or abandoned their former way of life and dress and joined the Lutheran community as parish priests, teachers, and layfolk, free to marry and raise families. Luther himself married a former nun and enjoyed a happy family life with the five children he had by her. In organizing the new Lutheran communities

---

* But he removed the priestly-sacrificial aspects of the Roman Mass, and may be said to have moved back toward the Lord's Supper as described in the New Testament.

he concerned himself most with three functions: the pastorate, charity, and the training and educating of the children. The monasteries that were appropriated by the town councilors or by princes were often turned, on his advice, into schools and universities.

Luther did not live to see the religious war which brought Germany during the mid-century years to the brink of chaos and resulted in the compromise Peace of Augsburg (September, 1555), by which equal rights were guaranteed to Catholics and Lutherans, but which left the religion of each province to the determination of its prince, on the principle *cujus regio, ejus religio* ("whose the rule, his the religion"). The Lutheran Reformation had really put the ruling prince where the bishop had formerly been, that is, in a position to exercise general jurisdiction over the churches.

The Swiss Reformation

A more radical Reformation came in Switzerland, when Ulrich Zwingli (1484–1531), a highly educated parish priest, whose sympathies lay from youth with the Humanists, especially in their war on superstition and irrationalism, advocated a return to the New Testament as the basic source of Christian truth. In Zurich, therefore, he began a systematic public exposition of the books of the Bible, beginning with the Gospels. By 1522 he reached the conviction that Christians are bound by and should practice only what is commanded in the Bible —a far more radical position than that of Luther, who held that Christians need not give up the elements in Catholic practice which are helpful and not forbidden in the Bible. In accordance with his convictions Zwingli persuaded the people of Zurich to remove all images and crosses from the churches, and to sing without organ accompaniment. In putting a stop to the celebration of the mass, he took the view that when Jesus said "This is my body," he meant "This *signifies* my body." It was irrational to suppose, he contended, that Christ's body and blood could be at once in heaven and with equal reality on ten thousand altars on earth all at the same time, as Luther argued. The bread and wine must be regarded as symbolic in character; they were blessed memorials of Jesus' sacrifice of himself upon the cross. The proper way to celebrate the Lord's Supper was to reproduce as nearly as possible the atmosphere and situation of the early Christian eucharist. Ritual should be at a minimum. And as to the regular church services, the sermon should be the central element in worship; it was the chief means by which the will of God could be made known. Local church government was to be reposed in the hands of the elders of each congregation, called collectively the spiritual council; for this seemed a close approximation to early Christian church organization.

The Zwinglian Reformation spread in his lifetime to Basle, Berne, Glarus, Mulhausen, and Strassburg. Ultimately it produced civil war between Catholic and Reformed forces, and Zwingli fell in one of the battles (1531).

In the southwestern part of Switzerland an intense young preacher called Farel won Geneva over to the Reformation. The task of producing a thorough-going religious reform proved so difficult that he prevailed upon a young French scholar by the name of John Calvin (1509–1564) to stay and help him. Calvin was at the time (1536) in flight from France, where he had just published, at twenty-six years of age, the first edition of the Reformation classic, *The Institutes of the Christian Religion,* a crystal-clear definition of the Protestant position, which was destined to lay the foundations of Presbyterianism.

Since the public policies of Calvin flowed logically from his religious convictions, it would be well to list at once the chief affirmations of the *Institutes.*

1. The central fact of religion is the sovereignty of God. God wills whatever happens in the physical world and in human history, and thereby assures His own glory. His will is inscrutable, and from the human point of view He may seem to follow merely His good pleasure; but His character is holy and righteous, and all His decisions are just.

2. Man is possessed of a certain natural knowledge of God as the moving spirit in Nature and history; but his understanding is dimmed by his innate depravity, inherited from Adam, and so his knowledge must be supplemented by the revelation of Holy Writ.

3. Man's depravity vitiates not only his understanding but his whole nature. With a conviction going straight back to St. Augustine, Calvin wrote:

Original sin may be defined as an hereditary corruption and depravity of our nature, extending to all parts of the soul, which makes us obnoxious to the wrath of God, and then produces in us those works which the Scripture calls "works of the flesh." . . . We are, on account of this corruption, justly condemned in the sight of God. And this liableness to punishment arises not from the delinquency of another; for when it is said that the sin of Adam has made us obnoxious to the justice of God, the meaning is not that we, in ourselves innocent and blameless, are bearing his guilt. The Apostle himself expressly declares, that "death has passed upon all men, for that all have sinned" (Rom. 5:12), that is, have been involved in original sin, and defiled.[38]

4. But not all men are lost. There is a justification by faith that saves some, and these go on to sanctification. Justification comes through the work of Christ in the believer's behalf, and is "the acceptance with which God receives us into His favor, as if we were righteous." [39] But God justifies only those believers in Christ whom He *elects* to receive into favor.

5. This idea of election leads into the Calvinistic doctrine of predestination. "By predestination we mean," wrote Calvin, "the eternal decree of God, by which he determined with himself whatever he wished to happen with regard to every man. All are not created on equal terms, but some are preordained to eternal life, others to eternal damnation." [40]

6. Like Augustine, Calvin considered the Church under two aspects. The Church invisible is constituted of all the elect of God in heaven and on earth; the Church visible is the company of professing believers on earth, organized in accordance with God's word in the Scripture. In the Church visible the believer is not saved by his works, since it is God's election alone that saves him; yet he is saved unto a righteousness abounding in good works; in fact, *his righteousness is the only assurance he has of his election.* "We are justified not without, and yet not by works," said Calvin.

This reasoning led Calvin to regard life with more than usual gravity and seriousness. Duty and self-discipline were to him uppermost. One must live as under God's eye. Frivolous people who spent their hours in worldly pleasures, light-heartedly preferring card-playing, dancing, and masquerades to sober reflection, reading the Bible, and doing God's will, might fear the worst; they were to be regarded as already the Devil's own, doomed to the fires of Hell. On the other hand, those who were moved by the Holy Spirit to go about the Lord's solemn business on earth were earnest, industrious, and thrifty, and valued these attributes in themselves as signs of their election to salvation. By this chastening logic, from which there seemed no escape, Calvin changed the mood of the citizens of Geneva to a puritanical righteousness. There was no room in Geneva for Luther's playfulness and laughter, his roaring, lusty voice raised in song around the organ; nor for his glad sense of the passing of God's wrath and the outpouring of his gracious love. Calvin's joy was a more secret thing, an inward peace and satisfaction, not expressed in the joviality of convivial fellowship; it was intellectual rather than emotional in quality and expression.

In Geneva arose a new kind of community. Working with the Small and General Town Councils, over which he gained increasing, if sometimes stormy ascendancy, Calvin instituted both a church life and an educational system that gave Geneva a trained ministry and a people sufficiently informed regarding their faith to be able to give a clear account of it. Refugee scholars and exiles from all over Europe flocked to Geneva as to an asylum, so that the city increased its original 13,000 population by 6,000. Among the brilliant men who came there were Beza, one of Europe's leading humanists; Cordier, perhaps the ablest of European educators; Caraccioli, an Italian noble; Michael Servetus, who scarcely reached Geneva before he was condemned to death in a public trial and burned at the stake for heretical unitarian views; and the Scottish refugee, John Knox.

The Reformation in France and the Low Countries

Beza and Cordier came to Geneva when the fires of affliction were being kindled for the Protestants of France. The Reformation had begun rather quietly in that land, yet with every prospect of soon sweeping the country. Then all at once it was very nearly drowned in blood. The forces on either side were brought into such violent conflict that civil war engulfed the country. Much more completely than in Geneva, the French Protestants, or Huguenots, adopted John Calvin's conception of church organization. The local congregation "called" its own ministers through the elders and deacons who formed the "consistory." * The Catholic clergy and the French court took alarm and resorted to suppression by fire and sword. When Catherine de Medici became regent, she first courted, then turned upon the Huguenots. It was she who persuaded the weakling king Charles IX to order the Massacre of St. Bartholomew (August, 1572), which is said to have brought death to 20,000 Protestants. But the Huguenots were served by great military leaders, notably Admiral Coligny, and after each renewal of the bitter

* T. M. Lindsay, in *A History of the Reformation* (Scribner's Sons, 1919), II, p. 165, gives the following clear summary: Calvin "proposed to revive the simple three-fold ministry of the Church of the early centuries—a congregation ruled by a bishop or pastor, a session of elders, and a body of deacons. This was adopted by the French Protestants. A group of believers, a minister, a 'consistory' of elders and deacons, regular preaching, and the sacraments duly administered, made a church properly constituted. The minister was the chief; he preached; he administered the sacraments; he presided at the 'consistory.' The 'consistory' was composed of elders charged with the spiritual oversight of the community, and of deacons who looked after the poor and the sick. The elders and deacons were chosen by the members of the congregation; and the minister by the elders and deacons." This was Christian democracy. Kings and bishops naturally opposed it.

civil war, they were able, howsoever reduced in numbers, to secure at least a measure of toleration, and at last by the Edict of Nantes (1598) won complete liberty of conscience, full civil rights, and the control of two hundred towns. Protestantism in France had not grown strong, but it had won the protection of the state. However, Louis XIV revoked the Edict of Nantes (in 1685), and made Protestantism illegal again! It was Napoleon who finally restored Protestant rights.

Bitter, too, was the struggle in the Low Countries. The Spaniards were in control there, and both the emperor Charles V and his son, Philip II of Spain, were determined to stamp out the Reformed faith wherever it showed itself. The people of the Low Countries were in some sense prepared for the Reformation by the Brethren of the Common Life, already described, who had expressed what was really a people's movement toward personal piety, accompanied by a strong love of biblical learning. Luther's writings were eagerly circulated when they appeared; later Zwingli won devoted adherents; and still later Calvin's conception of church organization was to prevail. Some Netherlanders were attracted to the radical Anabaptists (see below). Open rebellion against Spain came when Philip II sent the cruel Duke of Alva to suppress every form of heresy at any necessary cost of blood. The struggle was long drawn out; but at last William the Silent was able to form a group of northern states that won independence as the nation of Holland. Holland became a Calvinistic land, sturdy and self-reliant, with its churches (the Dutch Reformed) organized on the democratic principles already established among the French Protestants.

The Reformation in Scotland

If the antagonism of Philip II and William the Silent may be called dramatic, that of Mary Queen of Scots and John Knox was highly so; for the first two never met face to face, but Mary and John Knox confronted each other more than once, with decisive results.

In a sense, the case of Scotland was critical for the whole Reformation. To many at the time it seemed very possible that Mary, either by her marriage with Francis II of France (through which she became an adherent of the French Catholic party in European politics) or by making good her claim to the English throne as a Stuart (which she never was able to do), might bring both Scotland and England back to the Catholic fold.

But Mary's marriage to the French king actually gave the Protestants of Scotland a chance they were not slow to seize. She was long absent in France, and during that time John Knox led his Protestant colleagues in the rapid development of a Calvinistic church. Knox did not introduce the Reformation to Scotland; he was himself a product of it. Captured in youth by a French force sent to Scotland to apprehend a group of Protestant rebels there, he was carried to France, and compelled to row in the galleys for nineteen bitter months. On release he went to England, then under the Protestant government of Edward VI, and served in various towns as a royal chaplain. On the accession of Mary Tudor he escaped to the Continent, and made his way to Geneva, where he became an enthusiastic disciple of Calvin. Ultimately he returned to Scotland, and in 1560, not long after his return, had the great triumph of having the Scottish parliament ratify the "Confession of Faith Professed and Believed by the Protestants within the Realm of Scotland," which he and five others prepared, and which remained the creedal formula of the Church of Scotland until it was replaced by the Westminster Confession in 1647. A week later the parliament decreed that "the bishops of Rome have no jurisdiction nor authority in this realm," and forbade the saying, hearing, or being present at mass. Eventually, the Roman Catholic bishops and priests were expelled from the church lands, which then came largely into the possession of the Scottish nobles.

In subsequent developments the so-called Presbyterian system of church government was worked out on a national scale. In its complete form it established a representative democracy. The congregation elected and called the minister, who thereafter was alone responsible for the conduct of public worship. But this was his only unlimited prerogative. All local matters affecting the discipline and administration of the parish were entrusted to the kirk-session, composed of the minister, who presided, and the elders, chosen by election. Above the kirk-session was the presbytery, which consisted of the ministers of the parishes of a designated area and an equal number of elders representing each parish. Above the presbyteries was the Synod, with jurisdiction over certain groups of presbyteries; and over all was the General Assembly, the supreme judicatory of the national church, consisting of delegate ministers and an equal number of elders. The center of gravity of this system was the presbytery, which was small enough to be vitally representative of its locality and large enough to have plenty of fight in it when its survival was threatened.

It was a bad moment for the Scottish Reformers when the fascinating and calculating Mary Queen of Scots came back from France a widow. They knew she was a devout Catholic and meant to overthrow the Reformation in Scotland, if she could. When she first arrived, she pursued a moderate course, insisting only on having mass for her own household, but promising to maintain elsewhere the laws which made it illegal in Scotland. She summoned Knox to five interviews, in which she used all her skill to win him over; but he remained firm in opposition to any concession to the Papacy. In other quarters Mary had more success, and might have won all had she not fallen into disgrace through her intrigue with Bothwell and been deposed in favor of her year-old son, who later became James I of England. With her fall the Protestant forces recovered their strength, and Scotland was made secure for the Reformation.

In the meantime, the Reformation in England had won a similar firm footing.

The English Reformation

The English Reformation was one of those more or less inevitable outcomes that thrive upon accidents; a king's private whim opened the way for the religious revolution which the nation basically wanted. With the moderation so characteristic of them, the English leaders nourished a desire to enjoy at least the degree of religious self-determination which the Reformation had brought to the continental Protestants, and yet they bowed to the forms of legality in their national life, and patiently waited. Eventually they made their will felt, which was as soon as the opportunity presented itself.

The uninhibited Henry VIII, in the grip of a personal desire for a change in his marital status, vowed that, if the Roman curia would not annul his marriage to Catherine of Aragon in order that he might marry Ann Boleyn, he would break with the pope! The Roman curia turned him down, and Henry did not hesitate to act. Though much that he did and said shocked all shades of opinion in the nation, he had powerful elements among his people with him when he got Parliament to declare that "the bishop of Rome" had no more jurisdiction in England than any other foreign ecclesiastic; that the only true head of the Church of England was the king of England; that bishops in England were thenceforth to be nominated by the king and were to give their oath of obedience to him instead of to the pope; and that denial of the king's supremacy in the church was an act of high treason. Henry quickly won the support of his nobles by first suppressing the monasteries in his realm and then distributing generous grants of land to them from among the great possessions thereby confiscated. Besides winning these powerful supporters, he cut off the flow of papal taxes to Rome, and satisfied the growing desire of the English people for national self-determination in religion.

But Henry VIII was theologically conservative; he did not intend that there should be a doctrinal break with the past to match his jurisdictional break with the pope. In 1539 he had Parliament pass what is known as the "Bloody Statute." It declared the doctrine of transubstantiation to be the faith of the Church of England, and denial of it to be punishable by burning at the stake and confiscation of goods; it also forbade the marriage of priests, disallowed communion in both bread and wine, and enjoined private masses and auricular confession. The only considerable concession he made to liberal views, aside from his break with Rome, was in having a copy of the Bible in English placed in all the churches.* Many English followers of Luther and the Swiss Reformers were put to death under the Bloody Statute; more fled to the Continent, where they found their chief asylum in Switzerland.

These exiles returned when Henry was succeeded by his nine-year-old son, Edward VI; for then it became apparent that, under the protectorate established for the immature king, the national policy would shift religiously to the left. The young king's advisers, especially Somerset and Northumberland, strongly favored doctrinal as well as political changes. The Bloody Statute was repealed; communion in both kinds was allowed; private masses were brought to an end by the confiscation of the chapels where they were said; priests were permitted to marry; and images were removed from the churches as instances of papish idolatry. But Edward died when only fifteen, and was succeeded by his sister, Mary, an ardent Catholic, who loved and married the Spanish heir-apparent.† She led the return to Rome by restoring the pope's jurisdiction over the English churches; and herself earned the name of "Bloody Mary" by the ruthlessness with which leading Protestants were at her behest apprehended and burned at the stake. When she died after a reign as brief as Edward's, her sister Elizabeth, the daughter of Ann Boleyn, brought the nation finally to the Protestant fold. "Good Queen Bess," as her subjects affectionately called her, completed the unfinished work of her young brother's reign; the Prayer Book of Edward VI was revised so as to be made palatable to Catholics and Protestants alike, and under the name of "The Book of Common

---

* The so-called Great Bible, drawn largely from the translation of Tyndale, but with some parts taken from Coverdale's version.

† Charles V's son, soon to become the intolerant Philip II.

Prayer" was, by the Act of Uniformity of 1559, prescribed for use in all churches without alteration or deviation; and the beliefs of the church were stated clearly in the famous creedal statement "The Thirty-Nine Articles of the Church of England," which is to this day the finally authoritative summary of its doctrines. England remained Protestant henceforth, even when Catholic monarchs were on the throne.

The Protestant Radicals

While the national Reformation movements just described were coming to terms in one way or another with the civil powers, quiet searchers of the Scriptures all over Europe were finding their own way to a much more radical break with constituted authority. Some were *moved* by the Word of God alive within them; some followed *reason* solely.

Among the former were the *Anabaptists* (literally "rebaptizers"), groups largely recruited from the common people—peasants and artisans —and led in the first instance by immediate associates of Luther and Zwingli. Most took the New Testament literally and with great seriousness, determined to depart in no way from the manner of life they saw depicted in it. Others felt themselves not bound thus by the "letter" of Scripture, because the "Word" is a "living spirit" expressed in but not confined to Scripture nor present equally in all parts of it; the living Word of God is heard in prophetic personalities and in the inner consciousness of all who are justified by faith.

It seemed to all the Anabaptists that the first requisite of being a Christian is that one should grasp clearly in his own mind the meaning of each aspect of the Christian life and practice, and then act upon that understanding no matter what the cost. Ceremonies and rituals must, they thought, have a clear meaning to the participants, or cease being real and vital. Accordingly, they rejected infant baptism; plainly, the baby could not know what was being done, and so the rite could mean nothing. Those who had been baptized in infancy therefore baptized each other all over again (hence the name they bore). In the wider realm of conduct, clear understanding and sincerity, they held, are just as imperatively needed. The New Testament teaches the principle of overcoming evil with good, instead of resisting one injury with another. Most Anabaptists concluded that they should not join the armed forces of the state, contribute to warfare in any way at all, or even take part in the civil administration during peacetime, because of the policy of force all states adopt. They found New Testament warrant for never taking oaths; so, when taken to court, they insisted that their simple word be taken for truth: their yea was yea and their nay nay. Because they felt that priests and ministers were prone to please worldly powers and make compromises in vital areas, the Anabaptists were anti-clerical, and met outside the regular church circles in their own houses; churches were to them idolatrous "steeple-houses." They did not agree on all matters, but they made it a principle to exercise tolerance where differences as to the literal meaning of Scripture appeared. Some, for instance, took with greater literalness than others the apocalyptic or millenarian passages of the New Testament expressing the expectation that Christ would return on the clouds of heaven to be the judge on the Last Day. Others practiced the communism of the early Christian fellowship in Jerusalem. Occasionally an Anabaptist would proclaim himself a prophet, as did the noted Hans Hut, who won many of the working people of Austria and adjacent parts of Germany to the view that a Turkish invasion would be followed by the appearance of Christ to inaugurate the millennium.

The finality with which the Anabaptists separated themselves from the established churches and the state (whence the name Separatists which they also bore), and the radical views which many of them espoused, led to intense persecution. Luther parted company with them, or, rather, they with him. Zwingli engaged them in bitter public debates, which were usually followed by the decision of the Swiss cantonal authorities that his views were alone to be recognized as lawful. A few Anabaptist leaders were executed as criminals. In 1527 Felix Manz was put to death by drowning in Zurich, Michael Sattler was burned and his wife drowned at Rottenburg; the following year Balthasar Hubmaier and his wife met the same fates in Vienna; and a year later Georg Blaurock was burned in the Tyrol. One desperate group of millenarian Anabaptists seized control of the German town of Münster and so radically revolutionized both the religious and social life there that the Catholics and Lutherans joined forces in storming the city and putting the leaders to death by torture. The erratic behavior of these Anabaptist leaders, marked as it was by communism, polygamy, and violence, gave Anabaptism an undeserved bad name in Europe.

Later on, this bad name was partially redeemed by the gentle and reasonable Anabaptist leader Menno Simons (1492–1547), whose followers in the Netherlands and the United States were called, after him, Mennonites. They were pacifists, espoused an Arminian theology which softened the harshness of Calvinism,* and practiced a person-to-person tolerance that enabled individual Mennonites to house, with simple Christian charity, such exiles as the ostracized Spinoza and certain refugee English Separatists.

But the Anabaptist revolt was not the only expression of radical Christianity. The basis of *Unitarianism* was now laid. At a time so early in the period of the Reformation that the doctrines of the Reformers had not yet been fixed in set forms—such as the Augsburg Confession or the Heidelberg Catechism—and the extent of the doctrinal departure from Catholic dogma was not yet clear, excited minds, stirred by the possibilities opening up to a thorough-going *rational* test of Christian doctrines, proposed unrestricted reason as the sovereign guide to sound reconstruction in theology. Such a one was the Michael Servetus whom we saw burned at the stake in Calvin's Geneva. A Spaniard by birth, he was struck on a close reading of the New Testament, while traveling in the retinue of a Catholic prelate, by the fact that the Nicene doctrine of the Trinity, in whose name so many of his own countrymen were being burned at the stake or exiled, was not to be found in it; and that moreover, his reason found fault with the doctrine itself. So he wrote down his ideas secretly and audaciously, and in 1531 published his famous heretical treatise, *Concerning the Errors of the Trinity.* Hopeful of winning the Reformers to his views, he went to Switzerland, but found the leaders whom he met cool, though still not committed to any clear position. Servetus could not imagine how his reasoning failed to carry conviction. The doctrine of the Trinity he felt to be a Catholic perversion and himself to be a good New Testament Christian in combating it. He himself was far from denying the divinity of Christ. According to his conception, a Trinity composed of three distinct persons in one God is a rational impossibility; he proposed instead "a

---

* In the Reformed churches, especially in Holland, the harsh predestinarianism of the strict Calvinists—and no less of the "Formula of Concord" (1580), which was meant to unify the Lutherans—could not be stomached by many who felt that damnation was not due solely to God's determination but also to man's erring choices. In their heartfelt conviction (for "God is love"), God has elected not just some but *all* men to salvation through the atonement of Christ, which has saving efficacy for every member of the human race; but not all men reach the pitch of faith which makes forgiveness and justification available to them; hence they perish through their own lack. Those who held these views were called Arminians, after the Dutch theologian Arminius who gave expression to their convictions. The Reformed churches condemned their position at the Synod of Dort (1619), but it has spread through the Methodist churches and has gained more than a foothold in Presbyterian and other Reformed circles.

manifestation of the true substance of God *in* the Word (or Christ) and its *communication* in the Holy Spirit," * a view which seemed to him to preserve the full deity of Christ without destroying the unity of God. There seemed to be no good reason, he felt, to deny the Virgin Birth or miracles.

Finding himself in danger, Servetus now changed his name, went to France, studied and practiced medicine with success, and became the first scientist to advance the theory of the pulmonary circulation of the blood. Meanwhile he was being sought by the Inquisition, and, from motives of prudence, when he opened up an acrimonious, and to himself fatal, correspondence with Calvin, he wrote under his assumed name; but Calvin's friends looked him up, made his identity known, and thus obliged him to flee. At the moment, Calvin's position in Geneva was not altogether secure, and for this or some other reason Servetus went there; only to fall afoul of Calvin's supporters, have condemnation passed upon him with Calvin's assent, and perish at the stake (1553).

Servetus was associated with no organized group; he was something of an individualist and worked alone; but his writings stirred groups of already existent anti-Trinitarians, who, when made the object of persecution both by the Inquisition and Protestants, took refuge in the only areas which would at that time harbor them, Poland and Transylvania, now part of Roumania. Some asserted the Arian position, which maintained that long before the Incarnation Christ proceeded from the Father and was subordinate to Him; others denied Christ's pre-existence, but believed he should be adored as virgin-born and risen from the dead to God's right hand (whence they were called "Adorantes"); still others (the "Non-adorantes"), led by the great Transylvanian preacher, Francis David, would worship God only, for to them Christ was not God but a man born of Joseph and Mary, who grew into fulness of divine powers—a view shared with certain Anabaptists, and common to Unitarians today. The reconciliation of these divergent views was to a large degree effected by Faustus Socinus (1539–1604), an Italian, who, after living in Switzerland and in Transylvania, finally established himself in Poland. He denied the pre-existence of Christ, holding that he was only a man; but he asserted, more positively, that Christ's life was so exemplary and his consciousness so flooded with divine wisdom, that he was resurrected in triumph from the dead and elevated to God's right hand; and so one may adore, and address prayers, to him. In the Racovian Catechism (1605), published by his followers after his death, this median position was explained and proved widely acceptable, becoming known as Socinianism.

* "Verae substantiae Dei manifestatio in Verbo et communicatio in Spiritu."

Poland was then a hospitable refuge for the oppressed, and in the atmosphere of freedom of thought which there existed these views met with a warm reception. But after 1632 the Catholics returned to power, and the Unitarians were suppressed, together with all other Protestants in Poland. Driven into exile, they fled to eastern Germany, Holland, and England. When the English passed a law in 1648 making the denial of the divinity of Christ a crime punishable by death, some of the more liberal Unitarians were obliged to flee again to Holland. During the 18th century many of them quietly appeared in New England, and in the early 19th century, under the preaching of Ellery Channing and Theodore Parker, they grew in strength, formed the American Unitarian Association (1825), and received many Congregational ministers and churches into their organized fellowship.

The Nonconformists

The Anabaptists and Unitarians were generally considered to be too immoderate in their radicalism to be tolerated. The Nonconformists —a much larger group—were not so fiercely set upon by the duly constituted authorities of church and state. Not that there was no persecution of the more moderate radicals; we shall see there was plenty of it; but the authorities were unable to maintain the sterner attitude with unbending harshness.

The Nonconformists were in general neither as non-cooperative with the state as the Anabaptists nor as heterodox as the Unitarians. They were willing to render civil obedience as long as they were granted freedom of conscience in their religion. So far as their theological position was concerned, they generally subscribed to the ancient Creeds as standard interpretations of Holy Writ; hence their trinitarianism was never in question. But in matters of polity or denominational organization, they differed quite widely from the so-called established churches. In church administration they demanded self-determination as their Protestant right.

The Puritans

These Nonconformists got their name in the time of Queen Elizabeth. Her accession in 1558 brought back to England, as we have seen, many exiles who had fled from "Bloody Mary." Their residence abroad in Calvinistic areas had inclined them toward presbyterial forms of church government and simplicity of worship and life, but they had no wish to be separatists; rather they desired only to *purify* the worship of the Church of England of what they called its "Romish" elements * and to give emphasis to preaching the Word rather than to ritual and sacraments. Most of them resigned themselves, at least for the time being, to episcopacy—bishops, archbishops, archdeacons, and the like—provided locally they could be served by sympathetic parish ministers; but a few openly advocated a presbyterial system such as existed in Scotland. When these presbyterial Puritans increased in numbers, the Puritans became divided. Those who wished to reform the Church of England from within retained their membership in it in patience and hope; while those who could not wait broke away from time to time as Separatists—and found the government so determined to crush them that they emigrated to Holland. They were the first Congregationalists and Baptists; and we shall return to them shortly.

The Puritans still within the Church of England found the government hardening against them when James I became king. Charles I after him was more resolved even than his father, not only to make the English Puritans conform in full to the practices of the Established Church, but to carry further his father's attempt to force episcopacy on the Scots. It was a literally fatal attempt on his part. To his astonishment, he provoked the Scots (thousands of them as "Covenanters" sworn to a life and death struggle against him) to rebellion; and their success in arms brought him to such a pass that he had to summon Parliament, only to find that the Puritans were now in the majority in that body! The Puritans had not for some time been faring so well; they had fared ill, in fact, while Archbishop Laud was in power, and twenty thousand of them in the period from 1628 to 1640 crossed the Atlantic to settle in Massachusetts and Connecticut and become New England Congregationalists. But now in 1640 they were in such majority in Parliament, that they could cast Laud into prison. When the angered king opposed them, they as angrily rose to arms as representatives of the people driven by their sovereign's stubbornness to make war upon him. So came about Charles I's beheading, and the Puritan Revolution under Oliver Cromwell. For twelve years England was a Puritan land, and all the people were bound by a stern religion's purifying restraints.

Not only the Puritan way of life but also Presbyterianism seemed about to triumph in England; for in 1646 the Westminster Assembly, called to advise Parliament, and composed of English ministers and

---

* Such as kneeling to receive the bread and wine at communion services, the sign of the cross at baptism and confirmation, the use of the ring at weddings, and special clerical garb for ministers.

laymen, with Scottish commissioners sitting in an advisory capacity, presented to Parliament the "Westminster Confession"—the last of the great confessional standards of the Reformation and still the doctrinal norm of the Presbyterians throughout the world. The Parliament rather hesitantly adopted it, as well as the Larger and Shorter Catechisms prepared to accompany it. But as it happened, little came of the Parliament's action; for the return of Charles II to England in 1660 brought with it the Restoration; and reaction was thereafter so triumphant that by the Act of Uniformity of 1662 the Puritans were forced out of the Church of England into the ranks of the Dissenters, ultimately to become Congregationalists, Baptists, Quakers, Presbyterians, and Unitarians.

The Congregationalists and Baptists

Meanwhile, the Separatists who had left England prior to the Puritan Revolution had had an interesting and important history abroad. One group that settled at Amsterdam about 1607 was led by a John Smyth, formerly a Church of England minister; who, upon learning from Mennonite neighbors their views on adult baptism and being convinced by study of the New Testament that it was not the early Christian practice to baptize infants, rebaptized himself and his whole flock. Members of his congregation returned to London and established there about 1612 the first *Baptist* church in England that endured. This was the beginning of the Baptist denomination, soon to spread throughout the British Isles. Though some Baptists are Arminian and others Calvinist in theology, they finally found unity in one distinctive position: baptism of believers only, and that by total immersion. In 1639 a group of Baptists, to whose number Roger Williams belonged, founded a church in Rhode Island; Baptists subsequently appeared in all the American colonies, especially in the South.

Other emigrants in Holland passed their first years of exile there quietly enough. At Middelburg in 1582 Robert Browne, a Cambridge man, published the clearest definition of *Congregationalism* ever to be penned. His logic was firm. Said he, the church of Christ, in the view of true Christians, is not an ecclesiastical organization, but a local group of believers who have experienced union with Christ, the only real and permanent head of the Church, and by a voluntary covenant with each other have consented to be ruled by officers—pastor, elders, deacons, teachers—chosen by themselves as moved by the spirit of Christ. Each church is absolutely self-governing; none has authority over any other, but all are under the Christian obligation to extend each other brotherly help and good will.

But if all this was quietly done and said, a notable course in history was run by one group among them. In 1609 a Congregationalist group that had come over from Scrooby, England, under the leadership of John Robinson and William Brewster, with William Bradford of their number, settled in Leyden. Not content there, they made a momentous decision: to return to England and from there send their more adventurous and able-bodied members to America. On the *Mayflower*, then, in 1620, the Pilgrims crossed the Atlantic; and, in the spirit of their solemn covenant made at sea, founded the colony of Plymouth. Other immigrants, mostly Puritans from England, followed them over the waters, until the whole of New England, except Rhode Island, was won for Congregationalism. There it enjoyed the status virtually of a state religion for two centuries.

The Quakers

One more English nonconformist group of this period, the Quakers, requires our attention. They were in many respects the most radical of all. Founded during the civil war that resulted in the Puritan Revolution, the Quaker movement was in essence a revolt against formalism and sham. The Quakers were nicknamed so, but preferred to call themselves the Society of Friends. Their founder was George Fox (1624–1691), a religious genius who may be reckoned one of the world's great mystics. In a profound experience of conversion, which occurred in 1646, he came to a belief much like that of some of the early Anabaptists. True Christianity was to him not a matter of conforming to a set of doctrines or of believing in Scripture without having "a concern" as the result of so doing; nor was it going to a "steeple-house" to listen to a sermon or prayers read by a professional priest; it was being illuminated by an *inner light*. The Word of God is a living thing not confined to the Scriptures, though it is there; it comes directly into the consciousness of the believer whom God chooses for the purpose of speaking through him.

Fox would not hear of training a professional clergy; God speaks through whom He will when He will. Every man—or woman, for that matter—is potentially God's spokesman. Fellowmen are to be treated as friends, with infinite reverence for the divine possibilities in any personality. War and any violence are therefore thoroughly wicked. Slavery is abhorrent. The requirement to take an oath should not be imposed upon a Christian, for he always speaks soberly and truthfully.

At a religious meeting of Friends there were no sacraments (sacraments by their material symbolism are the occasion of leading the mind out of its subjective state of contemplation into the idolatry of fixation on an object) and no prepared discourses (God will stir up thought in someone present, at need). It was admitted that prayer is appropriate to begin with, but let it be followed by silent meditation, until the inner light illumines someone's understanding.

Fox and his followers promptly obeyed every prophetic impulse to action. Fox, for instance, would march boldly into a "steeple-house," if inspired to do so, interrupt the "priest" in the middle of his sermon, and denounce the proceedings, to the accompaniment of outcries and tumult. Consequently the authorities vigorously opposed Quakers as disturbers of the peace. Thousands were imprisoned or heavily fined. Fox himself was often jailed. But no persecution could quench his ardor.

During the intensely repressive persecutions of the Restoration period, William Penn (1644–1718) became a Quaker, and after obtaining in 1681 the grant of Pennsylvania from Charles II, he threw it open to colonization by all who might desire freedom of religion, the Quakers being especially invited to Philadelphia. In England, it was not until the "Glorious Revolution" which accompanied the accession of William and Mary (1689) that full religious toleration for the Quakers, and all other dissenting groups, was made into law.

Pietism

Common to most of the Nonconformists was a shift of emphasis from doctrinal orthodoxy (which was taken for granted) to conversion or new birth. Conversion seemed the one infallible test of the possession of true Christianity. Abandonment of the conception of human sin and depravity was not contemplated, nor were the standard Reformation theologies called in question; all that was sought was a heightened sense of reality in the emotional life. The accent lay on having *new life* in Christ. Everyone was dead in sin, lost, guilty before God, certain to be damned, until "reborn," made a "new man in Christ Jesus," by the quick inflow of divine grace, bringing joy and peace to the distracted sinner and a sense of divine forgiveness, crowned by reconciliation with God and personal communion with Christ. It cannot be overemphasized that to most of these men and women of deep personal piety Christ had the reality of a living presence, who, though he was a visitant from another world, was as real and near as any earthly person.

We see all this with particular clarity in Pietism, which was in origin a reaction from 17th century German doctrinalism, the latter being regarded by the Pietists as infected with moral unconcern and a cold indifference toward right *feeling* in religion. The cultivation of right feeling was held to lead, not to a coming to terms with the world, as worldings might expect, but to its opposite, an ascetic emphasis on purity and holiness of life. This is the reason why Pietism was initially separatist in tendency.

Two figures were important in the development of Pietism. One, Philipp Spener (1635–1705), was an earnest Lutheran minister who felt keenly the lack of "heart" and "life" in the current Lutheran absorption in "pure doctrine." He invited a group of similarly minded people to meet in his home as a "church within the church" (as he put it, as an *ecclesiola in ecclesia*) for Bible study, prayer, and the further discussion of Sunday sermons. The result was their common conviction that the world was too much with them: the state was too interfering; the clergy quarreled too much over theological matters to live a holy life; the clergy were even morally lax; and the laity were immoderate in eating, drinking, and dress, and spent too much time on worldly amusements, dances, the theater, and cards. In his writings Spener advocated the formation everywhere of similar study groups, and found immediate response in all German-speaking areas; but the movement, spreading rapidly, soon ran into stiff opposition on the part of the clergy, who did not relish a church within the church nor criticisms of their piety or morality. Their hostility increased when some of Spener's followers, against his wish, exhibited their separatist tendency by refraining from church attendance and the sacraments.

The other leader of Pietism was Hermann Francke (1663–1727), an instructor in the University of Leipsic, who introduced Pietism into German academic circles by establishing a *collegium philobiblicum* (a "gathering of Bible lovers"). Driven from the university by the opposition of his colleagues, he ultimately joined Spener and others at Halle, where the elector of Brandenburg, who was to become King Frederick I of Prussia, founded a university and encouraged, without becoming identified with, their activities. In this new environment Francke proceeded to demonstrate the implicit social consciousness of Pietism by successively founding a school for poor children, a Latin school, an orphans' home, and a Bible institute, all of which had great contemporary support. The Halle group also displayed a zeal for missions, a development of interest which prompted the earliest Protestant attempts to evangelize India.

After the time of Spener and Francke, Pietism gradually declined, perhaps because it had largely attained its initial objectives, but it survived as a special form of impetus in the revival of the *Moravian Brethren.* This occurred under the guidance of Count Zinzendorf, a landowner in eastern Saxony to whose estates came a group of refugee Moravian Hussites displaced by the turmoil of the Thirty Years' War. Zinzendorf had had a Pietist education at Halle, modified by law studies at Wittenberg, a center of orthodox Lutheran influence, and by travels in Holland and France. He had the compassion to allow the Hussites to establish a Moravian village on his estates, which they called Hernhut; and it was also in his nature to enter into their communal life; with the result that a communion service into which he entered with them led in 1727 to a revived and revitalized form of the Moravian church. Though Zinzendorf strove to keep it within the Lutheran fellowship, the new church gradually became a separatist sect with a special life of its own and a sense of mission to the world. Missions, in fact, became the hallmark of the movement. Zinzendorf himself inspired the first Moravian missionaries to go to the Danish West Indies, Greenland, and Georgia. When Lutheran opposition caused him to be expelled from Saxony, he traveled widely, first in the European areas to which the Moravians spread, including London, then in the West Indies and the American colonies. He also instituted missions among the American Indians. But he did not live to see the full extent of the far-flung missionary efforts of the Moravian church, the successful establishment of missions in Egypt, South Africa, Surinam, Guiana, and Labrador.

VII CATHOLICISM SINCE THE 16TH CENTURY

The Protestant Reformation resulted in intensifying latent Catholic self-criticism and stirred up a church-wide call for reform. The popes, however, were not among the motivating forces; they were too much on the defensive. It was the emperor Charles V, anxious like Constantine in the 4th century to reduce sources of disunity, who earnestly sought for reforms in the Church and a redefinition of Catholic doctrine in order to offset the effectiveness of Protestant critical propaganda. He came to this position only after his prolonged efforts to bring about a reconciliation of Catholics and Protestants on the basis of projected reforms had failed. It was he who brought pressure on Pope Paul III to call the Council of Trent.

This pressure was decisive, because it had behind it all the accumulated power generated by the cries for reform, both clerical and lay, which had been heard in Europe for centuries. John Wyclif, John Huss, Savonarola, and Erasmus, not to mention Luther and Zwingli before they left the Mother Church, were simply the more powerful figures among those who advocated reform. But the Catholic Reformation (by Protestants labeled the Counter-Reformation) did not get under way until momentum was imparted to it by the determined and militant forces for reform and enlightenment in Spain, where the expulsion of the Moors in the 15th century had been followed by the reform of the clergy under Ximenes, the great archbishop of Toledo and confessor to Queen Isabella. The Spanish church had been purified of unworthy monks and priests, universities for the training of the clergy had been founded, the union of Church and State under Ferdinand and Isabella had been made very close, and the means of keeping Church and State purified had been found in the reorganization of the Inquisition on a national basis, with inquisitors appointed by the Spanish monarchs. The result had been a revitalization of the Spanish church to match the rapid rise of Spain itself to the position of the first power in Europe. When therefore the Spanish king became the Holy Roman Emperor, in the person of Charles V, the drive for reform, all the more urgent because of the Protestant menace, had secured powerful support.

The Catholic Reformation

The wave of Catholic reform had three chief expressions.

A. THE COUNCIL OF TRENT. When Charles V got Pope Paul III to call the Council of Trent in 1545, he hoped first to get needed reforms and afterwards a redefinition of the Catholic position; it was thus that he planned to conciliate the Protestant leadership and follow up his military victories over the German Protestant princes with a psychological master-stroke that would bring the recalcitrants back into the Catholic fold; but the Catholic leaders insisted that doctrine be discussed alternately with reform, and soon made reconciliation with the Protestants impossible by firmly redefining the medieval Catholic doctrines. The Council met over a period of eighteen years (1545–1563), and during its course declared:

1. Catholic tradition is co-equal with Scripture as a source of truth and in authority over Christian life.

2. The Latin Vulgate is the sacred canon.

3. The Catholic Church has sole right of Scriptural interpretation.

4. The sacraments are the seven recognized by the medieval Church, not just the two of the Protestants. They are, as Thomas Aquinas declared, the visible forms of invisible grace bestowed through the Church on the worthy.

5. Justification rests on faith, but not on faith alone as the Protestants assert; good works also procure God's grace.

In the sphere of discipline and church management, the Council turned to the broad task of preserving morals and furthering education. It ordered stricter regulation of the issuance of indulgences and the veneration of saints; it limited the number of holy days observed during the year (in deference in part to demands of economic interests); and it ordered bishops and priests in the larger towns to make public expositions and interpretations of Scripture, and in general to preach and teach what is necessary for salvation. Of far-reaching effect was the Council's instruction to the pope to prepare an index of prohibited books—a step which helped to limit the reading of Protestant literature by Catholics.

B. THE REORGANIZATION OF THE INQUISITION FOR CHURCH-WIDE OPERATION. In 1542 Pope Paul III was persuaded by his advisers to reorganize the Inquisition on a scale which made its immediate use possible in any part of Europe where the civil authorities asked for it or were willing to support it. The "Counter-Reformation" thus acquired the instrumentality by which Catholic areas could quickly be purged of Protestants. The first country to be thus cleared was Italy.

C. THE JESUITS AND OTHER RELIGIOUS ORDERS. Of the greatest importance for the revival of Catholic spirit and zeal was the rise of new religious orders, the most famous of which has been the Jesuit Order founded by Ignatius Loyola.

The Jesuits

Loyola (1491–1556) was a Spanish nobleman, who after being a page at the court of Ferdinand and Isabella, became a soldier, and was seriously wounded in a battle with the French. During convalescence he read the lives of Christ, St. Dominic, and St. Francis, and resolved to become a "knight of the Virgin." He accordingly hung his weapons on the Virgin's altar at Monserrat, and at a Dominican monastery began the self-directed visualizations of the life and work of Christ and of Christian warfare against evil which he later systematized as the Jesuit spiritual "exercises." While on a pilgrimage to Jerusalem he came to feel the need of more education; so he hurried home to study in Spain and at Paris. Wherever he was, he gathered around him student associates with whom he practiced his spiritual exercises. It was thus that he attracted to himself Francis Xavier, who became the famous missionary to India and Japan, and men like Diego Lainez and Simon Rodriguez. In Paris in 1534 he organized these friends into a military "company of Jesus" vowed to go to Jerusalem, if possible, as missionaries to the infidel Moslems, or failing that, to offer their services to the pope. When war with the Turks barred the way to Jerusalem, they went to Rome, and in 1540 obtained the authorization of the pope, Paul III, to establish *The Society of Jesus,* with Loyola as the first General.

Known as the Jesuits, they bound themselves to a life of strict militia-like discipline, "spiritual exercises," and absolute obedience to their superiors short of sin. But "sin" was so defined that it was seldom confronted; for they held that there could be no sin in a course of action, unless its sinfulness were clearly known when the will consented to the doing of it; and one could even follow a doubtful course of action without hesitation, if "probable" grounds for it existed or it had been accepted by men of greater experience or had authority for it. Moreover, so sure were the military-minded Jesuits that a good end justifies secrecy about means, that they sanctioned "mental reservation" in the case of being required to tell the whole truth: one was not bound to give the whole truth even under oath. The main thing was absolute self-commitment to the aims of the Jesuit order and unreserved and complete surrender of self in doing what one's superiors ordered. This sacrificial devotion was intensively cultivated in each Jesuit during his novitiate, a regimen which included a unique and very effective four weeks of "spiritual. exercises" under the point-to-point direction of a spiritual drillmaster. On the basis of the capacities revealed during this period, each Jesuit was assigned by his superiors to the tasks he was judged best suited to; and when sent to some post, no matter how far away, he was under obligation to send back a continuous stream of reports to his superiors who had sent him.

The Jesuit order had spectacular success in the field of missions. Not only did Francis Xavier and his associates carry Catholicism to India, Japan, and China, but others during the 16th and 17th centuries won their way into South America, the St. Lawrence and Mississippi valleys, Mexico, and California.

Here it is important to observe that the natives sensed that the priests had come not to exploit and rob them, as the conquistadors often did, but to save them. In Europe itself Jesuits diligently and intelligently sought and occupied important commercial and governmental posts, which took them into far-flung places abroad as well as into the council chambers of kings and princes at home. Their political influence in France, Portugal, Spain, and Austria during the 16th and 17th centuries was very great. They led in checking the spread of Lutheranism into south Germany and were powerful factors behind the scenes when the Huguenots in France were fought and massacred. But they aroused the enmity eventually not only of all Protestant but also of many Catholic groups. In the 18th century they found Portugal, France, and Spain successively closed to them. At last they lost their temporal power; but they have continued to this day to promote the supremacy of the pope implied in the decrees of the Council of Trent.

The Jesuit was not the only new organization to witness to the forces of Catholic renewal. The 16th and 17th centuries saw the rise of the Oratorians, Theatines, Ursulines, Visitandines, and Lazaristes. The first two sought respectively the reform of the Breviary and the improvement of preaching; the last three were orders for women which laid emphasis on remedial social work.

These movements were both effects and causes. They sprang from the heightened Catholic sense of the seriousness of the Church's mission in the world, and they caused the older organizations in the Church to look into their ways and to replace their former laxity with greater earnestness. The Franciscan and Dominican orders were thus revitalized. Even the papal office was affected; the popes from this time forward were uniformly men of more austere character and earnestly Catholic aims.

Doctrinal and Ecclesiastical Developments since 1700

The 18th century saw much of the force of the Catholic Reformation wane. In France Louis XIV had already stemmed the power of the papacy by appropriating the income of vacant bishoprics and by encouraging the French clergy to assert openly their right to certain "Gallic liberties," which included the view that the pope was not infallible, since general councils are superior to him. The rise of the rationalistic spirit among great numbers of Frenchmen during the 18th century reached a climax in the French Revolution, when anticlericalism developed to the point of violence and Christianity itself was for a time "abolished." Although religious freedom for all men was later proclaimed, Napoleon, in coming to terms with the Catholic Church, was determined to keep it under government control. In Germany, the Catholics painfully recovered from the effects of the Thirty Years' War, which had reduced the population of the German states by sixty-five per cent without effecting any real changes in the lines separating Catholics and Protestants; not until after the Napoleonic wars, when Romanticism led the reaction against the rationalistic spirit of the 18th century, did the Catholic Church revive some of its old power.

In Europe generally, during the 19th century, the assertion of papal supremacy in the name of world-wide Catholic unity reappeared in Ultramontanism, or the movement among Catholics north of the Alps in favor of the view that final authority lay "beyond the mountains," that is, in the Vatican and the regularized channels of the papal government (the Roman Congregation). The popes for obvious reasons encouraged this opinion to the limit of their influence.

Two major doctrinal developments mark the 19th century. In 1854 Pius IX, after consulting with cardinals concerning a doctrine that had been discussed since the Middle Ages, proclaimed the Immaculate Conception of the Virgin to be a dogma of the Catholic Church. The meaning of this was, that all Catholics must believe that Mary, in order to be fitted to conceive Christ while still a virgin, was freed from original sin by the immaculate purity in which her parents conceived her. More important was the declaration in 1870, under the same pope, of the doctrine of papal infallibility. It was not said that *all* utterances of the pope are without error, but only those which he pronounces *ex cathedra* in exposition of "the revelation or deposit of faith delivered through the Apostles." The declaration affirms:

> The Roman pontiff, when he speaks *ex cathedra,* that is, when in discharge of the office of pastor and doctor of all Christians, by virtue of his supreme apostolic authority, he defines a doctrine regarding faith or morals to be held by the universal church, by the divine assistance promised to him in blessed Peter, is possessed of that infallibility with which the divine Redeemer willed that His church should be endowed.

This doctrine elevated the pope to a supreme height in the field of faith and morals. But it did not save him from the consequences of the rise of Italian nationalism in the wake of the agitations of Mazzini and Garibaldi; for no sooner had the Vatican Council made its declaration than King Victor Emmanuel came along to capture Rome, and after a plebecite of the inhabitants overwhelmingly directed him to do so, took from the pope the States of the Church, leaving only the Vatican, the Lateran, and Castel Gondolfo as the area where papal secular sovereignty could be exercised.

Some Recent Developments

Toward the end of the 19th century many thoughtful Catholics, both clerical and lay, began to see the need of taking into account the discoveries of modern historical and Biblical criticism and of modern science, especially in the realms of biology and geology, where the theory of evolution was applied. There thus came into being the short-lived movement called Catholic Modernism. It sought a reconciliation of Catholicism and modern scientific and critical knowledge. Modernist voices were heard suddenly in all parts of Europe. Notable were those of George Tyrrell in England, Alfred Loisy in France, and Hermann Schell in Germany. But Pope Pius X found their thought dangerous and firmly condemned it in an encyclical in 1907, which effectively brought the movement to an end.

More successful as an attempt to put Catholic doctrine into current thought-forms is recent Neo-Thomism—so-called because its representatives, Jacques Maritain and others, seek to state the entire philosophy of Thomas Aquinas in modern terms and to apply it to modern issues. But the pope is still the final arbiter of what is sound in theology and morals and what is not.

In fulfilling his theological responsibilities, the Pope (Pius XII) in 1950 proclaimed as a dogma of the Church the assumption of the uncorrupted body of the Virgin Mary to heaven after her death.

The pontiffs have also been conscious of world-wide responsibility in overseeing morals. Recent years have found them more and more disposed to make moral pronouncements, international in scope, in the name of God and the Church. Recent popes have taken a strong anti-Communist stand.

In like manner, the Catholic Church as a whole has become intensely aware of the value of action on an international scale. One of the significant new features of its effort is the institution of church-wide Eucharistic congresses, held every few years, when world conditions permit, in different parts of the Catholic world.

The concern throughout the Christian world with church unity has affected the Catholic Church. Pope John XXIII issued in 1959 a summons to an ecumenical council embracing the entire Catholic world; the council met in 1962 in Rome and was attended by the twenty-five hundred bishops of the Catholic Church. Furthermore, a special secretariat has been appointed to act as an advisory board in matters of liaison and possible unity with non-Catholic bodies such as the Eastern Orthodox and Protestant churches. Here compromise in matters of discipline and practice is not excluded, but there is to be no compromise in matters of doctrine.

VIII PROTESTANTISM IN THE MODERN WORLD

With perhaps one exception, the basic diversifications within the Protestant world all occurred before the 18th century. The exception might be Methodism. Methodism, however, was not really a Reformation movement; it was essentially an awakening in response to new conditions created by the development of science and the rapid rise of industrial capitalism, and it is therefore to be considered a phenomenon not immediately related to the Reformation. Methodism stands in fact at the beginning of the shifts and changes characteristic of modern times.

To these changes we now turn, in a final general survey.

Deism in the 18th Century

It was not until the 18th century that western science in its modern sense became generally diffused among thinking men. When it did, the 18th century Enlightenment came. Religion was for the first time in the Western world compelled to justify its case *inductively*. The empirically minded men of the 18th century were so little content with the dogmas of the Church that they asked themselves curiously what made primitives religious, or what "natural religion" was. The whole structure of revealed religion was abandoned, and in the estimation of many wide-eyed men of reason it came tumbling down. In their awe before the iron laws of the beautifully running mechanical universe, viewed as through the eyes of a Galileo or a Newton in mathematical terms, they ruled out all miracles and special divine providences. God was no longer invoked to explain immediate causes; He was not any longer necessarily *inside* the physical frame of Nature. He seemed distant both in space and time. The Deists, who adopted these views, "ushered God to the frontiers of the universe"; to them He was the Ancient of Days, who was to be revered as the Creator who made all; but they virtually "bowed Him out over the threshold of the world," courteously but firmly.

The Deists were representative of their age in avoiding a clash between religion and science by thus separating God from his creation, and conceiving that the latter ran by itself, and could therefore be a separate object of study.

A great many of the clergymen of the English churches, and many also on the Continent, highly educated as a class, held views similar to those of the Deists. Indeed they were at heart Unitarians, or even privately agnostic; and so lukewarm were their devotions, so utterly non-mystical their public utterances, that it was inevitable that something like Methodism should appear to bring heart and soul back into English Christianity. When this renewal of religious warmth among the clergy came to pass the people responded eagerly.

Methodism

The industrial revolution was in the making. Drawn from the land to the towns, the people had lost anchorage. Drunkenness was so widespread among them as to menace the national well-being. The spiritual hunger of the common people was not satisfied by the sceptical intellectualism of the sermons they heard in the Established Church—mere discourses, virtually essays, prepared as an accompaniment to the formal reading of the Book of Common Prayer. John Wesley and his associates, enhungered too, brought them the emotional fire and hearty conviction which they most needed.

The name Methodist was applied at first in sarcasm by Wesley's fellow-students at Oxford to the little group—also derisively called the "Holy Club"—of which he was a leader, and which met regularly for *methodical* study and prayer in their rooms, endeavoring to bring God down to them out of the skies to which He had been relegated by their Deist teachers. They strove to cultivate something of the sense of the immediacy of God's presence in human lives that the Quakers felt. In an unmistakably decisive experience since known as *conversion,* they underwent a complete change of life and faith and came to know that religion was real and vital for every act of existence. Afterwards, in seeking to "revive" their fellow-Christians of the churches, they had no intention of leaving the Church of England; they hoped only to reform that church from within. But when the Wesley brothers and George Whitefield began to preach up and down the British Isles, and the people flocking to them in all the towns were converted in astonishing numbers, it was natural to form a new denomination, and to call it the Methodist Church.

John Wesley had been born in an Anglican manse in 1703, the fifteenth child of Samuel and Susannah Wesley. His brother Charles was the eighteenth. After their years at Oxford, during which the most important accession to their Methodist Club was George Whitefield, the talented son of an innkeeper, John and Charles Wesley went as missionaries to Georgia, where neither met with much success, though John Wesley made fruitful friendships with Moravians. On return to England both brothers resorted to a Moravian, Peter Böhler, in London, who convinced them that they would not be true Christians until they had experienced genuine conversion. That experience subsequently came to both. Together with Whitefield, also changed, they were soon preaching in the open fields to tens of thousands of deeply stirred miners and workmen in England, Scotland, and Ireland. It was common for their hearers to exhibit their emotion in ecstasies, bodily excitement, cries and groans, and lapses of consciousness. Methodist "chapels" were soon erected for more orderly worship; and as circumstances showed the need for them, characteristically Methodist innovations appeared: "classes," "bands," "circuits," "stewards," "superintendents," and the like. On the devotional side, Charles Wesley contributed to the cause the highly emotional hymns which were to have the usefulness to evangelistic Christianity which the hymns of Isaac Watts and of the Lutherans and Moravians had to the older churches.

The new church spread to the American colonies. Whitefield had prepared the way by seven immensely successful visits which greatly extended the area swept by an earlier wave of revivals, also marked by the experience of conversion, which had begun under Jonathan Edwards' powerful preaching in Northampton, Mass., and was called "The Great Awakening." Systematic organizational work in behalf of Methodism was begun in New York by 1766; and the epic labors of Francis Asbury (1745–1816), the great "circuit-rider," secured the spread of Methodism across the Alleghanies into the vast spaces of the Middle West. Since then, the Methodist Church has become one of the great denominations of the United States.

The Missionary Movement

The 19th may be reckoned a great Protestant century. It opened with a second "great awakening" in the United States, a series of revivals that much increased the number of Baptists and Methodists in the midwestern states. In Great Britain, the Church of England was powerfully moved by a pietistic Evangelical Movement, which in later decades issued in the Oxford or Tractarian Movement, the formation of the Young Men's Christian Association (in London in 1844), and the organization of the Salvation Army (by William Booth in 1865). In Germany, the theologians Schleiermacher (1768–1834) and Ritschl (1822–1889) gave a new and liberal turn to Protestant religious thought. But perhaps the two most significant developments of the century were the organization of world-wide Protestant missions and the rapid expansion of the Sunday School movement, two developments to which we now turn.

In missionary activity the Catholics had long shown the way. The Protestants gathered momentum more slowly. When the Dutch established trading stations in the East Indies in the 17th century, they encouraged missionaries to follow behind them. In the same century the Church of England felt a responsibility for the American Indians, and organized the Society for the Propagation of the Gospel in New England, a group which at the beginning of the 18th century was largely superseded by the Society for the Propagation of the Gospel in Foreign Parts. The Quakers from the start sent missionaries to the West Indies, Palestine, and various parts of Europe. We have already seen how vigorously the Moravians fostered missions during the 18th century.

A new phase of missionary effort began with the publication of the journals of the globe-circling Captain Cook, whose vivid descriptions of the condition of the primitives of the many South Pacific islands which he visited from 1768–1779 stirred up William Carey to go to India as the first missionary of the Baptist Society for Propagating the Gospel among the Heathen, which he helped to organize in 1792. In 1795 an interdenominational group formed the London Missionary Society, which sent its first appointees to Tahiti. (This society has since been Congregationalist.) There followed the formation of the Edinburgh Missionary Society, the Glasgow Missionary Society, the Church Missionary Society (of the Church of England), and the Wesleyan Methodist Missionary Society.

To match these British efforts with like devotion to the expansion of the Christian world, a group of students at Williams College in Massachusetts joined in mutual commitments which led in 1810 to the birth of the famous missionary organ of American Congregationalism, the American Board of Commissioners for Foreign Missions. Subsequently, like organizations were formed in the other American churches.

Continental Europe was not idle. Similar societies appeared in Denmark, Germany, France, and Switzerland.

In the years that followed, the reports brought back by the missionaries from every part of the world had a pronounced quickening effect on the life of the churches at home. The whole tone of Christian life was raised. With the dawn of the 20th century, incalculable benefits to Christendom as a whole were seen to have sprung from the development of world-wide fellowship between Christians of every culture and color. Recent changes in missionary objectives have led to the concept of total service in every area of life. Indigenous church leadership is encouraged, and one missionary aim is now the eventual development of "two-way evangelization"—the mission fields producing interpretations and interpreters of Christianity to minister to the churches at home.

The Sunday School Movement and Religious Education

The older Protestant churches were conscious from the very beginning of the need to instruct their young people in the doctrines and duties of the Christian religion before confirming them as members of the church; this of course was the origin of catechetical instruction. But the religious education thus attempted was brief and of limited effect, and it did not embrace all the children of the community. There was therefore great need for more frequent instruction, and particularly for instruction open to the children of the religiously illiterate and the unchurched. Realization of this need came in Gloucester, England, to Robert Raikes, whose interest in prison reform led to his observing the conditions producing delinquency in city slums. In order to provide schooling for the neglected waifs of Gloucester, he organized in 1780 the first Sunday School, in part designed to teach them how to read the Bible.

Thus began the Sunday School movement which became so significant a feature of the religious life of the 19th century. It spread rapidly through the British Isles, in the Protestant areas of the European Continent, and on the other side of the Atlantic. The Sunday School Society of London, its analogues on the Continent, and the state Sunday School associations of the United States held, during a century of effort, numerous conventions to advance the cause. These societies actively fostered teacher-training programs, prepared and published lesson-materials, and worked with each other on an international basis. In 1907 they organized the World's Sunday School Association.

So valuable were the Sunday Schools and their teachers to the churches during this period, that no Protestant congregation could afford to be without them; indeed, they were the chief source of the new members brought into the churches by confirmation. Their altruistic purpose shone clear and strong. The teachers and superintendents, with very rare exceptions, served without salary, on a purely voluntary basis. The instruction was too often inadequate and ill-prepared, but it was always meant to supply the highest kind of moral and religious guidance.

The short-comings of the Sunday Schools of the 19th century have been clearly seen in the 20th. A better informed leadership has been seeking to turn them into an effective means of Christian education by applying the principles and techniques discovered in secular public instruction. The Sunday School has now acquired the more comprehensive and dignified name of the Church School.

No more serious and sustained educational effort to bring Christianity home to men's hearts and lives as a discipline for the whole of human life has ever been attempted in any period of the history of the Christian church.

Protestantism and Science

The 19th century dawned with little inkling of the hazards which science was to place in the way of faith; but long before the century was out a momentous struggle between orthodox religion and a naturalism bred by science was joined; and many a devout Christian felt his heart turn faint within him as he watched and listened.

One of the earliest controversies was precipitated by the development of historical criticism and the rewriting of history. Hume and Gibbon in the 18th century had cast doubt on many a feature of Christian belief, but they did not subject the life of Jesus, nor the Bible as a whole, to detailed examination. The 19th century was to supply such "Biblical criticism." David Strauss and Ernest Renan in epoch-making German and French works radically rewrote the life of Jesus. Lower (or textual) and higher (or historico-literary) criticism of the Bible demonstrated that its books were the work of many different authors at many different times. The Pentateuch was shown to have had a composite authorship stretching over at least five centuries. The New Testament was dissected into Q, M, L, and other strata of tradition. Violent controversy over these findings, as they were made, divided Protestantism into two camps, later to be called Fundamentalists (who rejected Biblical criticism as gross unbelief) and Modernists (who accepted it as sound).

But, though bitter and long-drawn-out, this controversy was all but overshadowed during the last half of the 19th century by the chorus of angry protest which followed the publication of Darwin's *Origin of Species*. For Darwin, and his predecessor in formulating the evolutionary theory, Lamarck, were interpreted, not only to deny the story of Creation in the first chapters of Genesis, but to rule out any theory of creation whatever. At the same time, some of the philosophic successors of Hegel had transformed his spiritual monism into materialism, and they loudly welcomed the support of the theory of evolution. Ludwig Büchner and Ernst Haeckel, particularly, sprang forward as champions of a mechanistic materialism which left no room for God. (Feuerbach had concluded thirty years earlier, in 1841: "Anthropology is the secret of theology. God is man worshipping himself. The Trinity is the human family deified." [41]) And in England, Thomas Huxley and Herbert Spencer increased the sense of outrage among the conservatives by rejecting the doctrine of an impassable gulf between man and the beasts and arguing instead for the theory that man has emerged by slow evolution from the anthropoid apes.

To all these views orthodox Christians entered a heated denial in the name of the immutability of the species God had separately created. When geologists had worked out Lyell's theory of gradual evolutionary change in the history of the earth, and presented fossils taken from the rocks as evidence of the biological evolution of the various species, the only reply the orthodox could make was that God had planted the fossils in the rocks on the day of creation to confound the judgment of unbelievers, whose rejection of God's truth was thus made manifest and their damnation justified. Confronted, by the end of the century, with bio-chemical theories which sought to explain away as nonexistent the vital principle in living things, and psychological theories which denied the existence of the soul (and later of the mind and consciousness as such), many devout believers felt they were faced by an inflexible choice between irreconcilable positions: one that science is true and religion is false, and the other that science is preposterous guess-work and the biblical revelation God's own infallible word, true from beginning to end exactly as it is contained in the Bible.

But, amidst the clamor, liberal Christians remained sure no such irreconcilability between science and religion existed. Men like Henry Drummond in Scotland (in his *Natural Law in the Spiritual World*) and John Fiske in New England (in *Outlines of Cosmic Philosophy* and *The Idea of God as Affected by Modern Knowledge*) endeavored to show that, on the theory that evolution is God's method of creation, religion and science can indeed be reconciled. The biblical story of creation has to be taken as devout, prescientific theorizing, poetically, if not literally true, its essence not disproved, though its form requires reinterpretation. With this beginning, the liberals proceeded confidently to a task of reconstruction, assured that the essentials of the Christian faith are never shaken by the findings of a careful, non-metaphysical (or "pure") science. Science itself, they pointed out, moves on assumptions which are beyond proof, and these are *its* faith. More recently the liberals have been saying that the dogmatic materialism of the 19th century is no longer tenable. Scientists, for lack of any definite indication of what electrons and protons are made of, must be more open-minded toward organic as against mechanistic conceptions of the universe. Even psychology, with its emphasis on integrations, configurations, or *gestalts,* can no longer be dogmatically sure about the detailed analyses which once seemed to destroy any evidence of the existence of the soul. The Christian faith is thus, say the liberals, unshaken in its major assumptions, and its adherents may give credence to the assured findings of science. For truth is one and indivisible; and to see life steadily and to see it whole is still to gain the pure heart of those who see God.

This liberal view, so confident and optimistic in its faith in God and man, was itself severely shaken by the catastrophe of the First World War. There emerged thereafter a Neo-Orthodoxy, which accepted the findings of science and of historical criticism, but insisted that God is not immanent in nature and history in the way in which the liberals say he is, but is transcendent, existing quite apart from Nature and man, indeed is the Wholly Other, the Absolute, who must break through the wall of human error and self-contradiction that separates him from men in order to appear in human history. Without such breaking through, man is lost. The dour champions—Karl Barth and Emil Brunner—of a going "beyond fundamentalism and modernism" to a theology resting on a dualism of God and the world have not yet won the field. It remains to be seen whether the liberals will yield to their attack, and abandon their faith in the divine in man, that is, in the eternal immanence of God in the nature of man.

The Social Gospel

With the advent of the era of "big business" and the onset of labor-capital tension, socialism took on new life. In Europe, as the 19th century approached and passed its half-way mark, it had great and increasing political significance. The social upheavals of 1848 brought sharply home to thoughtful churchmen the need of finding a Christian solution to poverty and social injustice. In England, Frederick Maurice and Charles Kingsley made a beginning of discussing the application of the Christian gospel to these social problems. Liberals in the Church of England were moved to form the Christian Social Union and the Church Socialist League (subsequently renamed the League of the

Kingdom of God). Bishops and archbishops associated themselves with these and later efforts to bring Protestantism to bear on social issues. In the United States, men like Francis G. Peabody, Washington Gladden, Shailer Mathews, and Walter Rauschenbusch searched the scriptures, and discovered a neglected theme in the teaching of Jesus—the Kingdom of God. They brought together all the sayings of Jesus referring to it, and found in the Carpenter of Nazareth a prophet of social justice whose principles seemed still the key to happier human relationships in every variety of social context. Here was a social gospel whose practice would solve modern man's economic, industrial, political, racial, and international problems; it could bring peace to the nations, justice among the peoples, and good will among the races.

A new note had been sounded in Protestant Christianity. In general the liberals rallied to the ardent exposition of the social gospel; the conservatives as generally drew back, decrying the dabbling in politics and the involvement in merely worldly matters which they declared was the pit into which the preachers of the social gospel fell. The critics complained that the New Testament contained no social message to speak of, the appeal of Jesus being almost exclusively to individuals that they might be saved one by one. But advocates of the social gospel replied that, although the redemption of the individual is a necessary aim of all religion, it is clearly impossible to bring about the *moral* redemption of individuals in an immoral society, and that the church will lose all relevance to modern life, as it seems to have already lost relevance for a large part of the laboring classes, unless the Christian religion is brought to bear on the moral redemption of society. If the Christian religion, they cried, has nothing to say and no program to offer on the chief problems of the hour, it is no longer of any use to men! Its day is over!

The critical question of how much social gospel there is in the New Testament is not yet settled, and may never be settled; but the great Protestant denominations, at least of the English speaking world, have all formulated detailed social policies and programs, and in all their major conferences devote a large part of their attention to questions of Christian social action. The determination of the social bearing of Christianity is indeed one of the principal factors now drawing Protestantism together.

Movements toward Union of the Churches

The fissions and separations within Protestantism have slowed down markedly in the last fifty years and have now virtually ceased. Rapprochement and union are now sought. In part this is due to the attitude of the liberals in all denominations who have stressed the fact of agreement on essentials as a basis for unity. But there are many other factors—the social changes which an economy marked by rapid communications and general interdependence have brought about; the fact that scientific skepticism and widespread secularism have tended to drive adherents of religion together; the very expansion of the Christian effort into all the world; the growing interchange between denominations of helpful literature, such as hymns, lesson materials, and devotional aids; the meeting and intermingling of ministers and laymen from many different denominations on interdenominational boards and committees and at conferences and camps; and, not least, the realization that a divided Protestantism is a weakened Protestantism, particularly in a day when the problems of society are no longer those of the frontier, nor yet those of the village or town, but those arising from the closely interwoven destinies of the peoples of the entire world; all these factors suggest that only a united church can effectively seek social redemption.

Union of the churches has been urged for over a century, both in Europe and America. Heads of states have frequently expressed a desire for it. A prime example of government initiated union was the Prussian national church formed in 1817 by the organic union of Lutheran and Reformed churches (the Evangelical Church of Prussia). But the steps toward union rising from within the churches have greater significance. The most natural expression of the urge to union has been the creation of interdenominational agencies and boards, like the American Tract Society, the American Bible Society, the Home Missions Council, and the Foreign Missions Conference of North America. Federation on a yet wider scale has long been urged, and has been in good part responsible for the forming of societies on both sides of the Atlantic looking toward united Christian action against evil.

From such beginnings the ecumenical movement (or the movement for world-wide unity of the churches) has grown into one of the most significant features of modern Protestantism. Just the bare rehearsal of the chief results of the trend to union is impressive. In the area of interdenominational cooperation, lesser and greater federations of churches (city, county, state, and nation-wide) have been organized. The outstanding example of a nation-wide federation was the Federal Council of Churches of Christ in America, organized in 1908, the predecessor of the present National Council of Churches. Although the latter body

meets only biennially, it functions constantly through standing committees dealing with home missions, race relations, international justice and
good will, mercy and relief, and relations with churches abroad. In Europe the first great achievements in unity were in the area of foreign
missions. The problems of interdenominational comity on the mission
fields led to the calling of the great Edinburgh Missionary Conference
of 1910, which resulted in the formation of the International Missionary
Council (1921) and the calling of the world conferences held at Jerusalem in 1928 and at Madras in 1938. Episcopal or Church of England
hopes of serving as the mediator between the Protestant and Catholic
worlds shone forth strongly in the Lambeth Conference of 1920, and the
World Conference on Faith and Order at Lausanne in 1927. But a
papal encyclical in 1928 dashed all hopes of reunion with Rome except
by "return" and submission to the Roman Church. The Eastern Orthodox Church, however, proved more open-minded, and its representatives participated in the World Conference on Faith and Order held
in Edinburgh in 1937, and the two world conferences on Life and Work
meeting in Stockholm in 1925 and in Oxford in 1937. Held in close
succession, for the sake of the delegates who came from all parts of
the world, the 1937 Oxford and Edinburgh conferences gave rise to the
World Council of Churches, designed to parallel on a world-wide scale
the Federal Council of Churches of Christ in America. The first assembly
of the World Council of Churches was held in Amsterdam, Holland, in
1948, the second in Evanston, Illinois, in 1954, and the third in New
Delhi, India, in 1961. The last of these meetings was significant for
three things especially: (1) the integration of the International Missionary Council with the World Council of Churches, (2) the admission
of the Orthodox churches of Russia, Roumania, Bulgaria, and Poland
to membership, an event signalizing the first organizational penetration
of the World Council behind the Iron Curtain, and (3) the presence
throughout the sessions of official observers from the Roman Catholic
Church.

Two separate methods of union have emerged: *federal* union of the
churches without abolishing the member denominations, as in the World
Council of Churches and certain proposed closer federal unions, and
(2) complete *organic* union through merger. Of the latter kind was
the organic union in Canada of Presbyterians, Methodists, and Congregationalists in the United Church of Canada (1925). Along denominational lines, separate branches of the Lutheran and also of the
Presbyterian churches in the United States have more recently united.
Ecumenically more significant was the organic union in 1961 of the

Congregational-Christian Church (itself the result of the union of the Congregational and Christian churches) and the Evangelical and Reformed Church (formed from the Reformed Church in the United States and the Evangelical Synod of North America), under the name of the United Church of Christ. Great interest is now being shown in a proposed union of this new denomination with the Presbyterian, Methodist, and Episcopal churches in the United States.

In many respects the most significant denominational mergers of all are those which have occurred on the mission fields. The transplantation of Christianity to new environments has made most of the differences between denominations seem of no real consequence. The new converts find these differences hard to grasp, and even extraordinarily irrelevant. The missionaries on their part tend to forget them when engaged in joint planning and day-to-day cooperation; and when they do so, they find their effectiveness at once increasing.

Our space is at an end. Perhaps the story here unfolded does this: suggests that basic Christianity is not a way of looking back into the past, but a way of going forward into the future; not an escape from the world into solitariness, but a way of spending one's life in order to find it; not a retreat into ultimate truth, but a redemptive mission, a way of salvation leading into the world and through the world, in the love of God and man.

SUGGESTIONS FOR FURTHER READING

Ayer, J. C. *A Source Book for Ancient Church History.* Scribner, 1913

Bainton, R. *Here I Stand, a Life of Martin Luther.* Abingdon-Cokebury, 1950. Available as Mentor pb

Brauer, J. C. *Protestantism in America: a Narrative History.* Westminster, 1954

Bultmann, R. *Theology of the New Testament.* 2 vols. Scribner, 1951 and 1955
———. *Primitive Christianity in Its Contemporary Setting.* Meridian Books pb 1956

Crump, C. G. and Jacob, F. *The Legacy of the Middle Ages.* Oxford, 1926

Deissman, A. *Paul.* 2nd ed. Hodder and Stoughten, 1926. Available in Harper Torchbooks, pb

Denzinger, H. J. D. *The Sources of Catholic Dogma.* Herder, 1957

Dibelius, M. and Kummel, W. G. *Paul.* Westminster, 1953

Elliott-Binns, L. *The Reformation in England.* Duckworth, 1957

Enslin, M. S. *Christian Beginnings.* Harper, 1938. Available in Harper Torchbooks pb, 2 vols.

French, R. M. *The Eastern Orthodox Church.* Hutchinson, 1951

Gilson, E. *History of Christian Philosophy in the Middle Ages.* Random House, 1954

Goodspeed, Edgar J. *Paul.* Winston, 1947

Kelly, J. N. D. *Early Christian Doctrines.* Harper, 1958

Klausner, Joseph. *From Jesus to Paul.* Macmillan, 1943. Available as Beacon pb (A Jewish view)

Latourette, K. S. *History of the Expansion of Christianity,* 7 vols. Harper, 1937–1945

Lietzmann, H. *The Beginnings of the Christian Church.* Scribner, 1950

————. *The Founding of the Church Universal.* Scribner, 1938

Lossky, V. *The Mystical Theology of the Eastern Church.* James Clarke, 1957

MacKintosh, H. R. *Types of Modern Theology.* Scribner, 1937

McGiffert, A. C. *A History of Christian Thought.* 2 vols. Scribner, 1932–1933

Nichols, J. H. *A History of Christianity 1650–1950.* Ronald, 1956

Parker, T. H. L. *Portrait of Calvin.* Westminster, 1954

Rouse, R. and Neill, S. C., eds. *A History of the Ecumenical Movement.* Westminster, 1954

Walker, Williston. *A History of the Christian Church.* Revised by Richardson, Pauck, and Handy. Scribner, 1959

Weiss, J. *The History of Primitive Christianity.* Ed. F. C. Grant in 2 vols. Wilson-Erickson, 1937. Available in Harper Torchbooks pb

16 Islam: Monotheism with an Arabian Coloring in Interaction with Various Cultures

IN ITS EARLY YEARS THE RELIGION OF MUHAMMAD HAD A SWIFT AND spectacular spread, often, where resistance occurred, to the terrible accompaniment of fire and sword; and so it made an unforgettable impression upon many peoples both of the East and West. In the 1st century of its existence it must have appeared to those who stood in the path of its advance like a devouring fire enlarging from its center, which rushed upon them with remorseless and inexorable speed; before they knew what to do, it was upon them. Most of those who were confronted by its authoritarian control, were, on condition of paying tribute, granted tolerance. Many, not caring to withstand the New Order, and half-convinced already, surrendered themselves and became Moslems ("Submitters").* Others welcomed it. Some resisted actively, and became dead men, incapable of counter-argument. There seemed to be no way to moderate the severity of the new faith's demands. In southwestern and southeastern Europe its impetuous rush was halted and its attack hurled back; but its advance continued toward the east and south, until its force was finally spent, deep in Asia and far to the west in Spain, a thousand and more miles from its starting point.

But though its severity appalled those who resisted it, its simplicity and clarity appealed to those who bowed to its teaching. Four hundred

* In the following pages it might be thought advisable, in the interests of consistency in orthography, to spell this word Muslim, as is common in the East. But long-prevailing habits are hard to break (!), and the Western custom is here inconsistently followed.

713

and fifty million people, by a conservative estimate, are now numbered among its willing adherents, and their number is increasing. They accept it as the absolute and final faith, and they are proud to be able to understand it. In general, it does not overburden them with a multitude of scriptures and a plethora of abstruse doctrines. It has kept to one basic scripture, preserved from the first in a state of textual purity such that comparatively few variant readings have arisen to confuse the commentators. What is in the Qur'an * all orthodox Moslems accept for absolute truth; for it is the word of God himself.

The Moslem's pride in his faith is not decreased by the convincing array of evidence that can be gathered to show that Muhammad's teaching was not new. It is Islam's proud boast that the Qur'an completes and fulfils the half-truths that other religions before it haltingly declared.

Anyone familiar with the world's religions will, of course, perceive at once on reading the Qur'an that Muhammad drew extensively from other religions. But though he relied heavily upon Jewish and Christian tradition for his conception of the relation of God to men in history, and borrowed also from Sabaeans and Zoroastrians, he gave to Allah, his deity, an Arabian character and personality. This will be evident as we proceed.

But in the study of Islam we are met by an initial difficulty. Though its doctrinal and ethical character is finally determined by one absolute standard or rule of faith—the Qur'an—it is not from the Qur'an that we get most of the information we possess concerning the life of Muhammad and the early spread of his religion. This information comes to us through the *Ahadith* or "Traditions" originating from the first generation of Moslems and handed down orally to those who finally committed them to writing. The Traditions contain great masses of palpably unreliable material, but as early reports of what Muhammad said and did, or was believed by his early followers to have said and done, they are extremely valuable to the discriminating historian.

I ARABIAN BELIEFS AND PRACTICES BEFORE MUHAMMAD

Racial and Economic Factors

The Arabians, like any other people that might be mentioned, were

* Or Koran, the traditional spelling, and therefore to be found in some of the quotations of this chapter, but Qur'an more accurately suggests the real pronunciation.

not racially homogeneous. The pure Semites among them outnumbered very greatly all the representatives of other ethnic groups; but a considerable proportion of the population had in their blood a mixture of both Semitic and non-Semitic strains. In the south, Ethiopians crossed the Red Sea to establish settlements along the coastal plain; on the northeast, conquests dating as far back as the second millennium B.C., somewhat altered the racial composition there by infusion of Sumerian, Babylonian, and Persian elements. From Egypt a Hamitic strain entered the population.

Divisive modes of thought produced further variations. Cultural differences that often proved irreconcilable were introduced when Semites who left the desert returned again after the passage of centuries. During periods of international convulsion many of these in lands to the north and west retreated into the desert wastes which their fathers had put behind them. In the time of Muhammad the western portions of Arabia contained considerable numbers of Jews who had fled from their enemies—Assyrian, Babylonian, Greek, and Roman. It was they who introduced the intensive cultivation of the oases in western Arabia. They were numerous in Medina (the ancient Yathrib) and in its neighborhood, and had even at times held this region under armed control. When Muhammad took over this city, he found it necessary to court the Jews there, until his power had grown sufficiently strong for him to express his anger at their lack of faith by crushing them.

There were some rather marked differences between Northern and Southern Arabs. The huge Arabian peninsula (natively and aptly called Jazirat al-'Arab, "the Island of the Arabs," because it is virtually isolated by its surrounding waters and its own sands) is geographically divided by a clam-shell-shaped tract of red sand, a third of a million square miles in extent, which even the bedouins avoid (it being known to them as Al-Rub 'al-Khali, "the Vacant Quarter"). To the north of this bad land are stretches of more habitable desert steppe, containing oases and arable valley-bottoms. This more hospitable territory extends like a wide band in nearly a full circle around another desert, the Great Nefud, lying in the northwest. The Nefud's shifting dunes of red and white sand stretch midway between Medina and Damascus. On the steppe-land the coarse soil supports a sparse hardy verdure which springs up when the infrequent winter rains fall, and provides grazing for the camels, sheep, goats, and horses of the bedouin tribes. South of the "Vacant Quarter" is the rain-bathed area of Yemen or South Arabia—the classical Arabia Felix—bounded on the southeast by the Gulf of Aden and on the southwest by the lower end of the Red Sea. This was the region so famed among the Greeks and Romans for its frankincense and spices. The geographical separation of north and south Arabia was paralleled by ethnic differences among the people. The North Arabians of Muhammad's day were long-headed, wiry nomads, who spoke a pure Arabic, and were by nature liberty-loving and imaginative. Thousands of years of hungry struggle had schooled them in predatory habits. They were quite different in speech and customs from their comfortable brethren below the "Vacant Quarter," the round-headed, hook-nosed Southerners, who were farmers and horticulturists, and spoke a Semitic dialect, with Ethiopic affinities, that sounded strange in northern ears. Before the time of Muhammad the North Arabians had no outside contacts and never knew a conqueror; but the South Arabians, blessed with fertilizing rain and sun, grew prosperous through trade, built cities and towns surrounded by green fields and gardens, and brought down upon themselves in consequence raids from the desert, wars from abroad, the expense of fortifications, heavy taxes, economic rivalries, commercial anxieties, and recurrent depressions coming close on the heels of boom times. And when the Ptolemies (and the Romans after them) learned how to sail past them to India, they went into permanent decline.

A third section of Arabia happens to be more important to us. It consists of the mountain range running parallel with the Red Sea from Yemen to the southeast to the Gulf of Aqaba in the northwest. Rising at some points over ten thousand feet above sea level, this range falls swiftly to the Red Sea; but its eastern slope declines gradually, through bare, volcanic lava-tracts, scoured with deep wadis or water-courses, toward the red sands of the central desert and the flat coastal plains bordering the far-away Persian Gulf. Although at places like Ta'if or Medina subterranean waters rising to the surface moisten an arable soil, this mountain range for the most part is dry and barren. Violent rain storms sometimes visit it, but then the water rushes off in floods which more deeply wash out the gullies or wadis. Yet it figures historically as the most vital part of the peninsula, for it once furnished a connecting link between the southern spice-lands and the markets of the Mediterranean world; on the cool hard surface of its uplands, caravans long before the time of Christ plodded their way through the trading posts of Ta'if, Mecca, and Yathrib (Medina), and at Petra forked off west or north to Egypt or Syria. The pre-Islamic prosperity of the communities of Al-Hejaz, this mountain home of Islam, was primarily due to the passage through them of the spice-laden caravans of the south.

Religious Conceptions

The religion of pre-Islamic Arabia was a development out of the primitive Semitic desert-faith already sketched in the chapter on Judaism. In some parts of Arabia that development had gone pretty far in one or another direction. In South Arabia, for example, a rather advanced astral cult (known as Sabaeanism) prevailed, centered in the moon god, and reflecting Babylonian and Zoroastrian influences. In other regions where Jews and Christians had secured a foothold (which was in most of the commercial centers of Arabia), the native converts to these faiths abandoned their primitive beliefs and espoused monotheism. But the great majority of Arabs, both in the towns and on the steppes, worshiped local gods and goddesses. Some of these deities were strictly tribal; others presided over certain geographical areas, and obliged all who entered their domains to worship them, like Hubal at Mecca and Dushara at Petra. There was also widespread veneration of certain astral deities. Some of these had names which were obviously foreign, Babylonian for the most part, and were readily identified by Greek and Roman visitors as local forms of Jupiter, Mercury, Canopus, and other deities. In Mecca three almost indistinguishable goddesses were adored, Al-Lat, a mother-goddess (perhaps the sun), Al-Manah, the goddess of fate, and Al-'Uzza, the morning star, a pale sort of Venus; their idols being the center of a phallic worship much like that accorded across the frontiers in olden times to Ishtar and Isis. They were reckoned to be "the daughters of Allah"—Allah * being vaguely conceived as the creator, a far-off high-god, venerated by Muhammad's tribe, the Quraysh.

In addition to these beings of the rank of high divinity, there were lesser spirits, scarcely less honored—namely, angels, fairies, and demonic jinn. It is interesting to mark the differences in character which seem to have existed between these lesser spirits. The angels were, of course, morally irreproachable and of a uniformly beneficent nature.† The fairies rivaled them in kindliness, but were not moral beings in the true sense, having no interest in morality as such; in fact, they were in all essentials children, living in a playworld of their own, without evil. In contrast, the desert-ranging jinn, a predominantly demonic group, struck terror to Arab hearts as active agents of evil; yet they too could be bent to good uses; for anyone who could control their movements might convert them into helpful agents to the attainment of beneficial ends, like finding treasure, building palaces, or whirling young men away on the wings of the wind to far places and new fortunes. Among the demonic beings who were always evil were the ghouls, who lay in wait where men were destined to perish, that they might satisfy their depraved

* Meaning "the deity," like the Hebrew El and the Babylonian Bel.

† It is likely that this concept was derived from Jewish and Zoroastrian sources, through the currency in Arabia of the stories of the Old Testament and the Avesta.

appetite for corrupt human flesh, or who robbed graves of their bodies to furnish the main dish for their midnight orgies. The ever-active imagination of the Arabs, which came to such colorful expression in after-times in the tales of *The Thousand and One Nights,* whiled away the hours, weaving innumerable stories out of these concepts.

Particularly among the bedouin, but in every part of Arabia, naive animism (and even animatism) existed. Pillar-like stones, and noteworthy rocks, caves, springs, and wells were held in great respect. In some districts there were sacred palm trees on which offerings of weapons and cloth were hung. Totemism may have been involved in the reverence paid to the gazelle, the eagle, the vulture, and the camel.

Mecca

Mecca offered the most conspicuous instance of veneration given to a stone—that offered to the meteorite built into the corner of the Ka'bah,* the holiest shrine in Arabia. The Roman historian, Diodorus Siculus (ca. 60 B.C.) already refers to it. In some far past the people of that part of Arabia had been startled by the rush of a meteor, which quenched its heaven-fire in Mecca's sandy glen. Afterwards the awed inhabitants worshiped it, calling it "the black stone which fell from heaven in the days of Adam." From far and near across the desert the tribes of Arabia, year after year, came on a *hajj* (pilgrimage) to offer sacrifices of sheep and camels and to run the circuit of the stone seven times and kiss it, in the hope of heaven's blessing on them. In the course of years the cube-shaped Ka'bah was erected in honor of the stone and to give lodgment to the gods associated with it by the pilgrims. The holy stone was placed in the southeast corner at a height which permitted it to be kissed by those who made the seven-fold circuit. Images of local and distant deities were placed in the dark interior. Borrowing from the stories of the Hebrews, the Meccans declared that the great patriarch Abraham, while on a visit to his son Ishmael, had built the Ka'bah and imbedded the Black Stone in it.†

Only a few steps away from the Ka'bah was the holy well Zamzam, whose water was sacred to the pilgrims who ran the circuit of the

* Literally "the cube," for it was a cubelike structure with no exterior ornament. To enhance its appearance, it was later covered with a tissue of black cloth.

† Tradition was not content with this legend, however; it asserted that the *first* Ka'bah was built by Adam from a celestial prototype, and was *rebuilt* by Abraham and Ishmael.

shrine. Meccan tradition endowed it with a curious history. In the 3rd century A.D., when the men of the Beni-Jurhum tribe were driven from Mecca by the Bani-Khuza'ah, their sheikh, so it was said, before giving up the town, threw down into the well some suits of armor, several swords, and two gazelles of gold; and then covered all up with tamped-down earth and sand so that, when the captors of the city entered it, the location of the well was not known to them. After the Quraysh came into control of Mecca, Muhammad's grandfather, 'Abd-al-Muttalib, the leading chief, relocated the well and restored its flow. The Meccans could not thank him enough; for they had an old tradition that after Hagar was expelled from Abraham's tent,* she came with her little son Ishmael to the future site of their city, at that time a barren valley; and because her child was dying of thirst, she left him lying on the hot earth while she searched despairingly for water; behind her the child, in a tantrum, kicked his heels into the ground, and the waters of Zamzam welled up into the depression and saved his life! In recognition of this supposed event, it was considered meritorious for pilgrims to add to the circling of the Ka'bah an exercise called the "Lesser Pilgrimage," which involved a rapid pacing back and forth seven times between two hills near the Ka'bah in imitation of Hagar's anguished search. And since Ishmael was declared to be the founder of the city, it was thought well to extend this exercise into something more arduous, called the "Greater Pilgrimage." This was performed during the holy month Dhu-al-Hijja, and included, besides the exercises of the lesser pilgrimage, a tour of the hills east of Mecca taking several days, and including in its scope visits to places celebrated for great events in Arabian history.

Within the Ka'bah itself a large number of idols were ranged around Hubal, the chief male deity. Next in importance to him were the three goddesses, Al-Lat, al-Manah, and Al-'Uzza. Together with their associates, including the far-off Allah, who was imageless, these deities constituted a sort of pantheon for Arabia, designed to draw to Mecca the people of every region. So holy did Mecca become, in fact, that the city and its immediate environs were declared sacred territory, and pilgrims were obliged to disarm when entering it.

By agreement throughout Arabia four months were reserved out of each year for pilgrimage and trade; during them no violence or warfare was permitted; and Mecca, along with many other places, profited by the fairs and markets which then sprang up.

In spite, however, of her pre-eminent station as the chief pilgrim center, and one of the chief crossroads towns, of Arabia, Mecca had a

* The Arabs learned this story also from the Hebrews.

hard struggle to keep going. There were three reasons for this, all rooted in long-standing conditions, the first geographical, the second economic, the third civic. The trouble with Mecca physically was that it lay in a barren mountain pass. In the words of William Bolitho: "Even the date palm, the only plant that can endure both freezing and scorching, will not grow there. After all these years that the riches of three continents have poured ceaselessly into this wretched place, there are no gardens, and a stunted bush is a civic pride." [1] Economically, the fortunes of Mecca steadily declined after the Arab monopoly in the spice trade was broken by the re-opening of the old Egyptian maritime route through the Red Sea. This was a serious blow not only to the Al-Hejaz transport towns but to South Arabia as well, for it forced down prices by bringing India and Somaliland into play as trade rivals. In the subsequent decline of Arab commerce, some hill towns had to fall back on agriculture for survival; but barren Mecca could have recourse to no such expedient and had mainly to rely for survival on her power to attract pilgrims to her Black Stone. That power alone saved her from the fate of Petra to the west, the marvelous rock-hewn city which by Muhammad's time had lain uninhabited for five centuries. The margin of security was none too large. Should the Ka'bah be endangered, a crisis of real magnitude would threaten. Tradition had it that such a crisis actually developed in the very year in which Muhammad was born. This was the year known in Arabia as "the year of the elephant," because the Abyssinian (and Christian) governor of South Arabia marched upon Mecca, in force, and with a battle elephant, professing a holy desire to destroy the heathen shrine; but he had to retreat, just when Mecca lay defenceless before him, because of an outbreak of smallpox among his troops.

Of course Mecca had been getting used to economic stringency through the years; what made her more unhappy was the civic tension between her rival factions. Civic peace was of that hair-trigger variety dependent on the precarious balance maintained by the law of vendetta. Exactly like the free-roaming bedouin tribes, the rival clans which camped together within the city's limits subscribed to the ancient principle that the murder of any member of one's own clan called for the answering death of a member of the murderer's clan. If the murder was done *within* a clan, the murderer would be without defence; if he was caught he was put to death, and if he escaped he became an outlaw, a member of no clan, with every man's hand against him. But when a member of a clan was murdered by an *outsider*, his whole clan rose up to avenge him. The principal deterrent to violent crime in Arabia and also the guarantee of civic order was, it is clear, the fear of blood vengeance.

At the time of Muhammad the two chief tribes that contended for mastery in Mecca were the Quraysh and Khuza'ah, the former having risen to dominance about the middle of the 5th century. But the Quraysh tribe was itself inwardly at tension between the Hashimite and Ummayad families or clans. Their rivalry for the prerogatives of civil and religious power was a competitive struggle of great consequence for the future of Islam, as the sequel will show.

II THE PROPHET MUHAMMAD

Perhaps the really determinative factor in making Muhammad a prophet was the fact that he early became an orphan. According to tradition, his father, a Hashimite, died before his birth and his mother when he was six years old; he then became a ward of two leading Quraysh chiefs, first of his grandfather 'Abd-al-Muttalib, and then of his uncle, Abu Talib. Under the guardianship of these two men, he grew up in an atmosphere of religious excitement and responsibility; for both men were prominent members of the Quraysh tribe, and that tribe held the position of trustee of the Ka'bah, its idols, its Black Stone, the nearby sacred well, and all the properties connected with them, and discharged the hospitable office of providing food and water, at a price, for the pilgrims who thronged to Mecca. But his loyalties were not fully enlisted; his orphaned state seems to have given him a certain objectivity and detachment of judgment. As he came to maturity, he began to look on many of the beliefs and customs of his community with a critical appraisal born of questioning and distaste. He was disturbed by incessant quarreling in the avowed interests of religion and honor among the Quraysh chiefs. Stronger still was his dissatisfaction with the primitive survivals in Arabian religion, the idolatrous polytheism and animism, the immorality at religious convocations and fairs, the drinking, gambling, and dancing which were fashionable, and the burial alive of unwanted infant daughters practiced not only in Mecca but throughout Arabia. He must have been puzzled by the senseless bloodshed and inter-tribal anarchy which accompanied the so-called "Sacrilegious Wars" that occurred during his youth. There was little to commend these conflicts, called sacrilegious because they broke out during the sacred month Dhu-al-Qa'dah, at the time of the fair annually held at Ukaz, three days east of Mecca. The Quraysh were involved, and Muhammad is said to have attended one of his uncles during one of the skirmishes. If so, he was not a fire-eater. In later years he produced, according to one tradition, this rather tepid reminiscence: "I remember being present with my uncles in the Sacrilegious War; I discharged arrows at the enemy, and I do not regret it." [2]

But he did not come to these views unaided. Some of his moral and spiritual emancipation from the more objectionable practices of his people are traditionally said to have come during caravan trips to Palestine and Syria. The first of these is said to have been made in the company of his uncle Abu Talib when he was twelve years old; a second journey to Syria when he was twenty-five years old is said to have been made as the business manager of the widow Khadijah, whom he later married. It is likely that even if he made these trips, they contributed little more than general impressions, hardly anything specific concerning either doctrines or rites. Greater importance should be attached, therefore, to the fact that some of his closest acquaintances in Mecca were well versed in the traditions of the Jews and Christians, and were perhaps critical of native Arabian beliefs. He also came into contact with Jews and Christians at commercial fairs, where representatives of these faiths used to address the crowds; as a matter of fact, the Qur'an contains references which indicate that his curiosity and admiration were aroused by the exposition of these faiths which he so heard. What he learned he acquired gradually and from heterodox sources; for, so far as Christianity is concerned, he was most influenced by Nestorian conceptions and popular traditions that reflected apocryphal as well as canonical Christian literature.

His need to resolve his religious perplexities only grew during the leisure which his marriage to Khadijah, a rich Qurayshite widow, brought him. Fifteen years his senior, she mothered as well as loved him, and encouraged his religious interests. The two sons, possibly three, she bore him died in infancy, to Muhammad's lasting grief; of their four daughters only Fatima survived him. [*]

Religious Awakening

Muhammad now entered a period of spiritual stress. He had apparently been struck by the belief common to both Jews and Christians

---

[*] Their four daughters lived long enough to marry associates of Muhammad, Zainab marrying Abu-al-'As, Ruqayyah Uthman, who became the third caliph, Fatima 'Ali, the fourth caliph, and Umm-Qulthum Utayba.

that there would be a Last Judgment and a punishment of idolaters by everlasting fire. The one true God, they said, could not be represented by any image, but only by prophetic spokesmen. Such spokesmen had in times past appeared in Palestine, but had not yet been sent to Arabia. But why not?

His private thought during this period was quickened by persons brought close to him by marriage. A cousin of Khadijah, the blind Waraqah, a wise old man who had some influence in her household, may have been a Christian, and though his information was apparently at many points misleading, Muhammad found him a useful source of knowledge concerning matters of faith and conduct. Less information was perhaps provided by a Christian slave boy called Zaid, whom Muhammad liberated and adopted as a son, just as he had already adopted 'Ali, the child of his uncle Abu Talib. The thought that the Last Day and the Last Judgment might be near at hand began to agitate him. He wandered off to the hills about Mecca to brood privately. He was now about forty years old.

Prophetic Call

According to Moslem tradition, he visited a cave near the base of Mount Hira, a few miles north of Mecca, for days at a time. Suddenly one night ("The Night Of Power and Excellence," Moslems call it) there rose in vision before him the archangel Gabriel, the Messenger of God, at about "two bows' length," crying "Recite!"

> RECITE thou in the name of thy Lord who created;—
> Created man from CLOTS OF BLOOD:—
> Recite thou! For thy Lord is the most Beneficent,
> Who hath taught the use of the pen:—
> Hath taught Man that which he knoweth not. . . .[3]

When the vision ended, Muhammad was able to reproduce the whole revelation (Sura 96 of the Qur'an, of which only the first lines are here given). He rushed home in great excitement, half doubting, half believing. Later, he was to defend the authenticity of his experience in these words (Sura 53):

> By the STAR when it setteth,
> Your compatriot erreth not, nor is he led astray,
> Neither speaketh he from mere impulse.
> The *Koran* is no other than a revelation revealed to him:
> One terrible in power taught it him,

Endued with wisdom. With even balance stood he
In the highest part of the horizon:
Then came he nearer and approached,
And was at the distance of two bows, or even closer,—
And he revealed to his servant what he revealed.
His heart falsified not what he saw.
What! will ye then dispute with him as to what he saw? [4]

Yet at first Muhammad's heart did nearly belie that which he saw. He had fears for his own sanity. Moslem tradition (in the words of Al-Waqidi) relates:

He hurried home to tell his wife. "Oh, Khadijah," he said, "I have never abhorred anything as I do these idols and soothsayers; and now verily I fear lest I should become a soothsayer myself." "Never," replied his faithful wife; "the Lord will never suffer it thus to be," and she went on to speak of his many virtues, upon which she founded the assurance. Then she repaired to her cousin Waraqah, and told him all. "By the Lord," cried the aged man, "he speaketh truth! Doubtless it is the beginning of prophecy, and there shall come upon him the *Great Namus* (the Great Law), like as it came upon Moses."

But Muhammad was not lightly to be comforted. The tradition adds:

After this he waited some time without seeing Gabriel. And he became greatly downcast, so that he went out now to one mountain, and then to another, seeking to cast himself headlong thence. While thus intent on self-destruction, he was suddenly arrested by a voice from heaven. He looked, and behold it was Gabriel upon a throne between the heavens and the earth, who said: "O Muhammad! thou art the Prophet of the Lord, in truth, and I am Gabriel." Then Muhammad turned to go to his own house; and the Lord comforted him, and strengthened his heart. And thereafter revelations began to follow one upon another with frequency. [5]

Other traditions somewhat vary this account, but, without attempting to straighten out the tangle of fact and tradition, we may conclude that Muhammad, after a period of self-questioning and discouragement, lasting for several months, finally came to look upon himself as being, miraculously enough, a true prophet (*nabi*) and apostle (*rasul*) of Allah, that is, a messenger of the real and only God, already known under other names to the Jews and Christians. When it began to appear that the strange experiences, in which rhapsodies in Arabic flowed across his lips, would continue to occur, almost without his willing them, he came to believe that Allah was using him as a mouthpiece; the verses he uttered, half in trance, were real revelations. His first doubts about them disappeared; he now saw what his wife and friends asserted was true, that they made sense. At last Arabia was being provided with a scripture—of later date and therefore greater authority than the scriptures of the Jews and Christians!

The Meccan Ministry

After a short period of consultation with relatives and friends, he appeared in the streets and in the courtyard of the Ka'bah, to recite "in the name of the Lord" the verses of the revelations. The listening Meccans gaped, and then, hearing strange doctrine, broke into ridicule. The man must be mad! The incredible substance of his preaching seemed to be a warning of some judgment day, or other, together with predictions of the resurrection of the body, and of a consuming fire! They gave him a poor reception; but in spite of that he kept coming back day after day to recite his rhythmically composed verses.

> When the sun shall be FOLDED UP,
> And when the stars shall fall,
> And when the mountains shall be set in motion,
> And when the she-camels shall be abandoned,
> And when the wild beasts shall be gathered together,
> And when the seas shall boil,
> And when souls shall be paired with their bodies,
> And when the female child that had been buried alive shall be asked
> For what crime she was put to death,
> And when the leaves of the Book shall be unrolled,
> And when the Heaven shall be stripped away,
> And when Hell shall be made to blaze,
> And when Paradise shall be brought near,
> Every soul shall know what it hath produced. . . .
> Whither then are ye going?
> Verily, this is no other than a warning to all creatures.[6]

Could much credence be accorded to such an utterance? his critics cried; or to what follows:

> They of God's right hand
> In their gardens shall ask of the wicked;—
> "What hath cast you into Hell-fire?"
> They will say, "We were not of those who prayed,
> And we were not of those who fed the poor,
> And we plunged into vain disputes with vain disputers,
> And we rejected as a lie, the day of reckoning,
> Till the certainty came upon us!" [7]

There was much in the revelations bearing on the Unity of God, and on the function of Muhammad as the Prophet of God. Often the verses quoted God as speaking in the first person (usually plural):

Surely in trouble have we created man.
What! thinketh he no one hath power over him? . . .
What! have we not made him eyes,
And tongue, and lips,
And guided him to the two highways?
Yet he attempted not the steep (path).
And who shall teach thee what the steep is?
It is to ransom the captive,
Or to feed in the day of famine
The orphan who is near of kin, or the poor that lieth in the dust;
Beside this, to be of those who believe, and enjoin stedfastness on
    each other, and enjoin compassion on each other.
These shall be the people of the right hand:
While they who disbelieve our signs
Shall be the people of the left.
Around them the fire shall close.[8]

Unimpressed though they were at first, his hearers, especially those of the Quraysh tribe, at last became seriously disturbed. They did not object so much to Muhammad's insistence that there is but one God and he (Muhammad) was God's prophet—that might be laughed off—but they stiffened with hostility at his forthright denunciation of the worship of their idols. He could talk all he liked about his belief in the resurrection of the dead, but when he condemned the religion of Mecca and the worship of the Ka'bah idols as leading to perdition, their ancient traditions (and the revenues of the Ka'bah) were thereby threatened.

It would not serve our purpose to go into the chronology of the ensuing trials and tribulations of Muhammad during a whole decade of disheartening community opposition. His following seemed doomed to be small. Khadijah was perhaps the first to accept his mission, believing in it even before he himself did; her faith was quickly echoed by his adopted sons, Zaid, the liberated slave-boy, and 'Ali, the son of Abu Talib. A very important convert, one of the first, and destined to be Muhammad's first successor, was Abu Bakr, a kinsman from the Quraysh tribe, a merchant and therefore a person of some prestige. Abu Bakr's proselyting for the new faith secured five other early converts, among whom Uthman, son of 'Affan (later the third caliph), was outstanding. But conversions came slowly; in the first four years they numbered only about forty, including wives of male believers and liberated slaves.

Muhammad's revelations were meanwhile continuing. When he appeared to recite them, the hostile members of the Quraysh did all they could to break up his gatherings; they scattered thorns about, threw filth and dirt on him and his hearers, and stirred up the rowdies to hurl insults and threats. They longed to be able to use violence; but from this they were deterred by the stout protection of his uncle Abu Talib. In an attempt to prevent his public appearances, the Ummayads, the hostile element of the Quraysh, issued a solemn ban against the Hashimites, the branch of the tribe to which Muhammad belonged, and forced them to retire to the quarter of the town where Abu Talib lived —a narrow defile among the hills—for over two years; but the rest of the community brought pressure to have the ban removed. Then greater blows were to fall on Muhammad. Khadijah, his greatest support, died; and five weeks later his protector, faithful Abu Talib, still unconverted, but loyal always, was taken. This severe double bereavement weakened the position of Muhammad in the eyes of his enemies, and though the vendetta law still shielded him, it was apparent that some of the Hashimites were becoming disaffected, and might be persuaded to consent to his imprisonment or execution.

He therefore began to look afield. An attempt to establish himself in Ta'if, some sixty miles to the southeast, proved abortive. His cause seemed almost hopeless. Then suddenly hope revived. During the truce period of 620 A.D., he held a lengthy conference at the Ukaz fair with six men from Yathrib (Medina), who thought he might be their man. Their native city, three hundred miles to the north, had not recovered from the effects of open dissension caused by blood feuds between two Arab tribes, the Aws and the Khazraj, and stood to benefit if someone could be brought in to impose a firm rule over them. They agreed to prepare their town for the Prophet's coming. By the next pilgrimage season they reported progress, and in the following year the preparations for Muhammad's assumption of undisputed leadership were complete.

The Hijra (622 A.D.)

Secrecy had been well maintained, but at the last moment the Meccans got wind of the matter, and the hostile Quraysh (chiefly Ummayads under the leadership of Abu Sufyan) determined to strike and strike quickly. But Muhammad and Abu Bakr escaped to a cave on Mt. Thaur, and when the pursuit died down, mounted camels, and successfully made the Hijra (the Migration) to Yathrib, ordinarily eleven days off, in the short time of eight days.

Establishment of the Theocracy at Medina

Given astonishingly unrestricted power over the town, whose name was changed in his honor to Medina (*Madina an nabi*, the City of the Prophet), Muhammad immediately set about the erection of a house of worship—the first mosque. Rapidly and simply, he evolved a new cultus. Weekly services on Friday; prostration during prayer (at first toward Jerusalem, but when the Jews in Medina withstood conversion, toward Mecca); a call to prayer from the mosque's roof (at first only for the Friday services, and then every day at the times for private prayer); the taking up of alms for the poor and for the support of the cause—these and other practices were soon established.

To supply his followers with arms and treasure, he led out a small force to waylay a Meccan caravan. War with Mecca was the result. In the first engagement Muhammad had the better of it, in the next

Muhammad and his Companions; at Medina. (After 17th century Indo-Persian miniature, Carfax Collection)

the Meccans; and then the Meccans prepared for a grand assault. With some ten thousand men they invested Medina; but Muhammad had taken the advice of a Persian follower and dug a trench around the town. The "Battle of the Ditch" which followed persuaded the Meccans that Muhammad was beyond their taking. In January, 630, Muhammad in his turn marched forth with ten thousand men. Mecca offered only token resistance. The Prophet of Allah, at a bound, reached the stature of the greatest chief in Arabia. As such he acted with great magnanimity toward his former fellow-townsmen, excluding only a handful of them from the general amnesty which he proclaimed.

One of his first acts was to go reverently to the Ka'bah; yet he showed no signs of yielding to the ancient Meccan polytheism. After honoring the Black Stone and riding seven times around the shrine, he ordered the destruction of the idols within it and the scraping of the paintings of Abraham and the angels from the walls. He sanctioned the use of the well Zamzam, and restored the boundary pillars defining the sacred territory around Mecca. Thenceforth no Moslem would have cause to hesitate about going on a pilgrimage to the ancient holy city.

Muhammad now made sure of his political and religious ascendancy in Arabia. Active opponents near at hand were conquered by the sword, and tribes far away were invited sternly to send delegations offering their allegiance. Before his sudden death in 632, he knew he was well on the way to accomplishing his divine mission of unifying the Arab tribes under a theocracy governed by the will of the one and only God, Allah. Since he was no longer so conscious of imminent Divine Judgment on the world, an immediate task absorbed him—the moral elevation and unification of the Arab tribes. On his last visit to Mecca, just before his death, tradition pictures him as preaching a memorable sermon, in which he proclaimed a central fact of the Moslem movement in these words: "O ye men! harken unto my words and take ye them to heart! Know ye that every Moslem is a brother unto every other Moslem, and that ye are now one brotherhood." [9]

Since he had oftentimes commissioned Abu Bakr to lead the prayers when he himself could not do so, it seemed natural that this devoted follower and companion should be proclaimed his temporal "successor" (or Caliph). Muhammad's death therefore only momentarily halted the rapid growth of his movement.

III THE CREED OF ISLAM

The teachings of Muhammad became the creed of Islam, with few alterations or additions. (The differences in interpretation and method which gave rise to the sects, still to be described, were in no case marked by consciousness of departure from the *ipsissima verba* of Muhammad.) The fundamentals of the faith as set forth in the Qur'an are not many in number and are within the mental reach of all. The simple believer feels no need to puzzle his head over theological and ethical subtleties. The way of life recommended to him has little to do with theory and much to do with practice—definite things to do that assure his salvation. He is not asked to agree, for there is not much to agree to, but rather to submit, and thereby become a *Moslem* or "submitter." His one obligation is to say, with many a character in *The Thousand and One Nights*, "I hear and obey." And this course seems to him both highly satisfactory for this life and promising for the life to come.

Moslem teachers usually subsume most of the articles of their faith under three heads: *īmān* or doctrine, *'ibādāt* or religious duty, and *ihsan* or right conduct.

A. DOCTRINE. In the famous Moslem credal formula, the first part reads: *la ilāha illa Allāh* "(There is) no god but Allah." This is the most important article in Moslem theology. No statement about God seemed to Muhammad more fundamental than the declaration that God is one and undivided, and no sin seemed to him so unpardonable as associating another being with God on terms of equality.* God stands alone and supreme. He existed before any other being or thing, is self-subsistent, omniscient, omnipotent ("All-seeing, all-hearing, all-willing"). He is the creator, and in the awful Day of Judgment he is the sole arbiter who shall save the believer out of the dissolution of the world and place him in Paradise.

But the Qur'an is not entirely consistent in its portrayal of the character of Allah. If we arrange the suras of the Qur'an as nearly as possible in their chronological order, we see between the earliest and the latest of them a difference of conception: Allah becomes less Jewish and more Arabian. More significant, he changes in that he governs men less loosely, guides them more rigorously. In the Meccan period, Muhammad was a long-suffering prophet who, under the influence of Jewish and Christian teaching, proclaimed on the one hand God's purpose to bring the world to judgment, and on the other the wilful wickedness of man in rebellion against the will of God. The underlying conception is that the God of mercy and love must in justice hold man responsible for the acts which he has freely committed in contravention of God's holy will. In the Medina days, when Muhammad had become the militant leader of a new religion clearly dis-

---

* The Arabian idolaters who worshiped many gods and goddesses represented by stocks and stones were obviously guilty of this sin of sins, but so also were the Christians who said, "God is the third of three."

tinguished from Judaism and Christianity, the suras stress the majesty and power of the God who had willed the surprising events of history and set the feet of the Moslems on the road to salvation while he sent the unbelievers astray to the damnation which their unbelief deserved. The latest suras imply that men have the freedom of obedience only, since Allah wills all, both good and bad. Allah is a being beyond all human questioning—the inscrutable determiner of men's destinies, who acts according to divine ends which no man can clearly know, and not according to the limited standards of justice discernible by man; in short, in his pursuit of over-all good, Allah appears in the latest revelations, to use R. E. Hume's vivid characterization, "like an Arab sheikh glorified and magnified to cosmic proportions." [10] He does not reason with his people; he leads them, through his commands, which they must hear and obey, toward the happiness which they must trust him to find for them. He wants his people to have the best of every good thing, since he loves those whom he has chosen to love him, and hates those whom he has rejected. God is the Compassionate, the Merciful—but only to the Moslem, the man who submits unquestioningly and enthusiastically to his holy will.* All such he guides and conducts toward their salvation.

Allah reveals his will and guides men in three very distinct ways: through Muhammad, his messenger; through the Qur'an, his revelation; and through the angels.

* Orthodox Moslems have no difficulty with this point that Allah rewards with his mercy those whom he has predestinated to love him, and condemns to everlasting punishment those whom he has predestinated to disobey him. It is outsiders, and those pious souls who presuppose that God is moved by an absolute justice and not simply by his own good pleasure, who raise questions. But it is possible to reconcile the earlier and later portions of the Qur'an satisfactorily, if one keeps the conditions of desert life in mind—that is, if one is properly anthropomorphic in the Arabian sense. For example, to follow Goldziher's illuminating comments: "If, in many passages of the Koran it is said, 'Allah guides whom he will, and lets whom he will go astray,' such passages do not imply that God directly brings the latter class into the evil path. The decisive word *adalla* is not to be taken in such a connection as meaning to 'lead astray,' but to allow to go astray, not to trouble about a person, not to show him the way out. . . . Let us conjure up the picture of a lonely wanderer in the desert,—it is from this idea that the language of the Koran concerning leading and wandering has sprung. The wanderer errs in a boundless expanse, gazing about for the right direction to his goal. So is man in his wanderings through life. He who, through faith and good works, has deserved the good will of God, him he rewards with his guidance. He lets the evildoer go astray. He leaves him to his fate, and takes his protection from him. He does not offer him the guiding hand, but he does not bring him directly to the evil path. . . . Guidance is a reward of the good. 'Allah does not guide the wicked.' (Sura 9, v. 110)." [11]

Muhammad's night journey to heaven on the mare Buraq. (Detail from Persian manuscript in Bibliotheque Nationale, Paris)

The second half of the Moslem creedal formula declares: *Muhammad rasūl Allāh*, "Muhammad is the messenger (or prophet) of Allah." It seems self-evident to Moslems that God must reveal himself through prophets, else men could not know him. God would not leave himself without witness, and so there has been a long line of such prophets, including Abraham, Moses, and Jesus. But Muhammad is the last and greatest of them all, the "seal" of those who appeared before him; none is his equal, either in knowledge or in authority; none has received or handed down so perfect a revelation. But though his authority is supreme, he was not a divine being appearing in the flesh: he was human like the rest of men; nor did he pretend to supernatural powers: he performed no miracles; instituted no mystical, deifying sacraments; ordained no holy priesthood; set apart none to a sacred office by ordination or a mystical laying on of hands. He was simply man at his best, and God was still the wholly Other, with whom he was united in will but not in substance. The only suggestion in Moslem tradition that Muhammad had any special relationship with heaven is to be found in the traditions (*ahadith*) concerning the Mir'aj or Night Journey of the Prophet to Paradise. These traditions are based on a passage in Sura XVII, 1, which says: "Glory be to Him Who took His servant by night from the sacred temple [at Mecca] to the more remote temple [at Jerusalem], whose precincts We have blessed, to show him some of Our signs." The traditions vary with those who tell or attest to them but they compose into something like this story: On a certain night while the Prophet still lived in Mecca (a night whose anniversary is celebrated each year throughout the Moslem world) Gabriel came, cleansed him within, and took him through the air (on the back of the winged steed Buraq) first to Jerusalem and then up through the seven heavens, where as he passed through he spoke successively with Adam, John the Baptist and Jesus, Joseph, Enoch, Aaron, Moses, and (in the seventh heaven) with Abraham. Finally, without Gabriel, who could go no further perhaps, he was lifted on a flying carpet (a *rafraf*) into the great space beyond to the very presence of Allah, who spoke with him about many unutterable matters and told him: "O Muhammad, I take you as a friend just as I took Abraham as a friend. I am speaking to you just as I spoke face to face with Moses." [12] Thus Muhammad is demonstrated to have a status in God's sight at least equal to that of any of his prophetic predecessors. But even with such a story to give it encouragement, no claim is made by Moslems that Muhammad was other than human, even though Allah viewed him with special favor.

The second way by which Allah guides men is through the Qur'an. The Qur'an, revealed to Muhammad, is the undistorted and final word of Allah to mankind. The Moslem doctrine asserts that the Qur'an is identical with a word of God written on a heavenly scroll, an uncreated archetype, which has existed from eternity in the seventh heaven. It is not a copy, a quotation, or a communication of the heavenly original; it is identical exactly with the heavenly original—the word of God in the language of heaven. Previous authoritative revelations, such as the Jewish and Christian scriptures, are good, but not complete and final like the Qur'an. *

---

* This conviction concerning the infallibility of the Qur'an must assume, of course, that the "Memorizers" (*huffaz*) who preserved part of the Qur'anic materials before they were reduced to writing, made no errors of recollection. This is by no means an assumption that a non-Moslem can make without some hesitation; but there can be little doubt that, even though Muhammad might have arranged the materials differently and made some revisions in the text had he seen it, there is no reason to think that the Qur'an as now preserved alters the original *content* he gave it. According to tradition, in the year which followed Muhammad's death Abu Bakr, on the advice of Umar, who feared the Memorizers might all die off or perish in battle, ordered Muhammad's secretary, Zaid ibn Thabit, to make a collection of the revelations. The collection was composed from "ribs of palm-leaves and tablets of white stone and from the breasts of men," we read. There is strong evidence that other collections were made that varied in containing more or less materials and to a certain extent in wording. The final canonical text resulted from the work of a committee appointed by the Caliph Uthman and headed again by Muhammad's secretary. Four identical copies were made and all previous texts were ordered destroyed. The Uthmanic text met some resistance, but finally prevailed. For a good brief discussion of this matter, see C. S. Braden, *The Scriptures of Mankind*, pp. 443–446.

The third means by which Allah makes known his will is through the angels. Of these the chief is Gabriel, the agent of revelation, who is described in terms reminiscent of Zoroastrian angelology as "the faithful spirit" and "the spirit of holiness." In Muhammad's imagination, Allah sits in the seventh heaven on a high throne, surrounded by angels who serve him exactly as kings are served by their ministers and attendants.

The Devil (called either *Iblis*, a contraction of Diabolos, or *Shaitin*, the Zoroastrian Satan) is an angel who fell through pride and is now an accursed tempter. He and his assistants busy themselves on earth to obstruct the plans of Allah and tempt men to go astray. This sounds worse than things really are; for—at least in the light of the later Medina suras—since Allah wills all, the scope of the Devil's operations is in fact restricted to Allah's permissive decrees and calculated noninterferences.

As to the Last Judgment, Muhammad used the stock phrases of Zoroastrian, Jewish, and Christian apocalypticism. There will be "signs" of its imminence: portents, ominous rumblings, strange occurrences in nature; then, the last trumpet, at whose sound the dead will rise, and all souls will assemble before Allah's judgment throne. During the Judgment itself, the books in which each man's deeds have been recorded will be read, and eternal judgment will be passed accordingly.

Heaven and Hell are concretely described.

After this sort will we recompense the transgressors.
They shall make their bed in Hell, and above them shall be coverings
of fire! . . .
And the inmates of the fire shall cry to the inmates of Paradise: "Pour
upon us some water!" . . .[13]

Oh! how wretched shall be the people of the left hand!
Amid pestilential winds and in scalding water,
And in the shadow of a black smoke,
Not cool, and horrid to behold. . . .
Then ye, O ye the erring, the gainsaying,
Shall surely eat of the tree Ez-Zakkoum. . . .[14]

It is a tree which cometh up from the bottom of hell;
Its fruit is as it were heads of Satans;
And, lo! the damned shall surely eat of it and fill their bellies with it:
Then shall they have, thereon, a mixture of boiling water. . . .[15]

Verily the tree of Ez-Zakkoum
Shall be the sinner's food:
Like dregs of oil shall it boil up in their bellies,
Like the boiling of scalding water.

"—Seize ye him, and drag him into the mid-fire;
Then pour on his head of the tormenting boiling water.
"—'Taste this:' for thou forsooth art the mighty, the honorable!
Lo! this is that of which ye doubted."

But the pious shall be in a secure place,
Amid gardens and fountains,
Clothed in silk and richest robes, facing one another. . . .[16]

On inwrought couches
Reclining on them face to face:
Aye-blooming youths go round about to them
With goblets and ewers and a cup of flowing wine;
Their brows ache not from it, nor fails the sense:
And with such fruits as shall please them best,
And with flesh of such birds as they shall long for:
And theirs shall be the Houris, with large dark eyes, like pearls hidden
  in their shells,
In recompense for their labors past. . . .
Of a rare creation have we created the Houris,
And we have made them ever virgins,
Dear to their spouses, of equal age with them.* [17]

B. RELIGIOUS DUTY. The prescribed religious acts of Islam are the so-called "Five Pillars" (*al-Arkan*).

1. Repetition of the Creed: *La ilāha illa Allāh; Muhammad rasūl Allāh*: "There is no god but Allah; and Muhammad is the prophet of Allah." Acceptance of this confession of faith and its faithful repetition constitute the first step in being a Moslem. These simple words are heard everywhere in the Moslem world, and come down as if out of the sky from the minaret in the muezzin's calls to prayer.

2. Prayer. The good Moslem reserves time each day for five acts of devotion and prayer. The first comes at dawn, the second at mid-day, the others at mid-afternoon, sunset, and at the fall of darkness. In town or country or on the desert, the devotee goes through a ritual of ablution, rolls out his prayer rug, and bows down toward Mecca, to offer to Allah less a petition than ascriptions of praise and declarations of submission to his holy will. It is common simply to repeat the Fatihah, the Arabian Lord's Prayer (Sura 1):

---

* It is an interesting fact that these promises of Houris in Paradise date from Muhammad's Meccan days when he had but one wife going on sixty years of age. But in Medina he more than once suggested that the Faithful take their *wives* with them to Paradise. E.g. Sura 13:23: "Gardens of Eden—into which they shall enter together with the just of their fathers, and their wives, and their descendants." [18]

Praise be to God, the Lord of the worlds!
The compassionate, the merciful!
King on the day of reckoning!
Thee only do we worship, and to thee do we cry for help.
Guide thou us on the straight path,
The path of those to whom Thou hast been gracious;—with whom
thou art not angry, and who go not astray.[19]

Friday is the special day of public prayer for all adult males, when the faithful assemble in the mosque, under the leadership of the *imam,* usually at noon, or perhaps at sunset. The service is in the mosque's paved courtyard.* The men have assembled at the call from the minaret, have left their shoes at the entrance, gone to the pool or fountain to perform their ablutions (of hands, mouth, nostrils, face, fore-arms, neck, and feet), have sat for a few minutes to hear a "reader" (*qari*) recite from the Qur'an, and then on the appearance of the *imam* have taken their places in long rows, facing Mecca and spaced so as to allow their throwing themselves forward in "prostration" on their prayer mats. During the ritual prayer (or *salat*) the *imam* recites all the necessary words and all the worshipers silently and as one follow him in his motions, standing erect when he does so, and inclining the head and body or dropping on their knees, placing their hands upon the ground a little in front of them and putting their foreheads to the pavement, in "prostration," at the exact moment they see him do so. After the prayers, the *imam* usually preaches a sermon having for its purpose the exposition of Moslem doctrine.

3. Almsgiving. This is called *Zakah* (or *Zakat*). Its general meaning is that of a free-will offering, consisting of gifts to the poor, the needy, debtors, slaves, wayfarers, beggars, and charities of various kinds. In the early days of Islam it was a "loan to Allah", exacted from believers, in money or kind. It was gathered by religious officials into a common treasury, and distributed in part as charity to the poor and in part to mosques and imams for repairs and administrative expenses. It was a fund quite apart from the tribute (the *jizyat*) exacted of non-Moslems for political and military expenses. The *Zakah* was once universally obligatory, although not, strictly speaking, a tax; it is now in most regions voluntary; yet even there no one is expected to neglect it, on pain of exciting contempt.

4. The fast during the sacred month of Ramadan. Except for the sick and ailing, this fast is laid upon all as an obligation, and is carried out in this manner: as soon as it becomes possible to distinguish be-

* If women attend, they ordinarily stay behind screens and are not seen.

tween a white thread and a black at dawn, no food and drink are to
be taken until at sundown the difference between the threads is no
longer distinguishable.

5. Pilgrimage. Once in a lifetime every Moslem, man or woman,
is expected, unless it is impossible, to make a pilgrimage (a *hajj*) to
Mecca. The pilgrim should be there during the sacred month Dhu-al-
Hijja so as to enter with thousands of others into the annual mass
observance of the circumambulation of the Ka'bah, the Lesser and
Greater Pilgrimages, and the Great Feast.

When war or other untoward conditions do not interfere, a great
part of the pilgrims nowadays go by rail and ship or by air to the
coast below Mecca or to Cairo or Jerusalem; but in ancient times they
joined far-traveling over-land caravans, which in the last stages of the
journey crossed the desert from Basrah in Iraq, or followed the trade
routes from Yemen, Cairo, or Damascus. Each such caravan had as an
indispensable part of its insignia (at least since the 13th century) a
camel bearing on its back an unoccupied *mahmil* or richly ornamented
litter, the resplendent symbol of the piety and sacrificial spirit of the
pilgrims.

Since Muhammad's day, all pilgrims have been required, whether
rich or poor, to enter the sacred precincts of Mecca wearing the same
kind of seamless white garments and practicing the proper abstinences:
no food or drink by day, continence, and no harm to living things,
animal or vegetable. This is the first of a long series of leveling practices
by which people of all countries and languages are made to mingle in
one unifying mass observance, without distinction of race or class.

The principal ceremonies in Mecca begin with circumambulation
of the Ka'bah. The pilgrims start at the Black Stone and run three
times fast and four times slowly around the building, stopping each
time at the southeast corner to kiss the Black Stone, or, if the crowd
is too great, to touch it with hand or stick, or perhaps just look keenly
at it. The next observance is the Lesser Pilgrimage, which consists of
trotting, with shoulders shaking, seven times between Safa and Mar-
wah, two low hills across the valley from each other—this in imitation
of frantic Hagar seeking in despair for water for wailing little Ishmael.

On the eighth day of Dhu-al-Hijja the Greater Pilgrimage begins.
The pilgrims in a dense mass move off toward Arafah, a day's foot
journey to the east. Some pass the night at Mina, the half-way point,
the rest go on. The next day the pilgrims, all arrived, stand or move
slowly about, from noon to sunset, over the Arafah plain, absorbed in
pious meditation. After sunset they begin running en masse, and with

the greatest possible noise and commotion, to Muzdalifah, a fourth of the way back to Mecca, where they pass the night in the open. At sunrise they continue to Muna, where each pilgrim casts seven pebbles down the slope below the mountain road, crying out at each throw: "In the name of God! Allah is almighty!" Those who are able to do so then make the Great Feast possible by offering as a sacrifice a camel, sheep, or horned animal, keeping in mind the injunction in the Pilgrimage sura of the Qur'an (Sura 22:37):

Make mention of the name of God over them when ye slay them, as they stand in a row; and when they are fallen over on their sides, eat of them, and feed him who is content and asketh not, and him who asketh.[20]

That is to say, the sacrificer eats part of the meat and gives the rest of it to the poorer pilgrims who stand by, whoever they may be.

The three days following are spent in eating, drinking, and merry-making; and then as a final act of the pilgrimage all return to Mecca and make the circuit of the Ka'bah once more.

C. RIGHT CONDUCT. Muhammad gave much thought to the behavior of his followers, and must be said to have legislated for them so comprehensively, and with such a uniform purpose of elevating their morals to a higher level than before—the high level of an inclusive

The Ka'bah with pilgrims. (Modern popular picture, Algeria; reproduced in Dermenghen, *Muhammad and the Islamic Tradition*)

brotherhood instead of the lower level of divisive tribal organization—that almost every act of the Moslems of his time, of either sex, from birth to death, was provided for. The following selection of some of the principal moral regulations of Muhammad will show how reformatory they initially were. The laws prohibiting wine and gambling, as well as the regulations covering the relations of the sexes and granting a higher status to women, must have meant to his early followers a considerable change in their way of life.

There is no piety in turning your faces toward the east or the west, but he is pious who believeth in God, and the last day, and the angels, and the Scriptures, and the prophets; who for the love of God disburseth his wealth to his kindred, and to the orphans, and the needy, and the wayfarer, and those who ask, and for ransoming; who observeth prayer, and payeth the legal alms, and who is of those who are faithful to their engagements when they have engaged in them, and patient under ills and hardships, and in time of trouble: these are they who are just, and these are they who fear the Lord.[21]

The Lord hath ordained kindness to your parents, whether one or both of them attain old age with thee: and say not to them, "Fie!" neither reproach them; but speak to them both with respectful speech;

And defer humbly to them out of tenderness; and say, "Lord, have compassion on them both, even as they reared me when I was little."

Kill not your children for fear of want: for them and for you will we provide. Verily, the killing them is a great wickedness.

Have nought to do with adultery; for it is a foul thing and an evil way.

And give full measure when you measure, and weigh with just balance.[22]

And give to the orphans their property; substitute not worthless things of your own for their valuable ones, and devour not their property after adding it to your own; for this is a great crime.

And make trial of orphans until they reach the age of marriage; and if ye perceive in them a sound judgment, then hand over their substance to them; but consume ye it not wastefully, or by hastily entrusting it to them.

Verily they who swallow the substance of the orphan wrongfully, shall swallow down only fire into their bellies, and shall burn in the flame!

Of women who seem good in your eyes, marry but two, or three, or four; and if ye still fear ye shall not act equitably, then one only. . . . Give women their dowry freely; but if of themselves they give up aught thereof to you, then enjoy it as convenient and profitable.[23]

When ye divorce women, and the time for sending them away is come,* either retain them with generosity, or put them away with generosity.

Mothers, when divorced, shall give suck to their children two full years, if the father desire that the suckling be completed; and such maintenance

* After four months of sexual abstinence.

and clothing as is fair for them, shall devolve on the father. . . . But if ye choose to have a nurse for your children, it shall be no fault in you.

And when ye divorce your wives, and they have waited the prescribed time,* hinder them not from marrying. . . . This is most pure for you, and most decent.[24]

And fight for the cause of God against those who fight against you: but commit not the injustice of attacking them first: God loveth not such injustice. . . .

Fight therefore against them until there be no more civil discord, and the only worship be that of God: but if they desist, then let there be no hostility, save against the wicked.[25]

They will ask thee concerning wine and games of chance, SAY: In both is great sin, and advantage also, to men; but their sin is greater than their advantage.[26]

O BELIEVERS! be faithful to your engagements. You are allowed the flesh of cattle other than what is hereinafter recited. . . . That which dieth of itself, and blood, and swine's flesh, and all that hath been sacrificed under the invocation of any other name than that of God, and the strangled, and the killed by a blow, or by a fall, or by goring, and that which hath been eaten by beasts of prey, unless ye make it clean by giving the death-stroke yourselves, and that which has been sacrificed on the blocks of stone, is forbidden you. . . . Woe this day on those who forsake your religion! And fear them not, but fear Me! [27]

Until the Arabs burst out of their home-land into strange surroundings, where situations that had not been foreseen by Muhammad were faced, these and other laws of the Qur'an seemed all-sufficient for Islam.

IV THE SPREAD OF ISLAM

It may be doubted whether the spread of Islam, at least in its early stages, was the result of calculation. Neither the devout Moslem view that it was a purely religious movement engaged in a far-sighted effort to save the world, by force if necessary, nor the medieval Christian view that it was the outgrowth first of pure imposture and then of greed, will bear scrutiny. Both religion and greed may be granted to have played their part as motivating impulses; but it would be closer to the mark to say that Muhammad unified the bedouins for the first time in their history, and thus made it possible for them, as a potentially powerful military group, to yoke together their economic need and their

* Three months.

religious faith in an overwhelming drive out of the desert into lands where plenty beckoned. They began with scarcely more than the hope of carrying out a gigantic raid for booty that might be brought back into the desert; but the weakness of the Byzantine and Persian empires, exhausted by years of strife with each other, made a permanent conquest of the Near East easy. Only then did calculated efforts to extend the spread of Islam make their appearance. On the whole, then, the Moslem conquests represent one more of the long succession of Semitic migrations—the last and the greatest.

Abu Bakr and the Unification of Arabia for Conquest

When Muhammad died so suddenly, he had designated no successor (caliph). His followers had to decide who should exercise that function. Should the principle of succession be that of heredity, or should the caliphs be elected by (and from) some properly qualified group? The answer to these questions was supplied differently at different times by the three major political parties of early Moslem history. The Companions (so-called because they were composed of Muhammad's closest associates, the Muhajirun or Emigrants and the Ansar or Supporters) assumed that the caliph should be elected from their number; a later group (the Legitimists), following the hereditary principle of succession, thought the caliphs should be Muhammad's descendants through Fatima and her husband, 'Ali, Muhammad's son-in-law and cousin; and, later still, the Ummayads, as the leaders of Muhammad's tribe, sought to be the sole determinants of the question who should occupy the caliphate.

The Companions were the first to act, and gained the initial decision. Abu Bakr was their choice for caliph, the first of four thus chosen. His caliphate lasted only a year, for he soon followed the Prophet in death; but his administration was notable for three things: the assembling of the Qur'an; great firmness in bringing to heel not only those sheikhs who took the opportunity provided by Muhammad's death to break away from control, but also those who had not yet "submitted" (which was accomplished by the so-called Riddah wars); and, finally, the fusing of these forces in the first organized assault on the outside world. Three armies, totaling 10,000 men, whose ranks were soon swollen to twice that number, took separate routes into Syria, in accordance, it was said, with Muhammad's own well-laid plans. Abu Bakr did not live to see their startling triumphs.

Umar and the Conquests

The second caliph, Umar (in office A.D. 634–644) dispatched, and from a distance directed, the great general Khalid ibn al-Walid, in the stroke which altered beyond all calculation the destiny of the Near East: the capture of the ancient city of Damascus after a six months' siege (635). Christian forces were at once summoned to restore the situation; but Khalid sagaciously retreated to a more favorable location, when the force of 50,000 men sent by the Byzantine emperor Heraclius came to drive him away; and on a day of smothering heat and dust, such as only bedouins could endure, he turned and won a decisive victory, in which Theodorus, brother of Heraclius and general of the Christian forces, fell. The whole of Syria, up to the Taurus Mountains, fell too, and the deeply agitated emperor, departing for good, is said to have exclaimed: "Farewell, O Syria, and what an excellent country this is for the enemy!"

But the Jewish and Christian inhabitants, even of Damascus, felt differently; they were not altogether displeased! They had felt oppressed by Heraclius in the aftermath of the wars of their liberation from the Persians. The Arabs were, moreover, comparatively magnanimous; they acted in the spirit of the Qur'anic injunction, "If they desist (from fighting), let there be no hostility," as the terms for the surrender of Damascus suggest:

> In the name of Allah, the compassionate, the merciful. This is what Khalid would grant to the inhabitants of Damascus if he enters therein: he promises to give them security for their lives, property, and churches. Their city wall shall not be demolished, neither shall any Moslem be quartered in their houses. Thereunto we give to them the pact of Allah and the protection of His Prophet, the caliphs and the believers. So long as they pay the poll tax, nothing but good shall befall them.[28]

It is historically sound to say, with Philip Hitti, that the "easy conquest" of Syria had its own special causes: "The Hellenistic culture imposed on the land since its conquest by Alexander the Great (332 B.C.) was only skin-deep and was limited to the urban population. The rural people remained ever conscious of cultural and racial differences between themselves and their masters," [29] that is, between themselves as the Semitic population of Syria and their Greek rulers. The Moslem historian Baladhuri attributed to the people of the Syrian town of Hims this confession to their Arab conquerors: "We like your rule and justice far better than the state of oppression and tyranny under which we have been living." [30]

The Moslem victories in Syria were decisive elsewhere. Jerusalem fell in 638, and Caesarea, relieved by sea and invincible until a Jew within the walls gave the necessary secret information, in 640. The whole of Palestine then surrendered to the Arabs. Cut off from needed aid, Egypt was the next conquest (639–641), and the Arabs pushed on rapidly through North Africa, to be in Spain within a century. Back in the Near East, the attack shifted to the Sassanids (Persians). First Iraq, with its fabulously rich cities (in 637), and then Persia (from 640 to 649), were subdued. Persia offered the stiffest opposition the Arabs had yet encountered; its conquest took longer because the population was non-Semitic, well unified, and firmly Zoroastrian. To the northwest, a twelve-year campaign (640–652) reduced the greater part of Asia Minor to subjection.

It may be asked in astonishment how the comparatively ill-equipped and outnumbered Moslem warriors, armed chiefly with bows and arrows and bamboo-shafted spears, and riding on camels and horses, could overthrow one after another the disciplined hosts, and even the navies, of the Byzantine world. The answer is to be found partly in the high mobility of their camel transport, but equally, perhaps, in their intense eagerness, which was fed on the one hand by their acceptance of the Prophet's word that if they survived the battle they could keep four-fifths of the booty and if they died they would go to Paradise, and on the other hand by their sense of wonder and discovery: they were invading countries that seemed to their scarcity-bred minds literally earthly paradises. No untraveled country lad ever felt more wonder-struck by a metropolis than these warriors of the desert felt when they beheld the richly appointed cities lying ready for their taking in the ancient lands which were the "cradle of civilization." And what also greatly animated the better minds among them was the exciting prospect of learning the Greek and Persian arts, philosophies, and sciences—ripe and beckoning fields of learning as yet unharvested by their hungry minds and spirits.

Subsequent campaigns took the Moslem armies, now no longer predominantly Arab, northeastward and to the back of the Himalayas into Chinese Turkestan and Mongolia, and southeastward into India; while, far to the west, the Spanish Moslems, but for Charles Martel, might well have overrun France; only the slender margin of the victory of the Franks in the Battle of Tours (732) turned them back into Spain. The resistance of the Byzantines in Asia Minor kept them also from crossing the Bosphorus for a long time.

But we must return to the caliphs and the internal history of the rapidly expanding Moslem empire.

Umar, who himself lived very simply, was soon in receipt of a swelling stream of tribute money, pouring into the treasury at Medina from all sides. Not even Muhammad could have dreamed of so much wealth. Umar determined to distribute it in the form of yearly stipends, first to Muhammad's widows and dependents,* next to others of the faithful, such as the Companions (the Emigrants and the Supporters), and finally, in lesser amounts, to all Arab warriors and tribesmen ($10–$30). In consideration of this income and in order to keep the Arabian Moslems together as a military unit, with home addresses, so to speak, always in Arabia, he forbade any Arab to acquire lands outside that peninsula. Simultaneously, he dispossessed and drove out all unconverted members of other religions, especially Jews, Christians, and Zoroastrians.

Appearance of the First Dissensions

In addition to the moneys distributed to them and their families as an annuity, the Arab warriors were, as has been noted, entitled to four-fifths of all the booty they gathered in the form of movable goods and captives. (All *moneys* seized during campaigns were kept in the common treasury.) The economic advantages of being an Arabian Moslem were obvious. It became a matter of first importance to the various Arab groups close to the seat of power to control the caliphate. Umar himself was incorruptible, but a Christian captive stabbed him one day with a poisoned dagger, and the road to political maneuvering at once lay open.

It was significant of the internal political situation beginning to develop, that Uthman, another of Muhammad's close associates, a son-in-law in fact, was next chosen (in office 644–656). An Ummayad, he yielded weakly to the pressures of his family, and appointed so many Ummayads to high office that the ensuing scandals led to his being assassinated in Medina by dissatisfied Moslems gathered to force his abdication.

'Ali, another of Muhammad's sons-in-law, an early believer, and father of the two boys who were Muhammad's only male descendants, became caliph in 656 A.D. over much opposition, including that of 'A'ishah, who never forgave him for thinking her unfaithful with a camel-driver on the day she failed to keep up with Muhammad while re-

* 'A'ishah, Muhammad's favorite wife, was assigned 12,000 dirhems, or about $2,400.

turning from a desert raid. He had had to triumph over two other aspirants, and after his assumption of office a third appeared in the person of the governor of Syria, Mu'awiyah, an Ummayad, the son of Abu Sufyan. So formidable did the movement to depose him become that 'Ali, who had moved the administrative capital from Medina to the Moslem camp at Kufah in Iraq, raised an army, marched west, and was about to defeat his rival, when he generously—to many it seemed over-generously—consented to arbitrate the issue. Disgusted followers, during the disturbances that followed, murdered him—a never-to-be-forgotten fact, as we shall see.

The Ummayads now seized the caliphate, Mu'awiyah declaring himself 'Ali's successor. Thus began the long Ummayad caliphate, ruling from Damascus. But in 750, the Abbasids overthrew them everywhere except in Spain, and moved the capital to Baghdad, which they built up into a great city, on the "cross-roads of the world," famous both in the Orient and the Occident for its wealth, culture, and gaiety, qualities all exemplified in the person of their most distinguished representative, the caliph Harun al-Rashid (736–809). Then came slow political decadence—and suddenly the Mongols (1258); whereupon the Moslem empire fell apart into separate states. Finally, the Ottoman Turks rose to power in the late 13th century, possessed themselves of Asia Minor, crossed the Bosphorus, took Constantinople, and fought their way as far as Vienna before they were forced back into the area near the Bosphorus that they could hold.

V   THE FIRST FIVE CENTURIES OF MOSLEM THOUGHT

That the simplicity and like-mindedness of the period of the first four caliphs did not long persist should afford no surprise. The caliph Umar's laws, designed to keep the Arabs permanently in Arabia as a land-owning and military unit, were soon and inevitably modified. Multitudes of Arabs thereafter migrated out of their barren home-land to enjoy the possession of richer holdings elsewhere—and were changed in the process. In many cases they were merged by assimilation into the subject peoples (the Mawali or non-Arabic Moslems) among whom they settled; in all cases they were won over, short of abandonment of the Five Pillars of the Faith, to Syriac, Hellenistic, Egyptian, or Persian ways, both of living and thinking.

The Formation of the Hadith Canons

Lines of divergence appeared early in the Moslem "Traditions." We have already referred, in the opening paragraphs of this chapter, to the *Ahadith* (pl.; *hadith*, sing.) or recollections of Muhammad's sayings and doings traced back through "attestors" or "authorities" to Muhammad himself or to a Companion in Medina. There were many of these, but they were not the only authenticated traditions. Many others dealt with the way things had been done in Medina, during Muhammad's lifetime, either by himself or with his "silent approval" (*taqrir*) —in short, they described the customs, usages, or precedents established in Muhammad's days. The whole body of material thus accumulated was called the *Sunna*. It soon swelled to formidable bulk, and much of it was self-contradictory. Some lines of tradition were suspiciously favorable either to the partisans of 'Ali (the Legitimists), or to the "orthodox" group which advocated the election of caliphs by the vote of duly qualified persons, or to the Ummayads, or, later on, to the Abbasids, and so on.* But not until over two centuries had passed after Muhammad's death were critical attempts made to select the more trustworthy traditions and bring them into a collection; and then the criterion used was an "external" one: authoritativeness (or as the Christians might have put it, the "apostolicity") of the contributors of each hadith, this was the sole measure of authenticity. The traditions had to have, as it were, a good pedigree. The authenticity and value of a tradition were judged by its *isnad* or chain of attestors, each of whom had to stand up under examination for veracity. The traditions were then declared either "genuine" or "fair" or "weak." At last six separate (and overlapping) collections made their appearance, and won general acceptance. Of these the most highly regarded is the book of al-Bukhari, a Persian Moslem who diligently visited all through Arabia, Syria, Egypt, and Iraq gathering a vast number of hadiths (reportedly

---

* Evidence even existed of outright invention or fabrication. One Ibn-abi-al-'Awja confessed before his execution 150 years after the Hijra that he had profited financially by fabricating 4,000 hadiths. There was evidence also (though orthodox Moslems were inclined to shut their eyes to it) of fertility of imagination and bias even among those who bore all the marks of trustworthiness. 'A'ishah's prejudice against 'Ali appeared in her 2,210 traditions; and there seemed to be a very ready remembrance indeed on the part of Abu-Hureira, one of the Companions, with his 5,300 traditions. There were others only slightly less voluble. And always there were those who had it from someone, who had it from someone else, that still another person had heard a Companion say: "Muhammad used to do so and so." It became a major concern of the Moslem scholars and theologians to sift and weigh this evidence.

numbering 600,000!) and then sifted them down to the 7,275 which he found "genuine." In influence this collection ranks next to the Qur'an itself.

But the interpretation and reconciliation of these "genuine" traditions (by their internal criticism) still allowed plenty of room for divergence of thought.

The First Controversies

Should expediency or political considerations have any weight in the choices of a Moslem? Was a Moslem to hew straight to the line of purely religious principle, without compromise or delay, or was he to let events sometimes take their course and leave the ultimate decision or action to Allah? These were the issues underlying the first Moslem controversies.

When 'Ali was chosen caliph, he was supported by fiercely anti-Ummayad elements who watched him narrowly to see if he would be as firm and decisive as Muhammad had been; but midway in the struggle with Mu'awiyah, he had, as we have seen, agreed to arbitrate the issues; whereupon twelve thousand disgusted warriors marched out of his camp, so disillusioned with him that some of them later assassinated him. They became the *Kharijites*—"separatists" or "secessionists." Viewing with hostile eyes the political developments occurring behind the scenes among the Moslem leaders, this group of Moslems concluded bitterly that the only sure way of getting the right caliph was to let the whole Moslem world have a say in his election, not just the Prophet's family nor just his tribe. The caliph need not come from either group, they said. Not enough of them were true Moslems! The Ummayads, for instance, had joined the Moslem movement at the last minute, just before it would be too late, obviously less from conviction than from expediency. No, the true caliph could be the choice only of true Moslems, men acting solely on the religious principle of doing the will of Allah in complete self-surrender. All those who had become Moslems for political or economic reasons, or who were "trimmers," or who went through the practices of Islam as a mere outward form, were not true Moslems at all, and must be destroyed in a great purge; this was imperative to save the cause of Allah and Muhammad from their hands! It was natural that these fierce puritans should find the full force of the Ummayads arrayed against them. The more radical and uncompromising were wiped out in bloody slaughter. Yet their beliefs spread in time to the utmost fringes of the Moslem empire, and still persist in Zanzibar and Algeria.

Opposed to them were the *Murjites*—the advocates of "delayed judgment." Their position was that only God can judge who is a true Moslem, and who is not. When one sees a believer sinning, he cannot call him forthwith an infidel. Therefore, believers should treat all practicing Moslems, tentatively at least, as real Moslems, leaving to the Last Judgment, that is, to Allah, the fixing of their final status. Hence, even the Ummayads were to be tolerated—not to mention the converted Christians and Jews who appeared to be only half-hearted in their "submission."

The Liberals

That the doctrines and duties of the Faith must be and are in accord with reason was the basic conviction of the first Moslem liberals, the *Mu'tazilites*. These vigorous defenders of the Faith appeared first in Syria and Iraq during the Ummayad caliphate among the converts to Islam who were familiar with Greek, Jewish, Christian, and Zoroastrian thought. In an attempt to find firm ground between the Kharijites and the Murjites, they laid emphasis upon the free response of men to the moral demands of Allah in the Qur'an, particularly when confronted by the "Promise and Threat" of Allah contained there. But they were also sure, and believed that they were acting in the spirit of Muhammad in affirming, that not only does Allah challenge the consciences of men; he also seeks their rational assent. Hence, the Mu'tazilites took it for granted that the theological doctrines which might be erected on the foundation supplied by the Qur'an, whose truth they never questioned, were subject to rational testing. Their reading of translations of works of Greek philosophy made it seem to them a foregone conclusion that no doctrine could be true which did not survive such a test. How could a true doctrine be contrary to reason?

Reason, for example, the Mu'tazilites argued, insists on the justice and unity of God. Doctrines which throw doubt on either his justice or his unity cannot be accepted. Hence the Mu'tazilites made a fundamental attack on the orthodox denial of freedom of the will, the doctrine that *all* men's doings are decreed by the inscrutable will of Allah, who "guides whom he will, and lets whom he will go astray." Since the inconclusiveness of the Qur'an on this point allowed some room for further clarification, the Mu'tazilites insisted that no final position ought to be taken which would put to the question the justice of Allah: Allah *must* be just; it would be monstrous to think him moved by arbitrariness alone or by mere good pleasure. How could it be just for God to predestine a man to commit mortal sin or to maintain an attitude of heresy or unbelief, and then punish him for non-submission? It would not be fair or right. Hence, Allah *must* allow men enough freedom to choose between right and wrong, truth and falsehood. Only then could men be held responsible for their actions.

That Allah *had* to do anything whatever, as of necessity, was a doctrine which the orthodox Moslems viewed with distaste and horror; but the Mu'tazilites nevertheless insisted, further, that, since Allah most certainly was the Merciful, the Compassionate, and desired the good of all creatures, he *had* to send down revelations to the Prophet to indicate the way of salvation—an act which showed both graciousness and an inner necessity to be just and merciful. Hence, a "necessary grace" is to be seen in the delivery to men of the Qur'an.

And this brought the Mu'tazilites to the declaration which stirred up the greatest dissension. They denied that the revelation—that is, the Qur'an—is eternal and uncreated. Allah created it when the need arose, and sent it down. To suppose that it was uncreated and eternal would destroy the unity of God by setting up beside him something else co-eternal with him; and this would be polytheism, which the Qur'an itself condemned.

So persuasive did this point seem to one of the Abbasid caliphs (Al-Ma'mun) that in 827 A.D. he proclaimed it a heresy to assert the eternity of the Qur'an, and went so far as to set up an inquisition to purge all government departments of those who held such a view. (But twenty years later another caliph thought the orthodox view the true one, called the Mu'tazilites heretical, and began a purge of them in turn!)

Before their final overthrow in the 10th century, the Mu'tazilites turned their rationalistic method upon the anthropomorphism inherent in the orthodox interpretation of the Qur'an. They refused to take literally the descriptions of Allah as sitting on a throne in heaven among the angels, and as having hands and feet, eyes and ears.* Allah is infinite and eternal and nowhere particularly in space. It endangered the unity of God, they said, to be too literal about his agents, or about his attributes, as though these last could be his "members," as some of the orthodox maintained. It would be consistent with the unity of

* Some of the ultraorthodox teachers said God is a being made of flesh and blood.

God only to speak of his attributes as being of his essence or as being his modes or states, not as being additions or accretions of an external kind. (Here the Mu'tazilites seemed to have profited by the reading of Christian theology; just as the orthodox seemed to be influenced by Zoroastrian conceptions.) This sort of reasoning was applied also to the language of the Qur'an about heaven and hell. The imagery was to be taken figuratively, or at any rate modified by the consideration that those who are intellectual or spiritual will not, in Paradise for example, go in for sensual delights, because they are above that. (The Hindus and Buddhists had long been saying this.)

But though the Mu'tazilites did manage to teach the orthodox theologians the value of using a rational method of exposition, the weight of opinion turned against them, and the 10th century saw their school come to an end.

The Sunnis or Traditionalists

The downfall of the liberals came about when the traditionalists— the orthodox defenders of the Sunna—adopted the methods of rationalism (the construction of logical systems) in order to confute them. It was a man trained in a Mu'tazilite school, named Ash'ari, who thus turned the tables on them.

Until the time of Ash'ari the orthodox Moslems had recoiled from the use of critical reason in interpreting the Qur'an and Tradition. The revelation contained in these sources of truth was not to be questioned; it was merely to be examined, analyzed reverently, and arranged into order or system. However, some use of "speculation" to fill in gaps or to meet new contingencies had to be allowed, provided it was speculation that built upon what had already been revealed. Here, however, divergences in reasoning became more than a possibility. Even though the method was no more than that of *assenting* reason, four orthodox "schools of the Law" came into existence during the two hundred years following Muhammad's death, one out of fear of going astray through speculation confining itself strictly to the letter of Tradition, the others using speculation guardedly, with varying boldness in building with its aid. All of them aimed at something comparable to what the rabbis achieved in providing guidance to the displaced Jews through the Talmud; only, here the motive was, to guide the Moslems in the great new areas of the world into which their extraordinary conquests admitted them. And each of them, curiously enough, has achieved a

Talmudic repute; each is accepted as orthodox and worthy to be followed, without danger of falling into error.

Of the four schools, the first in time, the *Hanifite*, was the most liberal in its use of speculation; by which, of course, is meant juridical, not theological, speculation. It was founded in Iraq by Abu Hanifa (died 767 A.D.), a Persian whose followers put down his teachings in Arabic. The essence of his position was that he began with the Qur'an (taking little notice of the Hadith) and asked himself how its precepts could be applied by *analogy* to the somewhat different situation in Iraq. If a particular situation for which Muhammad legislated was closely analogous to a situation existing in Iraq, he applied the Qur'an as it stood; if, however, the two situations differed widely, he developed by deduction an analogy applicable to Iraq, and if he ran into difficulties, he consulted "opinion" and "preference" drawn from the local situation, and then made a ruling. The ruling might in this last case even supersede the Qur'an! (For example, the Qur'an prescribes cutting off the hand for theft; but that was meant for a situation not analogous to the one obtaining in more advanced Iraq; hence it was not meant for Iraq! By analogical deduction from *other parts* of the Qur'an, we derive for Iraq other, more effective punishment, namely, imprisonment.) It was natural for the easy-going Abbasids, and the Ottoman Turks after them, to follow the Hanifite rulings on laws and religious rites. They are still followed in Iraq, Persia, Northern India, and Central Asia.

The second school, the *Malikite*, founded in Medina by Malik-ibn-Anas (ca. 715–795 A.D.) interpreted laws and rites in the light of the Qur'an and the Hadith together, and when in difficulty leaned heavily on the "consensus of opinion" (*ijma'*) which prevailed in Medina. For especially perplexing situations he used analogy, and when analogy conflicted with opinion, he fell back on "public advantage." This school is still generally followed in North Africa, parts of Egypt, and eastern Arabia.

The *Shafi'ite*, the third school, was founded by al-Shafi'i, an Arab born in Persia but descended from the Quraysh tribe. This school gives equal weight to the Qur'an and the Hadith, but sometimes, where one of the hadiths may be more specific and clear, prefers it even to the Qur'an. At times the traditions, it is held, represent the Moslem world in expansion and therefore the more developed situation; but, while liberal in this respect, the Shafi'ites reject "opinion" in any form, as using speculation in an unwarranted manner. The Shafi'ite school still prevails in Lower Egypt (Cairo), eastern Africa, southern Arabia, Palestine, southern India, and the East Indies.

The most conservative of the four schools is the *Hanbalite*. It was founded at Baghdad in the loose and merry days of Harun-al-Rashid by the shocked Ibn-Hanbal, a student of al-Shafi'i, who was even more uncompromising than his master toward opinion and reason. He seems to have been in special opposition to the Mu'tazilites, and adhered strictly to the letter of the Qur'an, with less reliance on the Hadith. For refusal to deny the eternity of the Qur'an, he was put in chains by the Abbasid caliph Al-Ma'mun, and by a succeeding caliph scourged and imprisoned. The Hanbalite laws and ritual are followed today in the Hejaz, notably in Mecca and Medina, and in Saudi Arabia as a whole, where the effects of the Wahhabi revival of two hundred years ago are still felt.

It is against this background that the achievement of Ash'ari is best seen. Born in Iraq about 873, he made his home in Baghdad, and died there in 935 (or 936). He became one of the two theologians most honored by orthodox Moslems, the other being Ghazzali. After studying and publicly advocating the Mu'tazilites' teachings, he found himself at the age of forty suddenly and violently disagreeing, and went on to develop a philosophy of religion which sought to reconcile the whole Sunna with reason.* He accomplished this by making God not only *one* but *all*. All life, all knowledge, power, will, hearing, sight, and speech—the seven divine attributes—no matter where or when experienced, are Allah in action; for Allah has created men *and all their acts*: men cannot see, hear, know, or will anything of themselves; it is Allah who causes what happens in and through them. This position (which echoes certain aspects of Indian philosophy) enabled Ash'ari to supply logical grounds for all the orthodox doctrines, whether drawn from the Qur'an or the Hadith. For example, since it is Allah who immediately causes all events, internal and external, it is he who determines men to think of him as he is described in the Qur'an. Allah, then, really sits on a throne, and literally has hands and feet, eyes and ears; the Qur'an says so; but since the Qur'an also declares that he is "not like anything" in the universe, men must believe what they are told "without thinking how" it may be so. Similarly, the concrete imagery of heaven and hell supplied by the Qur'an is to be taken as descriptive of reality; the believers in Paradise will really have a vision of Allah sitting on his throne, though it must not be supposed that the seeing or the sitting are to be compared with this world's seeing or sitting. As for the Qur'an, Ash'ari said that its words are, as ideas in the mind of Allah, eternal,

---

* He now swung all the way over to connection with the ultraconservative Hanbalite school of law.

but the letters on sheets of paper forming the words read and recited on earth are produced by men and are of temporal origin—a solution of the old puzzle as to the uncreated nature of the Qur'an which was immediately satisfactory to most Moslems. Finally, that the conception of Allah as being the immediate cause of every act made him responsible for evil as well as good did not daunt Ash'ari: it was just a fact that Allah created the unbelief of the infidel and damned him for it—a fact to be taken *bila kayf,* "without question." Allah has his own reasons, which men cannot know and should not have the temerity to seek to know.

The Mystics

But the juristic and rationalistic developments which we have been reviewing were excessively practical, or let us say, too concerned with externals, to suit millions of Moslems, who had within themselves the natural human need to *feel* their religion. This was true especially of converts from other religions and Moslems residing in areas where Christians, Jews, or Zoroastrians lived or had left an impress. The sight of Christian monks and ascetics in cells or caves set many to pondering. The knowledge of alien philosophies also drifted in—Neo-Platonism from the West, Hinduism and Buddhism from the East. An expression of response to these influences came early.

The first Sufis (meaning "wool-wearers," i.e., wearers of the ascetic's coarse undyed woolen robe) appeared with that name in the 8th century, but they were not the first ascetics. Early in the Ummayad caliphate, Syrian Moslems, influenced by Christian other-worldliness and passages from the New Testament, wandered about, neither begging nor yet working for a living, but endlessly reciting a litany of the "beautiful names" and titles of Allah, and resigning themselves to his care, in trustful dependence on such a promise as that contained in the saying of Jesus: "Take therefore no thought for the morrow: for the morrow shall take thought for the things of itself." Like some of the Taoists of China or like Mahavira in India (of whom they doubtless never heard), they practiced utter indifference toward hunger and illness or the abuse they received from men, saying that they must be under the hand of Allah "as passive as a corpse under the hand of him who washes it." [31] But the Sufis, as did the Taoists, soon developed intellectual and mystical interests that took them into directed contemplation. Neo-Platonism, Gnosticism, Buddhism, and Hinduism gave them philosophical foundations; Christian monasticism supplied them with hints toward organization. They adopted the monk's woolen robe, vowed celibacy, practiced long vigils and stated periods of meditation, and finally gathered into fraternities (this by the 12th century) with communal religious services, marked by rituals much like those of the Christian churches.* Their consuming interest was union with God now rather than after death. Since there were no distinctively Moslem lines of thought to guide them, they strained at the leash of Moslem orthodoxy toward theosophy and pantheism, largely under Neo-Platonic and Christian influences, though at a later stage Mahayana Buddhism and Vedantic Hinduism supplied both thought and motivation.

The first Sufis rested in the main on the mystical speculations of an Egyptian, who perhaps received the name he was known by, Dhu-al-Nun al Misri ("The Man of the Fish from Egypt," i.e., the Jonah of Egypt), because he said that individuality is a deadly sin, and the soul must be "swallowed up" in God and lost in him by complete mystic union. But neither he nor the Sufis in general thought that the swallowing up of the soul could be achieved at once without the soul being prepared for it. There were stages to pass through. To follow the figure of Harith al-Muhasibi of Basrah (died 857 A.D.), the Sufi was a pilgrim on the road that leads to "the Truth," and there were way-stations he must pass, under the guidance of a director, such as repentance, abstinence, renunciation, poverty, patience, trust in God, and satisfaction (the "seven stages" most commonly prescribed). Final entrance into the transcendental realm of Knowledge and Truth would crown the various "states" of longing, fear, hope, love, intimacy, and trust which Allah had bestowed; the climactic state would be experienced as an intoxicating and ineffable flash of divine illumination, bringing with it the certainty of divine love—the goal of the mystical theist in all lands.

But a few mystics were not theists. They substituted the Realm of Truth for Allah; and when the Buddhist influences penetrated Iraq, the Sufis there moved perilously close to atheism (as did some *zindiq* or free-thinking sufis), and emphasized self-annihilation as the entire goal.

These and others among the more extreme Sufis were recognized

---

* The Sufis claimed Muhammad as their example (witness his use of caves on Mount Hira), but they had to overlook the hadith quoting Muhammad as being critical of "monkery" (e.g., in the saying attributed to him: "Either you propose to be a Christian monk; in that case, join them openly! Or you belong to our people; then you must follow our custom [sunna]. Our custom is married life.").[32]

by the orthodox Moslems as heretics. There was even one martyrdom. A Persian Sufi called al-Hallaj was in 922 scourged, nailed to a cross, and then beheaded, for crying out publicly, "I am the Truth," by which his hearers, accustomed to hearing Allah named "The True," judged he was committing the ultimate in blasphemy. They were right in understanding that he felt he and his Creator were one; but he meant no blasphemy. He felt much as did the Persian mystic Bayazid, to whom the saying was attributed: "Thirty years the transcendent God was my mirror, now I am my own mirror—i.e., that which I was I am no more, for 'I' and 'God' is a denial of the Unity of God. Since I am no more, the transcendent God is His own mirror. I say that I am my own mirror, for 'tis God that speaks with my tongue, and I have vanished." [33] According to information gleaned from some of his recently recovered writings:

> Hallaj conceives the mystical union as union with the Creative Word (*Kun*, Be!),* which in the Koran is appropriated to the birth of Jesus and the Resurrection, a union obtained "by means of close and fervent adhesion of the understanding to the commandments of God." And the result of this permanent acceptance of the divine *fiat* is the coming into the mystic's soul of the divine Spirit, which proceeds "from the command of my Lord" (Koran, xvii. 87) and thenceforth makes of each of the acts of that man "acts truly divine." [35]

To Hallaj the union with the divine Spirit is like that of the lover with his beloved; and in his famous verses he bewails any absence of perfect harmony with the Great Beloved—or, when he can, celebrates its presence with intimacy and tenderness:

> Betwixt me and Thee there lingers an "it is I" that torments me.
> Ah, of Thy grace, take away this "I" from between us! [36]

> I am He whom I love, and He whom I love is I,
> We are two spirits dwelling in one body.
> If thou seest me, thou seest Him,
> And if thou seest Him, thou seest us both.[37]

Condemned for heresy though he was, Hallaj was to be echoed by

* There is an echo here of the first chapter of the Gospel according to St. John. Hallaj is described by R. A. Nicholson as "the nearest of all Moslem mystics to the spirit of Christ. For him, the saint in union with God is superior to the prophet charged with an external mission, and the model of saintly life is not Muhammad, but Jesus, the type of glorified humanity, the deified man whose personality, transfigured and essentialized, stands forth as the witness and representative of God, revealing from within himself *al-Haqq*, the creator through whom he exists, the Creative Truth in whom he has all his being." [34]

more than one of the Persian poets. Consider the words of the famous mystical poet Jalal al-Din Rumi, born in Balkh in 1207 A.D. (three hundred years later), the same who founded the Maulawi (Mevlevi) order of dervishes:

> When God appears to His ardent lover the lover is absorbed in Him, and not so much as a hair of the lover remains. True lovers are as shadows, and when the sun shines in glory the shadows vanish away. He is a true lover of God to whom God says, "I am thine, and thou art mine!" [38]

> Let me then become non-existent, for non-existence
> Sings to me in organ tones, "To him shall we return."
> Behold water in a pitcher; pour it out;
> Will that water run away from the stream?
> When that water joins the water of the stream
> It is lost therein, and becomes itself the stream.
> Its individuality is lost, but its essence remains,
> And thereby it becomes not less nor inferior. [39]

> In the world of Divine Unity is no room for Number,
> But Number necessarily exists in the world of Five and Four.
> You may count a hundred thousand sweet apples in your hand:
> If you wish to make One, crush them all together. [40]

> In the house of water and clay this heart is desolate without thee;
> O Beloved, enter the house, or I will leave it. [41]

For his dervishes Rumi wrote the famous "Song of the Reed Flute," celebrating both this sacred musical instrument of his dervish order and the love of God which the flute symbolized. It begins:

> Hearken to the reed-flute, how it discourses
> When complaining of the pains of separation—
> "Ever since they tore me from my osier bed,
> My plaintive notes have moved men and women to tears.
> I burst my breast, striving to give vent to sighs,
> And to express the pangs of my yearning for my home. . . ."

A central passage cries out in celebration of the ecstasy of the love of God:

> Hail to thee, then, o LOVE, sweet madness!
> Thou who healest all our infirmities!
> Who art the physician of our pride and self-conceit!
> Who art our Plato and our Galen!
> Love exalts our earthly bodies to heaven,
> And makes the very hills to dance with joy!

O lover, 'twas love that gave life to Mount Sinai,
When "it quaked, and Moses fell down in a swoon."

Did my Beloved only touch me with his lips,
I too, like the flute, would burst out in melody.[42]

The indebtedness of much of this to Indian philosophy would seem to be obvious. The fact is that the Sufis, and their off-shoots the dervishes, were hospitable to any point of view that lent aid to their quest. They felt the essential oneness of all seekers of union with God, no matter what their name or sign. Said Rumi:

If the picture of our Beloved is found in a heathen temple, it is an error to encircle the Ka'bah: if the Ka'bah is deprived of its sweet smell, it is a synagogue: and if in the synagogue we feel the sweet smell of union with him, it is our Ka'bah.[43]

And an earlier poet, Ibn 'Arabi (born 1165 A.D.) declared:

There was a time, when I blamed my companion if his religion did not resemble mine;
Now, however, my heart accepts every form: it is a pasture ground for gazelles, a cloister for monks,
A temple for idols and a Ka'bah for the pilgrim, the tables of the Torah and the sacred books of the Koran.
Love alone is my religion.[44]

But we have gone beyond our story, and must return now to the 11th century and the great synthesizer of Moslem theology.

The Synthesis of Ghazzali

After all the bickering of the traditionalists and the liberals, and the straining in different directions of the jurists and the mystics, the theology of Ghazzali, when it was understood, "came like a deliverance." [45] In recognition of the fact that he rescued the schools from the barren scholasticism into which they had fallen after Ash'ari, the Moslems have called him Muhyi al-Din, "The Restorer (or Reviver) of Religion."

And yet his value was not immediately recognized. It was only after his synthesis had been before them awhile that the Moslem schoolmen began to appreciate its balance and wisdom.

Born in a Persian village in 1058 A.D., he attained his fame elsewhere, but returned home before he died in 1111. After an education in jurisprudence in a Shafi'ite school, and in theology under a famous

Ash'arite imam, he was invited to Baghdad as a lecturer in the
Nizamiyah, a newly founded university where the Ash'arite doctrine
predominated. During his four years of teaching he reached a spiritual
crisis. Not satisfied with scholasticism, he veered to scepticism, then to
Sufism. His intellectual curiosity was great, but his desire to find himself left him physically and morally exhausted. Later in life, when he
was past fifty (and near his end), he wrote:

> Ever since I was under twenty (now I am over fifty) . . . I have not
> ceased to investigate every dogma and belief. No Batinite did I come across
> without desiring to investigate his esotericism; no Zaharite, without wishing
> to acquire the gist of his literalism; no philosopher (Neo-Platonist), without
> wanting to learn the essence of his philosophy; no dialectical theologian,
> without striving to ascertain the object of his dialectics and theology; no Sufi,
> without coveting to probe the secret of his Sufism; no ascetic, without trying
> to delve into the origin of his asceticism; no atheistic *zindiq*, without groping
> for the causes of his bold atheism and *zindiqism*. Such was the unquenchable
> thirst of my soul for research and investigation from the early days of my
> youth, an instinct and a temperament implanted in me by God through no
> choice of mine.[46]

The swing to Sufism proved decisive. He left the university, went
to Syria to find out for himself, under the Sufis there, whether their
way was the right path to religious certainty, and after two years of
meditation and prayer made a holy pilgrimage to Mecca, before returning to his home and children. He practiced mysticism thenceforth, and
began writing. Though at the command of the Sultan he returned to
teaching for a short time, he soon resumed his meditation and writing
in his native village until his death at fifty-three.

His greatest book was *The Revivification of the Religious Sciences*.
The essence of his achievement in this (and his other) works was that
he accepted the orthodox theology of Ash'ari, but purged it of its hard
intellectualism by "revivifying" (and modifying) it with Sufi mysticism.
As a fundamentally religious person, he was not satisfied with the legalism and intellectualism of the Sunnis; he had the same need that the
German Pietists were to have after Lutheran scholasticism had reduced
the German Reformation to a tough shell of theology and ritual; his
quietism, like theirs, was motivated by his sense of the unreality of
religion without *religious experience*. In fact, all human thinking, and
life itself, were flat and unprofitable without God; taken by itself, the
juristic casuistry of the law schools was irreligiously external and con-
tentious; and science and philosophy were of value only as an introduction to theology. He took the time to analyze in detail the philoso-

phies of certain Moslem followers of Aristotle, only to condemn them as self-contradictory and essentially irreligious rational systems. To him, the universe was not eternal; but was created out of nothing by the creative will of Allah. The relation between men and the great being who has produced them and the world about them should be fundamentally moral and experiential. It is not enough to observe the laws and rites of Islam or have a theology which one is ready to defend against all comers. A humble soul may be profoundly religious even though he be ignorant of the details of Qur'anic interpretation or theology. The core of religion—which may be practiced even by a non-Moslem—is to repent of one's sins, purge *the heart* of all but God, and by the exercises of religion attain a virtuous character. And here, he said, the Sufi methods of self-discipline and meditation, if practiced with common sense and wisdom, are of great value. Of priceless value, too, are the Five Pillars of the Faith, revealed as obligatory for all Moslems; yet they do not yield their full profit unless they are performed from the heart and with the right attitude of mind.° Only thus could the Moslem hope to escape punishment on the Last Day.

The vigor with which Ghazzali criticized the teachers of law, theology, and philosophy for their lack of religious fire and for encouraging sectarian tendencies caused his works to be bitterly assailed when they were first published; but on second thought, all but the more extreme sects in areas dominated by formalistic jurisprudence, like far-off Spain, acknowledged the sanity and general truth of his position. Ultimately, he was given the rank of the greatest of Moslem theologians, and was at last revered as a saint. And just as Catholic schoolmen have not gone

° The occasional difficulties Ghazzali had in charging with meaning and significance the Five Pillars and other prescriptions of the Qur'an, and his success in doing so, are well illustrated in the words of George Foot Moore: "Even for the rites of the pilgrimage to Mecca—that undigested piece of Arab heathenism which Muhammad incorporated in Islam—Ghazzali succeeded in finding religious meaning and profit. All the other prescribed observances, as he remarks, have some rational end, and are plainly useful to the soul; but the throwing stones into the valley of Mina and going in a circle around the Kaaba have no sense, no spiritual utility, in harmony with the natural inclination of the soul. And precisely therein consists the merit of the observance; man abdicates his reason in obedience to the law of God by performing acts which have no intelligible end. This is the value of the pilgrimage for the simple believer; but for the enlightened these seemingly meaningless acts have a deeper moral and spiritual significance, which is discovered by the way of allegory. Mecca is the symbol of Paradise; the Kaaba, of the abode of God; the circuit about the holy house is a figure of the continual adoration which the angels render to the Lord around his throne; the race back and forth between the hills of Safa and Merwa is an image of the perplexity of the soul before God's bar," etc.[47]

beyond the positions of Aquinas, so Moslem theologians have remained in the main content with Ghazzali's formulations, his word being taken as all but final.

VI. VARIATIONS ON THE STANDARD MOSLEM THEMES

It must be obvious by now that Islam is not, and never has been at any time, a monolithic faith. Deviation from the norm in doctrine and disturbances of a political nature have plenteously occurred. We turn first to a major deviation that goes back almost to the beginning.

The Shi'ites

The tragedy that befell the House of 'Ali, beginning with the murder of 'Ali himself and including the death of his two sons, has haunted the lives of "the partisans of 'Ali," something that they have brooded upon down the years as Christians do upon the death of Jesus. A major heretical group, they have drawn the censure and yet also have had the sympathy of the Sunnis and Sufis. They were among the sects which Ghazzali attacked as guilty of resting their claims on false grounds, and sinfully dividing Islam. And yet, although agreeing with this indictment, the Moslem world at large has suppressed its annoyance at them out of a kind of pity, because their movement goes back to the very beginnings of Islam and has a kind of perverse justification, even in orthodox eyes. Their critics agree that there is no sense in it, yet it has an appeal all its own.

The partisans of 'Ali only gradually worked out their final claims, asserted by the various Shi'ite sects. In the beginning there was little more than deviation (which the main body of Moslems called *ghuluw*, "exaggeration"). Such deviation was not adopted by the early Shi'ites for its own sake, but out of one or more of these sincere convictions: that Allah was determinedly behind 'Ali and his successors, that He would not be frustrated by death, and that He would surely conduct the Shi'ite cause to a final triumph, even if this might mean bringing a descendant of 'Ali back from death or "withdrawal" to be a messianic figure capable of accomplishing the aims that Muhammad and 'Ali had espoused when they were leaders of the Moslem world. Such expectations were at first scarcely more than hopes born of frustration and faith; but gradually the hope and faith became a matter of firm conviction.

In the eyes of the Shi'ites, Muhammad became the *Prophet* of Islam, and 'Ali, his cousin and son-in-law, the *Imam*, the divinely designated "leader" and commander-in-chief of the faithful, and also their "pattern"; for they came to believe that before his death Muhammad, the revealer of the Truth in Arabia, chose 'Ali as the Successor (caliph) who should establish this truth throughout the earth. For this conception of the divinely ordained Imamate of 'Ali (as contrasted with the humanly ordained and sinful non-Alid caliphates), they were to rely on the authenticity of a hadith, probably piously invented by 'Ali partisans, to the effect that Muhammad, on his return to Medina after his Farewell Pilgrimage to Mecca three months before his death, said to 'Ali: "I shall soon be called back to heaven; I leave you two important bequests, the Qur'an and my family." [48]

Here, certainly, much is suggested about both Muhammad and 'Ali which the orthodox cannot accept and which they say runs counter to the Qur'an. Muhammad is heard saying he will be "called *back* to heaven," as though he had come to earth from a state of pre-existence as a divine being. This saying, when construed, would suggest that his designation of 'Ali as his successor conferred on 'Ali the same kind of supernatural status as Catholics claim Jesus bestowed on Peter at Caesarea Philippi. Hence, the appointment of Abu Bakr, Umar, and Uthman as caliphs was a usurpation—a usurpation with disastrous consequences; for when 'Ali at last was elected caliph, the opposition had developed so much power, it was able to bring his caliphate to a tragic conclusion. So bitter are all but one of the Shi'ite sects about this great "betrayal," that to this day they curse Abu Bakr, Umar, and Uthman as usurpers, in their Friday prayers.

The Shi'ites found the same kind of tragedy overwhelming 'Ali's sons, who by heritage were endowed with his unique spiritual quality. Al-Hasan, the older of the two sons 'Ali had by Fatima, was led by the opposition to resign his imamship for a mere pension and shortly thereafter died; the younger son, Al-Husain, the third Imam according to this reading of history, fell a martyr (680 A.D.), together with his little son, in a night battle at Karbala during a futile attempt to establish himself as the rightful caliph over the Ummayad incumbent, Yazid.

While this interpretation of history was still in its formative stage, the Shi'ites struggled against the Ummayads and gave their support to the rebellions that led to the triumph of the Abassids. But the Shi'ites were no better treated by the Abbasids than by the Ummayads, and in seeking attainment of their aims broke up into different sects (which we shall examine shortly); nevertheless, they continued to regard the descendants of al-Hasan and al-Husain as "nobles" and "lords," and among their number distinguished, according to their various sectarian principles, certain individuals as divinely ordained Imams, who had inherited from 'Ali and the intermediate imams two extraordinary qualities: infallibility in interpreting the law and sinlessness. Historically it was not until about the time of the sixth Imam after 'Ali (Ja'far al-Sadiq) that these claims assumed a clear-cut form. Back of them were two principles: that of the *nass* (designation of the next Imam by the preceding one), a principle which was read back into history all the way to Muhammad, as we have seen; and that of the *'ilm* (special knowledge, such as would give an Imam the warrant to exercise authority, impose discipline, and make decisions of a binding character in cases at issue).

Eventually another belief was to be added. It came later and con-

Ali and his two sons, Hasan and Husain. (Modern popular picture, Algeria; reproduced in Dermenghen, *Muhammad and the Islamic Tradition*)

cerned the expected return of some one of the Imams as a "divinely guided" messianic personage, the <u>Mahdi</u>. Where their line of Imams ended, various sects were to believe that the last of these divine leaders had just "withdrawn" from sight, and would return again as the Mahdi before the Last Day, to gather his own about him once more.

Shi'ite loyalty to these Imams has been fanatical and stubborn. When persecution or compulsion proved too strong, they allowed themselves the leeway provided in their principle of dissimulation (*taqiyah*), which permitted them to conform outwardly to the requirements laid upon them by the persecuting authorities, while making a secret mental reservation. By this means they were able to survive as an underground movement in the areas where their views were proscribed. But though their fanaticism was sharpened by persecution in respect to their distinctive views, in other respects the very fact of their being in opposition to the orthodox Moslems made them sympathetic with liberal theological positions. Like the Mu'tazilites, they did not believe the Qur'an to be eternal, nor men to be without any freedom of the will; they believed, too, that Allah *must* be just and holds men responsible only for their own acts.

The Shi'ite Sects

The repressions suffered by the Shi'ites have had a result that might well have been expected. Underground sects and terrorist groups, often outlawed by the main body of the Shi'ites themselves, have kept forming. Some of them have preyed upon whole communities, or built states within states; some have seized large areas and ruled them as outlaw kingdoms; others have conspired secretly to annihilate their enemies by poison and dagger. These have, of course, been the violent minority.

Let us begin with the less extreme sects first. In order to do so without too much confusion, the reader is invited to consider the chart or tree* on the next page showing the family relationship of the successors of 'Ali who figure so largely in the thoughts of the Shi'ite world.

Following down the extreme left side of this chart, we find the three general groups that form the Shi'ite sects. A discussion of each follows.

A. THE ZAIDITES. These are the Shi'ites who approximate most closely to the Traditionalist (Sunnite) position. They differ with the other sects in considering Zaid (see chart) as the fifth Imam instead of Muhammad al-Baqir, the fifth Imam of the other sects. The Zaidites did not realize

* Adapted from Hitti, *History of the Arabs.*

1. 'ALI (died 661)

2. AL-HASAN (d. 669)

3. AL-HUSAIN (d. 680)

4. 'ALI ZAIN-AL-'ABIDIN (d. *ca.* 712)

ZAIDITES . . .→ZAID   5. MUHAMMAD AL-BAQIR (d. 731)
branch off
here

6. JA'FAR AL-SADIQ (d. 765)

ISMAILITES . . .→ISMAIL (d. 760)
stop here

7. MUSA AL-KAZIM (d. 797)

8. 'ALI AL-RIDA (d. 818)

9. MUHAMMAD AL-JAWAD (d. 835)

10. 'ALI AL-HADI (d. 868)

11. AL-HASAN AL-'ASKARI (d. 874)

TWELVERS . . .→   12. MUHAMMAD AL-MUNTAZAR (d. 878)
stop here

they were a separate sect until the time of Ja'far al-Sadiq, and have
quite generally shied away from the principle of the *nass,* especially if
it is interpreted as having a supernatural significance. It is typical for
them to assert that 'Ali, not having been designated as the first caliph by
Muhammad, freely gave Abu Bakr and Umar his allegiance when they
were chosen, and therefore these two caliphs are not cursed in the Friday
prayers. Some of them execrate Uthman for being an Ummayad who
displaced 'Ali as the third caliph, but not all the Zaidites feel the same
resentment, though all agree that the Ummayads who succeeded 'Ali
were usurpers of the lowest kind: they were and are accursed. As a
force in history the Zaidites have maintained a dynasty since the 9th
century in Yemen (South Arabia), and in the past have had dynasties
for periods varying from sixty to two hundred years in Tabaristan,
Dailan, Gilan, and Morocco.

B. THE TWELVERS. This sect claims the great majority of the Shi'ites as members. They get their name from reckoning through to the twelfth Imam, Muhammad al-Muntazar. This Imam is of great importance to them. They say that in 878 A.D. he "disappeared" or "withdrew" into the cave of the great mosque at Samarra, up the river from Baghdad. He had left no issue, but the Twelvers refused to believe that Allah could have let the divinely instituted line of Imams come to an end; the twelfth Imam therefore had simply gone into concealment; he had withdrawn from human sight, until the fulness of the time when he will return as the Mahdi, "the divinely guided one" who will usher in a period of righteousness and peace before the end of the world and the Last Judgment.° The "concealed Imam," while remaining in his hidden state, where death cannot touch him, has not left his waiting followers without guidance, many have said; he has selected representatives on earth to lead them. In Persia (now Iran), where almost the whole population of about twenty million is Shi'ite (and Twelver) and where Islam has been since the beginning of the 16th century the religion of the state, the shah was once regarded as such a representative. During the last two centuries this claim has not been made officially.

C. THE ISMAILITES OR SEVENERS AND THEIR OFFSHOOTS. While moderate as a group, the Ismailites have produced offshoots which have sometimes shocked and stirred the whole Moslem world. The Ismailites are so-called because they have remained loyal to Ismail, the first son of the sixth Imam. After being designated by his father as the next Imam (by the *nass*) Ismail was set aside for his younger brother, when his father learned of his drunkenness. But the Ismailites have refused to believe the accusation against their favorite; they have considered that the father must have yielded to a slanderous attack that was false; for Ismail, as Imam-designate, and therefore already infallible and sinless, simply could not have been guilty of the charge against him. The fact that Ismail was reported to have died (760 A.D.) five years before his father, excited the Ismailites all the more; they concluded that he was not dead but hidden: he would come again as the Mahdi.† In their fervid belief, Ismail was the very incarnation of God himself, and would soon

---

° A widely accepted hadith declares that Muhammad prophesied there would come in the last days a man of his own family who would do this. He would be known as the Mahdi. The Shi'ites seized upon the phrase "of his own family" and made the prophecy apply to the Alids, which meant the Imams.—But another hadith contradicts all this with the saying: "There is no Mahdi but Jesus the Son of Mary!" [49]

† Some admitted that he did die, but left a son, Muhammad ibn-Ismail, who "disappeared" in India, and would return as Mahdi.

return. In order to find support for these views in the Qur'an, they began to interpret it allegorically (as many Christian eschatologists today interpret the Bible), and arrived at an esoteric, hidden doctrine, which was so heretical that they spread it to others only through secret missionary activity.

This aspect of Ismailite thought attracted men disposed to rebellion against authority. An early and startling manifestation of the political effects which might flow from secret Ismailite activities occurred near the head of the Persian Gulf. There the ambitious Persian, 'Abdullah ibn-Maimum (d. ca. 874), claiming to be the earthly representative of the concealed Imam Muhammad ibn-Ismail, built up a secret society devoted to the cause of destroying the Abbasid caliphate and putting 'Abdullah or his descendants on the throne. Though this scheme was not carried out, because 'Abdullah had to flee for his life to northern Syria, his organization succeeded after his death in founding (909 A.D.) the Fatimid caliphate which for centuries ruled Egypt, Tunis, and Syria. This proved to be one of the major Shi'ite assumptions of temporal power.

Another group which developed from 'Abdullah's secret organization was the Qarmatians. They were led by one of 'Abdullah's disciples, a certain Hamdan Qarmat, from whom they took their name. His secret society, formed toward the close of the 9th century, was along communistic lines, and succeeded in setting up an independent kingdom on the western shore of the Persian Gulf, with complete control from Yemen to the borders of Iraq. This rebel state was able to defend itself successfully against the caliphs at Baghdad, and in one remarkable and hair-raising sortie dared to capture and loot Mecca during the pilgrimage season! In this astonishing assault on the holy city they carried off the Black Stone, and returned it after twenty years only because the Fatimid (fellow-Ismailite) caliph, the powerful al-Mansur, requested it. The Qarmatians cut the roads from Iraq to Mecca, and pilgrims over these routes either paid heavily for the privilege or were turned back. Before they finally fell, the Qarmatians set a record of a century of revolutionary violence and bloodshed—all at bottom a kind of vengeance of the Persians upon the Arabs who had conquered them, a vengeance disguised indeed, perhaps even to themselves, as religious obedience to the will of a divine Imam descended from Muhammad.

Actually less dangerous but even more dreaded were the mysterious Assassins, who as exponents of what they called "the new propaganda," developed to a high point the terrorist art of worming one's way in disguise into the presence of Moslem rulers and officials and striking them down with a poisoned dagger. It did not matter how public the occasion was—the Friday prayers at the mosque, the holding of court by a prince or king—the more people present the better; the assassin aimed and struck, and was himself struck down, or else seized and put to death after torture; but he endured all in the confident expectation of going directly to Paradise, the promised reward he was seeking.

The founder and first grandmaster of this order was Hasan Sabbah (d. 1124 A.D.), probably a Persian, though he claimed descent from a line of kings in south Arabia. It was he who had the inspiration to seize the mountain stronghold of Alamut, in Persia, perched on a high narrow ledge of rock three-quarters of a mile long and several hundred feet wide, which he and his men fortified so expertly that it remained impregnable for two centuries. Here they supported themselves by their own farming and gardening of the land beneath the heights of their fortress. By sorties in force from their mountain fortress, the Assassins captured other strongholds in northern Persia; and by sending missionaries into northern Syria, they were also able to start a vigorous movement there, which eventually led to the establishment of a powerful mountain kingdom with ten or more fortresses in the order's hands. It was here that the Crusaders came to know and to fear them, and to be in awe of their leader, Rashid-al-Sinan, whose title "sheikh al-jabah"— was translated for them into "The Old Man of the Mountain." It is said that 20,000 of them still survive as a now peaceful sect in the Lebanon mountains. In Persia (Iran) their order has declined. But they have continued to exist in greater numbers in Zanzibar, and especially in Pakistan and India, where they are about 250,000 strong.* Half of these have acknowledged as their rightful heads a fabulous line of Khans, their present head, the Agha Khan, being a Harvard graduate.

The Dervishes

The Sufi movement early gave rise, after observation in Syria of the value of certain types of Christian organization, to the nearest approach in Islam to church-worship and ecclesiastical organization. Under masters or guides, the devotees of Sufi mystical experiences drew apart into retreats or monastic houses, to live fraternally in something like communistic societies, and to enjoy social fellowship along with their mystical raptures. Those of them who began a wandering life, dependent on

* The total number of Moslems in Pakistan and India reaches the much larger figure of 70,000,000—the largest Moslem group in the world.

charity, came to be called dervishes (from the Persian *darwish*, meaning "one who comes to the door," i.e. to beg). Because of their distinctive dress, their begging baskets,* and their known addiction to ecstatic experiences, they excited great interest.

The poets celebrated them, some in fun, others in order to pay them grave respect. The "nightingale of Shiraz," the poet Sa'di, believed in the dervishes, and himself practiced meditation with them, but he warned them that a dervish is not made such by his clothes.

The dervish's course of life is spent in commemorating, and thanking, and serving, and obeying God; and in beneficence and contentment; and in the acknowledgement of one God and reliance on Him; and in resignation and patience. Everyone who is endued with these qualities is, in fact, a dervish, though dressed in a tunic. But a babbler, who neglects prayer, and is given to sensuality, and the gratification of his appetite; who spends his days till nightfall in the pursuit of licentiousness, and passes his night till day returns in careless slumber; eats whatever is set before him, and says whatever comes uppermost; is a profligate, though he wear the habit of a dervish.[50]

Since the 12th century a number of widespread dervish orders or brotherhoods have been founded, each with its own monastic retreats, special rites, and methods of inducing ecstasy. The Qadirites were the first of these orders. Founded in Baghdad by Abd-al-Qadar al-Jilani (1077–1166), it has spread, thinly to be sure, to Java in the East and Algeria in the West. The so-called Howling Dervishes (the Rifa'ites) came next, being founded in the second half of the 12th century by Ahmad al-Rifa'i; and the widely known Whirling Dervishes (the Maulawites) are members of an order founded by the Persian poet Jalal al-Din Rumi, whom we have quoted on a previous page, and who bequeathed to his followers not his verses only but also, to accompany them, a method of using music as an important and stimulating element in their rites, whereby they were made to whirl about in ecstasy.

The more extreme of the dervishes have turned out to be little more than shamans. They astonish the pious, in the manner of their Hindu prototypes, by swallowing live coals and snakes, and by passing needles, hooks, and knives through their flesh. Many wear special badges, use rosaries, and venerate the founders of their orders as saints.

The dervish orders parallel the Franciscans of Europe in admitting lay members, who live and work in the world but have stated times, usually in the evening, when they come to the monasteries to take part in religious exercises directed by a Master or Leader.

---

* Not all the dervishes beg, however. Many dervish orders raise their own food.

It should be added, perhaps, that though the sort of dervishes who have whirled, or howled, or lashed themselves into frenzy by using whips or knives, have given dervishes as a group much notoriety, the majority are content to practice their quiet devotional life in the fellowship of their houses and do not show themselves often in public. Their popular following is often quite large.

Veneration of Saints

The mention above of the practice by some dervish orders of the veneration of their founders as saints, brings before us yet another variation on the standard Moslem themes. Islam spread with such rapidity through the Middle East that in certain areas native customs and superstitions often survived with little change in spite of the conversion of the population to a faith that should have been seen to be logically at variance with them. Sacred places, holy stones and trees, the burial places of local heroes, the tombs of old-time saints and intercessors continued to receive their customary honors, howbeit under a new guise made possible by their being veiled over by Moslem beliefs. This was especially the case in places where Christians and Zoroastrians embraced Islam more or less superficially. Later on, the Sufis and Shi'ites had no great compulsion to discourage such practices.

Although the teachers and theologians of Islam continue to declare it highly unorthodox, the Sufis and the common people, fairly generally throughout the Moslem world, visit the tombs of Moslem saints to leave votive offerings, pray for the intercession of the saints, and ask their blessing (*barakah*) upon them personally. Some of these tombs are even found in the vicinity of mosques and may quite often be surrounded by the graves of those whose last wish it was to be buried nearby. Of course, to worship the sainted dead is in direct conflict with the Qur'an, which strongly condemns as polytheistic any ascribing of "partners unto Allah."

VII THE FEASTS AND FESTIVALS OF THE MOSLEM YEAR

Although the Sunnis, Sufis, and Shi'ites have tended at certain points to differ to the extent of irreconcilability, it must be said that powerful unitive forces have always been at work. Chief is the Qur'an itself; and running a close second are the Five Pillars, especially the observance of the five daily times of prayer and the pilgrimage to Mecca.

Not far behind in bringing a sense of over-all unity to the Moslem world are the recurring feasts and festivals of the Moslem year. They were gradually developed through the centuries to the number of five. (Five plays a role in Islam comparable to that of three in Christianity.) These feasts and festivals are observed differently in the various Moslem lands, but they have a common intention.

The feasts are two:

1. The so-called "little feast" at the end of the fast of Ramadan, called *'Id al-Fitr.* It is the occasion of great merriment, and occurs on the first day of the month Shawwal.

2. The Feast of Sacrifice (*'Id al-Adha*) or the Great Feast. It falls on the day (the 10th of the month Dhu-al-Hijja) when the pilgrims outside Mecca have returned halfway from the Great Pilgrimage and are making a Feast of Sacrifice by ritually offering up the allowed animals and joining in a joyous sharing of their flesh.

The festivals are three:

1. The New Year Festival (*Muharram*) observed during the first days of the first month. The Shi'ites take this occasion to commemorate the death of Husain and his little son in the night battle of Karbala; they do so by dedicating the first ten days to lamentation, at the end of which a passion play is performed with much attention to the suffering and death of the son and grandson of 'Ali.

2. The Festival of the Prophet's Birthday (*Mawlid an-Nabi*), held traditionally on the 12th day of the month Rabi'al-awwal. (In point of time this is the last of the festivals to be evolved.)

3. The Festival of the Prophet's Night Journey (*Lailat al-Mir'aj*), observed as a rule on the night preceding the 27th of the month Rajab. Mosques and minarets are lighted in honor of the famous "night journey," and the hadiths concerning the event are reverentially read.

VIII RECENT DEVELOPMENTS

That Islam has continued in the more recent past to give rise to powerful new movements within itself—movements even of a disruptive kind—is plain in the history of the last two centuries. An instance is provided by the 19th century activity of the Druses, a fanatical Syrian group of the Ismailite sect which originated from the adulation given the mad Fatimid caliph, Hakim abu Ali Mansur, the sixth of his line, by two of his ministers, who declared him to be a return in the flesh of the hidden Imam, and in fact an incarnation of God himself. In 1020 A.D.,

Hakim suddenly disappeared—probably as the result of his secret murder by a palace clique—and this disappearance was enough for the Druses: he was a divine Imam who had "withdrawn" in order to return in due time as Mahdi. Since then they have had more than one Mahdi pretender arise to lead them in revolt. In the 19th century, the famous British general, Lord Kitchener of Khartoum, fought one such Mahdi in the Sudan.

But other and better reasoned movements have appeared, and are still appearing, in the Moslem world.

Before we survey some of the more recent movements, a general observation needs to be made. It might be thought that the reformulations which have occurred within modern Islam must be the inevitable effect of the influx of new ideas and practices from Western Europe and America. There can be no doubt that this effect is mounting in significance; but it constitutes only part of the total situation. Moslems themselves find that the recent diversifications within their faith are principally due to two forms of Islamic self-searching: (1) revival and reform due strictly to internal causes reaching back to the 14th century, and (2) a defensive restatement of the essential and central elements in Moslem belief and practice, attempted in the face of the encroachment of the modern West and in order to render Moslem minds immune to foreign subversion. Western science and technology have begun to penetrate the Moslem defenses, but Western thought has not done so to the same extent. Alien modes of looking at life and the world, whether in the form of the universalism of missionaries seeking to convert the Moslems to a world Christianity or of Western philosophy from Thomas Aquinas to Marxian dialectical materialism, have had an extraordinarily widespread negative effect in alerting the whole Moslem community to the threat of disintegrative change.

The prime instance of the first form of Islamic self-searching is the reform begun in inner Arabia in the 18th century—the Wahhabi movement mentioned on a previous page. This was an iconoclastic puritan reform that grew to great strength through the support of the emirs of the House of Sa'ud. It represented a return to earlier Hanbalite theories of conduct and was greatly influenced by the anti-Sufism of the 14th century writer Ibn Taimiya. The movement took its name from its originator Muhammad ibn 'Abd al-Wahhab, whose aim was to lead Moslems in a return to Muhammad and the Qur'an. To this end he rejected all modifications of Moslem belief and practice owing to "the consensus of community opinion" (*ijma*'), except for those which went back authentically to the Medina community immediately after the death of Muham-

mad. "Sufi innovations" were especially frowned upon. Accordingly, the
Wahhabis (or *Ikwan*, "brothers") condemned all blood feuds and tribal
distinctions, and urged the utmost purity and simplicity of life, without
wine or tobacco. Through the years they have firmly emphasized Moslem
unitarianism, and so fierce has been their rejection of Sufi-inspired
intercessory prayers at the tombs and shrines of holy men and women
(which they denounce as saint-worship, and therefore polytheism), that
when they captured Mecca in 1806, they destroyed the tombs before
which pilgrims did reverence, and when again, in 1924–1925, the deposed Sultan ceded Mecca and Medina to Saudi Arabia, they turned the
birthplace of Muhammad himself into a camel's resting place and de-
molished the markers on the graves of Muhammad's family and of his
Companions. To accept as true any belief not confirmed by the Qur'an,
the authentic hadiths, or strict reasoning is an act of infidelity. Houses
and clothes must be plain; joking, music, and gold ornaments are forbidden. Such games as chess should be given up because they may make
the players forget the hours of prayer.

The extremism of the Wahhabis has been generally rejected by the
Moslem world, but their devotion to historic Islam pure and undefiled
has had pronounced reformative effects in North Africa, India, and the
East Indies.

Ironically enough, the Wahhabis in Saudi Arabia now find the outside world intruding mightily into their way of life. Their leaders have
concluded agreements and treaties with the great powers with respect
to the oil reserves under their sands; and Saudi Arabia has experienced
not only a quick inflow of vast wealth, but also the introduction in increasing measure of Western inventions and conveniences, such as auto-
mobiles, trailer-trucks, airplanes, air-conditioned housing, radios, movies,
hospitals, sanitary devices, artesian wells, and much else of a like kind.
It is a question whether the orthodox in Saudi Arabia can preserve
their puritan simplicity and conservatism much longer.

The Sufis, meanwhile, have had too great a measure of support
among the common people to worry overmuch because the Wahhabis assailed them. In the name of long-established religious experience, they
have continued to uphold the validity of personal religious response,
intuition, the practices of their religious orders, and reverence for sainted
leaders. This is true especially in the non-Arab areas and particularly
among the Berbers, Persians, and Turks. But even the Sufis have been
chastened by Wahhabi puritanism and orthodoxy; in fact, they have
abandoned many a practice to which they were once devoted.

When most of Africa and much of Asia came under the rule of the

European powers, it was inevitable that Western books and periodicals, Western-sponsored schools and academies, and still more the colonial administrations themselves, with all the political and economic changes that accompanied them, should introduce into the occupied areas new concepts of law and political organization, new forms of commercial and industrial enterprise, new modes of transport by land, sea, and air, improvements in agriculture, scientific medicine, and never-before-dreamed-of wealth through the exploitation of newly discovered natural resources, particularly oil. Conservatives who cling to the old Moslem way of life naturally view these developments with more than a little alarm.

But Moslems of all stripes, liberal or conservative, have discovered that they too can use the printed page. From about the middle of the 19th century there began to appear Moslem books and periodicals that have enjoyed wide circulation from West to East, their general aim being to save Islam by uniting the Moslem world to meet the challenge of the contemporary world, although the final effect has been to increase the diversity of opinion as to how this may be done. Perhaps the most important fact here is this: Moslems began to *reason* again as they had not done in centuries. Indeed, the *'ulama,* as the conservative scholars are called, have had some difficulty controlling the effects of this recovery of the use of reason, especially in the bold expression of private judgment.

In attempting here to cope with the vast amount of detail which has been accumulating concerning recent developments in Islam, perhaps the simplest and most clarifying thing to do is to review events in some of the major areas of the Moslem world.

The most startling political and cultural changes have occurred in *Turkey.* There the Young Turks, led by Mustapha Kemal, overthrew the Ottoman caliphate in 1924 and went on to revolutionary changes that were openly designed to westernize and secularize Turkey. The separation of church and state and new laws affecting marriage, divorce, the family, the status and dress of women, education, and public conduct in general have brought about drastic changes. The effect has been to remove Turkey from vital interrelationships with the rest of the Moslem world.

During the last hundred years *Egypt* has been the scene of religious and political developments that have had great importance in Moslem eyes. The revival of Egyptian influence began with the untiring efforts of Jamal al-Din al-Afghani (1839–1897), the founder of the Pan-Islamic movement, to unite the Moslem peoples against European domination and to incite them to rid themselves of certain religious and social errors and thus enable them to meet the challenge of the modern world. Concentrating upon the latter objective, his disciple Muhammad Abduh (1849–1905), a teacher and later a member of the administrative committee of the University of Cairo, urged not only the necessity of renewed study of the classical Arabic theological works but also the introduction into the university curriculum of courses in modern science, geography, and European history and religion. He was resolved to take seriously the orthodox position that reason cannot contradict revelation, for it can only confirm it. Reason is, moreover, of decisive importance not only in moral conduct and the quest of happiness, to which all men are entitled, but also in the understanding of the principles of the Qur'an.

One of the consequences of his teaching was the strengthening of tendencies toward a "modernism" that was very receptive of Western ideas, to the point of secularism; but, on the other hand, his return, in the spirit of Wahhabism, to Muhammad and the traditions of the early Medina community resulted in formation of a conservative religious group called the *Salafiya*, led by his Syrian disciple Rashid Rida, the editor of a periodical that was read from one end of the Moslem world to the other. The Salafi movement spread to India and the East Indies.

The Egyptian influence may be seen in another form: the rise of religious societies, such as The Young Men's Moslem Association (inspired by the Y.M.C.A.) and the Wahhabi-motivated Moslem Brotherhood, a powerful factor in Egyptian politics, before and since the independence of Egypt.

Potentially more decisive for Egypt abroad, as well as at home, is the military regime established by Jamal Abd al-Nasir ("Nasser"). In seizing the Suez Canal and in establishing the United Arab Republic, Nasser has attempted to achieve two aims: to rid Egypt of the last vestiges of colonialism and to seek pan-Islamic unity. He has succeeded in his first aim but not so far in his second, for Syria withdrew in 1961 from the U.A.R. and spiked his initial plans.

Turning now to *India* before its partition, we find among some of the Moslem leaders a liberal reaction that recalls that of the Hindu founders of the Brahmo Samaj. The readiness of the intellectuals in India through the centuries to consider openmindedly every variety of thought is reflected in the broadmindedness of Sir Sayyid Ahmad Khan (1817–1898). He was aided rather than hindered, curiously enough, by the spread of the Wahhabi movement among Indian Moslems, for, as we have seen, its rejection of Sufi emotionalism and its insistence on return to Muhammad and the early Medina community gave new importance to reason as a guide in religion. He took his stand upon the supreme authority of Muhammad, the Qur'an, and the early traditions, asserting that nature and reason both confirm any open-minded man in such a stand; since Allah supports nature as well as revelation, reason can find no real contradiction between them. Hence, science or the study of nature, when properly pursued, cannot conflict with the Qur'an but only confirm it. Accordingly, Sir Khan founded a Moslem university at Aligarh in 1875 with a curriculum which accompanied the study of the Moslem religion with courses in Western social and natural sciences (an advanced position from which the university, now in Pakistan, has since retreated).

Among the Indian intellectual leaders who were encouraged to take liberal positions influenced by Western throught was Sayyid Amir Ali, a Shi'ite, whose book *The Spirit of Islam* (first published in 1891 with the title *The Life and Teachings of Mohammad*) defends Islam as a liberal religion based on the perfect moral personality of Muhammad and the reasonableness of the Qur'an. This book is a classic among Moslem liberals and is widely used also by conservatives who wish to know what a modernist might believe. Even more liberal are the lectures delivered in English in 1928 by Sir Muhammad Iqbal and published under the title *The Reconstruction of Religious Thought in Islam*. A poet inspired by Sufi mysticism, Iqbal proposed a reconstruction of Moslem thought in quite non-Wahhabist terms: the validity of personal religious experience, the immanence of God, creative evolution a la Bergson, and the emergence of the superman a la Nietzsche. So radical is this position, that it is doubtful whether Iqbal has had many followers outside of India and Pakistan.

We should not exaggerate the influence of such intellectuals as these, for we need to be reminded, in the words of H. A. R. Gibbs, that "the illiterate Muslim, the villager, is in no danger yet of losing his faith, and, even if he were, the educated town-bred modernist would have no word to meet his needs. His spiritual life is cared for by the Sufi brotherhoods, regular or irregular, by the imam of the local mosque, or by the itinerant revivalist preacher." [51]

As to revivalist preachers, one such developed an organized religious movement that has distinctly heretical aspects in the eyes of the orthodox. Its leader, Mirza Ghulam Ahmad of Qadrian (d. 1908) accepted homage as a Mahdi in the closing decades of the 19th century. A reading of the Bible convinced him he was also the Messiah (Jesus in a second coming), and in 1904 he proclaimed himself an avatar of Krishna. But he remained a Moslem in the sense that he said he was not a prophet in himself but only in and through Muhammad. In his teaching he made it clear that holy war is not to be carried on by the use of force but only through preaching. His followers, the Ahmadiya, are therefore at once pacifists and ardent missionaries. The Ahmadiya have split into several branches. The original or Qadiani branch is consciously syncretist and all but outside the Moslem community. The Lahore branch is devotedly Moslem in character, and has rejected the extreme claims that Ahmad made for himself, although they consider him to be a genuine "renewer of religion." Ahmadiya missionaries of both these branches are active in England, America, Africa, and the East Indies, where they make considerable use of the printed page and regard Christian leaders as their chief adversaries. They often maintain, as for example on the outskirts of London, their own mosques, to which they cordially welcome all comers, including orthodox Moslems.

Persia (or *Iran*) has given rise to a markedly syncretistic movement, one which has, like Sikhism, become a separate and distinct faith. This is Bahaism. Its background is Shi'ite. Influenced by the teachings of a heretical Shi'ite to the effect that the Imams of the Twelver sect were "gates" by which the believers gained access to the true faith, and that the hidden Imam seeks further "gates" to conduct men to himself, a certain Mirza Ali Muhammad in 1844 added his name to the list and called himself Bab-ud-Din ("Gate of the Faith"). His followers were called after him Babis. He proclaimed that his mission was to prepare the way for a greater than himself who should come after him and complete the work of reform and righteousness which he had begun. When he said his writings were scripture equaling, if not superseding, the Qur'an, and on their basis advocated sweeping religious and social reforms, he was executed in 1850 as a heretic and disturber of the peace. Among his followers was a well-born youth who, following Babi custom, took the name of Baha'u'Llah ("Glory of God"). He was accused of complicity in an attempt by a fanatical Babi to assassinate the Shah in 1852 and was exiled to Baghdad. After some ten years there, when he and his followers were on the point of departure, he announced that he was the One-who-should-come of whom the Bab had spoken. Moving with his followers, who now called themselves after him Bahais, he sought asylum in the Moslem areas to the west and was finally imprisoned by the Turks in Acre, Palestine, for the balance of his life. His writings reached the outside world. They advocated a broad religious view upholding the unity of God and the essential harmony of all prophecy when rightly understood. He called upon all religions to unite, for every religion contains some truth, since all prophets are witnesses to the one

Truth, which Bahaism supremely represents. The human race is one under God, and will be united through His spirit when the Bahai Cause is known and joined. Outlawed in Iran, Bahaism, with headquarters in Haifa in Palestine, is active in many countries, and especially in the United States.

Although many observers have felt during the past quarter of a century that Islam has been yielding on all sides to the disintegrative influences of Western culture, it remains still to be seen whether or not the establishment of the state of Israel in Palestine will have the effect, for a period at least, of drawing the Moslem world together into a tighter unity and a heightening of resistance to change.

However that may be, one fact stands out in all Moslem history. Islam is no more immune to inner movements of change, growth, and diversification than the other religions of the world.

SUGGESTIONS FOR FURTHER READING

Adams, C. C. *Islam and Modernism in Egypt.* Oxford, 1933
Andrae, Tor. *Mohammed: the Man and His Faith.* Trans. Theophil Menzel. Allen and Unwin, 1936. Available as Harper Torchbooks pb
Arberry, A. J. *The Doctrine of the Sufis.* Cambridge, 1935
————. *Sufism.* Allen and Unwin, 1950
Arnold, T. W. *The Preaching of Islam.* Constable, 1913
————. *The Caliphate.* Oxford, 1924
Arnold and Guillaume, eds. *The Legacy of Islam.* 2nd ed. Oxford, 1948
Bell, R. *The Origin of Islam in its Christian Environment.* London, 1926
————. *The Qur'an.* 2 vols. Edinburgh, 1937–1939
Donaldson, D. M. *The Shi'ite Religion.* Luzac, 1933
————. *Studies in Muslim Ethics.* London, 1950
Faris, Nabih Amin, ed. *The Arab Heritage.* Princeton University Press, 1944
Gaudefoy-Demombynes, M. *Muslim Institutions.* Macmillan, 1951
Gibb, H. A. R. *Modern Trends in Islam.* University of Chicago Press, 1947
————. *Mohammedanism; an Historical Survey.* Oxford, 1949
Goldziher, I. *Mohammed and Islam.* Trans. K. C. Seelye. Yale University Press, 1917
Guillaume, Alfred. *Islam.* Penguin Books pb, 1954
————. *The Traditions of Islam.* Oxford, 1924
————. *Life of Muhammed.* Oxford, 1955
Hitti, P. K. *History of the Arabs.* 5th ed. Macmillan, 1951
Iqbal, Mohammed. *Reconstruction of Religious Thought in Islam.* 2nd ed. Oxford, 1934

Jeffery, Arthur, ed. *Muhammad and His Religion.* Liberal Arts Press pb, 1958

Levy, R. *The Social Structure of Islam.* Cambridge, 1957

Lewis, B. *The Arabs in History.* London, 1950

Margoliouth, D. S. *The Early Development of Mohammedanism.* London, 1914

Nicholson, R. A. *The Mystics of Islam.* London, 1914

————. *A Literary History of the Arabs.* 2nd ed. Cambridge, 1930

Smith, W. C. *Modern Islam in India.* Lahore, 1943

————. *Islam in Modern History.* Princeton, 1957. Available as Mentor pb, 1959

Tritton, A. S. *Islam: Belief and Practices.* Hutchinson, 1951

Von Grunebaum, G. E. *Muhammadan Festivals.* New York, 1951

————. *Islam: Essays in the Nature and Growth of a Cultural Tradition.* Menasha, 1955

Watt, W. M. *Free Will and Predestination in Early Islam.* Luzac, London, 1948

————. *Muhammed: Prophet and Statesman.* Oxford, 1961

Wensinck, A. J. *The Muslim Creed: Its Genesis and Historical Development.* Cambridge, 1932

Quoted References

REFERENCES are arranged in the order in which they are first quoted in the body of the text. The page numbers of the books from which quotations are taken are immediately preceded, in small type, by the number that is affixed to the end of the quotation in the body of the text. Where a book has been more than once quoted, as often happens when original sources are drawn upon, page numbers are arranged in the order of quotation in the text.

CHAPTER 1 RELIGION IN PREHISTORIC AND PRIMITIVE CULTURES

Paul Radin, *Primitive Man as Philosopher*. D. Appleton and Company, New York. 1927.   [1] p. 19. Reprinted by permission of Appleton-Century Company.

William A. Lessa and Evon Z. Vogt, editors, *Reader in Comparative Religion*, Row, Peterson and Company, Evanston, Illinois.   [2] p. 90.

E. B. Tylor, *Primitive Culture*, 2 vols. G. P. Putnam's Sons, New York, 1871.   [3] Vol. II, p. 185.

E. W. Hopkins, *The Origin and Evolution of Religion*. Yale University Press, 1923.   [4] p. 13.

Mabel Cooke Cole, *Savage Gentlemen*. D. Van Nostrand Company, New York, 1929.   [5] p. 15. Reprinted by permission of the publishers.

John L. Maddox, *The Medicine Man*. The Macmillan Company, New York, 1923.   [6] pp. 101–102 (condensing Catlin, *The North American Indian*, I, pp. 39–40). Reprinted by permission of the publishers.

Vergilias Ferm, ed., *Forgotten Religions*. Philosophical Library, New York, 1950.   [7] p. 275.

A. W. Howitt, *The Native Tribes of South-East Australia*. Macmillan and Company, London, 1904.   [8] p. 395;   [9] p. 798;   [10] p. 650;   [11] p. 661.

Rai Bahadur Sarat Chandra Roy, *The Birhors; A Little Known Jungle Tribe of Chota Nagpur*. Ranchi, India, 1925.   [12] pp. 70–76;   [13] p. 352;   [14] p. 241;   [15] pp. 284–285;   [16] p. 237;   [17] p. 369;   [18] pp. 378–384.

Hugh Stayt, *The BaVenda*. Oxford University Press, publishing for the International African Institute, London, 1928.   [19] p. 262;   [20] p. 276;   [21] p. 276;   [22] p. 162;   [23] p. 230. Reprinted by permission of the publishers.

CHAPTER 2   REPRESENTATIVE NATIONAL RELIGIONS OF THE PAST

J. H. Breasted, *The Dawn of Conscience*. Charles Scribner's Sons, New York, 1934.   [1] pp. 25, 27;   [7] p. 281;   [8] pp. 284–286. Reprinted by permission of the publishers.
The History of Herodotus. Trans. G. C. Macaulay. Macmillan and Company, London, 1914.   [2] Vol. I, p. 153. Reprinted by permission of the publishers.
J. H. Breasted, *Development of Religion and Thought in Ancient Egypt*. Charles Scribner's Sons, New York, 1912.   [3] p. 295;   [5] pp. 299–300. Reprinted by permission of the publishers.
Sir W. Flinders Petrie, *Religious Life in Ancient Egypt*. Constable and Company, Ltd., London, and Houghton Mifflin Company, Boston, 1924.   [4] p. 118. Reprinted by permission of the publishers.
W. F. Albright, *From the Stone Age to Christianity; Monotheism and the Historical Process*. Johns Hopkins Press, 1940.   [6] p. 166. Reprinted by permission of the publishers.
James B. Pritchard, ed., *Ancient Near East Texts*. 2nd ed., rev. and enl. Princeton University Press, 1955.   [9] p. 161;   [11] p. 162 f.;   [14] p. 107;   [15] p. 108;   [17] pp. 384–85.
R. W. Rogers, *The Religion of Babylonia and Assyria*. Eaton and Mains, New York, 1908.   [10] pp. 124–126;   [12] p. 201;   [13] pp. 202–204.
Morris Jastrow, *Aspects of Religious Belief and Practice in Babylonia and Assyria*. G. P. Putnam's Sons, New York, 1911.   [16] p. 374;   [18] p. 303. Reprinted by permission of the publishers.
Gilbert Murray, *Five Stages of Greek Religion*. Oxford, Clarendon Press, 1925.   [20] p. 87;   [21] p. 94. Reprinted by permission of the publishers.
Jane E. Harrison, *Mythology*. Marshall Jones, Boston, 1924.   [22] p. 94.
The Iliad of Homer. Trans. Edward Earl of Derby. Everyman's Library, J. M. Dent and Sons, London, 1910.   [23] p. 2 (Bk. I);   [25] p. 94 (Bk. V), substituting Hera for Juno in the translation;   [26] p. 212 (Bk. XIII);   [27] p. 239 (Bk. XIV);   [28] p. 281 (Bk. XVI).
Jane E. Harrison, *Prolegomena to the Study of Greek Religion*. Cambridge University Press, London, 1903.   [24] p. 321. Quoted by permission of the publishers.
Greek Religious Thought from Homer to the Age of Alexander. Ed. F. M. Cornford. J. M. Dent and Sons, London, and E. P. Dutton and Company, New York, 1923.   [29] p. 94;   [30] p. 50, arranging lines in verse form;   [31] p. 51, arranged as verse;   [37] p. 87;   [38] p. 85. Reprinted by permission of the publishers.
The House of Atreus, being the Agamemnon, Libation-bearers, and Furies of Aeschylus. Trans. E. D. A. Morshead. The Macmillan Company, London, 1901.   [32] pp. 18, 22 (Agamemnon, 380–385, 467–476).
The Plays of Euripides, translated into rhyming verse by Gilbert Murray. George Allen, London, 1914.   [33] "Hippolytus," 1347 ff.;   [34] Ibid., 1144 f.;   [35] Ibid., 1102 f.;   [36] "The Trojan Women," 884–888. Reprinted by permission of the publishers.

The Dialogues of Plato. Trans. ed. by Benjamin Jowett. Oxford University Press, London, 1893. [39] Book II, 378; [40] Book II, 364-365.

Carl Clemen, ed. *Religions of the World; Their Nature and History.* George G. Harrap and Company, London, and Harcourt, Brace and Company, New York, 1931. [41] p. 204; [45] p. 220. Quoted by permission of the publishers.

Cyril Bailey, *The Religion of Ancient Rome.* Constable and Company, London, 1907. [42] pp. 18–19. Reprinted by permission of the author.

George Foot Moore, *History of Religions.* 2 vols. Charles Scribner's Sons, New York, and T. & T. Clark, Edinburgh, 1913, 1919. [43] Vol. I, p. 541. Reprinted by permission of the publishers.

Cyril Bailey, *Phases of the Religion of Ancient Rome.* University of California Press, 1932. [44] p. 74.

CHAPTER 3   EARLY HINDUISM

Vedic Hymns. Trans. Edward J. Thomas. Wisdom of the East Series. John Murray, London, 1923. [1] p. 45 (Bk. I. 32.2, 3); [2] pp. 48–51 (II. 12.7–9, 15); [3] p. 70 (I. 114.7–9); [4] pp 65–66 (V. 57.4–5); [5] p. 31 (I. 113.7). Reprinted by permission of the publisher.

The Hymns of the Rig Veda. Trans. Ralph T. Griffith. E. J. Lazarus and Company, Benares, 1896. [6] I. 50.2; [7] X. 139.1; I. 35.11; [8] X. 14.1, 2, 7, 8; [9] V. 85.7, 8; [10] VI 23.6, 7; [12] VII. 98.7, 8; [16] I. 164.46. Reprinted by arrangement with the publishers.

Hymns from the Rig Veda. Metrically translated by A. A. Macdonell. Association Press, Calcutta. (Printed by the Wesleyan Mission Press, Mysore, without date.) [11] p. 80 (Bk. VIII. 48.3).

Sacred Books of the East, Vol. XLII, *The Hymns of the Atharva Veda.* Trans. by Maurice Bloomfield. Oxford, Clarendon Press, 1897. [13] p. 163 (Bk. VI. 26); [14] p. 31 (VI. 136). Reprinted by permission of the publishers.

Surendranath Dasgupta, *History of Indian Philosophy.* 3 vols. Cambridge University Press, 1932. [15] Vol. II, pp. 300–301. Reprinted by permission of the Syndics of the Cambridge University Press.

The Thirteen Principal Upanishads. Trans. R. E. Hume. Oxford University Press, London, 1934. [17] Svet. 6.17, p. 410; [18] Mait. 6.17, p. 435; [19] Chand. 3.14.1, p. 209; [20] Brih. 2.1–20, pp. 92–95; [21] Kath. 5.2, p. 356; [22] Mund. 2.2.11, p. 373; [23] Brih. 3.7.1–23, pp. 115–117; [24] Chand. 6.8.6, p. 246 f.; [25] Brih. 1.4.7, p. 82; [26] Chand. 3.14.3, p. 210; [27] Chand. 6.12, p. 247; [28] Tait. 2.4, p. 285; [31] Chand. 5.10.7, p. 233; [35] Mait. 1.4, p. 413; [36] Tait. 2.9, p. 289. Reprinted by permission of the author and publishers.

S. Radhakrishnan, *The Philosophy of the Upanishads.* George Allen and Unwin, London, 1924. [29] p. 36; [30] pp. 36–37; [37] p. 23. Reprinted by permission of the publishers.

Sir Charles Eliot, *Hinduism and Buddhism.* 3 vols. Edward Arnold and Company London, 1921. [32] Vol. I, lix. Reprinted by permission of the publishers.

George Foot Moore, *The Birth and Growth of Religion.* Charles Scribner's Sons, New York, and T. & T. Clark, Ltd., Edinburgh, 1923. [33] p. 118. Quoted by permission of the publishers.

Sacred Books of the East, Vol. XXV, *The Laws of Manu*. Trans. G. Buhler. Oxford, Clarendon Press, 1886. [34] pp. 484, 496–498 (XII. 9, 54–67). Reprinted by permission of the publishers.

CHAPTER 4 JAINISM

Sacred Books of the East, Vol. XXII, *The Gaina Sutras*. Trans. by Hermann Jacobi. Oxford, Clarendon Press, 1884. [1] pp. 192–193; [2] p. 250; [3] p. 194; [4] p. 194; [5] p. 200; [6] pp. 80, 79, 82, 79, 87; [7] pp. 82, 83, 86, 82, 86; [8] pp. 80, 84, 85; [9] p. 201; [10] p. 264; [11] p. 52; [12] p. 152; [13] p. 33; [14] pp. 202–210; [15] p. 21; [17] p. 81; [18] p. 264. Reprinted by permission of the publishers.

James Bissett Pratt, *India and Its Faiths*. Houghton Mifflin Company, Boston, 1915. [16] p. 255. Quoted by permission of the publishers.

Carl Clemen, ed., *Religions of the World: Their Nature and History*. George G. Harrap & Co., Ltd., London, and Harcourt, Brace and Company, New York, 1931. [19] p. 106, quoting Otto Strauss. By permission of the publishers.

CHAPTER 5 BUDDHISM IN ITS FIRST PHASE

Kenneth J. Saunders, *Gotama Buddha: A Biography Based on the Canonical Books of the Theravadin*. Association Press, New York, 1920. [1] p. 9 (quoting Anguttara Nikaya 1.45); [2] p. 8; [14] p. 21 (quoting Jataka 1.71); [40] p. 112 (Samyutta IV). Quoted by permission of the publishers.

Asvaghosa's Life of Buddha (Buddha Carita). Trans. Samuel Beal. The World's Great Classics, Colonial Press, New York, 1900. [3] p. 306.

Henry Clarke Warren, *Buddhism in Translation*. Harvard University Press, 1922. [4] p. 55 (Jataka 1.58.7); [23] p. 122 (Majjhima Nikaya 63); [25] p. 129 (Milindapanha 25.1); [26] p. 234 (Ibid. 71.16); [27] p. 239 (Vissudhi Magga 17); [28] p. 136 (Maha-Nidana-Sutta 256.21); [32] p. 436 (Vissudhi Magga 3). Reprinted by permission of the publishers.

Sir Charles Eliot, *Hinduism and Buddhism*. 3 vols. Edward Arnold and Company, London, 1921. [5] Vol. I, p. 135 (Anguttara Nikaya 3.35); [16] Vol. I, p. 139 (Majjhima Nikaya 1.22); [22] Vol. I, p. 160 (Maha-Parinibbana 5.25); [35] Vol. I, p. 227 n. (Puggala Pannati 1.39). Reprinted by permission of the publishers.

Further Dialogues of the Buddha. Trans. from the *Majjhima Nikaya* by Lord Chalmers. For the Pali Text Society. Oxford University Press, London, 1926. [6] I. 115 (1.163); [7] I, pp. 115–117 (1.163–166); [8] I, p. 117 (1.166); [9] I, p. 173 (1.240–241); [10] I, p. 174 (1.242); [11] I, p. 56 (1.80); [12] I, p. 176 (1.246); [15] I, p. 15 (1.22); [17] I, p. 17 (1.24); [18] I, p. 118 (1.167). Reprinted by permission of the publishers.

L. Adams Beck, *The Story of Oriental Philosophy*. Cosmopolitan Book Corporation, New York, 1931. [13] p. 133 (a condensation of a lengthy passage from the Buddha Carita of Asvaghosa, Bk. XII); [19] p. 136 (Majjhima Nikaya 1.171).

Sacred Books of the East, Vol. XIII, *Vinaya Texts*. Trans. T. W. Rhys Davids and Hermann Oldenberg. Oxford, Clarendon Press, 1883. [20] p. 94. By permission of the publishers.

Buddhist Scriptures. Trans. Edward J. Thomas. Wisdom of the East Series. John Murray, London, 1913. [21] p. 52 (Khuddaka Patha 2). Quoted by permission of the publisher.

George Foot Moore, *History of Religions*. 2 vols. Charles Scribner's Sons, New York, and T. & T. Clark, Ltd., Edinburgh, 1913–1919. [24] Vol. I, p. 296. Quoted by permission of the publishers.

Sacred Books of the East, Vol. XI, *Buddhist Suttas*. Trans. T. W. Rhys Davids. Oxford, Clarendon Press, 1881. [29] pp. 148–150. Quoted by permission of the publishers.

Sacred Books of the East, Vol. X, *The Dhammapada*. Trans. F. Max Müller. Oxford, Clarendon Press, 1881. [30] 16:211; [38] 1:2–5. Quoted by permission of the publishers.

James Bissett Pratt, *The Pilgrimage of Buddhism*. The Macmillan Company, New York, 1928. [31] p. 30 (Udana 8.8, following the German of Seidenstucken); [33] p. 30 (Samyutta 21, following Mrs. Rhys Davids); [39] p. 54 (Majjhima Nikaya, using chiefly French of La Vallee Poussin). Reprinted by permission of the publishers.

Mrs. T. W. Rhys Davids, *Psalms of the Brethren*. Published for the Pali Text Society by Henry Frowde, London, 1913. [34] p. 362 (CCLXI).

Sacred Books of the East, Vol. X, Part 2, *The Sutta Nipata*. Trans. V. Fausböll. Oxford, Clarendon Press, 1881. [36] p. 6 f. (Khaggavissana Sutta 1–13); [37] p. 25. Quoted by permission of the publishers.

CHAPTER 6   THE RELIGIOUS DEVELOPMENT OF BUDDHISM

Carl Clemen, ed., *Religions of the World: Their Nature and History*. George G. Harrap and Co., Ltd., London, and Harcourt, Brace and Company, New York, 1931. [1] pp. 308–309. Quoted by permission of the publishers.

Vincent A. Smith, *Asoka, the Buddhist Emperor of India*. Oxford, Clarendon Press, 1920. [2] p. 186; [3] pp. 150, 178. Reprinted by permission of the publishers.

Sir Charles Eliot, *Hinduism and Buddhism*. 3 vols. Edward Arnold and Company, London, 1921. [4] Vol. II, p. 30 (quoting the Lesser Sukhavati-vyuha); [6] Vol. II, p. 43 (quoting Nagarjuna); [10] Vol. III, p. 404; [12] Vol. II, p. 284 n. 2. Reprinted by permission of the publishers.

Sacred Books of the East, Vol. XLIX, *Buddhist Mahayana Texts*. Trans. E. B. Cowell, Max Müller, and I. Takakusu. Oxford, Clarendon Press, 1893. [5] pp. 153–154. Reprinted by permission of the publishers.

Heinrich Zimmer, *Philosophies of India*, ed. Joseph Campbell Bollinger Foundation, 1951. Reference here is to Meridian Edition (1956). [7] pp. 447–448, quoting *Majjhima Nikaya*, 3.2.22.135. [8] p. 485, quoting *Astsahasrika Prajnaparamita*, 1.

James Bissett Pratt, *The Pilgrimage of Buddhism*. The Macmillan Company, 1928. [9] p. 480 (quoting Coates and Ishizuka. *Honen, the Buddhist Saint*, pp. 185–187). Quoted by permission of the publishers.

Dwight Goddard, ed., *A Buddhist Bible*. Dwight Goddard, Thetford, Vermont, 1938. [11] *pp*. 497–498 (Sutra Spoken by the Sixth Patriarch). Quoted by permission of the Dwight Goddard estate.

Erik Haarh, "Contributions to the Study of Mandala and Mudra." *Acta Orientalia*, Vol. XXIII, nos. 1–2 (1958). [13] pp. 57–91.

CHAPTER 7   LATER HINDUISM

Sacred Books of the East, Vol. XII, *Satapatha-Brahmana*. Trans. Julius Eggeling. Oxford, Clarendon Press, 1882. [1] pp. 190–191 (1.7.2.5). Reprinted by permission of the publishers.

W. Crooke, *Ancestor-Worship (Indian)* Article in the Encyclopaedia of Religion and Ethics. T. & T. Clark, Edinburgh, and Charles Scribner's Sons, New York. [2] Vol. I, p. 453. Reprinted by permission of the publishers.

Sacred Books of the East, Vol. XXV, *The Laws of Manu.* Trans. G. Buhler. Oxford, Clarendon Press, 1896. [3] p. 195 (V. 148); [4] p. 196 (V. 154); [5] p. 196 (V. 157, 158); [6] p. 197 (V. 161, 164); [10] pp. 87–88 (III. 68–70); [11] p. 198 (VI. 2); [12] pp. 199–205 (VI. 3–6, 8, 16, 29, 33); [13] p. 213 (VI. 82); [14] pp. 206–213 (VI. 42, 43, 55, 56, 44, 45, 65, 81, 79); [36] p. 25 (I. 93, 98); [37] p. 398 (IX. 317–319). Reprinted by permission of the publishers.

R. E. Hume, *The Thirteen Principal Upanishads.* 2nd ed. Oxford University Press, London, 1934. [7] Svet. 1.6, p. 395; [8] Mun. 3.2.8, p. 376; [9] Mun. 2.2.8, p. 373; [15] Mait. 6.18, p. 435; [27] Svet. 4.9, p. 404. Reprinted by permission of the author and publishers.

Sir Edwin Arnold, *The Bhagavad Gita: The Song Celestial.* In any edition. [16] 1.13–23; [17] 1.24–26; [18] 1.28–47; [19] 2.11–20; [21] 2.47–51; 3.19, 30; [22] 6.10–15, 25–31; [23] 9.16–19; [24] 11.12; [25] 12.8–12; 18.64–66; [26] 9.28–30.

Swami Paramanda, *The Bhagavad Gita.* The Vedanta Center, New York. [20] III.5.

Bombay Census Report for 1911. [28] Part I, pp. 66–67 (as quoted by L. S. S. O'Malley, *Popular Hinduism,* 1935).

Sir Charles Eliot, *Hinduism and Buddhism.* 3 vols. Edward Arnold and Company, London, 1921. [29] Vol. II, p. 144. Reprinted by permission of the publishers.

Romain Rolland, *Prophets of the New India.* Translated by E. F. Malcolm-Smith. Albert and Charles Boni, New York, 1930. [30] pp. 42–43; [31] p. 43 n.

James Bissett Pratt, *India and Its Faith.* Houghton Mifflin Company, Boston, 1915. [32] p. 40. Quoted by permission of the publishers.

Mohandas Gandhi, *Young India, 1919–1922.* Huebsch, New York, 1923. [33] p. 804.

Sir Monier-Williams, *Brahmanism and Hinduism.* The Macmillan Company, London, 1891. [34] p. 318. By permission of J. Murray, author's publisher.

Gertrude Emerson, *Voiceless India.* Doubleday, Doran and Company, New York, 1931. [35] p. 110. Reprinted by permission of the John Day Company, publisher.

Wm. Theodore deBary and others, *Sources of Indian Tradition.* Columbia University Press, 1958. [38] p. 641 (quoting *Gospel of Ramakrishna,* Vedanta Society, 1907, pp. 158–160); [39] p. 639 (quoting ibid. pp. 207–214).

Charles S. Braden, *Modern Tendencies in World Religions.* The Macmillan Company, 1933. [40] p. 31.

E. A. Gait, *Caste.* Article in the Encyclopaedia of Religion and Ethics. T. & T. Clark, Edinburgh, and Charles Scribner's Sons, New York. [41] Vol. III, p. 231. Reprinted by permission of the publishers.

Paul D. Devanandan, "The Contemporary Attitude to Conversion." *Religion in Life,* Vol. XXVII (1958). [42] pp. 381–392.

CHAPTER 8   SIKHISM

M. A. MacAuliffe, *The Sikh Religion; Its Gurus, Sacred Writings and Anthems.* Oxford, Clarendon Press, 1909. 6 vols. Vol. I: [1] pp. 33–34; [2] p. 35; [3] p. 37; [4] p. 58; [5] p. 175; [6] pp. 190–191; [7] p. 213; [8] p. 219; [9] p. 377; [10] p. 328; [11] p. 40; [13] p. 60. Vol. II: [14] p. 238; [15] p. 70. Vol. IV: [17] p. 2 Reprinted by permission of the publishers.

Dorothy Field, *The Religion of the Sikhs*. Wisdom of the East Series. John Murray, 1914.   [12] p. 54;   [16] p. 19;   [18] p. 106. Quoted by permission of the publisher.

R. E. Hume, *The World's Living Religions*. Charles Scribner's Sons, New York, 1924.   [19] p. 103, as quoting Court, *History of the Sikhs*, pp. 43, 56.

Sir Monier-Williams, *Brahmanism and Hinduism*. The Macmillan Company, London, 1891.   [20] p. 177. By permission of J. Murray, author's publisher.

CHAPTER 9   *CHINESE RELIGION AND THE TAOISTS*

Tsui Chi, *A Short History of Chinese Civilization*. G. P. Putnam's Sons, New York, 1943.   [1] p. 3. Reprinted by permission of the publishers.

S. Wells Williams, *The Middle Kingdom*. Charles Scribner's Sons, New York, 1899.   [2] II, p. 139 (slightly condensed). Reprinted by permission of the publishers.

H. G. Creel, *Sinism: A Study of the Evolution of the Chinese World-View*. Open Court Publishing Company, Chicago, 1928.   [3] p. 21.

The Shi-King, metrically translated by James Legge. The World's Great Classics, Colonial Press, New York, 1900.   [4] pp. 195–199.

E. R. Hughes, *Chinese Philosophy in Classical Times*. Everyman's Library, No. 973. J. M. Dent and Sons, London, and E. P. Dutton and Co., Inc., New York, 1941.   [5] p. 308;   [17] p. 163;   [41] p. 154. Reprinted by permission of the publishers.

Sacred Books of the East, Vol. III, *The Texts of Confucianism, Part I*. Trans. James Legge. Oxford, Clarendon Press, 1879.   [6] p. 443 f., arranged in the form of verse. Reprinted by permission of the publishers.

L. A. Lyall, *China*. Ernest Benn, London, and Charles Scribner's Sons, New York, 1934.   [7-8] pp. 28–33 (translating G. E. Simon, *La Cité Chinoise*). Reprinted by permission of publishers.

The Analects of Confucius, etc. A translation by Charles A. Wong, published in China without imprint of publisher or date. (A partial American reprint is to be found in Robert O. Ballou, *The Bible of the World*, Viking Press, New York, 1939. P. 398 f.)   [9] Analects, Bk. XIII. 18.

Y. L. Fung, *History of Chinese Philosophy (From the Beginnings to circa 100 B.C.)*. Trans. by Derk Bodde. Henri Vetch, Peiping, 1937.   [10] pp. 133–134 (quoting Mencius and Huai-nan-tzu);   [11] p. 156 (quoting Chuang-tzu);   [12] p. 153 (Chuang-tzu);   [54] p. 237. Reprinted by permission of the publisher.

Lionel Giles, *The Sayings of Lao Tzu*. Wisdom of the East Series. John Murray, London, 1905.   [13] p. 20 (Chap. XXI);   [14] p. 43 (V);   [15] p. 23 (XXX);   [16] p. 25 (XXIV);   [29] p. 32 (LXIII);   [34] p. 46 (LXXVIII);   [36] p. 50 (L);   [39] p. 30 (XXXVII);   [40] p. 38 (LVII);   [42] p. 41 (XXXI);   [43] p. 34 (LXI). Reprinted by permission of the publisher.

Ch'u Ta-kao, *The Tao Te Ching*. A translation published by the Buddhist Society, London.   [18] Chap. LI;   [19] XXXVII;   [20] XVI;   [21] XL;   [25] XLII;   [27] XXII;   [30] II;   [31] XLVII;   [35] VIII;   [37] LV;   [38] XVI. Reprinted by permission of the publishers.

Arthur Waley, *The Way and Its Power*. Houghton Mifflin Company, Boston, and George Allen and Unwin, London, 1934.   [22] p. 152 (IX);   [24] p. 159 (XIV);   [33] p. 164 (XVII). Reprinted by permission of the publishers.

Lin Yutang, editor, *The Wisdom of China and India*. Random House, New York, 1942.

From the *Tao Te Ching:*   [23] p. 606 (XLI);   [26] p. 594 (XXII).

From *Chuang-tzu:*   [44] p. 686;   [46] p. 685;   [47] p. 686;   [51] p. 647;   [53] p. 664;   [58] p. 672;   [61] p. 660;   [62] p. 660–661. Reprinted by permission of the publishers.

Witter Bynner, *The Way of Life*. John Day Company, New York, 1944.   [28] p. 38 (XXIII). Reprinted by permission of the publishers.

Sacred Books of the East, Vol. XXXIX, *The Texts of Taoism*. Trans James Legge. Oxford, Clarendon Press, 1891.   [32] p. 91. Reprinted by permission of the publishers.

H. A. Giles, *Chuang Tzu: Mystic, Moralist and Social Reformer*. Kelly and Walsh, Shanghai, 1889.   [45] II. 4;   [48] XII. 2;   [49] II. 5;   [50] II. 5;   [56] XII 3; [57] VIII. 2;   [60] II. 6. Reprinted by permission of the publishers.

Edward J. Jurji, ed., *The Great Religions of the Modern World*. Princeton University Press, 1946.   [52] p. 27. Quoted by permission of the publishers.

Leon Wieger, *A History of the Religious Beliefs and Philosophical Opinions in China*, Trans. E. C. Werner. Hsien-hsien Press, China, 1927.   [55] p. 187;   [63] pp. 395–401 passim;   [64] p. 603.

Chan Wing-tsit, "The Story of Chinese Philosophy," in *Philosophy—East and West*, ed. Charles A. Moore. Princeton University Press, 1944.   [59] p. 45. Quoted by permission of the publishers.

CHAPTER 10 CONFUCIUS AND CONFUCIANISM

James Legge, *The Analects of Confucius*. Vol. I of *The Chinese Classics*, 2nd ed., Oxford, Clarendon Press, 1893–1895.   [1] XIV. 11;   [2] VII. 26;   [3] III. 7; [6] IX. 2;   [16] X. 1–17 (changing "king" to "duke" in the translation);   [49] XIV. 13. Reprinted by permission of the publishers.

Arthur Waley, *The Analects of Confucius*. Houghton Mifflin Company, Boston, and George Allen and Unwin, London, 1938.   [4] p. 127 (VII. 22). Reprinted by permission of the publishers.

Lin Yutang, *The Wisdom of Confucius*. The Modern Library, Random House, 1938. [5] p. 83;   [12] p. 13;   [13] p. 216 (LiKi XXVII);   [14] pp. 228–229 (LiKi IX); [15] p. 238;   [57] p. 14;   [85] p. 280 (Mencius VI. I). Reprinted by permission of the publishers.

Y. L. Fung, *A History of Chinese Philosophy (From the Beginnings to circa 100 B.C.)*. Trans. Derk Bodde. Henri Vetch, Peiping, 1937.   [7] p. 108 (quoting Sse-ma Ch'ien);   [11] p. 15;   [35] p. 59 (An. XIII. 3);   [41] p. 72;   [56] p. 58 (An. VI. 20);   [66] p. 106;   [79] p. 318;   [81] p. 327;   [92] p. 113;   [111] p. 17. Reprinted by permission of the publisher.

Brian Brown, *The Story of Confucius*. David Mackay Company, Philadelphia, 1927. [8] p. 94 (An. VII. 1);   [45] p. 137 (An. IV. 5);   [52] p. 94 (An. VII. 1);   [61] p. 100 (An. VII. 34). Reprinted by permission of the publishers.

Lin Yutang, *The Wisdom of China and India*. Random House, New York, 1942. [9] p. 816 (An. VII. 19);   [19] p. 828 (An. XIV. 36);   [38] p. 838 (Mencius); [40] p. 833 (An. III. 3);   [46] p. 835 (An. XIII. 21);   [63] p. 819 (An. III. 13); [64] p. 817 (An. IX. 5);   [67] p. 604 (Tao-Te-Ching, XXXVIII);   [68] p. 592 (Ibid. XVIII);   [69] p. 677 (Chuang-tzu);   [70] p. 665 (Chuang-tzu). Reprinted by permission of the publishers.

E. R. Hughes, *Chinese Philosophy in Classical Times*. Everyman's Library No. 973. J. M. Dent and Sons, London, and E. P. Dutton and Co., Inc., New York, 1941.

[10] p. 12;   [78] p. 87;   [80] pp. 265–266;   [82] p. 261;   [83] pp. 259–260;   [86] p. 101;   [87] pp. 100–101;   [97] p. 102;   [98] p. 102;   [112] pp. 294–295;   [114] p. 317;   [115] pp. 335–336;   [116] pp. 324–325. Reprinted by permission of the publishers.

Charles A. Wong, *The Analects of Confucius, The Great Learning, The Doctrine of the Mean, and the Works of Mencius.* Translation published in China without the imprint of a publisher or date. — A partial American reprint is to be found in Robert O. Ballou, *The Bible of the World* (Viking Press, New York, 1939). Because of the great rarity of the original work, the following references are made, for reader convenience, to this American reprint.   [17] p. 413 (An. XV. 23);   [30] p. 420 (Gr. Learn.);   [53] p. 399 (An. II. 4);   [58] p. 400 (An. III. 17);   [84] p. 451 (Men.);   [88] p. 444 (Men.);   [89] p. 455 (Men.);   [90] p. 452 (Mem.);   [91] pp. 431, 433, 434 (Men.);   [93] p. 458 (Men.);   [94] p. 459 (Men.);   [95] p. 460 (Men.).

Ku Hung Ming, *The Conduct of Life: A Translation of the Doctrine of the Mean.* Wisdom of the East Series. John Murray, London, 1906.   [18] p. 26 (XIII); [20] p. 28 (XV);   [25] p. 42 (XIX);   [31] p. 29 (XVI);   [32] p. 39 (XVII); [62] p. 53 (XXIX). Reprinted by permission of the publisher.

L. A. Lyall, *The Sayings of Confucius.* 3rd ed., Longmans, Green and Company, 1935.   [21] p. 2 (I. 11);   [22] p. 4 (II. 6);   [23] p. 5 (II. 7);   [24] p. 15 (IV. 19);   [33] p. 4 (II. 3, slightly modified);   [59] p. 10 (III. 12). Reprinted by permission of the publishers.

Ivan Chen, *The Book of Filial Duty.* Wisdom of the East Series. John Murray, London, 1920.   [26] *p.* 22 (Chap. VIII). Quoted by permission of the publisher.

Lionel Giles, *The Sayings of Confucius.* Wisdom of the East Series. John Murray, London, 1917.   [27] p. 41 (XII. 17);   [28] p. 42 (XII. 19);   [29] p. 45 (XIII. 11);   [34] p. 46 (XIII. 15);   [37] p. 69 (XVII. 6);   [39] p. 108 (XVII. 13); [42] p. 57 (IV. 10);   [43] p. 64 (XII. 20);   [44] p. 68 (XV. 17);   [47] p. 60 (VI. 27);   [50] p. 87 (VII. 33);   [51] p. 86 (VII. 27);   [54] p. 94 (II. 16);   [55] p. 102 (XI. 11);   [60] p. 95 (III. 11). Reprinted by permission of the publisher.

Hu Shih, *The Development of the Logical Method in Ancient China.* The New China Book Company, Shanghai, 1917.   [36] p. 26.

Ku Hung Ming, *The Discourses and Sayings of Confucius.* Kelly and Walsh, Shanghai, 1898.   [48] p. 46 (An. VI. 27).

James Legge, *Mencius.* Vol. II of *The Chinese Classics,* 2nd ed., Oxford, Clarendon Press, 1893–1895.   [65] III. 1, 4, 13. Reprinted by permission of the publishers.

Yi-pao Mei, *Motse, the Neglected Rival of Confucius.* Probsthain, London, 1929. [71] p. 80 f.;   [72] p. 89;   [73] p. 83;   [74] p. 87;   [75] p. 145;   [76] p. 142;   [77] p. 83. Reprinted by permission of the publisher.

Chan Wing-tsit, "The Story of Chinese Philosophy," in *Philosophy — East and West,* ed. Charles A. Moore. Princeton University Press, 1944.   [96] p. 30;   [113] p. 50;   [119] p. 57;   [120] p. 58;   [128] p. 63;   [129] p. 63–64;   [130] p. 64. Reprinted by permission of the publishers.

H. H. Dubs, *The Works of Hsüntse Translated from the Chinese.* Probsthain, London, 1928.   [99] p. 301   [100] pp. 301, 302;   [101] p. 310;   [102] pp. 113–114; [103] pp. 179, 181;   [105] p. 182;   [106] pp. 244–245;   [107] p. 237;   [108] pp. 236–237;   [109] pp. 232–233;   [110] p. 223. Reprinted by permission of the publisher.

Gung-hsing Wang, *The Chinese Mind*. John Day Company, New York, 1946.   [104] p. 46;   [122] p. 138;   [123] p. 139;   [124] p. 139;   [127] p. 145. Reprinted by permission of the publishers.

Tsui Chi, *A Short History of Chinese Civilization*. G. P. Putnam's Sons, New York, 1943.   [118] pp. 168–169. Reprinted by permission of the publishers.

John K. Shryock, *The Origin and Development of the State Cult of Confucius*. The Century Company, New York, 1932.   [117] p. 123. Reprinted by permission of Appleton-Century Company.

P. J. MacClagan, *Chinese Religious Ideas*. Student Christian Movement Press, London, 1926.   [121] p. 112.

Dagobert D. Runes, ed. *The Dictionary of Philosophy*. Philosophical Library, New York, 1942.   [125] p. 52 (article on Chinese Philosophy by Chan Wingtsit);   [126] p. 53 (Ibid.).

CHAPTER 11   SHINTO

The Ko-ji-ki, translated by Basil H. Chamberlain. 2nd ed., J. L. Thompson and Company, Kobe, 1932.   [1] pp. 17–51, 127–129.

D. C. Holtom, *The National Faith of Japan*. Kegan, Paul, Trench, Trubner and Company, London, 1938.   [2] p. 113;   [4] p. 49;   [6] p. 23;   [10] p. 73;   [12] pp. 81–82;   [13] pp. 133–134. Reprinted by permission of George Routledge & Sons, Ltd., London.

Wieman and Horton, *The Growth of Religion*. Willett, Clark and Company, Chicago, 1938.   [3] p. 88. Quoted by permission of the publishers.

Charles S. Braden, *Modern Tendencies in World Religions*. The Macmillan Company, New York, 1933.   [5] p. 169. Quoted by permission of the publishers.

Yoshito Tanaka, *The True Import of Shinto*. An article in The Universities Review, issued by the National League of Japanese University Professors, 1938.   [7] Vol. I, No. 2, p. 4.

N. Hozumi, *Ancestor-Worship and Japanese Law*. 6th ed., Hokuseido Press, Tokyo, 1940.   [8] pp. 107–108.

D. C. Holtom, *The Political Philosophy of Modern Shinto*. Vol. XLIX, Part II, of Transactions of the Asiatic Society of Japan, Tokyo, 1922.   [9] p. 73;   [11] p. 88;   [19] pp. 107–108.

Christopher Noss, *Tohoku, The Scotland of Japan*. Board of Foreign Missions of the Reformed Church in the United States, Philadelphia, 1918. ·   [14] pp. 87–88.

A. B. Mitford (Lord Redesdale), *Tales of Old Japan*. Reprint of 1928, The Macmillan Company, London.   [15] p. 13.

Tadayoshi Sakurai, *Human Bullets: A Soldier's Story of Port Arthur*, trans. Masujiro Honda and Alice M. Bacon. 9th ed., Teibo Publishing Company, Tokyo, 1911.   [16] p. 221;   [17] pp. 16–17;   [18] pp. 10–11.

CHAPTER 12   ZOROASTRIANISM

Carl Clemen, ed. *The Religions of the World: Their Nature and History*. George G. Harrap & Co., Ltd., London, and Harcourt, Brace and Company, New York, 1931.   [1] p. 142. Quoted by permission of the publishers.

A. V. Williams Jackson, *Zoroaster, the Prophet of Ancient Iran*. Columbia University Press, New York, 1898.   [2] p. 33;   [3] p. 41;   [4] p. 41;   [6] p. 52;   [18] p. 60. Reprinted by permission of the publisher.

James Hope Moulton, *Early Zoroastrianism*. Constable and Company (for Hibbert Trust), London, 1913. [5] pp. 365–366 (Yasna 43.7 f.); [7] p. 350 (Ys. 30.5); [8] p. 367 (Ys. 44.3–7); [10] pp. 98; [11] p. 349 (Ys. 30.3–5); [12] p. 370 (Ys. 45.2); [13] p. 354 (Ys. 31.18); [14] p. 53 (Ys. 31.10); [15] p. 373 (Ys. 45.4). Reprinted by permission of the publishers.

James Hope Moulton *The Treasure of the Magi*. Oxford University Press, London, 1917. [9] p. 24; [17] p. 37 (Yasna 46.11); [19] p. 87; [21] p. 89; [25] p. 142; [26] p. 149. Quoted by permission of Rev. H. K. Moulton.

George Foot Moore, *History of Religions*. 2 vols., Charles Scribner's Sons, and T. & T. Clark, Ltd., Edinburgh, 1913–1919. [16] Vol. I, p. 366 (Ys. 12). Quoted by permission of the publishers.

Sacred Books of the East, Vol. XXIII, *The Zend Avesta*, trans. J. Darmesteter. Oxford, Clarendon Press, 1883. [20] p. 183 (Ys. 13.12). Reprinted by permission of the publishers.

Jal Dastur Cursetji Pavry, *The Zoroastrian Doctrine of a Future Life*. Columbia University Press, New York, 1926. [22] pp. 92–93; [23] pp. 44–45 (from Sar Dar Bundahish 99.5–20). Reprinted by permission of the publishers.

Sacred Books of the East, Vol. V, *The Pahlavi Tests*, Part I, trans. E. W. West. Oxford, Clarendon Press, 1880. [24] p. 248 (Bundahis 30). Reprinted by permission of the publishers.

CHAPTER 13 JUDAISM

Smith and Goodspeed, *The Bible: An American Translation*. University of Chicago Press, 1935. [1] Ex. 1:8–10, 22; 2:1–10; [2] Ex. 3:1–15; [3] Ex. 34:1–8; [4] Ex. 34:17–26; [5] Ex. 24:3–8; [6] Ex. 32:1–24; [25] II Kings 23:4–14; [26] Deut. 24:16; [27] Jer. 1:4–9; [28] Jer. 20:7–18; [29] Jer. 26:5–24; [30] Jer. 28:10–14; [31] Jer. 23:16, 31–32; [32] Jer. 30:11; [33] Jer. 31:27–34; [34] II Kings 24:14–16; [35] Ps. 137; [36] Esther 3:8–9; [37] Jer. 44:17–18; [38] Ezek. 3:17; [41] Ezek. 36:22–23; [42] Is. 40:28; [43] Is. 43:10; [44] Is. 55:9; [45] Is. 57:15; [46] Is. 49:1–3; [48] Is. 42:25, [50] Is. 45:14–15; [51] Is. 49:22–23; [52] Ezra 1:5; [53] Neh. 9:38–10:39; [54] Neh. 13:15–21; [55] Neh. 13:25. Reprinted by permission of the publishers.

George A. Barton, *Archaeology and the Bible*. American Sunday School Union, 6th ed. revised, 1933. [7] p. 442, 444. (Substituting Habiru for Habiri.)

James Moffatt, *The Holy Bible: A New Translation*. Hodder and Stoughton, Ltd., London and George H. Doran Company, New York, 1922, 1924, 1926. [8] Hosea 4:11–14; [11] Amos 3:6–8; 5:7–11; 6:1–6; [12] Amos 5:4–6, 21–24; [13] Amos 7:1–17; [14] Hosea 2:2–19; [15] Hosea 10:7; [16] Is. 6:1–9; [17] Is. 30:15; [18] Is. 7:1–9; [19] Is. 3:2; 5:8, 11; 6:21–23; 1:23; [20] Is. 1:18–19; [21] Is. 2:1–5; [22] Is. 11:1–10; [23] Micah 3:5–12; [24] Micah 6:6–8; [47] Is. 42:6. Reprinted by permission of Hodder and Stoughton, Ltd., and Harper and Brothers, present publishers.

Max Loehr, *A History of Religion in the Old Testament*. Ivor Nicholson & Watson, Ltd., London, and Charles Scribner's Sons, New York, 1936. [9] pp. 51–52. Quoted by permission of the publishers.

Rudolph Kittel, *The Religion of the People of Israel*. The Macmillan Company, New York, 1925. [10] p. 71; [39] p. 162; [40] p. 162. Reprinted by permission of the publishers.

R. G. Moulton, *The Modern Reader's Bible*. The Macmillan Company, New York, 1907.   [49] Is. 53:3–6. Reprinted by permission of the publishers.

Abram Leon Sachar, *A History of the Jews*. Alfred Knopf, New York, 1930.   [56] p. 88;   [58] p. 89;   [61] p. 229;   [62] p. 265.

Gaalyahu Cornfield, ed. *Adam to Daniel*. Macmillan, New York, 1961.   [57] p. 381.

Lewis Browne, *Stranger than Fiction: A Short History of the Jews*. The Macmillan Company, 1931.   [59] p. 171;   [60] p. 249. Reprinted by permission of the publishers.

David Philipson, *The Reform Movement in Judaism*. The Macmillan Company, rev. ed., 1931.   [63] p. 54;   [64] p. 122;   [65] p. 363. Reprinted by permission of the publishers.

Oscar I. Janowsky, *The American Jew: A Composite Portrait*. Harper and Brothers, New York, 2nd ed., 1932.   [66] pp. 214–215. Quoted by permission of the publishers.

CHAPTER 14 CHRISTIANITY IN ITS OPENING PHASE

Abram L. Sachar, *A History of the Jews*. Alfred Knopf, New York, 1930.   [1] p. 117.

Smith and Goodspeed, *The Bible: An American Translation*. University of Chicago Press, 1935.   [2] Matt. 3:4;   [3] Matt. 3:12;   [4] Lk. 3:11;   [5] Mk. 1:9–11;   [6] Mk. 1:15;   [7] Mk. 4:1;   [8] Mk. 9:45;   [9] Gal. 5:17;   [10] Lk. 17:22–24; 26–27, 30;   [11] Mk. 9:1;   [12] Mk. 13:30–33;   [13] Lk. 13:24–30;   [14] Matt. 8:11–12;   [15] Lk. 4:18–21;   [16] Lk. 9:59–62;   [17] Matt. 5:22;   [18] Matt. 5:28;   [19] Matt. 5:43–48; 7:12; 22:37–40;   [20] Matt. 5:38–40;   [21] Matt. 7:1–5;   [22] Lk. 6:36–38;   [23] Mk. 2:27–28;   [24] Mk. 7:14–15;   [25] Mk. 6:4;   [26] Mk. 3:31–35;   [27] Mk. 3:24–26;   [28] Mk. 8:27–29;   [29] Mk. 11:17;   [31] Matt. 21; 31, 43;   [32] Mk. 14:22–24. Reprinted by permission of the publishers.

James Moffatt, *The Holy Bible: A New Translation*. Hodder and Stoughton, Ltd., London and George H. Doran Company, New York, 1922, 1924, 1926.   [30] Mk. 12:14–17. Quoted by permission of Hodder and Stoughton, Ltd., and Harper and Brothers, present publishers.

CHAPTER 15 THE RELIGIOUS DEVELOPMENT OF CHRISTIANITY

Smith and Goodspeed, *The Bible: An American Translation*. University of Chicago Press, 1935.   [1] I Cor. 15:1–8, 42–44, 50;   [2] Acts 2:1–4;   [3] Acts 5:29;   [4] Acts 5:35–39;   [5] Acts 6:1;   [6] Acts 8:1;   [7] Gal. 1:14;   [8] Acts 9:2–19;   [9] II Cor. 11:24–27;   [10] Col. 1:15–16;   [11] Eph. 2:1–19;   [13] John 1:14. Reprinted by permission of the publishers.

Joseph Cullen Ayer, Jr., *A Source Book for Ancient Church History*. Charles Scribner's Sons, New York, 1913.   [12] pp. 20–21;   [15] p. 319;   [17] p. 501;   [28] pp. 696–697. Reprinted by permission of the publishers.

Williston Walker, *A History of the Christian Church*. Charles Scribner's Sons, New York, 1918.   [14] p. 61. Reprinted by permission of the publishers.

The Ante-Nicene Fathers, edited by Alexander Roberts and James Donaldson. American reprint of the Edinburgh edition, revised and rearranged. Buffalo, The Christian Literature Publishing Company. 10 vols., 1885–1887.   [16] Praxeas 27 (Vol. III, p. 624);   [18] Letter 54.14 (Vol. V, p. 344).

A *Select Library of Nicene and Post-Nicene Fathers.* New York, The Christian Literature Company. First Series, 14 vols., 1886–1890.   [19] Confessions 2.5 (Vol. I, p. 62);   [20] Ibid. 8.7 (Vol. I, p. 124);   [21] Ibid. 8.12 (Vol. I, p. 127);   [22] On Trinity, Bk. 8, pref. (Vol. III, p. 115);   [23] Ibid. Bk. 4.20 (Vol. III, p. 84);   [24] Ibid. Bk. 10.11 (Vol. III, p. 142);   [25] On Original Sin, 2.34 (Vol. V, p. 249);   [26] Marriage and Concup., 1.27 (Vol. V, p. 275);   [27] Gift of Perseverance, 1 (Vol. V, p. 526 f.).

Isabel Florence Hapgood, ed. *Service Book of the Holy Orthodox Catholic Apostolic (Greco-Russian) Church.* Cambridge, Mass., 1922.   [29] pp. 455–456.

D. C. Somervell, *A Short History of Our Religion.* G. Bell and Sons, London, 1922.   [30] p. 190. Reprinted by permission of the publishers.

Froissart, *Chronicles,* trans. from the French by Thomas Johnes. Vol. I of revised edition. The World's Great Classics, Colonial Press, New York, 1901.   [31] pp. 212–213 (Chapter IX).

Henry Wace and C. A. Bucheim, *Luther's Primary Works.* Lutheran Publication Society, Philadelphia, 1885.   [32] pp. 194–196;   [33] p. 78;   [34] p. 53;   [35] p. 9;   [36] p. 21.

J. MacKinnon, *Luther and the Reformation.* 4 vols., Longmans, Green and Company, London, 1925–1930.   [37] Vol. II, pp. 301–302. Reprinted by permission of the publishers.

John Calvin, *Institutes of the Christian Religion,* trans. Henry Beveridge. 3 vols., Calvin Tract Society, Edinburgh, 1845.   [38] Bk. II, chap. 1.8 (Vol. I, pp. 292–293);   [39] Bk. III, chap. 11.2 (Vol. II, p. 303);   [40] Bk. III, chap. 21–25 (Vol. II, p. 534).

Alfred Weber, *History of Philosophy,* trans. Frank Thilly from 6th French edition. Charles Scribner's Sons, New York, 1896.   [41] p. 562, quoting Feuerbach, *Essence of Christianity,* 1841, in footnote 1.

CHAPTER 16 ISLAM

William Bolitho, *Twelve against the Gods.* Simon and Schuster, New York, 1929. Reader's Club edition (1941).   [1] p. 111.

Sir William Muir, *Life of Mahomet.* Smith, Elder and Company, London, 1878.   [2] p. 15;   [5] p. 132.

The Koran, trans. J. M. Rodwell. Everyman's Library, No. 380. J. M. Dent and Sons, London, 1909.   [3] XCVI, p. 19;   [4] LIII, p. 69;   [6] LXXXI, p. 45;   [7] LXXIV, p. 23;   [8] XC, p. 35;   [13] VII, pp. 297–298;   [14] LVI, p. 67;   [15] XXXVII, p. 81;   [16] XLIV, p. 90;   [17] LVI, p. 66;   [18] XIII, p. 335;   [19] I, p. 28;   [20] XXII, p. 456;   [21] II, p. 356;   [22] XVII, pp. 166–167;   [23] IV, pp. 410–412;   [24] II, p. 363;   [25] II, p. 358;   [26] II, p. 361;   [27] V, p. 485.

Philip K. Hitti, *History of the Arabs.* The Macmillan Company, New York, 1937.   [9] p. 120;   [28] p. 150;   [29] p. 153;   [30] p. 153;   [46] p. 431. Reprinted by permission of the publishers.

R. E. Hume, *The World's Living Religions.* Charles Scribner's Sons, New York, 1924.   [10] p. 225.

I. Goldziher, *Hohammed and Islam,* trans. K. C. Seelye. Yale University Press, 1917.   [11] pp. 97–98;   [43] p. 183;   [44] p. 183. Reprinted by permission of the publishers.

Arthur Jeffery, ed., *Islam: Muhammad and His Religion.* Liberal Arts Press, New York, 1958.   [12] p. 45.

George Foot Moore, *History of Religions.* 2 vols. Charles Scribner's Sons, New York, and T. & T. Clark, Ltd., Edinburgh, 1913–1919. [31] II, p. 442; [32] II, p. 441; [47] II, pp. 462–463; [49] II, p. 435. Reprinted by permission of the publishers.

The Legacy of Islam, ed. Sir Thomas Arnold and Alfred Guillaume. Oxford, Clarendon Press, 1931. [33] pp. 215–216; [34] p. 217; [35] p. 217; [36] p. 218; [37] p. 218. Reprinted by permission of the publishers.

The Persian Poets, ed. N. .H. Dole and Belle M. Walker. Thomas Y. Crowell, 1901. [38] p. 216; [39] p. 219; [40] p. 241; [41] p. 242; [42] p. 207-209; [50] p. 289.

Carl Clemen, ed., *The Religions of the World.* George C. Harrap & Co., Ltd., London, and Harcourt, Brace and Company, New York, 1931. [45] p. 454.

John C. Archer, *Faiths Men Live By.* Thomas Nelson and Sons, New York, 1934. [48] p. 447.

H. A. R. Gibb, *Modern Trends in Islam.* University of Chicago Press, 1947. [51] p. 69.

Index

The pronunciation of words which are not found in standard dictionaries (Oriental words in particular) is indicated by a system of diacritical marks which are to be sounded approximately like the italicized letters in the following words: ärtistic, ădd, ȧsk, bĕll, fāme, ēve, hĭt, pĭne, gō, ŏdd, ôr, fŏŏt, fōōd, oĭl, bŭt, menŭ, bûrn, ûnite, säuerkraut, chin, H like ch in German ach or Scotch loch. Where, however, pronunciation seems to present no difficulty, it is not suggested. This is especially true of Japanese words, which, besides being phonetically spelled, seldom have an accent. To avoid overburdening the index, names and topics only incidentally mentioned in the text are omitted, except where pronunciation might present a difficulty, in which case the word is included and the pronunciation indicated.

795

485; Hebrew, 524, 557, 559, 561; in teaching of Jesus, 603 f.; in Christianity, 616, 622, 684; in Islam, 725 f., 734 f.; *see also* Doomsday

Juno, goddess, 100, 102; and Jupiter, 102; as Juno Lucina, 102; as Hera, 102

juno, of Roman women, 97, 102, 104

Jupiter, 50, 75, 96, 100 ff., 104; as Pluvius, Tonans, Fulminator, Prodigialis, etc., 100; and Dyaus Pitar, 100; and Juno, 102; among Celts, 108; among Teutons, 111; in Arabia, 717; *see also* Zeus, Dyaus Pitar

Justin Martyr, 630 f.

ka, soul, 59 f.

Ka'bah: building, 718 f.; and Muhammad, 721, 726, 729; in Islam, 314, 737 f.

Ka'bah Stone, 18, 718, 721, 726, 729, 737, 766

Kabbala (kä'-bŭ-lŭ), 574 f.

Kabir (kŭ-bēr'), founder of sect, 311, 314, 317

Kagu-Tsuchi, fire-god, 430, 433

Kalacakra (kä-lŭ-kŭk'-rŭ), Wheel of Time in Buddhism, 183 f.

Kali, the Black, 283, 284 f.

Kalki, messiah of Vishnuites, 287

kalpa, world age, 145

Kama, pleasure, in Hinduism, 255

Kamasutra, of Vatsyayana, 255

kami, gods of Japan, 213 f., 431 f., 442 f.

kami-dana, god-shelf, 457

Kami-no-michi, "Way of the Gods," 430; *see also* Shinto

Kanada (kŭ'-nŭ-dŭ), philosopher, 276

Kanishka (kän-ĭsh'-kŭ), king of the Kushans, 205

Kao Tsu (gäu dzōō), Han emperor, 422

Kapila (kä'-pĭ-lŭ), philosopher, 273, 276

Karaites, 573

Karma, Law of: in Hinduism, 123, 146 f., 150; in Buddhism, 147 n., 181, 233; in Jainism, 158 f.; in Sikhism, 315 f.

Karma-Marga, *see* Way of Works

Kassapa (kä'-sŭp-ŭ), disciple of Gautama Buddha, 188 n., 197

Kedeshoth or "Consecrated ones," 513

Keshab Chandra Sen, Hindu reformer, 299

Kevala (kä'vŭ-lŭ), trance-state, 157

Khadijah, wife of Muhammad, 722, 723, 724, 727, 735 n.

khaibit, shadow-soul, 60

Khalsa, in Sikhism, 319 f.

Khan, Mirza Ghulam Ahmad, 775

Khan, Sayyid Ahmad, 774

Kharijites, 747

Kheprer, sun, 57

Kimmei, emperor, 213

Kingdom of God: in teaching of Jesus, 602 f., 605, 612; in Christian doctrine, 622; in recent Protestantism, 708

Kingsu, 70

Kitchener, Lord, of Khartoum, 771

Knox, John, 679 f.

Knummu, 54

Ko Hung (gō hŭng), Taoist, 362 f.

koan, in Zen Buddhism, 236

Kobo Daishi, founder of Shingon sect, 239

Kojiki, or *Record of Ancient Matters,* 430, 437, 439, 453

kokutai, national solidarity, 428

Koran; *see* Qur'an

Korê, 80; a name of Persephone, *q.v.*

Korea, 212 f., 412

kosher, clean, 551

Krishna, 267-272, 288 ff.; as object of separate worship, 288

Kronos, 81, 83

Kshatriyas (kshä'-trĭ-yŭz), 137, 147 f., 253 f., 267 f., 287; in Upanishads, 140, 141; in rise of Jainism, 153, 163, 167, 253; in rise of Buddhism, 167, 176, 178, 253

Kshitigarbha, heavenly bodhisattva, 220

Kublai Khan, 416

K'ung-fu-tzu (kŏōng-fōō'-dzŭ); *see* Confucius

Kuomintang (gwō-mĭn-dŭng), Chinese Nationalist Party, 424 f.

Kurus, princes, 266

kusa (kōō'-shŭ), grass, 155, 269

kusti or sacred thread, Iran, 468, 489; *cf.* Sacred cord

Kwan Yin (gwän yĭn), a female form of Avalokita, *q.v.*

kwei (gwā), evil spirits, 331, 336

Lakshmi, consort of Vishnu, 286

Lamaism, 243 n.; *see* Vajrayana, Tibetan Buddhism

lamas, priests, 246 ff.

Land of No Return, 71

Land of the Gods, Japan, 431

Lao Tan (läu dän), 344 and n.; *see also* Lao-tzu

Lao-tzu (läu'-dzŭ), 327, 344 f., 354, 361, 364, 365, 366

Lares, the, protective spirits, 97

Last Days or Last Judgment; *see* Judgment

Last Supper, 613

Latins, 94

Latium, 94

Law of Moses; *see* Torah

Lay-folk: in Jainism, 163; in Buddhism, 178, 200, 204

lectisternium, sacred festal banquet, 103 f.

Legalists, of China, 343, 377, 396, 400-403, 408

Leo I, pope, 640 f., 654

Lesser Pilgrimage, Islam, 719, 737 f.

Lesser Vehicle; *see* Hinayana Buddhism

Levites, 506, 548 n., 549; *see also* Zadok

Lhasa (lä'-sŭ), 248

li (lē), propriety, 379-381, 383, 388, 389 f., 396, 409 ff.; as cosmic principle, 419 f.

Li Chi (lē jē), The Book of Rites, 373, 375 n., 376, 378, 379, 383, 395

Li Erh; *see* Lao-tzu

The illustration inside the rear cover shows a Buddhist mandala of the Wheel of Time. For a description, see page 184.

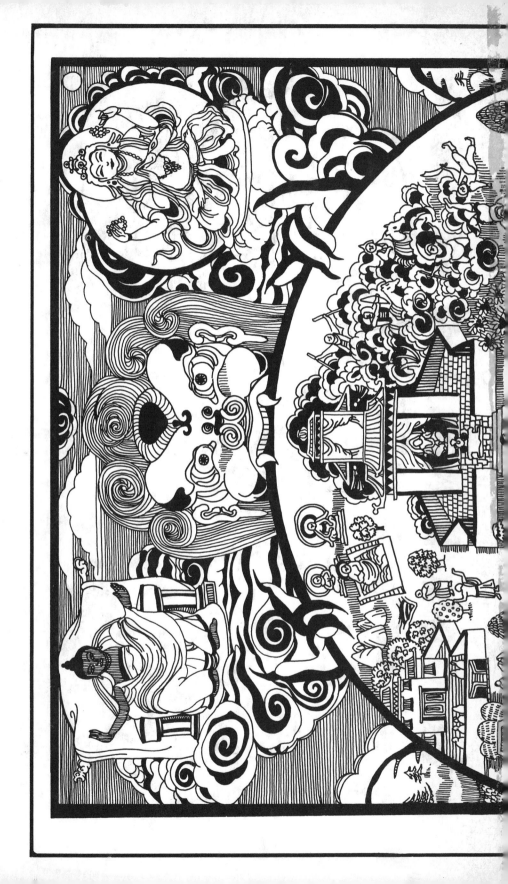